P9-CER-462

Dominican Republic Republic & Haiti

Paul Clammer

Michael Grosberg, Jens Porup

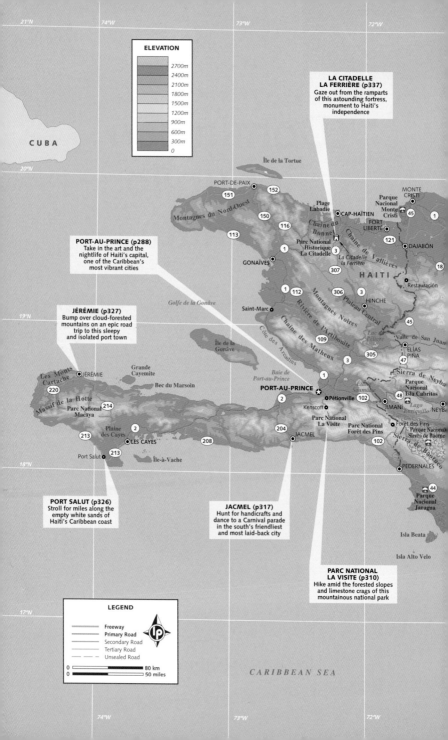

ELEVATION

2700m
2400m
2100m
1800m
1500m
1200m
900m
600m
300m
0

CUBA

Île de la Tortue

PORT-DE-PAIX

LA CITADELLE LA FERRIÈRE (p337)
Gaze out from the ramparts of this astounding fortress, monument to Haiti's independence

Montagnes du Nord-Ouest

Plage Labadie

CAP-HAÏTIEN

Chaîne du Bonne

MONTE CRISTI

Parque Nacional Monte Cristi

FORT LIBERTÉ

GONAÏVES

Parc National Historique La Citadelle

La Citadelle la Ferrière

DAJABÓN

PORT-AU-PRINCE (p288)
Take in the art and the nightlife of Haiti's capital, one of the Caribbean's most vibrant cities

Chaîne de Vallières

HAITI

Restauración

Golfe de la Gonâve

Saint-Marc

Montagnes Noires

Rivière de l'Artibonite

Plateau Central

HINCHE

JÉRÉMIE (p327)
Bump over cloud-forested mountains on an epic road trip to this sleepy and isolated port town

Lac Péligre

Valle de San Juan

ELÍAS PIÑA

Les Monts Cartache

JÉRÉMIE

Grande Cayemite

Bec du Marsoin

Île de la Gonâve

Chaîne des Matheux

Côte des Arcadins

Baie de Port-au-Prince

Sierra de Neyba

Parque Nacional Sierra de Neyba

Massif de la Hotte

Parc National Macaya

Plaine des Cayes

LES CAYES

PORT-AU-PRINCE

Pétionville

Kenscoff

JIMANI

Étang Saumâtre

Parque Nacional Isla Cabritos

Lago Enriquillo

NEYBA

Port Salut

Île-à-Vache

Parc National La Visite

Parc National Forêt des Pins

Foret des Pins

Parque Nacional Sierra de Baoruco

Sierra de Baoruco

JACMEL

PEDERNALES

PORT SALUT (p326)
Stroll for miles along the empty white sands of Haiti's Caribbean coast

JACMEL (p317)
Hunt for handicrafts and dance to a Carnival parade in the south's friendliest and most laid-back city

Parque Nacional Jaragua

Isla Beata

Isla Alto Velo

PARC NATIONAL LA VISITE (p310)
Hike amid the forested slopes and limestone crags of this mountainous national park

LEGEND

Freeway
Primary Road
Secondary Road
Tertiary Road
Unsealed Road

0 _____ 80 km
0 _____ 50 miles

CARIBBEAN SEA

151 152 150 116 113 1 112 306 307 3 305 109 3 1 2 204 208 213 214 220 2 213 102 48 47 45 18 1 45 121 44

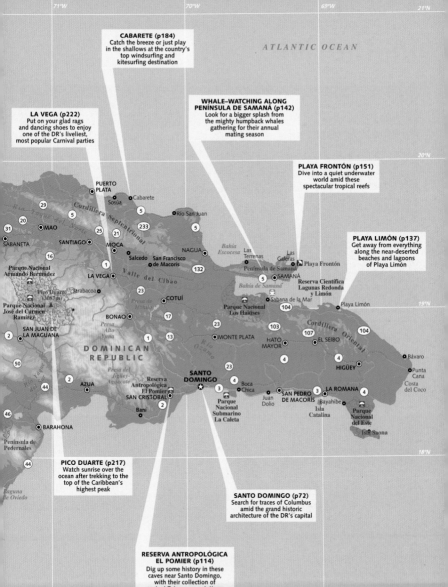

CABARETE (p184)
Catch the breeze or just play in the shallows at the country's top windsurfing and kitesurfing destination

WHALE–WATCHING ALONG PENÍNSULA DE SAMANÁ (p142)
Look for a bigger splash from the mighty humpback whales gathering for their annual mating season

LA VEGA (p222)
Put on your glad rags and dancing shoes to enjoy one of the DR's liveliest, most popular Carnival parties

PLAYA FRONTÓN (p151)
Dive into a quiet underwater world amid these spectacular tropical reefs

PLAYA LIMÓN (p137)
Get away from everything along the near-deserted beaches and lagoons of Playa Limón

PICO DUARTE (p217)
Watch sunrise over the ocean after trekking to the top of the Caribbean's highest peak

SANTO DOMINGO (p72)
Search for traces of Columbus amid the grand historic architecture of the DR's capital

RESERVA ANTROPOLÓGICA EL POMIER (p114)
Dig up some history in these caves near Santo Domingo, with their collection of ancient Taíno cave paintings

On the Road

PAUL CLAMMER Coordinating Author

Here I am near the end of my trip, at Fort Jacques (p309) in the clean air above Port-au-Prince, wondering how that little notebook is going to be transformed into a guide, and trying to calculate how many more rum punches I can fit in before I head for the airport…

JENS PORUP This photo was taken at the bird-watching platform on Cayo de las Iguanas in the middle of Laguna Oviedo (p236) in the southwest.

MICHAEL GROSBERG This photo was taken after a cramped six-hour ride on a *gua-gua* (local bus) from the Península de Samaná to Santo Domingo (p72). We were stranded with heavy bags, a scrum of people were pushing their way on and there were no cabs in sight, but a generous stranger grabbed our things, put them in his car and drove us to a café.

For full author biographies, see p372.

DOMINICAN REPUBLIC & HAITI

The Dominican Republic and Haiti show that a trip to the Caribbean isn't just all-inclusive resorts and Bob Marley. Yes, there are beaches to laze on (and what beaches!) and there's plenty of good music, but these are countries rich in their historical sites, noisy in their festivals and breathtaking in their mountains and lakes. For active types there are myriad sports, and for active minds an abundance of culture. The only trouble is finding the time to fit it all in.

Festivals & Religious Ceremonies

Think Caribbean, think Carnival, right? Music and dancing mark the Dominican Republic's and Haiti's big annual street parties, of course, but the festivities don't end there. Haiti in particular has rich traditions wrapped up in its Vodou heritage, from dazzling groups of white-clad pilgrims to raucous celebrations of the dead.

❶ Carnival, Haiti

If you thought Carnival was just a fancy parade, head for Jacmel (p322), where the bizarre procession of elaborately masked characters turns the whole town into one big street theatre. Raucous and Dionysian, it's Haiti at its wildest.

❷ Saut d'Eau Pilgrimage

Haiti's biggest Vodou pilgrimage finds thousands of adherents bathing in the sacred pools of the Saut d'Eau waterfall (p313) each July, drawn there by the prospect of visions of the Virgin Mary and her Vodou counterpart Erzuli Dantor.

❸ Vodou Ceremony

A world away from the Hollywood zombie clichés, it's worth checking out a Vodou ceremony (p279) to get an insight into this deeply spiritual culture. This is religion at its most raw.

❹ Carnival, Dominican Republic

Where's best to celebrate Carnival (p249) in the Dominican Republic? Santo Domingo certainly has the biggest party, but Santiago has the most elaborate masked parade, and La Vega has connoisseurs applauding its traditional celebration. Wherever you go, hit the party.

❺ Fet Gédé

At the start of November, Haitian cemeteries overflow with black- and purple-clothed Vodou celebrants marking Fet Gédé (All Souls Day; p346). Late-night offerings are made to the spirits of Baron Samedi and Maman Brigitte, the guardians of the dead.

❻ Latin Music Festival, Santo Domingo

Music in the Dominican Republic is more than just merengue – the enormous Latin Music Festival (p90) proves it in spades every October, showcasing everything from salsa and samba to jazz and Cuban *son*.

❼ Semana Santa

Semana Santa (Holy Week; p249), in March, is when the Dominican Republic takes a vacation. At this time the whole country seems to be on the move, heading for the nearest beach. A wild, packed and noisy time, it's the perfect picture of Dominicans at play.

Beaches & Scenery

When he landed here in 1492, Christopher Columbus was sure he'd discovered a corner of paradise. For its sweeping mountains, lush green forests and pure white beaches, Hispaniola is at the top of the scorecard. There's so much to see that you could almost tire of the parade of breathtaking landscapes. Almost…

① Playa Rincón

Tastemakers agree that Playa Rincón (p151) is one of the finest beaches in the Dominican Republic. Soft white sand meets turquoise waters, and a handful of beach bars serve seafood, cold beers and rum punch.

② Cabarete

Cabarete (p184) used to be a one-street, one-beach town. These days you're not restricted to lazing on the sands; you can enjoy the best water sports that the Dominican Republic has to offer, and finish your day at the best restaurants.

③ Playa Limón

The best beaches aren't simply the preserve of the all-inclusives. Isolated Playa Limón (p137) is a dream of endless sand, fringed with forests and lagoons and overlooked by rugged mountains.

④ Bassins-Bleu

Set in the wooded hills near Jacmel, these waterfall-fed pools (p321) are well worth the muddy hike. Once here you can plunge into crystal-clear waters in a grotto that'll have you believing the local stories that this place is home to magical spirits.

⑤ Parc National Macaya

One of the few remaining cloud forests on Hispaniola, Macaya (p327) is a true biodiversity hot spot. Difficult to access but immensely rewarding, it's a trip only for the most adventurous and self-sufficient.

⑥ Constanza

The fabulously fertile valley of Constanza (p220) is a popular weekend retreat for locals, and we can understand why. Hemmed in by rock walls and sweetened by the cool mountain air, it'll entice you to stay longer than you had originally planned.

⑦ Damajagua

How many waterfalls does anyone need to see in a single day? Damajagua (p196) has the precise answer: 27. Not only are they beautiful, there's great fun to be had leaping and canyoning into its glorious limestone pools.

Sports & Activities

Some people think that visiting the Caribbean is about doing little more than sitting on a beach with a rum punch. Well, you can do that, too, but if you want to get the blood flowing a little more, the Dominican Republic and Haiti have plenty to offer. Save that drink for when you've finished.

❶ Diving
Getting under the sea in the Dominican Republic is even more fun than splashing on the surface. Whether you're scuba diving or snorkeling (p61), there are coral, myriad fish and some good wrecks if you're looking for the life aquatic.

❷ Mountain Biking
With its dirt trails, green forests and cool mountain air, the Dominican Republic offers great opportunities for pedal power (p64) – and there's always a bar at the end, where you can buy yourself a cold beer as a reward for the day's efforts.

❸ Baseball, Santo Domingo
Dominicans don't just worship at Sunday Mass: baseball makes a solid claim for the country's *other* religion. While many dream of World Series glory, the place to catch a game is at the high church of the Estadio Quisqueya (p98) in Santo Domingo.

❹ Hiking, Pico Duarte
Hispaniola has some surprisingly rugged terrain, so take yourself up Pico Duarte (p217), the Caribbean's highest mountain (3087m). You'll need good shoes and several days, but the views out to both the Atlantic and the Caribbean are more than worth the blisters.

❺ Whale-Watching, Península de Samaná
Tourists aren't the only repeat visitors to the Dominican Republic. Every year, humpback whales congregate off the Península de Samaná (p145) to mate and give birth, watched (from a respectful distance) by boatloads of their human fans.

❻ Windsurfing & Kitesurfing, Cabarete
The strong Atlantic breeze makes the Dominican Republic's north coast heaven for both wind and wave. The beaches of Cabarete (p187) are the undisputed capital for windsurfers and kiteboarders alike.

❼ White-Water Rafting, Río Yaque del Norte
The Caribbean's only river, the Río Yaque del Norte (p213) in the Dominican Republic was designed to be plunged down, screaming, in a rubber raft. Perfect for when adrenaline levels need recharging after too much beach time.

❽ Hiking, Parc National La Visite
The limestone crags of Haiti's Massif de la Selle (p310) are sprinkled with pine forests. Easily reached from Port-au-Prince, they offer one of the best day walks on the island, with mountain views giving way to the blue of the Caribbean.

History

In many ways Hispaniola is a crucible for the history of the New World and there are plenty of notable footsteps for the traveler to follow in. Evidence of the early Taíno inhabitants, traces of Christopher Columbus and the after-shocks of the world's most successful slave rebellion are all here to be investigated.

① Catedral Primada de América, Santo Domingo

Consecrated in 1521, this cathedral (p79) is the oldest in the Americas. A rich blend of architectural styles (yet never finished), after nearly five centuries it remains the proud historic and spiritual heart of the country.

② Zona Colonial, Santo Domingo

Follow in the footsteps of Columbus with a tour around Santo Domingo's colonial quarter (p78). With its cobbled streets and historic buildings, this is the original staging post of the New World.

③ La Citadelle la Ferrière

Built to withstand an invasion by Napoleon that never came, the Citadelle (p337) sits high on its mountain crag. The most impressive fort in the Caribbean, it is an astounding testament to Haitian independence.

④ Gingerbread Architecture, Port-au-Prince

Dating back to the late 19th and early 20th centuries, Port-au-Prince's famed ginger-bread architecture (p297) is a delight to the eye, with its graceful balconies, delicate lattice woodwork and relaxed approach to tropical living.

Contents

Regional Map Contents

Destination Dominican Republic & Haiti

FAST FACTS: DOMINICAN REPUBLIC

Country area: 48,734 sq km

Population: 9.7 million

Population under 14 years old: 32%

Life expectancy at birth: 71.5 years

Adult HIV infection rate: 1.1%

Gross National Income per capita: US$2850

Percentage of population living on less than US$1 per day: 2.8%

Sharing the island of Hispaniola, the Dominican Republic (DR) and Haiti could be said to be two sides of the same coin. At first glance, culture seems to divide the two countries: while the DR is Spanish-speaking and obsessed with baseball, Haitians would rather watch the soccer World Cup and comment on the game in French, or the Creole that's derived from their slave ancestry. But shared history and a common border mean that the DR and Haiti are both dependent on and obsessed with each other.

As Dominicans prepared to head for the polls in presidential elections in mid-2008, the main issue debated up and down the country was, as always, the economy. Recent economic strictures have seen the peso further decline in value and, under guidance from the International Monetary Fund, governmental belt-tightening has been the order of the day. Manufacturing has been squeezed, and although there has been a growth in service industries (notably tourism), the economy as a whole is expected to be under even more pressure in the immediate future.

When the DR catches a cold, Haitians often get the sniffles. Haitians make up a significant (and unloved) proportion of the Dominican workforce, usually doing the lowest-paid jobs that others turn their faces from. The position of temporary Haitian workers, who are perennially discriminated against, is again an election issue. But poor relations can play out in other arenas too. When Haiti temporarily banned imports of Dominican chicken at the start of 2008 amid fears of bird flu, it saw reprisals from Dominican businesses and threats to close the border markets, where many Haitians shop for essentials unavailable at home. Such popular actions threaten the long-mooted free-trade agreement between the two countries.

FAST FACTS: HAITI

Country area: 27,560 sq km

Population: 9.5 million

Population under 14 years old: 42%

Life expectancy at birth: 52 years

Adult HIV infection rate: 5.6%

Gross National Income per capita: US$490

Percentage of population living on less than US$1 per day: 53.9%

Haiti's economy remains heavily dependent on foreign aid and remittances from the Haitian diaspora. On the political front, slow but steady progress has been made. The arrival of the heavily armed UN stabilization mission MINUSTAH in 2004 prompted dark jokes that Haiti was the only country in the world not at war that needed a peacekeeping mission, but the UN has overseen successful presidential elections and has largely tackled the problem of endemic gang violence. By all current indicators, Haiti now sees less violent crime than tourist-rich Caribbean destinations like Jamaica. In 2008 the Haitian government put tourism firmly back on its agenda, with plans to improve access to sites and even to launch a 'tourism awareness' program for a Haitian public who have largely forgotten what foreign visitors looked like.

Haiti's newfound sense of cautious optimism gives hope that this corner of the Caribbean could still turn out to be a success story. Travelers heading there now will have the country virtually to themselves and, although the road ahead is bumpy, could possibly discover one of the great secrets of Caribbean tourism. If your holidays are less about adventuring and more about, well, holidaying, the DR continues to play to its strengths, with an established infrastructure and a host of activities. When Columbus made landfall on Hispaniola, the island transfixed him, and whatever you're after, it continues to weave a spell on anyone who washes up on its shores.

Getting Started

Approaching a trip to Hispaniola, your planning is going to be very different depending on whether you're heading to the DR or Haiti. On the surface the two countries have many similarities. At any time of the year you can find great weather, beautiful beaches and a host of interesting sporting and cultural activities in either. Some events that are big draws – spotting humpback whales in the DR, Vodou festivals in Haiti and Carnival in both countries – take place at certain times; you may need to tailor your trip around these if they capture your particular interest. In the DR, there are also peak tourist seasons, which can mean higher prices and larger crowds, and some months across the whole island are rainier than others. These shouldn't be deal-breakers – the prices and weather don't vary *that* much – but are worth considering.

Neither country could truly be called a budget destination in backpacker terms, but Haiti is definitely more expensive to visit. The DR is not only cheaper to visit but often easier to travel in too, having a more stable economy and developed infrastructure ready to receive tourists by the planeload (with plenty of affordable all-inclusive resorts if all you're after is a beach). By contrast, Haiti offers a more unpolished experience, and visitors will do well to prepare themselves for the sometimes harsh realities of travel to a desperately poor country.

See Climate Charts for the DR (p247) and Haiti (p343) for more information.

Both countries are small enough to cover in a single trip – or possibly even hop between the two to get a full view of the diversity of this stunning island.

WHEN TO GO

Except in the central mountains, temperatures don't vary much in either the DR or Haiti, averaging a summery 28°C to 31°C (81°F to 87°F) in most places for most of the year. In the mountains, sunny days climb to 24°C (75°F) but can just as easily fall to single digits at night or on cloudy days. Tropical humidity can make the temperatures feel higher, though sea breezes help mitigate the effect. The rainy season is from May to October, though in

---

DON'T LEAVE HOME WITHOUT...

- passport and US cash – you'll need both
- valid travel insurance
- the latest news and government travel advice for Haiti
- a flashlight – blackouts are common in the DR and endemic in Haiti
- mosquito repellent – biting bugs are common, and malaria is present in some parts of Haiti (consult a doctor for current malaria travel advice)
- a universal washbasin plug
- biodegradable detergent and travel clothesline
- sunscreen, which can be expensive to buy locally
- an emergency stash of toilet paper and antibacterial hand-cleaning gel
- patience – things do get done, but the pace of life can be several steps slower than at home
- a taste for rum – essential for both countries!

Samaná and the North Coast in the DR it can last until December. Northern Haiti tends to be wetter from November to March. The hurricane season is during August to October.

With fewer visitors, Haiti doesn't have tourist seasons. In the DR, the peak times are from December to February, July to August, and Semana Santa (the week before Easter). Expect higher prices and more-crowded beaches during these times – Semana Santa is especially busy. Note that most water sports and activities, including scuba diving, jet-skiing and even kayaking are prohibited throughout the DR during Semana Santa – well worth noting if these are a key component of your trip.

Several popular events and attractions can only be enjoyed at certain times of the year. In both countries, Carnival is celebrated just before Lent (usually in February). The DR stretches events over several weekends, while the biggest Haitian Carnivals in Port-au-Prince and Jacmel run a week apart – the closest thing Haiti gets to a busy tourist season. February is also one of the best times for whale-watching in Samaná in the DR, although the season officially stretches from mid-January to mid-March. If you're interested in baseball, the Dominican professional season runs from October to late January. Those with a taste for Vodou may want to time their Haitian trips for festivals like Fet Gédé (November), Souvenance (Easter) or the Saut d'Eau pilgrimage (July).

COSTS & MONEY
Dominican Republic

The DR isn't an especially great destination for shoestring travelers, but most people will be able to get by on even a modest budget. As always, accommodation prices eat the largest portion of your money. A decent budget hotel will set you back about US$20 per night, but there's a marked improvement in quality when you move into the midrange bracket – say around US$40 per night. Only the most expensive hotels will top US$100. A reasonable daily budget for accommodation, food and transport would be around US$75, but if you plan on lots of activities like sailing or diving it's a good idea to budget these in separately. If you're heading to the DR with resorts in mind, a decent all-inclusive resort will cost around US$70 to US$100, but remember that many places run special offers, and rack rates for walk-in guests are always higher.

Eating in cheaper restaurants, you'll be able to fill up for about US$7 with a bottle of Presidente beer. For somewhere a little nicer you should double that, then add a further US$10 to US$20 for a high-class restaurant.

Transport won't be a major expense. First-class bus tickets shouldn't go beyond about US$15, while local transport such as *gua-guas* (small buses) and *motoconchos* (motorcycle taxis) are even cheaper. Hiring a car will cost between US$50 and $100 per day excluding fuel.

Haiti

Haiti is probably more expensive than you think. Taking into account the occasional taxi fare, a few beers with dinner and a willingness to stay in cheap hotels, those with an eye on their money could just about get by on around US$50 per day. At the other end of the scale, it's easy to spend over US$100 a day just on accommodation, especially in Port-au-Prince, where most of the best hotels are based, with another US$50 for the rest of the day's expenses. Prices for an average-quality midrange hotel hover around US$60.

Street food costs the equivalent of loose change. A meal in a cheap restaurant will set you back around US$4, and closer to US$10 in a midrange

HOW MUCH (DR)?

Internet access (per hour) US$0.80

100km bus ride US$3

Quality cigar US$4

Box of 25 premium cigars US$400

Bleacher seats at Quisqueya Stadium US$8

HOW MUCH (HAITI)?

Internet access (per hour) US$0.80

100km bus ride US$3

Moto-taxi ride US$0.40

Papite (fried banana chips) US$0.12

Bottle of five-star Barbancourt rum US$20

IS HAITI SAFE TO VISIT?

If you were planning a trip to the Caribbean 50 years ago, Haiti would probably have been top of your list. Together with Cuba, Haiti virtually invented tourism to the Caribbean, and Port-au-Prince was one of the most swinging destinations in the Americas. Even up to the 1980s, Haiti's tourism industry was a major earner. But the turmoil of recent years is more likely to have people asking – isn't Haiti too dangerous to visit?

While you should be aware that many government travel advisories continue to counsel against recreational travel to Haiti, the realities on the ground are actually far better than popular media coverage might lead you to expect. The presence on the ground of the UN peacekeepers of MINUSTAH allowed the 2006 elections to pass largely without incident and pave the way for improved political stability. It's still essential to keep your eyes on the news however; demonstrations over skyrocketing prices turned violent briefly in early 2008. But the biggest concern has always been the threat of violent crime and kidnapping. MINUSTAH operations since 2006 have tackled Haiti's gang problem head-on, breaking up the power of the gangs and largely staunching kidnappings (it's important to note that kidnappings were almost exclusively targeted against rich Haitians rather than foreigners.) At the start of 2008, Port-au-Prince and Haiti in general had a far lower violent crime and murder rate than nearby Jamaica, with its prosperous tourist industry. (For more-specific advice, see p293 and p344.)

One thing to bear in mind is that the country's poverty and broken infrastructure can make traveling here more akin to visiting a developing country than the Americas. But Haitians deplore the media image of their country as being in constant anarchy, and the vast majority of visitors are pleasantly surprised at how calm and welcoming Haiti really is.

---

place. At the best restaurants (such as those in Pétionville) it's easy to spend US$40 once you include wine.

Hiring a car is expensive. Roads are poor, so hire leans towards the 4WD end of the market. Typical prices are US$70 per day for a saloon, double that for a 4WD. Buses are cheap, however – the longest bus trip is never going to top US$12, although a comfortable ride isn't always guaranteed.

TRAVELING RESPONSIBLY

Since our inception in 1973, Lonely Planet has encouraged our readers to tread lightly, travel responsibly and enjoy the magic that independent travel affords. International travel is growing at a jaw-dropping rate, and we still firmly believe in the benefits it can bring – but, as always, we encourage you to consider the impact your visit will have on both the global environment and the local economies, cultures and ecosystems.

Many visitors to the DR will be staying in all-inclusive resorts. If you're among this number, it's definitely worth making the effort to eat and drink outside the resort if you can. Most all-inclusive places are foreign-owned, and most of the money spent at them is repatriated to the parent country rather than the DR. Wages inside the resorts can also be low. Tipping staff and spending money outside the resort ensures that more of your money benefits the local economy. When outside, it's best to have a relaxed attitude to being called a *gringo* or *gringa* – these are generic terms for foreigners, not an insult (the Haitian equivalent is being hailed as a *blanc,* no matter the color of your skin).

When on an excursion – whether that's diving, snorkeling, kayaking or hiking – ask your guide as many questions as possible about the environmental policies of the company, in order to persuade tour operators that these issues are of interest to tourists.

In Haiti, it is many years since the country enjoyed tourists visiting in any numbers, and 'sustainable tourism' is yet to make an appearance on the

---

CLIMATE CHANGE & TRAVEL

Climate change is a serious threat to the ecosystems that humans rely upon, and air travel is the fastest-growing contributor to the problem. Lonely Planet regards travel, overall, as a global benefit, but believes we all have a responsibility to limit our personal impact on global warming.

Flying & Climate Change

Pretty much every form of motor travel generates CO_2 (the main cause of human-induced climate change) but planes are far and away the worst offenders, not just because of the sheer distances they allow us to travel, but because they release greenhouse gases high into the atmosphere. The statistics are frightening: two people taking a return flight between Europe and the US will contribute as much to climate change as an average household's gas and electricity consumption over a whole year.

Carbon Offset Schemes

Climatecare.org and other websites use 'carbon calculators' that allow jetsetters to offset the greenhouse gases they are responsible for with contributions to energy-saving projects and other climate-friendly initiatives in the developing world – including projects in India, Honduras, Kazakhstan and Uganda.

Lonely Planet, together with Rough Guides and other concerned partners in the travel industry, supports the carbon offset scheme run by climatecare.org. Lonely Planet offsets all of its staff and author travel.

For more information check out our website: lonelyplanet.com.

---

radar. On one level, any form of tourism is worthwhile – injecting money into the local economy and, just as importantly, coming home and being able to challenge others' preconceptions of this so-called nightmare republic. On the ground, day-to-day challenges are more gritty. Haiti is in environmental crisis, and you might spend hours agonizing about throwing your trash in the street, only to find out that that's exactly what your hotel does with the rubbish you saved to dispose of in your room. At the very least, be aware that access to water and electricity can be problematic at the best of times, so try to avoid wasting these precious resources. Using the filtered drinking water provided by all hotels and restaurants does at least minimize adding to the country's plastic bottle mountain.

TRAVEL LITERATURE

The intrigues of its history and the attractions of Vodou have blessed Haiti with a richer body of travel literature than the DR.

A sobering novel by young Haitian-American writer Edwidge Danticat, *The Farming of Bones* takes as its backdrop the horrific slaughter of Haitians by Dominican soldiers in 1937 – excellent reading whichever country you're visiting. Danticat's *After the Dance: A Walk Through Carnival in Jacmel* is a charming and thoughtful meditation on growing up, Haitian history and finally attending Jacmel's most famous celebration after being banned as child.

Part travelogue, part memoir, *The Best Nightmare on Earth* by Herbert Gold recounts over 37 years of living in Haiti, from the rise of Papa Doc to the eve of Prosper Avril in 1990. It vividly captures Haiti with the charm and occasionally wearied air that only a deep love affair can produce.

Dead Man in Paradise by JB Mackinnon is an intriguing blend of travelogue, history and reportage with the author, the nephew of a priest murdered decades ago during the Trujillo regime, trying to piece together the stories of the surviving actors in this unsolved crime.

TOP**PICKS**

FESTIVALS

The DR and Haiti are full of wild festivals to watch or participate in, which are almost always accompanied by a great deal of drinking and dancing:

- Carnival in Jacmel, Haiti (January–February; p322) – enjoy the street theatre of the festival's masks and costumes

- Carnival parade in La Vega, Dominican Republic (January–February; p223) – the DR's biggest show

- International Sand Castle Competition in Cabarete, Haiti (February; p189) – more than just buckets and spades

- Carnival in Port-au-Prince, Haiti (February; p298) – the biggest and noisiest festival on the island

- Fet Gédé, Haiti (November; p346) – the Vodou festival of the dead is held in cemeteries across Haiti at midnight

- Saut d'Eau Vodou pilgrimage, Haiti (July; p313) – devotees bathe under a sacred waterfall

SHOPPING

Forget the cheap stuff that touts push to the crowds fresh off the cruise boat – you might find yourself worrying about your luggage allowance with the top-notch souvenirs that the DR and Haiti have to offer. Here's our list of top shopping items:

- A canvas by an upcoming Haitian artist from the vibrant galleries of Port-au-Prince (p305)

- Oil drums recycled into intricate sculptures by the carved-iron artists of Haiti's Croix des Bouquets (p311)

- The best in Dominican cigars from Santiago (p208), the stogie capital of Hispaniola

- Brightly painted papier-mâché boxes and masks from Jacmel (p324), the home of Haitian handicrafts

- Dominican amber – head for Puerto Plata (p173) to find out how to pick the best

- A bottle of rum (Brugal or Bermudez in the DR, Barbancourt in Haiti) to help you try to re-create those sunny Caribbean punches once you're back home

- Dominican merengue and Haitian *compas* CDs picked up at any street market to help with the ambience when pouring the aforementioned rum

BEACHES

The Caribbean is heaven for beach bunnies, and these are some of our favorite beaches to help you laze your holiday away:

- Playa Grande, Dominican Republic (p193) – one of the most beautiful (and undeveloped) beaches in the DR

- Bávaro and Punta Cana, Dominican Republic (p131) – home to the DR's top all-inclusive resorts

- Playa Limón, Dominican Republic (p137) – a short ferry hop and bus ride from Samaná, this deserted spot is still far enough from the action to let you indulge your Robinson Crusoe fantasies

- Cabarete, Dominican Republic (p184) – combine wind, sand and surf at this wind- and kitesurfing hot spot

- Playa Rincón, Dominican Republic (p151) – with kilometers of nearly white sand framed by huge coconut trees, this has been named one of the top 10 beaches in the Caribbean by *Conde Nast* magazine

- Cormier Plage, Haiti (p338) – enjoy gold sand and white Atlantic rollers while dining on the finest seafood

Alan Cambeira's *Azucar! The Story of Sugar* is a fascinating novel that portrays the human toll of sugar production in the DR, with much of the information, descriptions and events based on real events.

Ian Thomson's *Bonjour Blanc* is one of the most entertaining and well-researched travel books written about Haiti. Visiting during the turmoil of the early 1990s, this often hair-raising account offers meticulous historical detail and vivid portraits, making it an essential read.

For more reading suggestions, see the marginal reviews in the History, Culture and Environment chapters.

INTERNET RESOURCES

There are a number of excellent websites providing general information about the Dominican Republic and Haiti, and traveling there.

Debbie's Dominican Republic Travel Pages (www.debbiesdominicantravel.com) This popular site contains a wealth of detailed firsthand reviews of tourist destinations from resorts and golfing to dive sites.

Dominican Republic One (www.dr1.com) This portal is the first place to visit for all matters Dominican, from daily news and business reports to a broad selection of travel information.

Haiti Info (www.haiti-info.com) Pulling stories straight off the newswires, this website will keep you abreast of the current situation in Haiti prior to your visit.

Haiti Innovation (www.haitiinnovation.org) This blog, which runs a commentary on the state of development and aid in Haiti, makes fascinating reading for anyone volunteering in Haiti.

Lonely Planet (www.lonelyplanet.com) The dedicated Caribbean branch of our Thorn Tree forum is one of the best places to ask questions and get up-to-date traveler's reports on the DR and Haiti.

Itineraries
ONE ISLAND, TWO COUNTRIES

HISPANIOLA FULL CIRCLE
Three Weeks

Start in **Santo Domingo** (p72), exploring the old colonial center. Next take a car southwest to the Taíno cave paintings of **San Cristobal** (p113), then southeast to the beaches at **Bávaro** and **Punta Cana** (p131), the hub of Dominican tourism.

It's a fair way to **Península de Samaná** (p142), but **whale watching** (p145) is a definite highlight. Alternatively, hike or boat around the beaches of **Las Galeras** (p150), or explore the mangroves of **Parque Nacional Los Haitises** (p140).

Next up, the water-sports mecca **Cabarete** (p184). Unwind with a cigar in **Santiago** (p204), then bus directly to **Cap-Haïtien** (p331), Haiti's second city. From here visit the **Citadelle** (p337), Hispaniola's most remarkable historic site.

Bump over mountains and along the coast to **Port-au-Prince** (p288), taking a few days to explore this vibrant urban mass. It's a short drive to the pleasant southern port of **Jacmel** (p317), the handicrafts capital of Haiti, and a short hop from the waterfalls of **Bassins-Bleu** (p321).

Back in Port-au-Prince, freshen up with a day in the mountains in **Parc National La Visite** (p310). Finally, take a direct bus back to Santo Domingo, or break the journey with a spot of bird- and crocodile-watching on the cross-border **Lac Azueï** (p313)/**Lago Enriquillo** (p240).

This three-week odyssey covers the pick of Hispaniola, and will show you the great contrasts between the two countries. It can be done in either direction, but we'd recommend tackling the DR first, building up to the slightly tougher challenge of Haiti.

CLASSIC ROUTES

DOMINICAN CIRCUIT   Three Weeks

Start with a couple of days exploring **Santo Domingo** (p72), hitting the Zona Colonial, the Faro a Colón and the essential Dominican experiences of baseball, cockfighting and dancing to merengue.

On day three head to **Jarabacoa** (p212). Visit the waterfalls in the afternoon, with white-water rafting or canyoning the next day.

Head north to **Cabarete** (p184), which has world-class water sports and mountain biking. There's great diving and beaches in nearby **Sosúa** (p178) and **Río San Juan** (p192) – enough to keep you happy for two or three days.

Next you're off to the **Península de Samaná** (p142). If it's mid-January to mid-March, go whale watching (p145). Otherwise take a boat trip to **Parque Nacional Los Haitises** (p140) to see the mangroves and cave paintings, or visit the waterfall near **El Limón** (p145). Spend another two or three days hiking or boating to the beaches around **Las Galeras** (p150). For a bit more nightlife, base yourself in **Las Terrenas** (p155) instead.

Allow for some relaxing beach time. The southeast is perfect – we'd go for either deserted **Playa Limón** (p137) or perennially popular **Bávaro** and **Punta Cana** (p131).

Return to Santo Domingo. Renting a car lets you hit several sites easily. To the southwest there are Taíno cave paintings in **San Cristobal** (p113), a spectacular drive **south of Barahona** (p233), and crocodiles in **Lago Enriquillo** (p240). Spend a night or two before finishing in Santo Domingo.

Taking in the best the DR has to offer, this route follows a large clockwise loop, starting and ending in Santo Domingo, and hitting Jarabacoa, Cabarete, the Península de Samaná, Bávaro and Punta Cana, and the southwest.

HAITI UNCOVERED   Two Weeks

Everything starts in **Port-au-Prince** (p288). Spend several days here to take in everything that Haiti's capital offers, from the vibrant arts scene to the music and the best in tropical 'gingerbread' architecture.

Take a bus north to Haiti's second city, **Cap-Haïtien** (p331). From here it's a perfect day trip to the towering mountaintop **Citadelle** and **Sans Souci Palace** (p337), the most spectacular historic sights in the country. You can look for French colonial remains to the east at **Fort Liberté** (p339) or simply head back to Cap-Haïtien and the gorgeous Atlantic beaches of **Cormier Plage** (p338) and **Labadie** (p338).

To save time, you can fly back to Port-au-Prince, then stretch your legs with a hike through **Parc National La Visite** (p310). If you want, you can walk almost to the Caribbean Sea and catch onward transport to **Jacmel** (p317) – alternatively, it's just a couple of hours' drive from Port-au-Prince.

Jacmel is worth a few days, taking in the old port architecture, the myriad handicrafts shops and an excursion to the waterfalls of **Bassins-Bleu** (p321). If you can get here for Carnival in February, so much the better.

There's beach-lounging to be had further west along the coast, either at gorgeous **Île-à-Vache** (p325) or the vast sandy expanses of **Port Salut** (p326).

Wrap your trip up back in Port-au-Prince. Spend a morning seeing the iron sculptors of **Croix des Bouquets** (p311), picking up the last of the souvenirs with plenty of time for a final rum punch before heading to the airport.

To get the essential Haitian experience, this itinerary has you based in and out of Port-au-Prince, exploring the capital and surrounds, while heading further afield to take in both the historic northern coast and the laid-back charms of the south.

ROADS LESS TRAVELED

FAR FROM THE DOMINICAN CROWDS   Two Weeks

From **Santo Domingo** (p72), rent a car and drive southwest to **Barahona** (p231),
stopping in San Cristobal to see the Taíno **cave paintings** (p114). Spend the next
day visiting **Laguna Oviedo** (p236) or **Bahía de las Águilas** (p237) – the drive alone
is spectacular. The following day head to **Lago Enriquillo** (p240), the lowest point
in the Caribbean and home to iguanas, crocodiles and lots of bird life.

**Start and finish in
Santo Domingo for
this trip, which re-
veals the corners of
the DR that many
tourists ignore.
You'll take in less-
visited destinations
like the southwest
and Pico Duarte,
and where you do
follow the tourist
route, it's for less-
common sights and
activities.**

Returning to Santo Domingo, catch a bus to **Jarabacoa** (p212). Take a day
for rafting or canyoning, but you're really here to climb **Pico Duarte** (p217), the
highest peak in the Caribbean. The standard trip is three days, but consider
arranging a side trip to beautiful **Valle de Tétero** (p218), which adds two days.

From the mountains, head north and east along the coast to **Río San Juan**
(p192). There are two terrific beaches nearby, and some of the best snorkeling
and diving on the north coast. Alternatively, consider stopping at beach town
Cabarete (p184) along the way. Although touristy, Cabarete has more restaurants, hotels and outdoors options, and a livelier nightlife than Río San Juan.

Leave early so you can get across the bay to Sabana de la Mar and **Parque
Nacional Los Haitises** (p140) in one day. Visit the lodge at the entrance to the
park for a tour featuring mangrove forests and Taíno paintings.

Your last stop should be **Playa Limón** (p137), an isolated beach and lagoon
where you'll have kilometers of coastline to yourself. You'll return to Santo
Domingo feeling totally refreshed.

TAILORED TRIPS

DOMINICAN REPUBLIC FOR KIDS

All-inclusive resorts are tailor-made for families; if all you want to do is splash about in the water, you could do worse than book at the resorts at **Bávaro** and **Punta Cana** (p131). Many are particularly child-friendly, and activities include go-karts, bowling, sailing trips and parasailing. Resorts also offer tours to local sights; for more independence, rent a car and head out on your own.

Spend time in **Santo Domingo** (p72) first. There's a great children's museum and the national aquarium; the Columbus connection is great for inspiring games of explorers (see p89). From Santo Domingo it's an easy day trip to **Boca Chica** (p105), with its pretty beach of shallow, calm water that's ideal for youngsters. Further east, **Bayahibe** (p123) is a tiny town on the edge of a national park with a number of excursion options, from package tours of an island beach to snorkeling trips to get the kids 'finding Nemo.'

Further afield, kids and adults alike should adore shouting 'There she blows!' while **whale watching** (p145) in Samaná (between mid-January and mid-March). If it's more activity your family hankers for, the windsurfing schools in **Cabarete** (p184) offer special courses for children, while kiteboarding might engage the most truculent of teenagers. At **Jarabacoa** (p212) you can take the family white-water rafting and even dinosaur hunting at the spectacular waterfalls where part of *Jurassic Park* was filmed.

NATIONAL PARKS & RESERVES

Starting in the DR, head southwest from Santo Domingo to **Barahona** (p231), a good base for bird-watching trips to Laguna Oviedo in **Parque Nacional Jaragua** (p236), and spotting crocodiles and iguanas at Lago Enriquillo in **Parque Nacional Isla Cabritos** (p240).

Head north to Jarabacoa, gateway to **Parques Nacionales Armando Bermúdez** and **José del Carmen Ramírez** (p217). The two parks cover much of the DR's central mountain range, including Pico Duarte, the highest peak (3087m) in the Caribbean. From Pico Duarte continue northwest to **Parque Nacional Monte Cristi** (p200), where you can snorkel amid pristine coral reefs and spot rare manatees.

It's a long cross-country drive to **Parque Nacional Los Haitises** (p140), near Sabana de la Mar. Boat tours of the park take in mangrove forests and Taíno cave paintings. See more cave paintings at **Parque Nacional del Este** (p124) near Bayahibe, on the way back to Santo Domingo.

Traveling over the border to Haiti, base yourself in Port-au-Prince for the pine forests of **Parc National Forêt des Pins** (p313), then trek from mountains to sea through **Parc National La Visite** (p310). Finish the trip with a flight to Cap-Haïtien and take in the sweep of **Parc National Historique La Citadelle** (p337), with its breathtaking fortress of the Citadelle.

HISTORY'S FOOTSTEPS

Home to the first European settlements in the New World, both the DR and Haiti are rich in historical sites.

Almost overflowing with colonial history, Santo Domingo (p72) is the ideal place to start, and you can spend several days soaking up the Zona Colonial, the first cathedral in the Americas and more besides.

Just southwest of the capital is an area rich in cave paintings executed by Hispaniola's original Taíno inhabitants. **San Cristobal** (p113) is the more popularly visited site, although **Reserva Antropológica El Pomier** (p114) is more extensive. In the north, the **Parque Nacional La Isabela** (p198) hosts the site of Columbus' second attempt to settle in Hispaniola (the location of the first remains unknown).

Traveling from the DR to Haiti, the sites get richer still. **Port-au-Prince** (p288) has the anchor of Columbus' *Santa Maria* in its national museum, and although there's little evidence of the colonial period on offer, the richness of the Victorian **gingerbread architecture** (see boxed text, p297) is a joy to explore. Above the city, Fermathe (p309) has two forts impressively guarding the coastline.

Heading north, stop along the **Côte des Arcadins** (p314) to explore an old sugar plantation–turned-museum, before continuing north to **Cap-Haïtien** (p331). You've saved the best until last – the massive World Heritage–listed fortress of the **Citadelle** and the ruins of **Sans Souci** (p337), 200-year-old symbols of Haitian pride at independence, and a fitting point to end the trip.

Hispaniola History

Hispaniola's earliest inhabitants called their island Quisqueya – 'cradle of life.' From its role in the earliest settlement in the Americas, to becoming the richest colony in the world and home of the world's first black republic, the island has often played a key part in world history.

THE TAÍNOS

Hispaniola had been inhabited for three millennia before Christopher Columbus sailed into view. Hunter-gatherers from the Yucatan were the first to arrive, but their impact was marginal compared with that of the Arawak peoples who had island-hopped from South America. Of these, the last to arrive were the Taínos ('the friendly people'), who prospered on the island for around 700 years until the clash of civilizations with Europe brought their ultimate downfall.

The Taínos were both farmers and seafarers. The island was divided into half a dozen independent chiefdoms called *caciques,* with a total population of around 500,000 at the time of Columbus' arrival. Each chiefdom comprised several districts with villages of 1000 to 2000 people. These were often twinned, with a small coastal village linked to a larger settlement further inland. The Taínos were skilled fishermen and caught fish and turtles with nets, spears, traps, and hooks attached to lines – they even used a mild poison that slowed the reflexes of river fish, making them easy to grab. As farmers, the Taínos cultivated root crops such as yam, cassava and sweet potato, clearing land by fire and then using heaped mounds of earth called *conucos* to slow erosion and facilitate weeding and harvesting. Dogs were the only domesticated animals, and were used for hunting.

The Taínos believed in two supreme deities: Yúcahu, the lord of the cassava and the sea, and his mother, Atabey, goddess of fresh water and human fertility. They also believed in a plethora of lesser spirits, such as those of their ancestors as well as spirits who lived in trees and other features of the landscape.

Comparatively little of Taíno culture has survived to the modern age. Pottery and stone tools form the most common artifacts, along with jewelry of bone, shell, and gold that was panned from rivers. Clothing was made of cotton or pounded bark fibers, although early Spanish arrivals noted that the Taínos frequently went unclothed. A more widespread legacy is the crops that the Taínos bequeathed to the world. Tobacco quickly spread to be grown across the world, guavas and pineapples enliven fruit bowls everywhere, and when taken to Africa, yams and cassava cultivation revolutionized agriculture

A Brief History of the Caribbean: From the Arawak and Carib to the Present by Jan Rogozinski does an excellent job of placing Hispaniola into the larger currents of Caribbean history.

You can see hundreds of Taíno cave paintings preserved at the Reserva Antropológica El Pomier (p114) in the DR.

TIMELINE

4000 BC	1200 BC	AD 500–1000
Earliest evidence of human colonization of Hispaniola. Stone-flaked implements found at archaeological digs are thought to have been brought by hunter-gatherers migrating from the Yucatan peninsula in Mexico.	Ancestral Arawaks arrive in Hispaniola, having originated in South America and migrated through the Lesser Antilles. Dubbed 'the Saladoid culture,' they live in settled agricultural communities, and are best known for their sophisticated pottery.	A third wave of migrations arrives in Hispaniola with the Taínos, an Arawak-speaking group with a rich seafaring culture. The Taíno population expands rapidly, and is divided into a series of interdependent but competing chiefdoms.

on that continent. Hispaniola's inhabitants, however, were barely to survive their first encounter with Europe.

COLUMBUS' NEW WORLD

In 1492, Christopher Columbus sailed from Spain with 90 men in the *Pinta*, the *Niña* and the *Santa María,* bound for Asia. He sailed west rather than east, expecting to circumnavigate the globe. In one of the greatest miscalculations in history, he instead discovered the New World for the Old. After stops at the small Bahamian island of Guanahaní and present-day Cuba (which Columbus initially mistook for Japan), a mountainous landscape appeared before the explorers. Columbus named it 'La Isla Española,' 'the Spanish Island,' later corrupted to 'Hispaniola'. He made landfall at Môle St-Nicholas in modern Haiti on December 7, and days later ran the *Santa María* onto a reef. Here on Christmas Day he established Villa La Navidad, the first settlement of any kind made by Europeans in the New World.

'I cannot believe that any man has ever met a people so good-hearted and generous, so gentle that they did their utmost to give us everything they had.'

CHRISTOPHER COLUMBUS MEETS THE TAÍNOS

Columbus was greeted with great warmth by the Taínos, who impressed him further with their gifts of gold jewelry. Capturing a handful to impress his royal patrons, he sailed back to Spain to be showered with glory. He returned within a year, leading 17 ships of soldiers and colonists.

La Navidad had been razed by the Taínos in reprisal for kidnappings by the settlers, so Columbus sailed east and established La Isabela, named for Spain's queen. The first church in the Americas was erected here, and a replica of the church now stands in its place (Templo de las Américas, p198). However, La Isabela was plagued with disease, and within five years the capital of the new colony was moved to Santo Domingo, where it has remained.

Columbus' early administration was a disaster, and appointing his brother Bartholomé proved no better. Their haphazard rule soon had the colonists up in arms, and a replacement sent from Spain returned the brothers home in chains. The colony would now be run with military harshness.

The Taínos were the ones to bear the brunt of this. They were already stricken by European illnesses that sent their numbers crashing, but on top of this Spain introduced *encomienda,* forced labor requiring the natives to dig up quotas of gold. The Spanish broke up Taíno villages, killed their chiefs and put the entire population to work. Within three decades of their first meeting with Europeans, the Taínos were reduced to a shadow of their previous numbers.

When a slave ship docked at Santo Domingo in 1669, the colonists had become so impoverished they could hardly afford to buy one-third of the human cargo.

EUROPEAN COMPETITION & COLONIZATION

As Taíno civilization collapsed, so did the gold mines, and no amount of imported African slaves could make up the shortfall. Spain dropped Hispaniola as quickly as it had found it, turning its attention instead to the immense riches coming from its new possessions in Mexico and Peru. Santo Domingo

1492	1496	1503
Christopher Columbus makes landfall on Hispaniola on Christmas Day and founds the settlement of La Navidad (Nativity) near modern-day Cap-Haïtien in Haiti, before returning to Spain with Taíno captives.	Nueva Isabela is founded by the Spanish. Rebuilt as Santo Domingo after a hurricane in 1502, it quickly receives a royal charter, making it the oldest European city in the New World.	Queen Anacaona of the Taíno kingdom of Xaragua in central Hispaniola is arrested by the Spanish governor and publicly executed, effectively marking the end of Taíno independence on the island.

LOOKING FOR COLUMBUS

Although La Isabela and Santo Domingo in the DR are celebrated for their connections to Columbus, the site of La Navidad, the first attempted Spanish settlement in the Americas, remains unknown and a holy grail for archaeologists. It's believed to be close to Cap-Haïtien in Haiti, probably built on the site of a Taíno village around Bord de Mer de Limonade. If you don't want to dedicate yourself to archaeology, the easiest way to get close to La Navidad is at Musée du Panthéon National in Port-au-Prince (p295), where you can see the anchor of the *Santa María*, whose wood was salvaged to build the settlement in 1492.

was reduced to a trading post for gold and silver convoys, but couldn't even hold onto that position with the opening of new trade routes via Cuba. After the English admiral Sir Francis Drake sacked Santo Domingo in 1586, it was effectively abandoned for the next 50 years, further signaling the decline of Spanish Hispaniola.

For the next three centuries, Europe was riven by war. Imperial Spain slipped into a slow decline, and the English and French took advantage, competing not just in the Old World but in North America and the Caribbean. Hispaniola was considered a great prize. The colony was stagnating under Spanish rule. Both the English and French encouraged piracy against the Spanish, even licensing the pirates as 'privateers.' For security, the Spanish convoys sailed en masse once a year, a system that effectively cut Hispaniola off from trade with the mother country – not only were visiting ships far and few between, but the colonists were banned from trading with non-Spaniards. The colony shrank to the area around Santo Domingo, leaving the rest of the island open for the taking.

The 17th century was the golden age for Caribbean piracy, and the rugged coast and mountainous interior of Hispaniola made it an ideal base for operations. Although a few captains became notorious raiders, most divided their time between hunting the wild cattle and pigs that thrived on the island and plundering for booty. The lack of any governmental control also made the island a haven for runaway slaves.

Isolated pockets of settlers were followed by soldiers. The English attempted to come in through the front door in 1655, but their army of 13,000 soldiers was somehow repelled at the gates of Santo Domingo. The French were more successful, and won territory by demographics, with tobacco farmers grabbing more and more territory until France had formed a de facto colony. The Spanish could do nothing, especially as France was beating it on the battlefields of Europe. At the close of the 17th century, Paris had managed to grab the western two-thirds of Hispaniola, christening them the colony of St-Domingue.

First published in 1724 (and still in print!), *A General History of the Robberies and Murders of the Most Notorious Pirates*, by Charles Johnson, is full of gripping period details on this swashbuckling era.

1510	1586	1605
King Ferdinand of Spain issues the first royal charter to import slaves to Hispaniola. Demand booms, to supplement the Taíno workforce, which is rapidly crashing due to hunger, overwork and introduced European diseases.	Following the outbreak of war between England and Spain, Sir Francis Drake leads a devastating naval raid against Santo Domingo, leaving the city virtually razed.	Spain sends its army to relocate most of its colonists to Santo Domingo city by force of arms, to prevent their contraband trade with foreign merchants, effectively abandoning its claim to the west of Hispaniola.

ÎLE DE LA TORTUE – A REAL PIRATE'S ISLAND

When Captain Jack Sparrow (Johnny Depp) needs safe harbor in the film *Pirates of the Caribbean* he sets sail for the port of Tortuga. In the mid-17th century, so did a lot of other freebooters. Tortuga is the Spanish name for Île de la Tortue, named for its resemblance to a sea turtle. French settlers, who found it rich in timber and wild cattle, first made the island their home, and sold meat and hides to passing traders. From the 1620s, the settlers began supplementing their income by piracy and were christened 'buccaneers,' from the *boucan* grills they used to smoke the meat that they sold.

The French, then at war with Spain, welcomed the redistribution of wealth from Spanish galleons, and appointed a governor who strengthened the island's defenses against Spanish reprisals. He oversaw a peculiarly democratic attempt at creating a society, with loot shared out equitably, compensation paid to injured buccaneers and, due to a shortage of women, same-sex marriages with rights of inheritance.

The buccaneer experiment was relatively short-lived. It reached its peak in the 1660s, but as the French increased their stake on Hispaniola, raids began to be suppressed. A later governor imported prostitutes for the buccaneers, who eventually married and settled down, turning to growing sugar and tobacco. Those that couldn't give up the Jolly Roger moved to Petit-Goâve in southern St-Domingue, and Port Royal in Jamaica. Ironically, present-day Île de la Tortue is an important smuggling station for drugs heading from Colombia to the USA, showing that the lure of contraband is yet to fully disappear from the island.

BLOOD, SUGAR & SLAVES

Where the Spanish had allowed Hispaniola to turn into a backwater, within a hundred years the French had made St-Domingue the richest colony in the world. They key to their success was sugar. Even before the Industrial Revolution, St-Domingue was a model of industrial factory production, but rather than rely on technology, the boom was powered by a bloodier motor altogether: slavery.

The European taste for sugar had been growing steadily for years, and at the start of the 18th century the colonial powers turned much of the Caribbean over to its production. St-Domingue and British Jamaica were the lead producers, although the French colony managed to diversify its economy to include other important cash crops such as coffee and indigo. Molasses, a by-product of sugar production, was turned into cheap rum for export.

The fertile lowlands of northern St-Domingue were soon turned over to sugar plantations, centred on the port of Cap Français (modern Cap-Haïtien). Plantations were both farm and factory, huge fields of sugarcane with a mill and refining house at their heart. Surrounding quarters consisted of the planter's house, workshops, food crops and slave quarters.

Life was harsh for the slaves. From clearing the land to planting, weeding and harvesting, sugar cultivation was hard, labor-intensive work. Field slaves

When cheap French rum from St-Domingue flooded the market in the American colonies, the British government passed the *Sugar Act* (1764), another form of taxation without representation that helped fuel the American Revolution.

1640s	1640–70	1655
The sugar plantation system is introduced to the West Indies. Highly profitable and labor-intensive, it causes a massive increase in demand for slaves from Africa. France establishes a formal claim on Hispaniola.	Tortuga (Île de la Tortue) becomes a major base for Caribbean piracy. Nominally ruled by a French governor, its buccaneers effectively form an independent republic, plundering Spanish ships for treasure.	An English military expedition is dispatched by Oliver Cromwell to conquer Santo Domingo. Although beaten back, the navy saves face by managing to grab Jamaica as a permanent English foothold in the Caribbean.

THE ATLANTIC SLAVE TRADE

When the Portuguese first rounded the coast of Africa in the 1450s, they were astounded by the wealth of the continent. Gold was a driving force in their early interactions with Africa, but this was swiftly overtaken by a trade in slaves. The settlement of the Americas and development of the sugar industry turned this into an international money machine, mining Africa for its human resources.

The Atlantic slave trade was dubbed 'the triangular trade.' European merchants sailed to Africa with goods to exchange for slaves. From Senegal to Mozambique, domestic slavery was already an established part of most African societies. The demand for trade goods – horses, firearms and gunpowder being the most sought after – turned African states into asset-strippers for the Europeans, sucking in slaves in insatiable numbers.

Traders packed hundreds of captives – often shackled in pairs by the wrist and leg – into the bowels of their ships. Around one in eight died from dysentery and scurvy during the passage, which lasted two to three months. The slaves were sold for sugar, which was then exported back to Europe – the third profitable leg of the trade.

The Portuguese and the British were the most avid slave traders, followed by the French and Dutch. Lisbon, Liverpool, Bristol, Nantes, Marseilles and Bordeaux all boomed as a result of the trade. Some African kingdoms (such as Benin) also became rich, but the majority of societies were impoverished by the repeated harvest of their most economically productive members. During the lifetime of the trade, around 12 million slaves were brought to the Americas. Such was the reach of the trade's tentacles, slaves were often from tribes living 1000 miles from African slave ports. But few records were kept regarding the origin of the Africans brought to Hispaniola or nearby islands, and it remains almost impossible to trace the exact origins of most present-day African-Caribbeans.

worked in gangs, with even children required to work. Ten- and 12-hour days were the norm, and although Sunday was a rest day, slaves used any spare time they had to grow their own food – rations provided by owners were usually minimal. Huts were squalid, and clothes were provided by giving the slaves a bolt of cloth once a year. Punishments for stepping out of line were governed by the bloody *Code Noir*. Owners, who knew well they were outnumbered by the vast slave population, were never slow to apply the whip.

Mortality rates were high, as the sugar plantations consumed ever-increasing numbers of slaves. In non-sugar-producing slave countries (such as the USA), slave numbers increased due in great part due to birthrates. But the brutal conditions endured by sugar slaves meant that birthrates were low, and there was a constant decline in numbers that could only be met by importing more African captives. It's estimated that around one in five slaves (one in three in some areas) died within three years of arrival on a sugar plantation.

Slaves that lived in towns, such as the new colonial capital of Port-au-Prince, fared better. Wealthy planters ran extravagant numbers of servants,

The Musée Colonial Ogier-Fombrun near Port-au-Prince in Haiti (p314), built on an old sugar plantation, gives an insight into the harsh realities of sugar production.

1697	**1743**	**1749**
The Treaty of Ryswick settles the nine-year pan-European War of the Grand Alliance. As a result, Hispaniola's colonial borders are finally settled, dividing the island into Spanish Santa Domingo and French St-Domingue.	François Toussaint Breda is born into slavery near Cap Français. As Toussaint Louverture he becomes a key figure leading the Haitian Revolution, although he himself never lives to see full independence.	Port-au-Prince is founded by French governor Charles Burnier. Its wide bay and central location make it the ideal new candidate for the capital of increasingly prosperous St-Domingue.

while even poor whites kept a slave if they could afford it. Many slaves were highly skilled, but even those working as dockhands and builders were glad to be away from the sickly sweet aroma of the sugar fields.

PATHS TO INDEPENDENCE

If you were a white planter in St-Domingue in 1789, life was good. Around half the world's sugar and coffee came from the colony. The produce of 8000 plantations was providing 40% of France's foreign trade. More economically productive than even Britain's North American colonies, it was the envy of the European powers. Around 40,000 whites lorded it over half a million slaves, although there was an increasing number of free blacks and mulattoes (mixed race) who were allowed to own property but were forbidden many political and legal rights. By contrast, Spanish Santo Domingo had fared badly. Years of neglect had seen it miss out on the sugar rush (Spanish investors had preferred to put their money into booming Cuba). Its population had increased to around 125,000, but it still relied primarily on cattle ranching for its lifeblood. Slave imports had never been high, as they simply couldn't be afforded, and slaves made up less than one percent of the population.

The African population hadn't always taken placidly to being transported for forced labor. Newly imported captives often refused to work on plantations and small-scale revolts were common (and bloodily suppressed). Slaves regularly absconded and formed bands that sought refuge in the mountainous hinterland between the two colonies. Dubbed 'Maroons,' they set up their own communities to try to re-create the African life they had lost. Others were more ambitious yet. Charismatic Maroon leader François Mackandal set up a network to agitate among plantation slaves and poison the planters.

Mackandal's rebellion was short-lived, but the colonists refused to see that their system was ultimately unsustainable. By the advent of the 19th century, slavery would be swept from the island altogether and both colonies freed from colonial rule. The spark for these momentous events, however, came not from the Caribbean, but the French Revolution that was reshaping the map of Europe. But once again, Hispaniola would play a key role on the world stage.

To follow the histories of the DR and Haiti from the independence struggles to the present day, see p45 and p265 respectively.

The Slave Trade: History of the Atlantic Slave Trade by Hugh Thomas is one of the most impressive available histories of this dark period of human commerce.

In the decade leading up to the Haitian slave rebellion, St-Domingue was importing an average of 29,000 slaves *every year*.

1757	1779	1789
Following years of planning, François Mackandal leads a band of Maroons in open rebellion to gain freedom for the slaves of St-Domingue. Betrayed by a confidante, he is burned at the stake by the French.	Five hundred free black soldiers from St-Domingue fight the British army in Savannah, Georgia during the American War of Independence, including Henri Christophe, Haiti's second post-independence ruler.	Revolutionary fervor sweeps France, with the masses demanding *liberté, égalité* and *fraternité*. Calls for liberation are heard as far as St-Domingue, causing a chain reaction leading to eventual independence for the colonies in Hispaniola.

Hispaniola Environment

THE LAND

If wealth were measured by landscape, the DR and Haiti would be among the richest countries in the Americas. Hispaniola is the second-largest island in the Caribbean, after Cuba, with a landmass of around 76,000 sq km, a dynamic mass of high mountains, fertile valleys, watered plains and an amazing diversity of ecosystems.

The island's geography owes more to the Central American mainland than its mostly flat neighboring islands. The one thing that Hispaniola has in spades is an abundance of mountains, with Haiti even proclaiming itself more mountainous than Switzerland. Primary among mountain ranges is the Cordillera Central that runs from Santo Domingo into Haiti, where it becomes the Massif du Nord, fully encompassing a third of the island's landmass. The Cordillera Central hosts Pico Duarte, the Caribbean's highest mountain, at 3087m, which is so big it causes a rain shadow that makes much of southwest DR so arid.

Hispaniola has eight mountain ranges in total. In the DR these include the Cordillera Septentrional, rising dramatically from the coast near Cabarete, and the Cordillera Orientale, along the southern shoreline of Bahía de Samaná. In Haiti, the southwestern Massif de la Hotte is noted for the rich biodiversity of its cloud forests, with the Massif de la Selle containing some of the country's last remaining pine woodland.

Between the ranges lie a series of lush and fertile valleys. Coffee, rice, bananas and tobacco all thrive here, as well as in the plains around Santo Domingo, Cap-Haïtien and Les Cayes. In comparison, sections of southwest DR and Haiti's Côte des Arcadins are semi-desert and studded with cacti.

The unique landscape of Hispaniola is due to the 90 million year-old movements of the earth's crust. As it slowly ground past North America, the Caribbean Plate cracked and crumpled to form the islands stretching from Cuba to Puerto Rico. Further collisions formed the Lesser Antilles, the coastal mountains of Venezuela and much of Central America. The plate is still moving at 1cm to 2cm per year, and continues to elevate Hispaniola. For example, Haiti was once split from the rest of the island by a strait. When it became connected it left behind the Cul-de-Sac plain and the brackish lakes (once the ocean) of Lac Azueï and the DR's Lago Enriquillo.

The beaches of Hispaniola are justly famous. A combination of white-sand beaches lined with palm trees and deluxe accommodations seems so perfect they are nearly impossible to leave. Adding a touch of the exotic are sea cliffs that create countless hidden beaches. Beneath the ocean's surface, however, there are more surprises. The entire island of Hispaniola sits on top of a shallow underwater platform that extends far offshore and forms the foundation for bountiful coral reefs, multitudes of tiny islands and sheltered banks where, in the northwest DR, humpback whales gather to breed. We're not in the least surprised that when Columbus arrived in Hispaniola he wondered if he hadn't landed in paradise itself.

When British monarch George III asked one of his admirals to describe Hispaniola, he was given a crumpled piece of paper, to demonstrate how mountainous the island was

WILDLIFE

Hispaniola's rich landscape is matched by an equally rich biodiversity. There are over 5600 species of plants and close to 500 vertebrate species on the island, many of these endemic.

HURRICANE ALLEY

Caribbean hurricanes are born 3000km away off the west coast of Africa, where pockets of low pressure draw high winds toward them and Earth's rotation molds them into their familiar counterclockwise swirl. The storms start small but grow in strength as they cross the Atlantic, fed by warm moist air, as they bear down on the Caribbean and the North American eastern shore.

A low-level storm is called a 'tropical disturbance,' which may then grow into a 'tropical depression.' When winds exceed 64km/h, the system is upgraded to a 'tropical storm' and is usually accompanied by heavy rains. The system is called a 'hurricane' when wind speeds exceed 120km/h and intensify around a low-pressure center, the so-called eye of the storm. Hurricane systems can range from 80km in diameter to a devastating 1600km across. They travel at varying speeds, from as little as 10km/h to more than 50km/h.

The strength of a hurricane is rated from one to five. The mildest, Category 1, has winds of at least 120km/h. The strongest and rarest of hurricanes, Category 5, most typically build up in July and August and pack winds that exceed 250km/h. Hurricane Katrina, which devastated New Orleans in 2005, was a Category 5 hurricane.

Hispaniola has often been hit hard by hurricanes. In 1979 Hurricane David killed over a thousand people, while in 1998 the destruction wreaked by Hurricane Georges left around 340,000 people homeless in the two countries. Landslides and flooding are major causes of destruction. In 2007, Hurricane Noel was the deadliest hurricane of the season, arriving in November, well past the traditional hurricane season. Severe flooding, particularly in the DR, killed around 160 people, and knocked out electricity for a third of that country. Haiti got off comparatively lightly, with 400 houses destroyed.

If you're near the coast when a hurricane is approaching, head inland, preferably to a large city where there are modern buildings and emergency services. Large resorts in the DR have sturdy hurricane shelters and evacuation procedures. Stay away from the beach, rivers, lakes and anywhere that mudslides are a risk. Avoid standing near windows, as flying debris and sudden pressure changes can shatter the glass.

The **National Hurricane Center** (www.nhc.noaa.gov), run by the US National Oceanic and Atmospheric Administration, is the place to head for current tropical storm information.

The problems of colonizing an island are clear, with plants heavily reliant on seeds and roots arriving on floating rafts of vegetation, often with animal hitchhikers. Reptiles make the best long-distance voyagers and over 140 species are found on the island, compared to around 60 amphibians and 20 land mammals (only two of which survived the arrival of Europeans). The rest of the country's fauna is made up of a rich variety of birds, marine mammals and bats.

Animals

BIRDS

Over 250 species of bird have been recorded on Hispaniola, including several dozen species found nowhere else in the world. Abundant, colorful species include the white-tailed tropicbird, magnificent frigatebird, roseate spoonbill and greater flamingo, plus unique endemic species such as the Hispaniolan lizard-cuckoo, ashy-faced owl and Hispaniolan emerald hummingbird.

Travelers are most likely to encounter birds on beaches and coastal waterways – specifically herons, egrets, ibis, rails, pelicans and gulls. Some of the best spots for twitchers in the DR are Parque Nacional Jaragua, Parque Nacional Los Haitises, Parque Nacional Monte Cristi and Laguna Limón. In Haiti, binoculars are best pointed at Trou Caïman and Parc National la Visite. More-determined travelers taking the time to wander into some of the rich wildlife areas in the interior of the DR can expect to encounter a

Bird lovers will want A Guide to the Birds of the West Indies by Herbert Raffaele to answer all their ornithological questions.

tremendous variety of forest birds. Depending on the season and habitat, you will find a full range of North American warblers, or local birds like Hispaniolan trogons, woodpeckers, parakeets and parrots. Some of these are common and widespread, while others are highly secretive and require specialized knowledge or a guide to locate.

Favorites among birdwatchers include the DR's national bird – the odd palmchat, which builds large apartment-like nests in which each pair sleeps in its own chamber. The endangered La Selle thrush is a high-altitude species prized by visitors to Haiti.

LAND MAMMALS

The arrival of Europeans, who introduced many disruptive species of their own, proved disastrous for Hispaniola's land mammals. Rats, cats, pigs and mongooses all tore through the local wildlife with disastrous consequences.

Just two native mammal species remain, clinging to survival on scattered pockets throughout Haiti and the DR. These are the hutia, a tree-climbing rodent, and the endemic solenodon, an insectivore resembling a giant shrew. The solenodon is particularly threatened, and both species are nocturnal, making sightings extremely difficult.

MARINE MAMMALS

Hispaniola is world famous for its marine mammals, with manatees and humpback whales the star attractions. Travelers, however, are more likely to see dolphins unless they arrive in the right season or make a special trip to the right habitat.

Manatees feed on the seagrass meadows surrounding Hispaniola, hence their alternative name of 'sea cow' (their closest relative is in fact the elephant). Weighing up to 590kg and reaching 3.7m in length, manatees are shy, docile creatures; Parque Nacional Monte Cristi (p200) is the best place to try to spot them.

Several thousand humpback whales migrate south from frigid arctic waters to breed and calve in the tropical waters of the DR each winter (with their numbers peaking in January and February). The DR is one of the foremost places in the world to view whales, and it is one of few places where you can swim and snorkel (under supervision) with these truly magnificent creatures. Tourist boats make half-day excursions to the Banco de Plata (Silver Banks), located just beyond the Bahía de Samaná, to view the whales close up (p145).

FISH & MARINE LIFE

The shallow coastal waters and coral reefs that surround Hispaniola are home to a tremendous variety of sea life. So many species of tropical fish, crustaceans, sponges and corals can be found here that it takes a specialized field guide to begin to sort them out. Where they remain intact and unfished – such as at Sosúa (p180) and Monte Cristi (p200) – the reefs of the DR are stupendously beautiful. In Haiti, the Zombie Hole of Saint-Marc in the Gulf of Ganâves plunges 200m and is home to reputedly the world's largest seasponge, the Elephant's Ear. Some of the more colorful Caribbean reef fish include fluorescent fairy basslet, queen angelfish, rock beauty and blue tang, but each visitor will quickly find their own favorites.

The warm waters are also home to four species of sea turtle: green, leatherback, hawksbill and loggerhead. As well as encounters you might have while snorkeling, from May to October these turtles can be viewed coming ashore at night to lay their eggs on sandy beaches in places such as Parque Nacional Jaragua (p236) in the DR.

Bats are the only nonendangered, protected species on the island. They eat as many as 2000 mosquitoes a night, helping reduce the transmission of dengue and other mosquito-born diseases.

Most of the humpbacks visiting the DR spend the winter gorging on krill in the feeding grounds of the Gulf of Maine off the US coast – they don't take a bite to eat during their entire Caribbean stay.

An overview of Caribbean coral reefs can be found in the eye-opening *A Guide to the Coral Reefs of the Caribbean*, by Mark Spalding.

REPTILES & AMPHIBIANS

Reptiles were Hispaniola's most successful vertebrate colonists. You can expect to see lots of lizards (geckos in particular) but also keep your eye out for snakes and turtles and even the American crocodile (or caiman), found in sizable numbers in the brackish cross-border lake of the DR's Lago Enriquillo (p240) and Haiti's Lac Azueï (p313). There is also a Hispaniolan boa, its numbers now reduced by mongoose predation. At opposite ends of the spectrum are the Jaragua lizard, which is the world's smallest terrestrial vertebrate (adults measure only 2.8cm), and the massive 10kg rhinoceros iguana. Frogs are the most numerous amphibians. Haiti's Massif de la Hotte is a particular hot spot for frogs, with 13 species endemic to this area alone.

Want to put a name to that frog or gecko? Consult *Amphibians and Reptiles of the West Indies,* by Henderson and Schwartz.

ENDANGERED SPECIES

All of the island's large animals, and many of its smaller ones, could easily be considered as under threat. Environmental degradation is the main cause, and is especially acute in Haiti. Both Haiti and the DR have outlawed practices that endanger protected species, but enforcement is minimal or absent. Except for the creation of national parks, there are few practical steps being taken to protect threatened species, many of which are endemic.

Vertebrate species particularly endangered on Hispaniola include the Caribbean manatee, Caribbean monk seal, Atlantic spotted dolphin, American crocodile, rhinoceros iguana, Hispaniolan ground iguana, sea turtles, three species of freshwater turtle and dozens of bird species.

CONCH

What Dominicans call *lambí* (or *lambi* in Haiti) is known to scientists as *Strombus gigas,* in Taíno as *cohobo* and in English *queen conch* – yet no matter what you call it, this hefty snail-like creature is the largest mollusk in the Caribbean (growing 35cm long and weighing up to 3kg) and is a vital part of the underwater ecosystem and a staple of Hispaniola's cuisine.

Conch (pronounced 'konk') live in shallow waters near coral reefs and are found throughout the Caribbean, as well as along the Mexico, Florida, Bahamas and Bermuda coastlines, and as far south as Brazil. They feed on algae that can asphyxiate coral if not kept in check.

Conch has been an important food source on Hispaniola and throughout the Caribbean for centuries. Archaeologists have uncovered piles of conch shells near ancient settlements, including on Isla Saona and Isla Catalinita in the DR's Parque Nacional del Este. Conch shells were used in tool-making and carved into fine necklaces and other jewelry. Taínos also used ground conch shell as an ingredient for a hallucinogenic powder used in religious ceremonies. Centuries later, blowing the conch became the emblematic call to arms of the Haitian slave rebellion, still commemorated in popular art.

Lambí is found on almost every restaurant menu in both the DR and Haiti; typically it's chopped into small morsels and served in a spicy tomato sauce or with garlic. As a by-product, conch shells are still used in jewelry and other crafts. One out of every 10 thousand conches also forms a pearl, highly prized and ranging from pale pink to fiery red.

Conch take three to five years to mature, and are easily caught, as they prefer clear shallow water. A valuable fishery resource, conch populations have shrunk considerably in most areas of the Caribbean due to over-harvesting and degradation of the seagrass meadows used as conch nurseries. As a result, the Convention on International Trade in Endangered Species of Wild Fauna and Flora (CITES) introduced quota-based export restrictions on conch in 2003, but while the DR (previously the largest exporter in the Caribbean) has implemented these, instability across the border has seen Haiti lagging behind.

Plants

Hispaniola presents a bewildering assortment of plants. In every season there is something flowering, fruiting or filling the air with exotic fragrances, and it makes the place truly magical. Nearly a third of the 5600-odd species are endemic, spread across more than 20 discrete vegetation zones ranging from desert to subtropical forest to mangrove swamp.

Of these vegetation zones, by far the most prevalent is the subtropical forest, which blankets the slopes of many of the DR's valleys and is found throughout the Península de Samaná. This is a majestic landscape, dominated by royal palms with large curving fronds, and native mahogany trees.

True tropical rainforest is rare both because areas receiving enough rainfall are scarce and because the grand trees of this forest type have been extensively logged. Green-leaved throughout the year, these dense humid forests support a wealth of tree ferns, orchids, bromeliads and epiphytes. Examples can still be found in the Vega Real, which is located in the eastern end of the Valle de Cibao, adjacent to the Samaná region.

Above 1830m the habitat gives way to mountain forests characterized by pines and palms, in addition to ferns, bromeliads, heliconias and orchids. Although threatened by coffee plantations and ranching, large tracts still exist in Parques Nacionales Armando Bermúdez and José del Carmen Ramírez (p217) and Haiti's sublime Parc National Macaya (p327).

Thorn and cacti forests abound in the southwest corner of the DR. Parque Nacional Jaragua (p236), the country's largest protected area, consists largely of thorn forest, cacti and agaves, and receives less than 700mm of rain a year. The Massif de la Selle across the border is one of Haiti's few remaining areas of thick pine forest.

Mangrove swamps are a characteristic feature along the coast around the DR's Bahía de Samaná. They're a hugely important wildlife habitat, serving as nurseries for many marine species and nesting grounds for water birds. Mangrove stands also play a critical ecological role by buffering the coast from the erosive power of storms and tides.

> Thirty of the 133 orchid species found in Hispaniola are endemic to the cloud forests of Haiti's Parc National Macaya.

> Living in salt water is a challenge for mangroves, and some species require a healthy dose of fresh water at least once a year in order to survive. Their source? Hurricanes.

NATIONAL PARKS

The DR and Haiti are home to some of the largest and most diverse parks in all the Caribbean, but comparisons between the two countries are striking. The DR has set aside over 10% of its land as *parques nacionales* (national parks) and *reservas científicas* (scientific reserves) and is doing a reasonably good job of protecting these important local resources in the face of external pressures. This is especially important in coastal areas where beach resorts are devouring open spaces like they were candy and destroying fragile coral reefs with huge numbers of tourists in the process. Enforcement has been less effective in the DR's central mountains, where logging and encroachment by farmers continues in many areas.

In Haiti, the state has little power to prevent encroachment into its *parcs nationals* by local populations, where land clearance for farming and charcoal burning are major threats. Only the relative remoteness of Parc National Macaya in the southwest, which hosts Hispaniola's most intact cloud forest, has led to it avoiding the large-scale environmental devastation seen across the rest of the country.

> Introduced from the Indian Ocean, coconut palms have huge leaves divided into narrow segments so they don't tear like cotton sheets in powerful tropical storms.

ENVIRONMENTAL ISSUES

Hispaniola, like all islands in the Caribbean, is ultimately a tiny isolated speck of land with limited space and resources. It has a rapidly growing population and, in the DR, millions of tourists a year, all of whom put

HISPANIOLA'S NATIONAL PARKS

Covering most of the island's ecosystems, the 13 national parks in the DR and Haiti offer outdoor enthusiasts good options for adventure. Further details are given in related chapters.

Dominican Republic

- **Parque Nacional Armando Bermúdez** (p217) This 766-sq-km park in the humid Cordillera Central park is blanketed in pine trees, tree ferns and palm trees, and is home to the hawk-like Hispaniolan trogon.

- **Parque Nacional del Este** (p124) Located in the southeastern part of the country, it consists of dry and subtropical humid forest with caves featuring Taíno petroglyphs, as well as the sandy beaches of Isla Saona: look out for manatees and dolphins off the coast.

- **Parque Nacional Isla Cabritos** (p240) In the southwest, this park is a 24-sq-km island surrounded by the saltwater Lago Enriquillo. It is a refuge for crocodiles, iguanas, scorpions, flamingos, crows and cacti.

- **Parque Nacional Jaragua** (p236) At 1400 sq km, this is the largest park in the DR. It is made up of an arid thorn forest, an extensive marine area and the islands of Beata and Alto Velo. This southwestern park is rich in birdlife, particularly sea and shore birds, and its beaches are nesting grounds for hawksbill turtles.

- **Parque Nacional José del Carmen Ramírez** (p217) This 764-sq-km park is home to the Caribbean's tallest peak – Pico Duarte – and the headwaters of three of the DR's most important rivers: Yaque del Sur, San Juan and Mijo. Although there is occasional frost, the park is considered a subtropical humid mountain forest.

- **Parque Nacional La Isabela** (p198) Located on the north coast, this park was established in the 1990s to protect the ruins of the second European settlement in the New World. An on-site museum, however, contains many objects that were used by the earliest European settlers.

- **Parque Nacional Los Haitises** (p140) Situated on the Bahía de Samaná, this park's lush hills jut out of the ocean and are fringed with mangroves, tawny beaches and several Taíno caves. Bamboo, ferns and bromeliads thrive, along with the Hispaniolan parakeet.

- **Parque Nacional Monte Cristi** (p200) This 530-sq-km park in the extreme northwest contains a subtropical dry forest, coastal lagoons and seven islets. It is home to many seabirds, including great egrets, brown pelicans and yellow-crowned night herons. American crocodiles also inhabit the park's lagoons.

- **Parque Nacional Sierra de Bahoruco** (p239) Located in the southwest, this 800-sq-km park stretches from desert lowlands to 2000m-high tracts of pine. Along with the broad range of plantlife (orchids abound), it's rich in birds, including the endemic white-necked crow and the Hispaniolan parrot.

- **Parque Nacional Submarino La Caleta** (p105) Only 22km from Santo Domingo, this 10-sq-km national park is one of the country's most visited. Containing several healthy coral reefs and two shipwrecks, it is one of the top diving spots in the country.

Haiti

- **Parc National Historique La Citadelle** (p337) An hour from Cap-Haïtien, this small park hosts the imposing mountain fortress of Citadelle la Ferrière, one of the most stupendous historic sites in the Caribbean.

- **Parc National La Visite** (p310) Within easy reach of Port-au-Prince, this mountainous park offers good hiking through pine forests with views to the Caribbean.

- **Parc National Macaya** (p327) In the southwest Massif de la Hotte, this remote and hard-to-access park has Hispaniola's best cloud forest and some of its richest biodiversity.

severe pressure on the land. Water use, damage to marine ecosystems and, most of all, deforestation present the DR and Haiti with acute environmental challenges. Nowhere are these challenges more starkly illustrated than when flying between the two countries. The border cuts the two like a knife, dividing the green forested hills of the DR from the brown slopes of Haiti. Today, just 1% of Haiti's natural forest remains, compared with 28% across the border.

The loss of Haiti's forests is an ongoing chapter in centuries of human activity that have forever altered Hispaniola's landscape. Introduced mammal species from rats and mongooses to pigs have wreaked havoc on native ecosystems, while swaths of land were cleared for commercial plantations such as sugar (even the iconic coconut palm is an import from the Indian Ocean).

The political development of the different countries has greatly influenced their environmental outcomes. Land clearance was an early priority in French St-Domingue, while Spanish Santo Domingo languished as a colonial backwater, and at independence Haiti was economically far more developed than its neighbor. But the isolation it suffered in the 19th century saw it return to a largely peasant economy and increasingly unstable central government, a pattern extending to the present. Clearance for subsistence farming and charcoal burning (still the main form of fuel in Haiti) has wreaked an environmental disaster. Deforestation has led to erosion, decreased soil fertility and lower rainfall. Haiti's exploding population – two-thirds of the island's population in one-third of its space – creates its own pressure to clear further land. In the DR, stronger government, notably under the Trujillo dictatorship, allowed it to avoid Haiti's ruinous path, setting aside pristine land and at times banning commercial logging. Even here, however, parks and reserves remain chronically underfunded and illegal logging and agricultural encroachment remain a problem, especially in the central highlands.

Modern environmental issues stem from both local residents and foreign visitors. Locals, for example, utilize rivers and waterways as garbage and sewage dumps, and many rivers and beaches are strewn with trash and plastic bags. Garbage is even a problem in towns and cities, where trash bins are few and collection sporadic. The problem is especially pressing in Haiti, where even the majority of Port-au-Prince's population lacks adequate sanitation and access to clean water. Everywhere (and particularly in the DR's tourist areas), an insatiable appetite for disposable items results in many of them ending up in overflowing garbage pits or scattered elsewhere in the environment.

Coastal resorts and villages also have a tremendous impact on the very seas that provide their livelihood. Pollution, runoff and other impacts caused by massive developments have destroyed many of the island's foremost reefs. Overfishing and the inadvertent destruction caused by careless humans transform reefs into gray shadows of their former selves.

There is a growing awareness of the need to protect these diminishing resources, although the DR is better placed than Haiti to take action. In the DR – country of the megaresorts – there is an increased emphasis on low-impact tourism and environmental monitoring, while outside funding has helped support critical infrastructure for ecotourism and parks. In Haiti, environmental protection can only go hand in hand with social and economic development, aims toward which the country still continues to take baby steps.

Though written for the eastern Caribbean, Virginia Barlow's *The Nature of the Islands* is an excellent and highly readable introduction to the plants and animals of the entire region.

Dominican Republic

ALFREDO MAIQUEZ

44

DOMINICAN REPUBLIC

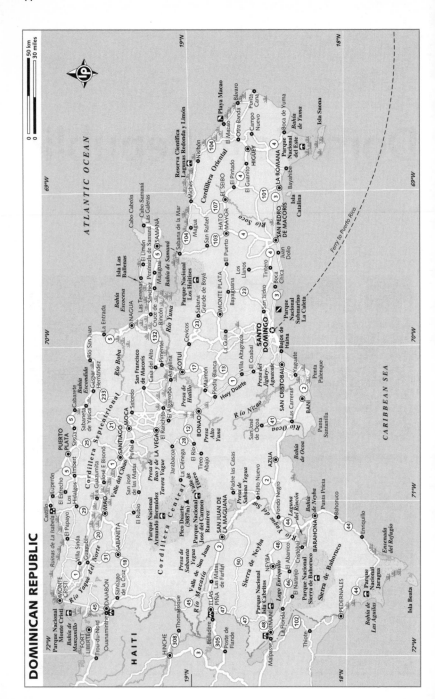

Dominican Republic History

One of the major if not most important strands winding its way through Dominican history, what has shaped its identity and self-understanding more than anything, is its relationship with Haiti, its neighbor sharing the island of Hispaniola.

SEPARATION ANXIETY

While France and Spain's power in Europe waxed and waned, so, too, did their imperialist ambitions. And conflict within the colonies became ways of waging proxy wars against their rivals. So when the enslaved African population of Saint-Domingue rose up in bloody revolt, Spain supported the revolution. However, once the French agreed to abolish slavery, the former slaves turned their attention to liberating the entire island – the Spanish colony had about 60,000 slaves of its own. Lacking an appetite, will and ability to forcefully oppose the uprising, Spain and France haggled over the details, one of which involved the injunction that Spanish colonists abdicate their lands in exchange for ones in Cuba.

In 1801, frustrated by the slow pace of negotiations, François Dominique Toussaint Louverture, a former slave and leader of the rebel forces, marched into Santo Domingo and, without French authority, declared that the abolition of slavery would be enforced throughout the island. At odds with French leaders, who now viewed him as a loose cannon, he was betrayed to the French who sent him in chains to France, where he died of neglect in a dungeon in April 1803. Jean-Jacques Dessalines, who had been one of Toussaint's chief lieutenants, crowned himself emperor of the Republic of Haiti with the clearly stated ambition of uniting Hispaniola under one flag.

For the Spanish colonists in Santo Domingo, this new imperialist threat compelled them to ask Spain to reincorporate them into the empire. But Spain completely bungled its administration of Santo Domingo and on November 30, 1821, the colony declared its independence once again. Colonial leaders intended to join the Republic of Gran Colombia (a country that included present-day Ecuador, Colombia, Panama and Venezuela) but never got the chance – Haiti invaded and finally achieved its goal of a united Hispaniola.

Dominicans chafed under Haitian rule for the next 22 years, and to this day both countries regard the other with disdain and suspicion. Resistance grew until February 27, 1844 – a day celebrated as Dominican Independence Day – when a separatist movement headed by Juan Pablo Duarte captured Santo Domingo in a bloodless coup. The Puerto del Conde in Santo Domingo

The *trinitaria,* a bougainvillea that blooms purple, red and magenta, also refers to Juan Pablo Duarte, Francisco de Rosario Sánchez and Ramón Mella, the three fathers of the republic, and to the secret cells of three that were organized in 1838 to struggle for independence from Haiti.

TIMELINE

1821–22	1844	1849
Colonists of Santo Domingo, known as Spanish Haiti, declare their independence from Spain in November 1821, only to be invaded by Haiti nine weeks later and incorporated into a united Hispaniola.	A coalition of Santo Domingo intellectuals and rebel Haitian soldiers spark a largely bloodless coup and the Dominican Republic declares its independence from Haiti, after 22 years of occupation.	Buenaventura Baez begins the first of his five terms – between 1849 and 1878 – as president of the Dominican Republic. One of his first acts was an attempt to have his country annexed by the USA.

marks the spot where Duarte entered the city. Despite the reversal of fortunes of the two countries in the 20th century, many Dominicans still view Haiti as an aggressive nation with territorial ambitions.

Fearing an invasion and still feeling threatened by Haiti in 1861, the Dominican Republic once again submitted to Spanish rule. But ordinary Dominicans did not support the move and, after four years of armed resistance, succeeded in expelling Spanish troops in what is known as the War of Restoration. (Restauración is a common street name throughout the DR, and there are a number of monuments to the war, including a prominent one in Santiago; see p208.) On March 3, 1865, the Queen of Spain signed a decree annulling the annexation and withdrew her soldiers from the island.

The zenith of the Haiti xenophobia was Trujillo's massacre of tens of thousands of Haitians in 1937. After hearing reports that Haitian peasants were crossing into the Dominican Republic, perhaps to steal cattle, Trujillo ordered all Haitians along the border to be tracked down and executed. Dominican soldiers used a simple test to separate Haitians from Dominicans – they would hold up a string of parsley (*perejil* in Spanish) and ask everyone they encountered to name it. French- and Creole-speaking Haitians could not properly trill the 'r' and were summarily murdered. Beginning on October 3 and lasting for several days, at least 15,000 – and some researchers say as many as 35,000 – Haitians were hacked to death with machetes and their bodies dumped into the ocean. (Guns would have too easily linked the massacre to the government, though there was never any doubt who had ordered it.) Trujillo never openly admitted a massacre had taken place, but in 1938, under international pressure, he and Haitian president Sténio Vicente agreed the Dominican Republic would pay a total of US$750,000 as reparation for Haitians who had been killed (a paltry US$50 per person). The Dominican Republic made an initial payment of US$250,000 but it's unclear if it ever paid the rest. What is clear is that none of the money went to the families of those killed.

POWER FROM THE NORTH

With no strong central government, the newly independent Dominican Republic was a fractured nation, divided up among several dozen caudillos and their militias. From 1865 until 1879 there were more than 50 military uprisings or coups and 21 changes in government. In 1869 after Buenaventura Báez, the leader of a coalition of plantation owners, mahogany exporters and a significant portion of residents of Santo Domingo, was installed as president, he attempted to sell the country to the US for US$150,000. Even though the treaty was signed by Báez and US president Ulysses S Grant, the agreement was defeated in the US Senate.

But the US was to involve itself once again in Dominican affairs, this time at he invitation of General Ulises Heureaux, who stabilized the musical chairs of political and military leadership from 1882 until his assassination in 1899.

Between 1844 and 1916, the Dominican Republic had 40 different governments.

Trujillo nicknames: Hot Balls, the Goat, the Chief, the Butcher.

Trujillo titles: Benefactor of the Fatherland, Founder and Supreme Chief of the Partido Dominicana, Restorer of Financial Independence, First Journalist of the Republic, Doctor Honoris Causa in the Economic Political Sciences

---

1861	1865	1916–24
Dominican president-cum–strong man Pedro Santana Familias, hoping to both defraud Spain and buttress its protection from Haitian military incursions, allows Spain to re-annex the Dominican Republic despite public protests.	Two years after an initial uprising in Santiago, triggered by the Spanish authority's continual erosion of Dominican rights, the Dominican Republic gains independence by defeating Spanish troops in the War of Restoration.	After years of civil wars, the US occupies the Dominican Republic under the pretence of securing debt payments owed by the defaulting Dominican government.

The general, known as Lilí, borrowed heavily from American and European banks to finance the army, infrastructure and the sugar industry. But after a sharp drop-off in world sugar prices, Lilí essentially mortgaged the country to the US-owned and -operated San Domingo Improvement Company just before his death. Because the Dominican government was bankrupt, the US government intervened in 1905 by taking control of the customs houses and guaranteeing repayment of all loans, stopping just short of ratifying President Theodore Roosevelt's plan to establish a protectorate over the DR.

Despite some economic growth, after the assassination of another president in 1911, Dominican politics mostly remained chaotic, corrupt and bloody. In 1916, under the pretext of quelling yet another coup, President Woodrow Wilson sent the marines to the DR – they remained for the next eight years. Though deeply imperialistic, the US occupation did succeed in stabilizing Dominican politics and the economy. Once the DR's strategic value to the US was no longer important, and a new strain of isolationism had entered American discourse, the occupation was ended and the troops sent home.

THE RISE OF THE CAUDILLO

Like the calm before the storm, the years from 1924 to 1930 were in many ways positive, led by a progressive president, Horacio Vásquez, whose administration built major roads and schools and initiated irrigation and sanitation programs. Vásquez did extend his four-year term to six, a constitutionally questionable move that was nevertheless approved by the Congress. When a revolution was proclaimed in Santiago, Rafael Leonidas Trujillo, chief of the former Dominican National Police (renamed the National Army in 1928), ordered in his troops to remain in their barracks, effectively forcing Vásquez and his vice president from office. After a sham election in which he was the sole candidate, Trujillo assumed the presidency. Within weeks, he organized a terrorist band, La 42, which roamed the country, killing everyone who posed any threat to him. An egomaniac of the first degree, he changed the names of various cities – Santo Domingo became Ciudad Trujillo, for example – and lavished support on San Cristobal, the small city west of the capital where he was born; a never-used palace Trujillo had built can still be visited (see p114).

Trujillo ruled the Dominican Republic with an iron fist from 1930 to 1961, lavishing over 21% of the national budget on the ever-expanding *Guardia Nacional* and creating a handful of intelligence agencies dedicated to suppressing any dissent. The torture and murder of political prisoners was a daily event in Trujillo's DR. Two of the more infamous incidents were the kidnapping and murder of a Spanish professor teaching in New York City, who had criticized his regime, and plotting to assassinate the Venezuelan president Rómulo Betancourt. Trujillo, in spite of being part black, was deeply racist and xenophobic; he sought to 'whiten' the Dominican population by

Life in Santo Domingo during the Trujillo regime was regimented: begging was only allowed on Saturdays, laborers were awakened with a siren at 7am while office workers were given an extra hour to sleep in; their siren was at 8am.

After losing power to revolutionaries led by Fidel Castro, Cuban dictator Fulgencio Batista fled to Trujillo City.

1930

After six years of relatively stable government, Rafael Trujillo, the chief of the Dominican National Police, declares himself president after an election in which he was the sole candidate.

1937

Perhaps the culmination of his xenophobia, paranoia, racism and tyranny, Dictator Rafael Trujillo orders the extermination of Haitians along the DR–Haiti border; from 15,000 to 20,000 are killed in a matter of days.

1945

Minerva Bernardino, the Dominican representative to the UN Charter in San Francisco and one of only four women present at the signing, would later be appointed to represent the country at the UN.

increasing European immigration and placing quotas on the number of Haitians allowed in the country. In 1937 he ordered the massacre of tens of thousands of Haitians living along the border.

During these years, Trujillo used his government to amass a personal fortune by establishing monopolies that he and his wife controlled. By 1934 he was the richest man on the island. Today there are many Dominicans who remember Trujillo's rule with a certain amount of fondness and nostalgia, in part because Trujillo did develop the economy. Factories were opened, a number of grandiose infrastructure and public works projects were carried out, bridges and highways were built, and peasants were given state land to cultivate.

In honor of the Mirabal sisters, Minerva, Paria and Maria Teresa, activists who were murdered by Trujillo's agents, the UN declared November 25, the day of their death, International Day for the Elimination of Violence Against Women.

FALSE STARTS

When Trujillo was assassinated by a group of Dominican dissidents with the help of the CIA on May 30, 1961, some hoped that the country would turn a corner. The promise of change however was short lived. Puppet President Joaquín Balaguer, merely a figurehead used by Trujillo, officially assumed the office – he did rename the capital Santo Domingo. After a groundswell of unrest and at the insistence of the USA, a seven-member Council of State, which included two of the men who'd taken part in Trujillo's deadly ambush, was to guide the country until elections were held in December 1962. The first free elections in many years in the DR was won by the scholar-poet Juan Bosch Gaviño.

The Dominican Republic: A National History by Frank Moya Pons is the most comprehensive book on the Dominican Republic's history.

Nine months later, after introducing liberal policies including the redistribution of land, the creation of a new constitution and guaranteeing civil and individual rights, Bosch was deposed by yet another military coup in September 1963. Wealthy landowners to whom democracy was a threat and a group of military leaders led by Generals Elías Wessin y Wessin and Antonio Imbert Barreras installed Donald Reid Cabral, a prominent businessman, as president. Bosch fled into exile but his supporters, calling themselves the Constitutionalists, took to the streets and seized the National Palace. Santo Domingo saw the stirrings of a civil war; the military launched tank assaults and bombing runs against civilian protesters.

Why the Cocks Fight by Michele Wucker examines Dominican-Haitian relations through the metaphor of cockfighting.

The fighting continued until the USA intervened yet again. This time the Johnson administration, after losing Cuba, feared a left-wing or communist takeover of the Dominican Republic despite the fact that Bosch wasn't a communist and papers later revealed US intelligence had identified a grand total of 54 individuals that were part of the movement fighting the military junta. The official reason was that the US could no longer guarantee the safety of its nationals and so over 500 marines landed in Santo Domingo on April 27, 1965. A week later and only 40 years since the previous occupation, 14,000 American military personnel were stationed in the Dominican Republic.

1961	1962–63	1965
Despite the support he has received over the years from the US as a staunch anticommunist ally, Rafael Trujillo is assassinated by a group of CIA-trained Dominican dissidents.	In the first democratic election in nearly 40 years, Juan Bosch, the leader of the left-leaning Dominican Revolutionary Party, is elected president and subsequently removed in a coup orchestrated by a three-person junta.	In April Lyndon Johnson sends almost 23,000 US Army and Marines to invade the Dominican Republic, ostensibly to prevent a civil war. The troops remain until October 1966.

AN UNLIKELY MAN OF LETTERS

Balaguer was a writer as well as a strong-man ruler. He published over 50 works of writing, from poetry to biographies to criticism and one novel. Maybe his most infamous work was his auto-biography *Memorias de un Cortesano de la Era de Trujillo* (Memoirs of a Courtesan in the Era of Trujillo; 1988). In it he includes a blank page, which refers to the murder of outspoken Dominican journalist Orlando Martinez Howley in 1975. Balaguer apparently meant the page as a memorial to Howley and assigned someone to reveal the details of the assassination – Balaguer denied he gave the orders – after his death. He died in 2002 and no one has come forward.

CAUDILLO REDUX

Elections were held in July 1966 – Bosch, the benevolent reformer against Balaguer, the Trujillo throwback. Balaguer won handily, in part because many voters feared a Bosch victory would lead to civil war since the right couldn't be expected to accept the results. Bosch would go on to contest elections in 1978, 1982, 1986, 1990 and 1994, always losing. Balaguer, meanwhile, would outlast every Latin American ruler except Fidel Castro. Not the typical authoritarian dictator, Balaguer was a writer and poet – in one book he argues against interracial marriage – who lived in the servant's quarters of his female-dominated home.

Taking a page from Trujillo's playbook, Balaguer curtailed opposition through bribes and intimidation and went on to win reelection in 1970 and 1974. Despite economic growth, in part fueled by investment and aid from the USA, who saw Balaguer as a staunch anticommunist ally, Balaguer lost the 1978 election to a wealthy cattle rancher named Silvestre Antonio Guzmán. The transfer of power wouldn't come easily, however; Balaguer ordered troops to destroy ballot boxes and declared himself the victor, standing down only after US president Jimmy Carter refused to recognize his victory.

As a result of plunging sugar prices and rising oil costs, the Dominican economy came to a standstill under Guzmán's corrupt administration; he committed suicide shortly after leaving office in 1982. His successor, Salvador Jorge Blanco, adhered to a fiscal austerity plan, measures that were far from popular with many ordinary Dominicans, but the economy slowly picked up and inflation was brought under control. But old dictators don't go easily and Balaguer, 80 years old and blind with glaucoma, returned to power, defeating Guzmán in the 1986 election.

For the next eight years Balaguer set about reversing every positive economic reform of the Blanco program; the result was five-fold devaluing of the Dominican peso and soaring annual inflation rates. With little chance of prospering at home, almost 900,000 Dominicans, or 12% of the country's population, had moved to New York by 1990. After rigging the 1990 and 1994 elections, the military had grown weary of Balaguer's rule and he agreed

The Dictator Next Door: The Good Neighbor Policy and the Trujillo Regime in the Dominican Republic, 1930-1945 by Eric Paul Roorda details the compromises the US government made with Trujillo's regime and its complicity in its survival.

The website of the US Library of Congress (http://lcweb2.loc .gov/frd/cs/dotoc.html) has in-depth historical, political and economic information about the DR that dates until 1989, as well as articles (somewhat dated but still useful for background) on its economy, society and environment.

1982	1986	1996
Distraught over revelations of financial corruption and improprieties, incumbent President Silvestre Antonio Guzman Fernandez commits suicide, with just over a month left in his term of office.	After an eight-year hiatus from power, Joaquín Balaguer, 80 years old and blind, is elected to his fifth term as president despite his previous administration's notorious corruption and dismal human rights record.	After massive election fraud and widespread national and international pressure, Balaguer agrees to step down after two years and Leonel Fernández, a 42-year-old lawyer who grew up in New York City, is elected president.

to cut his last term short, hold elections and, most importantly, not be a candidate. But it wouldn't be his last campaign – he would run once more at the age of 92, winning 23% of the vote in the 2000 presidential election. Thousands would mourn his death two years later, despite the fact that he prolonged the Trujillo-style dictatorship for decades. His most lasting legacy may be the Faro a Colón (see p86), an enormously expensive monument to the discovery of the Americas that drained Santo Domingo of electricity whenever the lighthouse was turned on.

The Last Playboy: The High Life of Porfirio Rubirosa by Shawn Levy tells the life story of the DR's most famous womanizer and Trujillo intimate.

BREAKING WITH THE PAST

The Dominican people signaled their desire for change in electing Leonel Fernández, a 42-year-old lawyer who grew up in New York City, as president in the 1996 presidential election; he edged out three-time candidate José Francisco Peña Gómez in a runoff. But would too much change come too quickly? Shocking the nation, Fernández forcibly retired two dozen generals, encouraged his defense minister to submit to questioning by the civilian attorney general and fired the defense minister for insubordination – all in a single week. In the four years of his presidency, he presided over strong economic growth and privatization, and lowered inflation, unemployment and illiteracy – endemic corruption, however, remained pervasive.

Hipólito Mejía, a former tobacco farmer, succeeded Fernández in 2000 and immediately cut spending and increased fuel prices, not exactly the platform he ran on. The faltering US economy and September 11 attacks ate into Dominican exports, as well as cash remittances and foreign tourism. Corruption scandals involving civil service, unchecked spending, electricity shortages and several bank failures, which cost the government in the form of huge bailouts for depositors, all spelled doom for Mejía's reelection chances.

Check http://lanic.utexas .edu/la/ca/dr for detailed information about past and current Dominican leaders and politicians as well as basic economic information.

Familiar faces reappear again and again in Dominican politics and Fernández returned to the national stage by handily defeating Mejía in the 2004 presidential elections. Though he's widely considered competent and even forward thinking, it's not uncommon to hear people talk about him rather unenthusiastically as a typical politician beholden to special interests. The more cynical observers claim that the Fernández administration is allied with corrupt business and government officials that perpetuate a patronage system different from Trujillo's rule in name only. In May 2008, despite the challenges like the faltering US economy, the devastation wrought by Tropical Storm Noel, the threat of avian flu and continued tension with Haiti, Fernández was reelected for another presidential term.

An excellent website www.hispaniola.com has historical information and up-to-date travel listings.

2003–04	2007	2008
A growing financial crisis sparks widespread public unrest and protests, including a general strike in which several people are killed and scores injured by police.	Tropical Storm Noel devastates much of the country, destroying roads and bridges, stranding communities for weeks and killing over 120 people. The government's response is questioned.	In May Leonel Fernández convincingly wins reelection to his third presidential term; a 2002 constitutional amendment allows him to again run for office.

Dominican Republic Culture

THE NATIONAL PSYCHE

History is alive and well in the Dominican Republic. With a past filled by strong-man dictators and corrupt politicians, the average Dominican approaches the present with a healthy skepticism – why should things change now? Whether it's the Santo Domingo taxi driver's outspoken disbelief that the metro will ever function or the local fisherfolks' acceptance that the new resort marina is going to take away their livelihood, Dominicans have learned to live through hardships. What is extraordinary to the traveler is that despite this, there's a general equanimity, or at the very least an ability to look on the bright side of things. Sure, people complain, they know unfairness and exploitation when they see it, but on the whole they're able to appreciate the good things: family, togetherness, music and laughter. It's not a cliché to say that Dominicans are willing to hope for the best and expect the worst – with a fortitude and patience that isn't common.

In May 2008 President Leonel Fernández won reelection for a second consecutive term (his third in total) despite a challenge from Miguel Vargas Maldonado of the Dominican Revolutionary Party, amongst other opposition candidates. Fernández, widely considered competent, if not especially courageous or willing to disrupt the ensconced patronage system that rewards established elite politicians and businesspeople at the expense of the general welfare (not an uncommon complaint the world over), doesn't elicit strong passions. In general, he's seen as being better than the alternative.

Fernández won without having to face a runoff, despite mounting criticism in late 2007. This included questions about the logic of spending US$700 million on Santo Domingo's subway system (see p103), rising gas prices, the fact that the DR still has one of the highest rates of income inequality in Latin America and the government's less than stellar response to the devastation wrought by Tropical Storm Noel in late October 2007 – all signs of Dominicans' comfort with the status quo.

The impact of Noel (Tropical Storm Olga in December 2007 only exacerbated the damage) is proving to be a particularly complicated and demanding challenge: over 66,000 people were displaced from their homes and around 100 communities were completely isolated, some for over two weeks, because of damaged roads and bridges and massive layoffs in the agricultural industry after crop production took a major hit.

So while over three million people, mostly foreign tourists, visited the country in 2007, more than any other island in the Caribbean, Dominicans continue to migrate in the other direction, seeking better lives abroad, mostly in the US. In 2006 the United States Coast Guard intercepted more than 1300 Dominicans attempting the crossing from the Mona passage to Puerto Rico; in the last several years alone dozens have lost their lives. The DR has also become a major transshipment hub for drugs; hundreds of flights and an even larger number of boats arrive yearly on the DR's shores, transporting mostly cocaine from elsewhere in South America, most notably Columbia, on its way to the US and Europe.

History in the DR can be foreshortened like an accordion to suit political arguments and buttress opinions. Some Dominicans still refer angrily to the Haitian occupation of their country over 160 years ago and many poor

The Devil Behind the Mirror: Globalization and Politics in the Dominican Republic by Stephen Gregory investigates the realities of the impact of global culture and capital on ordinary lives in the Dominican Republic, especially the towns of Boca Chica and Andrés.

Dominicans accuse Haitians of stealing jobs that are rightfully theirs. Like roommates with different lifestyles that share a too small space, Dominicans chafe when Haiti is in the news, looking to the past to explain current conflicts. Haitians are typically blamed for overburdened schools, insufficient health care and rising crime rates, especially guns, drugs and prostitution. If the country could just solve the 'Haiti problem' things would work out is not an unusual sentiment to hear. By the end of 2007 there were 200 UN soldiers, mostly from other Caribbean countries, to help buttress the DR army's attempts to stop the flow of drugs and arms across the Haitian border. In early 2008 there were increased tensions along the border over accusations of cattle rustling and reprisals, and Dominican chickens being turned away because of fears over avian flu.

Generally an accepting and welcoming culture, Dominicans' negative attitudes toward Haitian immigration have only become more pronounced as the country has received more and more international criticism over its treatment of the nearly one million Haitians in the DR. Ironically and sometimes tragically, both peoples tend to have more in common than not; both are from primarily poor countries with weak political legacies and share an origin story, not to mention an island. However, the average income in the DR is six times that of Haiti's and so Haitians risk losing all legal and civil rights, not to mention enduring terribly poor living conditions and the threat of violence, to earn more money working on the vast sugar plantations in the DR. Haitians have few legal protections; in 2005 the Dominican Supreme Court ruled that the children of visitors 'in transit' were not afforded citizenship. This ruling defines illegal immigrants, which virtually all Haitian workers are, as 'in transit', meaning that even those Haitians who were born in the DR and have lived their entire lives in the DR are denied citizenship.

Dominicans question the perspective of foreigners who focus exclusively on the plight of Haitians rather than on the welfare of poor Dominicans. And government officials are quick to claim that 30% of the DR's health-care budget goes toward caring for Haitians, even though they make up around 11% of the population; the DR provides jobs and income for Haitians, something the international community does not do; foreigners lecturing them about human rights abuses ignore the poor records of their own home countries; and finally that the DR has few resources to deal with border issues, let alone other pressing problems faced by all Dominicans. Nevertheless, in 2006 the government pledged to improve the living conditions on the *bateyes* (communities of Haitian sugarcane workers) and to provide labor contracts with a guaranteed minimum wage.

> *The Sugar Babies: The Plight of the Children of Agricultural Workers in the Sugar Industry of the Dominican Republic*, released in 2007, is a documentary depicting the plight of Haitian sugar-cane workers in the *bateyes* (communities of Haitian sugarcane workers) of the Dominican Republic.

LIFESTYLE

Like any country, it's difficult to generalize about Dominicans' lifestyles. That said, there is a certain amount of cohesiveness and continuity experienced from one part of the country to the other. The real differences, unsurprisingly, are in terms of income and gender. After all, one out of eight Dominicans in 2006 lacked electricity, while the remainder experience regular blackouts. Nearly 40% of the population lives below the poverty line, the average per capita income is US$2850, the unemployment rate is over 15% and the wealthiest 10% control 40% of the country's total economy.

> Two companies are responsible for 85% of the DR's total sugar production, in addition to numerous other investments. Romana is owned by the Fanjuls who also own Casa de Campo resort; Vicini also has partial ownership in two newspapers, *El Caribe* and *Diario Libre*.

Women make up less than one-third of the DR's paid workforce and the vast majority are employed as domestic workers or low-level office workers. Almost 30% of women are single mothers, and make up one of the largest groups of people living in poverty. Women are poorly represented in government and politics as well, making up just 10% to 15% of legislator and top- or middle-level cabinet officer positions.

Almost a quarter of Dominicans live in Santo Domingo, which is without question the country's political, economic and social center. But beyond the capital, much of the DR is distinctly rural, and a large percentage of Dominicans still rely on agriculture for their livelihood (or by fishing along the coast). This is evident if you drive into the DR's vast fertile interior, where you'll see cows and horses grazing alongside the roads, tractors plowing large fields, and trucks and burros loaded down with produce.

Dominican families, typical of the stereotypical Latin American kind, are large and very close knit. Children are expected to stay close to home and help care for their parents as they grow older. That so many young Dominicans go to the US creates a unique stress in their families. While Americans and Europeans commonly leave home to live and work in another city, this is still troubling for many Dominicans, especially for the older generation – it's no surprise that Dominicans living abroad send so much money home.

The DR is a Catholic country, though not to the degree practiced in other Latin American countries – the churches are well maintained but often empty – and Dominicans have a liberal attitude toward premarital and recreational sex. This does not extend to homosexuality though, which is still fairly taboo. Machismo is strong here but, like in merengue dancing, many Dominicans experience the traditional roles of men and women as more complementary than confrontational, as naturally separate spheres of influence. And the physical, mainly in the way a woman looks or dances, is appreciated unashamedly by both sexes.

Azucar! The Story of Sugar by Alan Cambeira is a fascinating novel that portrays the human toll of sugar production in the DR. Though the story is fictional, much of the information, descriptions and events are based on real events and detailed research by the author.

ECONOMY

The Dominican Republic earns more tourism dollars than any other country in Latin America – except Mexico and Brazil. Unsurprisingly, the service industry, primarily tourism but the newly exploding free-trade zone areas as well, is the largest employer and earner in the DR. Another major revenue source are remittances from Dominicans living abroad – more than one million people, principally in New York and the eastern US, collectively send over US$1 billion to the DR yearly. Mining operations – gold, silver, ferronickel and bauxite – are another big chunk of GDP. In fact, in early 2008 a Canadian mining company made the largest investment in the country's history, agreeing to a US$2.6 billion fee to reopen Pueblo Viejo, a formerly government-owned gold mine in the central DR. Agriculture, once the largest source of export dollars, is still significant. Sugar, coffee, cocoa, tobacco and tropical fruits are the primary crops.

More than 20,000 Haitians cross into the Dominican Republic yearly to work on the sugar plantations.

All Dominican sugar that is exported from the country is sold to the US.

Despite strong growth in many of these sectors, it would be difficult to call the Dominican economy healthy (for economic statistics, see opposite), but President Leonel Fernández's 2008 reelection can be interpreted as a vote of confidence on his administration's ability to steward the economy through a global economic downturn. With 72% of exports sold to the US, the US's own faltering economy, the devaluation of the dollar, rising oil prices and the impact of Tropical Storm Noel, the challenges ahead are significant.

POPULATION

The Dominican Republic has roughly 9.5 million residents. A little under three-quarters are of mixed ethnic or racial ancestry. Those who are of mixed European and African descent, the most common, are referred to as Indio, although this term popularized under the Trujillo administration intentionally elides their African heritage. The next largest group are *mestizo* or people of mixed European and indigenous descent. A minority of Dominicans are considered full Euro-Caucasian (16%) or of African (11%) ancestry.

There is a sprinkling of other ethnic groups, including Chinese, Japanese, Arab and Jewish (of mostly European descent), the result of various waves of immigrants. In addition to Spanish colonists and enslaved Africans, groups that have settled here over the centuries include Sephardic Jews from Curaçao, Canary Islanders, Germans, Italians, Cubans, Puerto Ricans, Lebanese, Syrians, Palestinians, Jewish refugees from Germany, Japanese, Hungarians, freed slaves from the US, and Protestant workers from Great Britain, the Netherlands and Denmark. Mainland Chinese came in small numbers in the early 20th century, but by the 1980s Chinese immigrants were the second-fastest-growing immigrant group in the Dominican Republic.

The Tropic of Baseball: Baseball in the Dominican Republic by Rob Ruck gives a comprehensive look at the DR's national obsession, and the impact of Dominican players on the US major leagues.

SPORTS

A number of sports and pastimes are popular in the Dominican Republic, including volleyball, basketball, soccer and horseracing. But two sports – baseball and cockfighting – are far and away the most popular and both have long, rich traditions.

Baseball

Not just the USA's game, *beísbol* is part of the Dominican social and cultural landscape. So much so that ballplayers who have made good in the US major leagues are without doubt the most popular and revered figures in the country. Over 400 Dominicans have played in the major leagues (in 2007 there were 99 Dominicans, around 10% of all major leaguers), including active players like David Ortiz, Moises Alou, Julio Franco, Pedro Martinez, Albert Pujols and most famously Sama Sosa, who is likely one day to be inducted into the Hall of Fame in Cooperstown, New York. Two dozen major league teams have training facilities here.

The documentary *The Republic of Baseball: The Dominican Giants of the American Game* (2006) profiles the careers of the first great Dominican stars of Major League Baseball.

The Dominican professional baseball league's season runs from October to January, and is known as the Liga de Invierno (Winter League; the winner of the DR league competes in the Caribbean World Series against other Latin-American countries). The country has six professional baseball teams: Licey and Escojido, both of Santo Domingo; the Águilas from Santiago; the Estrellas from San Pedro de Macorís; the Gigantes of San Francisco de Macorís; and the Azuqueros from La Romana. Because the US and Dominican seasons don't overlap, many Dominican players in the US major leagues and quite a few non-Dominicans play in the winter league in the DR as well (rookie teams play a second season from June to August). Needless to say, the quality of play is high, but even if you're not a fan of the sport, it's worth checking out a game or two. It's always a fun afternoon or evening. Fans are decked out in their respective team's colors waving pennants and flags, as rabidly partisan as the Yankees–Red Sox rivalry, and dancers in hot pants perform to loud merengue beats on top of the dugouts between innings.

Sugar, a feature film about baseball in the DR, follows the eponymous hero as his fastball takes him from his beloved family and country to the minor leagues in Iowa. Eventually, his alienation leads him to seek out the Dominican community in New York City.

Cockfighting

Cockfighting rings *(galleras)* look like mini sports arenas or ancient coliseums, which is appropriate since Dominicans approach these brutal contests between specially bred roosters as events worthy of the same enthusiasm. There are around 1500 official *galleras* throughout the country, but by far the most prestigious – and safe – is the Coliseo Gallístico Alberto Bonetti Burgos (p99), which regularly hosts international competitions. Gambling on fights is part of the sport, all conducted under a strict honor code. That said, some small-town rings are decidedly seedy and tourists should be alert for trouble.

It's said that fighting roosters first arrived on the island in 1492 with Columbus and that the sport is as much part of the Dominican culture as bullfighting is in Spain, maybe even more so. Perhaps it's no surprise that cockfighting – specifically the roosters' intensity and willingness to fight to the death – would resonate in a country that has endured so much civil strife and outside manipulation. Indeed, the fighting rooster is the symbol of a number of political parties and social organizations. It is an institution with deep roots in Dominican culture, which is why many Dominicans responded with amused outrage when several Dominicans playing in the US baseball major leagues, most prominently Pedro Martínez of the Mets, were the focus of attention and criticism when it came to light that they frequented *galleras* when in the DR. For those reasons, many travelers see cockfighting as a window to Dominican culture. Others cannot reconcile a night at the *gallera* with the concept of responsible tourism. It is impossible to argue that cockfighting is not a form of cruelty to animals – after all, the point is for one animal to kill the other, sometimes slowly and agonizingly, for the sake of entertainment and monetary gain. Both are justifiable points of view.

MEDIA

Unsurprisingly, Santo Domingo is the unrivaled media capital of the country with seven daily papers. Countrywide, there are over 300 radio stations and 42 TV stations. And like many countries, especially ones of such a relatively small size, a handful of large companies with diverse interests have controlling or partial ownership in a number of media outlets, prompting critics to question their independence.

RELIGION

Around 95% of Dominicans profess to be Roman Catholic. For a large majority though, religious practice is limited and formalistic. Few actually attend Mass regularly. As in many Latin American countries, evangelical Protestant Christianity has gained a strong foothold in Dominican culture, attracting adherents with dramatic faith healings and fiery sermons. Many Haitian immigrants and their descendants are Catholic in name and identity, but continue to practice elements of traditional Vodou spiritualism. Such practices are generally done in secret, as the Dominican government, Catholic church and much of the public view Vodou as pagan or even evil.

ARTS
Music & Dance

From the minute you arrive in the DR until the minute you leave, merengue will be coming at you at full volume. At a restaurant, in public buses or taxis – it's there. At the beach or walking down the street – yet more merengue. Merengue is the dance music of the Dominican Republic, and if you attend a dance club here and take a shine to the music, you may want to pick up some cassettes or CDs before leaving the country. There are many merengue bands in the DR; the nation's favorites include Johnny Ventura, Coco Band, Wilfredo Vargas, Milly y Los Vecinos, Fernando Villalona, Joseito Mateo, Rubby Perez, Miriam Cruz, Milly Quezada and, perhaps the biggest name of all, Juan Luis Guerra.

Dominicans dance merengue with passion and flair. It follows a distinctive 2-2 and 2-4 beat pattern typically played with drums, an accordion-like instrument known as a melodeon, and a *güira*, a metal instrument that looks a little like a cheese grater and is scraped using a metal or plastic rod. If you have a chance, go to a nightclub or dance hall where merengue is played. Even if you don't dance – something Dominicans will find very peculiar – you can't help but be impressed by the sheer skill and artfulness of even amateur dancers.

The 2007 documentary *The Price of Sugar* follows Father Christopher Hartley, a passionate advocate of the poor, as he confronts sugar-company authorities, politicians and ordinary Dominicans, pressing them to recognize the humanity of the Haitians who live and work in their midst in utterly deplorable conditions.

The website www.colonialzone-dr.com is not only an online guide to the Zona Colonial in Santo Domingo, but also a good source of information about Dominican art, history, myths, superstitions and language.

Since 1986 merengue and *bachata* superstar Juan Luís Guerra has won almost every major music award possible, including a Grammy, three more Grammy nominations, three Latin Grammys, five Billboard Latin Music Awards and two Premios Soberanos.

THE GÜIRA

The *güira* is a popular musical instrument that is used to infuse a song with a rhythmical rasping sound. It was originally used by Hispaniola's indigenous people – the Taínos – who used dried, hollowed-out gourds and a forked stick to produce music for their *areítos* (ceremonial songs). Today the *güira* has been modernized – but not by much. Instead of using vegetables, the modern *güira* is made of latten brass; it typically looks like a cylindrical cheese grater that is scraped with a long metal pick. The rasping sound is essentially the same – the modern-day instrument just lasts a little longer. The next time you hear a merengue or a *bachata* song, listen carefully – you're sure to hear this centuries-old sound.

Whereas merengue might be viewed as urban music, *bachata* is definitely the nation's 'country' music. This is the music of breaking up, of broken hearts, of one man's love for a woman or one woman's love for a man, of life in the country. The term initially referred to informal backyard parties in rural areas, finally emerging in Santo Domingo shanties. '*Bachata*' was meant as a slight by the urban elite, a reference to the music's supposed unsophistication. Among the big names of *bachata* are Raulín Rodríguez, Antony Santos, Joe Veras, Luis Vargas, Quico Rodríguez and Leo Valdez.

Bachata: A Social History of Dominican Popular Music by Deborah Pacini Hernandez and *Merengue: Dominican Music and Dominican Identity* by Paul Austerlitz are academic examinations of the Dominican Republic's two most important musical contributions and obsessions.

Bachata Roja is a new compilation of classic *bachata* from the early 1960s to late '80s, the pre-electric era when the music was entirely guitar based and drew on a bunch of musical traditions, including Mexican *ranchera*, Puerto Rican *jíbaro*, Cuban bolero, guaracha and *son*. It includes legendary musicians like Edilio Paredes and Augusto Santos.

Salsa, like *bachata*, is heard on many Caribbean islands, and it's very popular in the DR. If you like the music, it may interest you to know that the following individuals and groups enjoy particularly favorable reputations in the DR: Tito Puente, Tito Rojas, Jerry Rivera, Tito Gómez, Grupo Niche, Gilberto Santa Rosa, Mimi Ibara, Marc Anthony and Leonardo Paniagua.

Reggaeton, a mix of American-style hip-hop and Latin rhythms, is increasingly popular; Wisin & Yandel is a well-known reggaeton duo. Other names to look out for are Pavel Nuñez, an established star who's music is a mix between folk and Latin, and Kat DeLuna, a 19-year-old up-and-coming singer, whose music is a hodge-podge of styles and rhythms.

Literature

The Dominican Republic's literary history dates to the Spanish colonial period (1492–1795). It was then that Bartolomé de Las Casas, a Spanish friar, recorded the early history of the Caribbean and pleaded for fair treatment of the Taínos in his famous *Historia de las Indias* (History of the Indies). During the same era Gabriel Téllez, a priest who helped to reorganize the convent of Our Lady of Mercy in Santo Domingo, wrote his impressive *Historia general de la Orden de la Mercéd* (General History of the Order of Mercy).

During the Haitian occupation of Santo Domingo (1822–44), French literary style became prominent, and many Dominican writers who emigrated to other Spanish-speaking countries made names for themselves there. With the first proclamation of independence in 1844, Félix María del Monte created the country's principal poetic form – a short patriotic poem based on local events of the day.

During the late 19th and early 20th centuries, three literary movements occurred in the DR: *indigenismo*, *criollismo* and *postumismo*. *Indigenismo* exposed the brutalities the Taínos experienced at the hands of the Spaniards. *Criollismo* focused on the local people and their customs. And *postumismo* dealt with the repression that Rafael Trujillo's iron-fist leadership brought. Some writers, such as Manuel and Lupo Fernández Rueda, used clever metaphors to protest the regime. Juan Bosch Gaviño, writing from exile, penned numerous stories that openly attacked Trujillo.

Only a few Dominican novels have been translated into English. Viriato Sención's *They Forged the Signature of God,* winner of the DR's 1993 National Fiction award (after realizing that the book was critical of both Trujillo and himself, Balaguer rescinded the prize) and the country's all-time best seller, follows three seminary students suffering oppression at the hands of both the state and the church. Though slightly preachy, it provides another perspective on the Trujillo regime besides the exceptional *Fiesta del Chivo* (*Feast of the Goat*) by the Peruvian novelist Mario Vargas Llosa.

Ten years after publishing the short-story collection *Drown,* Junot Diaz received critical acclaim for his 2007 novel *The Wondrous Life of Oscar Wao,* a stylistically inventive story of a self-professed Dominican nerd in New Jersey and the tragic history of his family in the DR. Less well known than Diaz's novel, but maybe a more devastating picture of the Dominican diaspora's rejection of the conventional American Dream, is Maritza Pérez's *Geographies of Home.* For Spanish readers, other recommended young Dominican authors are Pedro Antonio Valdés (*Bachata del angel caído, Carnaval de Sodoma*), Rita Indiana Hernández (*La estrategia de Chochueca, Papi*) and Aurora Arias (*Inyi's Paradise, Fin del mundo, Emoticons*). *In the Time of the Butterflies* is an award-winning novel by Julia Álvarez about three sisters slain for their part in a plot to overthrow Trujillo. Also by Álvarez is *How the García Girls Lost Their Accents,* describing an emigrant Dominican family in New York. Other well-known contemporary Dominican writers include José Goudy Pratt, Jeannette Miller and Ivan García Guerra.

Death in Paradise by JB Mackinnon is perhaps the best contemporary account of the DR. The author, the nephew of a Canadian priest murdered by agents of the Trujillo government, travels the country, from the barrios of Santo Domingo to rural villages, trying to unravel how and why his uncle was killed.

Painting

The Dominican art scene today is quite healthy, thanks in no small part to dictator Rafael Trujillo. Although his 31 years of authoritarian rule in many ways negated the essence of creative freedom, Trujillo had a warm place in his heart for paintings, and in 1942 he established the Escuela Nacional de Bellas Artes (National School of Fine Arts). Fine Dominican artwork predates the school, but it really wasn't until the institution's doors opened that Dominican art underwent its definitive development.

If the artwork looks distinctly Spanish, it's because the influence is undeniable. During the Spanish Civil War (1936–39), many artists fled Franco's fascist regime to start new lives in the Dominican Republic. Influential artists include Manolo Pascual, José Gausachs, José Vela-Zanetti, Eugenio Fernández Granell and José Fernández Corredor.

The Dominican Republic has also produced many accomplished painters; if you visit any of the art galleries in Santo Domingo (see p99) or Santiago (p207), keep an eye out for paintings by Adriana Billini Gautreau, who is famous for portraits that are rich in expressionist touches; the cubist forms of Jaime Colson emphasizing the social crises of his day; Luis Desangles, considered the forerunner of folklore in Dominican painting; Mariano Eckert, representing the realism of everyday life; Juan Bautista Gómez, whose paintings depict the sensuality of the landscape; and Guillo Pérez, whose works of oxen, carts and canefields convey a poetic vision of life at the sugar mill.

The Eduardo León Jimenes Art Contest in Santiago began in 1964 and is the longest-running privately sponsored art competition in Latin America.

Also well represented is what's known as 'primitive art' – Dominican and Haitian paintings that convey rural Caribbean life with simple and colorful figures and landscapes. These paintings are created by amateur

DOMINICAN CINEMA

The Dominican Republic does not have a strong film industry of its own; only a handful of films made by Dominican directors have reached a wider audience. Two of the more interesting films of the past several years are *Sanky Panky* and *Yunior 2*.

But more than 60 films and TV shows ranging from *Miami Vice* to *The Godfather: Part II* have been shot in full or in part in the DR. Some of the famous river scenes in the 1979 classic *Apocalypse Now* by Francis Ford Coppola were filmed on the Río Chavón near La Romana. Several scenes from Steven Spielberg's 1993 *Jurassic Park* were shot at Salto Jimenoa Uno outside of Jarabacoa. The film, based on a Michael Crichton book about a scientist who extracts blood from a mosquito trapped in amber to clone dinosaurs, is credited with reviving interest in amber and amber jewelry across the world.

painters – some would say skilled craftsmen – who reproduce the same painting hundreds of times. They are sold everywhere there are tourists; you're sure to get an eyeful regardless of the length of your trip.

Architecture

The quality and variety of architecture found in the Dominican Republic has no equal in the Caribbean. In Santo Domingo and in Santiago you can see examples of Cuban Victorian, Caribbean gingerbread and Art Deco; in the Zona Colonial you'll also see plenty of the Gothic, which was popular in Europe during the colonial times. The buildings in Puerto Plata vary between the vernacular Antillean and the pure Victorian, sometimes English, sometimes North American. San Pedro de Macorís has late-Victorian style buildings that were created with concrete (in fact, it was the first city in the DR to use reinforced concrete in its construction). And rural clapboard homes have a charm all of their own: small, square, single story and more colorful than a handful of jelly beans, you'll find yourself slowing down to take a longer look.

Dominican Republic Outdoors

WATER SPORTS

If it involves standing on a board, the Dominican Republic's got it in spades – here you'll find world-class windsurfing, kitesurfing, surfing and wakeboarding. While there's a few scattered spots across the island if you're adventurous, the undisputed water sports capital of the DR is Cabarete (p184), on the North Coast.

WINDSURFING

Cabarete's bay seems almost custom-made for windsurfing, and it's here that the sport is most popular – although you'll also find a small windsurfing school in Las Terrenas (p155). The best time to come is generally in winter, when the wind is strongest – in general, windsurfing requires stronger winds than kitesurfing does.

The beach at Cabarete is lined with outfits small and large, renting windsurf equipment and offering lessons for beginners. Renting a board and sail will cost about US$35/65/300 per hour/day/week. Lessons range from just one hour (US$50) to a complete four-session course (US$200).

Bruce van Sant, the author of the boater's bible to finding the 'thornless path' from Florida through the islands, *The Gentleman's Guide to Passages South*, is something of a legend, and resides in Luperón, on the north coast of the DR.

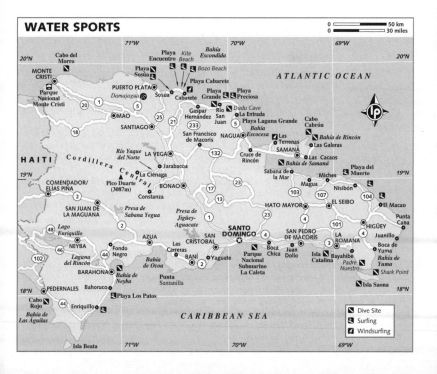

WATER SPORTS

In general, windsurfing is much easier to learn than kitesurfing, meaning you can be out on the water enjoying yourself within a few days' time. Lessons and equipment rentals are also significantly cheaper.

KITESURFING

www.cabaretekiteboard ing.com and www.cabar etewindsurfing.com focus on kitesurfing and windsurfing respectively with listings of schools, rental and retail outfits, plus reports on conditions and upcoming events.

Kitesurfing (also known as kiteboarding) is the sport *du jour*, and involves strapping a board to your feet and a powerful kite to your torso, which propels you through the waves at sometimes breakneck speeds.

The learning curve to get good enough to enjoy kitesurfing is quite steep – as much as a week's worth of lessons to go out solo, and weeks of practice to get comfortable at it. It's also an expensive sport – to make this a regular hobby, you'll end up investing at least US$5000 in lessons and gear. No wonder, then, that around 90% of students who take lessons don't generally advance to become regular kiteboarders.

Kitesurfers perform tricks such as 'kitelooping,' 'back-side handle passes,' 'mobius' and 'slim chance.'

That said, if you've got the time and the money, and you relish a challenge, the DR is one of the world's leading kitesurfing destinations – so much so that the **International Kiteboarding Organization** (www.ikointl.com) has its headquarters in Cabarete.

Unlike surfing or windsurfing, where risk increases with ability – you have to be good to get out to the reefline – kitesurfing is risky from the very beginning. The kite leads, pulled taught by the wind, are diving, swooping knife blades, and it's important you learn from qualified instructors, for your safety and for that of others.

Plenty of kitesurfing schools offer instruction in Cabarete. Most people need a minimum of four days of lessons at a cost of around US$350 to US$450. Schools and instructors vary considerably in personality, so spend some time finding one where you feel comfortable.

There's also a few good kitesurfing spots in Las Terrenas (p155) in Samaná, although the wind is lighter and the water shallower.

SURFING

www.activecabarete.com features listings, information and reviews about sporting activities in and around Cabarete.

Cabarete is also the top spot in the country for surfing, although the intrepid surfer traveling with boardbag in tow could easily explore many of the lesser-visited beaches along both the north and south coast. The best season to surf is December through March, when the region can get waves up to 4m high.

Playa Encuentro (p185), 4km west of Cabarete, has the best waves on the island, where awesome tubes often pound into shore. Other popular places for surfing are Playa Grande (p193) and Playa Preciosa (p194), both near Río San Juan.

There are a number of surf shops in Cabarete and on Playa Encuentro itself where you can rent boards or take surfing lessons. Rentals cost US$25 to US$30 for half a day; courses vary from three-hour introductory sessions

---

SORRY KAYAKERS

The DR holds great potential for both sea and river kayaking, a potential that is largely unfulfilled. While a few scattered shops and hotels around the country can rent you a sea kayak for a paddle along the beach, the activity remains unpopular. Probably the best sea kayaking you'll find is a kayaking tour of the mangroves in Parque Nacional Los Haitises (p140) – a pleasant morning's saltwater paddle. The tour operators in Las Terrenas (p158) can organize this for you.

Gung-ho river kayakers looking for some crazy rapids (and who don't mind traveling with a kayak in their luggage) should head up to Jarabacoa (p213), where Class III, IV and V rapids surge past on the nearby Río Yaque del Norte.

> **WHITE-WATER RAFTING**
>
> The Dominican Republic has the only navigable white-water river in the Caribbean, the Río Yaque del Norte. It's mostly a Class II and III river, with a couple of serious rapids, and the rest consists of fun little holes and rolls. The river winds through hilly countryside and makes for a fun half-day tour. Be aware that the water is frigid – you'll be issued a wetsuit along with your life vest and helmet. While you can make this a day trip from the north coast or Santo Domingo, it's a long journey in a bus – you'll enjoy yourself a great deal more if you spend a couple of nights in Jarabacoa (p213). Trips cost around US$50 per person.

(US$45 to US$50) to a full-blown five-day surf camp (US$200 to US$225 per person). You can also rent surf boards at Playa Grande.

Bodyboarding

For those not keen on hanging ten, the DR's beaches make ideal spots for this gentler pastime. Most resorts and larger hotels have a few bodyboards you can use for free, and on the more remote beaches you can sometimes find a beach-side shack where you can rent a board for a few bucks an hour.

WAKEBOARDING

Water skiing has gone the way of corduroy bellbottoms, and in its place is this new sport – the principle is the same but instead of 'water skis' you use a 'water board,' or 'wakeboard.' The sport has a small but passionate community of enthusiasts, and kiteboarders swear it's a great way to develop your board skills.

There's only one wakeboarding school in the country, at La Boca just outside Cabarete, where there's more than 2km of flat, straight river water to play with. The spot attracts devoted wakeboarders from around the world, and on windless days they are joined by kiteboarders looking to practice their bag of tricks.

DIVING & SNORKELING

The DR is not known as a diving destination, but it has some great places for underwater exploring all the same. The warm Caribbean waters on the southern coast have pretty fields of coral and myriad tropical fish that make for fun easy dives. Two national parks east of Santo Domingo – Parque Nacional Submarino La Caleta (p105) and Parque Nacional del Este (p124) – can be reached through dive shops in Boca Chica (p107) and Bayahibe (p124), respectively. La Caleta is an underwater preserve covering just 10 sq km but is one of the country's most popular dive destinations. The main attraction is the *Hickory,* a 39m salvage ship with an interesting past (see boxed text, p107) that was intentionally sunk in 1994. Parque Nacional del Este has a number of interesting dives, too, including another wreck – a massive 89m cargo ship – and a site ominously called Shark Point (p125).

The DR's north coast provides a very different diving experience. Facing the Atlantic, the water there is cooler and somewhat less transparent, but the underwater terrain is much more varied, making for challenging dives and unique profiles. Sosúa (p178) is the dive capital here, and from where excursions can be organized to all points along the coast. Las Galeras (p150) also has a few small dive shops.

Other off-the-beaten-track options are two diveable freshwater caves – Dudu Cave, near Río San Juan, and Padre Nuestro, near Bayahibe. Dudu, with two openings, three different tunnels and a spacious stalactite-filled chamber,

Divers exploring the waters near the Península de Samaná can sometimes hear humpback whales singing.

RESPONSIBLE DIVING

- Never use anchors on the reef and take care not to ground boats on coral.

- Avoid touching or standing on living marine organisms or dragging equipment across the reef. Polyps can be damaged by even the gentlest contact. If you must hold on to the reef, only touch exposed rock or dead coral.

- Be conscious of your fins. Even without contact, the surge from fin strokes near the reef can damage delicate organisms. Take care not to kick up clouds of sand, which can smother organisms.

- Practice and maintain proper buoyancy control. Major damage can be done by divers descending too fast and colliding with the reef.

- Take great care in underwater caves. Spend as little time within them as possible, as your air bubbles may be caught within the roof and thereby leave organisms high and dry. Take turns to inspect the interior of a small cave.

- Resist the temptation to collect or buy corals or shells or to loot marine archaeological sites (mainly shipwrecks).

- Ensure that you take home all your rubbish and any litter you may find as well. Plastics in particular are a serious threat to marine life.

- Do not feed fish.

- Minimize your disturbance of marine animals. *Never* ride on the backs of turtles.

is one of the most memorable cave dives in the Caribbean (although dive shops will want to see an Advanced Diver certificate, or at least 20 logged dives in order to take you out here). Located within the Parque Nacional del Este, Padre Nuestro is a challenging 290m tunnel that should be attempted only by trained cave divers. With the exception of the cave dives, most of the sites mentioned here also make for excellent snorkeling.

Dive prices vary from place to place, but average US$30 to US$40 for one tank, plus US$5 to US$10 for equipment rental (if you need it). Most people buy multidive packages, which can bring the per-dive price down to around US$25. You must have an Open Water certificate to dive with any of the shops recommended in this book; if you're new to the sport, all the dive shops also offer the Discover Scuba and Open Water certification courses. For snorkeling, trips cost around US$25 to US$40 per person.

> The home page of the federal Department of the Environment, www .medioambiente.gov.do (in Spanish), has information on national parks.

There are at least two functioning decompression chambers in the DR: the **Santo Domingo decompression chamber** (Map pp74-5; ☎ 809-593-5900; Base Naval, 27 de Febrero, San Souci Pier, Av España), located on the east side of Río Ozama, and the **Puerto Plata decompression chamber** (Map pp170-1; ☎ 809-586-2210; Hospital Dr Ricardo Limardo, cnr Av Manolo Taveres Busto 1 & Hugo Kundhart). The Santo Domingo chamber, though mainly used for military divers, is open to civilians and tourists in emergencies.

FISHING

Like most places in the Caribbean, there is good sport fishing to be had for those so inclined. Blue marlin peaks in the summer months, there's white marlin in springtime, and mahi-mahi, wahoo and sailfish in wintertime.

The best places to go deep-sea fishing are the north-coast region and Punta Cana. Expect to pay around US$70 to US$100 per person (US$60 to US$70 for watchers) for a group half-day excursion. Most captains will also gladly charter their boats for private use; expect to pay upwards of US$700/900 for a half/full day.

BEHOLD LEVIATHAN

Between mid-January and mid-March more than 80% of the reproductively active humpback whales in the North Atlantic – some ten to twelve thousand in all – migrate to the waters around the Península de Samaná to mate. The Bahía de Samaná is a favorite haunt of the whales, and one of the best places in the world to observe these massive, curious creatures. Most tours depart from the town of Samaná (p147), and you are all but guaranteed to see numerous whales surfacing for air, lifting their fins or tail, jostling each other in competition, and even breaching – impressive jumps followed by an equally impressive splash. Whale-watching season coincides with Carnival (every weekend in February) and Independence Day (February 27) – major holidays here – so you should make reservations well in advance.

SWIMMING

When you tire of sunbathing, go in the water for a dip – the water's warm, and nearly all the beaches in the DR are ideal for swimming and bodysurfing. (A few spots do have riptides, and we've mentioned those throughout the book.)

LAND SPORTS

CASCADING & CANYONING

Cascading – climbing up through a series of waterfalls, and then jumping and sliding down into the pools of water below – is hugely popular at the 27 waterfalls of Damajagua (see boxed text, p196), on the north coast. Lots of travelers told us it was their favorite thing in the DR – it was ours, too.

You'll be issued a life jacket and safety helmet, and guides will lead up, sometimes pulling you up bodily through the force of the water. Some of the jumps down are as much as 5m high.

The best way to visit the waterfalls is to go by yourself – foreigners pay only US$10 per person, and while a guide is mandatory, there's no minimum group size. Alternatively, you can come with a tour group, but all the package 'jeep safari' tours go only to the 7th waterfall – disappointing. Only one tour agency offers the trip to the very top (see p188).

Canyoning – often referred to as 'canyoneering' in the US – is cascading's technical, older brother, which involves jumping, rappelling and sliding down a slippery river gorge with a cold mountain river raging around you. You'll be issued a safety helmet and usually a shorts-length wetsuit. Canyoning is not especially popular in the DR, but if you're craving an adrenaline rush, there are a few spots in whichto indulge yourself near Cabarete (p184) on the north coast and Jarabacoa (p212) in the mountains.

HIKING
Pico Duarte

The most famous hike in the DR is the ascent of Pico Duarte (3087m; p217), the tallest peak in the Caribbean. It's a tough multiday hike, but involves no technical climbing, and most people hire mules to carry their supplies and equipment up the mountain. About 3000 hikers make it to the top yearly. There are two main routes to the summit (see p218) and several side trips you can take along the way, including hikes through two beautiful alpine valleys and up the Caribbean's second-highest peak, La Pelona, just 100m lower than Pico Duarte.

The website www .godominicanrepublic .com has a variety of information on outdoor activities, golfing and beach activities.

Pico Duarte was first climbed in 1944 as part of the 100th anniversary celebration of the Dominican Republic's independence from Haiti.

KEEP IT CLEAN, FOLKS

If you're headed up Pico Duarte, remember the following:

- Carry out *all* your garbage. Don't overlook easily forgotten items, such as candy bar wrappers, orange peel and cigarette butts. Empty packaging should be stored in a dedicated rubbish bag. Make an effort to carry out rubbish left by others.

- Never bury your rubbish: digging disturbs soil and ground cover and encourages erosion. Buried rubbish is likely to be dug up by animals, who may be injured or poisoned by it. It may also take years to decompose.

- Minimize waste by taking minimal packaging and no more food than you will need. Take reusable containers or stuff sacks.

- Sanitary napkins, tampons, condoms and toilet paper should be carried out despite the inconvenience. They burn and decompose poorly.

While the destination – the peak itself and the views – is stunning, the well-traveled walker may be disappointed by the journey required to get there. You pass quickly through the ferns and moss-bound rainforest of the lower elevations, and once you hit 2200m all you see are burnt-out forests of Caribbean Pine, spaced at regular intervals, with no animals and only cawing crows for company. Still, if it's clear at the top when you get there – and you have time to linger at the summit – then the hard work to get there may be worth it. You'll also enjoy the trip more if you spend part or all of it on the back of a mule.

Shorter Hikes

The DR is not a world-class hiking destination. Still, if you're keen, there are a couple of shorter walks about the place to get the blood moving. The Península de Samaná has some beautiful hikes near Las Galeras (p152), with picturesque deserted beaches as your reward at the end. In the southwest, there's some decent half-day and full-day hikes just outside Pariaíso, although they are best visited as part of a tour (p230). There are also a number of waterfalls around Jarabacoa (p213) that you can hike to.

One of the opening scenes of Steven Spielberg's *Jurassic Park* was filmed in Salto Jimenoa Uno outside of Jarabacoa in the central highlands.

No matter what hike you take, it's a good idea to have sturdy shoes. For Pico Duarte they are absolutely essential – boots are even better – while some of the coastal hikes can be managed in good sandals with heel straps.

MOUNTAIN BIKING

The Jarabacoa area (p215) is the best and most popular area for mountain-bike riding. Tucked into the mountains, there are a number of dirt roads and single-track trails offering challenging climbs and thrilling descents. The crisp air and cool climate make for ideal cycling, and thick forests and a number of waterfalls are within easy reach.

Cabarete (p189) also has a number of good rides and is home to the DR's best cycling tour operator, Iguana Mama (p188). It offers mountain-bike tours ranging from half-day downhill rides to 12-day cross-country excursions. It can also customize a trip to fit your interests, available time and experience level.

Tour prices vary widely depending on the length of the ride, but begin at around US$45 per person for half-day trips.

HORSEBACK RIDING

Those equestrian-inclined will find good riding on beaches and in the mountains. You may be somewhat disappointed in the horses, however –

Dominicans themselves tend to use mules, and the few horses on the island are principally for tourists and rich Dominicans. Don't expect to ride a thoroughbred.

A number of stables offer their services through the many tour agencies and resorts listed in this book. Expect to pay roughly US$50 to US$70 per person for a half-day ride. You can also ride a mule to the top of Pico Duarte.

Updated in 2006, *Birds of the Dominican Republic & Haiti*, by Steven Latta et al, is the most recent book on birds in the DR.

BIRD-WATCHING

The DR is a popular destination for gung-ho birders looking for the island's endemic bird species – 31 in all (depending on who you ask and how you count). The very best place to go birding is the southwest, especially the north slope of the Sierra de Bahoruco (p239), where you can spot nearly all the endemics, including the high-altitude La Selle's thrush, western chat tanager, white-winged warbler, rufous throated solitaire and Hispaniolan trogon.

The Jardín Botánico Nacional (National Botanic Gardens) in Santo Domingo (p86) are, surprisingly, also a good spot to look for birds, especially the palm chat, black-crowned palm tanagers, Hispaniolan woodpeckers, vervain hummingbirds and Antillean mangoes.

The 2003 birding manual *The Birds of the West Indies* by Herbert Raffaele et al covers birds across the West Indies, including migratory species you may see in the DR.

Parque Nacional Los Haitises (p140) is the only place you're likely to see the highly endangered Ridgway's hawk.

While numerous overseas birding groups brings enthusiasts here, there's only one birding tour company based in the DR (see p231).

GOLF

The DR's top courses all take advantage of the county's dramatic coastline, with holes hugging high cliffs and offering golfers incredible views of the deep-blue and turquoise seas, right along the fairway and greens. Two of the best courses include 'Teeth of the Dog' in La Romana (p121), designed by Pete Dye, and the Playa Grande Golf Course (p194), the last course designed by Robert Trent Jones Sr.

Although updated somewhat infrequently, www.golfguide-do.com provides golf-related listings for the Dominican Republic, including information on golf courses, clinics and convenient accommodations.

There are many more golf courses to choose from, scattered across the country. Green fees vary widely – from US$195 at Teeth of the Dog down to just US$25 for two laps around the hilly par 3 course at Jarabacoa Golf Club (p215), nestled among the pine trees in the central mountains. Most courses require either a caddie or a golf cart, typically US$10 to US$25 per round. All courses offer club rental.

Dominican Republic Food & Drink

Though not known as a culinary capital, eating in the Dominican Republic has its own pleasures. There aren't the same regional variations as you have in Indian, Mexican or French cuisines, but as much as dancing, the act of eating and drinking is the social glue that binds people together. A hybrid of Spanish, African and indigenous staples, flavors and styles, it has several major starches, including rice, potatoes, bananas, yucca and cassava, usually served in large portions – leave your low-carb diet at home.

STAPLES & SPECIALTIES

Dinner is the biggest meal, though neither breakfast nor lunch are exactly light. All three meals usually consist of one main dish – eggs for breakfast, meat for lunch and dinner – served with one or more accompaniments, usually rice, beans, salad and/or boiled vegetables.

The most typically Dominican meal is known as *la bandera* (the flag); it consists of white rice, *habichuela* (red beans), stewed meat, salad and fried green plantains, and is usually accompanied by a fresh fruit juice. It's not hard to see why it's so popular – it's good, cheap, easy to prepare and nutritionally balanced. Red beans are sometimes swapped for small *moros* (black beans), *gandules* (small green beans) or *lentejas* (lentils).

Bananas *(guineos)* are a staple of Dominican cuisine and served in a variety of ways, including boiled, stewed and candied. But the main way Dominicans eat bananas is boiled and mashed, like mashed potatoes. Prepared the same way, but with plantains, the dish is called *mangú;* with pork rinds mixed in it is called *mofongo*. Both are very filling and can be served for breakfast, lunch or dinner, either as a side dish or as the main dish itself.

It should be no surprise that seafood is a central part of Dominican cuisine, especially along the coast where it is sure to be fresh. The most common plate is a fish fillet, usually *mero* (grouper) or *chillo* (red snapper), served in one of four ways: *al ajillo* (with garlic), *al coco* (in coconut sauce), *al criolla* (with a mild tomato sauce) or *a la diabla* (with a spicy tomato sauce). Other seafood like *cangrejo* (crab), *calamar* (squid), *camarones* (shrimp), *pulp* (octopus) and *lambí* (conch) are prepared in the same sauces, as well as *al vinagre* (in vinegar sauce), a variation on ceviche and for many people the tastiest of the lot.

Two other common dishes are *locrio,* the Dominican version of paella – rice is colored with achiote – with a number of different variations, and Dominican sweet bean soup – *habichuela con dulce,* a thick soup with root vegetables. Goat meat is also extremely popular and is presented in many different ways. Two of the best are *pierna de chivo asada con ron y cilantro* (roast leg of goat with rum and cilantro) and *chivo guisado en salsa de tomate* (goat stewed in tomato sauce).

DRINKS
Nonalcoholic Drinks

One of the DR's favorite drinks, among locals and foreigners alike, is *batidas* (smoothies), made from crushed fruit, water, ice and several tablespoons of sugar. A *batida con leche* contains milk and is slightly more frothy. Though they can be made of just about any fruit, popular varieties include *piña* (pineapple), *papaya* (known as *lechoza*), *guineo* (banana) and *zapote* (sapote).

The website www.the worldwidegourmet.com /countries/westindies /dominican-r/dominican -r.htm provides recipes as well as background on Dominican cooking, especially as it relates to other Caribbean cuisine.

The website www.cook ingwithcaro.bizhosting .com provides an excellent resource for Dominican and Creole recipes.

CASABE

From ancient Taíno cooking fires to elegant presidential banquets, there is at least one common thread, a starchy bread known as *casabe*. High in carbs and low in fat – whatever would Dr Atkins say? – *casabe* is made from ground cassava roots (also known as manioc and a close relation to yucca). Cassava was one of the Taíno's principal crops, as it was for numerous indigenous peoples throughout the Caribbean and South America. Easy to plant – just bury a piece of the root or stalk into the ground – it's also fast growing. Europeans brought the hardy plant from the Caribbean to their colonies in Africa and Asia, where it was quickly and widely adopted. *Casabe* is still popular today, especially at traditional meals with soups and stews where it's great for soaking up every last drop. Rather tasteless on its own, *casabe* is best topped with butter, salt, tomato or avocado. A modern variation is the *catibía*, fried cassava flour fritters stuffed with meat.

Some *batidas* have strange local names, such as *morir soñando* (literally, 'to die dreaming'), made of the refreshing and tasty combination of orange juice, milk, sugar and crushed ice.

Juices (*jugos* or sometimes *refrescos*, although the latter also means carbonated soda) are typically made fresh right in front of you and are a great pick-me-up on a hot day. Popular flavors include *chinola* (passionfruit), *piña* (pineapple peel) and *tamarindo* (tamarind). Orange juice is commonly called *jugo de china*, although most people will understand you if you ask for *jugo de naranja*.

Coco, coconut juice from a *cocotero* (a street vendor who hacks out an opening with a machete), is available everywhere from the downtown streets of Santo Domingo to the most isolated beach. *Jugo de caña* (sugarcane juice) is another drink sold from vendors, who are usually on tricycles with a grinder that mashes the cane to liquid; equally popular are the sticky pieces inside that people chew on.

Coffee, grown in six different regions by over 60,000 growers, is a staple of any menu and most Dominicans' diets. It's typically served black in an espresso cup with sugar; a *café con leche* is a coffee with hot milk.

Other popular nonalcoholic Dominican drinks include *ponche de frutas* (fruit punch), *limonada* (lemonade) and *mabí*, a delicious drink made from the bark of the tropical liana vine.

Alcoholic Drinks

When it comes to *ron* (rum), it's tough to beat the Dominican Republic for quality. It is known for its smoothness and its hearty taste, as well as for being less sweet than its Jamaican counterparts. The earliest form of rum was created by accident after colonists left molasses (a by-product of sugar production) in the sun for several days. Adding a little water, they realized that it fermented into a sweet drink with a kick. Homemade rum rapidly gained popularity in the New World and by the 1800s businessmen began perfecting its production. Today over four million cases of rum are produced in the Dominican Republic yearly.

Dozens of local brands are available, but the big three are Brugal, Barceló and Bermudez. Within these three brands, there are many varieties from which to choose, including *blanco* (clear), *dorado* (golden) and *añejo* (aged), which contains caramel and is aged in special wooden casks to mellow the taste. Bermudez, established in 1852, is the oldest of the distilleries.

Most travelers will recognize a *cuba libre* (rum and Coke) but may not have tried a *santo libre* (rum and Sprite), which is just as popular among Dominicans. *Ron ponche* (rum punch) is what you'd expect it to be – a blend of rum and sweet tropical juices – but is more often ordered by foreigners than by locals.

Oranges in the DR are sometimes referred to as *chinas*. That's because in the early to mid-17th century Chinese oranges were the most popular variety in Europe, and the original Spanish settlers in the DR decided it was an easy word to remember.

Road signs throughout the country are sponsored by the Brugal Rum company.

Whiskey is popular in the Dominican Republic and a number of familiar brands, plus a few Dominican variations, are available at most bars – purists will want a *trago de etiqueta roja* (Johnny Walker Red Label) or *trago de etiqueta blanca* (Dewar's White Label). You can also always order Bloody Marys, margaritas, martinis and Tom Collins, and white and black Russians.

There are a handful of locally brewed beers, including Presidente, Quisqueya, Bohemia and Soberante. The best and most popular way to enjoy a beer is to share a *grande* (large) with a friend or two. A tall 1.1L beer is brought to your table in a sort of insulated sleeve, made from either wood or bamboo or from plastic and Styrofoam with a beer label emblazoned on the side, along with a small glass for each of you. There are few experiences more quintessentially Dominican than milking a couple of Presidente *grandes* at a plastic table on the sidewalk patio of a no-name restaurant.

Mujer 2000, a classic cookbook compiled by Silvia de Pou, a former television personality, remains one of the most popular in the DR and is now in its 24th edition.

Mamajuana, the DR's own homemade version of Viagra, is a mixture of herbs, dried bark, rum, wine and honey, which is then steeped for around a month. If you can keep it down, it's said to also cure various illnesses and, in general, is a substitute for vitamins.

CELEBRATIONS

There are a number of dishes usually reserved for special occasions, such as baptisms, birthdays and weddings: *puerco asado* (roast pork), *asopao de mariscos* (seafood) and the more modest *locrio de pica-pica* (spicy sardines and rice). Dishes like *sancocho de siete carnes* (seven-meat soup), made with sausage, chicken, beef, goat and several pork parts, all combined with green plantains and avocado into a hearty stew, are sometimes found on restaurant menus.

Christmas time in the Dominican Republic is associated with a few specialties: *jengibre,* a drink made of cinnamon, fresh ginger root, water and sugar; *pastelitos* (pastries with meat, vegetable or seafood fillings); *moro de guandules* (rice with pigeon peas and coconut milk); and *ensalada rusa* (basically, potato salad).

Dominican Cookbook by María Ramírez de Carias is a comprehensive and beautifully presented book on the culinary delights of the Dominican Republic.

WHERE TO EAT & DRINK

Restaurants are called just that – *restaurantes* – though more informal places may be called *comedores*. Most restaurants are open from 8am to 10pm daily, though a few are closed one day per week, typically Sunday, Monday or Tuesday. Reservations are rarely needed. There are very few places in the country where only tourists go, though certainly some cater more to foreigners (and their prices prove it). Most of the restaurants in this book are popular with locals and tourists alike, or even just locals.

Colmados, an institution in Dominican life, are combination corner stores, groceries and bars, and you can usually put together a meal here or, at the very least, grab a Presidente or two.

FOUR MOST ROMANTIC RESTAURANTS IN THE DOMINICAN REPUBLIC

- La Bricola (Santo Domingo; p94) – fine cuisine in an absolutely gorgeous setting on the patio of a mansion in the heart of the Zona Colonial

- Mare Nostrum (Bayahibe; p127) – a candlelit restaurant with water views and delicious, fresh seafood

- Camp David (Santiago; p210) – the balcony provides views of the twinkling city lights below and the food is equally enticing

- Hotel Atlantis (Playa Bonita; p163) – gourmet French food prepared by a master chef in beautiful and peaceful surroundings

---

TAXES & TIPPING

Diners sometimes experience sticker shock after receiving the bill. A whopping 25% is typically added to menu prices. The federal government requires restaurants to add a 16% sales tax and 10% service tax to all bills. The latter is designed to go to the restaurant staff, though it's hard to gauge how much of that the workers actually see. Some restaurants already include taxes in the prices, so be sure to check before ordering if it's a concern. Some people decide to leave an additional 10% tip for their waiter if the service is exceptional. If you're paying with a credit card, leave the tip in cash to make sure that your waiter gets it right away.

Car washes in the DR are rarely just car washes. Combining the passions of many men – automobiles and beer – these facilities, common throughout much of the country, serve drinks throughout the afternoon and evening. Of course, one has to question the wisdom of encouraging drinking and driving.

Quick Eats

By far the most common snack in the DR – one served at nearly every celebration – is the *pastelito* or closely related empanada. Empanadas typically have ham or cheese in them, while *pastelitos* usually contain beef or chicken, which have first been stewed with onions, olives, tomatoes and a variety of seasonings, and then chopped up and mixed with peas, nuts and raisins. Whatever the filling, it's tucked into a patty of dough and fried in boiling oil. *Pastelitos* are a tradition enjoyed by generations of Dominicans, and are made at home as well as by street vendors whose carts are fitted with burners to keep the oil hot. Other traditional Dominican snacks include *frituras de batata* (sweet-potato fritters), *fritos maduros* (ripe plantain fritters), *tostones* (fried plantain slices) and *yaniqueques* (johnny cakes). Dessert snacks include *frío-frío* – shaved ice and syrup, the local snow cone; *agua de coco,* fruits like oranges, bananas and pineapples mixed with sliced coconuts and sugarcane juice; and *helados* (ice cream).

Because most Dominican street food is fried, you can be relatively confident it's safe to eat (your arteries may disagree, however.) A small step up from street vendors are tiny cafeteria-style eateries where food is kept in heated trays under glass. These places can be more risky than street vendors, as the food may have been prepared a long while ago, or have even been recycled from the previous day. If something looks like it's been out all day, it probably has and you're better off avoiding it. That said, some of these eateries are very conscientious about freshness and hygiene, and are a great budget alternative to sit-down restaurants. The truth of the matter is you're more likely to contract food poisoning eating every meal at the buffet in an all-inclusive resort than you are anywhere else.

VEGETARIANS & VEGANS

Vegetarianism is not widely practiced in the Dominican Republic, and there are certainly a large number of Dominicans who view it as downright strange. Still, there are enough nonmeat side dishes in Dominican cuisine – rice, salad, plantains, eggplant, yucca, okra and more – to ensure that vegetarians and even vegans shouldn't have too much problem finding something to eat. Beans are another tasty and easy-to-find staple, though they are often made using lard. Pizza and pasta restaurants are ubiquitous in the DR and there is always at least one vegetarian option on the menu (and if not, it's easy enough to request). Of course, for those vegetarians who make an exception for fish and seafood, there is no problem

A Taste of the Caribbean: Remembrances and Recipes of the Dominican Republic, by Valerie Grullon and Susan Pichardo, has quirky food facts and illustrations amid the recipes and memories.

whatsoever. There is at least one vegetarian restaurant in the DR – a place called Ananda, in the Gazcue neighborhood of Santo Domingo – but virtually all the restaurants listed in this book will have at least some nonmeat alternatives.

HABITS & CUSTOMS

El Origen de la Cocina Dominicana: Historias y Recetes Tipicas Dominicanas, by Juan B Nina, traces Dominican cooking from its early beginnings to contemporary influences and includes recipes reflecting the cuisine's evolution.

Dominicans are essentially very polite, but observe relatively very few strict rules for dining and etiquette. Though formal restaurants certainly exist, a casual atmosphere with loud conversation and lively background music is the norm, especially during lunch, the most boisterous of Dominican mealtimes. It is not considered rude to call out or even hiss to get the waiter's attention. It *is* considered rude for a waiter to bring your bill before you've asked for it – the waiter isn't ignoring you, he's just being polite! This stems partly from the custom of lingering over meals, which are seen as much as a time to socialize as to fill one's stomach.

COOKING COURSES

Cooking classes are occasionally offered to students at Spanish-language schools (see p89). Ask about them when you sign up for a language course.

EAT YOUR WORDS

www.dominicancooking .com is a user-friendly website providing the history as well as the classic recipes of Dominican cuisine. *Aunt Clara's Dominican Cookbook,* sold on the site, is an excellent collection of recipes and source material on Dominican cuisine.

Food is one area of traveling where hand signals and a healthy sense of adventure usually suffice. Still, knowing just a few terms will prevent you from ordering *guinea* (guinea hen) when you meant *guineo* (banana) or *mangú* (mashed plantains) when you really wanted mango. For pronunciation guidelines, see p364.

Useful Phrases

The bill, please.
    La cuenta, por favor.   la *kwen*-ta por fa-*vor*

Is the tip included?
    ¿La propina está incluída?   la pro-*pee*-na es-*ta* in-cloo-*wee*-da

Do you have a menu in English?
    ¿Tiene carta en inglés?   *tye*-ne *kar*-ta en een-*gle*

I'm vegetarian.
    Soy vegetariano.   soy ve-khe-ta-ree-*ya*-no

May I have this dish without meat/chicken/ham?
    ¿Podría tener este plato sin   po-*dree*-ya te-*ner* es-te *pla*-to seen
    carne/pollo/jamón?   *kar*-ne/*po*-yo/*kha*-mon

What does this dish contain?
    ¿Qué contiene este plato?   ke-con-*tye*-ne *es*-te *pla*-to

What do you have to drink?
    ¿Qué tiene de tomar?   que *tye*-ne de to-*mar*

What types of juice/soda/beer do you have?
    ¿Qué tipo de jugos/refrescos/cervezas hay?   ke *tee*-po de *khu*-gos/re-*fres*-cos/ser-*ve*-sas ai

We need more time.
    Necesitamos más tiempo.   ne-se-see-*ta*-mos mas *tyem*-po

I haven't finished yet/I'm still eating.
    Todavía no he terminado.   to-da-*vee*-ya no e ter-mee-*na*-do

Would you bring me another fork/spoon/knife/napkin, please?
    ¿Me trae otro tenedor/cuchara/   me *tra*-ye o-tro te-ne-*dor*/koo-*cha*-ra/
    cuchillo/servieta, por favor?   koo-*chee*-yo/ser-*vye*-ta por fa-*vor*

Very good/tasty.
    Muy rico.   mooy *ree*-ko

Food Glossary

aguacate	a-gua-*ka*-te	avocado
ají	a-*hi*	pepper
arroz con leche	a-*ros* con *le*-che	rice pudding
arroz con pollo	a-*ros* con *po*-yo	steamed rice with chicken
asopao de camarones	*paro*a-so-o de ka-ma-nes	soupy rice with tomatoes and shrimp; also made with *lambí* (conch)
bacalao	ba-ca-*lao*	salted cod fish, usually broiled and served in a tuna salad-like form (sans mayo) with tomato and onion
bisteck	bis-*tek*	thinly sliced steak
camarones al ajillo	ka-ma-*ro*-nes al ah-*hi*-lo	garlic shrimp
camarones mariposa	ka-ma-*ro*-nes ma-ree-*po*-sa	butterflied shrimp
carne molida	*kar*-ne mo-li-da	ground beef
cazuela de mariscos	ka-*swe*-la de ma-*rees*-kos	seafood casserole
cerdo	*ser*-do	pork
chicharrones de pollo	chi-cha-*ro*-nes de *po*-yo	chunks of deep-fried chicken, also done with pork
chillo al horno	*chee*-yo al *or*-no	oven-baked red snapper
chivo al vino	*chee*-vo al *vee*-no	goat cooked in wine
chuleta al carbon	*chu*-le-ta al car-*bone*	grilled pork chop
chuleta de res	*chu*-le-ta de race	prime rib
ensalada de camarones	en-sa-*la*-da de ka-ma-*ro*-nes	shrimp salad
ensalada verde	en-sa-*la*-da *ver*-de	green salad
filete a la parrilla	fee-*le*-te a la pa-*ree*-ya	broiled steak
guineas al vino	gee-*ne*-as al *vee*-no	guinea hen in wine
guisada	gui-*sa*-da	any stew
helados	hey-*la*-dos	ice cream
mangu	*mahn*-gu	mashed plantains
medallon de filete	me-da-*yon* de fee-*le*-te	beef medallions
mero a la plancha	*me*-ro a la *plan*-cha	grilled grouper
mondongo	mo-*don*-go	stew of entrails and tripe
mofongo	mo-*fon*-go	mashed plantains with pork rinds
parillada	pa-*ri*-yada	barbecue
pechuga de pollo	pe-*choo*-ga de *po*-yo	breast of chicken, usually oven baked
pica-pollo	*pi*-ka *po*-yo	breaded fried chicken
pulpo	*pool*-po	octopus
queso frito	*ke*-so *free*-to	pan-fried thick slices of white cheese, sometimes with tomato and onion, served for breakfast
revueltos	re-*buel*-tos	scrambled eggs
ropo vieja	*ro*-po *bi*-eh-ha	beef, fried and shredded and served with rice and salad
sofrito	so-*free*-to	mixture of spices and herbs used to season dishes
sopa de mariscos	*so*-pa de ma-*rees*-kos	seafood soup
sopa de pescado	*so*-pa de *pes*-ka-do	fish soup
sopa de vegetales	*so*-pa de ve-khe-*ta*-les	vegetable soup
tocino	tos-*ti*-no	bacon
tostones	tos-*tone*-es	plantain slices fried like potato chips

Santo Domingo

This is a deeply Dominican city – an obvious statement but no less true. It's where the rhythms of the country are on superdrive, where the sounds of life – domino pieces slapped on tables, backfiring mufflers and horns from chaotic traffic, merengue and *bachata* blasting from corner *colmados* – are most intense. Santo Domingo (population 2.9 million), or 'La Capital' as it's typically called, is to Dominicans what New York is to Americans, a collage of cultures and neighborhoods, or what Havana is to Cubans, a vibrant beating heart that fuels the entire country.

At the heart of the city is the Zona Colonial. And at the heart of the Zona Colonial is Parque Colón. And across from the park is one of the oldest churches in the New World. And a block from the church is one of the oldest streets in the New World. And on this street is the oldest surviving European fortress. And so on and so on. Amid the cobblestone streets reminiscent of the French Quarter in New Orleans, it would be easy to forget Santo Domingo is in the Caribbean – if it weren't for the heat and humidity.

But this is an intensely urban city, home not only to colonial-era relics and New World firsts, but also to hot clubs packed with trendy 20-somethings; museums and cultural institutions, the best of their kind in the DR; and businesspeople taking long lunches at elegant restaurants. Santo Domingo somehow manages to embody the contradictions central to the Dominican experience: a living museum, a metropolis crossed with a seaside resort, and a business, political and media center with a laid-back casual spirit.

HIGHLIGHTS

- Wander the 500-year-old cobblestone **backstreets of the Zona Colonial** (p78)

- Enter the **Catedral Primada de América** (p79) – the first church in the New World – and imagine how 16th-century residents felt

- Root for the home team at raucous **Estadio Quisqueya** (p98), one of the premier places to watch a baseball game in the Dominican Republic

- Let the night slip away after a late dinner along romantic **Calle la Atarazana** (p94) off Plaza España

- **Merengue, bachata or salsa** (p97), or just plain-old grind down, at one of the capital's vibrant nightclubs

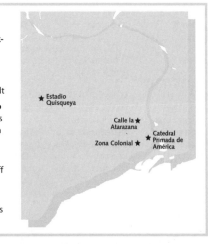

HISTORY

In a way it can be said that the founding of Santo Domingo was an act of desperation. Columbus' first settlement, Villa La Navidad in present-day Haiti, was burned to the ground and all settlers killed within a year. His second settlement, La Isabela, west of present-day Puerto Plata, lasted only five years and was beset from the beginning by disease and disaster. Columbus' brother Bartholomew, left in charge of La Isabela and facing rebellion from its disgruntled residents, pulled up stakes and moved clear around to the other side of the island. He founded Nueva Isabela on the east bank of the Río Ozama. The third time, evidently, was the charm as the city he founded, though moved to the west bank and renamed Santo Domingo, has remained the capital to this day.

That's not to say the city hasn't had its fair share of troubles. In 1586 the English buccaneer Sir Francis Drake captured the city and collected a ransom for its return to Spanish control. And in 1655 an English fleet commanded by William Penn attempted to take Santo Domingo but retreated after encountering heavy resistance. A century and a half later a brazen ex-slave and Haitian leader by the name of François Dominique Toussaint Louverture marched into Santo Domingo. Toussaint and his troops took control of the city without any resistance at all; the city's inhabitants knew they were no match for the army of former slaves and wisely didn't try to resist. During the occupation many of the city's residents fled to Venezuela or neighboring islands. It was in Santo Domingo on February 27, 1844 that Juan Pablo Duarte – considered the father of the Dominican Republic – declared Dominican independence from Haiti, a day still celebrated today.

ORIENTATION

For travelers, the Zona Colonial – home to streets that were once strolled by Christopher Columbus and Sir Francis Drake – is the heart of Santo Domingo. This is where most of the museums, churches and other historical sites are located. It has a number of hotels and restaurants in various price ranges and offers easy access to internet cafés, ATMs, shops and more. Río Ozama marks the eastern border of the neighborhood; several sights can be found not far on the other side. Just west of the Zona Colonial is a residential area of quiet,

tree-lined streets called Gazcue, which has a number of hotels, restaurants and some services. West of Gazcue between Av Tiradentes and Av Winston Churchill is a fairly high-end area of businesses, restaurants, apartment buildings and homes. South of Gazcue is the beginning of the Malecón, a portion of Av George Washington that contains most of the city's high-rise hotels and casinos and some nightclubs. The waterfront avenue runs the length of the city but the majority of activity takes place between Cambronal and Av Abraham Lincoln. On Sundays, the Malecón is closed to vehicular traffic and is a popular place to spend the day. The shantytowns that ring much of the city are known as Zona Apache – an allusion to the forbidden territory of the Old West in the US.

Maps

Located on the 3rd floor of an aging office building, **Mapas Gaar** (Map pp80-1; ☎ 809-688-8004; Espaillat; ⏰ 8:30am-5:30pm Mon-Fri) has the best variety and the largest number of maps in the Dominican Republic. Maps are designated by city or region (eg Santo Domingo and Environs, North, Central, South) and include a country map, as well as several city maps on the back of each. Road atlases are also sold here.

Also in the Zona Colonial, the **Instituto Geográfica** (Map pp80-1; ☎ 809-682-2680; Calle El Conde; ⏰ 8am-6pm Mon-Fri) produces mostly commercial use maps, but does sell a handsome five-panel, 1m-by-1.5m map of the Dominican Republic for US$35.

INFORMATION
Bookstores

Editorial Duarte (Map pp80-1; ☎ 809-689-4832; cnr Arzobispo Meriño & Mercedes; ⏰ 8am-7pm Mon-Fri, 8am-6pm Sat) This dusty shop in the Zona Colonial has a good selection of Spanish-language fiction books, foreign-language dictionaries and maps.

Librería Cuesta (Map pp74-5; ☎ 809-473-4020; www .cuestalibros.com; cnr Av 27 de Febrero & Abraham Lincoln; ⏰ 9am-9pm Mon-Sat, 10am-3pm Sun) This modern, two-story Dominican version of Barnes & Noble is easily the nicest and largest bookstore in the city.

Librería Pichardo (Map pp80-1; cnr José Reyes & Calle El Conde; ⏰ 8am-7pm Mon-Thu, 8am-5:30pm Fri, 8am-1pm Sun) Some early and antique Spanish-language books, mostly on colonial history and Latin American literature and poetry, plus some curios. Bargain to get a good price.

SANTO DOMINGO

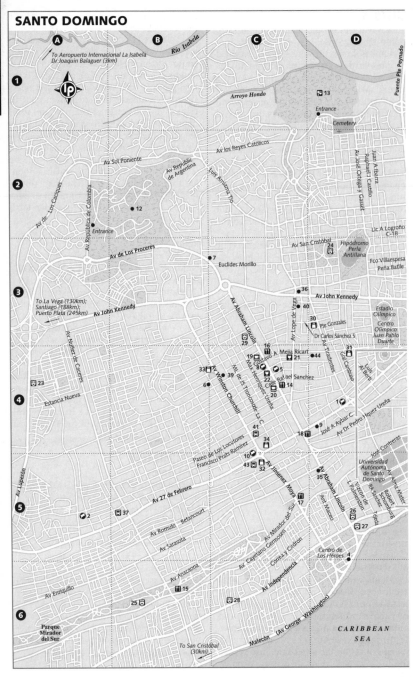

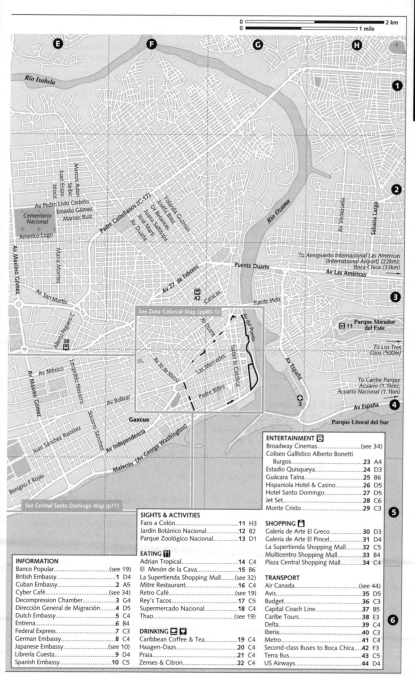

See Zona Colonial Map (pp80-1)

See Central Santo Domingo Map (p77)

INFORMATION

Banco Popular	(see 19)
British Embassy	**1** D4
Cuban Embassy	**2** A5
Cyber Café	(see 34)
Decompression Chamber	**3** G4
Dirección General de Migración	**4** D5
Dutch Embassy	**5** C4
Entrena	**6** B4
Federal Express	**7** C3
German Embassy	**8** C4
Japanese Embassy	(see 10)
Librería Cuesta	**9** D4
Spanish Embassy	**10** C5

SIGHTS & ACTIVITIES

Faro a Colón	**11** H3
Jardín Botánico Nacional	**12** B2
Parque Zoológico Nacional	**13** D1

EATING 🍴

Adrian Tropical	**14** C4
El Mesón de la Cava	**15** B6
La Supertienda Shopping Mall	(see 32)
Mitre Restaurant	**16** C4
Retro Café	(see 19)
Rey's Tacos	**17** C5
Supermercado Nacional	**18** C4
Thao	(see 19)

DRINKING 🍷🍸

Caribbean Coffee & Tea	**19** C4
Haagen-Dazs	**20** C4
Praia	**21** C4
Zenses & Citron	**22** C4

ENTERTAINMENT 🎭

Broadway Cinemas	(see 34)
Coliseo Gallístico Alberto Bonetti Burgos	**23** A4
Estadio Quisqueya	**24** D3
Guácara Taína	**25** B6
Hispaniola Hotel & Casino	**26** D5
Hotel Santo Domingo	**27** D5
Jet Set	**28** C6
Monte Cristo	**29** C3

SHOPPING 🛍

Galería de Arte El Greco	**30** D3
Galería de Arte El Pincel	**31** D4
La Supertienda Shopping Mall	**32** C5
Multicentro Shopping Mall	**33** B4
Plaza Central Shopping Mall	**34** C4

TRANSPORT

Air Canada	(see 44)
Avis	**35** D5
Budget	**36** C3
Capital Coach Line	**37** B5
Caribe Tours	**38** E3
Delta	**39** C4
Iberia	**40** C3
Metro	**41** C4
Second-class Buses to Boca Chica	**42** C5
Terra Bus	**43** C5
US Airways	**44** D4

Cultural Centers

Casa de Italia (Italian House; Map pp80-1; ☎ 809-688-1497; cnr Calle Hostos & General Luperón; admission free; ✆ 9:30am-9pm Mon-Thu, 9:30am-6pm Sat) Regularly hosting art exhibits in its 1st-floor gallery, this center also doubles as an Italian-language institute.

Casa de Teatro (Map pp80-1; ☎ 809-689-3430; www .arte-latino.com/casadeteatro; Arzobispo Meriño 110; admission varies; ✆ 9am-6pm & 8pm-3am Mon-Sat) Housed in a renovated colonial building, this fantastic arts complex features a gallery with rotating exhibits by Dominican artists, an open-air bar and performance space where music and spoken word shows are held every weekend, and a theatre that regularly hosts dance and stage productions. Call or stop by for a schedule of events.

Centro Cultural Español (Spanish Cultural Center; Map pp80-1; ☎ 809-686-8212; www.ccesd.org, in Spanish; cnr Arzobispo Meriño & Arzobispo Portes; admission free; ✆ 10am-9pm Tue-Sun) A cultural space run by the Spanish embassy, this institute regularly hosts art exhibits, film festivals and musical concerts, all with a Spanish bent. It also has 15,000 items in its lending library with both Dominican and Spanish newspapers, magazines, fiction and art books. For a listing of events, stop by for a brochure.

Emergency

The **Politur** (tourist police; Map pp80-1; ☎ 809-689-6464; cnr Calle El Conde & José Reyes; ✆ 24hr) can handle most situations; for general police, ambulance and fire dial ☎ 911.

Internet Access & Telephone

Abel Brawn's Internet World (Map pp80-1; ☎ 809-333-5604; Plaza Lomba, 2nd fl; per hr US$1; ✆ 9am-9pm Mon-Sat, 10am-4pm Sat) Fast internet access, as well as international phone and fax service.

Caribae (Map pp80-1; ☎ 809-685-2142; General Luperón 106; per hr US$1.40; ✆ 9am-9pm Mon-Sat) Quiet internet café.

Centro de Internet (Map p77; ☎ 809-238-5149; Av Independencia 201; per hr US$1; ✆ 8:30am-9pm Mon-Sat, 8:30am-3pm Sun) Internet and call center in Gazcue.

Codetel Centro de Comunicaciones (Map pp80-1; ☎ 809-221-4249; Calle El Conde 202; per hr US$1; ✆ 8am-9:30pm) Large call center and has internet access to boot.

Cyber Café (Map pp74-5; Plaza Central Shopping Mall, 3rd fl, Av 27 de Febrero; per hr US$1.75; ✆ 9am-7pm)

Cyber Red (Map pp80-1; ☎ 809-685-9267; Sánchez 201; per hr US$1; ✆ 9am-9pm Mon-Sat) Just off Calle El Conde, you can also make international calls here.

Internet/Phone Center (Map pp80-1; Calle El Conde; per hr US$1; ✆ 9am-10pm) On last block of Calle El Conde before you reach Parque Independencia.

Laundry

Many hotels do laundry, though they typically charge per piece, which adds up real fast. There are no laundromats in the Zona Colonial.

Library

Biblioteca Nacional (National Library; Map p77; ☎ 809-688-4086; Plaza de la Cultura, Calle César Nicolás Penson 91; ✆ 9am-5pm Mon-Sat) Santo Domingo's best library. Memberships are limited to scholars and persons with residency status, but there are no restrictions pertaining to use of the library's books on site.

Medical Services

Centro de Obstetricía y Ginoecología (Map p77; ☎ 809-221-7100; cnr Av Independencia & José Joaquín Pérez; ✆ 24hr) This hospital specializes in gynecology and obstetrics, but is equipped to handle all emergencies.

Clínica Abreu (Map p77; ☎ 809-688-4411; cnr Av Independencia & Burgos; ✆ 24hr) Widely regarded as the best hospital in the city, this is where members of many of the embassies go.

Farmacia San Judas (Map pp80-1; ☎ 809-685-8165; cnr Av Independencia & Pichardo; ✆ 24hr) Free delivery.

Farmax (Map p77; ☎ 809-221-2000; cnr Av Independencia & Dr Delgado; ✆ 24hr) Free delivery.

Hospital Padre Billini (Map pp80-1; ☎ 809-221-8272; Av Sánchez; ✆ 24hr) The closest public hospital to the Zona Colonial, service is free here but expect long waiting lines.

Money

There are several major banks with ATMs in the Zona Colonial. Gazcue also has a number of banks and others are scattered throughout the city, especially around major thoroughfares like Av 27 de Febrero and Av Abraham Lincoln. Large hotels, particularly those on the Malecón, all have at least one ATM.

Banco de Reservas Zona Colonial (Map pp80-1; cnr Isabel la Católica & Las Mercedes); Central Santo Domingo (Map p77; cnr Av Independencia & Máximo Gómez)

Banco Popular (Map pp74-5; cnr Av Abraham Lincoln & Gustavo Mejía Ricart)

Banco Progreso (Map p77; cnr Av Independencia & Socorro Sánchez)

Scotiabank (Map pp80-1; cnr Isabel la Católica & Las Mercedes)

Post

Federal Express (Map pp74-5; ☎ 809-565-3636; www.fedex.com; cnr Av de los Próceres & Camino del Oeste; ✆ 8:30am-12:30pm Mon-Fri) Recommended for important shipments.

CENTRAL SANTO DOMINGO

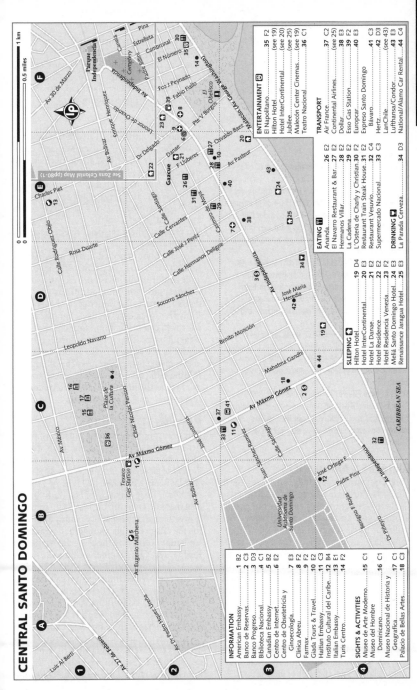

CARIBBEAN SEA

Post office (Map pp80-1; Isabel la Católica; ☺ 8am-5pm Mon-Fri, 9am-noon Sat) Facing Parque Colón in the Zona Colonial.

Tourist Information

Tourist office (Map pp80-1; ☎ 809-686-3858; Isabel la Católica 103; ☺ 9am-3pm Mon-Fri) Located beside Parque Colón, this office has a handful of brochures and maps. English and French spoken.

Travel Agencies

Colonial Tour & Travel (Map pp80-1; ☎ 809-688-5285; www.colonialtours.com.do; Arzobispo Meriño 209; ☺ 8:30am-1pm & 2:30-5:30pm Mon-Fri, 8:30am-noon Sat) A few meters north of the Calle El Conde promenade, this long-running professional outfit is good for booking flights, hotel rooms, and any and all excursions from mountain biking to rafting to whale watching. English, Italian and French spoken.

Giada Tours & Travel (Map p77; ☎ 809-686-6994, 809-264-3704; giada@verizon.net.do; Hostal Duque de Wellington, Av Independencia 304; ☺ 8:30am-6pm Mon-Fri, 9am-2pm Sat) Friendly professional outfit arranges domestic and international plane tickets, and also conducts area tours.

Tody Tours (☎ 809-686-0882; www.todytours.com) Former Peace Corps volunteer who specializes in tropical birding tours all over the country and at the National Botanical Gardens in Santo Domingo (three hours per person US$10).

Turis Centro (Map p77; ☎ 809-688-6607, 809-689-2714; turiscentro@hotmail.com; Av George Washington 101; ☺ 8:30am-12:30pm & 2-6pm Mon-Fri, 9am-2pm Sun) Another reputable travel agency, located on the Malecón.

DANGERS & ANNOYANCES

Pick-pocketing, especially on buses or in clubs, is the main concern for visitors to Santo Domingo. Being alert to the people around you and being careful with your wallet or purse (or even leaving them in the safety deposit box back at the hotel) is the best defense. Muggings are less common, especially of tourists, but they do happen occasionally. The Zona Colonial is generally very safe to walk around, day or night. The Malecón is safe as well, but be extra cautious if you've been drinking or you're leaving a club or casino especially late. Gazcue is a mellow residential area, but street lights are few and far between. If you have a long way to walk or you're unsure of the neighborhood, play it safe and call or hail a taxi.

SIGHTS

The highest concentration of sights are conveniently located within walking distance of one another in the Zona Colonial. A few sites, like the Faro a Colón and the Jardín Botánico Nacional, are in the surrounding neighborhoods.

Zona Colonial

For those fascinated by the origin of the so-called New World – a dramatic and complicated story of the first encounter between native people of the Americas and Europeans – the Zona Colonial, listed as a Unesco World Heritage site, is a great place to explore. It is 11-square blocks, a mix of cobblestoned and paved streets, on the west bank of the Río Ozama, where the deep rivers meets the Caribbean Sea.

As might be expected, many of the structures in the Zona Colonial that still have their 16th-century walls have more recently altered façades and structural additions like new floors and roofs. The western end of Arzobispo Portes is especially attractive, a quiet leafy avenue with colonial homes, stone churches and pleasant parks. Keep your eyes open for the little nooks and crannies – the small pedestrian alleys, men playing dominos at an aluminum folding table set on the street. These scenes, as much as the historical sites and buildings, make the Zona Colonial unique.

MUSEUMS

One of the more interesting museums, partly because of its history and the high quality of its exhibits, is the **Museo de las Casas Reales** (Museum of the Royal Houses; Map pp80-1; ☎ 809-682-4202; Las Damas; adult/student US$1/0.15; ☺ 9am-5pm, closed Mon), near Plaza España. Built in the Renaissance style during the 16th century, it was the longtime seat of Spanish authority for the entire Caribbean region, housing the Governor's office and the powerful Audiencia Real (Royal Court), among others. It showcases colonial-period objects, including many treasures recovered from Spanish galleons that foundered in nearby waters. Several walls are covered with excellent maps of various voyages of European explorers and conquistadors. Each room has been restored according to its original style, and displays range from Taíno artifacts to dozens of hand-blown wine bottles and period furnishings. Also on display is an impressive antique weaponry collection acquired by dictator/president Trujillo from a Mexican general (ironically, during a 1955 world peace event); you'll see samurai swords, medieval armor, ivory-inlaid crossbows and even a pistol/sword combo.

Designed in the Gothic-Mudéjar transitional style, the **Museo Alcázar de Colón** (Museum Citadel of Columbus; Map pp80-1; ☎ 809-682-4750; Plaza España; admission US$2; ⏰ 9am-5pm Tue-Sat, 9am-4pm Sun) was used as a residence by Columbus' son, Diego, and his wife, Doña María de Toledo, during the early 16th century. Recalled to Spain in 1523, the couple left the home to relatives who occupied the handsome building for the next hundred years. It was subsequently allowed to deteriorate, then was used as a prison and a warehouse, before it was finally abandoned. By 1775 it was a vandalized shell of its former self and served as the unofficial city dump. Less than a hundred years later, only two of its walls remained at right angles.

The magnificent building we see today is the result of three restorations: one in 1957, another in 1971 and a third in 1992. Great pains were taken to adhere to the historical authenticity of its reconstruction and decor. Today it houses many household pieces said to have belonged to the Columbus family. The building itself – if not the objects inside – is definitely worth a look.

Museo Mundo de Ambar (World of Amber Museum; Map pp80-1; ☎ 809-682-3309; www.amberworldmuseum.com; 2nd fl, Arzobispo Meriño 452; admission US$2; ⏰ 9am-6pm Mon-Sat, 9am-1pm Sun) has an impressive collection of amber samples from around the world, and excellent exhibits explaining in Spanish and English its prehistoric origins, its use throughout the ages, Dominican mining processes, and its present-day value to the science and art worlds. The collection includes fine amber jewelry and various samples containing a wide array of critters and bugs. The 1st-floor shop sells jewelry made from amber, larimar and more ordinary stones. Not nearly as impressive as its competitor is the **Museo de Ambar** (Map pp80-1; ☎ 809-221-1333; Calle El Conde 107, Parque Colón; admission free; ⏰ 9am-6pm Mon-Fri, 9am-4pm Sat); it has a few decent exhibits and high-quality samples, plus an exhibit on larimar, a beautiful blue stone only found in the Dominican Republic.

A better place to learn about larimar is the **Larimar Museum** (Map pp80-1; ☎ 809-689-6605; www.larimarmuseum.com; 2nd fl, Isabel la Católica 54; admission free; ⏰ 8:30am-6pm Mon-Sat), equal to the Museo

Mundo de Ambar in terms of the thoroughness of its exhibits. Signage is in Spanish and English. Of course, the museum is meant to inspire you to make a purchase from the strategically located jewelry store on the 1st floor.

Located in the Casa de Tostado – the beautifully restored 16th-century home of the writer Francisco Tostado – is the **Museo de la Familia Dominicana** (Museum of the Dominican Family; Map pp80-1; ☎ 809-689-5000; cnr Padre Billini & Arzobispo Meriño; admission US$1.50; ⏰ 9am-4pm, closed Sun). It's as interesting as much for its architectural features (it has a double Gothic window over the front door – the only one of its kind in the Americas), as for its exhibits displaying well-restored 19th-century furnishings and household objects. Ask to go up the spiral mahogany staircase for a rooftop view of the Zona Colonial. Tours in Spanish only.

The small **Quinta Dominica** (Map pp80-1; cnr Padre Billini & 19 de Marzo; admission free; ⏰ 9am-6pm Mon-Sat, 9am-2pm Sun) art gallery, located in a renovated colonial home, features ever-changing exhibits of colonial art. A shady courtyard at the back with tables and chairs provides a great place to just sit and relax. BYO snacks and drinks.

CHURCHES

Diego Columbus, son of the great explorer, set the first stone of the **Catedral Primada de América** (Primate Cathedral of America; Map pp80-1; Parque Colón; admission free; ⏰ 9am-4pm) in 1514, but construction didn't begin in earnest until the arrival of the first bishop, Alejandro Geraldini, in 1521. From then until 1540, numerous architects worked on the church and adjoining buildings, which is why the vault is Gothic, the arches Romanesque and the ornamentation baroque. It's anyone's guess what the planned bell tower would have looked like: a shortage of funds curtailed construction, and the steeple, which undoubtedly would have offered a commanding view of the city, was never built.

Although Santo Domingo residents like to say their cathedral was the first in the Western hemisphere, in fact one was built in Mexico City between 1524 and 1532; it stood for four decades, until it was knocked down in 1573 and replaced by the imposing Catedral Metropolitano. It *can* be said that Santo Domingo's cathedral is the oldest cathedral in operation, which is something for sure, but its current interior is a far cry from

SANTO DOMINGO

ZONA COLONIAL

To Second-
class Buses
to Higüey,
Puerto Plata,
La Romana,
Santiago,
Sosúa (20m)

To State Tourism Office (800m);
Caribe Tours (1.5km);
Estadio Quisqueya (4km);
Metro (5km); Terra Bus (5.5km);
Parque Zoológico Nacional (6km);
Jardín Botánico
Nacional (7.5km)

To Guácara Taína (6.5km);
Coliseo Gallístico (8km)

Parque
Independencia

Cemetery

To Gazcue (250m); Car-
Rental Agencies (2km);
Malecón (2km)

See Central Santo
Domingo Map (p73)

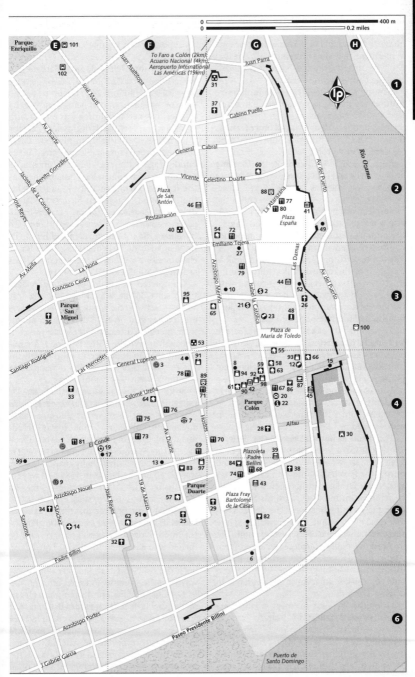

the original – thanks to Drake and his crew of pirates, who used the basilica as their headquarters during their 1586 assault on the city. While there, they stole everything of value that could be carried away and extensively vandalized the church before departing.

Among the cathedral's more impressive features are its awesome vaulted ceiling and its 14 interior chapels. Signs in English and Spanish beside each chapel and other features describe their rich histories. Shorts and tank tops are strictly prohibited.

Built in 1510 by Charles V, the **Convento de la Orden de los Predicadores** (Convent of the Order of Preachers; Map pp80-1; cnr Av Duarte & Padre Billini; admission free; ☉ varies) is the first convent of the Dominican order founded in the Americas. It also is where Father Bartolomé de las Casas – the famous chronicler of Spanish atrocities committed against indigenous peoples – did most of his writing. Be sure to take a look at the vault of the chapel; it is remarkable for its stone zodiac wheel, which is carved with mythological and astrological representations. On the walls are various paintings of religious figures, including Pope Saint Pius V.

The Gothic-style **Capilla de Nuestra Señora de los Remedios** (Chapel of Our Lady of Remedies; Map pp80-1; cnr Las Damas & Las Mercedes; admission free; ☉ varies) was built during the 16th century by alderman Francisco de Avila and was intended to be a private chapel and family mausoleum. Early residents of the city are said to have attended Mass here under its barrel-vaulted ceiling. It was restored in 1884.

The **Iglesia de Nuestra Señora de las Mercedes** (Church of Our Lady of Mercy; Map pp80-1; cnr Las Mercedes & José Reyes; admission free; ☉ varies), constructed during the first half of the 16th century, was sacked by Drake and his men and reconstructed on numerous occasions following earthquakes and hurricanes. The church is remarkable for its pulpit, which is sustained by a support in the shape of a serpent demon. The intricate baroque altarpiece is carved from tropical hardwood. Of the group of buildings that pay homage to the Virgin Mary, only the cloister adjacent to the church is in original condition.

Home to the first nunnery in the New World, **Iglesia de Santa Clara** (Map pp80-1; cnr Padre Billini & Isabel la Católica; admission free; ☉ morning Sun) was built in 1552. Years after being sacked by Drake and his men (who apparently hated all things Catholic), it was rebuilt with

funds from the Spanish Crown. This simple, discreet church has a severe Renaissance-style portal with a gable containing a bust of St Claire.

The baroque **Iglesia de Santa Bárbara** (Map pp80-1; cnr Gabino Puello & Isabel la Católica; admission free; ☉ varies) was built in 1574 to honor the patron saint of the military. After being done over by Drake, however, the church was rebuilt with three arches – two are windowless and the third frames a remarkably sturdy door. These additions proved invaluable in protecting the building against pirates and hurricanes alike.

Paid for by a woman who donated her entire fortune to construct this monument for the cloistered Dominican Sisters, the **Iglesia de la Regina Angelorum** (Map pp80-1; cnr Padre Billini & José Reyes; admission free; ☉ varies) was built toward the end of the 16th century. In addition to its imposing façade, the church is known for its elaborate 18th-century baroque altar, which is crowned with the king's coat of arms.

Completed in 1650, but altered several times since, **Iglesia de San Lázaro** (Map pp80-1; cnr Santomé & Juan Isidro Pérez; admission free; ☉ varies) was erected beside a hospital that treated people with infectious diseases. The church was constructed to give the patients hope – a commodity that no doubt was in short supply for patients with tuberculosis, leprosy and other common diseases of colonial times.

Since 1596 the **Iglesia de Nuestra Señora del Carmen** (Map pp80-1; cnr Sánchez & Arzobispo Nouel; admission free; ☉ varies) has served as a hospital, a jail and an inn, but is now famous for its carved-mahogany figure of Jesus, which is worshipped every Holy Wednesday during Easter Week. The small church, originally made of stone, was set aflame by Drake in 1586 and was rebuilt using bricks. During colonial times its small square was used to stage comedies.

In 1784 Spain ordered that the **Iglesia de San Miguel** (Church of Michael the Archangel; Map pp80-1; cnr José Reyes & Juan Isidro Pérez; admission free; ☉ varies) be turned into a hospital for slaves. The decree, however, was never followed. Note the appealing juxtaposition of its rectangular stone doorway with the structure's curved exterior.

The Chapel of the Third Dominican Order, or the **Capilla de la Tercera Orden Dominica** (Map pp80-1; cnr Av Duarte & Padre Billini), was built in 1729 and is the only colonial structure in Santo Domingo to reach the present fully intact. Today the building is used by the office of the archbishop of Santo Domingo. It's not open to the general public, but the graceful baroque façade is worth a look.

HISTORICAL SITES
Being the first colonial city in the New World, the Zona Colonial boasts several historical 'firsts,' including the first church, paved road and hospital.

Beside the Catedral Primada de América is the historic **Parque Colón** (Map pp80–1; cnr Calle El Conde & Isabel la Católica), containing several shade trees and a large statue of Admiral Columbus himself. It's the meeting place for local residents and is alive with tourists, townsfolk, hawkers, guides, taxi drivers, shoeshine boys and tourist police all day long. El Conde Restaurant (p96), at the corner of Calle El Conde and Arzobispo Meriño, has seating inside and out and is the premier people-watching corner in the Zona Colonial.

In front of the Alcázar de Colón, the **Plaza España** (Map pp80–1) has been made over many times, most recently during the early 1990s in honor of the 500th anniversary of Christopher Columbus' 'discovery' of the New World. The plaza is a large, open area that makes for a lovely stroll on a warm afternoon. Running along its northwest side is Calle la Atarazana, fronted by numerous restaurants and bars in buildings that served as warehouses through most of the 16th and 17th centuries. The street is occasionally closed to vehicular traffic and every afternoon much of it is lined with tables set up by the restaurants and bars. This is a popular place to have a drink around sunset and look out across the plaza to the Alcázar and beyond.

The **Fortaleza Ozama** (Map pp80–1; ☎ 809-686-0222; Las Damas; admission US$1; ☼ 9am-6:30pm Mon-Sat, 9am-4pm Sun) is the oldest colonial military edifice in the New World. The site of the fort – at the meeting of the Río Ozama and the Caribbean – was selected by Fray Nicolás de Ovando. Construction of the fortification began in 1502 under the direction of master builder Gómez García Varela and continued in various stages for the next two centuries. Over the course of its history, the fort has flown the flag of Spain, England, France, Haiti, Gran Columbia, the US and the DR. Until the 1970s, when it was opened to the public, it has served as a military garrison and prison.

As soon as you walk into the site, you'll see the oldest of the buildings here – the impressive Torre del Homenaje (Tower of Homage).

Its 2m-thick walls contain dozens of riflemen's embrasures and its roof-top lookout offers 360-degree views of the city. To its right, solid and windowless, stands El Polvorín – the Powder House – which was added in the mid-1700s; look for the statue of St Barbara over the door, the patron saint of the artillery.

Running along the riverside wall are two rows of cannons: the first dates from 1570, the second was added in the mid-1600s. Both served as the first line of defense for the city's port. The living quarters, now almost completely destroyed, were added along the cityside wall in the late 1700s. On the esplanade is a bronze statue of Gonzalo Fernández de Oviedo, perhaps the best-known military chronicler of the New World.

Near the door you'll find several guides, whose knowledge of the fort generally is quite impressive. Although the fee for a 20-minute tour is around US$3.50 per person, be sure to agree on a fee before you use their services. Tours are offered in Spanish, English and French, and there is occasionally a guide who speaks German, Italian or even Japanese.

Originally constructed in 1747 as a Jesuit church, the **Panteón Nacional** (National Pantheon; Map pp80–1; Las Damas; admission free; ☼ 9am-5pm, closed Mon) was also a tobacco warehouse and a theater before dictator Trujillo restored the building in 1958 for its current usage. Today many of the country's most illustrious persons are honored here, their remains sealed behind two marble walls. The entire building, including its neoclassical façade, is built of large limestone blocks. As befits such a place, an armed soldier is ever present at the mausoleum's entrance – along with a powerful fan since it does get hot. Shorts and tank tops are discouraged.

Connecting Las Damas and Isabel la Católica, the **Plaza de María de Toledo** (Map pp80–1) was named in honor of Diego Columbus' wife and is remarkable for two arches that were once part of the Jesuits' residence in the 17th century. Note the buttresses that support the Panteón Nacional: they are original, dating back to the construction of the Jesuit church in 1747, and a likely reason the building has survived the many earthquakes and hurricanes since.

Heading north and south in front of the fortress is **Las Damas** (Calle de las Damas, the Ladies' Street; Map pp80–1), the first paved street in the Americas. Laid in 1502, the street acquired its name from the wife of Diego

Columbus and her lady friends, who made a habit of strolling the road every afternoon, weather permitting.

Across from the Museo de las Casas Reales, the **Reloj del Sol** (Sundial; Map pp80–1) was built by Governor Francisco Rubio y Peñaranda in 1753 and positioned so that officials in the Royal Houses could see the time with only a glance from their eastern windows.

The **Monasterio de San Francisco** (Map pp80–1; Calle Hostos) was the first monastery in the New World and belonged to the first order of Franciscan friars who arrived to evangelize the island. Dating from 1508, the monastery originally consisted of three connecting chapels. It was set ablaze by Drake in 1586, rebuilt, devastated by an earthquake in 1673, rebuilt, ruined by another earthquake in 1751 and rebuilt again. From 1881 until the 1930s it was used as a mental asylum until a powerful hurricane shut it down – portions of chains used to secure inmates can still be seen. The buildings were never repaired. Today the monastery is a dramatic set of ruins that is occasionally used to stage concerts and artistic performances.

Standing next to a bright, white Iglesia de la Altagracia are the **Ruinas del Hospital San Nicolás de Barí** (Map pp80–1; Calle Hostos), ruins of the New World's first hospital. They remain in place as a monument to Governor Nicolás de Ovando, who ordered the hospital built in 1503. So sturdy was the edifice that it survived Drake's invasion and centuries of earthquakes and hurricanes. It remained virtually intact until 1911, when after being devastated by a hurricane, public-works officials ordered much of it knocked down so that it wouldn't pose a threat to pedestrians. Even today visitors can still see several of its high walls and Moorish arches. Note that the hospital's floor plan follows the form of a Latin cross.

The **Puerta del Conde** (Gate of the Count; Map pp80–1; Calle El Conde) owes its name to the Count of Peñalba, Bernardo de Meneses y Bracamonte, who led the successful defense of Santo Domingo against an invading force of 13,000 British troops in 1655. The gate is the supreme symbol of Dominican patriotism because right beside it, in February 1844, a handful of brave Dominicans executed a bloodless coup against occupying Haitian forces; their actions resulted in the creation of a wholly independent Dominican Republic. It also was atop this gate that the very first Dominican flag was raised. Just west of the gate inside

Parque Independencia (Map pp80–1) look for the **Altar de la Patria** (Map pp80–1), a mausoleum that holds the remains of three national heroes: Juan Pablo Duarte, Francisco del Rosario Sánchez and Ramón Matías Mella. The park itself has a few benches but little shade.

Downhill from the Alcázar de Colón is the imposing **Puerta de San Diego** (Map pp80–1; Av del Puerto), built in 1571. For a time it was the main gate into the city. Beside it you can still see some of the original wall, which was erected to protect the city from assaults launched from the river's edge.

The Gate of Mercy, or **Puerta de la Misericordia** (Map pp80–1; Arzobispo Portes), was erected during the 16th century, and for many decades served as the main western entrance to the city. The gate obtained its name after a major earthquake in 1842, when a large tent was erected beside it to provide temporary shelter for the homeless.

Said to be not only one of the first European residences in the Americas, but also one of the first residences in the Western hemisphere with two floors, **Casa del Cordón** (House of the Cord; Map pp80–1; cnr Isabel la Católica & E Tejera; ✆ 8:15am-4pm) was briefly occupied by Diego Columbus and his wife before they moved into their stately home down the street. Named after its impressive stone façade, which is adorned with the chiseled sash-and-cord symbol of the Franciscan order, it is also believed to be the site where Santo Domingo's women lined up to hand over their jewels to Drake during the month he and his men held the city hostage. Today the structure is home to Banco Popular, and while you can go in to exchange money, visiting the house beyond the main lobby is not permitted.

The **Casa de Francia** (French House; Map pp80–1; Las Damas 42) was originally the residence of Hernán Cortés, conqueror of the Aztecs in what is today central Mexico. It was in this building that Cortés is believed to have organized his triumphant – and brutal – expedition. Built in the early 16th century and sharing many elements with the Museo de las Casas Reales, experts theorize that these buildings were designed by the same master; both have a flat façade and a double bay window in the upper and lower stories, repeating patterns of doors and windows on both floors, and top-notch stone rubblework masonry around the windows, doors and corner shorings.

Although the Casa de Francia served as a residence for nearly three centuries, it has had several incarnations since the beginning of the 19th century: a set of government offices, the Banco Nacional de Santo Domingo, a civil courthouse and the headquarters of the Dominican IRS. Today it houses the French embassy. While visitors are not permitted past the lobby, this marvel of masonry is worth a walk by, if only to check out its façade.

Originally the residence of Governor Nicolás de Ovando, **Hostal Nicolás de Ovando** (Map pp80-1; Las Damas) is a handsome building with a Gothic façade that was built in 1509. Ovando is famous for ordering Santo Domingo rebuilt on the west bank of the Río Ozama following a hurricane that leveled most of the colony. Today it houses the posh Sofitel hotel (p92).

Fuerte de Santa Bárbara (Map pp80-1; cnr Juan Parra & Av Mella), built during the 1570s, served as one of the city's main points of defense. It proved no match for Drake, however, who along with his fleet of 23 pirate-packed ships captured the fort in 1586. Today the fort lies in ruins at the end of a lonely street. There isn't much to see here anymore, mostly rooftops and occasionally a cruise ship in the distance.

Plaza de la Cultura

Near the city center, the **Plaza de la Cultura** (Map p77; Av Maxímo Gómez) is a large park area with three museums, the national theater (p98) and the national library (p76). The land was once owned by the dictator Trujillo, and was 'donated' to the public after his assassination in 1961. At least two of the museums are worth visiting, though the plaza itself is mostly a sun-baked expanse and fairly unkempt; the theater and library will appeal to travelers with specific interests.

The permanent collection at the **Museo de Arte Moderno** (Map p77; admission US$3; 🕙 10am-6pm Tue-Sun) includes paintings and a few sculptures by the DR's best-known modern artists, including Luís Desangles, Adriana Billini, Celeste Woss y Gil, José Vela Zanetti, Dario Suro and Martín Santos. The temporary exhibits tend to be fresher and more inventive – more installation and multimedia pieces. Note that the entrance is on the 2nd floor – don't miss the artwork on the bottom level, accessed by a set of stairs just past the ticket counter.

The most extensive of the museums is the **Museo del Hombre Dominicano** (Museum of the Dominican Man; Map p77; ☎ 809-689-4672; admission US$0.75; 🕙 10am-5pm Tue-Sun). Highlights are the

impressive collection of Taíno artifacts, including stone axes and intriguing urns and carvings, and the small but interesting section on Carnival, with the masks and costumes used in various cities around the country. Other sections focus on slavery and the colonial period, African influences in the DR (including a small section on Vodou) and contemporary rural Dominican life. Unfortunately, the explanations are all in Spanish and the displays very old-fashioned. English-speaking guides can be requested at the entry – the service is free, but small tips are customary.

At the time of research the **Museo Nacional de Historia y Geografíca** (Map p77; ☎ 809-686-6668; admission US$0.20; 🕙 10am-5pm Tue-Sun) was closed and an opening date was uncertain. When it reopens, expect exhibits on the battles between Haitians and Dominicans; General Ulises Heureaux, the country's most prominent dictator during the 19th century; and Trujillo, the country's most prominent dictator during the 20th century – exhibits include his personal effects such as combs, razor, wallet etc.

The Dominican seat of government, the **Palacio Nacional** (Map pp80-1; ☎ 809-687-3191; cnr Av México & Av 30 de Marzo) was designed by Italian architect Guido D'Alessandro and inaugurated in 1947. The palace is built of Samaná roseate marble in a neoclassical design and is outfitted in grand style with mahogany furniture, paintings from prominent Dominican artists, magnificent mirrors inlaid with gold, and a proportionate amount of imported crystal. Of special note is the Room of the Caryatids, in which 44 sculpted draped women rise like columns in a hall lined with French mirrors and Baccarat chandeliers.

The Palacio Nacional sits on most of a city block and is primarily used as an executive and administrative office building. It has never been used as the residence of a Dominican president, who is expected to live in a private home. Unfortunately, the palace is not regularly open to the public, but you may be able to wrangle a VIP tour; they are offered free of charge and by appointment only on Monday, Wednesday and Friday. Dress appropriately – no flip-flops, shorts or T-shirts – if you are granted a tour.

Palacio de Bellas Artes (Palace of Fine Arts; Map p77; ☎ 809-687-9131; Av Máximo Gómez) was undergoing a complete and massive facelift when we stopped by. This huge neoclassical building was used infrequently in the past for exhibitions and

EIFFEL TOWER OR WHITE ELEPHANT?

The idea of commemorating Columbus' landing with a lighthouse wasn't Balaguer's: the **Faro a Colón** (see below) was suggested as early as the middle of the 18th century and later revived at the Fifth International American conference in Santiago, Chile, in 1923. The site of the memorial was always Santo Domingo. An international design competition was launched in 1929 and after sorting through hundreds of submissions from dozens of countries, the reward of US$10,000 eventually went to JL Gleave, a young British architect. Trujillo finally broke ground for the project in 1948, though one that incorporated his own design plans, but financial pledges from other Latin American governments never materialized and the project was scrapped.

Balaguer took up the issue again in 1986, appointing Nicolas Lopez Rodriguez, archbishop of Santo Domingo and a friend, as head of a commission for the celebration of the centenary of the 'discovery and evangelization of America' (he had also recently provided a blessing for the inaugural test run of the Santo Domingo metro). More than 50,000 shantytown dwellers were moved from their homes and tens of millions of dollars were spent on the project (some estimate the final cost to be around US$100 million) so that the beacon could project light visible 320km to the east in Puerto Rico – this in a city and country that at the time was often without power because of a poorly maintained electrical grid and high gas prices. The joke, not without some basis in fact, was that when the lighthouse was switched on the rest of the country went black.

Balaguer pulled the switch for the first time on October 12, 1992, with Pope John Paul II and King Juan Carlos and Queen Sofia of Spain in attendance – contemporary representatives of the dual powers that initiated the historic journey over 500 years ago. When responding to critics, supporters of the project – government officials at the time and some Dominicans – compared the lighthouse to the Eiffel Tower, explaining that both are in essence function-free white elephants.

performances. Check the weekend edition of local papers for events.

Outlying Neighborhoods

Some of these sights are worthwhile as much for the taxi ride there and back, a chance to see the Santo Domingo where ordinary people live and work.

Resembling a cross between a Soviet-era apartment block and a Las Vegas version of an ancient Mayan ruin, the **Faro a Colón** (Columbus Lighthouse; Map pp74-5; ☎ 809-592-1492, ext 251; Parque Mirador del Este; admission US$2.25; ⏰ 9am-5:15pm Tue-Sun) is worth visiting for its controversial and complicated history (see boxed text, above). Located on the east side of the Río Ozama, the Faro's massive cement flanks stretch nearly a block and stand some 10 stories high forming the shape of a cross. High-power lights on the roof can project a blinding white cross in the sky, but are rarely turned on because doing so causes blackouts in surrounding neighborhoods.

At the intersection of the cross' arms is a tomb, guarded by stern white-uniformed soldiers, that purportedly contains Columbus' remains. Spain and Italy dispute that claim, however, both saying *they* have the Admiral's bones. Inside the monument a long series of

exhibition halls display documents (mostly reproductions) related to Columbus' voyages and the exploration and conquest of the Americas. The most interesting (though deeply ironic) displays are those sent by numerous Latin American countries containing photos and artifacts from their respective indigenous communities.

The lush grounds of the **Jardín Botánico Nacional** (National Botanic Garden; Map pp74-5; ☎ 809-385-2611; Av República de Colombia; admission US$1.25; ⏰ 9am-6pm, ticket booth 9am-5pm) span 2 sq km and include vast areas devoted to aquatic plants, orchids, bromeliads, ferns, endemic plants, palm trees, a Japanese garden and much more. Great care is taken to keep the grounds spotless and the plants well tended, and it's easy to forget you're in the middle of a city of over two million people. In fact, birders can contact Tody Tours (see p78) for an expert eye on the many species found here. The garden hosts a variety of events, including an orchid exhibition and competition in March and a bonsai exhibition in April. The on-site **Ecological Museum** (Map pp74-5; admission US$0.35; ⏰ 9am-4pm, ticket booth 9am-5pm) exhibits and explains the major ecosystems found in the DR, including mangroves and cloud forests, plus a special display on Parque Nacional

Los Haitises (p140). Once inside you can stay until 6pm. An **open-air trolley** (admission US$1.25; every 30min until 4:30pm) takes passengers on a pleasant half-hour turn about the park and is especially enjoyable for children. A taxi from the Zona Colonial costs around US$4.

One of the larger zoos in all Latin America, the **Parque Zoológico Nacional** (Map pp74-5; 809-562-3149; Av los Reyes Católicos; admission US$5; 9am-5pm Tue-Sun) is a dismal collection of cramped, bare enclosures that will leave you fearing for the future of the natural world. The collection of animals is extensive: rhinos and chimps, flamingos and the endangered solenodon, an extremely rare, rat-like creature endemic to the island. Located in a somewhat seedy neighborhood in the northwest corner of the city (the makeshift homes of the slum perched just above the zoo appear as if they're likely to collapse onto the property at any moment), it's a bit hard to find. A taxi here from the Zona Colonial costs around US$6; definitely be sure to arrange a return trip with the driver, as you won't find many taxis out here.

A long tree-filled corridor atop an enormous limestone ridge, **Parque Mirador Del Sur** (Southern Lookout Park; Map pp74-5; Av Mirador del Sur) is riddled with caves, some as big as airplane hangars. One of the caves has been converted into a restaurant (p95), another into a dance club (p97). The park's seemingly endless paths are a popular jogging spot for 30-something professionals, many of whom live in the middle- and upper-class neighborhoods north of the park. Av Mirador del Sur is closed to traffic from 6am to 9am and 4pm to 8pm daily, when it fills with men and women jogging, rollerblading and bicycling up and down the broad avenue, and mobile juice bars and snack stands for anyone who's hungry.

Consisting of three very humid caverns with still, dark lagoons inside and connected by stalactite-filled passages, **Los Tres Ojos** (The Three Eyes; Map pp74-5; Parque Mirador del Este; admission US$1.75; 9am-5pm) is a mildly interesting site frequented by organized tours. The caves are limestone sinkholes, carved by water erosion over thousands of years. The entrance is a long stairway down a narrow tunnel in the rock; once at the bottom, cement paths lead you through the caves or you can visit them by boat for another US$0.35. Unfortunately, the tranquility of the setting is usually upset by vendors aggressively hawking their postcards and jewelry to tourists at the entrance.

WALKING TOURS

Even if there weren't a number of interesting historical sites, some of the firsts in the New World, the cobblestone streets of the Zona Colonial are a pleasure to wander around in their own right.

Walk One

Start by visiting beautiful **Catedral Primada de América** (1; p79), the oldest working church in the New World. From the southeastern corner of the park take Alfau, a small pedestrian street, one block to the entrance to the **Fortaleza Ozama** (2; p83), the oldest military structure in the New World. If you have kids, stop in the **Museo Infantil Trampolín** (3; p89). Continuing north on Calle Las Damas, check out the lovely façades of the **Hostal Nicolás de Ovando** (4; p85) and the **Casa de Francia** (5; p84). If it's a Sunday, stop at the great **antiques flea market** (6; p100) at the Plaza de María de Toledo. Further down Calle Las Damas, you'll pass the **Capilla de Nuestra Señora de los Remedios** (7; p82) and the **Panteón Nacional** (8; p83). Next you'll come upon the interesting **Museo de las Casas Reales** (9; p78) before reaching Plaza España (10; p83), a large stone-paved plaza overlooking the Río Ozama, with the **Museo Alcázar de Colón** (11; p79) on one side. Head to one of the restaurants lining the northwestern edge of the plaza for a well-earned drink.

Walk Two

Start by visiting beautiful **Catedral Primada de América** (1; p79), the oldest working church in the New World. From there, turn south on Isabel la Católica – within a block you'll see the **Larimar Museum** (2; p79) and a short distance further the simple **Iglesia de Santa Clara** (3; p82). Turn west on Padre Billini and walk a block to the **Museo de la Familia Dominica** (4; p79), with its famous Gothic window. Turn left (south) onto Arzobispo Meriño and you'll pass **Casa de Teatro** (5; p76), where you can check out an art exhibit or find out about upcoming performances.

Continue south to the corner of Arzobispo Portes, where you'll bump into the **Centro Cultural Español** (6; p76), which also has exhibits and a full calendar of events. Head west on Arzobispo Portes, one of the Zona Colonial's prettiest streets, with tidy colonial homes and plenty of shade trees. Turn right onto Av Duarte, which down here has cobblestones and is for pedestrians only. Av Duarte opens

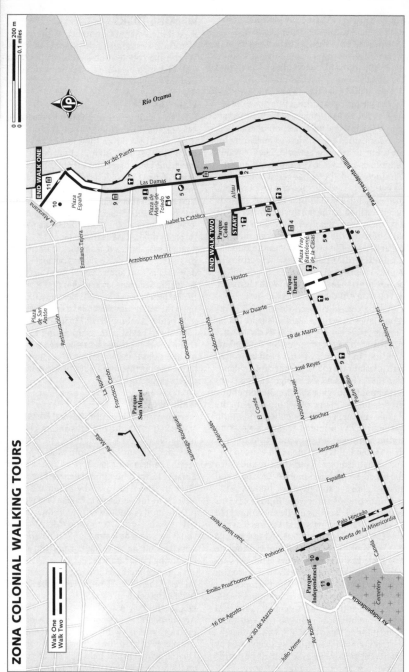

ZONA COLONIAL WALKING TOURS

Walk One
Walk Two

onto a plaza with two churches on either side – the spectacular **Convento de la Orden de los Predicadores** (7; p82) and the baroque **Capilla de la Tercera Orden Dominicana** (8; p82). Right in front is Parque Duarte, a pleasant and popular spot for locals and their families. Turn left (west) onto Padre Billini and continue to José Reyes, where you'll see the **Iglesia de la Regina Angelorum** (9; p82), notable for its ornate façade and baroque-style altar.

Continue west on Padre Billini for four long blocks past ordinary homes and shops until you reach Palo Hincado. Turn right and walk a block to the **Puerta del Conde** (Gate of the Count; 10; p84), the supreme symbol of Dominican patriotism. Just inside the gate is Parque Independencia and the **Altar de la Patria** (11; p84), a mausoleum that holds the remains of three national heroes. Backtrack back past the gate; Calle El Conde, the Zona Colonial's busy commercial walkway, begins right in front of the park entrance. Take your time wandering down Calle El Conde until you reach the leafy and cozy confines of Parque Colón.

COURSES

For those wishing to study Spanish, Santo Domingo has three excellent schools that offer a wide variety of programs, from private hourly classes to months-long homestays. Two of the institutes also offer cooking and dance lessons.

The **Instituto Intercultural del Caribe** (Map p77; ☎ 809-571-3185; www.edase.com; Aristides Fiallo Cabral 456, Zona Universitaria) was founded in 1994 and is the Spanish Department of Edase, a German-Dominican Language and Culture Institute. It offers Spanish courses of 20 and 30 hours per week in small classroom settings. There are more than a dozen price combinations, depending on the length and intensity of instruction and whether or not accommodations are included. Call for current course listings and prices. It also offers merengue dance lessons (eight hours of private lessons US$55) and maintains a language school in Sosúa (p181).

Providing Spanish-language instruction since 1982, **Entrena** (Map pp74-5; ☎ 809-567-8990; www.entrenadr.com; Calle Virgilio Diaz Ordoñez 42, Ensanche Julieta) has a long list of former clients, ranging from Peace Corps volunteers to professional baseball players. Its base program is a four-week intensive Spanish and Dominican

Culture course, which includes six hours of one-on-one instruction, competency-based language training and a homestay (US$1650). Programs can also be coordinated on a per-hour basis (US$8 to US$13) allowing students to take as many or as few classes and hours as they wish.

Offering six levels of Spanish-language instruction, the **Hispaniola Academy** (Map pp80-1; ☎ 809-688-9192; www.hispaniola.org; Arzobispo Nouel 103) is the only language school in the Zona Colonial. A week-long course – the shortest of those offered – consists of 20 lessons per week (ie four 50-minute classes per day) and your choice of accommodations. Prices begin at US$260 (with a homestay) and rise to US$580 (with hotel accommodations). Private classes available. Cooking (private US$48) and dance classes are also offered.

SANTO DOMINGO FOR CHILDREN

Santo Domingo isn't particularly kid-friendly. Outside of the Zona Colonial, it doesn't cater for pedestrians, there are no beaches and few parks, or at least ones that are well maintained and shady. **Parque Colón** (Map pp80-1; cnr Calle El Conde & Isabel la Católica) and **Parque Duarte** (Map pp80-1; cnr Padre Billini & Av Duarte) in the Zona Colonial are basically flagstone plazas where you can sit on a bench and feed pigeons. There are, however, several sights that will keep youngsters occupied.

Museo Infantil Trampolín (Map pp80-1; ☎ 809-685-5551; www.trampolin.org.do, in Spanish; Las Damas; adult/child US$3.50/1.75; ☺ 9am-6pm Tue-Fri, 10am-7pm Sat & Sun) is a high-tech, hands-on natural history, biology, science, ecology and social museum all wrapped into one. Enthusiastic guides (most are Spanish speaking) lead kids through the touchy-feely exhibits: the earthquake machines and volcano simulations are big hits, less so the exhibit on children's legal rights.

If the kids won't have a chance to snorkel and see underwater creatures in their natural habitat, the **Acuario Nacional** (National Aquarium; Map pp74-5; ☎ 809-766-1709; Av España; admission US$1; ☺ 9:30am-5:30pm Tue-Sun) can substitute. It's quite run-down in parts however, and algae often covers the viewing windows. That said, the long, clear underwater walkway where you can watch sea turtles, stingray and huge fish pass on the sides and overhead can be exciting. Signs in Spanish only. Across the street is **Caribe Parque Acuario** (Map pp74-5; Av España; adults/children US$6/4.50; ☺ 11am-7pm Wed-Sun), a not very well taken care of water park. It's a lot of concrete and safety probably isn't the best but…

Restaurants in general are probably more relaxed and kid-friendly than elsewhere, but Adrian Tropical (see p95) is especially good for loud youngsters. Hotels with pools, all those along the Malecón (see p93), are especially recommended and will allow you and the kids to take a break from the sightseeing for several relaxing hours.

TOURS

Interesting and informative walking tours of the Zona Colonial are offered on a daily basis by a number of official guides – look for men dressed in khakis and light-blue dress shirts, but always ask to see their official state tourism license. Tours cover the most important buildings in the zone and can be tailored to your specific interests. Walks typically last 2½ hours and cost US$20 to US$30 depending on the language that the tour is given in (ie Spanish and English are less expensive). To find a guide, head to **Parque Colón** (Map pp80-1; cnr Calle El Conde & Isabel la Católica) – you'll find a number of them hanging out under the trees. Also be sure to agree upon a fee before setting out.

If you want to hook up with a bus tour that may include outlying sights in addition to the Zona Colonial, try one of the local agencies that provide city tours to guests of all-inclusive resorts. A few popular ones include **Omni Tours** (☎ 809-565-6591; Roberto Pastoriza 204), **Prieto Tours** (☎ 809-685-0102; Av Francia 125) and **Turinter** (☎ 809-226-5342; Plaza Las Bromelias, Av Duarte). This isn't a bad option if you're short on time.

FESTIVALS & EVENTS

Carnival (or *Carnaval,* in Spanish) Celebrated throughout the country every Sunday in February, culminating in a huge blowout in Santo Domingo during the last weekend of the month or first weekend of March. Av George Washington (the Malecón) becomes an enormous party scene all day and night. Central to the celebration are the competitions of floats, and costumes and masks representing traditional Carnival characters.

Latin Music Festival Held at the Estadio Olímpico (Olympic Stadium; Map pp74-5) every October, this huge three-day event attracts the top names in Latin music – jazz, salsa, merengue and *bachata* (popular guitar music based on bolero rhythms). Jennifer Lopez and Marc Anthony have performed in the past.

Merengue Festival The largest in the country, a two-week celebration of the DR's favorite music held yearly at the

end of July and beginning of August. Most of the activity is on the Malecón, but there are related events across the city.

SLEEPING

The Zona Colonial is the most distinctive part of the city and therefore where most travelers prefer to stay. All of the sights and restaurants are within walking distance and there's an excellent choice of midrange and top-end hotels to choose from, some in attractive restored colonial-era buildings. Budget travelers have fewer options. Gazcue, a quiet residential area southwest of Parque Independencia, has several hotels in the midrange category, though there are far fewer eating options and you're likely to have to rely on taxis, especially at night. The high-rise hotels on the Malecón are best if you're looking for resort-style amenities like swimming pools, health clubs and tennis courts, and on-site entertainment like nightclubs and casinos.

Zona Colonial
BUDGET

Bettye's Exclusive Guest House (Map pp80-1; ☎ 809-688-7649; bettyemarshall@hotmail.com; Isabel la Católica 163; dm per person US$22, r US$44; ❄ 💻) Look for the nondescript iron doorway opening onto Plaza de María de Toledo around the corner from Isabel la Católica. Don't be discouraged by the messy gallery space overflowing with paintings and souvenirs; there's some method to the madness. The owner, originally from Tennessee, hopes to attract travelers who appreciate the eclectic, laid-back vibe. There are several dorm rooms (one only has a fan) with five to six beds, and while the spaces seem hectic, a mash of antiques with colorful modern art, they get good light and there's access to a common kitchen and bathroom. For those seeking privacy but not quiet, there's a private room with similar decor that opens directly onto Isabel la Católica – the bathroom is extremely small. During the low season the owner occasionally rents the whole dorm room out to pairs. Reservations are definitely recommended at other times. Wi-fi is available throughout, though the strength of the signal varies.

Hotel Freeman (Map pp80-1; ☎ 809-688-4263; www.hostalfreeman.com; Isabel la Católica 155; s/d US$30/40; ❄) Only half a block from Parque Colón, it's difficult to spot the entrance to the Freeman, and once you do you might want to turn around. The lobby desk does double service as a small car-rental agency and the stairwell has all the ambience of a police station. The six rooms themselves are spare and clean and have cable TV, and there's a 2nd-floor sitting area looking out over the street – the value here is location, location, location.

MIDRANGE

Hostal La Colonia (Map pp80-1; ☎ 809-221-0084; hostal lacolonia@yahoo.com; Isabel la Católica 110-A; s/d US$50/60; 🌐) Ideally located just around the corner from Parque Colón, newly opened La Colonia is a good choice. In addition to shiny, polished floors and large rooms with cable TV and refrigerator, each of the three floors has its own spacious street-side sitting area and balcony with armchairs. It's a lively and noisy block but the rooms are mostly shielded from the noise.

ourpick El Beaterío Guest House (Map pp80-1; ☎ 809-687-8657; http://elbeaterio.fr; Av Duarte 8; s/d US$50/60, with air-con US$60/70; 🌐 🖳) Take thee to this nunnery – if you're looking for austere elegance. It's easy to imagine the former function of this 16th-century building, the heavy stone façade, the dark and vaulted front room – now a beautiful reading room and dining area – giving way to a lush and sunny inner courtyard, all inspiring peace and tranquility. Each of the 11 large rooms is sparsely furnished, but the wood-beamed ceilings and stone floors are truly special; the bathrooms are modern and well maintained. Breakfast is included in the rate, and wi-fi is available.

Hotel Atarazana (Map pp80-1; ☎ 809-688-3693; www .hotel-atarazana.com; Calle Vicente Celestino Duarte 19; s/ d with fan US$50/70, with air-con US$70/90; 🌐 🖳) A newly opened boutique hotel for the design conscious only a few meters away from Plaza España. Housed in a beautifully renovated building from the 1860s, all six rooms sport custom-made furniture from native materials along with high-concept fixtures and textiles you'd find in a magazine. Each of the light and airy rooms has a balcony. Complimentary breakfast buffet is served in a secret garden-like patio shaded by lush vegetation; there's even a small Jacuzzi to relax in. Another option is the rooftop, which has fabulous views of the Zona Colonial and river. High-speed internet access in rooms.

Hotel Conde de Peñalba (Map pp80-1; ☎ 809-688-7121; www.condepenalba.com; cnr Calle El Conde & Arzobispo Meriño; s/d US$60/70; 🌐 🖳) There's no more desirable location in Santo Domingo. Rooms in this 20-room hotel overlook the Parque Colón, some with balconies with chairs and potted flowers, making for a perfect spot to watch the bustle down below; the downside is that noise can be an issue, especially from the ever-popular hotel restaurant on street level. Rooms have high ceilings and cable TV, but the furnishings have seen better days. Look for the entrance on Arzobispo Meriño and take the flight of stairs up to the 2nd-floor lobby. Internet access is via an old stand-alone computer.

Antiguo Hotel Europa (Map pp80-1; ☎ 809-285-0005; www.antiguohoteleuropa.com; cnr Arzobispo Meriño & Emiliano Tejera; r US$65; 🅿 🌐 🖳) Considering the impressive-looking façade of this hotel only two blocks west of Plaza España, the rooms are a letdown. Entering the spacious lobby, checking in at the professionally staffed front desk and having your luggage carried by uniformed bellboys, you'd expect the rooms to be more luxurious and modern. Other than the tile floors, the rooms are ordinary and aging. Ask for one with a balcony to ensure your room receives light. Continental breakfast is included in the rate and is served in a classy rooftop restaurant with a spectacular view of the Zona Colonial.

TOP END

Coco Boutique Hotel (Map pp80-1; ☎ 809-685-8467; www .cocoboutiquehotel.com; Arzobispo Portes 7; s/d US$70/90; 🌐 🖳) There's little traffic on this block in the southeastern corner of the Zona Colonial, which makes this hotel, four rooms in a renovated home, a particularly peaceful refuge. It doesn't have the old-world character of some of the other renovated hotels, but the owners have designed each room individually with particular color schemes and themes; the black-vanilla room is probably the nicest. All have beautifully polished wood floors and wi-fi access. The real draw is the rooftop lounge with a Balinese-style bed.

Hotel Doña Elvira (Map pp80-1; ☎ 809-221-7415; www.dona-elvira.com; Padre Billini 209; loft US$70, r US$85-95, ste US$105; 🅿 🌐 🖳 🎵) Tucked away on a quiet block far from the bustle around Parque Colón, the Doña Elvira is housed in a renovated colonial building, which is a plus. Unfortunately, much of the character seems to have been renovated out as well; the cramped loft room especially is in bad shape with peeling paint and a curtain serving as a bathroom door. There are 13 rooms, most are fairly modern looking, though the exposed stone walls and tile floors in the suite are attractive. It's a friendly place and geared toward travelers; you can hang out in the inner courtyard, take a dip in the pool (it's too small for swimming), lounge on the rooftop solarium or read in the lobby/dining area. Full breakfast is included.

Hotel Palacio (Map pp80-1; ☎ 809-682-4730; www .hotel-palacio.com; Av Duarte 106; s US$78-88, d US$88-98; P ✖ ☐) Cross colonial with a little touch of medieval and you have the Palacio, a maze-like hotel occupying a 17th-century mansion only a block north of the Calle El Conde pedestrian mall. Service is exceptional and you'll need it to find your way past the charming nooks and crannies, which include reading areas, a small bar, a lush interior courtyard and stone-walled walkways. Room design is strictly German conquistador minimalist with a few large imposing pieces of furniture – a heavy wrought-iron chandelier looks like a cage. Bathrooms are modern and comfortable. A stand-alone computer with internet access sits in the lobby and rooms have cable hook-up. An additional wing and a rooftop pool were under construction at the time of research.

Hodelpa Caribe Colonial (Map pp80-1; ☎ 809-688-7799; www.hodelpa.com; Isabel la Católica 159; r US$85; P ✖ ☐) A new boutique-style hotel only a block from Parque Colón, the Hodelpa Caribe is a convenient choice for those seeking modern comforts without the colonial ambience. There are some interesting design touches, from the blue fluorescent tube lighting to the blue drapery dropping from the 4th floor to the lobby, but the rooms themselves are attractive. White flowing drapes surround the beds, which are especially comfortable, and service is excellent. A rooftop solarium has several lounge chairs and good views, though daytime temperatures make it feel like a sauna. Wi-fi access is available in the lobby and there's a stand-alone computer for guests' use. An excellent breakfast buffet is included in room rates.

Sofitel Francés (Map pp80-1; ☎ 809-685-9331; www .accorhotels.com; cnr Las Mercedes & Arzobispo Meriño; s/d US$150/170; P ✖ ☐) It's hard living up to family expectations. Of course, the Francés suffers by comparison to its sister property, the Nicolás de Ovando, but what hotel wouldn't? Taken on its own merits, the Francés is a charming throwback to the same era. Housed in a colonial mansion only a few blocks away, rooms with high ceilings, stucco walls and tasteful decor surround a handsome stone patio. Some of the rooms are larger and quieter than others, so ask for layout specifics. Guests can access the pool at the Ovando, and a Continental breakfast is included. A nice bar and restaurant are on site.

Sofitel Nicolás de Ovando (Map pp80-1; ☎ 809-685-9955; www.sofitel.com; Las Damas; s US$220-336, d US$238-354; P ✖ ☐ ☎) Even heads of state must thrill when they learn they're sleeping in the former home of the first Governor of the Americas. Oozing character, Old World charm and a historic pedigree tough to beat, the Nicolás de Ovando is as far from a chain hotel as you can get. Indisputably one of the nicest hotels in the city, if not the nicest, the 107 rooms are definitely 21st century – flat-screen TVs, recessed Jacuzzi, internet cable hookup, luxurious boutique-style fixtures and linens. However, all this modernity is offset by beautifully crafted wood and stone interiors, cobblestone walkways, lushly shaded courtyards and a commanding view of the Río Ozama – the fabulous pool probably didn't exist during the governor's time. An excellent buffet breakfast is included in the rate; La Residence, the hotel's superb and elegant restaurant (mains US$17 to US$35), has a separate entrance down the street and opens for lunch and dinner.

Gazcue

Hotel La Danae (Map p77; ☎ 809-238-5609; www.hotel danae.com; Calle Danae 18; r US$24-30; ✖) Dominican-owned La Danae is the best of a number of similar small hotels located on this quiet residential street. Choose from the older, cheaper rooms in the front building and the newer, more modern ones in the back annex. The former have higher ceilings, but are subject to street noise. All have cable TV, and there's a kitchen area for common use.

Hotel Residence (Map p77; ☎ 809-412-7298; www .hotelresidencia.com; Calle Danae 62; r with fan US$25-30, with air-con $30-40; ✖) This family-run hotel, not to be confused with the Residencia Venezia, compensates for slightly cheesy room decor with its friendly enthusiasm. All rooms have cable TV and ceiling fan, and a 2nd-floor balcony for relaxing; rates drop for extended stays.

Hotel Residencia Venezia (Map p77; ☎ 809-682-5108; www.residence-venezia.com; Av Independencia 45; s/d US$45/58; P ✖ ☐) Within walking distance of the Zona Colonial and the Malecón, the Venezia is a logical and good-value option if you choose to stay in Gazcue. While the interior decorator may have gone a little crazy with the color green, rooms are immaculate and have large bathrooms; a couple of suites come with balcony and kitchenette, and obviously get more sunlight than the somewhat dim standard rooms. A pleasant surprise is a tiny bistro-bar off the 1st-floor lobby, good for a coffee and snack. Two internet-ready computers are available for guests.

Hostal Duque de Wellington (Map p77; ☎ 809-682-4525; www.hotelduque.com; Av Independencia 304; s/d US$45/90; P ⊠ ☐) With such an old-fashioned name, it's not surprising this hotel isn't fashionably modern. In fact, it's downright conservative, with room furnishings and decor that try terribly to be tasteful but are in the end fairly dowdy. Rooms on the 2nd floor have higher ceilings, and more expensive ones have balconies that provide more light. Guests can access the internet (per hour US$2) from an old computer in the lobby, and there's a travel agency on the 1st floor. It's a short walk to the Malecón.

Malecón

Less appealing than you might otherwise expect considering its waterfront Caribbean setting, Santo Domingo's Malecón, a long expanse of baking concrete, has several highrise hotels. The upside is that many rooms have views, all have pools and health clubs, and most have casinos and nightclubs. The downside is you'll have to take a taxi almost everywhere you go – you'll sweat just walking from the street to the hotel entrance – and the accommodation is very much bland international-chain style, with nothing particularly Dominican about it. The Malecón is closed to cars every Sunday, when it fills with locals, tourists, vendors and general revelry.

Meliá Santo Domingo Hotel (Map p77; ☎ 809-221-6666; www.solmelia.com; Av George Washington 365; r from US$75; P ⊠ ☐ ☑) The curiously designed and cavernous lobby at the Meliá doesn't inspire confidence, but this hotel does have the nicest pool area on the Malecón. Rooms are about as comfortable as the average chain hotel but no more.

Renaissance Jaragua Hotel (Map p77; ☎ 809-221-2222; www.renaissancehotels.com; Av George Washington 367; r from US$90; P ⊠ ☐ ☑) A middle of the road hotel, from its floral-print and wicker-furniture design scheme to its very ordinary restaurants, the Jaragua does have a popular nightclub and resort-style facilities and amenities.

Hotel InterContinental (Map p77; ☎ 809-221-0000; www.intercontinental.com/santodomingo; Av George Washington 218; r from US$120; P ⊠ ☐ ☑) Other than the Hilton, the InterContinental has the plushest lobby of the hotels on the Malecón and an even more hip bar-lounge area. Like all the big hotels on the waterfront, the hotel also has a pool, spa, tennis courts and casino, popular both with tourists and Dominicans on weekends.

Hilton Hotel (Map p77; ☎ 809-685-0000; www.hiltoncaribbean.com/santodomingo; Av George Washington 500; r from US$130; P ⊠ ☐ ☑) Easily the nicest of the luxury hotels on the Malecón, the Hilton is part of a huge complex, including a casino, movie theaters and several restaurants (however, much of it still remains vacant). The highest of the high-rises, it's a long elevator ride in the atrium to the top. Rooms are nicer and newer than its nearby competitors, and there's a bar and restaurant with stunning ocean views.

EATING

Unsurprisingly, Santo Domingo is the culinary capital of the country. It offers the full range of Dominican cuisine, from *pastelitos* (pastries with meat, vegetable or seafood fillings) sold from the back of street-vendors' carts to extravagantly prepared meals in picturesque colonial-era buildings. The Zona Colonial has some of the best restaurants and is most convenient for the majority of travelers. Pick any block and you're bound to find several to choose from. Seafood is always recommended, from the most ordinary *comedor* (informal restaurant) to top-end gourmet kitchens. Gazcue, only a short walk from the Malecón, has a number of good choices; the area west of Gazcue, between Av Tiradentes and Av Winston Churchill, is another fine area for dining with a good number of restaurants, many catering to a business crowd.

Zona Colonial
BUDGET
El Taquito (Map pp80-1; ☎ 809-687-1958; Emiliano Tejera 105; mains US$1.25-2.75; ⏲ 9am-1am Mon-Thu, 9am-3am Fri & Sat, 5pm-1am Sun) Tired of the same menu of 'international standards' – cooked from the same kitchen? Head over to this stamp-sized restaurant, really a stall, for tacos, burgers or sandwiches. It's especially good for a late-night snack.

La Cafetera Colonial (Map pp80-1; ☎ 809-682-7122; Calle El Conde; mains US$2-5; breakfast, lunch & dinner) Everyone knows everyone else's name here. That can seem intimidating at first, especially because the narrow entranceway means new customers can't pull up a stool at the long lunch counter unnoticed. It's a classic greasy-spoon menu: eggs and toast, simple sandwiches and super-strong espresso.

Restaurant Mariscos (Map pp80-1; Calle El Conde; mains US$2.50-5; lunch & dinner) Literally a hole-in-the-wall. There's only room for a few cramped tables, but there's no better lunchtime deal around. A plate of rice with your choice of seafood goes for only US$2.50. More substantial meals like grilled shrimp are slightly more expensive.

Expreso Pekin (Map pp80-1; ☎ 809-688-0499; cnr Calle El Conde & 19 de Marzo; mains US$3) Fast, cheap and good Cantonese-style Chinese food. Even delivers, which might be a good idea since the fluorescent lighting makes you feel like you're in an incubator.

MIDRANGE

El Meson de Luis (Map pp80-1; Calle Hostos; mains US$5-13; lunch & dinner) This simple and unpretentious restaurant is a downscale version of Mesón D'Bari across the street. Mostly loyal locals line up at the small bar or in the open-air dining room for filling plates of seafood and meat. Even though service isn't with a smile, it's a good choice, especially at dinnertime when it's not uncommon for a trio of musicians to serenade your table.

Mesón D'Bari (Map pp80-1; ☎ 809-687-4091; cnr Calle Hostos & Salomé Ureña; mains US$6-12; lunch & dinner) A Zona Colonial institution popular with tourists and sophisticated *capitalinos* on weekends, Mesón D'Bari occupies a charmingly decaying colonial home covered with bright, large paintings by local artists. The menu has Dominican and international standards, different versions of grilled meats and fish; the long attractive bar is equally appealing. Live music on some weekend nights.

Dajao Restaurant & Bar (Map pp80-1; ☎ 809-686-0712; Arzobispo Nouel 51; mains US$9-20; lunch & dinner) There are two Dajaos: a sleek, small, modern side, resembling a European café, and an older, basic side, much like an ordinary *comedor*. The former outshines the latter, not only in terms of style but in menu, too: it has specials like conch-meat croquettes (US$10), shrimp crepes (US$9) and grilled octopus (US$10).

Pasatiempo (Map pp80-1; ☎ 809-689-4823; Isabel la Católica 206; mains US$10-15; lunch & dinner Mon-Sat) This small Italian bistro boasts a preservative- and additive-free menu and handmade pastas. The dining room is a little cramped but it's a pleasant and romantic restaurant on a quiet block of the Zona Colonial. Especially recommended is risotto with seafood (US$15) and osso buco (US$13).

TOP END

A handful of restaurants share a corner of Plaza España. It's gets especially happening on weekends, but it's always a fun scene despite the high price tag.

Mesón del Jamón (Map pp80-1; ☎ 809-688-9644; Calle la Atarazana; mains US$10-20; lunch & dinner) Part of Plaza España's restaurant row, Mesón del Jamón is distinctive for its elegant 2nd-floor balcony. Only four or so tables for two fit out here, but they provide wonderful views of the goings on below – it's hard to give up the spot even after several hours. Along with grilled sirloin (US$17), pasta dishes (US$10) and fish (US$13), Jamón has an extensive menu of hot and cold tapas, like cured ham (US$12) and mussels in vinaigrette sauce (US$9).

Pat'e Palo (Map pp80-1; ☎ 809-687-8089; Calle la Atarazana 25; mains US$12-22; 4:30pm-late Mon-Thu, 1:30pm-late Fri-Sun) Another of Plaza España's eateries, Pat'e Palo is for gourmands and anyone tired of the same old bland pasta and chicken. Everything here is special but two personal recommendations are the grilled angus rib eye with rocket and parmesan with potato fricassee, mushrooms and bacon, and the Chilean sea bass served over Spanish sausage risotto in a creamy beer sauce.

our pick La Bricola (Map pp80-1; ☎ 809-688-5055; Arzobispo Meriño 152; mains US$13-22; lunch & dinner) La Bricola embodies romance. From the candlelit open-air patio to the soft melodic piano, a meal here is the perfect place to pop the question. While the setting in a restored colonial-era palace can't help but trump the food, the international- and Italian-inspired mains, including fresh fish specials, won't disappoint.

Café Bellini (Map pp80-1; ☎ 809-686-3387; Plazoleta Padre Bellini; mains US$12-30; noon-3am, closed Sun) This stunning restaurant off Plazoleta Padre Bellini (look for the statue of Don Francisco X Bellini) serves haute cuisine – interpretations of Italian meat, seafood and pasta with Dominican flourishes – like you'd find in the toniest restaurants in Paris or New York. A beautiful interior courtyard leads into an elegant and modern dining room that is designed to the hilt.

El Grand Charolais Steak House & Grill (Map pp80-1; ☎ 809-221-2052; Calle Hostos 151; mains US$15-22; ◷ noon-midnight) El Grand Charolais has all the hallmarks of a classic steakhouse – red checkerboard tablecloths, chalkboard specials, huge slabs of meat – and is a popular spot for long business lunches. The rib eye (US$21) is especially juicy and there are nonmeat options, like the fettuccine del mar (US$15).

GROCERIES

La Despensa (Map pp80-1; cnr Calle El Conde & Av Duarte) Largest grocery store in the Zona Colonial, which means lines can be long especially around closing time. Load up on cheap water, soda, alcohol and juice.

Gazcue, Malecón & Outlying Neighborhoods

BUDGET

Hermanos Villar (Map p77; ☎ 809-682-1433; cnr Av Independencia & Av Pasteur; mains US$2-9; ◷ breakfast, lunch & dinner) This bustling Dominican-style diner serves cafeteria food up front and deli/groceries at the back. The hot, grilled baguettes with a variety of fillings are popular. It's tough to find an empty table during the heavy lunchtime traffic, so getting things to go is always an option.

Ananda (Map p77; ☎ 809-682-7153; Casimiro de Moya 7; mains US$3-10; ◷ lunch & dinner Mon-Sat, lunch Sun) Hard-core vegetarians will want to try out this cafeteria-style restaurant-cum-yoga center run by the 'International Society of Divine Realization.' They may not find the offerings enlightening but more the equivalent of a downward facing dog. Dominican dishes like brown rice and roast beans outnumber the Indian offerings.

MIDRANGE

Adrian Tropical (Map pp74-5; ☎ 809-566-8373; Av Abraham Lincoln; mains US$5-8; ◷ breakfast, lunch & dinner) A huge sign of a smiling boy (Adrian?) announces this popular chain's kid-friendly credentials. However, from the road the lush jungle landscaping and waterfalls obscure its function – to serve as many hungry families as possible. Waiters scurry throughout the two floors and outdoor dining area doling out Dominican specialties like yucca or plantain

mofongo (mashed yucca or plantains with pork rinds; US$5) and standard meat dishes (US$8). An inexpensive buffet (US$6) is another option and the fruit drinks (US$1.50) hit the spot. There are three other outposts in Santo Domingo.

L'Osteria de Charly y Christian (Map p77; ☎ 809-333-6701; Av George Washington 47; mains US$6-12; ◷ noon-midnight) A favorite hangout for local expats and Dominicans alike, L'Osteria is a casual open-air restaurant on the Malecón. Aging albeit with character, it's as much a good place for a drink as a serving of homemade pasta or other Italian and French standards.

El Navarro Restaurant & Bar (Map p77; ☎ 809-689-3888; Av Independencia 302; mains US$7-15; ◷ lunch & dinner) This restaurant suffers a bit from a split personality. The dining room is richly and elegantly appointed, but much of the menu is mediocre bar food like hamburgers (US$4.75) and wraps (US$6). Higher-end items such as grilled meats and lobster thermidor (US$18 per lb) are available as well.

Restaurant Train Steak House (Map p77; ☎ 809-686-5961; Av Pasteur 100; mains US$12; ◷ 11:30am-midnight Tue-Sun) Not quite a chop house, not quite a sports bar, this restaurant combines a little of both. In the front bar there are several TVs tuned to international sporting events, while uniformed waiters and the enthusiastic owner hustle about the brick-walled dining room serving delicious cuts of meat as well as grilled seafood and tapas.

TOP END

Mitre Restaurant (Map pp74-5; ☎ 809-472-1787; Av Abraham Lincoln 1005; ◷ lunch & dinner) This sleek restaurant, located in a nondescript building in a an upscale business and residential district, serves a creative fusion of Asian, Italian and Dominican cuisines. The results are satisfying to both the eye and stomach; an outdoor patio and 2nd-floor lounge are more casual than the white-tableclothed dining room.

Restaurant Vesuvio (Map p77; ☎ 809-221-1954; Av George Washington 52; mains US$12-17; ◷ lunch & dinner) An upscale Italian restaurant on the Malecón, Vesuvio is a Santo Domingo institution that unfortunately has seen better days. The old-fashioned decor is fading and the wheeled cart displays of food are looking a little tired, but the Neapolitan owner still prides himself on serving the freshest seafood and homemade pasta dishes. Next door is a more casual pizzeria under the same ownership.

lonelyplanet.com

El Mesón de la Cava (Map pp74-5; ☎ 809-533-2818; Av Mirador del Sur; mains US$10-20; ✆ noon-1am) This is where Batman would take a date – this craggy stalactite-filled limestone cave is home to a unique and romantic restaurant. However, the formally clad waiters and soft merengue and salsa music don't entirely make up for only average food, primarily grilled meats and fish.

GROCERIES
La Cadena (Map p77; cnr Calle Cervantes & Casimiro de Moya; ✆ 7:30am-10pm Mon-Sat, 9am-2:30pm Sun) In Gazcue, La Cadena is within walking distance of hotels in the neighborhood and carries produce, meats and everything you should need.

La Supertienda Shopping Mall (Map pp74-5; cnr Av Jímenez Moya & Av 27 de Febrero) and **Supermercado Nacional** (Map pp74-5; Av 27 de Febrero) live up to their names, the latter (an enormous megastore occupying several city blocks) especially so; it's located at one of the busiest intersections in the city. There's another branch in Gazcue.

DRINKING
Santo Domingo has a lively bar and club scene, much of it located conveniently in the Zona Colonial. Otherwise many of the nicer bars are in strip malls around the city, and whatever neighborhood you're in you can always strap on a few Presidentes at the *colmado* (combination corner store, grocery store and bar).

Cafés
ourpick **El Conde Restaurant** (Map pp80-1; ☎ 809-688-7121; Hotel Conde de Peñalba, cnr Calle El Conde & Arzobispo Meriño; mains US$3-16; ✆ breakfast, lunch & dinner) Hands down, the place for an afternoon drink. As much a restaurant as a café, El Conde's appeal isn't it's large varied menu of decent food, but its commanding location at the busiest corner in the Zona Colonial. Crowded with tourists and locals alike, it seems like all of Santo Domingo passes by here. Nothing hits the spot more than a *morir soñando* (literally 'to die dreaming'), a combination of orange juice, milk, sugar and chopped ice.

Segafredo Zanetti Espresso (Map pp80-1; ☎ 809-685-9569; Calle El Conde 54; ✆ 9am-1am Mon-Thu, 9am-3am Fri & Sat) One of a number of cafés lining this cobblestoned alleyway, Segafredo stands out because of its cool indoor bar, which wouldn't be out of place in a trendy neighborhood of New York or Paris. You can lounge around with a mixed drink (US$4.50) on one of the

day beds or retreat to a nook in the back. Crepes, paninis and other morsels are also served inside and out.

Caribbean Coffee & Tea (Map pp74-5; Av Gustavo A Mejia Ricart; ✆ 8.30am-midnight) Tucked into Plaza Andalucia, a small strip mall, this café is popular with a young upscale crowd from the surrounding Los Angeles–like neighborhood. While there's nothing to see other than a busy intersection, sitting at one of the outdoor tables sipping a cappuccino (US$2) or tea (US$1.50) is a pleasant way to while away an afternoon. Wraps (US$10), paninis (US$7) and salads (US$6) are also available.

Haagen-Dazs (Map pp74-5; ☎ 809-566-4950; Av Abraham Lincoln; ✆ 11am-11pm) We know it's a Haagen-Dazs, but this modern, sleek and most importantly air-conditioned place is an oasis for those foolhardy enough to walk along this sun-baked stretch of asphalt. Shakes ($5), ice-cream sodas ($4), ice coffees ($3) and, of course, plain old ice cream are available.

Bars
1492 (Map pp80-1; ☎ 809-686-6009; Arzobispo Meriño 105; ✆ Tue-Sat) The horseshoe-shaped wood bar is conducive for conversation; the dim lighting is flattering and the barkeep-owner is friendly; located on a quiet street in the Zona Colonial, appropriately enough, 1492 feels like a discovery.

Double's Bar (Map pp80-1; Arzobispo Meriño; ✆ 6pm to late) Good-looking 20-somethings grind away to loud pop and Latin music at Double's. Others lounge around in groups downing bottles of Presidente, while the classic long wood bar is better for conversation.

La Parada Cervecera (Map p77; Av George Washington 402; ✆ 8am-midnight) This classic Dominican joint, a combination carwash-bar, isn't exactly a good advertisement against drinking and driving. It's an open-air place directly on a busy intersection of the Malecón; the loud music barely drains out the backfiring and honking traffic.

Los Tres Mosqueteros (Map pp80-1; ☎ 809-689-1114; Calle El Conde 56; ✆ lunch-late) This bar-café is one of several lining a cobblestone alleyway a few steps from Parque Colón. In addition to outdoor seating, it has an elegant indoor space with high ceilings and overhead fans. For those looking to make an afternoon of it, there's free wi-fi and a full menu.

Praia (Map pp74-5; ☎ 809-540-8753; Gustavo A Mejia Ricart 74; ✆ 10pm-2am) A bar and wine lounge à la

Soho – either NYC or London – Praia attracts a well-heeled Dominican clientele. The drinks are expensive, and the music, suitable for the modern minimalist decor, is electronica.

Zenses & Citron (Map pp74-5; ☎ 809-542-1111; Av Abraham Lincoln 958; ☺ noon-1am Sun-Thu, noon-3am Fri & Sat) The draw at this sophisticated bar and lounge, besides the extensive drink and food menu and occasional live music, is the attractive outdoor deck perfect for a sundowner.

Bicicleta Café Bar & Restaurant (Map pp80-1; cnr Arzopispo Nouel & Av Duarte; ☺ Mon-Thu 4pm-1am, Fri & Sat 4pm-3am, Sun 12:30pm-1am) Basically a step up from a corner *colmado*, this bar is a good place to rub shoulders with locals and sample Dominican drinks at reasonable prices.

ENTERTAINMENT

Santo Domingo has the country's best entertainment scene, from glitzy hotel nightclubs and casinos to small bars and dance spots. And lest you scoff, hotel nightclubs are hugely popular, especially among Santo Domingo's rich, young and restless. Merengue and *bachata* are omnipresent, but house, techno, and American and Latin rock are popular as well. A number of clubs in town cater to gays and lesbians, or at least offer a welcoming mixed atmosphere. *Ocio* and *Aquí* magazines both have listings of bars and restaurants of all sorts – the former is definitely cooler, but both are useful. Look for them at the tourist office or shops in the Zona Colonial. Newspapers are another good place to find out about upcoming concerts and shows, and if your Spanish is good, radio stations hype the capital's big events.

Live Music & Nightclubs

Nightclubs come and go, change names and ownership; however, those in hotels on the Malecón tend to have longer life spans. Most of the clubs have both live music some nights and DJs others. Some of the venues attract the wealthiest and hippest in Santo Domingo, but wherever you go, expect people to be dressed to the nines, so definitely no T-shirts, runners or sandals. Admission is up to US$5 when there's a DJ (most nights) and US$10 when there's a band.

Guácara Taína (Map pp74-5; ☎ 809-533-2151; Av Mirador del Sur 655; admission US$9; ☺ 9pm-3am Thu-Sun) A somewhat legendary nightclub, now maybe at least as popular with cruise-ship passengers as Dominicans, Guácara Taína is still an in-

teresting place to party. Located inside a huge underground cave in the Parque Mirado del Sur, this club hosts everything from raves to live merengue and hip-hop acts.

Jubilee (Map p77; Renaissance Jaragua Hotel, Av George Washington 367; ☺ 9pm-4am Tue-Sat) A long-standing hot spot, this nightclub in the Jaragua Hotel continues to draw in good-looking, well-heeled and well-dressed hordes looking to get down to live merengue music; most nights it doesn't get hopping until around midnight. Drink bills can be pretty steep at the end of a long evening.

El Napolitano (Map p77; ☎ 809-687-1131; www .hotelnapolitano.net; Av George Washington 101; admission US$3.50; ☺ 9pm-4am Thu-Sun) A smaller and less glamorous version of the Jubilee is the nightclub at this fairly run-down hotel. But because of its proximity to the Zona Colonial and its more reasonable drink prices, it still gets packed on weekends.

Atarazana 9 (Map pp80-1; ☎ 809-688-0969; Atarazana 9; admission free, open bar Thu US$7; ☺ 8pm-3am) Just off Plaza España on a cobblestone alleyway, Atarazana 9 feels like a cool neighborhood bar where regulars get served their favorite beers without asking; tourists wandering in after a meal in the Zona Colonial are equally welcome. There's a stage as well, where live music is sometimes performed.

Nowhere (Map pp80-1; ☎ 809-877-6258; Calle Hostos 205; admission free; ☺ 9pm-4am Wed-Sat) This club, just steps from Parque Colón, has had a long shelf life for the here today–gone tomorrow world of Santo Domingo nightspots. Once past the doorman, a maze of bars and dance floors are scattered over two floors. It doesn't get busy till late; ladies' night on Thursday.

Monte Cristo (Map pp74-5; ☎ 809-542-5000; Av Jose Armado Soler; ☺ 6pm-5am) This sophisticated club doubles as a cigar lounge with good wine and mixed drinks thrown in as well. There's a dance floor for merengue and salsa and live music on Wednesday. Weekends tend to be a hodge-podge of salsa, merengue, reggaeton and Latin rock.

Jet Set (Map pp74-5; ☎ 809-535-4145; Av Independencia 2253; admission US$7; ☺ 9pm-late) A trendy, good-looking crowd flocks to this 7th-floor disco. Besides offering great views of the city, there's live music – salsa, merengue – most nights of the week and *bachata* on Mondays. Happy hour from 5pm to 9pm.

Thao (Map pp74-5; Plaza Andalucia) and **Retro Café** (Map pp74-5; Plaza Andalucia) are across from one another in the same strip mall in a business/residential neighborhood west of the city center. Thao is at the higher end of the two, reflected by its drink prices, but both have reggaeton and merengue, and sometimes techno.

Gay & Lesbian Venues

Much like the straight scene, gay and lesbian venues in Santo Domingo don't tend to last for too long. The following were open at the time of research.

Amazonia (☎ 809-412-7629; Dr Delgado 71; ☽ 8pm-late Fri-Sun) A mostly lesbian bar in Gazcue.

CHA (Av George Washington 165; ☽ 6pm-3am Fri & Sat, 6pm-1am Sun) A fun place with good music, shows and strippers.

Esedeku (Map pp80-1; ☎ 809-869-6322; Las Mercedes 341; ☽ Tue-Sun 8pm-late) Only a block from Calle El Conde, Esedeku is an intimate bar, with a huge selection of cocktails; not for hustlers.

Jay-Dee's (☎ 809-333-5905; José Reyes 10; admission US$4; ☽ Thu-Sat) Tourists aren't unusual at this raucous club, which gets crowded on weekends when there are drag shows and strippers. Admission buys you a drink as well.

Cinemas

Recent Hollywood movies are screened at **Broadway Cinemas** (Map pp74-5; ☎ 809-872-0171; Plaza Central Shopping Mall; tickets Mon-Thu US$2, Fri-Sun US$2.50), **Malecón Center Cinemas** (Map pp74-5; ☎ 809-685-2898; Av George Washington 500; tickets Tue & Wed US$1.75) and **Hollywood Diamond** (☎ 809-565-2898; Diamond Mall; tickets Mon-Wed US$3, Thu-Sun US$4.50), among others.

Centro Cultural Español (Spanish Cultural Center; Map pp80-1; ☎ 809-686-8212; www.ccesd.org, in Spanish; cnr Arzobispo Meriño & Arzobispo Portes; admission free; ☽ 10am-9pm Mon-Sat) There are no cinemas in the Zona Colonial, although this cultural center periodically showcases alternative films, mostly by Spanish and Dominican filmmakers. The theatre is actually a gallery with a big white wall where DVDs are projected – unfortunately the acoustics aren't the best. Stop by for a current schedule.

Theaters

Teatro Nacional (National Theater; Map p77; ☎ 809-687-3191; Plaza de la Cultura; tickets US$4-15) Hosts opera, ballet and symphonic performances. Tickets for performances at this 1600-seat theater can be purchased in advance at the box office from 9:30am to 12:30pm and 3:30pm to 6:30pm daily. For show dates and times, call or check the weekend editions of local newspapers.

Casinos

After baseball and cockfighting, gambling is one of the DR's favorite pastimes. All of the large hotels on the Malecón have casinos, including the **Hilton Hotel** (Map p77; ☎ 809-685-0000; www.hiltoncaribbean.com/santodomingo; Av George Washington 500), **Hotel InterContinental** (Map p77; ☎ 809-221-0000; www.intercontinental.com/santodomingo; Av George Washington 218), **Hotel Santo Domingo** (Map pp74-5; ☎ 809-221-1511; cnr Av Indepencia & Av Abraham Lincoln) and **Hispaniola Hotel & Casino** (Map pp74-5; ☎ 809-221-7111; cnr Av Independencia & Av Abraham Lincoln). They generally open at 4pm and close at 4am. Bets may be placed in Dominican pesos or US dollars. Las Vegas odds and rules generally apply, though there are some variations; it doesn't hurt to ask the dealer what differences he or she is aware of before you start laying down money. All of the dealers at these casinos speak Spanish and English.

Sports
BASEBALL

The boys of summer play in the winter here, in this *béisbol*-mad city. Soon after the US major-league season ends in October, the 48-game Dominican season kicks off. From mid-November until early February the top players from the DR with a handful of major and minor leaguers from the US compete all over the country.

There is also a Liga del Verano (Summer League) if you're in the DR outside of regular season. Various major-league franchises – the San Francisco Giants, the Toronto Blue Jays, Arizona Diamondbacks, NY Yankees, to name a few – maintain farm teams in the DR, and summer league play is a semiformal tournament between these teams. Games are held at smaller stadiums around town.

Estadio Quisqueya (Map pp74-5; ☎ 809-540-5772; cnr Av Tiradentes & San Cristóbal; tickets US$2-18; ☽ games 5pm Sun, 8pm Tue, Wed, Fri & Sat) One of the better places to see a game and experience the madness is at the home field for two of the DR's six professional teams, Licey (www.licey.com) and Escogido (www.escogido). You can get tickets to most games by arriving at the stadium shortly before the first inning; games between rivals Licey and Escogido or Licey and the Águilas sell out more quickly. Asking for the best seats available at the box office is likely to cost US$18 and put you within meters of either the ballplayers or the between innings dancers. Scalpers also congregate along the road to the stadium and at the entrance.

COCKFIGHTING

Coliseo Gallístico Alberto Bonetti Burgos (Map pp74-5; ☎ 809-565-3844; Av Luperón; admission US$7-17.50; ☾ matches 6.30pm Wed & Fri, 3pm Sat) The Madison Square Garden of the Dominican cockfighting world, this is where the best and the fiercest roosters are brought to fight. If you have any interest in experiencing this traditional Dominican spectator sport (for more about cockfighting see the Culture chapter, p54), this *gallera* (cockfighting ring) is a good choice. Its largest events draw rooster handlers from as far away as Colombia, Brazil, Panama and Peru. Matches are held from November to June, but December to April is the busiest season (the roosters' plumage is fullest then) and a match could have 30 or 40 fights and last into the wee hours. Handler entry fees are higher on Saturdays, so the roosters tend be better and the stakes higher. Betting on cockfights is an intense and complex art – experts bet with dozens of people at high speed using only hand signals – but a good place to start is simply betting the guy next to you which rooster will win. Opposing cocks are designated blue or white – colored tape is used to indicate which is which. There is always a favorite, so bets involve odds that can change even as the fight is in progress. Above all, there is a powerful honor system that allows huge amounts of money to change hands peacefully with no oversight whatsoever. Those who renege on bets can be barred for life from the ring. Fights are to the death – some are quick, others are torturous bloody affairs that can last up to 15 minutes (the official limit before a fight is called off) and so obviously aren't appropriate for everyone.

SHOPPING

More than anywhere else in the country, shopping in Santo Domingo runs the gamut from cheap tourist kitsch to high-end quality collectibles. The easiest – and best – neighborhood to shop in is the Zona Colonial where you'll find rows of shops offering locally made products at decent prices. Large, American-style malls scattered around the city have good selections of clothing, music and shoe stores.

Amber & Larimar

If you're considering buying something in amber or larimar, shop around since these stones, considered national treasures, are virtually ubiquitous in Santo Domingo. Typically they're presented as jewelry, but occasionally you'll find figurines, rosaries and other small objects. For help on choosing amber, see boxed text (p173). Quality and price vary greatly and fakes aren't uncommon. For a sure thing, try the Museo de Ambar (p79) or Larimar Museum (p79), or one of the following shops.

Swiss Mine (Map pp80-1; ☎ 809-221-1897; Calle El Conde 101; ☾ 9am-6pm Mon-Fri, 10am-4pm Sat) English, French, Italian and German are all spoken at this shop, which is notable for its high-quality design work; it now also has an excellent selection of artwork by contemporary Dominican painters.

Flor Ambar Gift Shop (Map pp80-1; ☎ 809-687-3793; Las Damas 44; ☾ 9am-6pm) Amid cheap souvenirs, Flor Ambar offers a nice selection of amber and larimar jewelry.

Art

Walking around Santo Domingo you'll see sidewalk displays of simple, colorful canvases of rural life and landscapes. This so-called Haitian or 'primitive art' is so prevalent that it's understandable if you mistake it for the country's de facto wallpaper. Most of what you see on the street is mass-produced, low-quality amateur pieces with little value. For unique and interesting Dominican pieces, there are a number of more formal galleries in Santo Domingo.

The best resource on Dominican art and artists is still the authoritative *Enciclopedia de las Artes Plásticas Dominicanas* (Encyclopedia of Dominican Visual Arts) by Cándido Gerón. Illustrations and Spanish text are followed by English translations; look for copies at used bookstores in the Zona Colonial.

Bettye's Galería (Map pp80-1; ☎ 809-688-7649; Plaza de María de Toledo; Isabel la Católica 163; ☾ 9am-6pm, closed Tue) Browse through this gallery, connected to the guesthouse of the same name, if you like antiques, jewelry, and quirky souvenirs and paintings.

De Soto Galería (Map pp80-1; ☎ 809-689-6109; Calle Hostos 215; ☾ 9am-5:30pm Mon-Fri, 9am-noon Sat) This is a small gallery specializing in Dominican and Haitian painters. A rambling array of antiques is also for sale.

Galería de Arte María del Carmen (Map pp80-1; ☎ 809-682-7609; Arzobispo Meriño 207; ⏰ 9am-7pm Mon-Sat, 10am-1pm Sun) In business for over two decades, this place has been selling art long enough to attract a wide range of talented Dominican painters.

Outside of the Zona Colonial are dozens of other galleries that feature Haitian and Dominican art. **Galería de Arte El Greco** (Map pp74-5; ☎ 809-562-5921; Av Tiradentes 16; ⏰ 8am-noon & 2-6pm Mon-Fri) and **Galería de Arte El Pincel** (Map pp74-5; ☎ 809-544-4295; Av Gustavo Mejía Ricart 24; ⏰ 8am-noon & 2-6pm Mon-Fri) are good options.

Cigars

Dominican cigars are widely respected by aficionados around the world, so much so that the DR is one of the leading exporters. To try one for yourself, stop into one of the many cigar stores around Santo Domingo – you'll see several just strolling down Calle El Conde. Typically, prices vary from US$2 to US$6 per cigar and boxes can run as high as US$110.

La Leyenda del Cigarro (Map pp80-1; ☎ 809-686-5489; Calle Hostos 402) This small shop several blocks north of Parque Colón has a good selection of premium cigars, but equally importantly, the helpful staff are more than willing to answer the naive questions of cigar novices.

If you want to see *tabacos* being rolled, drop by the **Boutique del Fumador** (Map pp80-1; ☎ 809-685-6425; Calle El Conde 109; ⏰ 9am-7pm Mon-Sat, 10am-3:30pm Sun) or the **Museo del Tabaco** (Map pp80-1; ☎ 809-689-7665; Calle El Conde 101; ⏰ 9:30am-8pm); both are located on Parque Colón and are owned by the same tobacco company – Monte Cristi de Tabacos. At either one you can watch as one or two workers roll cigars in the shop window – a sampling of the 45 workers who roll away the day on the 2nd floor of the Boutique del Fumador. Montecristo, Cohiba and Caoba brand cigars are sold at both shops.

Handicrafts

Felipe & Co (Map pp80-1; ☎ 809-689-5812; Calle El Conde 105; ⏰ 9am-8pm Mon-Sat, 10am-6pm Sun) This shop on Parque Colón is stocked with charming high-quality handicrafts, like ceramics, jewelry and handbags, with also a good selection of paintings. Some of the best finds are stocked way in the back of this deep shop, easily one of the best in the Zona Colonial.

Muñecas Elisa (Map pp80-1; ☎ 809-682-9653; Arzobispo Nouel 54; ⏰ 9am-6pm Mon-Sat) Specializing in Dominican faceless dolls, this spacious shop sells the highest-quality figurines in town. Dolls are handcrafted in-house and are made of porcelain; all are also dressed in late-18th-century garb. Prices vary widely according to the size and detail of each and run from US$10 to US$550.

Markets

Mercado Modelo (Map pp80-1; Av Mella; ⏰ 9am-5pm) Housed in an aging two-story building just north of the Zona Colonial near a neighborhood of Chinese restaurants and stores, bargain hard at this local market, which sells everything from love potions to woodcarvings and jewelry. The more you look like a tourist, the higher the asking price. It's best not to dress too sharply or wear any fine jewelry yourself, in part to get a fair deal and in part because this isn't the best neighborhood to wander around, especially after dark.

Pulga de Antigüedades (Map pp80-1; Plaza de María de Toledo, Calle General Luperón; ⏰ 9am-4pm Sun) Poke around the clothes, shoes, handicrafts and antiques at this open-air flea market, held every Sunday on a small plaza a block north of Parque Colón.

GETTING THERE & AWAY
Air

Santo Domingo has two airports: the main one, **Aeropuerto Internacional Las Américas** (SDQ; off Map pp74-5; ☎ 809-549-0081), is 22km east of the city. The smaller **Aeropuerto Internacional La Isabela Dr Joaquin Balaguer** (JBQ, aka Higuero; off Map pp74-5; ☎ 809-567-3900), north of the city, handles mostly domestic carriers and air taxi companies. **Aerodomca** (☎ 809-826-4141/4242), **Caribair** (☎ 809-542-6688) and **Take Off** (☎ 809-552-1333; www.takeoffweb.com) service both airports.

Most international flights come into and depart from Las Américas. The major carriers:
Air Canada (Map pp74-5; ☎ 809-541-2929; Av Gustavo Mejía Ricart 54)
Air France Central Santo Domingo (Map p77; ☎ 809-686-8432; Plaza El Faro, Av Máximo Gómez 15); Airport (☎ 809-549-0311) The city branch shares its office with KLM.
American Airlines Zona Colonial (Map pp80-1; ☎ 809-542-5151; Calle El Conde); Airport (☎ 809-549-0043)
Continental Airlines Airport (☎ 809-549-0757); Central Santo Domingo (Map p77; ☎ 809-221-2222; www .renaissancehotels.com; Renaissance Jaragua Hotel, Av George Washington 367)
Copa (☎ reservations 809-549-2672, airport 809-472-2672)

FIRST-CLASS BUSES FROM SANTO DOMINGO

Destination	Fare (US$)	Duration (hr)	Distance (km)	Frequency (per day)
Azua	4.00	1¼	120	8
Barahona	6.70	3½	200	4
Castillo	5.50	1½	150	11
Dajabón	8.50	5	305	4
Jarabacoa	5.40	3	155	4
La Vega	4.50	1½	125	every 30min, 6am-8pm
Las Matas de Santa Cruz	7.50	2½	250	4
Monte Cristi	8.50	4	270	6
Nagua	7.60	3½	180	11
Puerto Plata	8.20	4	215	hourly 6am-7pm
Río San Juan	8.20	4½	215	5
Samaná	7.50	4	245	6
San Francisco de Macorís	6.70	2½	135	every 30-60min, 7am-6pm
San Juan de la Maguana	6.70	2½	163	4
Sánchez	7.50	4	211	6
Santiago	6.70	2½	155	every 30min, 6am-8pm
Sosúa	8.50	5	240	hourly 6am-7pm

Delta (Map pp74-5; ☎ 809-200-9191; Plaza Comercial Acropolis Center, cnr Av Winston Churchill & Andres Julio Aybar)

Iberia Santo Domingo (Map pp74-5; ☎ 809-686-9191; Av Lope de Vega 63); Airport (☎ 809-549-0205)

Jet Blue (☎ 809-549-1793) Located at the airport.

LanChile (Map p77; ☎ 809-689-2221; Av George Washington 353)

Lufthansa/Condor (Map p77; ☎ 809-689-9625; Av George Washington 353)

US Airways Santo Domingo (Map pp74-5; ☎ 809-540-0505; Av Gustavo Mejía Ricart 54); Airport (☎ 809-549-0165)

For more details on international air travel to and from the Santo Domingo area, see p255.

Boat

The DR's only international ferry service, **Ferries del Caribe** (Map pp80-1; ☎ in Santo Domingo 809-688-4400, in Santiago 809-724-8771, in Mayagüez, Puerto Rico 787-832-4400, in San Juan, Puerto Rico 787-725-2643), connects Santo Domingo with Mayagüez, Puerto Rico. The ticket office and boarding area are on Av del Puerto opposite Fortaleza Ozama in the Zona Colonial. The ferry departs Santo Domingo at 8pm on Sunday, Tuesday and Thursday and returns from Mayagüez at 8pm on Monday, Wednesday and Friday. The trip takes 12 hours and costs around US$129/189 one way/return in an airplane-style seat, or around US$182/311 (single/double) one way per person or US$295/474 (single/double) return in a private cabin with an exterior window.

Bus

Santo Domingo has no central bus terminal. Instead, the country's two main bus companies – **Caribe Tours** (Map pp74-5; ☎ 809-221-4422; www.caribetours.com.do; cnr Av 27 de Febrero & Av Leopoldo Navarro) and **Metro** (Map pp74-5; ☎ 809-227-0101; www.metroserviciosturisticos.com; Calle Francisco Prats Ramírez) – have individual depots west of the Zona Colonial. Caribe Tours has the most departures, and covers more of the smaller towns than Metro does.

Both lines use large, comfortable and fairly modern passenger buses; some even have TVs and screen movies. Air-conditioning on both lines is sometimes turned up to uncomfortable levels. In any case, all but a few destinations are less than four hours from Santo Domingo.

It's a good idea to call ahead to confirm the schedule and ticket price, and always arrive at least 30 minutes before the stated departure time. Both bus lines also publish brochures (available at all terminals) with up-to-date schedules and fares, plus the address and telephone number of their terminals throughout the country – handy if you'll be taking the bus often.

Expreso Santo Domingo Bávaro (Map p77; ☎ in Santo Domingo 809-682-9670, in Bávaro 809-552-0771; cnr Juan Sánchez Ruiz & Av Máximo Gómez) has a direct 1st-class service between the capital and Bávaro, with a stop in La Romana. Departure times in both directions are 7am, 10am, 2pm and 4pm (US$9, four hours).

There also are four 2nd-class bus depots near Parque Enriquillo in the Zona Colonial. All buses make numerous stops en route. Because the buses tend to be small, there can be a scrum for seats, especially for destinations with one to a few departures a day. *Caliente*, literally 'hot' buses, refer to those generally without air-con; *expreso* buses stop less often. Destinations include the following:

Baní (US$2.75, 1½ hours, every 15 minutes, 5am to 10pm)

Boca Chica (caliente/expreso US$1/1.25, 45 minutes, caliente every 15 minutes, expreso hourly, 6am to 8pm)

Higüey (caliente/expreso US$4.25/5, 2½ hours, caliente every 20 minutes, expreso hourly, 6am to 7pm)

Juan Dolio (US$2.10, one hour, every 30 minutes, 6am to 9:30pm)

La Romana (caliente/expreso US$2.75/4, two hours, caliente every 20 minutes, expreso hourly, 5am to 9pm)

Las Galeras (US$8, six hours, daily between 11:30am and 12:30pm depending on when bus arrives from Las Galeras)

Puerto Plata (US$5.25, 4½ hours, take any Sosúa bus)

San Cristóbal (US$1.40, 45 minutes, every 15 to 30 minutes, 6am to 10pm)

San Pedro de Macorís (US$2.30, one hour, every 30 minutes, 6am to 9:30pm)

Santiago (US$2.80, 2½ hours, take any Sosúa bus)

Sosúa (US$5.65, five hours, nine departures from 6:30am to 3:30pm)

To get to Haiti, **Capital Coach Line** (Map pp74-5; ☎ 809-530-8266; www.capitalcoachline.com; Av 27 de Febrero 455), Caribe Tours (p101) and **Terra Bus** (Map pp74-5; ☎ 809-531-0383; Plaza Lama, cnr Av 27 de Febrero & Av Winston Churchill) offer daily bus services to Port-au-Prince. Capital Coach Line has one departure daily at 10am, and Caribe and Terra at 11am and 11:30am respectively. All three use comfortable, air-con buses, and the trip takes from six to nine hours and costs US$40; that said, Capital and Caribe are more reliable and recommended. If possible, reserve at least two days in advance as the buses are frequently full.

Car

Numerous international and domestic car-rental companies have more than one office in Santo Domingo proper and at Las Américas International Airport – the majority have a booth in a small building just across the street from the arrivals exit. All are open daily roughly from 7am to 6pm in Santo Domingo (sometimes later) and from 7am to 11:30pm at the airport. For more information about costs, rental requirements etc, see p259.

Recommend car-rental companies:

Advantage Rent-a-Car (☎ 809-549-0536; Las Américas International Airport)

Avis Central Santo Domingo (Map pp74-5; ☎ 809-535-7191; cnr Av Abraham Lincoln & Av Sarasota); Airport (☎ 809-549-0468)

Budget Santo Domingo (Map pp74-5; ☎ 809-566-6666; cnr Av John F Kennedy & Av Lope de Vega); Airport (☎ 809-549-0351)

Dollar Central Santo Domingo (Map p77; ☎ 809-221-7368; Av Independencia 366); Airport (☎ 809-549-0738)

Europcar Central Santo Domingo (Map p77; ☎ 809-688-2121; Av Independencia 354); Airport (☎ 809-549-0942)

Hertz Central Santo Domingo (Map p77; ☎ 809-221-5333; Av José Ma Heredia 1); Airport (☎ 809-549-0454)

National/Alamo Central Santo Domingo (Map p77; ☎ 809-221-0805; Av Independencia at Máximo Gómez); Airport (☎ 809-549-8303)

Nelly Rent-a-Car (☎ 809-549-0505; Las Américas International Airport)

Thrifty (☎ 809-549-0930; Las Américas International Airport)

GETTING AROUND
To/From the Airport

There are no buses that connect directly to either of Santo Domingo's airports. From Las Américas, a taxi into the city costs US$25 to US$35, with only a little room for negotiation. The trip is a solid half-hour. If there are any other travelers arriving when you do, try sharing a ride. Taxis are available at the airport 24 hours a day. Many taxis, including Apolo Taxi, may be willing to take you from the city to the airport for much less.

The fare from La Isabela is more reasonable at US$10 to US$15. There's no permanent taxi stand there, but at least one or two taxis meet every flight. If, for whatever reason, there are no taxis around when you arrive, call one of the companies mentioned in the Taxi section (opposite).

Car

Driving can be difficult in Santo Domingo due to heavy traffic and aggressive drivers, especially taxis and buses. Drive with caution and whenever possible have a passenger help you navigate the streets. Finding parking is not typically a problem, though if you are leaving your car out overnight, ask around for a parking lot. Many midrange and top-end hotels have parking with 24-hour guards. In any case, be sure not to leave any valuables inside your car.

ISLAND METRO

'Centro de Héroes to Mamá Tingó.' Not exactly the same ring as 'Times Square to Broadway,' but functional nevertheless. Caribbean islands and underground metros usually don't appear to go together. But Santo Domingo is joining San Juan, Puerto Rico, as the second city in the region to have a commuter train system. By the time this book goes to print, Dominicans will be riding to work on the 14km track from the northern suburbs to downtown (16 stops, 10 underground). Whether this will have any impact on the city's disastrous traffic is another matter. And whether this is a misguided and even cynical project that will only benefit politicians and contractors, a white elephant on par with the Faro a Colón, or whether it's a much needed modernization of Santo Domingo's failing transportation system is up for debate.

Ask any taxi driver in the city what they think of the project and they're likely to respond skeptically, doubtful that it will ever actually start running. After all, it's opening date keeps getting pushed back, and at US$700 million it's US$230 million over the initial cost estimate. Many will question whether this is a good use of public funds in a country with substandard education and health care. And the big dig certainly isn't doing anything to help traffic in the meantime. Pop culture has weighed in on the debate: 'Now we have a Metro' is the sarcastic refrain for a song about the country's failures by the Dominican rap group La Krema.

Keeping his promise that he would ride the train by Independence Day 2008, President Leonel Fernandez boarded one of the French-manufactured three car trains – air-con, CCTV, sorry, no wi-fi – for a nonstop trip on elevated Line 1, which runs from Villa Mella in the north to La Feria. The fact that stations are named after well-known Dominicans (and foreigners like John F Kennedy and Abraham Lincoln) rather than streets may be inconvenient, but it may also lead some to brush up on their history. The Santo Domingo metro: convenient and educational.

Public Transportation

The city's bus system is simple to use and very cheap – the cost of a bus ride from one end of the city to the other is around US$0.25. Official public buses started using fixed bus stops in 1998, when a fleet of Brazilian-made buses was inaugurated and the president himself took the bus to work. Most stops are marked with a sign and the word *parada* (stop), but it took several years and a major public service campaign to get locals to actually use them. The routes tend to follow major thoroughfares – in the Zona Colonial, Parque Independencia is where Av Bolivar (the main westbound avenue) begins and Av Independencia (the main eastbound avenue) ends. If you're trying to get across town, just look at a map and note the major intersections along the way and plan your transfers accordingly.

Even more numerous than buses are the *públicos* – mostly beaten-up minivans and private cars that follow the same main routes but stop wherever someone flags them down. They are supposed to have *público* on their license plates, but drivers will beep and wave at you long before you can make out the writing. Any sort of hand waving will get the driver to stop, though the preferred gesture is to hold out your arm and point down at the curb in front of you. The fare is US$0.35 – pay when you get in. Speaking of getting in, be prepared for a tight squeeze – drivers will cram seven or even eight passengers into an ordinary two-door car.

Taxi

Taxis in Santo Domingo don't have meters, so you should always agree on the price before climbing in. The standard fare is a low US$3.50, even to the other side of the city. Within the Zona Colonial it should be even cheaper. Taxi drivers don't typically cruise the streets looking for rides; they park at various major points and wait for customers to come to them. In the Zona Colonial, Parque Colón and Parque Duarte are the best spots.

You can also call for a taxi or ask the receptionist at your hotel to do so. Service is usually quick, the fare is the same, and you don't have to lug your bags anywhere. Many of the top hotels have taxis waiting at the ready outside, but expect to pay more for those. Reputable taxi agencies with 24-hour dispatches include **Aero-Taxi** (☎ 809-685-1212), **Apolo Taxi** (☎ 809-537-7771), **Super Taxi** (☎ 809-536-7014) and **Taxi Cacique** (☎ 809-532-3132).

Around Santo Domingo

One of the pleasures of city living is leaving it. And like residents of large cities the world over, residents of Santo Domingo regularly feel the urge to flee the traffic, pollution and chaos of the capital city's streets for stress-free weekend escapes. Boca Chica, within commuting distance not far to the east and just past the airport, isn't far enough removed from the urban milieu – despite the white sand, bathtub-calm waters and seaside restaurants. When the sun goes down, so do the town's inhibitions, and its seedy side – still alive after many years – becomes hard not to notice. Only a little further east is Juan Dolio, more relaxing and comfortable and blessed with a long stretch of soft white sand and several resorts just outside town. For a chance to experience Dominican life in the streets outside of Santo Domingo, head to San Pedro de Macorís, a baseball player–producing factory only a short drive further east.

Basically an extension of Santo Domingo's creeping sprawl to the west, San Cristobal is noteworthy as the birthplace of dictator Rafael Trujillo and the gateway to an anthropological reserve with Taíno cave paintings. For those traveling to the southwestern part of the country, Baní makes a convenient stop. Known as the birthplace of Generalísimo Máximo Gómez y Báez, leader of Cuba's struggle for independence from Spain, Baní is also the turnoff to reach the dunes around Las Salinas or to start the climb north to the mountain village of San José de Ocoa. This route west of the city passes through a textured DR, one not defined by foreigners' needs and tastes but by the lives of ordinary people.

HIGHLIGHTS

- Relax on the soft white sand and mellow seas of **Juan Dolio** (p110), the best beach resort near Santo Domingo

- Cheer for the home team at **Estadio Tetelo Vargas** (p112) in San Pedro de Macorís, the baseball capital of the country

- Slide around the wind-blown sand hills of the **Dunas de las Calderas** (p115) near Las Salinas

- Explore the mountain scenery around **San José de Ocoa** (p116)

- Marvel at the hundreds of Taíno cave paintings at **Reserva Antropológica El Pomier** (p114), outside San Cristobal

GETTING THERE & AROUND

Because several of the destinations in this chapter are best visited as a day or overnight trip, a rental car is the most convenient option and allows you flexibility. This is especially recommended if you're traveling west of Santo Domingo, because many of the sights otherwise would involve multiple trips on multiple versions of public transportation – the effort and trouble would be of questionable value. That being said, it's easy to reach all of the towns by *gua-gua* (local bus) or taxi (the latter option is pricey).

EAST OF SANTO DOMINGO

Cross Río Ozama, the eastern border of the Zona Colonial in Santo Domingo, and the claustrophobia fades, the horizon opens and you remember that you're in the Caribbean. The highway hugs the coast for some time with promising views but then retreats inland once again, passing service stations and shops hugging the roadside until the turnoff for the beach resorts of Boca Chica and Juan Dolio a little further on.

PARQUE NACIONAL SUBMARINO LA CALETA

In the past this underwater park was a park in name only; little was done to protect the 12 sq km of underwater acreage in front of the Aeropuerto Internacional Las Américas. As a result of lax controls and the damage from Hurricane Jean in 2004, the number of coral and fish species here is very low. Only recently has the Ministry of Environment teamed up with Reef Check, a non-profit environmental organization, to try to halt the damage and restore the marine life. It is also the resting place of the *Hickory*, a salvage ship that was scuttled in 1984, the year the park was founded (see boxed text, p107) and now a popular dive site. If you're interested in diving here, contact one of the dive shops in Boca Chica (see p107) or any of the resorts in Juan Dolio.

BOCA CHICA
pop 58,200

Boca Chica is a survivor. After weathering development boom–bust cycles and being overshadowed by resorts further east, it staggers on, albeit with a healthy trade in sex tourism. It held a certain amount of cachet when the moneyed class built vacation homes here during Trujillo's regime, and in the 1960s when a few bayside hotels were built, and even again in the early 1990s during another construction boom, . These days, however, aside from its proximity to the capital and the airport, there's not a lot to recommend it; after all it's not much further to nicer resorts to the east. It does, however, have a long white, sandy beach with waters so calm and shallow it resembles a lagoon.

Orientation

Boca Chica comprises a 10-by-15-block area between Hwy 3 and Bahía de Andrés. From the highway there are three main avenues – 24 de Junio, Juan Bautista Vicini and Caracol – that lead downhill to the oceanfront streets of Av San Rafael and Av Duarte. It's only 8km to Aeropuerto Internacional Las Américas and 33km to Santo Domingo, both to the west.

Information
INTERNET ACCESS & TELEPHONE
Codetel Centro de Comunicaciones (Av San Rafael near Av Caracol; ⏲ 8am-10pm) International telephone service; the main entrance is on Av Duarte.

QK Internet Center (Av Duarte near Calle Sánchez; ⏲ 9am-10pm Mon-Sat, 9am-6pm Sun) Inexpensive international telephone rates and decent internet rates, too (per hour US$2.80).

Safe Power Contact (SPC; Av Juan Bautista Vicini; ⏲ 9am-10pm) Only a block south of Av Las Américas, this small shop has several computers in good condition with high-speed internet (per hour US$1); cheap international calling rates as well.

MEDICAL SERVICES
Farmacia Boca Chica (☎ 809-523-4708; Av Duarte near Av Juan Bautista Vicini; ⏲ 8:30am-9pm Mon-Sat, 8:30am-8pm Sun)

MONEY
Banco Popular (cnr Av Duarte & Av Juan Bautista Vicini; ⏲ 8am-3pm Mon-Fri, 9am-1pm Sun) Opposite the southwest corner of Parque Central. One ATM.

BanReservas (cnr Av San Rafael & Calle Juanico García; ⏲ 8am-5pm Mon-Fri, 9am-1pm Sat)

POST
Post office (Av Duarte near Av Juan Bautista Vicini; ⏲ 8am-5pm Mon-Fri, 8am-noon Sat)

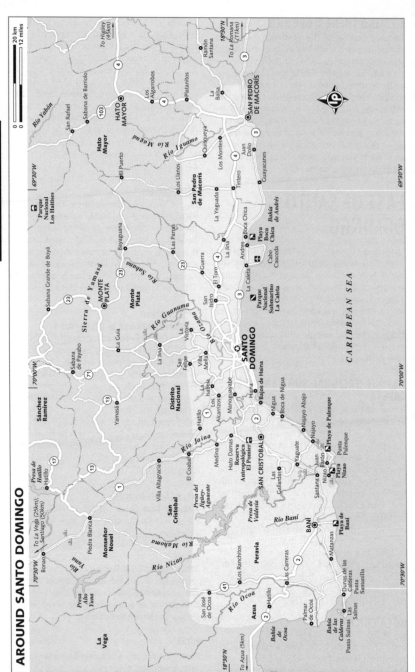

AROUND SANTO DOMINGO

AROUND SANTO DOMINGO

CARIBBEAN SEA

Sights

The thing about the beach at Boca Chica is that it's in Boca Chica. This means that despite the powdery white sand and tranquil waters, it's unlikely to be a relaxing experience. Flanked by Av Caracol and Av 24 de Junio, **Playa Boca Chica** is lined with coconut palms and food stands, restaurants and bars. During the day, the beach is filled with locals and foreigners, and vendors selling everything from fruit to cigars to large canvases of Haitian paintings. The view, not exactly a picture postcard, is of loading cranes and a sugar refinery in the distance.

The beach is effectively divided into three sections: the eastern side has a tiny half-moon section backed by the Hotel Oasis Hamaca that leads past a rusty children's swing set to a narrow stretch clustered with restaurants and bars only a few body lengths from the water; the central area – which is the best place for sunbathing; and the western end, where it widens out and eventually gives way to a sandy parking lot and a row of food stalls selling cheap local food.

Activities

There are over 25 dive sites in the area; most are located in the Parque Nacional Submarino La Caleta, with its two shipwrecks and myriad coral heads. The water is warm – averaging 25°C – and the visibility ranges between 5m and 28m, depending on the season. Dive trips to a nearby cave are also offered, as are trips to the waters near Bayahibe and Isla Catalina.

There are two reputable dive shops in town – **Treasure Divers** (☎ 809-523-5320; www.treasurediv ers.de; Av Abraham Nuñez; ⏱ 8:30am-5pm), on Playa Boca Chica near Don Juan Beach Resort, and **Caribbean Divers** (☎ 809-854-3483; www.caribbeandiv ers.de; enter at Av Duarte 28; ⏱ 8:30am-5pm), also on the beach. Dives average US$40 with equipment, but multidive packages bring the prices down a little. PADI courses (open water diver US$425) are also offered. English, French and German are spoken at both.

Tours

Cigua Tours (☎ 809-877-1689; www.erika-cigua-tours .com; cnr Av Duarte & Calle Domínguez; ⏱ 9am-noon & 4-6pm), a German-run tour company operating out of a clapboard kiosk, also has an office in Juan Dolio. Trips on offer include Santo Domingo (per person US$30), Isla Saona (per person US$65), Isla Catalina (per person US$65) and Los Haitises National Park (per person US$65).

Sleeping

Villa Marianna (☎ 809-523-4679; Av Juan Bautista Vicini 11; r with/without air-con US$45/35; ❄ 🔊) Old

AROUND SANTO DOMINGO

THE HUNTER BECOMES THE HUNTED

For divers, the main attraction in the Parque Nacional Submarino La Caleta is the *Hickory*, a 39m-long steel ship that was scuttled in 1984. Once a vessel that carried treasure hunters, the tables have now turned and the *Hickory* has become a sought-after underwater destination.

The *Hickory* was the primary vessel used in the recovery of artifacts from the Spanish galleons *Nuestra Señora de Guadalupe* and *El Conde de Tolosa*, both of which sank in the Bahía de Samaná on 25 August 1724. Both of these galleons were en route to Mexico when a violent storm forced them away from the shore and towards a treacherous coral reef. The captains were unable to steer the galleons to safety and the ships were torn apart and sank, taking the lives of over 600 passengers.

The remains of the ships – and their cargo – were left untouched until 1976 when fishermen discovered the *Guadalupe*. Curious about the wreck, the Dominican government hired Tracy Bowden, president of the Caribe Salvage Company of Texas, to explore the sunken galleon using the *Hickory*.

Bowden and his crew spent over a year digging through the sediment that had accumulated over the galleon before recovering any artifacts. Spanish records also indicated that the *Tolosa* had sunk within hours of the *Guadalupe*; knowing that it had to be nearby, the salvagers searched the Bahía de Samaná for six months before finding it just northwest of Miches.

Among the thousands of items discovered at the two wreck sites were hundreds of silver and gold coins minted in Spain during the early 18th century, a cache of jewelry and hundreds of crystal glasses.

AROUND SANTO DOMINGO

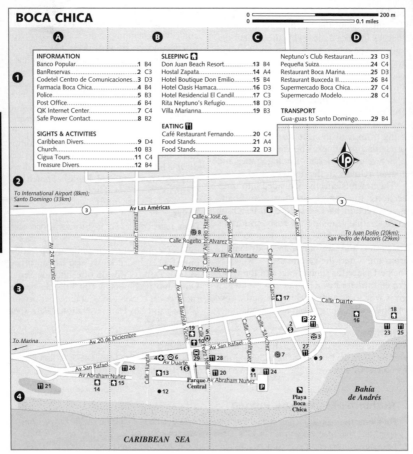

BOCA CHICA

0 ————— 200 m
0 ————— 0.1 miles

INFORMATION
Banco Popular................................**1** B4
BanReservas.....................................**2** C3
Codetel Centro de Comunicaciones...**3** D3
Farmacia Boca Chica.......................**4** B4
Police..**5** B3
Post Office......................................**6** B4
QK Internet Center..........................**7** C3
Safe Power Contact.........................**8** B2

SIGHTS & ACTIVITIES
Caribbean Divers.............................**9** D4
Church...**10** B3
Cigua Tours...................................**11** C4
Treasure Divers.............................**12** B4

SLEEPING
Don Juan Beach Resort...................**13** B4
Hostal Zapata................................**14** A4
Hotel Boutique Don Emilio.............**15** B4
Hotel Oasis Hamaca.......................**16** D3
Hotel Residencial El Candil.............**17** C3
Rita Neptuno's Refugio..................**18** D3
Villa Marianna...............................**19** B3

EATING
Café Restaurant Fernando...............**20** C4
Food Stands...................................**21** A4
Food Stands...................................**22** D3

Neptuno's Club Restaurant............**23** D3
Pequeña Suiza................................**24** C4
Restaurant Boca Marina.................**25** D3
Restaurant Buxceda II....................**26** B4
Supermercado Boca Chica..............**27** C4
Supermercado Modelo....................**28** C4

TRANSPORT
Gua-guas to Santo Domingo.......**29** B4

To International Airport (8km);
Santo Domingo (33km)

To Juan Dolio (20km);
San Pedro de Macoris (29km)

To Marina

CARIBBEAN SEA

Bahía de Andrés

Playa Boca Chica

Parque Central

---

mismatched furniture and less-than-spotless towels and linens aren't great calling cards, but the Marianna is friendlier than others and there's a small pool in the front yard. It's a white two-story building at the top of a steep slope several blocks from the beach.

our pick **Rita Neptuno's Refugio** (☎ 809-523-9934; Calle Duarte; www.dominicana.de/hotel-neptuno .htm; r US$40-50, 1-bedroom apt US$50-60, penthouse US$120; P ✗ ▢ ▣) Refuge (n.): protection or shelter from danger or hardship. This friendly hotel meets the dictionary definition – perched on a hill with views of the Caribbean in a quiet part of town, Neptuno's is the place to go for a long stay. Relaxed but efficient service and a nice, small pool are bonuses to the comfortable, cozy rooms.

Apartments come with fully equipped kitchens and private balconies. Breakfast isn't included in room rates, but is available for US$5.

Hotel Residencial El Candil (☎ 809-523-4252; www .comdata.nl/hotel-boca-chica-candil; cnr Calle Juanico García 2 & Av 20 de Diciembre; r from US$50; P ✗ ▢ ▣) Although it's located several blocks up from the beachfront on a residential street, El Candil is nevertheless good value. There are 24 apartments in several three-story buildings surrounding a small but well-kept pool and garden area. Each apartment comes with a fully equipped kitchenette, but the old wicker furniture in the sparsely decorated bedrooms feels dated. Wi-fi internet is available throughout the complex.

Hostal Zapata (☎ 809-523-4777; www.hotelzapata.com; Av Abraham Nuñez 27; s US$60-85, d US$70-95; **P** **X** **⌨**) Even a top-end all-inclusive place would envy the Zapata's beachfront real estate – and the private sandy backyard, a retreat from the hassles only a few feet away, is especially valuable. Not much attention is paid to the room furnishings; they're adequate enough but the lighting is dim and the small TVs have flickering pictures. Rooms with balconies facing the ocean obviously get more light and are worth the extra cost. Unfortunately, all of the upside is marred by a management attitude that is all business.

Hotel Boutique Don Emilio (☎ 809-523-4992; donemilio@hotmail.com; Av Abraham Nuñez; r from US$80; **P** **X**) Location, location, location. This real estate mantra is never truer than when talking about this purple behemoth. Rising four stories over the nicest stretch of beach in Boca Chica, the aging Don Emilio rests on this laurel and not much else. True, the modern rooms are clean enough, but the common areas and stairwell need a paint job and the vibe is more mercenary than friendly. Probably not the place for a family. Prices are negotiable.

Hotel Oasis Hamaca (☎ 809-523-4611; www.hotel esoasis.com; Calle Duarte near Av Caracol; s/d US$140/190; **P** **X** **⌨** **⌨**) The nicest of Boca Chica's resorts, the Oasis Hamaca occupies a strategic piece of beachfront property on the eastern edge of town. It's a bit of a fortress-like complex, with all amenities and facilities including tennis courts and a popular disco.

Don Juan Beach Resort (☎ 809-687-9157; www.donjuanbeachresort.com; Av Abraham Nuñez 8; s/d per person US$160/185; **P** **X** **⌨** **⌨**) The kind of Dominican all-inclusive that looks better from a distance, Don Juan is best appreciated with a discount – otherwise the bland food and mediocre rooms, not to mention the lack of privacy on the beach, will feel overpriced.

Eating

Café Restaurant Fernando (☎ 809-523-4939; Calle Pedro Mella near Av Duarte; mains US$5-11; ☻ lunch & dinner Mon-Sat) The food here is unremarkable – the typical menu of Italian-style and international standards and sandwiches – but it's a more organized and reliable choice than other similar restaurants in town.

Restaurant Buxceda II (☎ 809-527-5320; cnr Av Duarte & Calle Hungria; mains US$7-10; ☻ breakfast, lunch & dinner) This simple and unpretentious restaurant is willing to please: any fish, any style,

well within reason. Chow down family style at one of the long white tables in the open-air dining room.

Pequeña Suiza (☎ 809-523-4619; Av Duarte 56; mains US$9-20; ☻ breakfast, lunch & dinner) One of the better places to eat any time of day – English breakfast in the morning (US$7) and fondue (US$15), the house specialty at night – the Suiza isn't so *pequeña* (little). It has a great café/bar right on busy Av Duarte and an elegant dining room in the back on the beach.

Restaurant Boca Marina (☎ 809-523-6702; Calle Duarte 12A; mains US$10-24; ☻ breakfast, lunch & dinner) This restaurant on the eastern edge of town is perched over the water – you're even welcome to take a dip in between courses. And you just might want to cool off, since the service can be frustratingly slow and the fish and international standards only mediocre. Then again, with sunset views like this, there isn't much of a hurry.

Neptuno's Club Restaurant (☎ 809-523-4703; Calle Duarte 12; mains US$16-25; ☻ breakfast, lunch & dinner) Miami Beach comes to Boca Chica. This swank restaurant/club across the street from Rita Neptuno's Refugio is set on a platform overlooking the water. Lounge-style beds and all-white mini-cabanas set the mood for the party scene. Of course it's also an excellent restaurant, with above-average seafood specialties like lobster lasagna (US$16) and seafood casserole (US$25).

For a classic Dominican culinary experience, head to the **food stands** (cnr Av San Rafael & Caracol; ☻ 10am-6pm Fri-Sun) along the parking lot on the eastern end of Av Rafael or those set up on the beach on the western side of town. The former is open weekends only, when Dominican beachgoers line up to order fried whole fish, *plátanos* (fried green plantains) and *casabe* (flat round bread made of cassava). A meal costs US$5.50 and is often big enough for two.

Supermercado Boca Chica (cnr Av Duarte & Calle Juanico García; ☻ 9am-8pm Mon-Sat, 9am-6pm Sun) is the largest grocery store; **Supermercado Modelo** (Av San Rafael) is at the corner of Av Duarte.

Drinking

Boca Chica's reputation for seedy nightlife is well deserved. That being said, there are several pleasant places to kick back with a drink and dance in perfectly salubrious surroundings. Av Duarte is closed to cars from around 7pm and restaurants and bars set up tables on the street; many of the tables are taken up by older foreign men and younger Dominican women. Any single person, male or female, walking down the street is sure to receive attention.

Getting There & Away

Second-class buses service Boca Chica to Santo Domingo (*caliente/expreso* US$1/1.25, 30 minutes, *caliente* every 15 minutes, *expreso* every hour, from 6:30am to 8:30pm). *Gua-guas* stop on the north side of Parque Central and along Av San Rafael.

If you're heading east, *gua-guas* stop at the intersection of the highway and Av Caracol. Destinations include Juan Dolio (US$1.10, 15 minutes, every 30 minutes from 6:30am to 10pm), San Pedro de Macorís (US$1.30, 30 minutes, every 30 minutes from 6:30am to 10pm), La Romana (*caliente/expreso* US$1.75/2, 1½ hours, *caliente* every 20 minutes, *expreso* every hour, from 6:30am to 7:30pm) and Higüey (*caliente/expreso* US$3.25/4, two hours, *caliente* every 20 minutes, *expreso* every hour, from 6:30am to 7:30pm).

If you prefer taxis, you can often find one near the intersection of Av San Rafael and Av Caracol. Alternatively, you can get door-to-door service by calling the **Taxi Turístico Boca Chica** (☎ 809-523-4797). One-way fares include: Aeropuerto Internacional Las Américas (US$20), Santo Domingo (US$23), Juan Dolio (US$20), San Pedro de Macorís (US$50), Higüey (US$100) and La Romana (US$75).

Getting Around

Boca Chica is small and easily covered on foot. Despite this, you'll likely by asked if you need a ride by every passing *motoconcho* (motorcycle taxi). When not cruising the streets, they can be found congregating near the Parque Central. Rides around town cost US$1.

JUAN DOLIO

Juan Dolio has had its ups and downs, the natural byproducts of real estate speculation and investors hoping to cash in on the next Caribbean hot spot. Much younger, though, in terms of its evolution, the area remained undeveloped as recently as the late 1980s. Today, the small community is in a state of limbo: while the public beach itself is fairly small and cramped, the area in front of the resorts to the east of town is wider and softer than in nearby Boca Chica.

Most tourists stay at one of the several all-inclusive resorts east of town, however there's enough of a trickle of guests, independent travelers, loyal expats and Dominicans to keep a handful of bars and restaurants in town in business.

Orientation

Juan Dolio consists of a long narrow sliver of land between Hwy 3 (aka Boulevard) and the beach. From Hwy 3, there's an access road called Entrada a los Conucos just east of a large Shell gas station. Take this one short block towards the beach to Carretera Local, the main street through town. The intersection of Entrada a los Conucos and Carretera Local is the main area in town, with a number of restaurants, bars, shops and services clustered nearby. The hotels, including all of the resorts, are east of there, and not within walking distance if you're carrying baggage. The exception is the Hotel Fior di Loto, which is 500m west of the main intersection.

Information

The Shell gas station on the boulevard west of Entrada a los Conucos has a 24-hour Banco León ATM. There are also two ATMs on the property of the Coral Costa Caribe Resort.

Banco Popular (Plaza Turística, Carretera Nueva; ☽ 9am-5pm Mon-Fri, 9am-1pm Sun) Located 400m east of the Barceló Capella Beach Resort.

Cigua Tours (☎ 809-526-2077; Plaza de la Luna, Carretera Local; ☽ 8am-11pm) This small travel agency can book domestic and international air tickets, reserve rental cars, and book hotels around the DR. It also organizes day trips to Santo Domingo (per person US$30), Isla Saona (per person US$65), Isla Catalina (per person US$65), Parque Nacional Los Haïtises (per person US$65) and whale watching (per person US$95).

Farmacia Boulevard (☎ 809-526-2041, ext 223; Plaza Turística, Carretera Nueva; ☽ 8am-8pm Mon-Fri, 8am-7pm Sat & Sun) Affiliated with, and next door to, the Tourist Medical Service.

Ilsa (☎ 809-526-2777; Plaza de la Luna, Carretera Local; internet per hr US$4; ☽ 8am-11pm) Internet access and international calls. It's near the Coral Costa Caribe Resort.

Internet Center (Plaza Chocolate, Carretera Local; per hr US$2; ☽ 8am-8pm) Internet access.

Politur (☎ 809-526-1048; Av Boulevard; ☽ 24hr) For emergencies; next to the National Police building.

Rossy Call Center (Carretera Nueva; internet per hr US$3; ☽ 7am-8pm) Several computers with high-speed access; international call center. Barber shop in front.

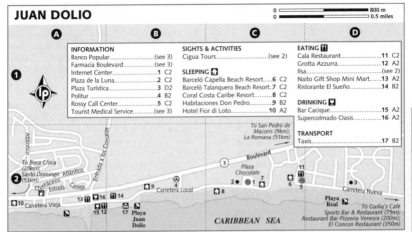

JUAN DOLIO

0			800 m	
0			0.5 miles	

INFORMATION
Banco Popular..........................(see 3)
Farmacia Boulevard................(see 3)
Internet Center........................1 C2
Plaza de la Luna.......................2 C2
Plaza Turística.........................3 D2
Politur.....................................4 B2
Rossy Call Center.....................5 C2
Tourist Medical Service...........(see 3)

SIGHTS & ACTIVITIES
Cigua Tours..............................(see 2)

SLEEPING
Barceló Capella Beach Resort.....6 C2
Barceló Talanquera Beach Resort..7 C2
Coral Costa Caribe Resort.........8 C2
Habitaciones Don Pedro...........9 B2
Hotel Fior di Loto....................10 A2

EATING
Cala Restaurant.......................11 C2
Grotta Azzurra........................12 A2
Ilsa...(see 2)
Naito Gift Shop Mini Mart........13 A2
Ristorante El Sueño..................14 B2

DRINKING
Bar Cacique............................15 A2
Supercolmado Oasis................16 A2

TRANSPORT
Taxis......................................17 B2

To San Pédro de
Macoris (9km);
La Romana (51km)

Atlántico
Cut-saceos
To Boca Chica
(20km);
Santo Domingo Atlántico
(53km)
Entrada Cenrejo

Entrada a los Conucos

Boulevard
Plaza
Chocolate

Carretera Local

Carretera Nueva

Playa
Real

Carretera Vieja

Playa
Juan
Dolio

CARIBBEAN SEA

To Guilia's Café
Sports Bar & Restaurant (75m);
Restaurant Bar Pizzeria Venezia (200m);
El Concon Restaurant (350m)

AROUND SANTO DOMINGO (sidebar)

Tourist Medical Service (☎ 809-526-2041; Plaza Turística, Carretera Nueva; ☺ 24hr) General and specialized medical services. English, German and French spoken.

Sleeping

Hotel Fior di Loto (☎ 809-526-1146; www.fiordilotohotel .com; Carretera Vieja; d US$10-20, tw US$30, apt with kitchen US$40) A little ashram on the Caribbean, this small idiosyncratic place about 500m west of the main intersection in Juan Dolio is for the traveler looking to mellow out in a backpacker-style hotel. That's not to say the rooms aren't comfortable; they're the equivalent of any mid-range place nearby and have clean, tile floors and overhead fans. And no other place offers regular meditation and yoga classes – and some of the proceeds from the hotel go to supporting a girls foundation in India. Hang out in the heavily cushioned front dining area draped with tapestries, or lounge on the 2nd-floor patio.

Habitaciones Don Pedro (☎ 809-526-2147; Carretera Local; r with fan/air-con $24/36; P ☒) There's little to recommend the dark and uninspiring rooms here over the Fior di Loto, other than the fact that the Don Pedro is directly across from the town beach. A detached apartment with small sitting area and kitchen is a good deal. The bar across the street is part of the Don Pedro family.

Barceló Talanquera Beach Resort (☎ 809-526-1510; www.barcelo.com; Carretera Local; s/d per person US$59/89; P ☒ ☐ ☒) Popular with the college crowd, this resort has a definite party feel to it: pool volleyball, packed bars and scantily clad guests are the norm. Rooms have seen better days;

ask for one in the 400 and 500 series, which are the most recently renovated. The beach is small and jam-packed with beach chairs, so if you're looking for some quiet time it's best to head east towards the Capella.

Barceló Capella Beach Resort (☎ 809-526-1080; www.barcelo.com; Carretera Nueva; s/d per person US$120/80; P ☒ ☐ ☒) Larger and more glamorous than its all-inclusive sister, rooms at the Capella are spread out around lush grounds with reflecting pools and the occasional flamingo and peacock. Inevitably for a resort this size, room quality is a bit uneven and the paint on the Caribbean-inspired architecture is peeling. The pool area is a little small considering the number of guests, but it's generally less of a party scene than the Coral Costa Caribe.

Coral Costa Caribe Resort (☎ 809-540-2008; www .coralcostacaribe.com; Carretera Local; s/d US$150/240; P ☒ ☐ ☒) Certainly every day isn't spring break but this all-inclusive place does have a party scene. Loud music is pumped from giant speakers around the pool area – the center of the action – and though the beach here is nice, it's small for the size of the resort. This high-rise property has fairly good motel-style rooms and several restaurants to choose from. Five bars and a disco round out a lively atmosphere.

Eating & Drinking

Don't worry if you're staying at an all-inclusive with less-than-stellar buffet food – Juan Dolio has several decent restaurants, both in town near the main intersection and strung out along Carretera Nueva east of the main resort area.

JUAN DOLIO

Ristorante El Sueño (☎ 809-526-3903; Carretera Local; meals US$4-12; �✆ noon-3:30pm & 7-11pm) Another casual open-air eatery, El Sueño is just east of Habitaciones Don Pedro. Pizzas and standard international mains round out the menu. Good spot for a drink as well.

Grotta Azzurra (☎ 809-526-2031; Carretera Vieja; mains US$5-10; �✆ lunch & dinner, closed Tue) Boasting a beachfront location – some tables are on the back porch with enviable views – this centrally located restaurant does good grilled fish. Also a good place for a sundowner.

Bar Cacique (Carretera Local; �✆ 9am-3am) This basic bar is popular with German expats and Dominicans alike.

Naito Gift Shop Mini Mart (cnr Carretera Local & Entrada a los Conucos; �✆ 8:15am-7pm) is the largest market in the center of town, with basic groceries and supplies. **Supercolmado Oasis** (cnr Blvd & Entrada a los Conucos) is good for a snack or a drink while waiting for onward transport.

CARRETERA NUEVA

Guilia's Café Sports Bar & Restaurant (Carretera Nueva; sandwiches US$3/9; �✆ breakfast, lunch & dinner) Juan Dolio's interpretation of a sports bar, Guilia's offers a flat-screen TV and pool table and serves up burgers (US$3).

Restaurant Bar Pizzeria Venezia (☎ 809526-1815; Carretera Nueva; pizzas US$5; �✆ lunch & dinner) Opposite the beach among the shells of condo developments, this restaurant has nice outdoor seating and a good selection of pizzas.

El Concon Restaurant (☎ 809-526-2562; mains US$6; �✆ lunch & dinner, closed Wed) Mostly locals go to this beachside thatched-roof restaurant. Pizza, pastas and grilled fish are served, and there's live music on Saturday nights.

ourpick Cala Restaurant (☎ 809-526-1108; Carretera Nueva; mains US$7-20; �✆ lunch & dinner) This sleek and modern restaurant across the street from the Barceló Capella Beach Resort looks like it belongs in a trendy neighborhood in New York City or London. Dining here puts the resort restaurants to shame; the experienced chef serves up delicious interpretations of Dominican specials and Italian cuisine.

Getting There & Around

Gua-guas pass through Juan Dolio all day every day, going westwards to Boca Chica

(US$1.10) and Santo Domingo (US$2.10), and east to San Pedro de Macorís (US$0.75), La Romana (US$2) and Higüey (US$3.50). No buses originate here, so there is no fixed schedule, but they pass roughly every 15 minutes from 6am to 7pm – stand on Blvd at the corner of Entrada a los Conucos and flag down any one that passes.

Taxis can be found in front of any of the resorts in town, and at a taxi stand on Carretera Local near the public parking lot for Playa Juan Dolio. Fares for one to four people range from US$25 (to Boca Chica), US$40 (Aeropuerto Internacional Las Américas), US$55 (to Santo Domingo) and up to US$130 (to Bávaro). You can also call **Juan Dolio Taxi** (☎ 809-526-2006) for door-to-door service.

When driving from Santo Domingo on Hwy 3, take the turnoff marked Playa Guayacanes.

SAN PEDRO DE MACORÍS
pop 251,900

It's hard to believe, as you drive past the harbor's crumbling balustrades, that only 50 years ago San Pedro was a cultural showplace of the Caribbean, with an opera hall where Jenny Lind (the 'Swedish nightingale') sang. Nineteenth-century locomotives carried millions of tons of sugarcane from the dense fields that ringed the city to giant grinders that mashed the cane into pulp, which was then refined into sugar. Today the same relentless humidity that converted the locomotives to heaps of rusting parts has transformed the elegant wooden homes into monuments of dry rot for termites to feast upon.

Sugar is still the basis for San Pedro's existence, but this provincial capital 65km east of Santo Domingo is most famous for producing more major-league baseball players per capita than any other city in the country. It's truly worth coming here to attend a baseball game (mid-November to early February) in the city's most prominent building, Estadio Tetelo Vargas, on the north side of Hwy 3.

Approaching San Pedro de Macorís from the west, you see the steeple of the **Catedral San Pedro Apostol** (�✆ 8am-8pm; Calle Charro near Av Independencia) from the bridge leading into town. It's notable only for the fact that the original church built in 1856 was destroyed by a hurricane nine years later, and again after being rebuilt, this time by a fire in

---

THREE BEST ROADS TO TAKE YOUR FOOT OFF THE ACCELERATOR

Santo Domingo traffic is enough to give the coolest driver road rage. Leave the bumper-to-bumper city behind and open your eyes to the world outside. Here are a few drives that are worth slowing down for:

■ San José de Ocoa (p116) to Baní (p115) – open the windows and poke your head out, taking in the beautiful views of the ocean from this mountain road; cycling is even better.

■ The Malecón of San Pedro de Macorís (opposite) – crawl slowly along the waterfront, seeing and being seen by Dominicans out for a stroll.

■ Around Las Salinas (p115) – plantations, ranches and small villages make up this area, a peninsula southwest of Baní; any of these are a good place to pull over and take in the fresh air and whatever is growing nearby.

1885. The version you see today has been standing for over 120 years.

WEST OF SANTO DOMINGO

Heading west from the city takes you not only in the opposite cardinal direction as the beach resorts to the east but also to a different DR – one whose landscape isn't defined by tourism but by the more haphazard demands of ordinary life. From Santo Domingo Hwy 2 cuts inland to the provincial capital of San Cristobal and from there it continues south to the city of Baní. Hwy 41, north to San José de Ocoa, takes you into the foothills of the Cordillera Central.

SAN CRISTOBAL
pop 220,000

During his authoritative and brutal rule, which lasted from 1930 until his assassination in 1961, Rafael Trujillo showered his hometown with generosity and monuments to his excess, including a never-lived-in mansion and a US$4 million dollar church, a paragon of Latin American Caudillo high kitsch (see boxed text, p114). The city's name was officially changed in 1934 to 'Meritorious City.' (It was changed back after Trujillo died.) An appropriate symbol and reminder of Trujillo's regime is the empty pedestal across from the church – it used to support a statue of the *commandante* on horseback but was pulled down by enraged Dominicans after Trujillo's death.

Today, this traffic-clogged provincial capital just 30km west of Santo Domingo,

is passed through by most visitors heading west from the capital. There are a few beaches nearby – Playa Palenque and Playa Najayo, popular with families on weekends – and it's also the nearest town to Reserva Antropológica El Pomier, a series of caves that contain the country's largest collection of Taíno cave paintings.

Because of its proximity to Santo Domingo and dearth of quality accommodation, San Cristobal is not a popular choice for staying overnight. The nearby **Rancho Campeche** (☎ 809-686-1053; www.ranchocampeche.com; Calle Leonor de Ovanda 1; tent & 3 meals per person US$22), however, offers one of the few opportunities to camp in the country. At the end of rough road west of San Cristobal, you can set up tents on this property overlooking the Caribbean. Toilets and shower facilities as well as meals are provided. Definitely arrange in advance since it's not uncommon for the property to be booked by groups or reserved for special occasions. Playa Palenque and Playa Najayo are nearby.

The culinary claim to fame of San Cristobal is the *pastelito en hoja,* literally 'pastry in paper,' basically a doughy empanada stuffed with cheese or meat wrapped in a piece of butcher paper. They cost around US$0.50 a piece and can be found at most eateries. San Cristobal's main **market**, along Calle María Trinidad Sánchez, is two blocks west of Av Constitución. All of San Cristobal's services are on those two streets, most within a few blocks of Parque Colón, where you'll be dropped if you arrive by bus.

Buses for San Cristobal leave Santo Domingo from Parque Enriquillo. In San Cristobal, *gua-guas* for the capital (US$1.40, 45 minutes) leave every 15 to 30 minutes from a stop at the southeast edge of the park.

CAUDILLO KITSCH

San Cristobal's strangest sight is not technically open to the public, but the soldiers guarding the **Castillo del Cerro** are usually happy to take the padlock off the door and let you look around. Trujillo had the structure built for himself and his family in 1947 (at a cost of US$3 million) but he reportedly hated the finished product and never spent a single night there. The name means 'Castle on the Hill,' which is pretty accurate – it overlooks the city – but the imposing concrete-and-glass structure looks like a medieval office building. Inside, though, huge dining rooms, ballrooms and numerous bedrooms and salons have fantastic ceilings and wall decorations made of plaster and painted in gaudy colors. The bathrooms – of which there must be 20 – have tile mosaics done in reds, blues and even gold leaf. There are six floors in all, and you can spend a half-hour or more just wandering through the abandoned structure.

Any taxi driver or *motoconchista* (motorcyle taxi driver) can take you there – it probably makes sense to ask the driver to come back in 30 to 60 minutes to pick you up. If you've got a vehicle, from Parque Independencia take Calle María Trinidad Sánchez west for 500m. Take a left onto Calle Luperón near the Isla gas station. Follow Calle Luperón for 800m until you reach a fork in the road. There, Calle Luperón veers right and an unsigned street veers left and uphill. Take the unsigned street and proceed another 500m to the top. There are signs saying 'Do Not Enter,' but you can disregard those and pull right into the parking area facing the front doors. A soldier is always posted there.

Atop another hill on the other side of San Cristobal is the house that Trujillo and his family actually used. It is called **Casa de Caoba** (House of Mahogany) and was clearly once splendid, but has been completely gutted since. There's often a caretaker on the premises who will open up a few rooms for a small tip, though there isn't much to see. It's believed it was here that Trujillo confronted the Spanish Columbia University professor Jesús Galíndez, who he had kidnapped from New York City; Galíndez was later murdered. The road to the house is rough, so a SUV is recommended.

Also interesting and slightly strange is the informal **Museo Jamas El Olvido Será tu Recuerdo** (☎ 809-474-8767) in the home of local resident José Miguel Ventura Medina, known to some as 'El Hippi.' The museum's name translates literally to 'Forgetfulness will never be your remembrance,' or simply 'You will never be forgotten.' The 'you' in this case is none other than Generalísimo Trujillo, who, along with John F Kennedy, was Ventura's favorite world leader. Most will not agree with Ventura's assessment of Trujillo as a 'good dictator,' but the extensive collection of photos and other memorabilia – plus a slew of random antiques, from old corn and coffee grinders to early typewriters – is worth poking around. Ventura, who speaks Spanish and English, has plenty of stories to go along with them. The museum is free and open whenever Ventura is home; if he's not there, give him a call. It's located on Calle General Leger several blocks north of the park – look for a small white car perched on the rooftop.

For towns west of San Cristobal, you have to go out to the main highway – under the overpass is a popular place – and flag down a passing bus (to Baní US$1.40, 45 minutes) to Barahona (US$3.80, three hours). At the time of research there was extensive road construction west of San Cristobal slowing traffic down significantly.

There are taxis and *motoconchos* in the vicinity of Parque Independencia from sunrise until late at night.

RESERVA ANTROPOLÓGICA EL POMIER

Visiting the Reserva Antropológica El Pomier is like reading a history book written in stone. There are 57 limestone **caves** (🕒 8am-5pm; admission US$3.50) in the area just 10km north of central San Cristobal, five of which (containing almost 600 paintings) are open to the public. The caves contain thousands of drawings and carvings that constitute the most extensive example of prehistoric art yet discovered in the Caribbean, including works by Igneri and Caribs as well as the Taínos. The faded drawings, painted with a mix of charcoal and the fat from manatees, depict birds, fish and other animals, as well as figures that may be deities. Relatively little is known about Hispaniola's earliest inhabitants, though the paintings here, believed to be as much as 2000 years old, provide some tantalizing clues. The principal cave was first discovered in 1851 by Sir Robert Schomburgk, who left his name and that of his companions on the wall. Unfortunately, the caves seem to be consistently closed for renovations; until recently they were also closed as a safety precaution because of nearby explosives blasting, part of a marble-mining operation. Local guides have fought to protect the site, though its future remains uncertain still to this day.

It's a challenge to get to the caves on your own – there are almost no signs marking the road to the caves, and the entrance, also unmarked, is several hundred meters down a mine access road. The easiest way there is to take a taxi or *motoconcho*. Round-trip with an hour wait should cost around US$5 on a *motoconcho* or US$15 in a taxi. If you're driving, follow Av Constitución north to La Toma, a small community across the highway from San Cristobal, where there is one easy-to-spot sign. From there, it's another 2.5km to a prominent but unmarked T-intersection, where you turn left and proceed up the hill for several more kilometers to the entrance. Ask as you go, as the turnoffs are easy to miss. Be alert for giant dump trucks coming down the road from the mine – there are a number of blind curves.

BANÍ
pop 73,800

Notable mainly as a convenient stopping point for those driving between Santo Domingo and Barahona, Baní also marks the turnoff for the beach and sand dunes of **Las Salinas** 20km to the southwest. Its historical claim to fame is as the birthplace of Generalísimo Máximo Gómez y Báez who, after serving in the Spanish army in Santo Domingo, moved to Cuba to become a farmer. During the 1860s, Gómez joined the insurgents opposed to Spanish rule and the heavy taxation it imposed, rose to the rank of general of the Cuban forces and, together with José Martí, led the revolution of 1868–78 that culminated in Cuba's independence from Spain.

Orientation

Baní's heart is Parque Duarte and you'll find all relevant services within a few blocks of here. To reach it from the east, turn right just after crossing the Río Baní, just in front of the oncoming one-way street that greets you almost at the foot of the bridge. Go two blocks and make a left onto Calle Máximo Gómez. Go six or seven blocks and make a left onto Calle Mella. After half a block you'll be at the intersection of Calle Sánchez and Calle Mella,

in front of the Iglesia Nuestra Señora de Regla (the city's main church).

To get to Parque Duarte from the west, turn right where Hwy 2 (also known as Sánchez Hwy) confronts an opposing one-way street. Turn left on Calle Sánchez – the first left you can make – and head six blocks to Parque Duarte.

Information

Banco León (cnr Hwy Sánchez & Calle Mella)
Banco Popular (Gómez at Duarte)
Centro Médico Regional (☎ 809-522-3611; Presidente Billini at Restauración) A recommended hospital four blocks east of Parque Duarte.
Farmacia Meniño (☎ 809-522-3344; Gómez btwn Duarte & Mella; ☽ 7:30am-9pm, 8am-noon Sun) A pharmacy on the other side of the church from the park.
Flash Point Cíber Café (☎ 809-522-2436; ☽ 9am-11pm) On Calle Mella, a half-block south of the park; internet access for US$1.50 per hour, and also operates as a calling center.

Sights

Baní's only tourist attraction, such as it is, is the **Casa de Máximo Gómez** (Calle Máximo Gomez; ☽ 8am-5pm; admission free), essentially a small park built on what was the site of the leader's birthplace and childhood home. Flags of Cuba and the DR, and a mural of Gómez watch over a marble bust of the man in the middle of the park. The site is located two blocks east of Parque Duarte.

Dunas de las Calderas, part of the Península de las Salinas, is 20 sq km of gray-brown sand mounds, some as high as 20m. The brown sandy beach near here gets crowded with Dominican families and windsurfers on Sundays and is not kept especially clean. Weekdays, you'll have it all to yourself. To get to Las Salinas, take any road from Parque Duarte south; eventually they all lead to a single paved though potholed road that passes through several small 'towns', at least one of which has an ATM. There's a naval station at the end of the road; continue past the guard's pillbox and turn left. Follow this road to town and the Salinas Hotel & Restaurant.

Sleeping & Eating

Hotel Caribani (☎ 809-522-3871; orencio2@hotmail .com; cnr Calles Sánchez 12 & San Tomé; s/d US$33/45; ☒) Adequate as a place to lay your head for the night, the Caribani is conveniently located only one block from the northwestern edge of

Parque Duarte. The basic dim rooms have cable TV, air-con and the standard safe box in the bathroom – the last place anyone would look, right? Pizzería Yarey is around the corner.

Salinas Hotel & Restaurant (☎ 809-866-8141; www .hotelsalinas.com; 7 Puerto Hermosa; per person US$75) Not many foreign travelers make it out here, almost the literal end of the road on the peninsula southwest of Baní. If you do, you'll likely be surprised by this hotel, not your standard all-inclusive resort – rates include breakfast, lunch, dinner and drinks. All the rooms in this four-story building with thatched roof have stunning views of the mountains across the bay, as does the restaurant – easily the best place to eat in town: lobster (US$18), seafood (US$12) and chicken (US$6). Rooms are large and comfortable, though the furnishings are fairly dated, and considering there's no beachfront the value is questionable. Sailboats are docked at the attached marina and the hotel has its own helipad, in case you plan on flying in. Otherwise you'll need your own vehicle to make a trip out here worthwhile.

Restaurant y Pizzería Yarey (☎ 809-522-3717; Calle Sánchez 10; mains US$7-10; ☺ breakfast, lunch & dinner) Waiters in bow ties, and a large open-air dining area make this restaurant one of the best in Baní. The pizza is mediocre but there are seafood and meat dishes to choose from as well. Yarey can be found on the north side of Parque Central, directly across from the Palacio del Ayuntamiento.

Supermercado Daneris (☎ 809-522-3410; cnr Calle Mella & Vladislao Guerrero), a small grocery for food and other supplies, is two blocks south of Parque Central.

Getting There & Away

There are express *gua-guas* to Santo Domingo (US$2.75, 1¼ hours, every 15 minutes from 3:40am to 8pm) leaving from a terminal a half-block west of the main park. Regular *gua-guas* leave even more frequently – every five minutes – and cost US$0.50 less, but take a half-hour longer to get there.

Gua-guas to San José de Ocoa (US$1.80, 45 minutes, hourly from 7am to 8pm) leave from a terminal about a kilometer west of the park on Av Máximo Gómez. Buses to Barahona (US$4.25, two hours) pass by the same terminal roughly every 30 to 60 minutes – they're coming from Santo Domingo and don't have a fixed schedule for Baní. They don't linger long here, so be sure to be on the lookout.

SAN JOSÉ DE OCOA
pop 21,900

San José de Ocoa is a collection of small colorful houses set in the foothills of the Cordillera Central. Ocoa, as it's known to locals who are descendants of Arab immigrants who arrived in the 19th century, is famous for its candied figs and its cooperative farming methods. The road here winds through undeveloped countryside, rising from 200m to nearly 2000m and was ruined after Tropical Storm Noel in October 2007, which cut the town off from the outside world for nearly two weeks.

The area is rich with spring water and a few *balnearios* (swimming holes), including filtered and chlorinated **Rancho Francisco** (☎ 809-558-4099; admission US$1; ☺ 8am-11pm), 1km south of town. A huge dining area serves standard fish, chicken and meat dishes for around US$7 to $10. It's quite busy on weekends, but is all but empty during the week.

There are two banks with ATMs, a post office and pharmacy around the town park. A few basic guesthouses can be found several blocks north of the park; the best is **Casa de Huéspedes San Francisco** (☎ 809-558-2741; cnr Calle Andrés Pimentel & Imbert; s/d US$18/22; ☼) with clean rooms and cable TV and hot water.

For a chance to get off the road, both in terms of a place to sleep and to explore the surrounding countryside, head to the German-owned **Rancho Cascada** (☎ 809-890-2332; www.ranchocascada.com; per person US$25; P ☻), a collection of six thatched-roof bungalows on the Río Nizao. Meals (US$5) are available, as are half- and full-day canoeing, horseback-riding, hiking and biking trips.

Getting There & Away

The bus stop (Calle Duarte between 16 de Agosto and Andrés Pimentel) is a half-block west of the park, across the street from the post office. *Gua-guas* for Santo Domingo (US$4, two hours) leave every 15 minutes from 4:15am to 5:30pm. If you're headed to Barahona, San Juan or other points west, take the Santo Domingo bus to the main highway (US$1.80) and flag a westbound *gua-gua* there.

For Constanza, pickup trucks make the tough, bumpy trip around three times per week. There is no fixed schedule or bus line, but either hotel can call around to see when the next truck is leaving. They typically leave very early – 5am or 6am – and charge from US$3 to $5 for the three- to four-hour trip.

The Southeast

This iconic region, synonymous with sun, sand and binge eating, is rightly popular with the hundreds of thousands of visitors who make the southeast the economic engine of the tourism industry in the DR. Sprawling resort developments, some like city-states unto themselves, line much of the beachfront from Punta Cana to Bávaro. However, the result is less like the high-rise congestion of Cancun or Miami and more like low-slung retirement communities, albeit ones populated by families, young and old, and couples and singles of all ages looking for a hassle-free holiday in the Caribbean.

Beyond the gated luxury enclaves, there's a vast landscape of sugar plantations dotted with *bateyes*, the small communities where many of the workers live. La Romana, a bustling city hugging the Río Chavón, anchors the sugar economy, but for travelers it's the nearby fishing village of Bayahibe that is of interest. Besides being the departure point for trips to the nearby islands in the Parque Nacional del Este, Bayahibe's seaside restaurants and bars feed a close-knit community of Dominicans and loyal expats.

Only a few miles north of Bávaro, the resorts thin out and the road leads inland past plantations and through small villages where horses are the preferred mode of transportation. Further up the coast, down a rutted and rough road is Playa Limón, an isolated stretch of beach backed by palm trees but also, more unusually, a lagoon and several mountain peaks. Those committed to carrying on west to Sabana de la Mar are rewarded with the Parque Nacional Los Haitises, a protected maze of caves and mangroves.

HIGHLIGHTS

- Stroll along the seemingly endless soft white beaches around **Bávaro** and **Punta Cana** (p131)
- Glide in a kayak through the mangrove forests of **Parque Nacional Los Haitises** (p140)
- Sit at the helm of a local fishing boat cruising the coastline near **Bayahibe** (p123)
- Escape the all-inclusive places by heading to **Playa Limón** (p137), a deserted beach paradise next to a protected lagoon
- Plunge into crystal-clear waters on a snorkeling or diving trip in the waters around **Parque Nacional del Este** (p124)

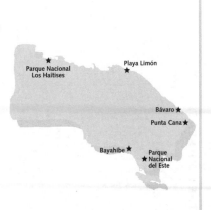

THE SOUTHEAST

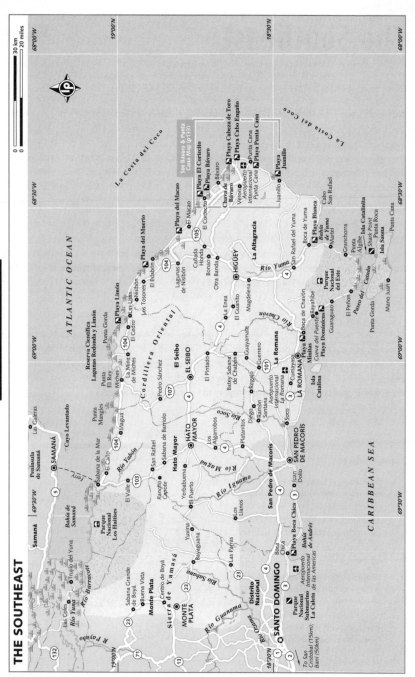

HISTORY

Before sugar, it was cattle ranching and the cutting and exporting of hardwoods that drove the region's economy. But Cuban planters, fleeing war in their country, began to arrive in the southeast in the 1870s and established sugar mills with the Dominican government's assistance (this migration also explains baseball's popularity and importance in the region). Rail lines were built and La Romana and San Pedro de Macorís, formerly sleepy backwaters, began to prosper as busy ports almost immediately as world sugar prices soared. Hundreds of families from the interior migrated to the area in search of jobs. In 1920, after peasants were dispossessed of their land during the US occupation, many fought a guerilla war against the marines in the area around Hato Mayor and El Seibo. Until the 1960s, the economy in the southeast was still strictly driven by sugar despite fluctuations in the world market and agriculture in general. However, when the US company Gulf & Western Industries bought La Romana's sugar mill, invested heavily in the cattle and cement industries and, perhaps most importantly, built the Casa de Campo resort, tourism became the financial engine of the southeast, and remains so to this day.

GETTING THERE & AROUND

The majority of international visitors to this region fly directly to the airport in Punta Cana (see p136) and then are whisked away in private vehicles to their respective resorts. Otherwise, it's anywhere from a 2½- to four-hour drive, depending on your destination, from Las Americas airport in Santo Domingo (see p100. La Romana has an airport as well, though it mostly handles charter flights (see p123).

Traffic between the resort centers can be surprisingly heavy and it's difficult to navigate much of the road system, which is being revamped and expanded. Though the distances aren't great, travel in the region, especially along the coast north of Bávaro all the way to Sabana de la Mar, can be slow and unreliable because of the poor condition of the roads. It's now possible to fly between Punta Cana and the Península de Samaná (see p144).

LA ROMANA TO HIGÜEY

LA ROMANA

pop 230,000

This traffic-congested and bustling city is a convenient stop for those traveling between Santo Domingo, 131km to the east, and the beach resorts further west. Surrounded by vast sugar plantations, the industry that bolsters its economy and the enormous Casa de Campo resort a few kilometers to the east, La Romana feels slightly more prosperous than neighboring cities. Modeled after the George Washington monument in Washington, DC, **El Obelisco** (The Obelisk; Av Libertad btwn Calles Márquez & Ducoudrey) is a much smaller version, painted on all four sides with contemporary and historical depictions of Dominican life.

Orientation

The coastal highway, which separates and changes names numerous times on the way from Santo Domingo, is named Hwy 3 when it reaches La Romana. Entering town, you'll see the baseball stadium for the local team, Toros del Este, on your left, and shortly thereafter the highway splits – the left (northern) fork is Av Padre Abreu, while the right (southern) fork is Av Gregorio Luperón. Take the left fork if you're driving and just passing through, but veer onto Luperón if you want to reach downtown La Romana. La Romana has a main town square (Parque Central) from which you can easily walk to most hotels, restaurants, internet cafés, post office and more. Aeropuerto La Romana/Casa de Campo is located 8km east of town.

Information

CULTURAL CENTERS

BoMana (☎ 809-757-6195; bomana@gmail.com; Calle Diego Avila 42; voluntary donation; ♥ 9am-7pm) A cultural center/art gallery/small theatre space; traditional Dominican dances for groups of tourists twice weekly. Shows are at 3pm on Tuesday and Sunday.

EMERGENCY

Politur (tourist police; ☎ 809-550-7112; cnr Calle Francisco Ducoudrey & Av Libertad; ♥ 24hr)

INTERNET ACCESS

Both internet cafés also operate as telephone centers for national and international calls.
Cyber N@utas.net (Av Santa Rosa; per hr US$1; ♥ 9am-11pm)

THE SOUTHEAST

THE SOUTHEAST

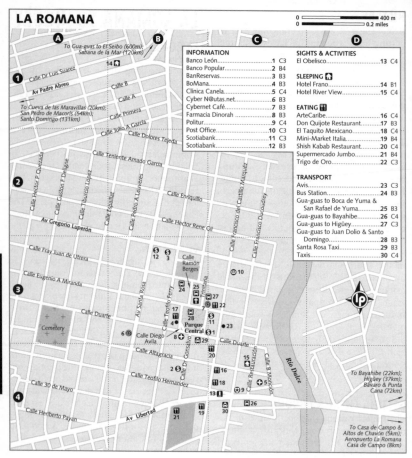

LA ROMANA

0 — 400 m
0 — 0.2 miles

Cybernet Café (Calle Eugenio A Miranda; per hr US$1.50; 8:30am-10pm)

MEDICAL SERVICES
Clínica Canela (☎ 809-556-3135; www.clinicacanela .com; cnr Av Libertad 44 & Restauración) A private 70-bed hospital with 24-hour pharmacy and emergency room.
Farmacia Dinorah (☎ 809-556-3231; Calle Duarte; 7am-8pm Mon-Sat, 8am-noon Sun) Free delivery available.

MONEY
Ban Reservas (Av Gregorio Luperón)
Banco León (Calle Duarte; 8:30am-5pm Mon-Fri, 9am-1pm Sat) Located at southeast corner of the main park.
Banco Popular (Calle Dr Gonsalvo)

ScotiaBank (cnr Av Gregorio Luperón & Santa Rosa; 8:30am-4:30pm Mon-Fri, 9am-1pm Sat)
ScotiaBank (Calle Eugenio A Miranda; 8:30am-4:30pm Mon-Fri, 9am-1pm Sat)

POST
Post Office (Calle Francisco del Castillo Marquéz near Av Gregorio Luperón; 9am-3pm Mon-Fri)

Sights & Activities
CUEVA DE LAS MARAVILLAS
More than 500 pictographs and petroglyphs can be seen on a tour of **Cueva de las Maravillas** (Cave of Wonders; ☎ 809-951-9009; cueva.maravillas@ medioambiente.gov.do; adult/child US$6/1.50; 9am-5pm Tue-Sun), an enormous cavern complex on the

highway some 20km west between San Pedro de Macorís and La Romana. Extending for 840m between Río Cumayasa and Río Soco, this massive underground museum is lighted and well marked. The entrance fee includes a 45-minute guided tour (some English is spoken) so there's little reason to wander around on your own. Coming from San Pedro de Macorís, look for the easy-to-spot entrance on your left not far past the Bahia Principe La Romana Resort. Best way to get here is to take your own car, though taxi is also an option.

ALTOS DE CHAVÓN

While a trip to a faux 15th-century southern Italian/Spanish village created by a Paramount movie set designer won't exactly give you a window onto Dominican culture, **Altos de Chavón** (☎ 809-523-3333) has some redeeming qualities, especially the excellent views of the Río Chavón (a scene from the film *Apocalypse Now* was filmed here). A visit to this little slice of the Old World created in the 1970s is de rigueur for many tourists, who arrive by the busload packing the cobblestone streets, restaurants, galleries and shops – it's more Times Square than a Roman piazza. There's a handsome church, an impressive pre-Columbian museum and a 5000-seat amphitheater, which attracts big-name performers – Frank Sinatra did the inaugural gig here.

Part of the Casa de Campo resort complex (see p122), Altos de Chavón is equally difficult to visit for nonguests, at least ones that are traveling independently. You'll have to arrange at least a day in advance and pay a US$5 entrance fee. Most people visit in the morning and early afternoon as part of a group tour from resorts around Bayahibe and Bávaro/Punta Cana.

Motoconchos (motorcycle taxis) are prohibited from entering the area. If you're driving from La Romana, take the main road past the gated entrance to Casa de Campo and continue for 5km until the turnoff on your right, marked with a small 'Altos de Chavón' sign. A cab from La Romana costs around US$7 one way, or US$18 round-trip with an hour's wait. Others arrive at the end of a group tour to Isla Catalina; the 250 steps from the pier to the top of the bluff can be challenging for some.

ISLA CATALINA

In the 15th century pirates, including Francis Drake, would lurk around Isla Catalina wait-

---

PIRATES OF THE CARIBBEAN

The purported remains – mostly pieces of cannons, anchors and wood – of the *Quedagh Merchant*, which belonged to the Scottish privateer Captain William Kidd, were found in the waters off Isla Catalina near the shores of the Casa de Campo resort. The ship was scuttled and set on fire after Kidd returned to England to face charges of piracy. Despite the fact that he was often acting under the authority of the English navy, he was convicted of piracy and hanged in London in 1699.

---

ing to pounce on Spanish ships on their way to and from Santo Domingo. Today, this island ringed by fine coral reefs teeming with fish in shallow water is a popular destination for groups from nearby Casa de Campo; the resort has frequent shuttles making the 2km trip, as do large cruise ships. Combine this traffic with the bar and restaurant and you won't feel like you've found paradise lost. Most groups spend a couple hours for snorkeling and lunch, and divers head to a steep drop-off called 'The Wall.' With enough people or cash it's possible to charter a boat (most tour companies in the area, from Bayahibe to Romana to Punta Cana and Bávaro, would probably be open to this for the right price) to an infrequently visited beach on the far side of the island. In order to camp on the island you must gain permission from the Parque Nacional del Este office in Bayahibe (see p124) – Isla Catalina is officially part of the park protected area.

GOLFING

Within the grounds of the Casa de Campo (p122) are four Pete Dye–designed **golf courses**, including 'The Teeth of the Dog' (greens fees US$196), open since 1971, which has seven seaside holes. 'Dye Fore' (greens fees US$175) and 'Links' (greens fees US$140) are also highly recommended. All of the courses are open to guests and nonguests alike, but you should make reservations as far in advance as possible. Tee times can be reserved by email (t.times@ ccampo.com.do) or fax (☎ 809-523-8800) only; phone reservations are not accepted.

Sleeping

Hotel River View (☎ 809-556-1181; hotelriverview@ gmail.com; Calle Restauración 17; r US$35; P ✕ ▯)

THE SOUTHEAST

The only hotel in La Romana proper that has a pleasant enough location, this multistory hotel is perched a block from the Río Dulce. You can have a coffee in the tiny patio area out back overlooking the parking lot – not exactly taking full advantage of its 'river view.' The rooms are clean and have modern amenities like cable TV and free wi-fi internet access, though some feel dark and forlorn; ask to look at several with windows.

Hotel Frano (☎ 809-550-4744; Av Padre Abreu 9; s/d US$36/45; P ⚒) Far from the beach and located on an extremely busy and loud thoroughfare, the Hotel Frano is popular with Dominican businessmen, but hardly a logical choice for tourists. On the 1st floor, the bustling restaurant (mains US$4 to US$7; open from 7am to 3pm and again from 6pm till 10pm) serving Dominican dishes and good seafood keeps the atmosphere lively, which is a plus, as the rooms themselves, though fairly modern, tend to be dark and drab, with or without windows.

Casa de Campo (☎ 800-877-3643; www.casadecampo.com.do; Av Libertad; r US$178-375, all-inclusive per person US$216-386; P ⚒ 🖳 🛎) Known as much for its celebrity guests and villa owners as for its facilities and wealth of activities, this enormous, sprawling complex truly resembles a city-state, albeit one with the security paranoia of a G8 conference ringed by anarchist protesters. Casa de Campo is an all-inclusive super-sized place, and while there's a wealth of accommodation options – from tropical-themed hotel rooms with mahogany furnishings and views of the Caribbean to luxurious villas complete with private gardens, a pool, a housekeeper and a cook – the decentralized nature of the resort makes navigation confusing and the service less reliable than you should expect at this price. All-inclusive rates, in addition to the standard food and drink, include unlimited horseback riding, tennis, one round of skeet/trap shooting and non-motorized water sports at the beach. Other available activities include horseback riding trips with dinner (per person US$74), kayak trips down the Río Chavón (per person US$35) and afternoon cycling tours (per person US$15). Four Pete Dye–designed golf courses (see p121) and Altos de Chavón (p121), a Tuscan-style 'village' and a Mediterranean-style piazza overlooking a massive marina round out the resort's offerings.

Day passes (US$40) are available for non-guests and can be purchased at the information office on the right before the entrance gates. Whether this is good value is debatable: you are allowed to enter the property, access the beach (towel included) and have a meal (alcohol extra) at the beachside restaurant. El Tour pass (US$20) includes a visit to Altos de Chavón and the marina – no lunch or beach access.

Most guests arrive at the resort by air, either at the private landing strip or the airport that serves La Romana, and are then driven onto the property. If arriving by private vehicle, follow Av Libertad east across the river, and stay in the right lane for 4km until you see the entrance on your right.

Eating

our pick **Trigo de Oro** (☎ 809-550-5650; Calle Eugenio A Miranda 9; mains US$1-4; ☺ 7am-9pm Mon-Sat, 7am-1pm Sun) There's no better oasis from the heat, exhaust fumes and backfiring *motoconchos* than the charming, shaded courtyard of this French café and bakery – hours can slip away sipping one of the specialty coffee drinks. The bakery has freshly made pastries like flan (US$3) and cheesecake, and a good selection of wines. You can choose from sandwiches, baguettes and other light eats from the café menu.

ArteCaribe (☎ 809-556-3436; cnr Calles Altagracia 15 & Francisco del Castillo Marquéz; mains US$1-8; ☺ lunch & dinner) From cheap and tasty snacks like chicken and beef empanadas (US$1.25) to sandwiches, salads and more-filling meat and vegetarian dishes (US$6), this casual postage stamp–sized café is an ideal place to get your bearings when walking through town. A fan-cooled garden dining area is attached and it gets a strong wi-fi signal no less.

El Taquito Mexicano (☎ 809-556-3851; Calle Francisco del Castillo Márquez 13; mains US$3; ☺ lunch & dinner) Cheap Mexican combo meals are served up fast-food style at this centrally located eatery with pleasant outdoor seating. Get a burrito, nachos and drink all for only US$5.50.

Shish Kabab Restaurant (☎ 809-556-2737; Calle Francisco del Castillo Marquéz 32; mains US$5-18; ☺ lunch & dinner, closed Mon) An entire wall is covered with photos of famous guests, including baseball players Pedro Martinez and George Bell, attesting to the popularity of this local institution. Middle Eastern dishes like hummus and baba ganoush round out an eclectic menu that also includes fish (US$8), grilled meats (US$8) and pizza (US$8). The modern dining area is open to the street and the service is prompt and professional.

Don Quijote Restaurant (☎ 809-556-2827; Calle Diego Avila 44; mains US$6-18; ☺ lunch & dinner, closed Mon) A modern and elegant restaurant – silverware, white tablecloths, soft lighting – on Parque Central, Don Quijote is where to go for fine dining in La Romana. Menu items like goat with pepper sauce (US$6), sea bass (US$9) and filet mignon (US$11) are served up in one of the few completely enclosed aircon dining areas in town.

Occupying a full city block, the **Supermercado Jumbo** (Av Libertad; ☺ 8am-9pm Mon-Sat, 9am-7pm Sun) is a massive grocery selling everything imaginable; there are several fast-food outlets and an office of American Airlines inside. Nearby **Mini-Market Italia** (Av Libertad) carries high-end European brands and fresh meat and cheeses.

Getting There & Away

AIR

Aeropuerto La Romana/Casa de Campo (☎ 809-556-5565) is 8km east of town. There are a few regularly scheduled flights, but most of the traffic here is chartered. Carriers include **American Airlines** (☎ 809-813-9080), with flights from Miami; **USA 3000 Airlines** (☎ 809-221-6626; www.usa3000airlines.com), with direct flights from Baltimore, Maryland; and charter flights arranged by **IAS** (☎ 809-813-9114) and **Swissport** (☎ 809-813-9080).

BUS

Gua-guas (small buses) to Bayahibe (US$1, 20 minutes, every 20 minutes from 6am to 7pm) depart from a stop on Av Libertad at Restauración. *Gua-guas* for other destinations leave from stops near or on Parque Central.

Boca de Yuma (US$2.75, 1 hour, every 20 minutes from 7am to 6pm)

Higüey (*caliente/expreso* US$2/3, 1¼ hours, every 20 minutes from 5:30am to 10pm)

Juan Dolio (US$2, 1 hour, every 10 minutes from 5am to 9pm)

San Rafael de Yuma (US$2, 45 minutes, every 20 minutes from 7am to 6pm)

Santo Domingo (*caliente/expreso* US$3/4, 1½ hours, *caliente* every 10 minutes, *expreso* every 20 minutes, from 5am to 9pm)

Getting Around

Motoconchos and taxis are typically found near the southeast corner of Parque Central. *Motoconcho* rides within the city cost US$1

to US$3; taxis cost between US$3 and US$6. You can call **Santa Rosa Taxi** (☎ 809-556-5313; Calle Duarte) or **Sichotaxi** (☎ 809-550-2222) for a pickup, or wait for the latter at a stop across the street from El Obelisco on Av Libertad. A taxi to or from the airport costs about US$8.

To rent a car, try **Avis** (☎ 809-550-0600; cnr Calles Francisco del Castillo Márquez & Duarte).

BAYAHIBE
pop 2000

Bayahibe, originally founded by fishermen from Puerto Rico in the 19th century, is like an actor playing many roles in the same performance. In the morning it's the proverbial tourist gateway, when busloads of tourists from resorts further east hop into boats bound for Isla Saona. Once this morning rush hour is over it turns back into a drowsy village. There's another buzz of activity when the resort tourists return, and then after sunset another transformation. What sets Bayahibe apart is that it manages to maintain its character despite the continued encroachment of big tourism, including the imminent opening of a large casino complex nearby.

A short drive from Bayahibe is Dominicus Americanus, an upscale Potemkin village of resorts, hotels and a few shops and services centered around a terrific public beach. Listings for Dominicus Americanus appear along with those for Bayahibe – be sure to double-check the address of the listings you're interested in.

Orientation

A single road not more than 2km long connects the coastal highway with the town of Bayahibe, 22km east of La Romana. The road splits about 1km south: the right fork heads to the village of Bayahibe, the left is a well-paved road that takes you to Dominicus Americanus.

Headed towards Bayahibe, the road eventually forks again: the right fork heads into a large parking lot next to the ocean, where the national park office is located and where fleets of tour buses are parked during the day; the left turns to dirt and continues east into the center of town past a few hotels and restaurants. Several small, winding sand roads lead from here to villagers' homes.

Dominicus Americanus itself contains only a handful of streets that are laid out in a grid, making it easy to negotiate. The Viva Wyndham Dominicus Beach resort lies at the center of the complex; access to the public beach is at the far eastern end.

Information

At the time of our research there were no internet facilities in town. Some of the listings below are in Dominicus Americanus.

Agencia de Cambio Sánchez (☎ 809-833-0201; Bayahibe; ◷ 8am-10pm Mon-Sat, 8am-6pm Sun) Moneychanger next to the Hotel Llave del Mar. Traveler's checks, cash dollars and euros accepted.

Banco Popular (Dominicus Americanus; ◷ 24hr) Has an ATM located just outside the Viva Wyndham Dominicus Beach Hotel.

BanReservas (Bayahibe) Next to Hotel Bayahibe. Small hole-in-the-wall branch of the bank; no ATM as yet.

El Mundo de la Hispaniola (Dominicus Americanus; ◷ 8am-1pm & 2:30-8pm) Day-old editions of the *New York Times* and *Miami Herald,* plus souvenirs, basic groceries and snacks.

Farmacia Job (☎ 809-833-0453; ◷ 8am-9pm Mon-Sat, 8am-10pm Sun) Pharmacy across from Restaurant La Bahia.

Western Union (Bayahibe; ◷ 8am-6pm) Has telephone services; also changes cash dollars and euros.

Sights & Activities

One advantage of staying in Bayahibe is that virtually every water-related activity is right out your front door, so you avoid the long commute that most travelers make here daily from resorts further east.

BEACHES

Much of **Playa Bayahibe**, the town beach to the right of the parking lot, is occupied by dozens of motorboats waiting to ferry tourists to Isla Saona. There's a relatively small, uninviting and narrow stretch of sand between the last of these and the start of the all-inclusive Sunscape Casa del Mar – the beach here is restricted to guests of the resort.

The advantage of staying in Dominicus Americanus is being able to walk to **Playa Dominicus**, a beautiful stretch of thick, nearly-white sand, and good water for swimming. It does tend to get crowded, especially because there's easy public access via a parking lot (free parking) at the far eastern end of the enclave, which means no cutting through hotels or restaurants to get to the beach. You can rent beach chairs for US$3 or eat at one of various food stands or restaurants.

SNORKELING & DIVING

Bayahibe is arguably the best place in the country to dive or snorkel, featuring warm, clear Caribbean water, healthy reefs and plenty of fish and other sea life. The diving tends to be 'easier' (and therefore ideal for beginners) than it is on the DR's north coast, where the underwater terrain is less flat, the water cooler and the visibility somewhat diminished. There are about 20 open-water dive sites; some favorites include **Catalina Wall** and an impressive 85m ship in 41m to 44m of water, known as **St Georges Wreck** after Hurricane Georges. Deep in the national park, **Padre Nuestro** is a weaving 290m tunnel flooded with freshwater that can be dived, but only by those with advanced cave diving training. See Tours, opposite, for details. In town you can also snorkel in the waters around La Punta.

PARQUE NACIONAL DEL ESTE

More than simply Isla Saona, which is all that most people see on a group tour, the Parque Nacional del Este includes eight emerged reef terraces, 400 or so caverns, some with pictographs and ceramic remains, and Islas Catalinita and Catalina, in addition to Saona. Designated a national park in 1975, it stretches for over 310 sq km of territory, the majority of which is semihumid forest.

The park is also home to 539 species of flora, 55 of which are endemic. There is also a good variety of fauna: 112 species of birds, 250 types of insects and arachnids, and 120 species of fish. There are occasional sightings of West Indian manatees and bottlenose dolphins, and the much rarer Haitian solenodon (p37), a small bony animal with a long snout and tiny eyes.

There's a **park office** in the parking lot in Bayahibe. One entrance is at Guaraguao, a ranger post 5km past Dominicus Americanus. The other entrance is in the town of Boca de Yuma (p128), on the eastern side of the park. There is a ranger station there but no formal services. A road leads along the coast for several kilometers and has a number of nice vista points.

Isla Saona

There's a reason why boatloads of tourists descend upon this island daily. The powdery, white-sand beach doesn't seem real from afar, and a dip in the aquamarine surf is a gentle restorative, like the waters of the most luxurious spa; palm trees provide a natural awning from the intense sun. All of this would be perfect if it weren't for the fact that ear-splitting dance music is blasted from competing sound systems and vendors wander the beach in search of buyers in need of hair braiding, shells and other knick-knacks. There isn't much coral to speak of, much of it damaged by heavy boat traffic and inexperienced snorkelers. Much of this 12km x 5km island is taken over by various companies and all-inclusive resorts who have set up lounge chairs, small dance floors, bars and buffets. **Mano Juan** (population 500) is the only established community on this island separated from the mainland by the narrow Catuano Passage.

The majority of visitors are ferried to Bayahibe early in the morning from resorts further east expecting a booze cruise–like experience, and they usually aren't disappointed. Most trips include a catamaran ride out to the island and then a speedier motorboat trip back or vice versa. A stop at the **piscina natural**, a shallow sandbank that extends far from the shore and has crystal-clear water, often includes young Dominican men and women wading through the water serving up glasses of rum and soda to tourists in need of a drink. The buffet lunch tends to be large and quite good. Unless you specifically request a trip that avoids the standard stops, don't expect a peaceful paradise, much less a protected national park. The dive shops in Bayahibe tend to offer more-rewarding trips that stop for lunch at Isla Saona, but only after visiting other spots for hiking, snorkeling or both (see right). Every hotel, restaurant and shop advertises Saona trips with little variation in quality and price (US$75).

Isla Catalinita

This tiny uninhabited island on the eastern edge of the park is a common stop on snorkeling and diving tours. Arriving on the island's western (leeward) side, it's about a half-hour hike to the other side, where a lookout affords dramatic views of the powerful open-ocean waves crashing on shore. There is a coral reef in about 2m of water that makes for great snorkeling, and a good dive site called 'Shark Point,' where sharks are in fact often seen.

Cueva del Puente

The park also has over 400 caves, many of which contain Taíno pictographs (cave paintings) and petroglyphs (rock carvings). Archaeologists have found several structures and artifacts inside and around the caves, including what appears to be the remains of a large Taíno city (perhaps the largest) and the site of a notorious massacre of indigenous people by Spanish soldiers.

Only one of the caves that contain Taíno pictograms, **Cueva del Puente**, can be easily visited. Cueva del Puente is partially collapsed, but has a modest number of Taíno pictures, mostly depicting animals and humanlike figures that may represent people or deities. The cave also has some impressive stalagmites and stalactites.

To visit Cueva del Puente, you must first drive to the national park entrance at Guaraguao, a well-marked ranger post about 5km past Dominicus Americanus. There you will pay the US$3.50 entrance fee and the guard will guide you to the cave – it's a little over 3km, about a 40-minute walk; you'll need a flashlight and good shoes. South of here is **Cueva Penon Gordo**, a smaller cave but with more pictograms.

LA PUNTA DE BAYAHIBE

This short, pleasant walk (10 minutes) follows a path beginning just past the Bamboo Beach Bar. It passes by the attractive Iglesia de Bayahibe, a small green, wooden structure, and signs in both English and Spanish outline interesting facts about the town's history and flora and fauna.

Tours

Virtually every hotel in Dominicus Americanus offers a wide variety of tours. Most are more expensive than those arranged through one of the two dive shops in Bayahibe or from **Captain Pat Tours** (☎ 809-609-2793; www.captain-pat-excursions.new.fr), a tour company based in town; locals can also arrange things for independent travelers. Both of the dive shops listed here have multilingual guides and instructors, with Spanish, English, German, French and Italian spoken, and can accommodate mixed groups (that is, both snorkelers and divers).

Swiss-run **Casa Daniel** (☎ 809-833-0050; www.casa-daniel.de; ☻ 8am-6pm), 100m from center across from Mare Nostrum, offers one-tank dives with/without equipment rental for US$39/33. Packages of six dives are US$210/182, 10-dive packages are US$325/292. Full-day snorkel and beach trips to Isla Catalinita and Isla Saona are US$68, including brief stops at Cueva Penon Gordo and a swing through the mangrove forest. Isla Catalina trips with snorkeling, lunch on the beach and a stop at Altos de Chavón are US$59. PADI certification courses are available. Ask about accommodation packages.

In operation for over nine years and located on the main strip in the middle of town is **Scubafun** (☎ 809-833-0003; www.scubafun.info; Calle Principal 28; ✆ 7:30am-6pm). This PADI dive center offers two-tank dives in nearby reefs (US$65) and dive/day trips to Isla Catalina (US$110) and Isla Saona (US$125). Full equipment rentals are an additional US$5. Beginner and advanced PADI courses are also offered.

One of the more enjoyable ways of spending a few hours exploring the coastline is to take a **sail** on a local's fishing boat. No doubt you wouldn't have to ask many people before finding a taker; one particularly nice man who can read the winds like a soothsayer is **Hector Julio Brito** (☎ 829-210-2437), who charges US$60 for one to four people for a two-hour trip. A longer outing, from 9am to 4pm to the piscina natural, will run around US$100.

A de facto mayor and general man about town that knows just about everyone and can help arrange any tour or trip with a local is **Rafael Antonio** (☎ 829-0740-4624). Ask for him at Restaurant La Bahia.

Festivals & Events

Every year on the Saturday of Semana Santa (late March/early April), Bayahibe hosts a **regatta** of handmade fishing boats. The race runs from the town cove to Catalina Island and back.

Sleeping

Bayahibe proper has several good budget hotels all within walking distance of one another; locals can point you in the direction of a family willing to take on temporary boarders. A stay here affords you excellent eating options and the chance to experience the rhythms of the town away from the masses. The enclave of Dominicus Americanus has several midrange and top-end options – the advantage here is that it's a short walk to an excellent beach.

BUDGET
All of the places listed here are in Bayahibe proper.

Hotel Bayahibe (☎ 809-833-0159; www.hotel bayahibe.com; r incl breakfast US$35; P ✖ ▣) The Bayahibe has the best budget rooms in town. This three-story modern building is easily noticeable, since it's the biggest around. Large comfortable rooms with cable TV and balconies, some with good views, surround an inner atrium. Breakfast is served in a 3rd-floor dining area and there's a computer in the lobby with internet access, the only such access in town, that's free for guests.

Cabañas Trip Town (☎ 809-833-0082; fax 809-883-0088; cabins with/without air-con US$28/21; P ✖) and **Cabañas Francisca** (☎ 809-556-2742; r with/without air-con US$28/21; P ✖) are comparable budget choices located across the dirt road from one another near the center of action in town. Pop your head into both before making a decision. Both have simple rooms with old furnishings, small porches and private bathrooms with hot water. Some have cable TV.

MIDRANGE
The first listing here is in Bayahibe proper and the rest are in Dominicus Americanus.

Villa Iguana (☎ 809-833-0203; www.villaiguana.de; Calle 8; r with/without air-con US$39/29, 1-bedroom apt US$69-150, penthouse US$120) If the Hotel Bayahibe is booked, or if you prefer a more homey atmosphere, walk on over to the Villa Iguana – it's only a few blocks away. This friendly German-owned hotel has seven well-kept rooms, though there's little character and the mattresses are soft in the middle (and no TV in standard rooms). A simple complimentary breakfast in served in a covered-over indoor patio area. The apartments are nicer and more deserving of a long-term stay, as is the penthouse, with its own small rooftop pool.

Hotel Bocayate (☎ 809-920-7966; hbocayate@ verizon.net.do; Av Eladia, Dominicus Americanus; r US$50) The Bocayate won't win any awards for service and there are few amenities. What it does have, though, is a certain unkempt charm. Seven attractive two-story bungalows surround a palm-shaded inner courtyard – guests will have to fight for the single burlap hammock. Find it across from the Viva Wyndham Dominicus Palace; the beach is a short walk down the road.

Cabaña Elke (☎ 809-689-8249; www.viwi.it, in Italian; Av Eladia, Dominicus Americanus; r US$55; P ✖ ✆) Sandwiched between the road and a high wall marking the boundary of the Viva Wyndham

THE SOUTHEAST

Dominicus Beach (below) property, Elke's rooms are arranged in two long narrow rows. Rooms are airy, especially the split-level apartments with kitchenettes, however the furnishings are aging. There's a nice pool area with lounge chairs, but unfortunately no view.

Hotel Eden (☎ 809-688-1856; www.santodomingovillage.com; Av La Laguna 10, Dominicus Americanus; r US$65; P ✗ ☐ ☢) This addition to the enclave is a good choice for those seeking hotel-style comfort, amenities and service. Because it's located on the access road to the resort area, you might confuse the Eden for a hotel somewhere in Arizona or Florida, just not necessarily on a Caribbean beach. The pool area and grounds are attractive and a good restaurant (see right) is attached.

TOP END

There is a string of all-inclusive resorts in Dominicus Americanus and along the road between there and Bayahibe; only Sunscape Casa del Mar is within walking distance of town.

Sunscape Casa del Mar (☎ 809-221-8880; www.sunscaperesorts.com; r US$135; ✗ ☐ ☢) This all-inclusive place is a good compromise for those who want to be within walking distance of Bayahibe but don't want to give up their creature comforts. Contiguous with the town beach, Sunscape's own isn't as nice as the one at Dominicus Americanus, but the low-slung complex includes two above-average pools and enthusiastic and friendly staff. Many of the rooms have seen better days and are in need of a paint job and update.

Iberostar Hacienda Dominicus (☎ 809-688-3600; www.iberostar.com; Playa Dominicus; r from US$150; P ✗ ☐ ☢) An impeccably maintained resort popular with European travelers, the Iberostar Hacienda Dominicus has beautifully landscaped grounds – most of the buildings surround quiet interior courtyards and some have ocean views. It fronts a beautiful beach with OK snorkeling just offshore. Four specialty restaurants receive better-than-average reviews from guests.

Viva Wyndham Dominicus Beach (☎ 809-686-5658; www.vivaresorts.com; Playa Dominicus; r from US$190; P ✗ ☐ ☢) This resort, the centerpiece of the enclave 5km east of Bayahibe, commands excellent beachfront property lined with thick, soft sand. Rooms with ocean views are pricier but well worth it – all have balconies. It's a typically sprawling property with several

pools, bars, a theater and a disco. There's a variety of specialty restaurants to choose from, even if the quality of the food gets mixed reviews. Next door is the sister resort, the Viva Wyndham Dominicus Palace (with the same contact and pricing details as Dominicus Beach), a step up in terms of room and food quality and the overall maintenance of the property. Pay attention to the location of your room since several buildings are located on the opposite side of the access road to the beach and may feel more like a stay at a retirement home community than a Caribbean beach holiday.

Eating

Bayahibe has a surprising number of good restaurants for a town of its size. Most offer relaxing waterfront seating and fresh seafood. Dominicus Americanus has a number of modern tourist-ready restaurants serving a mix of international standards and fish, though none has views.

Esperanza Grill (Bayahibe; mains US$5-12; ☽ lunch & dinner) Nothing more than a charcoal oven and a few plastic tables, this restaurant nevertheless is a charming place for a meal. The friendly owner/chef/waitress grills up tasty meat and seafood dishes – surprisingly, it's best to make reservations for dinner.

Cafecito de la Cubana (Playa Bayahibe; mains US$5-15; ☽ 9am-3pm & 6-11pm, closed Tue) One of several little kiosks set up around the parking lot and beach area in town, la Cubana is particularly charming and serves coffee and fruit drinks, sandwiches (US$3.25) and more-substantial meat and fish mains (US$8).

Restaurant El Eden (Dominicus Americanus; mains US$6-15; ☽ breakfast, lunch & dinner) Attached to the Hotel Eden on the entrance road to the enclave, with nice outdoor dining area, wine selection, Caesar salad (US$6), pasta, meat and fish dishes.

our pick **Mare Nostrum** (☎ 809-833-0055; Bayahibe; mains US$9-25; ☽ lunch & dinner, closed Mon) A sophisticated and elegant restaurant, the Mare Nostrum's 2nd-floor location affords it beautiful nighttime views of the darkening water. Lanterns and tablecloths add a romantic ambience and the food is equal, offering excellent Italian dishes. Pastas are all homemade and the chef offers delicious daily specials – the shellfish is super fresh and the risotto just melts in your mouth. A good selection of wines is also offered.

THE SOUTHEAST

Bamboo Beach Bar Restaurant & Grill (Bayahibe; mains US$7-18; ☺ lunch & dinner), **La Bahia** (☎ 809-352-5098; Bayahibe; mains US$8-18; ☺ lunch & dinner) and **La Punta** (☎ 809-833-0080; Bayahibe; mains US$10-25; ☺ lunch & dinner) are three more excellent open-air eateries near the beach in town, serving freshly caught fish and shellfish.

Drinking

our pick **Barco Bar** (☺ closed Thu) The aptly named boat-shaped bar can be found near the southern end of the dirt road that leads through Bayahibe proper. It generally opens in the afternoons, the best time for sunset views from the homemade tree house.

Big Sur (☺ nightly) Swiss-owned open-air disco located on the beach in Bayahibe proper. Friday nights, when the locals visit, are the best.

Super Colmado Bayahibe (☺ 7:30am-10pm Mon-Sat, 7:30am-7pm Sun) Town square, town bar and town grocery rolled into one, this *colmado* is where locals gather to talk, drink and listen to music all day long. Foreigners are welcome to pull up a stool and down a bottle or two of Presidente.

Getting There & Away

Gua-guas are the only means of public transportation to and from Bayahibe. **Servicio de Transporte Romana-Bayahibe** (☎ 809-833-0206) *gua-guas* leave from a stand of trees across from Super Colmado Bayahibe in the center of town, a block north of the Hotel Bayahibe near Super Colmado Bayahibe. Services run to La Romana (US$1.50, 25 minutes, every 20 minutes from 6am to 7pm) and Higüey (US$2, 40 minutes, irregular hours).

Sichotuhbared (☎ 809-833-0059) is the local taxi union, with a stop in front of Viva Wyndham Dominicus Beach. Rates are for one to five people and are for return trips: La Romana airport (US$55), Casa de Campo (US$60), Higüey (US$65), and Bávaro resorts (US$90). Be sure to agree upon a price before you get in the car.

To rent a car, look for the aptly named office for **Rent-A-Car** (☎ 809-258-9340) across from the Hotel Eden in Dominicus Americanus.

BOCA DE YUMA

pop 2300

Off the beaten track in terms of mass tourism, Boca de Yuma is a ramshackle little town with rough, unpaved roads and half-finished buildings, but also a quiet seaside promontory where waves crash dramatically into the rocky shore. At the far end of the ocean road the Río Yuma serves as the town border; several kilometers in the other direction is a cave with Taíno paintings and further on the same road is an entrance to Parque Nacional del Este, the start of a good nature walk. Other than several restaurants, a hotel and a gas station just outside town, there are no services in Boca de Yuma.

Sights & Activities

Several kilometers west of town on the way toward the entrance of the national park is **Cueva de Berna** (☺ 7am-6pm; adult/child US$3/0.75), a large cave with scattered Taíno pictograms (and graffiti) and stalactite and stalagmite formations. A caretaker usually sits outside the entrance and will gladly accompany you up the rickety ladder and deep into the cave (a small gratuity is appreciated). To find the cave, follow the paved road that runs along the ocean wall west (away from the mouth of the river); you need no more than 15 minutes inside.

A few kilometers further west down the same road, past several ranches with grazing cows and horses, is the eastern entrance of **Parque Nacional del Este** (admission US$3). A park ranger sleeps at the small cabin just past the gate, and should be around for much of the day, but there's little formality or information as few people enter here. A long easy-to-follow road hugs the coast for many kilometers and involves some hiking up a moderately steep slope to make it to the top of the rugged bluffs with beautiful views of the ocean. There is good bird-watching here if you're out early enough.

While **Playa Blanca** is a pretty, mostly deserted beach about 2km east of town on the other side of the river, the hassles of getting here may not make the trip worth it. The easiest and most expensive option is to hire a boat from one of the boatmen congregated at the mouth of the river at the east side of town (round-trip US$40). One alternative is to have them ferry you to the other side of the river and walk to the beach; however, the path is hard to find and follow and the sharp rocks are a hazard. In theory it's possible to drive, with an SUV, but the nearest bridge is well upriver and the route also difficult to navigate.

A COUNTRY RETREAT IS KIND OF LIKE A FOUNTAIN OF YOUTH...

Outside the small town of San Rafael de Yuma, just east of the two-lane highway linking Higüey to Boca de Yuma, is a fine rural Dominican town surrounded by fields in all directions, with dirt roads. Spanish explorer Juan Ponce de León had a second residence built in the countryside near San Rafael del Yuma during the time he governed Higüey for the Spanish crown. Still standing nearly 500 years later, **Casa Ponce de León** (Ponce de León House; admission US$1.40; ☼ 7am-5pm) is now a museum to this notorious character of the Spanish conquest.

Born in 1460, Ponce de León accompanied Christopher Columbus on his second voyage to the New World in 1494. In 1508 he conquered Boriquén (present-day Puerto Rico) and served as governor there from 1510 to 1512. While there, he heard rumors of an island north of Cuba called Bimini, which had a spring whose waters could reverse the aging process – the fabled fountain of youth. Setting off from Puerto Rico, Ponce de León reached the eastern coast of present-day Florida on 2 April 1513, Palm Sunday, and named it Pascua Florida (literally 'Flowery Easter'). He tried to sail around the peninsula, believing it to be an island, but after realizing his mistake he returned to Puerto Rico. When he resumed his quest eight years later, landing on Florida's western coast, he and his party were attacked by Indians. Wounded by an arrow, Ponce de León withdrew to Cuba, where he died shortly after landing.

The residence-turned-museum contains many original items belonging to Ponce de León, including his armor and much of his furniture. Also original are the candelabra and his bed; his coat of arms is carved into the headboard. Signs are in Spanish only.

There are no signs to the museum, oddly enough. If you have a car and are entering from the north, you'll encounter a fork in the road right past the police station. Bear left and then turn left onto a dirt road just before the cemetery (it's surrounded by a tall white wall). After almost 2km you'll see a long access road on your right with a boxy stone building at the end, which is the museum.

Sleeping & Eating

El Viejo Pirata (☎ 809-804-3151; nancy.felix@hotmail.com; Calle Duarte 1; r US$18; ❂ ▣ ▣) Can a place be both forlorn and inviting at the same time? Somehow El Viejo Pirata, an Italian-owned hotel with eight clean modern rooms and the equal of many all-inclusive places, produces these contradictory feelings. Off the tourist trail, Boca del Yuma receives few overnight visitors, hence the sometimes low occupancy rate here, but the well-maintained pool and patio with good ocean views makes it feel like a well-kept secret.

Almost a dozen restaurants are lined up along the road overlooking the ocean. Two of the better ones, both with wonderful views, are **Restaurant La Bahia** (mains US$6), owned and operated by a friendly Dominican family, and the Italian-owned **El Arponero** (☎ 809-292-9797; mains US$5-8; ☼ lunch & dinner) in the center of town. The latter has pizza (US$5) and pasta (US$6) in addition to the grilled fish and seafood.

HIGÜEY

pop 151,000

Famous throughout the country for its giant concrete basilica, Higüey, which is surrounded by a sea of sugarcane fields, is best visited as a day trip or as a stop along the way to points further north and south – in fact you're bound to end up here at some point traveling around the southeast. Thousands of Dominicans who work in the resorts around Bávaro and Punta Cana commute to this busy, concrete, traffic-clogged city daily.

Information

All of the internet places listed here operate as call centers as well.

Banco León (cnr Av Duarte & La Altagracia) Has an ATM.

Banco Popular (Calle Cleto Villavicencio) Has an ATM.

Cyber Station Internet (Av La Altagracia; per hr US$1; ☼ 8am-10pm) Internet access.

Internet Center (Av La Altagracia; per hr US$1.25; ☼ 9am-10pm Mon-Sat, 9am-5pm Sun) Internet access. Part of Plaza Barcelona, next to the Esso gas station.

Scotiabank (Calle Cleto Villavicencio) Has an ATM.

Spider Cíber Café (☎ 809-554-9903; Av La Altagracia; per hr US$1; ☼ 9am-noon & 2-10:30pm) Internet access.

Sights

From the outside, the **Basilica de Nuestra Señora de la Altagracia** (☼ 8am-6pm Mon-Sat, 8am-8pm Sun) is a strange mixture of the sacred and profane. A utilitarian concrete façade, not far removed from a military bunker, is topped by an elongated arch reaching high into the sky. But it's one of the most famous cathedrals in the country because of the glass-encased image of the Virgin of Altagracia housed inside. According to the story, a sick child in Higüey was healed when an old man thought to be an Apostle asked for a meal and shelter at the city's original church, the **Iglesia San Dionisio** (cnr Calle Agustín Guerrero & T Reyes; ☣ varies). On departing the following day, he left a small print of Our Lady of Grace in a modest frame. Since that day the 16th-century image has been revered by countless devotees, upon whom the Virgin is said to have bestowed miraculous cures. Originally housed in the handsome Iglesia San Dionisio, the image of the Virgin has been venerated in the basilica since the mid-1950s. Designed by Frenchmen Pierre Dupré and Dovnoyer de Segonzac, and completed in 1956, the long interior walls consist mostly of bare concrete and approach each other as they rise, connecting at a rounded point directly over the center aisle. The entire wall opposite the front door consists of stained glass and is quite beautiful, especially in the late afternoon when the sunshine casts honey-colored shadows across the floor.

Festivals & Events

Thousands of people travel to Basilica de Nuestra Señora de la Altagracia in a moving and intense homage to the Virgin every January 21. Pilgrims, dressed in their finest, file past the Virgin's image, seeking miracles and giving thanks. The church's bells chime loudly throughout the day.

Sleeping & Eating

Hotel Don Carlos (☎ 809-554-2344; cnr Calle Juan Ponce de León at Sánchez; r old/new bldg US$28/35; ▣ ☢) Only a block west from the basilica, Don Carlos is a maze of rooms. It's friendly and professional, but deserving of only a night when passing through. Ask to stay in the newer annex, whose rooms are clean, large and modern; rooms in the older building are cramped and dark. A restaurant (mains US$5 to US$8; open for breakfast, lunch and dinner) is attached, serving large portions of Dominican dishes.

Restaurant Doña Esmerelda (☎ 809-554-7432; Av La Altagracia; mains US$5-15; ☣ lunch & dinner) Unlike the casual snack shacks and bars lining the median, this open-air restaurant has an elegant ambience, with tablecloths and silverware and uniformed wait staff. Lobster (US$15), paella (US$18) and less-expensive fare like pasta (US$5) and fish (US$7) are on the menu.

El Meson de Cervantes (☎ 809-554-2506; Av Labuna Llana; mains US$8-15; ☣ lunch & dinner) Spanish themed to the hilt, El Meson de Cervantes has the brick walls, vaulted doorways and bullfighting posters expected in every Madrid knock-off. One of the nicer places to eat in town despite only ordinary Dominican and international dishes, this restaurant was also a piano bar in its glory days – an unused electronic keyboard still sits forlornly in the corner.

Blue Rain Restaurant (☎ 809-554-3016; 2nd fl, Plaza Barcelona, Av La Altagracia; mains US$6-20; ☣ lunch & dinner) Higüey and sushi aren't often used in the same sentence, but Blue Rain delivers. On the 2nd floor of a mini plaza a few blocks from the cathedral, this modern restaurant does Japanese specials, including a wide variety of sushi rolls (US$6) and sashimi (US$5). An even larger number of international and Dominican dishes like pasta al mare (US$7), baby back ribs (US$18) and a New York strip steak (US$16) are on the menu.

Mercado Municipal (Av de la Libertad btwn Guerrero del Rosario & Las Carreras; ☣ 7am-3pm) is a crowded market, packed to the gills with people and vendors selling mostly fresh fruits and vegetables.

There is also a number of snack shacks and bars with tables on the first several blocks of Av La Altagracia's leafy median, east of the basilica. You can get sandwiches, empanadas and other light fare, plus beer, soda or juices. Great place for a drink.

Getting There & Away

Gua-guas to Santo Domingo (US$4.25, 2¾ hours, every 15 minutes from 4:30am to 7:30pm) leave from a large busy terminal on Av Laguna Llana at Colón.

For Samaná take a *gua-gua* to Hato Mayor (US$4, 2½ hours, every hour from 4:40am to 8pm) or El Seibo (US$1.75, one hour, every 20 minutes from 4:30am to 8pm) and transfer to the bus for Sabana de la Mar, where there are ferries across the bay. Buses for Hato Mayor and El Seibo use the same stop on Av La Altagracia at Av Laguna Llana. Be sure to tell the driver that you are planning to connect to another bus, as they will often drop you right at the next terminal.

Gua-guas to Bávaro and Punta Cana (US$2, 1½ hours, every 15 minutes from 4:55am to 10pm; express air-con service US$3, 1¼ hours, every hour at the top of the hour) and Miches (US$2.75, 2½ hours, every 30 minutes from 5am to 6:20pm) leave from two side-by-side terminals on Av de la Libertad past Calle Luperón.

PUNTA CANA TO SABANA DE LA MAR

BÁVARO & PUNTA CANA

Ground zero of DR tourism. The epicenter of the all-inclusive resort. Where buffet items seem to outnumber grains of sand. If you were to tell a Dominican anywhere in the world that you visited their country, this is where they would assume you came. Deservedly popular because its beaches do rival those anywhere else in the Caribbean, both in terms of their soft, white texture and their warm aquamarine waters, a trip here nevertheless involves as much a love for swim-up pool bars and rubbing sun-tanned elbows with likeminded people. Over 24,000 hotel rooms from Punta Cana to El Macao, with more on the way, are crowding out the impressively tall coconut trees that fringe the shoreline. Punta Cana, shorthand for the region as a whole, is actually somewhat of a misnomer. The majority of resorts are scattered around the beaches of Bávaro, really nothing more than a series of small commercial plazas, and Cortecito, a short strip of shops along a 'town beach.' Punta Cana (Grey-Haired Point), the easternmost tip of the country and where the airport is located, has some of the more luxurious resorts and Caribbean-hugging golf courses.

Orientation

Most of Bávaro's services are located in one of several outdoor plazas (malls) just north of El Cortecito, the small one-road enclave where there's another cluster of shops and tour companies.

The area known as Plaza Bávaro is the largest, an open-air square surrounded with shops selling the same cheap Haitian paintings and kitschy souvenirs, several high-end cigar and jewelry shops, money exchanges and a Banco Popular. In addition there are one or two bars/snack shops in the middle.

West of Plaza Bávaro you'll come across two more small commercial centers – Plaza Las Brisas with a bank, gym and two good restaurants, and Plaza Riviera/Estrella – before reaching an intersection with a gas station and the main bus terminal and police station.

Punta Cana actually refers to the area just east and south of the airport. It's much more isolated than Bávaro as there is really only one coastal road, which eventually peters out further south and doesn't connect with the highway to Higüey. There are few services here and no towns in the immediate area. At the time of research there were several new roads being paved, which may make this area more accessible or at least ease the traffic between Punta Cana and Bávaro.

Information

EMERGENCY

Politur (tourist police; ☎ 809-686-8227) There are 24-hour stations next to the bus terminal in Bávaro and at Plaza Bolera in Punta Cana.

INTERNET & TELEPHONE

Cone Xion.com (Plaza Punta Cana, Bávaro; per hr US$2; ⏰ 8am-11pm Mon-Sat, 9am-11pm Sun) A small dual internet/call center.

Cyber Cafe (Plaza Riviera/Estrella, Bávaro; per hr US$2; ⏰ 10am-10pm) Towards the back of Plaza Estrella; a call center as well. Generally closes earlier Sunday evenings, depending on customers.

Tricom/Cyber Beach (El Cortecito; per hr US$3; ⏰ 8am-11pm) Along the main beach road in Cortecito proper.

LAUNDRY

Laundry Euro (☎ 809-552-1820; Plaza Riviera/Estrella, Bávaro; ⏰ 8am-8pm Mon-Sat, 8am-5pm Sun) Charges by the piece, with same-day service if you drop off in morning.

MEDICAL SERVICES

All-inclusive hotels have small on-site clinics and medical staff, who can provide first aid and basic care. Head to one of several good private hospitals in the area for more serious issues.
Centro Médico Caribe Bávaro (☎ 809-552-1415; www.caribeasistencia.com/cmcb; Plaza las Brisas, Bávaro; ⏰ 8:30am-6pm) Open 24 hours for emergencies.
Centro Médico Punta Cana (☎ 809-552-1506; btwn Plaza Bávaro & the bus terminal, Bávaro) The name notwithstanding, this is the main private hospital in Bávaro, with a multilingual staff, 24-hour emergency room and in-house pharmacy.

Farmacia El Manglar (☎ 809-552-1533; Plaza Punta Cana, Bávaro; ☽ 8am-midnight) Offers free delivery service to local hotels (until 10pm).

Farmacia Estrella (☎ 809-552-0344; Plaza Riviera/ Estrella, Bávaro; ☽ 8am-10pm)

Hospitén Bávaro (☎ 809-686-1414; bavaro@hospiten .com; btwn airport & turnoff to Bávaro) Best private hospital in Punta Cana, with English-, French- and German-speaking doctors and a 24-hour emergency room. The hospital is located on the road to Punta Cana, 500m from the turnoff to Bávaro.

Pharma Cana (☎ 809-959-0025; Plaza Bolera, Punta Cana; ☽ 9am-10pm Mon-Sat, 8am-11pm Sun) Punta Cana's main pharmacy.

MONEY

Almost every major Dominican bank has at least one branch in the Bávaro area. All of the following have ATMs.

Banco BHD (Plaza Caney 1, Bávaro)

Banco Popular (Plaza Bávaro, Bávaro; ☽ 9am-4pm Mon-Fri)

Banco Progreso El Cortecito (inside El Cortecito supermarket; ☽ 9am-9pm Mon-Sat); Plaza Bolera, Punta Cana (☽ 9am-4pm Mon-Fri)

Scotiabank (Plaza Las Brisas, Bávaro; ☽ 9am-5pm Mon-Fri, 9am-1pm Sat)

Sights

BEACHES

Superlatives describing the beaches here are bandied about like free drinks at a pool bar, but they're mostly deserved; keep in mind, however, that the best pieces of property have been claimed by developers and are either already occupied by all-inclusives and condos or will be in the near future. This means you will not be alone. In fact, you will be part of a beach-lounging crowd.

Public access is ingrained in the law, so you can stroll from less-exclusive parts like **Playa El Cortecito**, which tends to be crowded with vendors, to nicer spots in front of resorts – but without the proper color wrist bracelet you won't be able to get a towel or chair. Playa El Cortecito is a good place to **parasail** (12-15min US$40), though, or to find a boat operator to take you fishing or snorkeling.

North of El Cortecito is **Playa Arena Gorda**, lined with all-inclusive resorts and their guests, many topless, riding around on banana boats, parasailing or just soaking in the sun. A further 9km north of here is **Playa del Macao**, a gorgeous stretch of beach best reached by car. It's also a stop-off for a slew of ATV (All-Terrain Vehicle)

tours that tear up and down the beach every day – there's less noise at the far northern end of the beach. Roco Ki, a massive new resort development in the area, is scheduled to open in winter or spring 2009.

In the other direction, south of Bávaro and El Cortecito, is **Playa Cabo Engaño**, an isolated beach that you'll need a car, preferably an SUV, to reach.

PUNTA CANA ECOLOGICAL PARK

Though development may eventually cover every inch of the Dominican coastline, for now there are still large areas of pristine coastal plains and mangrove forests. A half-kilometer south of Punta Cana Resort and Club, the **Punta Cana Ecological Park** (☎ 809-959-8483; www .puntacana.org; ☽ 8am-4pm) covers almost 8 sq km of protected coastal and inland habitat and is home to some 80 bird species, 160 insect species and 500 plant species. Visitors can take very worthwhile 90-minute **guided tours** (adult/ child US$10/5) taken in English, French, German or Spanish through a lush 18-hectare portion of the reserve known as Parque Ojos Indígenas (Indigenous Eyes Park), so named for its 11 freshwater lagoons all fed by an underground river that flows into the ocean. The tour also includes a visit to the park's botanical and fruit gardens, iguana farm (part of a breeding program) and a farm-animal petting zoo. The visitor center has a great collection of insects that was compiled by entomology students from Harvard, and interesting maps and photos of the area. One or two-hour **Horseback riding tours** (US$20/30) through the park and along the coast can also be arranged with advance notice. The park is operated by the Punta Cana Ecological Foundation, a nonprofit foundation created in 1994 that works to protect the area's ecosystems – including 8km of coral reef along the reserve's shoreline – and to promote sustainable tourism and hotel practices. Nearly 4 hectares of the reserve are dedicated to the Cornell biodiversity laboratory, a joint project with other American universities to inventory and study native plants, birds and insects. Unfortunately, there is no hotel pickup service; a cab here will cost around US$25 each way from Bávaro or El Cortecito.

Activities

WATERSPORTS

Virtually every water activity is available but some involve a long commute to the actual

BÁVARO & PUNTA CANA

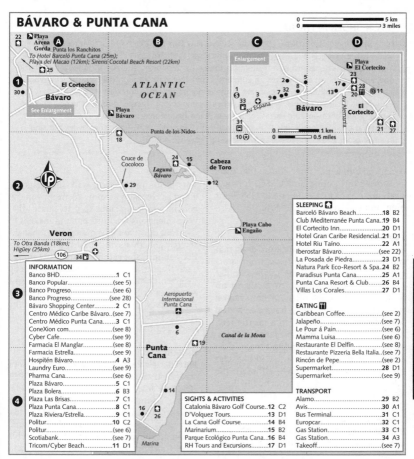

INFORMATION
Banco BHD	**1** C1
Banco Popular	(see 5)
Banco Progreso	(see 6)
Banco Progreso	(see 28)
Bávaro Shopping Center	**2** C1
Centro Médico Caribe Bávaro	(see 7)
Centro Médico Punta Cana	**3** C1
ConeXion com	(see 8)
Cyber Cafe	(see 9)
Farmacia El Manglar	(see 8)
Farmacia Estrella	(see 9)
Hospitén Bávaro	**4** A3
Laundry Euro	(see 9)
Pharma Cana	(see 6)
Plaza Bávaro	**5** C1
Plaza Bolera	**6** B3
Plaza Las Brisas	**7** C1
Plaza Punta Cana	**8** C1
Plaza Riviera/Estrella	**9** C1
Politur	**10** C1
Politur	(see 6)
Scotiabank	(see 7)
Tricom/Cyber Beach	**11** D1

SIGHTS & ACTIVITIES
Catalonia Bávaro Golf Course	**12** C2
D'Volquez Tours	**13** D1
La Cana Golf Course	**14** B4
Marinarium	**15** B2
Parque Ecológico Punta Cana	**16** B4
RH Tours and Excursions	**17** D1

SLEEPING
Barceló Bávaro Beach	**18** B2
Club Mediterranée Punta Cana	**19** B4
El Cortecito Inn	**20** D1
Hotel Gran Caribe Residencial	**21** D1
Hotel Riu Taíno	**22** A1
Iberostar Bávaro	(see 22)
La Posada de Piedra	**23** D1
Natura Park Eco-Resort & Spa	**24** B2
Paradisus Punta Cana	**25** A1
Punta Cana Resort & Club	**26** B4
Villas Los Corales	**27** D1

EATING
Caribbean Coffee	(see 2)
Jalapeño	(see 7)
Le Pour á Pain	(see 6)
Mamma Luisa	(see 6)
Restaurante El Delfín	(see 8)
Restaurante Pizzeria Bella Italia	(see 2)
Rincón de Pepe	(see 2)
Supermarket	**28** D1
Supermarket	(see 9)

TRANSPORT
Alamo	**29** B2
Avis	**30** A1
Bus Terminal	**31** C1
Europcar	**32** C1
Gas Station	**33** C1
Gas Station	**34** A3
Takeoff	(see 7)

THE SOUTHEAST

site. Every hotel has a tour desk offering snorkeling, diving and boat trips to destinations such as Isla Saona. Parasailing is done from the beach all over Punta Cana and Bávaro. A popular family outing is a snorkeling trip to the **Marinarium** (www.marinarium .com; adult/2-12yr US$72/36), a natural offshore pool near Cabeza de Toro, which is arguably more ecofriendly than other excursions. Rays, nurse sharks, tropical fish and patches of coral are all on hand.

GOLF

La Cana Golf Course (☎ 809-959-2262; www.puntacana .com; Punta Cana Resort & Club, Punta Cana; ⏲ 7:30am-6pm) is Punta Cana's top golf course and is located at the area's top resort. The 18-hole course,

designed by Pete Dye, has several long par fives and stunning ocean views. Green fees are guest/nonguest US$115/156 for 18 holes or guest/nonguest US$71/96 for nine, including a golf cart. Club rental is US$30 for 18 holes or US$18 for nine, and golf cart costs US$40 per round. A new Tom Fazio–designed course is scheduled to open in summer 2008.

Nearby **Cap Cana** (☎ (809-955-9501; www.capcana .com; Punta Cana), the site of an enormous development project in the works, has three Jack Nicklaus Signature golf courses already complete and open for play (greens fees June to October US$220, November to May US$320).

If you'd like to get in a round but La Cana is too upmarket, the **Catalonia Bávaro Resort** (☎ 809-412-0000; Cabeza de Toro; ⏲ 8:30am-5pm) has a

DOWN UNDER IN THE DR

For something down'n'dirty, check out **Cueva Fun Fun** (☎ 809-553-2812; www.cuevafunfun.com; Rancho Capote, Calle Duarte 12, Barrio Puerto Rico, Hato Mayor; adult/child US$106/55), which runs spelunking trips to one of the largest cave systems in the entire Caribbean. The day includes a horseback ride, a walk through a lush forest, a 20m abseil and 2km walk through the cave, which involves a good deal of splishing and splashing in the underground river. Breakfast is provided, as is the equipment, including boots, harness, crash helmet and colorful jumper outfits – the overall effect is of a group of disposable extras for a James Bond baddie in a missile silo. Trips are generally booked as groups from hotels in the Bávaro/Punta Cana area, a 2½-hour drive away, but singles or small groups can piggyback on with enough advance notice.

decent nine-hole par-three course that costs US$45 for one round and US$60 for two. Carts are US$25 for 18 holes and US$20 for nine, and club rental just US$10.

Tours

Every resort has a separate tour desk that can arrange all variety of trips, from snorkeling and deep-sea fishing to the popular Isla Soana trip. A handful of locals set up on El Cortecito beach offer 2½-hour **snorkel trips** (per person US$20-25) and 2-hour **glass-bottom boat rides** (per person US$25-30) to a nearby reef. Most also offer **deep-sea fishing trips** (min 4 people, per person US$80-90) for marlin, tuna, wahoo and barracuda. There are a few kiosks near the north end of the beach, although the odds are that you'll be approached by touts as soon as you set foot in town and on the beach.

If you're looking to explore the region, **D'Volquez Tours** (☎ 809-552-1861, 809-776-3823; www.dvolquez.com; El Cortecito) and **RH Tours & Excursions** (☎ 809-552-1425; www.rhtours.com; El Cortecito; ☼ 9am-7pm) both offer a number of decent day trips for tourists. Popular excursions include exploring Parque Nacional Los Haitises (US$88), boat trips to Isla Saona (US$79) and tours of Santo Domingo's Zona Colonial (US$58). Most trips include lunch and drinks. English, German and French are spoken.

Bávaro Runners (☎ 809-466-1122; www.bavarorunners.com; adult/children US$85/43) offers all-day trips taking in a sugarcane plantation, cigar museum, beach and horseback riding (price includes lunch and drinks).

For a bird's-eye view of the area, **Helidosa** (☎ 809-732-8809; www.helidosa.com; Aeropuerto Internacional La Isabela) offers sightseeing trips from 10 minutes (per person US$74) to 40 minutes (per person US$289).

Sleeping

For resorts in the area, walk-in-guests are about as common as snowstorms; if you can convince the suspicious security guards that your intentions are innocent and make it to the front desk, you'll be quoted rates that absolutely nobody staying at the resort is paying. Book all-inclusive vacations online or through a travel agent, as they can offer discounts of up to 50% off rack rates. Bear in mind that most resorts cater to a particular niche, whether it's families, honeymooners, golfers or the spring break crowd. For help on your decision, see p244.

BÁVARO

Hotel Barceló Punta Cana (☎ 809-476-7777; www.barcelopuntacana.com; Playa Arena Gorda; r from US$150; P ✸ ▣ ✧) Ideally located at the end of a strip of all-inclusive places, but only a short drive from the commercial plazas of Bávaro, this resort, also known as Barceló Premium, is a good choice considering the reasonable rates. Catering to a mix of young families and singles, the Premium exudes a Club Med-like atmosphere – 'activity specialists' glide around on Segways and lead get-to-know-one-another games on the beach. There's a climbing wall, trapeze and tennis courts for the active, plus a big casino complex was in the works when we were there. Some of the bathrooms of this huge complex could stand an update, but the rooms are comfortable nevertheless – each has a balcony. Wireless internet access is US$10 per day. Don't confuse this place with the several other Barceló resorts in the area. Note also that it's not in Punta Cana, despite the name.

Natura Park Eco-Resort & Spa (☎ 809-221-2626; www.blau-hotels.com; Cabeza de Toro; d per person US$150; P ✸ ▣ ✧) Located midway between Bávaro and Punta Cana, Natura Park has a narrow beach outside the village of Cabeza de Toro. This is an isolated area nowhere near as busy as El Cortecito and Bávaro, so not the best choice for people looking to hop in and out of different resort clubs at night. Egrets and flamingos wander the property, which has won awards for its efforts to reduce its environmental impact. Large glass doors open out onto balconies or terraces. The pool is a bit small, but the beach quite nice.

Several other recommended resorts include the **Paradisus Punta Cana** (☎ 809-687-9923; www .solmelia.com; Playa de Bávaro; d US$275; P ⊠ 🖳 🕃), which attracts singles as well as families – topless sunbathing is not uncommon and there's an 'action park' with batting cages, archery and a climbing wall for kids. A sister golf and country club is only a few minutes away. The **Iberostar Bávaro** (☎ 809-221-6500; www.iberostar .com; Playa Bávaro; d US$195; P ⊠ 🖳 🕃) is a large complex popular with Europeans. While the nightly entertainment is reminiscent of high-school musical productions, there's no denying the beauty of the crystal-clear water and immaculate grounds. For those who truly crave size and choice in terms of food, try the **Barceló Bávaro Beach** (☎ 809-686-5797; www .barcelobavarobeach.com; Playa Bávaro; d per person US$110; P ⊠ 🖳 🕃), part of a complex of five all-inclusive resorts with more than a dozen restaurants and grills, 18 bars, a casino and two dance clubs. The Barceló Bávaro Beach has a party vibe, which for some may excuse its relatively small and ordinary rooms.

While the rooms at the **Hotel Riu Taíno** (☎ 809-221-2290; www.riu.com; Punta Arena Gorda; d per person US$120-180; P ⊠ 🖳 🕃) are showing their age and the buffet food is less than stellar, the grounds themselves and the beach are top quality. Same goes for the **Sirenis Cocotal Beach Resort** (☎ 809-688-6490; www.sirenishotels.com; Playa de Uvero Alto; d from US$150; P ⊠ 🖳 🕃), which tends to have a windier beach than others and, while not exactly unusual for all-inclusives, only early risers get beach chairs here.

PUNTA CANA

Even though it's commonly used as shorthand for the vacation area of the southeast, Punta Cana only has a few resorts, though all of them are upscale. Keep in mind that if you stay here, you are definitely not within walking distance of much else.

Club Mediterranée Punta Cana (☎ 809-686-5500; www.clubmed.com; Punta Cana; d per person US$125-240;

P ⊠ 🖳 🕃) The Club Med brand is identifiable the world over. You get young, enthusiastic international staff and activities galore; it's especially good for parents looking to outsource care for their kids and teenagers. The Ramp is a new two-story lounge area for 14- to 17-year olds, with foosball, skateboarding, inline skating – a hangout where parents aren't allowed. Parents can snorkel, kayak, windsurf, waterski, play tennis etc. Neither the rooms nor the food is spectacular – and pay attention to room location, since it's a big property and you can feels stranded in some parts.

Punta Cana Resort & Club (☎ 809-959-2262; www .puntacana.com; Punta Cana; d incl breakfast US$140; P ⊠ 🖳 🕃) Famous for its part-time residents like Julio Iglesias, Oscar de la Renta and Mikhail Baryshnikov, this resort is also notable for its environmental efforts, especially the associated ecological park across the street from the entrance to the resort. Newly opened Tortuga Bay, an enclave of 15 luxurious villas, is part of the main resort property of 60 sq km and 400 rooms. Three-story buildings line a beautiful beach and there are nine restaurants to choose from, though unlike the typical resort lunch, dinner and drinks aren't included in rates. It's a low-key resort for people happier to read a book on the beach rather than do aqua-aerobics to loud disco music in the pool.

RESORT ALTERNATIVES

La Posada de Piedra (☎ 809-221-0754; www.laposadade piedra.com; El Cortecito; r with/without bathroom US$45/25) The only budget accommodation with a beachfront location, this privately owned stone house is smack in the middle of busy Cortecito. Those with only primitive needs will be happy in one of the two primitive beachfront cabanas – expect little quiet during the day and a fairly dark room at night. Inside the owner's home are two comfortable rooms with private bathrooms and a shared balcony with views of the ocean. There's no common space inside, as the first floor is basically a souvenir shop and office. Breakfast, drinks and sandwiches are served at a few small tables set up on the street in front of the house.

Hotel Gran Caribe Residencial (☎ 809-552-1039; www.grancaribe.it, in Italian; Playa Bávaro; s/d incl breakfast from US$45/90; P ⊠ 🖳 🕃) Advertised as a boutique hotel, the Gran Caribe boasts none of the luxury or attention to detail implicit in

THE SOUTHEAST

that description. The small rooms are plain if comfortable and the modest pool area is pleasant enough. It's a good choice for those seeking some quiet. Guests can use the facilities at a local beach club just 150m away free of charge

El Cortecito Inn (☎ 809-552-0639; cortecitoinn@ codetel.net.do; s/d incl breakfast US$55/60; P X R) A forlorn, lonely looking complex across the street from the beach in El Cortecito, this hotel nevertheless is one of the few independent, reasonably priced choices in the area. There are some loyalists who apparently aren't bothered by the service without a smile, the aging furniture or the unlandscaped concrete pool area. The complimentary buffet breakfast is rather uninspiring.

Villas Los Corales (☎ 809-221-0801; www.los-cor ales-villas.com; Playa Bávaro; r US$115; P X R) This small Italian-owned development has none of the grandiose ambitions of the nearby all-inclusives to be all things to all people. For those seeking more modest surroundings and a community feel, Los Corales will do. Of the 30 or so apartments, all have small private patios and balconies, and private kitchenettes; some have ocean-front views. There's an Italian restaurant, bar and small swimming pool, and it has its own 'beach club' – basically another restaurant and bar. Weekly and monthly rates are available.

Eating & Drinking

Most visitors are hardly hungry after gorging themselves at their resort's buffets, but there are enough condos and villas and locals to support a handful of eateries. Most are in various shopping centers in the area, easily reached by *motoconcho* or taxi.

Le Pour á Pain (Plaza Bolera, Bávaro; mains US$6; 10am-10pm) This small, pleasant café with outdoor patio seating is in Plaza Bolera, not exactly a picturesque location but a good spot if you're in town. Good coffee as well as crepes (US$6), salads (US$8) and sandwiches (US$6) are served.

Mamma Luisa (☎ 809-959-2013; Punta Cana Shopping Mall; mains US$8-15; lunch & dinner Mon-Sat) Though the setting resembles any mini-mall USA, this friendly restaurant serves up excellent Italian meat, fish and pasta dishes – the paella for two (US$35) is recommended. Checkerboard tablecloths, formally clad waiters and an extensive wine collection allow Mamma's to rise above its location a half-kilometer west of the airport.

For light and casual fare like salads, wraps and crepes try **Caribbean Coffee** (Bávaro Shopping Center, Bávaro; mains US$9-14; breakfast, lunch & dinner). Around the corner is **Rincón de Pepe** (☎ 809-552-0603; Bávaro Shopping Center, Bávaro; mains US$8-15; lunch & dinner Mon-Sat), for tasty Spanish dishes – the paella (US$23 for two) comes in seafood, rabbit, beef and chicken varieties. **Restaurante El Delfín** (Plaza Punta Cana, Bávaro; mains US$5-10; breakfast, lunch & dinner) is popular with Dominicans and serves fish, chicken and meat dishes with rice, beans and a side of loud music. For ersatz Mexican cuisine à la Tex-Mex and interpretations of fajitas and enchiladas head to **Jalapeño** (☎ 809-552-1033; Plaza Las Brisas, Bávaro; mains US$8-12; breakfast, lunch & dinner) and its open-air dining area. **Restaurante Pizzeria Bella Italia** (☎ 809-552-0493; Plaza Las Brisas, Bávaro; mains US$5-15; breakfast, lunch & dinner, closed Tue) definitely cooks up better pies than you'll find at your hotel's buffet.

The two best supermarkets are in plazas right next to each other: Plaza Riviera and Plaza Estrella. There's another supermarket, open from 9am to 9pm, in El Cortecito.

Getting There & Away

AIR

Several massive thatched-roof huts make up the complex of the Aeropuerto Internacional Punta Cana, located on the road to Punta Cana about 9km east of the turnoff to Bávaro. The arrival process, including immigration, purchase of a tourist card (US$10), baggage claim and customs, moves briskly.

American Airlines (☎ 809-959-2420), **Air France** (☎ 809-959-3002) and **LAN** (☎ 809-959-0144) all have offices at the airport. Other airlines serving the Punta Cana airport include US Airways, Air Canada, Air France, Continental, Northwest, Corsair, LTU, Iberworld and USA3000. See the Transportation chapter (p352) for airlines information.

For domestic air connections, the airline/ travel agency **Takeoff** (☎ 809-552-1333; www.take offweb.com; Plaza Las Brisas; 6am-8pm) has daily direct flights on 10- and 19-seat planes between Punta Cana and Santo Domingo (8:45am, one way $115), El Portillo (Samaná; 8:45am, one way $115) and La Romana (one way $23). It also serves Puerto Plata via Romana (one way $170) and El Catey (Samaná; one way $170) via Santo Domingo.

There is a Banco Progreso ATM located in the arrivals area, as well as a **Codetel Centro de Comunicaciones** (☎ 809-688-1153; internet per hr US$2;

(Y) 8am-6pm). None of the international rental car agencies have booths here; a representative will pick you up upon arrival if reservations are made in advance – otherwise you may have a long wait.

Resort minivans transport the majority of tourists to nearby resorts, but taxis are plentiful. Fares between the airport and area resorts and hotels range between US$10 and US$35 depending on the destination.

BUS

The bus terminal is located at the main intersection in Bávaro, near the Texaco gas station, almost 2km inland from El Cortecito.

Expreso Santo Domingo Bávaro Bávaro (☎ 809-552-1678); Santo Domingo (Map p77; ☎ 809-682-9670; cnr Juan Sánchez Ruiz & Máximo Gómez) has direct first-class service between Bávaro and the capital (US$9, four hours), with a stop in La Romana. Departure times in both directions are 7am, 10am, 2pm and 4pm.

Also at the same terminal is Expreso Romana, with departures to La Romana at 8am and 4pm (US$4.75). To all other destinations, take a local bus (marked Sitrabapu) to Higüey and transfer there. (You can also get to/from Santo Domingo this way, but it's much slower than the direct bus.) *Caliente* buses to Higüey leave Bávaro's main terminal (US$2.50, 1½ hours, every 20 minutes from 5am to 9pm), as does the express service (US$3, 1¼ hours, every hour from 3am to 9pm).

If you have questions, keep in mind that the terminal office is only open from 6:30am to 4pm (and is closed noon to 1pm for lunch).

Getting Around

Local buses start at the main bus terminal, passing all the outdoor malls on the way to El Cortecito, then turn down the coastal road past the large hotels to Cruce de Cocoloco, where they turn around and return the same way. Buses have the drivers' union acronym – Sitrabapu – printed in front and cost US$0.75. They are supposed to pass every 15 to 30 minutes, but can sometimes take up to an hour.

Daytime traffic is sometimes gridlocked between the resorts clustered just north of Bávaro and El Cortecito. Despite the stop-and-go pace of driving, renting a car for a day or two is recommended if you prefer to see the surrounding area independently. Consider

paying more for extra insurance coverage, especially if you'll be driving north toward Playa Limón, Miches and Sabana de la Mar. Some agencies allow you to drop off the car in Santo Domingo, usually for an extra charge, but check in advance. Rental agencies include **Avis** (☎ 809-688-1354; Plaza Caney, Carr Arena Gorda), **Europcar** (☎ 809-686-2861; near Plaza Punta Cana, Bávaro) and **Alamo** (☎ 809-466-1083; Carr Bávaro Km 5).

Otherwise, there are numerous taxis in the area – look for stands at El Cortecito, Plaza Bávaro and at the entrance of most all-inclusive places. You can also call a cab – try **Siutratural taxi** (☎ 809-221-2741) or **Arena Gorda taxi** (☎ 809-552-0786). Fares vary depending on distance, but are typically from US$5 (pretty much minimum charge on a short trip within Bávaro) to US$35 (to the airport). Water taxis also can be found on El Cortecito beach and cost between US$10 and US$50 per ride. *Motoconchos* congregate around Plaza Punta Cana in Bávaro and along the beach road in El Cortecito, and you can generally find one or two parked in front of the entrance to most resorts. Fares, while negotiable (US$2 to US$4 from El Cortecito to Bávaro), are always cheaper than taxis but the ride can be uncomfortable over long distances and at night.

PLAYA LIMÓN

The drive alone justifies the trip to **Playa Limón**. Hwy 104 passes through rolling mountain scenery, past bucolic ranches, where any unrecognized vehicle is sure to turn the heads of locals; it practically qualifies as an event in the sleepy villages along the way. Playa Limón itself, about 20km east of Miches and just outside the hamlet of El Cedro, is a 3km-long, isolated beach lined with coconut trees leaning into the ocean – coveted property that you're likely to have to yourself for much of the time. Horseback riding tours descend upon it a few hours a day, generally from late morning to early afternoon.

The rugged area surrounding Playa Limón has two important wetland areas, including **Laguna Limón**, a serene freshwater body of water surrounded by grassy wetlands and coastal mangroves. The lagoon feeds into the ocean on the eastern end of Playa Limón and is known for bird-watching; tours are organized by Rancho La Cueva (p138). The other lagoon – Laguna Redonda – is just 5km away, but is more commonly visited from Punta El Rey.

THE SOUTHEAST

Sleeping & Eating

our pick **Rancho La Cueva** (☎ 809-470-0876; www.lac uevalimon.com; r US$30; P 🖳) Horses roam this rural property surrounded by a lush palm-tree forest and a short walk from an isolated beach. But despite its out-of-the-way feel, this hotel 3km down a dirt road at the eastern end of El Cedro, doesn't lack in terms of modern convenience – it even has a strong wi-fi signal throughout. The eight large spick-and-span rooms are sparsely furnished and what furniture there is tends to be fairly fragile (beds excluded). An open-air restaurant hosts daily tour groups for a seafood buffet, but breakfast and dinner are more simple affairs – guests need to check in advance to see what's available. The hotel can arrange a trip that includes a visit to a cockfighting *gallera*, a coffee plantation, a ride in the mountains, seafood buffet and a boat ride across the lagoon for US$60 per person.

Harley's Heaven (☎ 809-476-8682; www.lagunalimon .com; r US$30, 2-/4-person apt US$40/50; P 🖳) Located directly above and behind Rancho La Cueva, this is another excellent option. Harley's friendly German owner is a good host and will arrange meals for groups with advance notice; otherwise there's no regular dining area as yet. One of the buildings is perched on a hill with a makeshift outdoor gym – well, three pieces of equipment – and great views of the area, and the other has a bar. All of the rooms, whether the hotel style ones or apartments with basic kitchenettes (refrigerator, hotplate, dining table) are immaculate, well kept and have satellite TV.

Getting There & Away

The road to Playa Limón, though severely potholed in parts, is empty and passes through beautiful scenery. From Higüey or other parts south, take Hwy 104 until you reach the very eastern edge of El Cedro. Head north on a rough dirt road (an SUV is recommended, especially after a heavy rain) – look for the sign reading 'Ecotourismo Playa Laguna de Limón' and painted with a beach scene. The hotels are about 3km down this road and the beach only another half-kilometer.

Keep in mind that the only gas station between Otra Banda (the start of Hwy 104) and Miches is in the town of Lagunas de Nisibón. From Playa Limón it's only 27km to Miches, about a 35-minute drive in your own vehicle.

Gua-guas running between Higüey (US$2, two hours) and Miches (US$1, 30 minutes) also stop in El Cedro every 30 minutes from 5:30am to 6pm. If arriving, be sure to let the driver know that you want to get off in El Cedro; it's easy to miss.

A *motoconcho* from town should cost around US$1.50, though this is far from comfortable, especially if you're carrying luggage.

PUNTA EL REY

Robinson Crusoe would feel at home here. The beach follows the curve of a large round bay east of Miches and a grassy point at the eastern end is Punta El Rey proper. Around the corner is a basic nipa-palm hut where tour groups visiting Laguna Redondo stop for lunch and a break usually between 10:30am and 3:30pm.

Punta El Rey, a worthwhile detour between Playa Limón and Miches, isn't the easiest to find. To get here from El Cedro, continue driving east on Hwy 104 towards Miches. Look for a sign on the right reading 'Playa Costa Esmerelda' just before the eastern edge of the small barrio La Mina de Miches. Take this turnoff and continue for 2km until you reach a fork; go left and after 3km more there's an intersection, where you take a right. After another 4km of very rough road, past a ranch with signposts cautioning you not to continue because you're on private property (if there is a guard on hand he'll be happy to wave you through), you finally reach Punta El Rey.

MICHES

pop 9200

From the surrounding hills, Miches, on the southern shore of the Bahía de Samaná, is fairly picturesque. A slim 50m-high radio tower marks the geographic center of what appear to be well-ordered streets, and Playa Miches, just east of the town proper, looks inviting. Upon closer inspection, however, it's a fairly tumbledown place and the beach, though long and wide, is not very attractive. The water isn't good for swimming, mainly because the Rió Yaguada empties into the ocean here. Miches sometimes makes national headlines as the launching point for Dominicans hoping to enter the USA illegally, via the Mona Passage to Puerto Rico.

Orientation

From Playa Limón, Hwy 104 descends to a bayside basin floor where it crosses a short bridge. On the other side of the bridge is *la bomba* – literally 'the pump.' This is the local gas station and the terminal for *gua-guas* heading to and from Higüey. If you're driving, take the next right and an immediate left to get onto the main west-bound street; at the end is the terminal for *gua-guas* to and from Sabana de la Mar. Shortly past here is a sign and turnoff for El Seibo, San Pedro de Macorís and Santo Domingo; at the top of the hill the rutted roadway turns into smooth blacktop. If you continue past this turnoff there is a sign indicating the road to Hotel La Loma on the left. Ignoring both turnoffs and continuing west out of town will take you to Sabana de la Mar – the mostly dirt road is in extremely poor condition. SUV is highly recommended.

Information

BanReservas (cnr Calle Fernando Deligne & Gral Santana; ☽ 9:30am-3pm Mon-Fri) is at the western end of town, one block south of Calle Mella; there's an ATM accessible 24 hours. **Banco Agricola** (☽ 8:30am-4pm), a fairly primitive affair, is two blocks north of Calle Mella and can change cash and traveler's checks in a pinch.

International calls can be made from **Codetel Centro de Comunicaciones** (Calle Mella; ☽ 8am-7pm).

Sleeping & Eating

Hotel La Loma (☎ 809-553-5562; fax 809-553-5564; Miches; s/d US$40/50; P ⊠ ⊠) Perched atop a hill at the end of an incredibly steep driveway, Hotel La Loma has commanding views of the city and bay below. It's a convenient place to stop for the night on your way to Sabana de la Mar, and it's certainly the best place to stay in town. Room furnishings are simple and old (wicker chairs, a single piece of Haitian art) but they're large and have equally spectacular views. There's a small pool, though it's buffeted by strong winds. Open for breakfast, lunch and dinner, the restaurant (mains US$4 to US$10) serves very mediocre food, not to mention weak coffee, but you can get a workman-like interpretation of spaghetti, steak or fish.

Getting There & Away

Gua-guas to Higüey (US$4, 2½ hours, every 30 minutes from 5am to 5:30pm) leave from a terminal at the Isla gas station at the east end of town just before the bridge. The terminal for *gua-guas* going to and from Sabana de la Mar (US$2.50, 1¼ hours, every 25 minutes from 6:55am to 6pm) is at the western edge of town.

If you are simply passing through town, whether from Sabana de la Mar to Higüey or vice versa, let the driver know you want to catch an onward bus and he will most likely drop you at the next terminal, saving you a *motoconcho* or taxi ride between the two.

An SUV is absolutely necessary to continue west to Sabana de la Mar in your own vehicle.

SABANA DE LA MAR
pop 14,800

The literal and figurative end of the road, this small, ramshackle and largely forgotten town is the gateway to Parque Nacional Los Haitises. However, until the roadways in the area are improved, especially Hwy 104 east to Miches, Sabana will continue to miss out on sharing a slice of the economic pie from the growing number of tourists visiting the bay for whale-watching and Los Haitises tours. Sabana is the departure point for the passenger ferry across the bay to Samaná, as well as for the dangerous Mona passage crossing to Puerto Rico, the first stop for many Dominicans hoping to make their way to the US.

Orientation

Hwy 103 from Hato Mayor descends from the hills straight into Sabana de la Mar, turning into Calle Duarte, the main street, and eventually bumping right into the pier where the Samaná ferry leaves and arrives. The road from Miches intersects with the Higüey highway just outside (south) of town. *Gua-guas* to Miches, Hato Mayor, El Seibo, Higüey and Santo Domingo all congregate at or near that intersection. The turnoff to Caño Hondo and Parque Nacional Los Haitises is a short distance north of the Miches intersection – look for a large sign pointing west. There's a gas station 2km south of town on the road to Hato Mayor.

Information

Sabana de la Mar is a small town with relatively few services. **BanReservas** (Calle Duarte; ☽ 8am-5pm Mon-Fri, 9am-1pm Sat) is three blocks south of the ferry pier and has an ATM. **Codetel Centro de Comunicaciones** (Calle Duarte; ☽ 8am-10pm), two blocks south of the southernmost roundabout in town, offers international telephone service.

Tours

Brigado Verde (☎ 809-232-8121; bvsabana@yahoo.com) is a guide association that runs boat and walking tours of Parque Nacional Los Haitises that typically last 3½ hours and include sailing around land formations and through mangroves, exploring Taíno caves and relaxing on the beach. The cost per person is US$35 for four or more people, or US$45 per person for smaller groups. **Whale-watching** trips also are offered between January 15 and March 15 (see boxed text, p148). The cost per person is US$60 for a group of four or more, and US$80 per person for smaller groups. English and French are spoken.

Paraíso Caño Hondo (☎ 809-248-5995; www.paraiso canohondo.com), a highly recommend hotel 9km west of town and 1km past the park entrance, offers good tours inside Parque Los Haitises as well. Boat excursions range between US$50 and US$85 for groups of two to four depending on the extent of the tour, and **hiking trips** (per guide US$18) through the park's Bosque Humedo (humid forest) also can be arranged. During the humpback season, Paraíso organizes whale-watching tours (per person US$56) in the waters near Samaná.

At the entrance to Los Haitises, town **boatmen** also offer to take visitors on tours of the park (per person US$17). While the excursions are similar to those offered by the tour operators, background information on the sights is often less detailed.

Sleeping & Eating

ourpick **Paraíso Caño Hondo** (☎ 809-248-5995; www .paraisocanohondo.com, in Spanish; r incl breakfast US$48) This is one of the more special places to stay anywhere in the DR, even though a stay here couldn't be farther from the typical beach resort experience. Coming upon Paraíso Caño Hondo so far out of the way after a long and rough road feels like an epiphany. The Río Jivales, which runs through the property, has been channeled into 10 magical waterfall-fed pools, perfect for a soak any time of the day. Rooms are large and rustic, made mostly of wood, though extremely comfortable. Bathroom ceilings are made of dried palm fronds and energy-saving light fixtures are used throughout. Easily unique, the most interesting room is the one in the upper building with a small balcony with hammocks and a sitting area perched on top of a large rock. The restaurant here is the best place to eat in

the area any time of day; try the shrimp creolestyle (US$12) or delicious steak (US$7). Signs from the center of Sabana de la Mar direct you to the turnoff for the hotel – the same one as for the entrance to Parque Los Haitises. Weekends are often packed with student groups, so best plan a midweek visit.

A block north of the *gua-gua* station is the **Hotel Riverside** (☎ 809-556-7465; r with/without air-con US$15/10; ❄), a place to lay your head for the night; a family rents out several rooms on the second floor of their home.

Getting There & Away

Gua-guas are the only means of public transportation out of town. They leave from the entrance of town, at the crossroads of Hwy 104 and Hwy 103. *Gua-guas* headed to Santo Domingo (US$4, 3½ hours, every 30 minutes from 6am to 4pm) stop along the way in Hato Mayor (US$1.40, one hour) and San Pedro de Macorís (US$2.50, two hours). *Gua-guas* also provide service to Miches (US$1.25, 1¼ hours, every 25 minutes from 6:45am to 6pm).

Transporte Maritimo (☎ 809-556-7000) provides a passenger ferry service across the Bahía de Samana to Samaná (US$4.25, 1¼ hours, 9am, 11am, 3pm and 5pm). From there you can catch *gua-guas* to Las Galeras, Las Terrenas or puddle-jump to other destinations on the north coast. Bad weather means rough seas and frequent cancellations, and some of the boats are rickety, making even a voyage under sunny skies a potentially seasickening experience for those with sensitive stomachs. The ticket office is on the pier.

PARQUE NACIONAL LOS HAITISES

Eight kilometers west of Sabana de la Mar, **Parque Nacional Los Haitises** (admission US$3.50; ❧ 7am-8pm) is certainly the best reason to visit this small bayside town. Its name meaning 'land of the mountains,' this 1375-sq-km park at the southwestern end of the Bahía de Samaná contains scores of lush hills jutting some 30m to 50m from the water and coastal wetlands. The knolls were formed one to two million years ago, when tectonic drift buckled the thick limestone shelf that had formed underwater. The turnoff to the park is near the crossroads of Hwys 104 and 103, at the south end of town (near the bus stop). The road is partially paved but still rough in parts.

The area receives a tremendous amount of rainfall, creating perfect conditions for subtropical humid forest plants such as bamboo, ferns and bromeliads. In fact, Los Haitises contains over 700 species of flora, including four types of mangrove, making it one of the most highly biodiverse regions in the Caribbean.

Los Haitises also is home to 110 species of birds, 13 of which are endemic to the island. Those seen most frequently include the brown pelican, the American frigate bird, the blue heron, the roseate tern and the northern jacana. If you're lucky, you may even spot the rare Hispaniolan parakeet, notable for its light-green and red feathers.

The park also contains a series of limestone caves, some of which contain intriguing Taíno pictographs. Drawn by the native inhabitants of Hispaniola using mangrove shoots, the pictures depict faces, hunting scenes, whales and other animals. Several petroglyphs (images carved into the stone) can also be seen at the entrance of some caves and are thought to represent divine guardians. Las Cuevas de la Arena, La Cueva del Templo and La Cueva de San Gabriel are three of the more interesting caves and shouldn't be missed.

Land and boat excursions inside the park leave from Sabana de la Mar (see opposite) and Samaná across the bay (see p147). Las Terrenas (see p158), also on the Península de Samaná, has the largest number of tour companies arranging trips here.

THE SOUTHEAST

Península de Samaná

The Península de Samaná is a small sliver of land – just 40km long and 15km wide – of rolling mountains, a sea of hillocks pushing their way to a long coastline of protected beaches and picturesque coves. A new international airport and a new highway to the capital, either ominous signs of development or economic lifelines to the rest of the country and the world, suggest that Samaná's character, defined in part by its relative inaccessibility, is trending more to the mainland and the mainstream. However, for now it's still a place where the stereotypical image of a vacation in the DR need not apply; where the European vibe is as strong as an espresso at a Las Terrenas café; where escape – both from the workaday, urban milieu of New York or Paris and from Santiago or Santo Domingo – is the operative word; where French and Italian are at least as useful as Spanish; and where it's only a short *motoconcho* ride from a luxurious second home to an open-air disco pumping merengue.

Tens of thousands of tourists, following the migratory pattern of the North Atlantic humpback whale, bus and fly in to Samaná from mid-January to mid-March, seeing little else of the peninsula – though if there's time for only one thing, this is definitely it. More urban and more Dominican than either Las Terrenas or Las Galeras, Samaná is also the transport hub for bus connections to Puerto Plata and Santo Domingo, and for the ferry across the bay to Sabana de la Mar and the southeast. Las Terrenas, the most developed in terms of tourism, is the place to base yourself if you crave a lively social scene, and Las Galeras, a sleepy one-road town, boasts several of the best beaches in the DR, their beauty enhanced by the effort it takes to get there.

HIGHLIGHTS

- Feel small – very small – after witnessing the majesty of 30-ton humpbacks breaching and diving on a **whale-watching trip** (p145) in Bahía de Samaná

- Take a long walk, and we mean *long*, on the gorgeous sand of **Playa Rincón** (p151)

- Snorkel undisturbed around some of the best reefs the peninsula has to offer at **Playa Frontón** (p151)

- Down a cocktail at an oceanside restaurant in cosmopolitan **Las Terrenas** (p160)

- Take in the rugged mountain scenery of Samaná's interior on a trip to 52m-high **Cascada El Limón** (p145)

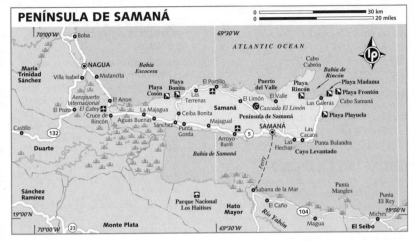

HISTORY

Because of Bahía de Samaná's fortuitous geography – its deep channel, eastward orientation and easy-to-defend mouth, perfect for a naval installation – the Península de Samaná has been coveted, fought over and bought several times over. At least six different countries, including Haiti, France, Spain, the US and Germany, have either occupied the Samaná area or sought to do so.

Founded as a Spanish outpost in 1756, Samaná was first settled by émigrés from the Canary Islands, but the political turmoil of Hispaniola – the sale of the island to the French, a Haitian revolution and two British invasions (see p29) – kept Samaná town's population growing and changing. It was deemed a prize even as early as 1807 during the brief French possession of Hispaniola. France's commander in Santo Domingo, an ambitious leader no doubt, proposed building a city named Port Napoleon in Samaná, but France was dispossessed of the island before the plan could move forward.

After its independence from Spain, the DR was taken over by Haiti, which controlled Hispaniola from 1822 to 1844. During this period Haiti invited more than 5000 freed and escaped slaves from the US to settle on the island. About half moved to the Samaná area. Today, a community of their descendents still speaks a form of English.

During Haitian rule, France pressured its former colony to cede the Península de Samaná in return for a reduction in the debt Haiti owed it. Incredibly, Haiti had been forced to pay restitution to France for land taken from French colonists in order to gain international recognition. Of course, France never paid restitution to former slaves for their ordeal.

After Dominican independence from Haiti in 1844, the new Dominican government feared Haiti would reinvade, so sought foreign assistance from France, England and Spain. The DR eventually resubmitted to Spanish rule in 1861, and Spain immediately sent a contingent of settlers to the Samaná area and reinforced the military installations on Cayo Levantado, a large island (and site of a luxury all-inclusive resort today) near the mouth of the bay.

Even after independence in 1864, the Península de Samaná remained a tempting prize for other countries. Beginning in 1868, the US, under President Ulysses S Grant, sought to purchase the peninsula from the DR in order to build a naval base there. Dominican president and strongman Buenaventura Báez agreed to the sale in order to obtain the money and weapons he needed to stay in power. However, the US Senate, under pressure from Dominican exile groups and strong opposition from France and the UK, rejected the proposal in 1871. A year later, Báez arranged to lease the area to the US-based Samaná Bay Company for 99 years. To the relief of most Dominicans, the company fell behind on its payments and Baez's successor, Ignacio María González, rescinded the contract in 1874. The US revisited the idea of annexing Samaná in 1897 as the Spanish–American war loomed, but decided to build its Caribbean base in Guantánamo Bay, Cuba after it quickly defeated Spain.

German intentions toward the Península de Samaná are less clear, but US documents from the 1870s suggest that Germany was also seeking to establish a military base in the Caribbean. In 1916, during WWI, the US occupied the DR in part because it feared that Germany was seeking to establish itself here.

GETTING THERE & AROUND

Península de Samaná is now more easily accessible by air because of the new Aeropuerto Internacional El Catey, on the highway between Nagua and Sánchez. It receives international flights from San Juan, Puerto Rico (American Eagle) and various cities in Europe (Air Comet, Condor, LTU, CanJet, Corsair, Skyservice, Neos, Sunwing and Air Transat). Tourism on the peninsula is likely to be transformed by this airport.

Two other airports – 'international' by name only – serve the peninsula. Several small domestic airlines have regularly scheduled flights to Aeropuerto Internacional El Portillo, several kilometers west of Las Terrenas, and during the height of whale-watching season less frequently to the otherwise charter-only Aeropuerto Internacional Arroyo Barril near Samaná.

Other than arriving by cruise ship, the only sea option is the regular ferry service between Samaná and Sabana de la Mar in the southeast. Cars are not allowed, the boats themselves vary from rickety and untrustworthy to serviceable, and the schedule is subject to the weather.

A new highway, said to cut the travel time from Santo Domingo to Samaná to a mere two hours, was scheduled to open in early 2008 but financing and construction hiccups have meant delays. As is their wont in the DR, some drivers have already begun to use portions of the new blacktop even though other parts are impassable. From Santo Domingo, it will pass through Los Merenas, Malta Moreno, Boya, Los Mapolos, Las Coles, Rincón Molinillos and finally Cruce de Rincón, which is almost 20km west of Sánchez; once the highway is operational, expect heavy traffic. Until then, it's a four- to five-hour drive from Santo Domingo. Take Hwy Duarte north to San Francisco de Macorís, Castillo, Nagua, Sánchez and finally

> **FIVE WAYS TO GET A NEW PERSPECTIVE ON THE PENÍNSULA DE SAMANÁ**
>
> Other than trains (well, and hovercrafts), just about every mode of transportation is available on the Península de Samaná. Each provides a unique way of seeing and understanding this compact and varied land.
>
> - By plane – Approach Samaná from the air for a bird's-eye view of the rugged interior.
> - By boat – Arrive on the ferry from Sabana de la Mar to get a sense of the peninsula's isolation.
> - By horse – Head out on a trail around Las Galeras to reach remote beaches and coves.
> - By ATV – Rumble around Las Terrenas like a European expat out for their daily bread.
> - By foot – Make your way with foot power along kilometer after kilometer of uninterrupted beach.

Samaná. From Puerto Plata, it's a three- to four-hour drive east along Hwy 5.

For more information, see p255.

EASTERN PENÍNSULA DE SAMANÁ

SAMANÁ
pop 12,500

For much of the year, Samaná follows the slow daily rhythms of an ordinary Dominican town: not much happens; fishermen's days are lived on the water; people pass through on their way to Las Terrenas and Las Galeras or to the mainland via the daily ferry; and the Malecón (main street; literally 'sea wall') takes on a somnolent air. It's a compact place built on a series of bluffs overlooking Bahía de Samaná, with little to distinguish it from other more charming towns on the peninsula. In fact, it remained an isolated fishing village until 1985, when the first whale-watching expedition set out. Because North Atlantic humpbacks find the bay water particularly suitable for their annual version of speed dating from mid-January to mid-March, Samaná is transformed by tens of thousands of tourists who flock here to go on a whale-watching tour, a natural spectacle with few equals.

Orientation

Arriving in town from the direction of El Limón or Sánchez, it's about a kilometer downhill past the municipal market where the *gua-gua* (small bus) station is, around several traffic circles and along a newly built faux Caribbean village to the main street – Av Malecón or Av la Marina. Most of the restaurants, banks and bus stations are located here. The port is across the street from a small shady park near where the buses leave from. Several of the hotels are all reachable by foot, but are a bit far if you're carrying bags.

Information

EMERGENCY

Politur (tourist police; ☎ 809-754-3066; Av Francisco de Rosario Sánchez; ☮ 24hr) On the traffic circle near Av Circunvalación.

INTERNET ACCESS & TELEPHONE

CompuCentro Samaná (☎ 809-538-3146; cnr Calles Julio Labandier & Santa Barbara; per hr US$2.10; ☮ 9am-noon & 3-6pm Mon-Fri)

LAUNDRY

Lavandería Santa Barbara (Calle Santa Barbara; ☮ 8:30am-6pm Mon-Sat) Same-day or overnight service available at US$1.50 per lb (450g).

MEDICAL SERVICES

Clinic Assist (Av Francisco de Rosario Sánchez) Doctors on call 24 hours. Located in the pastel faux village.

Farmacia Giselle (☎ 809-538-2303; cnr Calles Santa Barbara & Julio Labandier; ☮ 8am-10pm Mon-Sat, 8am-noon Sun) Good selection of meds and toiletries.

Farmacia Maritere (Av Francisco Rosario de Sánchez) On the second traffic circle up from the Malecón, on the road to Sánchez.

Hospital Municipal (Calle San Juan; ☮ 24hr) A very basic hospital near the Palacio de Justicia.

MONEY

Banco Popular (Av Malecón; ☮ 8:15am-4pm Mon-Fri, 9am-1pm Sat) Located on the Malecón across from the ferry dock.

BanReservas (Calle Santa Barbara; ☮ 8am-5pm Mon-Fri, 9am-1pm Sat) One block north of the Malecón.

Scotiabank (Av Francisco Rosario de Sánchez; ☮ 8am-4pm Mon-Fri, 9am-1pm Sat) Closest ATM to the *gua-gua* terminal and the municipal market.

POST

Post office (cnr Calles Santa Barbara & 27 de Febrero; ☮ 8:30am-5pm Mon-Fri)

Sights & Activities

WHALE-WATCHING

For sheer awe-inspiring, 'the natural world is an amazing thing' impact, a whale-watching trip is hard to beat. Around 45,000 people travel to Samaná every year from January 15 to March 15 to see the majestic acrobatics of these massive creatures. Try to avoid coming here during Carnival (celebrated throughout February) and on February 27, which is the Independence Day holiday for Dominicans, making it the busiest day of the year.

Most of the whale-watching companies have a morning and afternoon trip. There's little difference in terms of your likelihood of seeing whales, and although the water may be slightly rougher in the afternoon, it also tends to be quieter, with fewer boats out. There are around 43 vessels in total: eight companies, all owned or at least partly owned by Dominicans from Samaná, and around 12 independent operators. A co-management and self-regulation agreement was established in 1994 between the boat owners and various departments of the Dominican government, including the Ministry of Tourism and the Ministry of the Environment. A manual of rules and responsible behavior was created and every year all the stakeholders sign it to renew their commitment. One of the more important objectives is ensuring a minimum boat size of 8.7m: in big seas small boats are low to the water and sometimes aren't aware of the whales until they're too close. See boxed text, p148 for more about the whales, and p147 for information about how to see this amazing spectacle.

Private vessels are strictly prohibited from whale-watching; this applies to yachts and boats of any size. They can only transit into or out of the bay.

CASCADA EL LIMÓN

A trip to this 52m-high **waterfall**, a short distance from the town of El Limón, is a chance to experience Samaná's rugged interior and revel in some breathtaking mountain scenery. Travel agencies in Samaná offer trips here for around US$45, including transport, horses, guide and lunch. However, it's perfectly easy and much cheaper to do the trip yourself by

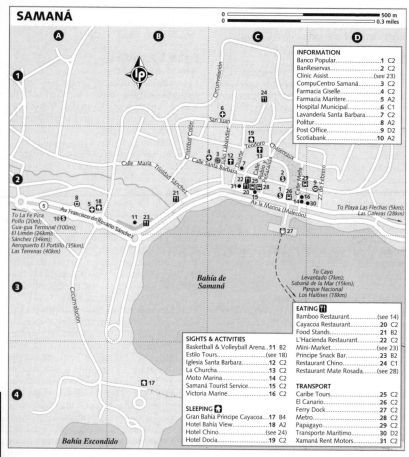

SAMANÁ

INFORMATION
Banco Popular	**1** C2
BanReservas	**2** C2
Clinic Assist	(see 23)
CompuCentro Samaná	**3** C2
Farmacia Giselle	**4** C2
Farmacia Maritere	**5** A2
Hospital Municipal	**6** C1
Lavandería Santa Barbara	**7** C2
Politur	**8** A2
Post Office	**9** D2
Scotiabank	**10** A2

SIGHTS & ACTIVITIES
Basketball & Volleyball Arena	**11** B2
Estilo Tours	(see 18)
Iglesia Santa Barbara	**12** C2
La Churcha	**13** C2
Moto Marina	**14** C2
Samaná Tourist Service	**15** C2
Victoria Marine	**16** C2

SLEEPING
Gran Bahía Principe Cayacoa	**17** B4
Hotel Bahía View	**18** A2
Hotel Chino	(see 24)
Hotel Docia	**19** C2

EATING
Bamboo Restaurant	(see 14)
Cayacoa Restaurant	**20** C2
Food Stands	**21** B2
L'Hacienda Restaurant	**22** C2
Mini-Market	(see 23)
Principe Snack Bar	**23** B2
Restaurant Chino	**24** C1
Restaurant Mate Rosada	(see 28)

TRANSPORT
Caribe Tours	**25** C2
El Canario	**26** C2
Ferry Dock	**27** C2
Metro	**28** C2
Papagayo	**29** C2
Transporte Maritimo	**30** D2
Xamaná Rent Motors	**31** C2

Bahía de Samaná

Bahía Escondido

taking a *gua-gua* to El Limón. See p156 for more details.

PARQUE NACIONAL LOS HAITISES

This national park, with its tiny, jungly islands and thick mangrove forests, makes for great exploring by boat or kayak. Victoria Marine and other outfits in town offer trips there for around US$55 per person, including a guide and transport to and inside the park; see opposite. For more information on the park see p140.

CAYO LEVANTADO

Only the western third of this lush island 7km from Samaná is open to the public; the eastern two-thirds is now occupied by a five-star hotel development (see opposite). The public

beach here is gorgeous – white sand and turquoise waters – but the idyll is somewhat marred by the Disneyfication of the experience. Large cruise ships dock here regularly, and the facilities, including a restaurant and bar and two thousand lounge chairs, don't offer much peace and quiet. Touts wander the beach looking for tourists who want to have their photographs taken with exotic animals, some endangered and on leashes, such as parrots, boa constrictors, monkeys and even sea lions – not a practice to be encouraged. If you choose to visit, try going in mid- to late afternoon, when most of the activity is winding down. Boatmen at the pier make the trip for US$10 to US$15 per person round-trip; if you have a group of six to eight people you can negotiate the round-trip for US$60. Another option is to travel to Carenero, a village 8km east of Samaná where there are 10 boats with permits (round-trip US$35 per person) or wait at Gran Bahía Principe Cayo Levantado's mainland wharf, where guests are ferried to and from the resort, only 1km further on, and join a group for around US$9 per person.

PLAYA LAS FLECHAS

This small beach several kilometers east of Samaná is thought by many historians to be the site of a small and short battle between Columbus' crew and the Ciguayos, a Taíno *cacique* (chiefdom), in which the Spaniards were driven back to their ship. A week later, somehow their differences were reconciled and they formed an alliance against the rival *caciques*.

Tours

Victoria Marine (☎ 809-538-2494; www.whalesamana .com; cnr Calle Mella & Av Malecón; adult/under 5yr/5-10yr US$55/free/30; ☒ 9am-1pm, 3-6pm) is Samaná's most recommended whale-watching outfit. It's owned and operated by Canadian marine biologist Kim Beddall, who was the first person to recognize the scientific and economic importance of Samaná's whales, back in 1985 (see boxed text, p148). Victoria Marine tours use a large two-deck boat with capacity for 60 people (though most tours have around 40). The skilled captains religiously observe the local boat-to-whale distance and other regulations – most of which Beddall helped create – while on-board guides offer interesting facts and information in five languages over the boat's sound system. Sodas and water are provided free of charge. Tours leave at 9am and last three to four hours. There is also a 1:30pm trip when demand is high, and tours can include a stop at Cayo Levantado on the way back.

Several other agencies also offer whale-watching excursions, as well as trips to El Limón waterfall and Parque Nacional Los Haitises, both for about US$55 per person. Most of these will generally have a tour guide as part of a larger group who can often answer questions, though there are no permanent naturalists associated with these operators.

Estilo Tours (☎ 809-538-2782; estilotour_sam@ verizon.net.do; Av Malecón 1; ☒ 8:30am-6pm) Next to Hotel Bahía View.

Moto Marina (☎ 809-538-2302; motomarina@yahoo .com; Av la Marina 3; ☒ 8am-6pm)
Samaná Tourist Service (☎ 809-538-2848; samana .tour@codetel.net.do; Av la Marina 6; ☒ 8:30am-12:30pm & 2:30-6pm Mon-Fri, 8:30am-12:30pm Sat)

Sleeping

There's little reason to stay in Samaná proper and most people booking whale-watching or Los Haitises trips do so from Las Terrenas, Las Galeras or further afield.

Hotel Docia (☎ 809-538-2041; cnr Teodoro Chasereaux & Duarte; r per person US$15; **P**) The rooms at this concrete hotel on a hill are certainly no-frills, with not much other than a bed and nightstand, but for budget travelers that might be enough. Complimentary coffee in the morning and use of the fridge in the kitchen are pluses.

Hotel Bahía View (☎ 809-538-2186; Av Circunvalación 4; r with/without air-con US$27/24; ☒) A longstanding popular hotel, the Bahía View unfortunately doesn't have great views of Bahía. Definitely ask for a room with a balcony anyway (construction has obstructed some sight lines). Each of the 10 rooms is arranged differently, with multiple beds, but all have high ceilings and clean, modern bathrooms.

Hotel Chino (☎ 809-538-2215; Calle San Juan 1; s/d US$60/75; **P** ☒) Located above a Chinese restaurant on top of a hill, Hotel Chino's rooms have balconies with fantastic views of town and the waterfront. But while the rooms are shiny and clean, with cable TV and air-con, there's no lounge area or other amenities, and not a beach within walking distance.

Bahía Principe has two resorts in the area. The older of the two, **Gran Bahía Principe Cayacoa** (☎ 809-538-3131; www.bahiaprincipeusa.com; r per person US$100; **P** ☒ 🖳 🖳) is perched on a cliff 6km east of Samaná with spectacular views of the bay; maybe even of humpbacks during whale season. Food and rooms, however, are mediocre. If the beach here, accessed via an outdoor elevator, isn't to your liking, there are free daily shuttles from this resort to the **Gran Bahía Principe Cayo Levantado** (☎ 809-538-3131; www.bahiaprincipeusa.com; Cayo Levantado; r from US$200; ☒ 🖳 🖳) and its beautiful beach. This new five-star resort is a step above the Cayacoa in every category, including cuisine and room décor. The downside is you're on an island and need to take a boat (provided by the hotel) to get there… Well, that's the upside too.

A WHALE OF A TIME

Canadian Kim Beddall, a marine mammal specialist since 1983 and pioneer of the whale-watching industry in the DR, has devoted herself to maintaining a healthy environment for the whales and a healthy living for the people of Samaná.

How many North Atlantic humpbacks come to these waters every year? The estimated population is 10,000 to 12,000, and almost all of these whales spend part of the winter in Dominican waters. During the peak months here from January to March, there are maybe 200 to 300 whales in the bay itself, but they don't hang out in large groups – they're spread out and others are in transit.

Why do the humpbacks come to these waters? It's like the world's largest singles bar: they come to mate and calve – we see an average of 12 new calves a year in Bahía de Samaná. We think humpbacks come specifically to Samaná because they like certain depths, around 60 feet to 80 feet; within 2km outside the bay it drops to 600m to 700m – good sound transmission. The wind conditions are right, as is the salinity of the bay mouth; it seems that one of the reasons they may enter the less saline waters inside the bay is to cleanse themselves of parasites – adult humpbacks carry with them on average around one ton of parasites.

Are the humpbacks found in other waters around the DR? The Bahía de Samaná is part of the National Marine Mammal Sanctuary of the Dominican Republic, covering approximately 27,000 sq km. It's one of the largest [such sanctuaries] in the world, and includes Silver Bank, Navidad Bank and Bahía de Samaná. Silver Bank is around 70 miles north of Puerto Plata and Navidad Bank is 45 miles northeast of Cape Samaná. The rest of the year these whales can be found feeding anywhere from the eastern seaboard of the US to the Arctic Circle, including Greenland and all the way to Norway.

What is the DR's official position concerning the whale-watching industry? The DR has no whaling history and promotes responsible whale watching as an economic alternative to whaling

---

Eating & Drinking

The majority of restaurants are located along Av Malecón.

La Fe Pica Pollo (Av Francisco de Rosario Sánchez; mains US$3.50; ☻ lunch & dinner) A small hole in the wall close to the gua-gua terminal and the municipal market, serving tasty fried chicken and rice plus a few other Dominican dishes.

Principe Snack Bar (Av Malecón; mains US$4-6; ☻ 10am-midnight) Part of the brightly painted fake village that stretches along the western part of Av Malecón, this place is a snack bar dressed up as an elegant restaurant. Owned and operated by the resort chain of the same name, Principe Snack Bar has an indoor dining area that is the nicest in town and perfect for a drink, which makes the menu of chicken fingers (US$4) and hamburgers (US$5.50) something of a surprise. The outdoor patio is pleasant, especially at night when the air cools and a breeze blows in from the bay.

Restaurant Chino (☎ 809-538-2215; Calle San Juan 1; mains US$4.50-15; ☻ 11am-11pm) Up a steep flight of stairs several blocks north of the pier, this restaurant has commanding views of the bay and town below. There's indoor and outdoor seating and the eclectic menu includes Dominican and standard international dishes along with pages of Cantonese-style specialties.

There are a number of restaurants along the Malecón with similar menus – fish, meat and pasta – and equally excellent vantages from which to watch the world go by very slowly, or for a drink late into the evening. Try the following places:

L'Hacienda Restaurant (Calle Santa Barbara; mains US$3-12; ☻ breakfast, lunch & dinner)

Restaurant Mate Rosada (Av Malecón; mains US$4-11; ☻ lunch & dinner)

Bamboo Restaurant (Av Malecón; mains US$5-9; ☻ breakfast, lunch, dinner) Near Calle Mella.

Cayacoa Restaurant (Av Malecón; mains US$6-12; ☻ lunch & dinner)

You can also get cheap eats at a series of food stands that line Av Malecón near Calle Maria Trinidad Sánchez. Beginning around 6pm and lasting until the early hours of the morning, fried chicken is served up with Presidente beers for Dominican and foreign customers alike. If you have trouble finding the party – which you probably won't – just listen for the bachata (Dominican music) blasting from the west side of town.

in the wider Caribbean. The country is in the process of becoming a pro-conservation member of the International Whaling Commission (IWC). To date six countries vote with Japan in favor of reinstating commercial whaling: Antigua, St Lucia, St Kitts, St Vincent and the Grenadines, Commonwealth of Dominica, and Grenada. These countries' waters are part of the general migratory area for North Atlantic humpbacks. These countries receive economic assistance from Japan – the assumption of many people is that they are being rewarded for their vote. Starting in 1982, there was a 10-year moratorium on whale hunting, this was extended in 1992, but there's no real way to enforce the ban other than through voluntary compliance.

What's the most immediate threat to the health of the North Atlantic humpback population? Considering that humpbacks are coastal species, and so brush up against humans and everything that comes with us, they are surprisingly tolerant and resilient animals, but they are still classified as a vulnerable species by the Convention on International Trade in Endangered Species (CITES). They like to occupy shallow waters close to shore, areas of intense human activity. Entanglement in fishing gear, contamination of feeding and reproductive habitats, uncontrolled coastal development, high concentrations of vessel traffic, unregulated whale-watching and the rapidly developing cruise ship market in the Caribbean, along with sound contamination, may all have impacts on humpbacks that we do not yet fully understand. Global warming and climate change may affect migratory routes, feeding and reproductive grounds, forcing species to move to other areas they previously have not occupied.

What's your advice for tourists? Whale watch responsibly everywhere you go on vacation; only in this way can you give local communities an economic alternative to whaling. Only whale watch with permitted vessels. Here in Samaná, all have numbered yellow flags from the Ministry of the Environment, and a permit they can show you. Learn what the regulations are and ask your captain to comply. Ask if there is a naturalist on board and also ask as many questions as possible to reinforce the idea that tourists are concerned and want people with expertise.

Getting There & Away

AIR

The nearest airport in regular operation is **Aeropuerto Internacional El Portillo** (EPS; ☎ 809-248-2289), just outside of Las Terrenas (p161). The new **Aeropuerto Internacional El Catey** (AZS; ☎ 809-338-0094), 40km west of Samaná, receives international flights. The closest airstrip to Samaná, Aeropuerto Internacional Arroyo Barril, receives mostly charter flights only. For details of domestic and international airlines servicing the DR, see p352.

BUS

Facing the pier, **Caribe Tours** (☎ 809-538-2229; Av Malecón) offers services to Santo Domingo at 7am, 8:30am, 10am, 1pm, 2:30pm and 4pm (US$8.50, 4½ hours, daily). The same bus stops along the way at Sánchez (US$2, 30 minutes), Nagua (US$2.15, one hour) and San Francisco de Macorís (US$3, 1½ hours). A block west, **Metro** (☎ 809-538-2851; cnr Av Malecón & Calle Rubio y Peñaranda) offers a similar service (US$8, 4½ hours, twice daily at 7:30am and 3:30pm). Like its competitor, it stops at Sánchez (US$2.30, 30 minutes), Nagua (US$2.30, one hour) and San Francisco de Macorís (US$3.50, 1½ hours).

Tickets are sold in the small Western Union office next door to Caribe Tours.

For direct service to Puerto Plata 210km to the west, there are two options. **El Canario** (☎ 809-291-5594; Av Malecón) buses (US$7, 3½ to four hours) leave at 10am beside the Banco Popular. **Papagayo** (☎ 809-970-2991) (ask for Salvador) has a service at 1:30pm from under the mango tree on the eastern side of the little park next to Banco Popular on the Malecón. Locals say the latter is a safer though slightly slower ride. Arrive 30 to 45 minutes early to reserve a seat.

For service to towns nearby, head to the **gua-gua terminal** (Av Malecón) at the *mercado municipal*, 200m west of the Politur station, near Angel Mesina. From here, trucks and minivans head to Las Galeras (US$2, 45 minutes to one hour, every 15 minutes from 6am to 6pm), El Limón (US$3, 30 minutes, every 15 minutes from 6am to 6pm) and Sánchez (US$1.75, 45 minutes, every 15 minutes from 6am to 4:30pm). You can also hail *gua-guas* on the main drag, but more often than not they're packed with passengers, boxes and chickens, so you'll either have to hang off the side or sit on one cheek to catch this ride.

PENÍNSULA DE SAMANÁ

UNDERWATER CEMETERY

The Bahía de Samaná is a veritable graveyard of ships, some ripped apart by hurricanes, others plundered by pirates. On one occasion the pirate Roberto Cofresí sank his own ship laden with treasure near the throat of the bay when he found himself cornered by Spanish patrol boats. Cofresí and his crew escaped the advancing Spaniards by boarding small skiffs and rowing their way into the area's maze of marshes. To this day the vessel has never been found.

Two other famous sunken ships in Bahía de Samaná – the Spanish galleons *Nuestra Señora de Guadalupe* and *El Conde de Tolosa* – remained untouched for more than 250 years until they were discovered in 1976 and 1977, respectively (see boxed text, p107). Both ships were en route to Mexico from Spain loaded with mercury when hurricane-whipped waves flung them into coral reefs, where they broke apart and sank within hours of each other.

FERRY

Transporte Maritimo (☎ 809-538-2556; Av Malecón) provides the only ferry service – passengers only, no vehicles – across the Bahía de Samaná to Sabana de la Mar (US$4.25, one hour plus, daily at 7am, 9am, 11am and 3pm). From there, it's possible to catch *gua-guas* to several destinations in the southeast and then on to Santo Domingo, though the road network in this part of the country is rough and public transportation is not so comfortable.

Getting Around

Samaná is walkable, but if you're carrying luggage, catch a *motoconcho* (motorcycle taxi) – they're everywhere. 4WD vehicles are your only option in terms of car rental – roads on the peninsula are bad enough to warrant the extra expense. Rates run from US$70 to US$90 per day (tax and insurance included) and discounts are typically given for rentals of a week or longer. Try **Xamaná Rent Motors** (☎ 809-538-2380; Av Malecón; ☺ 8am-noon & 2-6pm).

LAS GALERAS

The road to this small fishing community 28km northeast of Samaná ends at a fish shack on the beach. So does everything else, metaphorically speaking. One of the great pleasures of a stay here is losing perspective on the great big world beyond – even a trip to one of the beautiful and isolated outlying beaches seems far away. But Las Galeras, as much as anywhere else on the peninsula, offers terrestrial and subaquatic adventures for those with a will strong enough to ignore the pull of inertia and overcome the temptation to do nothing more than lie around your bungalow or while away the day at a restaurant watching others do the same.

Orientation

The road coming from Samaná winds along the coast and through lovely, often-forested countryside before reaching the outskirts of Las Galeras. There's one main intersection in town (about 50m before the highway deadends at the beach) and most hotels, restaurants and services are within walking distance from there.

Information

You'll find most of the relevant services are located in or around the main intersection, just a short walk to the beach. The only ATM in town is at the Grand Paradise Samaná resort; it's open to the public and situated close to where the path from town enters the resort property.

Ashley Communications (☎ 809-538-0053; internet per hr US$2; ☺ 8am-7:30pm Mon-Sat, 8am-noon Sun) Internet and telephone access.

Consultoria Las Galeras (☎ 829-918-3233; ☺ 8:30am-noon & 3-6pm Mon-Fri, 3-6pm Sat) The most convenient place to receive medical attention.

Farmacia Joven (☎ 809-538-0103; Calle Principal; ☺ 8am-9:30pm Mon-Sat) Near the main crossroad; has basic meds and supplies.

Grand Paradise Samaná (☎ 809-538-0020; ☺ 24hr) Has a small clinic that nonguests can use in emergencies.

Hermanos Cruz Agente de Cambio and Rent-A-Car (☎ 809-341-4574; Calle Principal; ☺ 8am-6pm Mon-Sat, 8am-noon Sun) Exchanges cash dollars and euros; also rents cars.

Internet Las Galeras (Calle Principal at main intersection; internet per hr US$2.75; ☺ 8:30am-1pm & 2:30-7:30pm Mon-Sat) Internet and telephone access; 30-minute minimum.

Plaza Lusitania Internet & Call Center (internet per hr US$2.50; ☺ 8:30am-8pm Mon-Sat) Internet and telephone access.

Sights & Activities

Las Galeras has a number of natural attractions that can be visited by boat, foot, car or horseback. All can be reached on your own, provided you're in decent shape or have a sturdy vehicle.

BEACHES
Playa Rincón

For those who are connoisseurs of such things, Playa Rincón is a pitch-perfect beach. Stretching uninterrupted for nearly 3km of nearly white, soft sand and multihued water good for swimming, there's even a small stream at the far western end, great for a quick freshwater dip at the end of a long, sunny day. Some historians claim that it's here, not Playa las Flechas, where Columbus and his crew landed. Consistently rated one of the top beaches in the Caribbean by those in the know – people who courageously brave heatstroke and sunburn in a quest for the ideal – Rincón is large enough for every day-tripper to claim their own piece of real estate without nosy neighbors peeking over the seaweed and driftwood. A thick palm forest provides the backdrop.

Several small restaurants serve mostly seafood dishes and rent beach chairs, making this a great place to spend the entire day. Most people arrive by boat; the standard option is to leave Las Galeras around 9am and be picked up at 4pm – it's around 20 minutes each way. If you join up with other beachgoers, it costs about US$12 to US$15 per person. You can also drive there, though the last kilometer or so is too rough for small or midsize cars. The turnoff to Playa Rincón is 7km south of Las Galeras on the road to Samaná. A taxi to Rincón should cost US$55 round-trip.

Playas Madama & Frontón

Preferred by some locals over Playa Rincón, Playa Frontón boasts some of the best snorkeling in the area. Apparently it's also popular with drug smugglers, Dominicans braving the Mona Passage on their way to Puerto Rico, and reality show contestants – in 2002, *Expedición Robinson*, Colombia's version of the reality show *Survivor*, was filmed here. Playas Madama is a small beach framed by high bluffs; keep in mind there's not much sunlight here in the afternoon.

The trail to both begins at the far eastern end of the Grand Paradise Samaná beach, about 200m past the resort's entrance, near a private house that most people know as 'La Casa de los Ingleses' (House of the English) after its original owners. Coming from town, the house and the trail will be on your right. In the first kilometer you'll pass a German beer garden and the turnoff to the Museo Taíno (actually the home and private collection of a quirky Frenchwoman named Ivette 'La Bruja' Durrieu) before reaching the first of two cut-offs to Playa Madama. If you turn left there (or at the next cut-off a kilometer later) you'll walk another 2km until you reach Madama. If you continue on the main trail, you'll pass a second cut-off to Playa Madama (not indicated) and a few kilometers later the cut-off to Playa Frontón (there's a small house just past the turnoff, so if you see this, turn around and retrace your steps, only about 10m, until you see the trail); from here it's another four winding kilometers to Frontón itself. It's much simpler to take a boat to either of these beaches, for around US$15 per person round-trip, with a pickup in the afternoon.

Playita

Better than the beach in town, Playita (Little Beach) is easy to get to on foot or by *motoconcho*. It's a swath of tannish sand, with mellow surf and backed by tall palm trees. There are two informal outdoor restaurants, basically thatched-roof shelters, where you can get grilled fish or chicken, plus water, soda and beer. On the main road just south of Las Galeras, look for signs for Hotel La Playita pointing down a dirt road headed west. Or if you're OK with clambering, follow the road that goes west at the main intersection, past Villa Serena until you reach a gated development; let yourself in and follow the path until you reach the remains of a barbed wire fence. It's easy enough to get over and the beach is just on the other side.

BOCA DEL DIABLO

'Mouth of the Devil' is an impressive vent or blowhole, where waves rush up a natural channel and blast out of a hole in the rocks. Car or motorcycle is the best way to get here – look for an unmarked dirt road 7km south of town and about 100m beyond the well-marked turnoff to Playa Rincón. Follow the road eastward for about 8km, then walk the last 100m or so.

PENÍNSULA DE SAMANÁ

PENÍNSULA DE SAMANÁ

WATER SPORTS

For experienced divers, **Cabo Cabrón** (Bastard Point) is one of the North Coast's best dive sites. After an easy boat ride from Las Galeras, you're dropped into a churning channel with a giant coral formation that you can swim around; you may see dolphins here. Other popular sites include Piedra Bonita, a 50m stone tower good for spotting jacks, barracudas and sea turtles; Cathedral, an enormous underwater cave opening to sunlight; and a sunken 55m-container ship haunted by big morays. Several large, shallow coral patches, including Los Carriles, a series of underwater hills, are good for beginner divers.

Grand Paradise Samaná Dive Center (Dive Samaná; ☎ 809-538-2000; www.lacompagniadeicaraibi.com; Casa Marina Bay resort; ☀ 7am-6pm) is located at the far end of Grand Paradise Samaná's beach. One-/two-tank dives including all equipment cost US$60/114 (US$5 to US$12 less if you have your own). Four- and six-dive packages bring the rate down to US$48 to US$52 per dive, including gear. Various PADI certification courses can also be arranged. Also on offer are snorkeling trips (US$12), whale-watching tours (US$49), trips to Playa Rincón (US$10), and windsurf and sailboat rental and instruction (US$10 to US$15 per hour), all available to guests and nonguests alike. It's easy enough to walk to the dive shop here by following the path along the beach from town; resort security will let you through.

HIKING

The spectacular El Punto lookout is a 5km walk from Bungalows Karin y Ronald (see right). To get there, simply continue past the turnoffs to Playas Madam and Frontón and keep climbing up, up and up. Allow at least an hour to get to the top.

HORSEBACK RIDING

The Belgian owners of Bungalows Karin y Ronald (see right) offer well-recommended **horseback riding tours** (from US$52) to various spots around Las Galeras, including Boca del Diablo, El Punto lookout and Playas Madama and Frontón. Grand Paradise Samaná resort (opposite) offers similarly priced but somewhat less-personalized horseback tours as well.

Tours

While you can visit many of the beaches and sights on your own – or hire a *motoconcho* driver to act as your chauffeur and guide. Organized tour operators include **ATM-Tours** (☎ 809-324-1696; Calle Principal), **R-azor Tours** (☎ 809-538-0218; www.azortour.eu; Calle Principal) and Grand Paradise Samaná resort (opposite). Numerous day trips include whale watching in Bahía de Samaná (US$80 per person), land and boat excursions through Parque Nacional Los Haitises (US$70 per person) and hikes to the area's isolated beaches (US$20 per person). Village tours that include a cockfight and stops in a typical home and primary school, as well as overnight trips further afield, can also be arranged.

Sleeping

With the exception of a few, all of the hotels and bungalows in Las Galeras are within walking distance of the main intersection.

BUDGET

El Cabito (☎ 829-697-9506; www.elcabito.net; campsites per person US$7.50, cabin incl breakfast US$60) For those looking to rough it, this property in lush farmland 4km east of the main intersection in town has one of the few campgrounds in all the DR. If you like the out-of-the-way location but want a little more comfort, there's an all-wood guestroom on the 2nd floor of the friendly owner's home. Stunning views are to be had all around, including from the restaurant area perched over crashing waves below. It's also a short walk to Playa Madama. Pickup from Las Galeras is available if arranged in advance.

Bungalows Karin y Ronald (☎ 829-878-0637; www.larancheta.com; r/bungalow US$30/54; P) Buried in the lush jungle, 2.5km from the main intersection, is this hotel with a number of funky and simple two-storied bungalows that can accommodate between four and six people comfortably. Semioutdoor rustic kitchens lend an eclectic cabin-in-the-woods feel to this out-of-the-way hotel. Take advantage of Karin, an expert tour guide, who leads day and overnight hiking and horseback riding trips to out-of-the-way beaches and mountaintops (left).

Casa Por Qué No? (☎ /fax 809-712-5631; s/d incl breakfast US$32/45; closed May-Oct; P) Pierre and Monick, the charming owners of this B&B, rent out two rooms on either side of their cozy home – each room has a separate entrance and hammock. Only 25m or so north of the main intersection on your right as you're walking towards the beach, the house is fronted by a long, well-groomed garden where delicious breakfasts are served (US$6 breakfast for nonguests).

MIDRANGE

Casa Dorado (☎ 829-221-2493; www.casadoradodr.com; r US$40-$80; 🖳) This house, about a kilometer from town, looks like a McMansion, but the Mexican-style décor, tropical garden and terrace-borne hammocks remind you that you're on vacation. Three rooms are available; the largest and most expensive comes with a Jacuzzi. The English-speaking owner runs sport fishing trips (up to four people from US$250 to US$400) and snorkeling excursions to Rincón and Fronton. Wi-fi is available throughout the property.

Juan y Lolo Bungalows (☎ 809-875-1423; www.juanylolo.com; bungalows US$40-120; 🅿) An especially good choice for groups and long-term stays, this disparate group of bungalows west of the main intersection has something for everyone. Whatever the size or price, all come with outdoor patios, serviceable kitchen and fans. Most are simply furnished and have thatched roofs, but there's also a stone fortress-cum-monastery–like building available. It's best to see several – if vacant – before deciding. The owners also run Xamaná Rent Moto (p155) and may be easier to find there.

our pick **Todo Blanco** (☎ 809-538-0201; www.hoteltodoblanco.com; r US$75; 🅿 🍴 🖳) In a wash of white, Todo Blanco, a well-established inn run by a cheerful Dominican–Italian couple, sits atop a small hillock a short walk from the end of the main drag in Las Galeras. The multilevel grounds are nicely appointed with gardens and a gazebo, all with views of the ocean below. The rooms are large and airy, with high ceilings and private terraces overlooking the sea. However, decorated sparsely and in need of a new paint job and minor repairs, they offer little more than a spacious place to rest your head. A homey living room area has a TV and DVD player and wi-fi internet access. Breakfast of fruit and eggs is available for an extra US$5, and dinner can also be provided if arranged ahead of time.

Plaza Lusitania Hotel (☎ 809-538-0093; www.plazalusitania.com; r incl breakfast US$60, 1-bedroom apt incl breakfast US$75-100; 🅿 🍴 🖳) This hotel is in downtown Las Galeras. Situated on the main intersection on the 2nd floor of a tiny mall complete with internet and telephone center, a good Italian restaurant (p154), medical office and shop, Plaza Lusitania is as urban as Las Galeras gets, which is to say not at all. Rooms are large and extremely comfortable and even boast small balconies and kitchenettes; check out several, since the layout and number of beds and price vary.

TOP END

Casa Calliope (☎ 829-929-8585, 829-448-1498; www.feeneyhayes@hotmail.com; r US$140) Located near El Cabito, around 4km east of town, this two-bedroom hilltop villa offers funky luxury in beautiful surroundings. Each of the two large bedrooms has a full bathroom and terrace, and there's a fully equipped kitchen for guests' use – vegetarian and healthy meals can be ordered up as well. The owners, a friendly couple from Boston, are a great source of information on the area. Two-night minimum stay generally required.

Villa Serena (☎ 809-538-0000; www.villaserena.com; r with/without air-con incl breakfast US$150/140; 🅿 🍴 🖳 🛱) A cross between a Victorian England manor home and a Caribbean villa, this hotel, 300m east of the main intersection, has gorgeous ocean views and is probably the nicest place in Las Galeras. That being said, the room furnishings are a little worn and kitschy, and while every one of the 21 rooms is different, it's mostly in terms of the shower curtain pattern and rug color. Each has a balcony, some face the ocean directly and others open on to the meticulously landscaped garden and swimming pool area. Off the main lobby, where there is a strong free wi-fi signal, is a peaceful terrace with rocking chairs. There's an excellent snorkeling spot just offshore and the hotel provides bikes and kayaks for guests.

Grand Paradise Samaná (☎ 809-538-0020; www.amhsamarina.com; r per person US$140-210; 🅿 🍴 🛱) Doing its best to remain relatively unobtrusive, Las Galeras' only all-inclusive resort (formerly Casa Marina Bay) is tucked into a forest of palm trees 2km west of town. Occupying a wide cove with calm waters and a thin but pleasant beach, much of the property, including lounge chairs and volleyball courts, is set on a somewhat messy lawn studded with palm trees. True to the low-key nature of the town, this resort is far from luxurious and rooms are your standard, bland typical all-inclusive type. Bungalows with full living rooms and terraces are a better bet. More than at other resorts of this category, guests tend to be active, leaving for excursions around Las Galeras, on their own or on a tour; it's only a short walk (500m) to town along a beach trail.

Eating

For a town of its size, Las Galeras has an abundance of restaurants and they're mostly all located at the single intersection on the main street. Several of the hotels also offer meals when ordered in advance.

El Kiosko (Calle Principal; mains US$5-7; ☺ 7am-midnight) Chow down on freshly caught fish, seafood and grilled meats at this basic thatch-roofed restaurant on the beach at the end of the main road.

L'Aventure Pizzeria (Calle Principal; mains US$5-10; ☺ dinner) More modern than other restaurants in town, L'Aventure is at least as popular for its bar and backroom disco as for its large menu. Besides the standard pasta, grilled chicken and fish, milkshakes (US$4.25) are served up and there's a TV at the bar for sports lovers.

Plaza Lusitania Italian Restaurant (☎ 809-538-0093; Calle Principal; mains US$6-12; ☺ breakfast, lunch & dinner, dinner only May-Oct, closed Wed) Easily the nicest restaurant in town both in terms of cuisine and ambience, Plaza Lusitania has a varied menu of Italian dishes; an extensive selection of pastas; excellent, large pizzas; grilled fish; and even a Chinese dish or two (chicken fried rice US$8). A fruit shake (US$3) and a banana split (US$4.25) can round out a nice meal.

Coconut Ray's Paradise Restaurant (Calle Principal; mains US$7-12; ☺ lunch & dinner) Meals at this restaurant in front of Paradiso Bungalows at the main intersection in town are a good deal in terms of portion size. Besides standard pasta and meat dishes like barbecued chicken (US$7.50), with a little foresight – two to four days' notice –you can get a 4lb to 6lb giant crab (US$7.50 per lb) or slow-smoked whole pig (US$6 per lb).

Grigiri (Calle Principal; mains US$5.75-11; ☺ breakfast, lunch & dinner) and **Chez Denise** (☎ 809-538-0219; Calle Principal; mains US$4-14; ☺ 9am-10pm Mon-Sat), two other restaurants located at the main intersection, have similar menus including crêpes with various toppings. Grigiri is a better value than Chez Denise, where service can be very slow.

Walking toward the beach, take a left at the main intersection and you'll find **L'Epicerie d'Armelle** (☺ 10am-7pm, closed Sun), a little storefront next to Caribe Fun Rentals selling gour-

met French meats, cheeses, wines and other delicacies. There's a **mini-market** (☺ 8am-10pm) at the Grand Paradise Samaná resort. The largest grocery store is **Supermercado £1** (Calle Principal; ☺ 7:30am-9:30pm); it's not uncommon for a power outage to occur here in the middle of the day. The 2nd-floor pool hall makes it easy to spot on the main drag.

Entertainment

Much of the nightlife involves drinks at one of the restaurants in town – the bar and disco at **L'Aventure Pizzeria** (Calle Principal) especially. Further up on the road on the way out of town is **La Indiana** (Calle Principal), an open-air bar/disco popular with locals that also has a big-screen TV that shows sports, music videos and movies. A little further up the road is **V.I.P.** (Calle Principal), an open-air disco that gets loud after 10pm.

The open-air **pool hall** (Calle Principal; per game US$0.20; ☺ 10am-10pm) above Supermercado £1 is an all-male affair at night, but more egalitarian during the daytime.

Shopping

Two good crafts and souvenir stores face one another on the main road: **Talisman Gift Shop** (Calle Principal), which accepts credit cards, and **Tribal Boutique** (☺ 9:30am-12:30pm & 4-6:30pm Mon-Sat).

Getting There & Around

Gua-guas head to Samaná (US$2, 45 minutes, every 15 minutes from 7am to 5pm) from the beach end of Calle Principal, but also cruise slowly out of town picking up passengers. There's also a daily 5:30am bus with service to Santo Domingo (US$8, six hours). Locals refer to it as the 'Bluebird Express,' though it's neither blue nor express. To guarantee a seat on this cramped air-con minivan, wait at the main crossroads in town in the pre-dawn hours. It's best not to sit in the front row unless you prefer a stranger on your lap; the aisle is filled with passengers in makeshift seats for most of the ride.

You can pretty much walk everywhere in Las Galeras proper. For outlying areas, a *motoconcho* ride costs around US$0.50 to US$1 – consider arranging with the driver to pick you up if you know when you'll be returning.

Taxis (☎ 829-380-0775) are available as well. Some sample fares are Aeropuerto Catey

(US$85), Las Terrenas (US$85), Samaná (US$30) and Santo Domingo (US$200). You may be able to negotiate cheaper fares, especially to Samaná.

Renting a car is an excellent way to explore the peninsula on your own. Prices are generally around US$85 per day. Try **RP Rent-A-Car** (☎ 809-538-0249; Calle Principal; ☺ 8am-7pm Mon-Sat, 8am-1pm Sun), **Caribe Fun Rentals** (☎ 809-912-2440; ☺ 9am-1pm & 3-6:30pm Mon-Sat, 9am-noon Sun) or **Xamaná Rent Moto** (☎ 809-538-0208; motorcycles per day US$25; ☺ 9am-noon & 3-6pm Mon-Fri, 9am-noon Sat & Sun). The latter two are located 50m west of the intersection; Xamaná Rent Moto also rents motorcycles.

You can rent a mountain bike at **Piccola Italia** (☎ 809-325-4018; Calle Principal; per day US$12.50; ☺ 8am-noon & 3-7pm Mon-Sat), a shop near the entrance to town. Most bicycles are 21-speed and in good condition.

WESTERN PENÍNSULA DE SAMANÁ

LAS TERRENAS
pop 8400

No longer a rustic fishing village, today Las Terrenas is a cosmopolitan town, seemingly as much French and Italian as Dominican. Fashionable-looking European women in designer sunglasses ride their personal ATVs with a bag of baguettes in tow. It's a balancing act between locals and expats – one that has produced a lively mix of styles and a social scene more vibrant than anywhere else on the peninsula. Either way you walk along the beach road leads you to beachfront scattered with hotels, high palm trees and calm aquamarine waters. Just east of town is Playa Punta Popy, not an especially beautiful beach but a popular spot for kiteboarders and windsurfers.

Orientation

The main road in town, Calle Principal (also known as Av Juan Pablo Duarte or Av Duarte for short – both names are used in official addresses and on maps and other information), begins at the beach and passes several small shopping plazas, restaurants, stores, banks etc before leaving the resort area. Tourist facilities thin out, replaced by Dominican *colmados* (small bars), hairdresser shops and tire repair kiosks before

turning into the highway to Sánchez. Calle del Carmen, a dirt-road version of Calle Principal, runs parallel to the latter until it, too, ends at the beach and veers left to Pueblo de Los Pescadores (Fishermen's Village), a collection of beachside bars and restaurants. Many hotels are located along the beach west of here. Turning east at the intersection of Calle Principal and Calle 27 de Febrero (also known as Carretera a Portillo) takes you past another cluster of restaurants, bars and hotels and eventually leads to El Portillo airport, an all-inclusive resort, El Limón and finally Samaná. A large golf resort complex covering much of the area east of the road to Playa Bonita is up and running with the official opening scheduled for some time in 2008.

Information

BOOKSTORES

Prensa International (El Paseo shopping center, Calle Principal; ☺ 9am-1pm & 4-7:30pm Mon-Sat, 9am-1pm Sun) Towards the rear of the El Paseo shopping mall, this shop sells a variety of international newspapers and magazines – most are a day or two old and the majority are in French, though the *International Herald Tribune* is available.

EMERGENCY

Politur (tourist police; ☎ 809-7240-6595; Av Emilio Prud'Homme; ☺ 24hr)

INTERNET ACCESS

A&M Communications (Calle del Carmen; per hr US$2.25; ☺ 8am-9pm Mon-Sat, 8am-3pm Sun) Part of same small building as El Pan de Antes.

Internet Point (Plaza Taína, Calle Principal; per hr US$3.75; ☺ 8:30am-1pm & 3-7pm Mon-Sat, 9am-1pm Sun) Fast internet connections, fax, CD burns, copies etc, and international telephone service.

Tup@ryn.com Internet (Calle Principal; per hr US$1.75; ☺ 8am-10pm) South of the main tourist strip.

LAUNDRY

Lavandería Ami (Calle Principal; ☺ 8am-6pm Mon-Sat) Located next to Plaza Rosada. Wash per load US$2.25, dry per cycle US$3.50; detergent and fabric softener each US$0.75; drop-off service extra US$1. Same-day service if you drop off early; heavy clothes may require two dry cycles.

Lavandería Tu Net (Lavandería Pat y Memo; ☎ 809-848-1661; Centro Colonial, Calle del Carmen; ☺ 8am-6pm Mon-Fri, 8am-3pm Sat) Wash and dry US$1.50 per lb; same-day service not always available. An internet café and call center (internet per hour US$2.25; open 9am to 1pm and 2pm to 9pm Monday to Saturday) is next door.

MEDICAL SERVICES
Centro de Especialidades Medicas (☎ 809-240-6817; Calle Principal; ⌚ 24hr) Small private hospital.
Hospital Pablo A Paulino (☎ 809-274-6474, ext 24; Calle Matias Mella; ⌚ 24hr emergency room)
Super Farmacia del Paseo (El Paseo shopping center, Calle Principal; ⌚ 9am-7pm Mon-Fri, 9am-noon & 4-7pm Sat) Well stocked but not cheap.

MONEY
Banco Leon (Calle Principal) Has a 24-hour ATM.
Banco Popular (Calle Principal; ⌚ 9am-5pm Mon-Fri, 9am-1pm Sat) Located just east of the river. Has a 24-hour ATM.
BanReservas (Calle Principal; ⌚ 9am-6pm Mon-Fri, 9am-1pm Sat) Across the street from Banco Popular. Has a 24-hour ATM.
Fort Knox Money Exchange (☎ 809-240-6719; El Paseo shopping center, Calle Principal; ⌚ 8am-1pm & 4-8pm Mon-Sat, 10am-1pm Sun)

POST
Post office (El Paseo shopping center, Calle Principal; ⌚ 9am-1pm & 3-5pm Mon-Fri)

TELEPHONE
Codetel Centro de Comunicaciones (Calle Principal; ⌚ 8am-10pm) An old facility near the intersection with Calle Salomé Ureña.

TRAVEL AGENCIES
Bahia Tours (☎ 809-240-6088; www.bahia-tours.com; Calle Principal 237; ⌚ 9am-1pm & 3:30-7pm Mon-Fri, 9:30am-1pm & 4:30-6:30pm Sat) Full-service travel agency that can handle airline, hotel and car-rental reservations. Area excursions are also organized, and English, French and Spanish are spoken.

Sights & Activities
PARQUE NACIONAL LOS HAITISES
Since so few independent travelers make it to Sabana de la Mar, the closest entrance to Parque Los Haitises across the bay on the mainland, Las Terrenas has become a popular place to book tours to the park. **Tortuga** (☎ 829-808-2233; tropicodoelsol@yahoo.fr; El Paseo, Tortuga) offers tours of Los Haitises by catamaran and kayak. Virtually every tour operator in town (see p158) offers trips to Los Haitises (US$60), though only twice a week unless you're part of a group of six or more, in which case you can arrange things at your own convenience.

There should be at least one company with a tour on offer five days a week, but schedules change, so it's best to book as soon as you arrive in town. For more info on the park, see also p140.

CASCADA EL LIMÓN
Tucked away in surprisingly rough landscape, surrounded by peaks covered in lush greenery is the 52m-high **El Limón waterfall**. A beautiful swimming hole is at the bottom, though it's often too deep, cold and rough for a dip except for the committed; other times it's an absolutely perfect place to wash off the sweat and mud from the trip there. The departure point is the small town of El Limón, only a half-hour from Las Terrenas.

Just about everyone who visits does so on horseback, and almost a dozen *paradas* (horseback-riding operations) in town and on the highway toward Samaná offer tours. (It is not recommended to hire someone off the street, as there's little saving and the service is consistently substandard.) All outfits offer essentially the same thing: a 30- to 60-minute ride up the hill to the waterfalls, 30 to 60 minutes to take a dip and enjoy the scene, and a 30- to 60-minute return trip, with lunch at the end. Your guide – who you should tip, by the way – will be walking, not riding, which can feel a little weird but is the custom.

Of course, horses are fully part of the workforce in the DR. In much of the country children learn to ride early on, and it is commonplace to see little ones bouncing along, racing atop ponies down the street at breakneck speed, often in and out of traffic. However, many of the horses are undernourished and many are abandoned, which is to say you should try to pick the operation with healthy, well-cared for horses. After heavy rains, the path to the falls becomes fairly treacherous even for these sure-footed animals. Falls are certainly few and far between but even the strongest horse struggles mightily step by step on this giant rock/mud slide. Most of them aren't work horses and not meant for such trail riding, especially with heavy passengers on board.

Otherwise, it's a minimum 40-minute walk (from the main intersection in El Limón its roughly 5.6km), sometimes up a very steep trail over rough terrain and even a river or two to ford. It's not difficult to follow the path

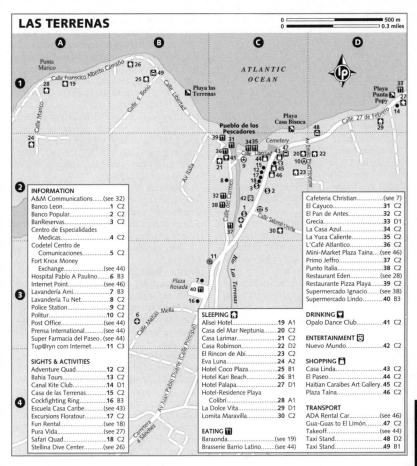

LAS TERRENAS

0 ────── 500 m
0 ────── 0.3 miles

ATLANTIC OCEAN

once you find it, though, especially if there are groups out on the trail.

Spanish-owned **Santí** (☎ 809-343-0776; limon santi@terra.es; rides per person with/without lunch US$23/14; ☙ 8am-7pm), at the main intersection in El Limón, is the most popular of the *paradas* and also the most expensive. The lunch is excellent and the guides and staff (all adults) are better paid than elsewhere. If you book with a tour company in Las Terrenas, transportation to/from El Limón is not included (*gua-gua* US$1.50). Typically the tour (horse, guide and lunch) costs per person from US$22 to US$24. Most other operators charge around US$14/7 with/without lunch; try **Parada la Manzana** (☎ 809-360-9142; ☙ 8am-4pm), 5km east of El Limón towards Samaná, or **Parada María**

y Miguel (☎ 809-282-7699; ☙ 7am-5pm), 2km east of El Limón towards Samaná. A *motoconcho* to either costs US$1 to US$2.

DIVING & SNORKELING
Las Terrenas has reasonably good diving and snorkeling and at least three shops in town to take you out. Favorite dive spots include a wreck in 28m of water and Isla Las Ballenas, visible from shore, with a large underwater cave. Most shops also offer special trips to Cabo Cabrón (p152) near Las Galeras and Dudu Cave near Río San Juan (p194). Standard one-tank dives average US$45 with equipment, and around US$35 if you have your own. Four-, 10- and 12-dive packages bring the per-dive costs to around US$26 to US$35, including

equipment. Two-tank Cabo Cabrón and Dudu Cave trips run from about US$80 to US$100, including gear, lunch and transport.

Snorkelers also go to Isla Las Ballenas, which has good shallow coral flats (one hour; US$20 per person). A popular full-day snorkel trip is to Playa Jackson, several kilometers west of town, reached by boat with stops in two or three locations along the way (US$60 per person including lunch, minimum six people).

Recommended operators:

Las Terrenas Divers (☎ 809-889-2422; www.lt-divers .com; Hotel Bahía las Ballenas, Playa Bonita; ◐ 9am-noon) Well-respected German-run operation.

Stellina Dive Center (☎ 809-868-4415; www.stellina diving.com; Hotel Kari Beach; ◐ 9am-noon)

KITESURFING & WINDSURFING

Second to only to Cabarete, Las Terrenas is a good place to try out a wind sport in the DR. The beach at Punta Popy, only a kilometer or so east of the main intersection, is a popular place for kitesurfers and windsurfers. Two recommended outfits, near one another and Punta Popy, are the long-established **Pura Vida** (☎ 809-878-6640; www.puravidacaraibes.com; Hotel Palapa, Calle 27 de Febrero; ◐ 10am-5:30pm) and **Canal Kite Club** (☎ 809-240-6556, 829-933-9325; www.canalkite.com; Calle 27 de Febrero), run by a friendly Italian who speaks Spanish, French and English. Both rent windsurf boards, bodyboards, surfboards, kitesurfing equipment and provide lessons for all these activities. Six hours of kitesurfing lessons (really the minimum needed to have a sporting chance of making it work) at Canal Kite Club cost US$200; a two-hour windsurfing lesson is US$60, the same time for surfing is US$40.

COCKFIGHTING

For those interested in one of the quintessential Dominican experiences, Las Terrenas has a **gallera** (cockfighting ring; admission US$3; ◐ 2-7pm Sun), located on Calle Principal just past Plaza Rosada. There are around a dozen matchups per night. Tourists are welcome, but the fights are certainly not watered down and betting is still an integral part of the event. Volunteers help explain the rules, strategy and wagering to cockfight neophytes. For more about cockfighting in the DR, see p54.

Tours

Along with booking airline tickets, hotels and car rentals, the full-service travel agency **Bahia**

Tours (☎ 809-240-6088; www.bahia-tours.com; Calle Principal 237; ◐ 9am-1pm & 3:30-7pm Mon-Fri, 9:30am-1pm & 4:30-6:30pm Sat) organizes many area tours. Popular day trips include whale watching in Bahía de Samaná (US$70 per person), excursions to Parque Nacional Los Haitises (US$60 per person), jeep tours to Playa El Rincón (US$70 per person) and horseback riding to Cascada El Limón (US$25 per person). Overnight trips include rafting, canyoning and trekking in Jarabacoa (p213) as well as climbing Pico Duarte (p217), the highest peak (3087m) in the Caribbean. English, French and Spanish are spoken.

Aerodomca (☎ 809-240-6571; www.aerodomca.com) offers helicopter sightseeing flights of the peninsula leaving from El Portillo airport. Prices vary according to season, number of passengers and length of flight.

There are several other recommended tour companies in town:

Aventure Quad (☎ 809-657-8766; aventurequad@ hotmail.com; Calle Principal 165) Half-day excursions; one 4WD for two people US$80.

Casa de las Terrenas (☎ 809-240-6251; www.laster renas-excursions.com; Calle Principal 280) Small, friendly, French-run operation run out of a little kiosk in front of Plaza Taína.

Excursions Floratour (☎ 809-360-2793; floratour@ caramail.com; Calle Principal 262)

Fun Rental (☎ 809-240-6784; www.funrental.fr; Plaza Creole, Calle Principal 258) Quad rentals (US$55 per day) and trips to Los Haitises (US$58).

Safari Quad (☎ 809-240-6056; Calle Principal; www .safari-quads.com) Trips to sites all over the peninsula with guides for all skill levels; rentals also available.

Tortuga (☎ 829-808-2233; tropicodoelsol@yahoo.fr; El Paseo shopping center, Calle Principal) In addition to trips to Los Haitises, Tortuga offers catamaran excursions to Playa Rincón, Playa Jackson and elsewhere.

Courses

To hold your own on the dance floor, or at the very least to avoid embarrassment, stop by the **Escuela Salsa Caribe** (☎ 809-880-4609; back of Casa Linda shopping center, Calle Principal; ◐ 9am-7pm Mon-Fri, 9am-noon & 4-7pm Sat) for private (US$18 per hour) and group merengue or salsa classes.

Sleeping

The majority of accommodation options in Las Terrenas are located along the beachfront roads to the east and west of the main intersection in town. Those to the east are across from the beach on the paved highway, while the small sandy road to the west means the area is quieter and feels more secluded. Prices drop dramatically in the low season, but at any time of the year discounts are negotiable for long-term stays.

BUDGET

Casa Robinson (☎ /fax 809-240-6496; www.casarobinson .it; Av Emilio Prud'Homme; r/studio/apt US$27/33/43; P) Set in leafy grounds down a side street a block from the beach, this hotel offers privacy on the cheap. Fan-cooled rooms in the all-wood buildings are simple and clean and the little balconies have rocking chairs – albeit old ones. Bathrooms, however, are more modern and some rooms have kitchenettes. Service doesn't always happen in a flash but it's friendly when it does finally arrive.

El Rincón de Abi (☎ 809-240-6639; www.el-rincon -de-abi.com; Av Emilio Prud'Homme; r incl breakfast US$32-60; P X 🖳 🕿) Just a block further down the road from Casa Robinson and Mar Neptunia, this French-owned hotel is well maintained, if a bit sterile. Rooms in the whitewashed two-story building topped with a thatch roof are clean and sparsely furnished; tiling in the bathrooms gives it some color and character. A small pool and outdoor kitchen with grill are for guests' use. Breakfast is Continental style.

Casa del Mar Neptunia (☎ 809-240-6617; www .casas-del-mar-neptunia.com; Av Emilio Prud'Homme; s/d incl breakfast US$35/45; P X) This whitewashed hotel across from Casa Robinson is equally homey and quiet with 12 large, airy rooms. Maybe the only downside is that each of the little porches faces a lush interior garden and so they lack privacy and views. Breakfast can be served here or in the comfortable lounge area in front.

MIDRANGE

Hotel Coco Plaza (☎ 809-240-6172; www.hotelco coplaza.net; Calle F Bono 2; r US$45, studio US$60-80, apt US$85-100; P X 🖳) This rambling four-story Mediterranean-style hotel is across the street from the beach west of town on the way to Playa Las Ballenas. You should see several rooms before deciding, since they vary in layout and size, although all are colorful and comfortable with cable TV and motel room–style décor. Many are tucked behind stairwells and other rooms with no views to speak of. Breakfast (extra charge) is served in an open-air dining area downstairs. Wi-fi available throughout.

Casa Larimar (☎ 809-240-6539; www.casa-larimar .com; Pueblo de los Pescadores; r incl breakfast US$50-55; P 🖳 🕿) This French-owned hotel, the first you come to walking west along the path in Pueblo de los Pescadores, is more notable for its spectacular rooftop patio and Jacuzzi and charming little garden pool than for its rooms. The latter are sparsely furnished with concrete floors; check several to find the one with the most sunlight. Cable TV and wi-fi are included. Not much Spanish is spoken here, so bring your French dictionary.

Hotel Kari Beach (☎ 809-240-6187; www.karibeach .com; Calle Libertad; s/d incl breakfast US$52/58; P X 🖳) Most of the rooms at the Kari Beach have large balconies with ocean views, an important difference from the Coco Plaza next door. However, rooms here don't stack up well against its neighbor – they're basic fan-cooled cement affairs. Air-con and TV are available upon request and wi-fi is available throughout. But it's a friendly, casual place with a beachside bar and dive shop.

Hotel Palapa (☎ 809-240-6797; www.palapabeach .com; cnr Calle 27 de Febrero & Av España; r/q incl breakfast US$65/85; P 🖳 🕿) Across the road from Punta Popy, a good stretch of town beach, the Palapa is a study in monochromatic simplicity. Mostly everything is white, other than the thatched roofs of the bungalows, which surround a little pond – in the far back is a peaceful pool area. This hotel is especially good for families and groups because the rooms are large and have loft spaces serving as an extra bedroom. Look for the hotel behind Pura Vida, the watersport activity company.

Hotel-Residence Playa Colibrí (☎ 809-240-6434; www.playacolibri.com; Fransisco Câmaño Deño; apt US$75-130; P X 🖳 🕿) One of the last hotels along this stretch of Playa Las Ballenas, Playa Colibrí is a good option for those seeking peace and quiet. Regardless of the room layout you choose, all are spacious, include fully equipped kitchens and furnishings out of a Caribbean Pottery Barn catalogue. Split-level apartments are especially good for families. Each has a terrace that overlooks a palm tree–shaded pool area. DSL internet available in apartments. Restaurant Eden (p160) and a bar are on the premises.

La Dolce Vita (☎ 809-240-5069; www.ladolcevitaresi dence.com; Av 27 de Febrero; r US$85; P X 🖳 🕿) Less 'dolce vita' than Fellini had in mind, the apartments at this pastel-colored seafront complex are nevertheless good long-term rentals. Rooms come with fully equipped kitchens, wicker furniture and the kind of Haitian artwork sold on the streets. A nice pool and landscaped grounds front the property. Rates vary significantly by length of stay and season.

TOP END

ourpick Lomita Maravilla (☎ 809-240-6345; www.lomitamaravilla.com; Calle Salome Ureña; villas US$100, with private Jacuzzi US$150, with private pool US$200; P ✗ ⬛ ⬛) A short walk down a dirt road – often muddy – off Av Duarte, you'll find one of the gems of Las Terrenas. This European-inspired boutique hotel consists entirely of thatched-roof private bungalows set along palmed paths and a center swimming pool. Rooms verge on swanky, with TVs, DVD players, and fully loaded kitchens ready for a make-it-yourself Caribbean meal. Enjoying your morning cup of Joe at your own private coffee bar on your porch might make you forget that you're still a 10- or 15-minute walk from the sea, the only downside to this hotel.

Alisei Hotel (☎ 809-240-5555; www.aliseihotel.com; Calle Franscico Alberto Cāmano; r US$130; P ✗ ⬛ ⬛) This hotel is a newer and more luxurious version of Hotel-Residence Playa Colibrí only a short walk away. Think flat-screen TVs, wi-fi internet, DVD and MP3 players, stylish and high-end linens, fully stocked kitchens, an on-site spa, swim-up pool bar…and you have a sense of how far you'd be moving on up with a stay here. Of the 54 apartments, several are villas that can sleep up to six and there's an even more luxurious honeymoon suite. The attached restaurant, Baraonda, is elegantly designed and sophisticated, with a large round open-air dining room supported by gnarled tree trunks – a hip-looking bar is in the center.

Eva Luna (☎ 809-978-5611; www.villa-evaluna.com; Calle Marico, Playa Las Ballenas; villas for 2/4 people US$150/300; P ✗ ⬛) A paragon of understated luxury, Eva Luna is a collection of five Mexican-style villas west of town and 200m from Playa Las Ballenas. Set around a beautiful pool and garden area, and with excellent service, this truly is a refuge. Each villa has a fully equipped kitchen, living room and terrace where a delicious gourmet breakfast is served.

Gran Bahía Principe El Portillo Beach Resort (☎ 809-240-6100; www.bahia-principe.com; d US$240; P ✗ ⬛ ⬛) Doing its best to fit in with the area's anti–big tourism vibe, this resort, the only all-inclusive near Las Terrenas, is actually 4km west directly across from the airstrip. It's a fairly low-key affair set on a nice stretch of beach with placid waters, good for swimming and kayaking. The property stretches all the way to the highway – if your room is near the entrance it's a long walk to the beach and your view will be of the parking lot. All the amenities you'd expect are included and a free shuttle takes guests to and from Las Terrenas.

Eating

The best restaurants in Las Terrenas are in Pueblo de los Pescadores, a cluster of fishermen's shacks-cum-waterfront restaurants just west of the river on what was the original site of the town. Virtually every restaurant has an entrance facing the road and an open-air dining or bar area out back, overlooking the ocean and narrow beach.

El Pan de Antes (☎ 809-994-3282; Calle Carmen; ⏲ 8am-7pm Tue-Sat, 8am-5pm Sun) Delicious pastries are made fresh daily at this French-owned patisserie. Croissants go fast Sunday mornings.

Cafeteria Christian (Calle Principal) A step up from the usual *colmado*, this place south of town is where locals eat and grab a pastry or two if they're on the run.

Primo Jeffro (☎ 829-352-7654; Calle del Carmen 143; mains US$2-7; ⏲ breakfast, lunch & dinner) For a change of pace, both in terms of cuisine and décor, head to this no-nonsense American-owned Mexican eatery. The open-air dining room couldn't be simpler and unpretentious but the hearty tacos (US$1.25), burritos and chimichangas hit the spot. *Almuerzos* (set lunches; US$4) and combo dinners (US$4.75) are great deals.

Brasserie Barrio Latino (☎ 809-240-6367; El Paseo shopping center, Calle Principal; mains US$2-10; ⏲ breakfast, lunch & dinner Mon-Sat) Occupying the busiest corner in town, this casual open-sided eatery has a large menu of international standards like sandwiches, burgers, pastas and meat dishes. Breakfast may be the best meal of the day here and there's a small bar that in addition to beer and alcoholic drinks mixes up smoothies and a delicious *morir soñando* (tasty combination of orange juice, milk, sugar and crushed ice). Enter from Calle Libertad.

Restaurant Eden (Hotel-Residence Playa Colibrí; mains US$7-12) Part of the Hotel-Residence Playa Colibrí, this pleasant outdoor restaurant is close to the end of the sandy beachside path from town, making it a perfect break before heading back. The menu and specials, from grilled salmon (US$10) to juicy burgers (US$7), are displayed on a chalkboard.

Grecia (Playa Punta Popy, Carretera a Portillo; mains US$10; breakfast, lunch & dinner) A step up from the average beachside shack, Grecia is a combo restaurant, café and bar located steps from a popular beach. Picnic tables and cushions are set out on the sand and it can get crowded when Dominicans, expats and tourists hunker down for the afternoon with sandwiches and drinks.

La Yuca Caliente (809-240-6634; Calle Libertad 6; mains US$10-23; lunch & dinner) A definite step up from the neighboring cookie-cutter restaurants, La Yuca Caliente is sophisticated and serene. Spanish, Italian, fish dishes and excellent pizzas are served by a professional and courteous staff. Tables are set out on the beach amid swaying palm trees and the low-key sound system is conversation friendly. Wi-fi internet is available.

A handful of restaurants line Pueblo de los Pescadores, the beachfront just west of Calle del Carmen. Most have pleasant ocean views and offer the same standard menu – pizza, pasta, grilled fish and meat – and do little to distinguish themselves from one another. The almost 40 types of pizzas at **Restaurante Pizza Playa** (809-240-6399; Pueblo de los Pescadores; mains US$2-10; lunch & dinner) are generally better than the competition. **El Cayuco** (Pueblo de los Pescadores; mains US$5-12; noon-11pm) serves Spanish cuisine with excellent tapas and **La Casa Azul** (Calle Libertad; mains US$3-12; 9am-11pm) is known for its seafood dishes.

Mini-Market Plaza Taína (7:40am-8:40pm Mon-Sat, 8am-1:30pm Sun) has snacks and basic necessities. **Punto Italia** (Calle del Carmen; 9am-7:30pm), a small Italian-owned grocery, is a vital resource for expats who demand high-quality meat, cheese, bread and brand-name European exports. Next door is **Supermercado Ignacio** (Calle del Carmen), which carries basics. Easily the largest and best supermarket in town, **Supermercado Lindo** (809-240-6003; Plaza Rosada, Calle Principal; 8:30am-1pm & 3-8pm Mon-Sat, 9am-1pm Sun) is the place to go for canned foods, pastas, produce, snacks and any other supplies.

Drinking

Most of the restaurants have bars and stay open well after the kitchen has closed. Bar hopping could scarcely be easier, as it takes

about 45 seconds to walk (or stagger, depending on the time of night) from one end of Pueblo de los Pescadores to the other. There are a few notable spots outside of Pueblo de los Pescadores as well.

Opalo Dance Club (829-604-4935; Pueblo de los Pescadores; Mon-Wed 8pm-midnight, Thu-Sun 9pm-2am) A stylish addition to the Las Terrenas nightlife scene, Opalo is a hip lounge-bar that ups the cosmopolitan quotient with plasma screens and the occasional DJ.

Paco Cabana Restaurant/Bar (Calle Libertad; 6pm-late) Located just west of the main intersection in town, Paco Cabana makes great use of its beachside location. Beds and comfortable couches piled with pillows make for a breezy and beautiful place to lounge late into the night. The vibe is sophisticated Miami and, while drinks are the draw, there's a kitchen that serves everything from basics such as hamburgers (US$8.50) to lobster (US$18).

Entertainment

Nuevo Mundo (Calle Principal; 9pm-4am Wed-Sun) This discotheque, close to the heart of the tourist enclave, is popular with locals and is a good place to get down to merengue and *bachata* in a typically Dominican way.

Shopping

Calle Principal and around are virtually wallpapered with the typical Haitian art found everywhere in the DR. The three shopping centers a stone's throw away from one another on Calle Principal – Plaza Taína, Casa Linda and El Paseo – have several high-end boutiques, eateries and a few shops selling basic tourist kitsch. All are open from 9am to 8pm Monday to Saturday and from 9am to 3pm Sunday. For more of a selection of paintings, other than the ubiquitous cookie-cutter mass-produced ones, stop by the **Haitian Caraïbes Art Gallery** (/fax 809-240-6250; Calle Principal 159; 9am-1pm & 4-8pm Mon-Sat); it also sells interesting crafts, jewelry and typical batiks and sarongs.

Getting There & Away

AIR

Domestic airlines service **Aeropuerto Internacional El Portillo** (EPS; 809-248-2289), a one-strip airport located a few kilometers east of Las Terrenas along the coastal road in the hamlet of El Portillo. In theory, an occasional flight from Europe gives it international credibility, but that's even less likely now with the opening of **Aeropuerto Internacional El Catey** (AZS; ☎ 809-338-0094), located 8km west of Sánchez and a 35-minute taxi ride (US$50) to Las Terrenas.

Takeoff (☎ 809-552-1333, 809-481-0707; www.take offweb.com; El Paseo shopping center, Las Terrenas) and **Aerodomca** (☎ 809-240-6571, in Santo Domingo 809-567-1195; www.aerodomca.com) operate propeller planes between El Portillo and Santo Domingo. Takeoff flies directly from Aeropuerto Las Américas (US$80, 30 to 50 minutes), while Aerodomca flies to La Isabela airport in Higuero, north of Santo Domingo (US$85).

Both also offer an air taxi service – as long as you have enough people or are willing to pay the total amount, flights leave whenever the passengers choose. Regular or air taxi tickets can be arranged through Bahia Tours (see p156).

There are minivan taxis (US$9) waiting at El Portillo for arriving flights.

BUS
Las Terrenas has two *gua-gua* stops at opposite ends of Calle Principal. *Gua-guas* headed to Sánchez (US$1.40, 30 minutes, every 25 minutes from 7am to 6pm) take on passengers at a stop 500m south of Calle Luperón. From Sánchez you can connect to an El Caribe bus to Santo Domingo or to a Bahia Tours bus (see p156) to Puerto Plata that leaves Sánchez at 2:30pm daily.

Those going to El Limón, 14km away (US$1.75, 20 minutes, every 15 minutes from 7am to 5pm), leave from the corner of Calle Principal and the coastal road; for an onward connection to Samaná, a further 26km, wait at the main intersection in El Limón.

TAXI
The local **taxi consortium** (☎ 809-240-6391) offers rides for one to six passengers to just about everywhere. Some sample fares are Playa Cosón (US$15), El Limón (US$25), Samaná (US$50), Las Galeras (US$80), Cabarete (US$120), Santo Domingo (US$170) and Punta Cana (US$360).

Getting Around
You can walk to and from most places in Las Terrenas, though getting from one end to the other can take a half-hour or more. Taxis charge US$10 each way to Playa Bonita and El Portillo and US$15 to US$20 to Playa Cosón

and El Limón. *Motoconchos* are cheaper – US$1.75 to Playa Bonita and US$7 to Playa Cosón – but are less comfortable. There are taxi and *motoconcho* stops in front of El Paseo shopping center and *motoconchos* are plentiful on Calle Principal and around Pueblo de los Pescadores. A bike can be handy for getting around town.

There are several local rental car agencies but rates are exorbitant (around US$80 per day). One of the more established and reliable ones is **ADA Rental Car** (☎ 809-704-3232; Plaza Taína; ☷ 9am-1pm & 2:30-7pm Mon-Sat).

PLAYA BONITA
A getaway from a getaway, this appropriately named beach only a few kilometers west of Las Terrenas is a better alternative for those seeking a more peaceful, reclusive vacation. Playa Bonita (Pretty Beach) is not without its imperfections – the half-moon-shaped beach is fairly steep and narrow, and parts are strewn with palm tree detritus. However, backed by a handful of tastefully landscaped hotels, many with well-manicured lawns that rival the beach in terms of attractiveness, this is an enticing spot.

Sights & Activities
Surfers and bodyboarders hit the waves around the eastern part of Playa Bonita near Calle Van der Horst. Just around the southwestern bend is the secluded, 6km-long **Playa Cosón**. The sand here is tan, not white, and the water greenish, not blue, but nevertheless it's a good place to pack a lunch and lose the bathing suit for a day. There are two small rivers that run through the thick palm-tree forest and open onto the ocean; the easternmost is said to contain agricultural runoff.

Las Terrenas Divers (☎ 809-240-6066; www.lt-divers .com; Hotel Bahía las Ballenas; ☷ 9:30am-noon & 3-5pm) offers dive trips and courses (one tank US$34, equipment US$7, five tanks US$155, open-water certificate US$345) as well as snorkel trips to Isla Las Ballenas (US$15, one hour) and Playa Jackson (minimum three people, US$25 to US$30 per person). You can also rent kayaks, bodyboards and surfboards by the hour or the day.

Sleeping & Eating
Coyamar (☎ 809-240-5130; www.coyamar.com; cnr Calles F Peña Gomez & Van der Horst; s/d US$45/60; P ☷) Located at Calle Van der Horst and

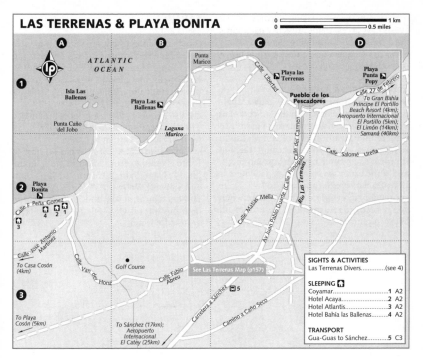

LAS TERRENAS & PLAYA BONITA

SIGHTS & ACTIVITIES
Las Terrenas Divers..............(see 4)

SLEEPING
Coyamar.................................1 A2
Hotel Acaya...........................2 A2
Hotel Atlantis........................3 A2
Hotel Bahía las Ballenas.........4 A2

TRANSPORT
Gua-Guas to Sánchez...........5 C3

the beach road, Coyamar is the least luxurious of the Playa Bonita hotels. The vibe is casual and friendly, especially good for families, and the restaurant near the front of the property and the pool are good places to hang out. Batiks and bright colors rule the day here and the fan-cooled rooms are simple and comfortable.

Hotel Acaya (☎ 809-240-6161; www.hotelacaya.com; Calle F Peña Gomez; r US$65-85; P ⊠ 🖳) Evocative of a more genteel era, the Acaya's two-story colonial building sits back from the beach on a finely manicured lawn. This French-owned hotel is understated and tastefully furnished and there's a relaxing lounge-restaurant on the property. Air-con rooms are available for US$10 extra; wi-fi is available throughout.

Hotel Atlantis (☎ 809-240-6111; www.atlantis-hotel.com.do; Calle F Peña Gomez; s incl breakfast US$60, d US$70-100, air-con extra US$10; P ⊠ 🖳) This rambling and charming hotel is straight out of a children's fairy tale – all twisting staircases, covered walkways and odd-shaped rooms. The furnishings are comfortable, not luxurious, and each of the 18 rooms is different – some

have balconies and fine ocean views. There's a palm tree–covered patio and fine French restaurant on the premises. Breakfast is included in the rate and wi-fi is available.

ourpick Hotel Bahía las Ballenas (☎ 809-240-6066; www.bahia-las-ballenas.net; Calle José Antonio Martínez; d incl breakfast US$95-130; P 🖳 🖾) Occupying a large swath of Playa Bonita property, this hotel combines the virtues of a luxurious resort and private retreat. Each one of the 32 huge airy villas scattered over the meticulously manicured lawn and garden is inspired by a Mexico–south of France aesthetic – pastel stucco walls, high thatched ceilings, tile floors and even roofless toilet and shower areas. Large wooden decks look out to an especially nice pool area lined with towering palm trees. An open-air restaurant serves creative Dominican dishes. There's an on-site dive shop as well.

Casa Cosón (☎ 809-374-2993; www.casacoson.com; Playa Cosón; r incl breakfast US$133; P) If Playa Bonita is just too congested for your liking, then this small colonial-style house on Playa Cosón is a good choice. It's fairly isolated, tucked away in a palm forest, but that's the appeal. Three

PENÍNSULA DE SAMANÁ

of the rooms have sea-facing balconies but all guests have access to the attractive back patio, great for a day of lounging. The only thing between you and a beautiful stretch of beach is a well-manicured lawn.

Getting There & Away

By car, Playa Bonita is reachable by a single dirt road that turns off from the Sánchez–Las Terrenas highway. In theory it's possible to walk from Playa Bonita to Playa Cacao in Las Terrenas via a coastal dirt/mud trail, but it requires clambering over a steep pitch, and some water wading. A taxi ride here is US$10, a *motoconcho* around US$1.75. There are usually a few *motoconchos* there when you're ready to return but it's best to set out before nightfall.

SÁNCHEZ
pop 11,800

Sánchez is a nondescript town that is notable mainly as a transportation hub. Buses to and from Santo Domingo and Puerto Plata stop here briefly, and pickups wait nearby to take passengers on the gorgeous, winding road over the coastal mountains to La Terrenas. There are also frequent *gua-gua* services to Samaná. There's at least one bank with an ATM if you need to pick up cash on the way.

Caribe Tours (☎ 809-552-7434) has services to Santo Domingo from Sánchez (four hours plus, 7:30am, 9am, 10:30am, 1:30pm, 3pm and 4:30pm). **Metro** (☎ 809-552-7332) has capital-bound buses at 9am and 5pm. The fare on both bus lines is US$7.50 and the trip takes around four hours.

North Coast

Within two hours' drive of Puerto Plata's international airport, you'll find all the best that the north coast has to offer – water sports and beach nightlife in Cabarete, mountain biking in the coastal hills, the celebrated 27 waterfalls of Damajagua, sleepy little Dominican towns where it's still possible to escape the tourist hordes, and mile after mile of that famous Caribbean sand.

Puerto Plata's all-inclusive resorts continue to draw a steady stream of package tourists, but it's Cabarete that shines as the north coast's center for independent travelers. This one-street town hit the big time when the winds were judged world class for kitesurfing, and up and down the street you'll hear half a dozen languages chasing the latest adrenaline-pumping activities – kitesurfing, of course, but also surfing, wakeboarding, windsurfing, mountain biking, and followed always by dinner and drinks on the beach.

Those looking for less action and more beach time – and who don't mind renting a condo – will find Cofresí or Costambar to their taste. Both sit just a few kilometers outside of Puerto Plata, and their large, condo-dwelling expat populations have the beaches almost entirely to themselves. Theme park fans will enjoy Ocean World, on Cofresí beach, where you can swim with the dolphins, but still gamble at the casino till dawn.

The north coast is bookended by two completely different towns: Río San Juan to the east and Monte Cristi to the west. Set amid the dry desert scrub near the border, Monte Cristi is the obvious launching pad for an expedition to Haiti, but otherwise holds little of interest. Río San Juan is a sleepy little town that sees few tourists, and yet is a good base for spending time on Playa Grande, one of the most beautiful beaches on the island.

HIGHLIGHTS

- Climb up through the **27 waterfalls of Damajagua** (p196), then leap and slide down into crystal-blue pools

- Dig your toes into the sand and your fork into some great grub while dining on the beach in **Cabarete** (p184)

- Marvel at the many shades of amber in Puerto Plata's **Museo del Ambar Dominicano** (p168), the museum that inspired the movie *Jurassic Park*

- Find tranquility in the typical small-town Dominican atmosphere of **Río San Juan** (p192)

- Worship the sun as the waves crash nearby on beautiful **Playa Grande** (p193)

NORTH COAST

HISTORY

Cabarete is the tourism capital of the north coast, but until about 20 years ago, the town existed only as a small farming hamlet. It was only the discovery by a pioneering windsurfer in the 1980s that the wind and waves were perfect for the sport that marked the beginning of Cabarete as we know it today.

Sosúa, Cabarete's seedy neighbor, was populated in 1940 by around 350 Jewish families fleeing Germany and other parts of Europe. Most left after just a few years, but not before building many fine homes and establishing what is to this day the DR's most recognizable cheese and dairy company.

Puerto Plata, the largest city on the coast, has a much older past – Columbus founded the city in 1493. As he approached the bay, the sunlight reflected off the water so brilliantly it resembled a sea of sparkling silver coins. Columbus named the bay Puerto Plata (Silver Port). He also named the mountain that looms over the city Pico Isabel de Torres (799m), in honor of the Spanish queen who sponsored his voyages.

An important port for the fertile north coast, Puerto Plata – and, indeed, the entire north coast – was plagued by pirates. It eventually became more lucrative for colonists to trade with the pirates (who were supported by Spain's enemies, England and France) rather than risk losing their goods on Spanish galleons. Such trade was forbidden and enraged the Spanish crown. In 1605 the crown ordered the evacuation of Puerto Plata – as well as the trading centers of Monte Cristi, La Yaguana and Bayajá – rather than have its subjects trading with the enemy.

The north coast remained virtually abandoned for more than a century, until the Spanish crown decided to repopulate the area to prevent settlers from other countries – namely the French from present-day Haiti – from moving in. Puerto Plata slowly regained importance, suffering during the Trujillo period, but eventually reinvented itself as a tourist destination. The early 1990s were golden years for the city, and for the first time tourism revenues surpassed those of its three main industries – sugar, tobacco and cattle hides – combined.

GETTING THERE & AROUND

Aeropuerto Internacional Gregorío Luperón is the second-largest airport in the country, and within two hours' driving distance from almost everywhere on the north coast. It's also your best place to rent a car, although you'll probably want an SUV, considering the state of the roads. Buses and *gua-guas* (small buses) offer frequent service all along this coast – it's as easy as sticking your hand in the air – although you may find the cost of the fare to be inversely proportional to your Spanish language ability.

PUERTO PLATA

pop 147,000

A wag in a bar put it this way: Puerto Plata is a charmless city, yes, but it's a city full of charming people. We agree.

While the Puerto Plata region boasts some of the best the country has to offer, the city itself is a working port town. It has a few interesting museums, and the cable car ride to the nearby bluff is worth the trip, but the accommodation options are poor – make Puerto Plata a day trip, and stay elsewhere, in the many welcoming towns along the coast.

A 2006 city project saw new sand dredged in and deposited along the coast, making the city beach and the beaches at Playa Dorada and Cofresí significantly more attractive. In a less welcome development, the government kicked all the street vendors off the oceanside boulevard and bulldozed the beach shacks at Long Beach, laying down pretty new paving stones but producing a character-free, sterile beach environment.

ORIENTATION

The center of town is Parque Central, which was under rigorous renovation when we were there – the park had been torn out and new, sterile red pavers were being laid. Most of the trees had been cut down too, but there might be some flowers and benches when they finish. Five blocks north of the park is the Malecón (main street; literally 'sea wall') and beyond that the ocean. The Malecón (also known as Av General Luperón and Av Circunvalación Norte) runs along the shore – Long Beach, the main city beach, is located 2km east along the center, but is nothing special. The other main east-west street is Av Beller (pronounced, oddly, 'Bell-AIR'), which runs along the north side of the park and feeds onto Av Luis Ginebra.

NORTH COAST

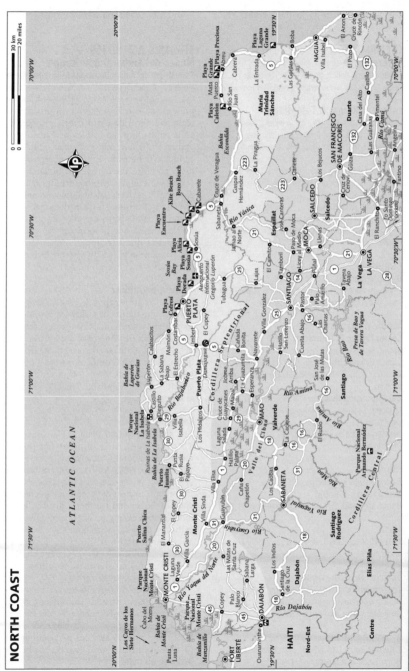

Take this road to go to the airport, Playa Dorada and beyond.

INFORMATION
Emergency
Politur (tourist police; ☎ 809-582-2331; cnr Av Hermanas Mirabal & Malecón; ☺ 24hr) Near Long Beach.

Internet Access & Telephone
Codetel (☎ 809-586-4393; cnr Av Beller & Padre Castellanos; per hr US$1) Doubles as a call center.
Dot Com (☎ 809-261-6165; Calle 12 de Julio 69; per hr US$0.70)
Internet Flash (cnr Separación & Margarita; per hr US$1.25) Friendly service and a relatively fast connection.

Internet Resources
Puerto Plata Report (www.popreport.com) Regional news and travel information from the north coast of the DR.

Laundry
D'Cast Lavandería (☎ 809-261-5900; Calle Camino Real 6) Per piece only – expect to pay as much as US$10 for a small load of washing. Also does dry cleaning.

Medical Services
Centro Médico Dr Bournigal (☎ 809-586-2342; Antera Mota; ☺ 24hr) A highly recommended clinic.
Clínica Brugal (☎ 809-586-2519; José del Carmen Ariza; ☺ 24hr) The heart specialist here is recommended by many.
Decompression chamber (☎ 809-586-2210; Hospital Dr Ricardo Limardo, cnr Av Manolo Taveres Busto 1 & Hugo Kundhart)
Farmacia Carmen (☎ 809-586-2525; Calle 12 de Julio) Offers free delivery.

Money
Banco BHD (JF Kennedy)
Banco León (JF Kennedy)
Banco Mercantil (Separación) On Parque Central.

Post
Post office (cnr Calle 12 de Julio & Separación) Two blocks north of Parque Central.

Tourist Information
Tourism office (☎ 809-586-5059; cnr Av Hermanas Mirabal & Malecón) On Long Beach, on the second floor of the Politur station. Moderately helpful.

Travel Agencies
Cafemba Tours (☎ 809-586-2177; cafembatours@ hotmail.com; Calle Separación 12) Half a block north of Parque Central, Cafemba can arrange plane tickets and package tours.

SIGHTS & ACTIVITIES
Museo del Ambar Dominicano
The **Museo del Ambar Dominicano** (Dominican Amber Museum; ☎ 809-586-3910; www.ambermuseum.com; Calle Duarte 61; admission US$1.50; ☺ 9am-6pm Mon-Fri) presents an excellent exhibit on this prized resin. Guides walk visitors through the display, explaining the origins and history of amber and answering any questions. They claim a visit here by Steven Spielberg was the inspiration for the movie *Jurassic Park*. The collection is impressive and includes valuable pieces with such rare inclusions as a small lizard and a 30cm-long feather (the longest one found to date). Tours are offered in English and Spanish. A gift shop on the ground floor has a fine selection of amber jewelry, but is open only in high season (December to March).

Galería de Ambar
Equally as impressive as the Museo del Ambar, the **Galería de Ambar** (☎ 809-586-6467; www.ambercollection.itgo.com; Calle 12 de Julio; admission US$1; ☺ 8:30am-6pm Mon-Fri, 9am-1pm Sat), near José del Carmen Ariza, would be almost indistinguishable from its competitor were it not for its exhibits on rum, sugar, tobacco and coffee. Guides speak English, French, German and Spanish.

Teleférico
Just south of Puerto Plata is Pico Isabel de Torres (799m), an enormous flat-topped mountain Columbus named in 1493. A **teleférico** (cable car; ☎ 809-586-2122; Camino a los Dominguez; US$3 one way; ☺ 8am-5pm, closed Wed) takes visitors to the top. On clear days there are spectacular views of the city and coastline – go early, before the mountain clouds up. The botanical gardens at the top are good for an hour's stroll. There's also a large statue of Christ the Redeemer (similar to but smaller than its counterpart in Río de Janeiro), an overpriced restaurant, and aggressive knick-knack sellers.

Board the *teleférico* at its base at the southern end of Camino a los Dominguez, 800m uphill from Av José Ginebra. A *motoconcho* (motorcycle taxi) here costs US$1.30, a taxi US$7. The ride is notorious for opening late or closing early, so cross your fingers before heading up there.

You can also walk up (or down) the mountain, paying only a one-way fare to return. Follow the trail under the cable-car lines up to the midpoint tower (there is only one), then turn right and follow the ridgeline to the right. It's a tough two- to three-hour walk (we estimate about 7km) uphill – leave granny at home. **Iguana Mama** (see p188) offers this tour. Alternatively, on weekends local guides sometimes hang out at the ticket office (US$10).

Cockfighting

There's a small **club gallistico** (US$10), with fights most Saturdays and Sundays at around 2pm. Expect crowds of 300 and more to elbow their way into this tiny space near the Malecón. There's no bookie – bets are shouted across the room based on the color of the corner the bird's fighting from. Ask any *motoconcho* if it's on.

Fuerte de San Felipe

Located right on the bay, at the western end of the Malecón, **Fuerte de San Felipe** (San Felipe Fort; admission US$1.20; 9am-5pm) is the only remnant of Puerto Plata's early colonial days. Built in the mid-16th century to prevent pirates from seizing one of the only protected bays on the entire north coast, the fort never saw any action. For much of its life its massive walls and interior moat were used as a prison. Today there's a small museum, but its exhibits – a few rusty handcuffs, a handful of bayonets and a stack of cannonballs – are far from remarkable. The views of the bay are impressive, though, and a large grassy area in front of the fort makes for a restful stop.

Also at the fort is Puerto Plata's **lighthouse**, which first lit up on September 9, 1879, and was restored in 2000. The white-and-yellow tower – 24.4m tall, 6.2m in diameter – is a melding of neoclassical style with industrial construction.

Casa de la Cultura

In addition to dance and music workshops, the **Casa de la Cultura** (Cultural Center; ☎ 809-261-2731; Parque Central, Calle Duarte; admission free; 9am-noon & 3-5pm Mon-Fri) often showcases work by Dominican artists in its first-floor gallery. It was closed for renovation when we were there, but should be open by the time you read this.

Iglesia San Felipe

The twin-steepled **Iglesia San Felipe** (Parque Central, Calle Duarte; 8am-noon & 2-4pm Mon-Sat, 7am-8pm Sun) had been completely gutted and was under renovation when we passed through, but should be spiffied up by the time you get there. The principal attraction here is the Italian stained-glass windows. Small but beautiful, they were donated to the church by area families in 1998 after Hurricane George blew through town and devastated the church. At the base of each window is the name of the family that contributed it.

Brugal Rum Plant

The local joke has it that everyone wants to be the quality-assurance tester here at this **rum distillery and bottling facility** (☎ 809-586-2531; Carretera a Playa Dorada; admission free; 8am-4pm Mon-Fri). Lots of package tours come through here, but it's a pretty underwhelming 15-minute tour from a 2nd-floor gangway. Of more interest are the complimentary rum-based cocktails at the end.

TOURS

There are no tour operators based in Puerto Plata, for the simple reason that almost no tourists stay in the city itself. All the nearby all-inclusive resorts listed in this book organize tours for their guests. For independent travelers: tour operators in Cabarete and Sosúa are generally happy to pick you up or provide transportation for you.

That said, there is one recommended deep-sea fishing company based in Puerto Plata, **Gone Fishing** (www.gonefishingdominicanrepublic.com). There's no office, or telephone – it's a boating business after all – but it does come highly recommended. You'll pay around US$100 (US$70 for watchers) per half-day trip in larger groups, or you can charter a boat for US$700/900 per half/full day. Gone Fishing also operates out of Punta Cana.

FESTIVALS & EVENTS

The third week in June brings a week-long **cultural festival**, which features merengue, blues, jazz and folk concerts at Fuerte de San Felipe. Troupes from Santo Domingo perform traditional dances that range from African spirituals to sexy salsa tunes. At the same time, the town hosts an arts-and-crafts fair for local artisans at nearby Parque Central.

NORTH COAST

PUERTO PLATA

INFORMATION
Banco BHD...**1** E1
Banco León.......................................**2** E1
Banco Mercantil................................**3** E2
Centro Médico Dr Bournigal **4** C5
Clínica Brugal....................................**5** E1
Codetel..**6** F2
D'Cast Lavandería............................**7** B5
Decompression Chamber (Hospital
    Dr Ricardo Limbardo).............**8** E5
Dot Com..**9** F2
Farmacia Carmen............................**10** E1
Internet Flash..................................**11** F1
Politur......................................(see 13)
Post Office.......................................**12** F1
Tourism Office.................................**13** F6

SIGHTS & ACTIVITIES
Cafemba Tours.................................**14** E2
Casa de Cultura...............................**15** E2
Club Gallistico.................................**16** D4
Fuerte de San Felipe.......................**17** B3
Galería de Ambar............................**18** E1
Iglesia San Felipe............................**19** E2
Museo de Arte Taíno......................**20** E1
Museo del Ambar Dominicano..**21** E2

SLEEPING
Aparta-Hotel Lomar.......................**22** E5
Hotel Altantico...............................**23** E1
Hotel Ilra...**24** F2
Hotel Mountain View.....................**25** C5
Portofino Guest House...................**26** F6

EATING
Aguaceros Bar & Grill.....................**27** F1
Barco's...**28** E1
Heladería Mariposa.........................**29** E2
Jamvi's...**30** C4
La Parrillada.....................................**31** F6
Mercado Municipal.........................**32** C5
Restaurant Pizzería Portofino.....**33** F6
Sam's Bar & Grill.............................**34** E1
Tropical Supermarket.....................**35** D4

DRINKING
Irish Tavern......................................**36** E1
Terraza Las Almendras...................**37** E5

ENTERTAINMENT
Cine Teatro Roma..........................**38** F2

SHOPPING
La Canoa..**39** E1
Museo del Ambar Dominicano
    Gift Shop..............................(see 21)

TRANSPORT
Caribe Tours.....................................**40** B5
El Canario Buses to Samaná...........**41** C5
Europcar...**42** F6
Gua-guas to Sosúa, Cabarete &
    Río San Juan..............................**43** E2
Javilla Tours.....................................**44** B5
Metro..**45** D4
Taxi Stand...**46** E1
Texaco Station.................................**47** B5
Texaco Station.................................**48** E6

Monumento á
General Gregorio
Luperón

17

Bahía de
Puerto Plata

Av Colón
Mella
Malecón
(Av General Luperón)
12 de Julio
JF Kennedy
Beller
Duarte
Antera Mota
José de Carmen Ariza
Señalación
Padre Castellanos
Emilio Prud'homme
Villa Nueva

30

Mella
Sánchez
Margarita
Calle del
Carmen
Malecón
(Av Circunvalación Norte)

Av Colón
Calle 2
Calle 4
Calle 6
Arroyo Los Muñoces
Av Penetración Portuaria
Calle 1

See Enlargement

45

35

16
Hugo Kunhardt
Vista Alegre
Pedro Haris
Paul

To Costambar (2km);
Cofresí (5km);
Imbert (20km);
Luperón (54km);
Santiago (71km);
Navarrete (75kms)

Cemetery
La Rosarios
La Rosarios
Altagracia
Teresa Suárez
Av Colón
Av José Ginebra

32

López
20 de Diciembre
Doctor Zafra
Av Virginia Ortega
Iglesia San Felipe
Francisco J Peinado
El Morro

Av Luis Alegre

47
7
44
40

Av Pedro Clisante
Camino Real
J Kunhardt
1 Kunhardt

25

Av Isabel de Torres

Calle 2
Av 27 de Febrero
Presidente Vásquez
Rafael Aguilar

Diagonal
Calle A
Calle C

5

To Teleférico
(450m)

41

Juan Lafitte
Calle 5
Gregorio de Lora
Av 27 de Agosto

Av Circunvalación Sur

NORTH COAST

Puerto Plata hosts a popular **merengue festival** in early November. During the festival the entire length of the Malecón is closed to vehicular traffic, food stalls are set up on both sides of the oceanside boulevard and a stage is erected for merengue performances.

SLEEPING

Unless you're after budget accommodation there's no real reason to spend the night in Puerto Plata, considering that there are much better options elsewhere on the coast.

Hotel Ilra (☎ 809-586-2337; Calle Villanueva 25; r with fan per person US$14) Housed in a Victorian-style home that's over a century old (and starting to show it), rooms here have whitewashed wood walls and mosquito nets over the beds. All share a large but aging bathroom. There's a small sitting room downstairs, and a restaurant (mains US$4 to US$8; open for breakfast, lunch and dinner Monday to Saturday) downstairs occupies the cheeriest room in the house and is a pleasant place to start your day.

Hotel Atlantico (☎ 809-586-6108; Calle 12 de Julio 24; r with fan US$15, with air-con & TV US$20; 🔀) The beds here have seen better days, and having padlocks instead of doorknobs is always a red flag, but the Atlantic remains a reliable and popular budget hotel. There are eight very basic rooms organized around a narrow interior courtyard; all have high ceilings and wood walls, and tolerable private bathrooms. Several rooms have air-con and cable TV.

Portofino Guest House (☎ 809-586-2858; Av Hermanas Mirabal 12; r US$26/32; 🅿 🔀 🔊) About a block from Long Beach, you get the feeling you're out in the boonies – this is a long way from the center. There are 20 clean rooms here – they're fading fast, but have hot water, air-con and cable TV. A well-tended swimming pool under a flourishing mango tree is a plus. An excellent pizzeria (p172) by the same name is next door.

Hotel Mountain View (☎ 809-586-5757; www .mountainviewdr.com; cnr J Kunhardt & Villanueva; r US$36; 🅿 🔀 💻) Indisputably the best hotel in Puerto Plata, the Mountain View (which does, incidentally, have an excellent view of the mountains) offers super standard motel rooms with firm mattresses, cable TV and spanking-clean bathrooms. There's free wi-fi, a computer in the lobby, plus a bar and restaurant on site. The location is not walking distance to the center, but is accessible by *motoconcho* and taxi.

NORTH COAST

Aparta-Hotel Lomar (☎ 809-586-3966; Malecón 8; s/d US$35/43, 1-bedroom apt US$55-70; P ❄) Rooms and apartments in this hotel are spacious and clean, and feature cable TV and telephones. Kitchens in the apartments are small but adequate. Some also have balconies with ocean views. For the outlay, this place is excellent value, and your best choice on the Malecón. Same owners as the Portofino (p171).

EATING

The best restaurants in the area cluster in and around Cofresí (see p178).

Heladería Mariposa (☎ 809-970-1785; Av Beller; mains US$3-8; ❄ 8am-11pm) A block north of the park, this cute ice-cream shop and bakery serves simple but good sandwiches and homemade ice cream.

Barco's (☎ 829-210-3922; Malecón 6; mains US$3-15; ❄ 8am-12midnight) On the Malecón, this restaurant has a breezy, open-sided dining room, but the mostly expat clientele prefers the sidewalk tables in front. The menu has a little of everything, from Dominican-style egg breakfasts to sandwiches and burgers, to pasta and pizza. There are also seafood dishes, of course, and daily specials that are a good deal off the regular prices. Main dishes come with a choice of potatoes, fries or *mangú* (mashed plantains).

Sam's Bar & Grill (☎ 809-586-7267; www.samsbar.tk; Calle José del Carmen Ariza 34; mains US$4-9; ❄ 8am-9pm Mon-Sat, 9am-5pm Sun; 🖳) With ragged flags flying over a clapboard façade, Sam's is the favored watering hole of the area's heavy-drinking resident gringos. The food here is great value, though – there's French toast, chicken Kiev, Mexican scramble, Philly cheese steak and Tijuana-style chili – all reliable. Free wi-fi (for you internet addicts) with purchase.

Jamvi's (☎ 809-320-7265; cnr Malecón & Calle López; mains US$5-12; ❄ 10am-late) This gargantuan open-air pizza joint sits above street level on the Malecón, offering a pleasant sea breeze and great views. Good for a pizza and wine fix (there's a decent wine list); from 10pm onwards it pumps the merengue and reggaeton till late.

Restaurant Pizzería Portofino (☎ 809-261-2423; Av Hermanas Mirabal 12; mains US$7-11; ❄ breakfast, lunch & dinner) Near the eastern end of the Malecón, Portofino's is a thatch-roofed, open-sided restaurant that offers excellent pizzas. Pasta dishes are also quite good. Handy if you're hanging out on Long Beach and want some grub.

ourpick Café Cito (☎ 809-586-7923; www.cafecito .info; mains US$7-15; ❄ lunch & dinner; 🖳) Just 500m west of Playa Dorada and an easy walk from your resort, this laid-back eatery is your salvation from bad buffet food. The kitchen serves up solid American (or rather, Canadian) food, including hearty breakfasts, Philly cheese steak, pork chops, and for homesick Quebecers, *poutine*. There's free wi-fi with your meal, the bar does drink specials till late, and the cigar-chomping owner (who is also the Canadian consul) sells good smokes at budget prices. Ask about his 'Nite on the Town' bar-hopping tours.

El Manguito Restaurant & Liquor Store (☎ 809-586-4392; mains US$7-18; ❄ lunch & dinner) Nestled at the side of the highway just east of the Costa Dorada complex (and just west of Playa Dorada) is this great-value seafood joint, a short walk from your resort. Beers here are only US$2, and the lobster (US$14) is great value. Service is excellent, and there's also a variety of desserts.

La Parrillada (☎ 809-586-1401; cnr Av Luís Ginebra & Circunvalación Sur; mains US$8-18; ❄ lunch & dinner) At the eastern end of town, this popular meat-lovers' restaurant serves quality grilled dishes in a classy, understated setting. Iron tables are covered with tablecloths and set with ceramic plates and wine glasses, either on an open-air patio or in the small, comfortable dining area. The *churrasco* (grilled or barbecued beef) is a house favorite, as is the shrimp, and on Sundays an outdoor barbecue brings flocks of people, locals and foreigners alike.

Aguaceros Bar & Grill (☎ 809-586-2796; Malecón 32; US$10-15; ❄ lunch & dinner) This open-sided, thatch-roofed, fan-cooled bar and grill is pleasant for its casual-Caribbean, low-light ambience and its location on the Malecón. Tex-Mex is the specialty here, including fajitas, burritos and a combo plate with nachos, quesadillas, soft tacos, chimichangas, flautas and more for under US$15. Great for a Mexican fix if you've been without for awhile.

The monster-sized **Tropical Supermarket** (☎ 809-586-6464; cnr Av 27 de Febrero & Beller) is the best place in the center for groceries.

Mercado Municipal (cnr Calles 2 & López; ❄ 7am-3pm Mon-Sat) is housed in what looks like an enormous, crown-shaped, reinforced-concrete gas station from the 1960s. Here you'll find a large variety of meat and vegetables, and pushy salesmen selling tourist knick-knacks.

IS IT REALLY AMBER & IS IT REALLY DOMINICAN?

Dominican amber is widely regarded as the finest in the world. It not only exhibits the largest range of colors – from clear and pale lemon to warm oranges, gold, brown, and even green, blue and black – but it contains the greatest number of 'inclusions': insects, tiny reptiles and plant matter that became trapped in the resin before it fossilized. Such inclusions add character to a piece of amber and increase its value.

Fake amber (made of plastic) is occasionally sold in the DR, especially by street and beachside vendors. You're advised to buy only from a reputable shop, which will always permit you the following tests to satisfy yourself that it is genuine:

- Examine the amber under a fluorescent lamp. If the glow changes, it's amber; if it doesn't, it's plastic.

- Rub the piece against cotton and bring it close to your hair. If the hair moves, it's real. Amber acquires static electricity; plastic doesn't.

- Place unadorned amber in a glass of salt water. If it floats, it's amber. If it sinks, it's plastic. Remember: this won't work if the piece is in a setting.

- Ask the salesperson to hold a match to the amber. Heated amber gives off a natural resin, plastic smells like a chemical.

Be aware also that a significant amount of the amber sold in the DR is actually imported from Europe, especially Poland. This amber is often good value, and will satisfy all of the above tests. While only experts can tell for sure where a particular piece comes from, one thing to look for is 'spangles' – flashes of light embedded inside the amber. This is typical of Polish amber and normally absent from the Dominican gem.

Finally, blue amber is mined exclusively in the DR. It is the most spectacular and most expensive form of amber, and if it passes the above tests you can be sure it is, in fact, Dominican.

DRINKING & ENTERTAINMENT

our pick **Irish Tavern** (☎ 809-708-5205; irish. tavern@comcast.com; Calle 12 de Julio 22; ☺ 8am-8pm Mon-Sat) This friendly Irish-owned bar does the best US$2.50 Dominican lunch in town. It also does fish and chips and shepherd's pie. A Guinness will set you back a mere US$4, and there's sometimes Bushmill's behind the bar. It has one of the best book swaps in the country.

Terraza Las Almendras (☎ 809-854-0092; www .puertoplatalasalmendras.info; cnr Malecón & Calle A Brugal Montanez; ☺ 8am-late) With pleasant outdoor seating under bright umbrellas, this sea-facing restaurant makes a good place to kick back and drink a couple of beers. The food consists almost entirely of *pinchos* – if it once roamed the earth (or sea), you can get it here served on a stick.

Cine Teatro Roma (☎ 809-320-7010; Av Beller 39; admission US$5) The only movie theater convenient to the center.

SHOPPING

La Canoa (☎ 809-586-3604; Av Beller 18; ☺ 8am-6pm Mon-Sat, 10am-1pm Sun) This rambling gift shop is the biggest and best in town. There's an enormous amber exhibit – almost a museum – and a good selection of amber and larimar jewelry. It also sells the usual acrylic Haitian paintings, boxes of cigars, and postcards.

GETTING THERE & AWAY
Air

Puerto Plata is served by **Aeropuerto Internacional Gregorío Luperón** (☎ 809-586-0107), 18km east of town along the coastal highway (past Playa Dorada), and just a few kilometers west of Sosúa. Numerous charter airlines use the airport, mostly in conjunction with the all-inclusive resorts. A taxi to or from the airport costs US$25. Cheapskates can also walk 500m from the terminal to the main highway, where they can flag down a *gua-gua* to Puerto Plata (US$1.20, 45 minutes) or Sosúa (US$0.30, 10 minutes).

Some of the airlines with international service here include:

Air Canada (☎ 809-541-5151; www.aircanada.com)
American Airlines (toll free ☎ 809-200-5151; www .aa.com)

NORTH COAST

Continental (toll free ☎ 809-200-1062; www.conti
nental.com)
Delta (☎ 809-586-0973; www.delta.com)
LTU (☎ 809-586-4075; www.ltu.com)
Lufthansa (toll free ☎ 809-200-1133; www.lufthansa
.com)
Martinair (toll free ☎ 809-200-1200; www.martinair
.com)

Car

Your best bet for renting a car is to pick one up
at the airport when you arrive. There are also
a couple of international rent-a-car agencies
on the road leading east out of town toward
Playa Dorada. Rates start at US$50 to US$60
per day, with taxes and insurance included.
Discounts are available in low season (May
to October) and if you rent for several days
or weeks.

All of the following also have offices at the
airport, where they are open 7am to 10pm
(and are usually on call overnight, but charge
extra for late pickup or delivery).
Alamo (☎ 809-586-1366, airport 809-586-0285; www
.alamo.com; ☙ 8am-6pm) East of town on the road to
Playa Dorada.
Avis (☎ 809-586-4436, airport 809-586-7007; www.avis
.com; ☙ 8am-6pm) Located next to Café Cito restaurant,
500m west of Playa Dorada.
Europcar (☎ 809-586-7979, airport 809-586-0215;
www.europcar.com; cnr Av Hermanas Mirabal & Luis Ginebra; ☙ 8am-6pm) Located near the state tourism office.
National (☎ 809-586-1366, airport 809-586-0285;
www.nationalcar.com; Playa Dorada; ☙ 8am-5pm) In the
Playa Dorada shopping center.

Bus

Caribe Tours (☎ 809-576-0790; btwn Real and Kunhardt)
has a depot 1km south of Parque Central.
The terminal provides hourly service, on the
hour from 6am to 7pm, to Santo Domingo
(US$8.20, four hours), and stops along the
way at Santiago (US$6.70, 1¼ hours) and La
Vega (US$4.55, two hours).

Metro (☎ 809-586-6062; Calle 16 de Agosto) is located eight blocks east of Parque Central, between Beller and JF Kennedy. The company
serves Santo Domingo (US$8.65, 3½ hours)
with a stop in Santiago (US$6.80, 1¼ hours).
Buses depart daily at 6am, 7am, 9am, 11am,
2pm, 4pm and 6:30pm. There are additional
departures on Sunday at 9:30am and 3pm.

Javilla Tours (☎ 809-970-2412; cnr Camino Real &
Av Colón; ☙ every 15min, 5am-7:30pm) provides bus
service to Santiago (US$5.30, 1½ hours) with

stops along the way at Imbert (US$1.20, 20
minutes) and Navarrete (US$2.20, 50 min-
utes). To get to Monte Cristi, take Javilla's
bus to Navarrete and tell the driver to let you
off at the junction, where you can change for
the **Expresos Linieros** bus (US$2.10, 1½ hours)
to Monte Cristi.

El Canarío (☎ 809-291-5594) is a Spanish-
operated bus that leaves daily for Samaná
(US$6.05, 3½ to four hours) at 5am from
near the public hospital. This is your only
option, as neither Metro nor Caribe Tours
has direct service to Samaná. Make two calls
the day before – one to the bus line to reserve
a spot and the other to a taxi line to arrange
an early-morning pickup.

For points east and west of town, *gua-guas*
are a cheap and reliable option. Eastbound
gua-guas leave from a stop on the north side
of Parque Central, passing by the entrance of
Playa Dorada and through Sosúa (US$0.60, 30
minutes), Cabarete (US$2.10, one hour) and
Río San Juan (US$3.50, two hours). From Río
San Juan, you can catch another van to Nagua
and then another to Samaná.

GETTING AROUND

Puerto Plata looks temptingly small on our
map – until you get here and realize just how
big the place really is. While you can walk
around the old town and parts of the Malecón,
you're going to have to either get comfortable
taking *motoconchos*, or rent a car – locals generally don't use regular taxis, and taxi fares can
easily wind up costing as much as a rental car,
especially if you're doing a lot of sightseeing.

The main trunk roads in Puerto Plata are
serviced by *gua-guas* following lettered routes,
which cost US$0.30. Lines C and F will be
of most interest to you: they run from as far
west as Cofresí, through town and past Playa
Dorada in the east. Line C runs direct; line
F makes lots of twists and turns as it barrels
through town.

Taxi & Motoconcho

Motoconchos rule the streets here. Thankfully,
a successful effort is underway to tame Puerto
Plata's once-infamous motorcycle taxis.
Drivers must now be licensed and pass a
driving test and inspection of their motorcycle – these drivers wear numbered, colored
vests. Licensed *motoconchos*, in our experience, were noticeably more cautious in traffic.
If you're going to take a *concho*, do yourself

a favor and take one wearing a vest. The in-town fare was between US$0.65 and US$1.40 when we were there.

For those squeamish of helmetless motorcycle joy, you'll find taxi fares priced almost exclusively for tourists – the in-town fare is around US$5 to US$8. Taxis don't generally cruise the streets looking for customers, so either ask your hotel to call you one, or try **Taxi Pollito** (☎ 809-261-2995). There's normally a taxi stand on the main park, but it had shifted to the western end of the Malecón when we were there – it may have resumed its normal location by the time you read this.

AROUND PUERTO PLATA

Just outside Puerto Plata proper lies Playa Dorada, a string of all-inclusive resorts. To the west of town, the beach hamlets of Costambar and Cofresí are home to many expat condo-dwellers (principally Canadians escaping their winter heating bills). Both have a good community feel, but regular hotels are in short supply – you'll get better value renting a condo by the week or month.

PLAYA DORADA & COSTA DORADA

These two adjacent beaches string together a total of 16 all-inclusive resorts and one five-star hotel. If you're after an all-inclusive, also check out Sun Village and Hacienda resorts in Cofresí. For a complete list of resorts and businesses in the area see www.playadorada.com.do.

Most of the all-inclusive places on Playa Dorada and Costa Dorada offer both day and night passes (US$45 to US$60), which entitle you to unlimited access to their facilities for either a buffet lunch, drinks and beach/pool access, or buffet dinner and access to their bars and disco (if they have one).

Activities

Playa Dorada Golf Club (☎ 809-320-3472; www.playadoradagolf.com; ☉ 7am-7pm), designed by Robert Trent Jones, is an attractive 6218m, par-72 course that is the centerpiece of the massive Playa Dorada hotel complex (which incorporates 14 resorts). The greens fee for nine holes is US$50, for 18 holes, US$75; caddies (US$8/15 for nine/18 holes) are obligatory,

golf carts (US$20/25 for nine/18 holes) are not. Some resorts offer discounted rates for their guests – be sure to ask at your hotel before you reserve your tee time.

Sleeping & Eating

Prices listed are rack rates.

Grand Oasis Marien Resort (☎ in the US 888-774-0040; www.oasismarienresort.com; s/d US$131/169) Also part of the Costa Dorada complex, this newish resort gets rave reviews for its well-manicured grounds, friendly staff and better-than-average food. It often offers specials that take the price well below the rack rate listed here. An additional two buildings were under construction when we passed through.

Hotel Iberostar Costa Dorada (☎ 809-320-1000; www.iberostar.com; s/d US$135/165; P ⊠ ☐ ☒) Consistently well rated by travelers, this is one of the best-value all-inclusive places in the Puerto Plata region. There's a certain Disneyland cheesiness about the place – you'll be greeted at reception by a porter wearing a pith helmet, for instance – but the grounds are enormous and well kept, the pool is immense, and the food (always a sticking point) is definitely better than average. The rooms are not luxurious, but for what you're paying, still good value.

Occidental Allegro Playa Dorada (☎ 809-320-3988; www.occidentalhotels.com; per person US$150/216; P ⊠ ☒) This satisfactory option has more than 500 rooms, half of which have sea views. There's an enormous pool with a small island in the middle, five restaurants, plus a tennis court, a Jacuzzi, and a beauty parlor.

Gran Ventana Beach Resort (☎ 809-320-2111; www.granventanahotel.com; s/d US$180/260; P ⊠ ☐ ☒) Part of the VH Hotels and Resorts chain, the Gran Ventana is a decent midrange option on Playa Dorada. There are 506 tastefully decorated rooms, all with balcony or terrace, and there's direct beach access under a string of almond and beach grape trees.

our pick **Casa Colonial Beach & Spa** (☎ 809-320-3232; www.casacolonialhotel.com; r US$450-1450; P ⊠ ☐ ☒) This extraordinary hotel is arguably the best in the country. It offers 50 indulgent suites, each with marble floors, sparkling fixtures, canopied beds, ample balconies, a cedar-lined closet, plus plush bathrobes and slippers. There's even a claw-foot bathtub on some of the balconies, should you want a romantic bubble bath with a view. The grounds are set in a sprawling mansion and boast a tropical garden with orchids growing at seemingly every turn. An infinity pool with four Jacuzzis is located on the roof, providing a spectacular view of the blue ocean beyond. A high-end spa and two elegant restaurants are also on site. Unlike those of its neighbors, the rates at the Casa Colonial are not all-inclusive.

Getting There & Around

The taxi association of Playa Dorada gouges guests for many times the price you'd pay if you hailed a regular taxi on the street. Don't let management at your hotel scare you with stories of danger lurking outside the complex – this is complete rubbish.

Taxis can be found at any of the hotel entrances and also in front of Playa Dorada Plaza. A taxi to the airport will cost you US$50, to Sosúa US$45, to Cabarete US$55, and within the hotel complex US$10. If you're going into Puerto Plata (US$25), refuse the taxi's invitation to wait for you, and take a regular taxi home (US$8).

For a taste of local life, walk to the front entrance and hail down a *gua-gua* to Puerto Plata (US$0.60) – when you want to get off, just bang on the side of the van.

COSTAMBAR

Less a traveler's destination than an expat hideaway, Costambar is still worth a look – it's got a beautiful, secluded beach (with a view of the ships leaving harbor to the east), and a couple of good restaurants. It's finding a hotel that's the challenge – this is a private community (see www.apc-costambar.com) that consists entirely of time-share units and vacation homes, many occupied for six months of the year by Canadians on the run from winter.

Some of the condo associations will rent by the week and occasionally by the night in low season, though, and you'll find a grocery store here, plus internet access (but no ATM). If you decide to come here you'll enjoy your stay a great deal more with a car – Costambar is a little spread out. A local monthly newsletter (www.costambarmonthly.com) can keep you up to date with the goings-on.

Information

All of Costambar's main services are in the small village just past the gated entrance. There is no hospital in town.

Aqua Marina Tours (☎ 809-970-7615; www.domini can-holiday.com) Provides tourist information and also manages several rental properties and arranges area tours.
Farmacia de los Trópicos (☎ 809-970-7607) Advertises Viagra, Cialis and Levitra (and presumably sells aspirin as well).
Jenny's Market (☎ 809-970-7503; Calle Principal; internet per hr US$1.70) Offers internet and phone services.

Sleeping & Eating

There are no standard hotels in Costambar, which is instead dominated by condos and time-share places. If you're after up-to-the-minute eating and sleeping info, log on to www.incost ambar.com.

Club Villas Jazmin (☎ 809-970-7010; www.villas jazmin.com; apt up to 4 people US$100; P X ⬛ ⬛) A small time-share club with an extremely loyal clientele, the Jazmin will rent apartments to independent travelers during the low season, roughly April to June and September to December. Like many time-share places, the units are large and comfortable if not exactly alluring, including full kitchens, cable TV, CD players and firm beds. The club, a five- to 10-minute walk from the beach, has a small pool, tennis court and even a resident tennis pro.

Aqua Marina Tours (☎ 809-970-7615; www.do minican-holiday.com) This company manages a number of condos and vacation homes of various sizes and prices in Costambar. Contact them for information on renting.

Pizza Plus (☎ 809-970-7497; Calle Central; mains US$7-14; ⏰ 24hr) As the name suggests, you can get pizzas here – there are a dozen different varieties, all reasonably priced – plus a slew of other Dominican and international dishes. There's also a full bar, and karaoke on Sundays at 9pm.

Harley y Rock Ristocafé (☎ 829-447-3704; mains US$5-15; ⏰ lunch & dinner) *Easy Rider* posters and Harley Davidson paraphernalia litter the walls of this groovy, beachside eatery. It does a quality set meal for US$5 to US$7, and Fridays draws crowds for the popular barbecue (US$12). There's a small pool that customers can dip into, and an apartment upstairs that's occasionally for rent.

Jenny's Market (☎ 809-970-7503; Calle Principal) is a medium-sized market located just as you enter town. There's also a call center and internet café, and a small fast-food eatery that pumps out good drunk food – fried fish, club sandwiches, tacos and burritos. Delivery available.

Getting There & Around

You'll be happiest in Costambar if you have your own vehicle. If not, a *motoconcho* from Puerto Plata will cost you US$3, and a taxi US$7. If you're already in Costambar, try the local **taxi association** (☎ 809-970-7318).

Gua-gua lines C and F from Puerto Plata pass the front gate (every 15 minutes from 6am to 6pm), although the village is a good kilometer from the highway, and the beach another kilometer past that.

PLAYA COFRESÍ

Five kilometers west of Puerto Plata lies the quiet, condo-dwelling hamlet of Cofresí. You'll see no sign of the town's namesake – a Puerto Rican pirate who ravaged this coast – although some of the locals may remind you of extras in the movie *Love Wrecked* (2005), which was filmed here.

At one end of town sprawl two enormous (and excellent) all-inclusive resorts; at the other, Ocean World. In the middle, sandwiched between the two on a 500m stretch of beach road, is a tiny community of expats and condo dwellers, and a small, beautiful beach. It's a pleasant stop for a day or two, and also a tranquil place to base yourself for exploring Puerto Plata and the surrounding region.

Information

ATMs and exchange booths are located at the entrance of both all-inclusive resorts.

Medical center (☎ 809-970-7518; Sun Village Resort & Spa; ☻ 8am-1pm & 1:30-6pm, 24hr emergency service) Clearly visible from the main road into town; staff are multilingual and will treat nonguests.

Plaza Taína (☎ 809-970-7504) Has an internet café (per hour US$3), and sells hats, sunscreen and film. It's right on the main beach road.

Tourist Medical Services (☎ 809-586-1227; ☻ 24hr) A medical clinic affiliated with the Hacienda resorts. There's a pharmacy (open 9am to noon and 1pm to 6pm) next door. Has multilingual staff and serves guests and nonguests alike; for more serious cases.

Sights & Activities

With an enormous sign at the western end of the beach, it's impossible to miss Cofresí's main attraction, **Ocean World** (☎ 809-291-1000; www.oceanworld.net; adult/4-12yr/under 4yr US$60/45/free; ☻ 9am-6pm). The main attractions are the sea lions, dolphins, sharks and manta rays, the aviary, and the tiger pool and show. You can also swim with the dolphins (per person

US$140) or the sharks (US$60). There are several restaurants, a disco, and a casino on site, and boaters who tie up at the new marina get free entrance to the park as part of their mooring fee. The all-you-can-eat Sunday brunch (US$35) includes prime rib and lobster, and is reportedly excellent.

The **Dominican International Film Festival** (www.dominicaninternationalfilmfestival.com) is hosted each year in early November at Sun Village resort. It attracts a sizable gaggle of Hollywood B-list actors, and although admission is not cheap – US$35 for a day pass, up to US$250 for the VIP 'All-Access Pass' – the price includes buffet dinner and open bar.

Sleeping

There are two good all-inclusive resorts in Cofresí, but no hotels as such. There are plenty of condos for rent by the week, though, and a local restaurant rents rooms to independent travelers.

Chris & Mady's (☎ 809-970-7502; www.chrisandmadys.com; r US$50-80, apt US$120) The focal point of social life in Cofresí, Chris & Mady's now rents rooms in the building next door to the restaurant. The larger rooms have kitchens, living rooms, and oceanfront balconies, and are excellent value, and the best option for the independent traveler looking to check out Cofresí. There was also a large luxury condo development underway nearby when we were there, and Chris will be handling the rentals; two- and three-bedroom apartments will go for around US$1000 to US$1500 per week.

Lifestyle Hacienda Resorts (☎ 809-586-1227; www.hacienda-resorts.com; r per person US$150; P ☒ ☐ ☒) This enormous resort is so large you'll need a golf cart to get around. It's bright and shiny and new and completely over the top – but then that's the idea, right? There are four hotel buildings and some cabins and villas, and style and price vary widely. More downscale than Sun Village, Hacienda is also going the timeshare route – expect a salesperson to hassle you at some point during your stay.

Sun Village Resort & Spa (☎ 809-970-3364; www.sunvillageresorts.com; r per person US$210-260; P ☒ ☐ ☒) One of the best all-inclusive places on the north coast, Sun Village sprawls over the hillside, with the lobby, bar-restaurant and main pool area perched well above the beach. Pathways lead down past large units where biggish rooms have red-tile floors, air-con and comfortable beds; some have ocean views.

NORTH COAST

At the beach are another two pools and a children's area. Part of the resort has been redeveloped as fractionalized five-star condos, which you can rent by the week.

Playa Villas Management Company (☎ 809-970-7821, in the US 800-390-1138; www.puerto-plata.com; ⊠) This enterprise manages around 10 houses in Cofresí, ranging from two-bedroom cottages to seven-bedroom houses. Some have an ocean view and/or swimming pools. A housekeeper is assigned to each house and will help with cooking, cleaning, laundry and even shopping. Prices range from US$600 to US$6000 per week in high season (December 15 to April 30) and drop considerably in low season. With many repeat guests, the houses can get booked up months in advance – call or email for availability.

Eating

Rancho Esmeralda (☎ 809-396-5087; mains US$6-10; ⊗ breakfast, lunch & dinner) Standing on Playa Cofresí, you could be forgiven for not knowing this place even existed – it's hidden amid a stand of coconut palms on the spit of land that juts out at the eastern end of the beach. It's about a 10-minute walk along to the strand to this homely Swiss-German restaurant, which serves typical German fare – pork chops and sausages, of course – and cold, cheap beer.

ourpick **Chris & Mady's** (☎ 809-970-7502; www.chrisandmadys.com; mains US$8-20 ⊗ 8am-11pm) This pleasant sea-facing restaurant run by a Canadian-Dominican couple is in many ways the hub of Cofresí, where long-time visitors congregate for good food and conversation, and newcomers stop for friendly information and directions. Under an open-air thatched roof with tile floors and sturdy wooden tables, the restaurant serves some of the best seafood around, including fettuccine with shrimp, grilled catch of the day, and lobster, all at reasonable prices. On Sunday there's a barbecue that sees most of the community show up.

Los Tres Cocos (☎ 809-993-4503; Las Rocas; mains US$8-20; ⊗ dinner, closed Tue) Located 800m east of Cofresí in the Las Rocas neighborhood is this excellent Austrian-owned restaurant. Hidden away down a side street off the highway, this is a favorite of expats and locals alike – there's gourmet food (like duck breast in orange sauce, US$17), and Teutonic favorites like liver dumpling soup (US$5).

Beach House (☎ 809-970-7672; mains US$15-30; ⊗ noon-late; ⊠) Surround-sound speakers in outdoor 'rocks' greet you as you come up the walk. Ribs are the specialty here, and they ain't cheap – but then, where else can you lick gooey sauce from your fingers with your toes in the sand and the waves 5m away? The big-screen TV shows every sporting event known to humanity, and there's free wi-fi for customers. Tuesday night is two-for-one wings night.

Le Papillon (☎ 809-970-7640; mains US$15-30; ⊗ dinner, closed Mon) This German-run restaurant, 100m east of Cofresí up a small hill, serves excellent meals in a large palapa-roofed dining area with dark-wood tables, a checkerboard floor and seafaring decor, including a tank of sea turtles. Favorites include leg of rabbit, smoked yellowtail or dorado, pepper steaks and vegetable curry. Daily specials are usually a good deal.

Getting There & Away

Take the *gua-gua* C or F (US$0.30) from Puerto Plata. Going back to town take only the C – the F does lots of twists and turns in the city and take twice as long to get you to the center. It's a steep downhill walk of about 700m to the main beach area. There's *gua-gua* service until about 7pm. If you're driving, simply follow the main highway west.

There's also a taxi stand located just outside Ocean World.

EAST OF PUERTO PLATA

Cabarete long ago stole the crown of tourism capital of the north coast – here you can fill your days with surfing and mountain biking but still dig into great seafood at a beachside restaurant. Sosúa, Cabarete's seedier neighbor, has a pretty beach, and a good selection of restaurants and hotels. Further east, Río San Juan is a typical Dominican small town that sees few tourists, and is a good base for visiting nearby Playa Grande.

SOSÚA
pop 45,000

The inescapable fact of Sosúa is the prostitution – it's the sex tourism capital of the north coast. Bar after bar is full of sex workers, and men both single and in groups can expect to be accosted and propositioned, on the street, on the beach, and even in restaurants.

If you don't mind this sort of thing, or are happy to look the other way, Sosúa does

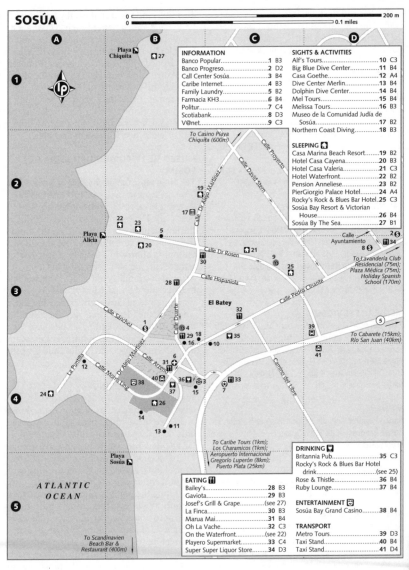

SOSÚA

offer a pretty, yellow-sand beach on a calm bay, ideal for swimming and snorkeling, plus some decent diving nearby. There's a good selection of hotels and restaurants, on average cheaper than trendy Cabarete, just 20 minutes away. Despite its more confronting qualities, Sosúa is a good base for exploring the north coast.

Orientation

As it passes along the south edge of Sosúa, the coastal highway becomes Carretera Gregorio Luperón. The main street into town off the highway is Calle Duarte, although Camino del Libre also works. Calle Pedro Clisante is Sosúa's main drag and is lined with shops, restaurants and bars.

NORTH COAST

The heart of the town is the intersection of Calles Duarte and Pedro Clisante. From there the beaches and most hotels, restaurants, bars and other services are a short walk away.

Information

INTERNET ACCESS

Alf's Tours (☎ 809-571-1734; www.alftour.com; Calle Pedro Clisante 12; per hr US$1.50; ⊗ 9am-6pm) This internet café runs by the tour operator next door.

Caribe Internet (☎ 809-915-2688; Calle Duarte 5; per hr US$2) The biggest and most modern email café in town; it also has webcams and scanners.

V@net (☎ 809-571-1708; Calle Dr Rosen 24; ⊗ 9:30am-midnight; per hr US$1.30) Inside a small supermarket.

LAUNDRY

Family Laundry (☎ 809-324-7922; cnr Calles Dr Rosen & Dr Alejo Martínez; per load US$5) 'Mores cheaper (sic) than your own house,' this family-owned and -run laundromat charges US$8 per load or US$1.30 per kilo.

Lavandería Club Residencial (per load US$6.80) Same-day service US$3 extra. Located behind Plaza Médica, near Calle Pedro Clisante.

MEDICAL SERVICES

The best medical center on the coast is 20 minutes away in neighboring Cabarete.

Farmacia KH3 (☎ 809-571-2350; Calle Pedro Clisante)

Plaza Médica (☎ 809-571-3007, emergency 809-854-1633; Calle Pedro Clisante 30; ⊗ 24hr) Medical clinic staffed by a general practitioner. Spanish-speaking only.

MONEY

Banco Popular (cnr Calles Dr Alejo Martínez & Sánchez)

Banco Progreso (Calle Pedro Clisante)

Scotiabank (Calle Pedro Clisante)

TELEPHONE

Call Center Sosúa (☎ 809-571-3464; Beachway Plaza; ⊗ 8am-7pm Mon-Fri, to 6pm Sat & Sun)

TRAVEL AGENCIES

Melissa Tours (☎ 809-571-2567; www.melissatours .com.do; Calle Duarte 2) A long-time locally owned agency, and one of the few bricks-and-mortar places left for you old-school types wanting to buy plane tickets.

Sights & Activities

BEACHES

Sosúa has two beaches. **Playa Sosúa** is the main beach, a long stretch of tawny sand backed by palm trees and often crowded with Dominican families and long-term visitors staying in local hotels and condos. To get there take the

downhill road between the Ruby Lounge and La Roca. A much better beach is **Playa Alicia**, located just around the corner at the end of Calle Dr Rosen. A broad half-moon of yellow sand lapped by blue water, it began to appear spontaneously around 2003 below the Hotel Waterfront – it's named after that hotel owner's mother. To get there, walk to the Sosúa By The Sea hotel and enter the parking lot. At the end on the left is a door, and a narrow alleyway provides beach access to the public.

MUSEO DE LA COMUNIDAD JUDÍA DE SOSÚA

The **Museo de la Comunidad Judía de Sosúa** (Jewish Community Museum of Sosúa; ☎ 809-571-1386; Calle Dr Alejo Martínez; admission US$3; ⊗ 9am-1pm, 2-4pm Mon-Fri), near Calle Dr Rosen, has exhibits describing the Jewish presence in the DR. At the multinational Evian conference in 1938 the DR was the only country to officially accept Jewish refugees fleeing Nazi repression in Germany. Around 350 families of refugees were settled in and around Sosúa. Most stayed only a few years – few were farmers by trade – but those who remained have been very successful in the dairy business, and Sosúa cheese is well known throughout the country. The museum has signs in Spanish and English, and is worth a stop.

DIVING & SNORKELING

Sosúa is generally considered the diving capital of the north coast. In addition to the dozen or so dive sites within boating range of Sosúa Bay, dive shops also organize excursions as far afield as Río San Juan and Cayo Arena. There's a good variety of fish here – 200 different kinds, according to some – plus hard and soft corals, drop-offs and sponges.

Among the popular dive spots nearby are Airport Wall, featuring a wall and tunnels in 12m to 35m of water; Zíngara Wreck, an upright 45m ship sunk in 1993 as an artificial reef in around 35m of water; and Coral Gardens and Coral Wall, both offering excellent coral formations in depths ranging from 14m to 53m.

Prices vary somewhat from shop to shop, but are generally US$30 to US$35 for a one-tank dive, plus US$5 to US$10 for rental equipment. Booking a dive package brings the price down considerably – with a 10-dive package, the per-dive price can be as low as US$25 if you have your own gear. All of Sosúa's shops offer certification courses. Snorkeling trips are available at all shops, and cost US$30 to US$45 per person, depending on the length and number of stops; equipment is always included.

One big difference among the shops is that the predominant language among the staff is German, though English and Spanish are spoken by all. Some of Sosúa's most established dive outfits:

Big Blue Dive Center (☎ 809-571-2916; Playa Sosúa; ⊗ 9am-5pm) At the end of the road to Playa Sosúa. Also does mountain-biking trips.

Dive Center Merlin (☎ 809-571-2963, 809-571-4309; www.divecenter-merlin.com; Playa Sosúa; ⊗ 9am-5pm) At the end of the road to Playa Sosúa. Offers PADI (Professional Association of Diving Instructors) certification courses.

Dolphin Dive Center (☎ 809-571-3589; www.dolphin divecenter.com; Playa Sosúa; ⊗ 9am-5pm) This operation has its office at the Sosúa Bay Resort (p182).

our pick Northern Coast Diving (☎ 809-571-1028; www.northerncoastdiving.com; Calle Pedro Clisante 8; ⊗ 8am-6pm) This well-respected dive shop is one of the best, and the most willing to create customized excursions to little-visited dive sites (although it'll cost you).

Courses

There are two places in town you can learn Spanish. Expect to pay roughly US$10 to US$12 per hour depending on the length of the course.

our pick Casa Goethe (☎ 809-571-3185; www.edase .com; La Puntilla 2; ⊗ 9am-5pm Mon-Fri) offers German and English classes to locals, and Spanish classes to foreigners. This German-run outfit has private and group classes, both on ordinary (four hours per day) and intensive (six hours per day) schedules. Classes are held in the mornings, and the center can organize activities like scuba diving or salsa-dancing classes in the afternoon. Long-term housing can be arranged either at the center itself or in area hotels, and rates usually include breakfast.

Spanish classes by the week are offered at **Holiday Spanish School** (☎ 809-571-1847; www .holiday-spanish-school.com; Calle Pedro Clisante 141) in El Colibrí Resort, a small hotel east of the town center. Lessons are offered to beginners and advanced students alike and are given in two-hour increments; the first hour typically focuses on grammar and vocabulary, the second is centered around speaking. Prices vary according to the length of the course and the number of students. Housing packages are available.

Tours

There are a lot of cheesy package tours on offer at numerous agencies along the north coast. Many involve spending the majority of your day on a bus getting to and from your destination. Be especially wary of any tour that purports to show you 'Dominican culture' – the 'local school' you'll visit will be more a Potemkin village than an authentic place of youth learning.

Tours that are most worth doing include rafting in Jarabacoa (four hours each way, US$70 to US$80), Cayo Arena for snorkeling (three hours each way, US$50 to US$60), whale-watching in Samaná (from mid-January to mid-March, four hours each way, US$120 to US$140), and anything involving a boat – catamaran tours (US$70 to US$80) and deep-sea fishing (US$70 to US$100) are hard to fake, and are generally good value.

Alf's Tours (☎ 809-571-1734; www.alftour.com; Calle Pedro Clisante 12) Run by a friendly operator with staff who speak Spanish, French, English and German.

Melissa Tours (☎ 809-571-2567; www.melissatours .com.do; Calle Duarte 2) Also sells plane tickets.

Mel Tours (☎ 809-571-2057; ww.mel-tour.com) On the road to Playa Sosúa.

Sleeping

BUDGET

Rocky's Rock & Blues Bar Hotel (☎ 809-571-2951; www.rockysbar.com; Calle Dr Rosen 22; r US$22; ✷ ▯) Basic but comfortable, the five rooms at Rocky's are a great deal. All are spotless, breezy and have cable TV. A mellow lounge with couches and tables spills into the bar/restaurant area, where locals and travelers hang out most of the afternoon and evening. The free wi-fi attracts laptop-laden loungers throughout the day. The Canadian owner is friendly and especially knowledgeable about the area.

Pension Anneliese (☎ 809-571-2208; Calle Dr Rosen; s/d US$35/50; ▯ ▯ ▩) If parrots were cats, then the crusty German widow who runs this aging hotel at the western end of Calle Dr Rosen would surely be an old cat lady. She's been renting 10 rooms in this sprawling house for nearly 30 years, and still maintains a certain Teutonic spotlessness. The rooms all have fans and either one king- or two queen-sized beds, and there are ocean views from the front terrace. A small pool mitigates the lack of air-con.

MIDRANGE

Hotel Casa Valeria (☎ 809-571-3565; www.hotelcasavale ria.com; Calle Dr Rosen 28; unit with/without kitchen US$50/45; ❄ 🏊) All nine rooms at this cozy hotel are slightly different, whether in size, furnishings or decor. Three units have kitchens (with gas burners), the others are hotel-like rooms with comfortable beds, brand-new furnishings and painted pink. Rooms are set around a leafy courtyard with a kidney-shaped pool in the middle; all have cable TV, fans and new ceramic-tiled bathrooms. The new Dutch owners have opened a tasty tapas bar next door.

Hotel Waterfront (☎ 809-571-2670; www.hotel waterfrontdr.com; Calle Dr Rosen 1; s/d/t US$45/50/55, with air-con US$55/60/65; ❄ P 🏊) The Waterfront offers 27 plain but comfortable rooms – 10 in stand-alone bungalows, the rest in a two-story building. All have a terrace or balcony, overhead fan, clean hot-water bathroom, fridge and up to three firm beds. All rooms are in a leafy garden tucked behind the inviting pool, with a great seaside restaurant and Sosúa's best beach right in front. Who cares if there's no TV?

Hotel Casa Cayena (☎ 809-571-2651; www.hotel casacayena.com; Calle Dr Rosen 25; s/d US$65/85; P ❄ 🖵 🏊) This hotel contains 24 rooms on two floors, connected by broad breezy corridors. All rooms have red-tile floors, clean modern bathrooms with hot water, cable TV and security boxes. It's a bit faded – think shiny motel bedspreads – but there's a pretty L-shaped pool, and Playa Alicia is just down the street. A small outdoor restaurant serves breakfast.

our pick **Sosúa By The Sea** (☎ 809-571-3222; www .sosuabythesea.com; cnr Calles B Phillips & David Stern; s/d/ ste incl breakfast US$70/120/165; P ❄ 🖵 🏊) This crisp, beautiful, eye-dropping resort has the best lodging in Sosúa. Set on a coral spit on the aptly named Playa Chiquita, rooms are recently renovated in a minimalist style – think black and white, and shiny chrome. In addition to its 58 studios, there are 33 fully equipped apartments with kitchen. All-inclusive service is available for a US$20 surcharge. One of Sosúa's best restaurants, Josef's Grill & Grape (see opposite), is part of the complex.

PierGiorgio Palace Hotel (☎ 809-571-2626; www .piergiorgiopalace.com; Calle La Puntilla; s incl breakfast US$85-105, d US$85-195, penthouse US$295; ❄ P 🏊) Popular with wedding planners, the PierGiorgio is built on a rocky cliff overlooking the ocean. It's lavishness – red carpet, ostentatious deco-

ration, grand wooden staircase – will appeal to some, but others may find it a bit tacky. The rooms are spotless, though, and the sea views magnificent – ask for a room on the 3rd floor. Room rate includes breakfast, and the cliffside restaurant (mains from US$7 to US$32) is an undeniably romantic spot.

TOP END

Sosúa boasts two all-inclusive resorts. Both are on the beach, a short stroll into town – the best of both worlds.

Sosúa Bay Resort & Victorian House (☎ 809-571-4000; www.sosuabayresort.com; Calle Pedro Clisante; s US$95-130, d US$130-210; P ❄ 🖵 🏊) Set on a bluff jutting out into the ocean, the Sosúa Bay Resort is directly in the middle of town, at the end of Calle Pedro Clisante. Two adjacent buildings offer distinctly different grades of accommodation – the Victorian House half sports boutique rooms at boutique prices. The reception area greets you with sweeping vistas of the ocean. A casino was opened here in early 2008.

Casa Marina Beach Resort (☎ 809-562-7475; www .amhsamarina.com; Calle Dr Alejo Martínez; s US$150-165, d US$200-220; P ❄ 🖵 🏊) Where the Sosúa Bay Resort has little in the way of grounds, the Casa Marina is a huge leafy complex with three pools, five restaurants and almost 400 rooms arranged in three-story buildings. The rooms are classic all-inclusive: clean and comfortable but not memorable in any way, with cable TV and a balcony, and most looking onto the pool. The hotel has direct access to Playa Alicia and a more rustic beach about 150m to the east.

Eating

Sosúa has a good selection of top-notch restaurants, and several quite acceptable midrange eateries.

Gaviota (☎ 809-603-4611; Calle Duarte; set meals US$4; ☾ breakfast, lunch & dinner) If you're after a typical Dominican meal, this is the place to go – meals come with rice, savory beans, a good portion of chicken and a half-hearted attempt at a salad. There is a menu but order from it at your peril – readers are recommended to order the plate of the day, except perhaps at breakfast time.

Rocky's Rock & Blues Bar Hotel (☎ 809-571-2951; www.rockysbar.com; Calle Dr Rosen 22; mains US$4-15; ☾ 7am-late; 🖵) Rocky's is a Sosúa institution. The sign outside says 'World Famous Ribs,'

WHERE EVERYBODY KNOWS YOUR NAME

Nearly 200 restaurants, bars and gift shops line the shady Sosúa beach promenade. One has drawn quite a following. The **Scandinavien Beach Bar and Restaurant** (☎ 809-399-8321; Playa Sosúa 152; ☿ 9:30am-6pm) is famous for its great burgers, cold beers, and, more importantly, the cleanest bathroom on the beach.

Then disaster struck – in 2006 a fire gutted the restaurant. The owner, Tom Nilsson, thinks it may have been arson. He sustained more than US$100,000 in losses, and was preparing to return to Norway when a miracle happened.

Sosúa's many repeat visitors told him they wouldn't let him leave. Customers flew down from New York with suitcases full of plates and cups and knives and forks. A DJ donated a laptop; another customer bought the hardwood picnic tables. In total he received donations upwards of US$50,000.

These days you'll find Nilsson grilling burgers to English rock music and joking with his customers. And the bathroom? Still the cleanest on the beach.

---

but that's just the beginning – the breakfasts are great value, the steaks are Dominican beef (not imported), and the beers some of the cheapest in town. The music, like the name suggests, is pure rock and blues.

Oh La Vache (☎ 829-860-8317; Calle Pedro Clisante; pizzas US$8-15; ☿ lunch & dinner) Decorated whimsically in a cow theme, this pizza joint makes some of the best crispy-crust pizzas on the north coast. Owned by a French couple, this is also a pleasant place to while away the early evening with a beer.

Bailey's (☎ 809-571-3085; Calle Dr Alejo Martinez; mains US$8-20; ☿ breakfast, lunch & dinner) A favorite among expats, this Austrian-owned restaurant is set around a large, horseshoe-shaped bar, and its specialties include chili burgers (US$9) and enormous schnitzel sandwiches (US$11). The decor includes lots of rattan furniture, and there's a small play area with a slide and jungle gym to keep the kids amused.

Marua Mai (☎ 809-571-3682, cnr Calle Clisante & Arzeno; mains US$8-25; ☿ breakfast, lunch & dinner) Right smack in the middle of things, this two-level, tropical-themed restaurant is a solid, midrange choice. Its burgers are great, but it also does lobster by the kilo and sometimes has seafood specials. There's a pleasant bar to sit for a quiet drink before or after. Good breakfasts, too.

On the Waterfront (☎ 809-571-3024; Hotel Waterfront; Calle Dr Rosen 1; mains US$10-30; ☿ breakfast, lunch & dinner) Set on a bluff overlooking Playa Alicia – and with waiters who wear big red firemans' suspenders – what's not to like about the Waterfront? It does great seafood options – like almond-brandy grouper – and

the steaks are recommended. Come at sunset for an aperitif.

La Finca (☎ 809-571-3925; www.restaurantelafinca .net; mains US$12-50; ☿ lunch & dinner) If you're after the very best money can buy in Sosúa, then La Finca is a must visit. Steak and seafood are the rock stars here – there's chateaubriand (US$18), surf and turf (US$24), and a mixed seafood platter for two (US$50). It has an amazing cocktail list, and the menu is in five languages, including Russian.

our pick **Josef's Grill & Grape** (☎ 809-571-3222; cnr Calles B Phillips & David Stem; mains US$35-40; ☿ dinner Thu-Sat) Set in the grounds of Sosúa by the Sea (see opposite) with the ocean waves crashing just meters from your table, Josef's offers a different menu every week from its gourmet chef – expect creative variations on the usual steak-and-seafood theme, and tasty, tropical-influenced desserts.

Playero Supermarket (☎ 809-571-1821; ☿ 8am-10pm), on the main highway, offers a good selection of local produce and imported, hard-to-find delicacies. **Super Super Liquor Store** (☎ 809-571-3862; cnr Calles Pedro Clisante & Ayuntamiento; ☿ 8am-8pm Mon-Sat) is where you can pimp your vice at a rock-bottom price. It has a good selection of cigars, too.

Drinking

Sosúa's nightlife is packed with bars and clubs catering to prostitutes and their customers. If this is not your scene, the following may be decent options.

Britannia Pub (☎ 809-571-1959; britanniabarsosua@ yahoo.com; Calle Pedro Clisante; ☿ 10am-late) Popular with the many expats who live in town, this pleasant retreat is a reliable spot for a quiet drink. There's a good book exchange at the back, and the bar food ain't bad, either – go for the US$3 burger and wings specials after 4pm.

Rose & Thistle (☎ 809-935-9203; Beachway Plaza; 9am-late) Owned by an expat English couple, this small bar is in the narrow alleyway that leads down to Ruby Lounge. It does an excellent all-day English breakfast, and mouthwatering homemade sausage rolls and pork pies. The owner cures his own ham and bacon – worth asking about, if you're in town for a while.

Ruby Lounge (cnr Calles Pedro Clisante & Arzeno; 1pm-late) Just outside the entrance to the Sosúa Bay Resort, this hip Canadian-owned bar has happy hours every day from 1pm to 8:30pm, live shows and music every Friday, and karaoke on Sunday. The bar and tiny stage area are downstairs (where the party sometimes spills onto the sidewalks) and there's a mellow lounge area upstairs.

Entertainment
There are two casinos in town.

Casino Playa Chiquita (☎ 809-571-2591; Calle Dr Alejo Martínez; 8pm-4am Mon-Thu, 4pm-4am Fri-Sun) If you're up for a little Texas hold 'em or just want to try your luck on the slot machines, then this casino is a decent place to spend an evening. Located about a kilometer from town, at the eastern end of Calle Dr Alejo Martínez, it's best to take a cab there and back. Free drinks for all players.

Sosúa Bay Grand Casino (☎ 809-571-4000; www .sosuabayresort.com; end of Calle Pedro Clisante) Part of the Sosúa Bay Resort, this new casino is right in the center of town. It was still under construction when we passed through, but will be one of the largest casinos on the coast when finished, and should be open when you get there.

Getting There & Away
AIR
Sosúa is much closer to the **Aeropuerto Internacional Gregorio Luperón** (☎ 809-586-0107) than Puerto Plata, although it's commonly referred to as 'Puerto Plata airport.' We're guilty of the same bias – see the Puerto Plata section (p173) for more info. A taxi from the airport to Sosúa is US$15. You can also walk 500m from the terminal to the highway and flag down a passing *gua-gua* (US$0.30, 10 minutes).

BUS
Caribe Tours (☎ 809-571-3808; Carretera a Puerto Plata) has a bus depot on the highway at the edge of Las Charamicos neighborhood, 1km southwest of the city center. It offers hourly service, on the hour, from Sosúa to Santo Domingo (US$8.50, five hours, hourly from 6am to 7pm).

If your final destination is Sosúa, you'll find **Metro Tours** (☎ 809-571-3480; Av Luperón) much more convenient – its depot is right in the middle of town. It runs services to Puerto Plata, Santiago, and onwards to Santo Domingo, at 8:20am, 10:20am, 1:20pm and 5:50pm. Buy tickets at the pharmacy in the Texaco gas station in the middle of Sosúa.

El Canario (☎ 809-291-5594) is a Puerto Plata–based bus that leaves daily to Samaná (US$5.20, 2½ to three hours) at 7am from the main *parada* (bus stop). This is your only option, as neither Metro nor Caribe Tours has direct service there. Be sure to call the day before to reserve your seat.

For destinations along the coast, go to the highway and flag down any passing *gua-gua*. They pass every 15 minutes or so, with services to Puerto Plata (US$0.60, 30 minutes), Cabarete (US$0.30, 20 minutes) and Río San Juan (US$2.10, 1½ hours).

Getting Around
You can walk just about everywhere in Sosúa, except the hotels east of the center, which are better reached by *motoconcho* or taxi. The former are easy to find around town, while shared taxis for intercity travel along the coast can be located at a **taxi stand** (☎ 809-571-3027) on the corner of Calles Pedro Clisante and Dr Rosen.

To rent a car, make your way to the airport (8km away).

CABARETE
pop 17,000
Cities gentrify; surf towns grow up. So it has been in Cabarete. This one-time farming hamlet is now the adventure-sports capital of the country, booming with condos and new development. You'll find a sophisticated, grown-up beach town, with top-notch hotels, and a beach dining experience second to none (not to mention the best winds and waves on the island).

Cabarete is an ideal spot to base yourself for exploring the north coast – you're within two hours' drive of the best that the coast has to offer, and if you want to go surfing, or windsurfing, or kitesurfing, heck, you don't even need to leave town.

You'll hear a babble of five or six languages as you walk Cabarete's single street. So strong is the foreign flavor that Dominicans from the capital come here on weekends just to tourist-watch – tourists themselves become a tourist attraction.

Orientation

Cabarete is a one-street town, built up around the highway, which runs right through the middle. Virtually all hotels, restaurants and shops are on the main drag, making it a congested, though easy-to-navigate place.

To the southeast of town lies the Pro Cab neighborhood, where a number of budget hotels congregate. To the southwest, a single street leads through the principally Dominican neighborhood of Callejón de la Loma, and dead-ends at the Caves of Cabarete (right).

Information

Banco Progreso is located right in the center of town, while Scotiabank is at the eastern end of town; there are exchange offices that accept major currencies and traveler's checks on the main drag. There is no post office in Cabarete, but hotels often post mail for guests. At the time of research, there were also no travel agencies; for plane tickets and other services, try Melissa Tours in Sosúa (p180).

Active Cabarete (www.activecabarete.com) A website with a range of information including activities and events, weather, and 'special stuff.'

All City (☎ 809-571-0112; per hr US$1; ◷ 9am-9pm Mon-Sat, 10am-6pm Sun) One of the best internet cafés on the north coast, with fast connection and headphones for VOIP calls. There's also a small bank of phones for domestic and international calls.

Family Lavandería (per kg US$2; ◷ 8am-7pm Mon-Sat) This laundry is at the eastern end of town, opposite Janet's Supermarket.

Fujifilm Digital (☎ 809-571-9536; fujifilm02@hotmail .com; per hr US$1) Next to No Work Team, this photo shop has a fast internet connection and headphones.

Politur (tourist police; ☎ 809-571-0713) At the eastern entrance to town.

Servi-Med (☎ 809-571-0964; ◷ 24hr) Four MDs, one dentist and a chiropractor. Highly recommended by expats and travelers alike, this is one of the best medical centers on the coast. The foreign-trained practitioners speak English, German, and Spanish, and do house calls.

Sights
BEACHES

Cabarete's beaches are its main attractions, and not just for sun and sand. They're each home to a different water sport, and are great places to watch beginner and advanced athletes alike.

Playa Cabarete, the main beach in front of town, is the best place for watching windsurfing, though the very best windsurfers are well offshore at the reef line. Look for them performing huge high-speed jumps and even end-over-end flips.

Bozo Beach is the western downwind side of Playa Cabarete, and so named because of all the beginner windsurfers and kiteboarders who don't yet know how to tack up wind and so wash up on Bozo's shore. There are more kiteboarders at Bozo and the surf here is better for boogie boarding.

Kite Beach, 2km west of town, is a sight to behold on windy days, when scores of kiters of all skill levels negotiate huge sails and 30m lines amid the waves and traffic. On those days there's no swimming here, as you're liable to get run over.

Playa Encuentro, 4km west of town, is the place to go for surfing, though top windsurfers and kiteboarders sometimes go there to take advantage of the larger waves. The beach itself is OK, but the strong tide and rocky shallows make swimming here difficult.

La Boca, at the mouth of the Río Yásica, 7km east of town, is an ideal spot for wakeboarding – more than 2km of straight, flat river water to practice your latest trick.

CAVES OF CABARETE

Part of **Parque Nacional El Choco**, the caves are walking distance from town, 1.3km from the entrance to Callejón de la Loma. Here you can take a two-hour **tour** (US$15; ◷ 9am-3:30pm) of a number of privately managed caves. Bring a swimsuit – you can swim in a small pool in a crystal-stalactite cave 25m below the surface. The current tour operator was making plans to move abroad when we were there, and it was unclear what will happen to the caves after that. The caves are padlocked by management and cannot be visited independently.

Activities

More information on all of these activities can be found in the Outdoors chapter (p59).

NORTH COAST

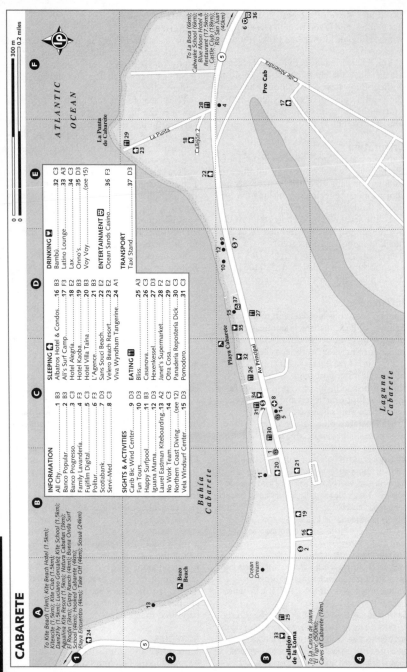

NORTH COAST

CABARETE

INFORMATION
All City.....................................1	B3
Banco Popular.........................2	B3
Banco Progresso.....................3	C3
Family Lavandería...................4	F3
Fujifilm Digital.........................5	C3
Politur......................................6	F3
Scotiabank...............................7	D3
Servi-Med................................8	C3

SIGHTS & ACTIVITIES
Carib Bic Wind Center............9	D3
Fun Tours...............................10	D3
Happy Surfpool......................11	B3
Iguana Mama.........................12	D3
Laurel Eastman Kiteboarding..13	A2
No Work Team.................(see 12)	
Northern Coast Diving...........14	C3
Vela Windsurf Center............15	D3

SLEEPING
Albatros Hotel & Condos.......16	B3
Ali's Surf Camp......................17	F3
Hotel Alegría.........................18	E2
Hotel Kaoba..........................19	B3
Hotel Villa Taína....................20	B3
L'Agence...............................21	B3
Sans Souci Beach..................22	E2
Velero Beach Resort..............23	D3
Viva Wyndham Tangerine......24	A1

EATING
Bliss......................................25	A3
Casanova...............................26	C3
Hexenkessel..........................27	D3
Janet's Supermarket..............28	F2
Otra Cosa..............................29	E2
Panadería Repostería Dick.....30	C3
Pomodoro.............................31	C3

DRINKING
Bambú...................................32	C3
Latino Lounge........................33	A3
Lax...34	C3
Onno's...................................35	D3
Voy Voy............................(see 15)	

ENTERTAINMENT
Ocean Sands Casino...............36	F3

TRANSPORT
Taxi Stand..............................37	D3

FOUR BEST TIME-FOR-A-BEER MOMENTS

The north coast has enough adrenaline-surging activities to keep your heart rate permanently elevated. Sometimes an ice-cold Presidente beer is medically necessary.

- Wiping out while surfing on Playa Encuentro (p188), under 4m-high waves – oh yeah, time for a beer.

- Screaming as you jump down as far as 5m into crystal-blue pools at the waterfalls at Damajagua (p196). *Dos cervezas, por favor.*

- Barreling down the hills outside of Cabarete (p189) on a mountain bike, and hitting a rock. *Si, Señor* Presidente.

- Reaching lift-off velocity while kitesurfing (below) for the first time – yee-haw! This cowboy's got a thirst.

WINDSURFING

The combination of strong, steady winds, relatively shallow water and a rockless shore creates perfect conditions for windsurfing here.

Board and sail rentals average US$30 to US$35 per hour, US$60 to US$65 per day or US$280 to US$300 per week. For a bit more, shops offer 'nonconsecutive rentals' so you get multiday prices but you don't have to go out every day. Renters are usually required to purchase damage insurance for an additional US$50 per week. Private lessons cost around US$50 for an hour, US$200 for a four-session course, with discounts for groups.

Carib Bic Wind Center (☎ 809-571-0640; caribwind .com) With more than 20 years' experience, the Bic Center is the oldest in town. It also rents bodyboards and Lasers (for those of you who prefer an actual boat attached to your sail).

Happy Surfpool (☎ 809-571-0784; www.happy cabarete.com; Villa Taína Hotel) This friendly shop also sells quality windsurfing equipment.

Vela Windsurf Center (☎ 809-571-0805; velacaba rete.com) One of the best choices for windsurfing in Cabarete. On the main beach, it uses excellent gear, and can also rent sea kayaks (per hour US$10 to US$15). Works in conjunction with kitesurfing school, Dare2Fly (see right).

KITESURFING

Cabarete is one of the top places in the world for kitesurfing, and the sport has eclipsed windsurfing as the town's sport *du jour.* Kite Beach, 2km west of town, has ideal conditions for the sport, which entails strapping yourself to a modified surfboard and a huge inflatable wind foil then skimming and soaring across the water. Bozo Beach at the west end of the city beach is also a good spot and typically less crowded. A number of kitesurfing schools offer multiday courses for those who want to learn – just to go out by yourself you'll need at least three to four days of instruction (two to three hours' instruction per day). The learning curve for the sport is quite steep – you'll need several weeks to get good enough to really enjoy yourself.

Expect to pay US$50 to US$70 per hour for private instruction, or roughly US$400 to US$500 for a three- to four-day course. Schools and instructors vary considerably in personality, so spend some time finding one where you feel comfortable. Kitesurfing is a potentially dangerous sport and it is extremely important that you feel free to ask questions and voice fears or concerns, and that you receive patient, ego-free answers in return. The **International Kiteboarding Organization** (www.ikointl.com) has a new feature listing student ratings for schools and instructors.

About half of the schools are located on Kite Beach.

Dare2Fly (☎ 809-571-0805; main street, Cabarete) Owned by Vela Windsurf Center, Dare2Fly has a center next to Agualina Kite Resort (p190) on Kite Beach. You can also inquire at Vela about classes and equipment.

Kite Club (☎ 809-571-9748; www.kiteclubcabarete .com) This well-run club is at the top of Kite Beach, and has a fantastic atmosphere for hanging out and relaxing between sessions. The tiny kitchen delivers delicious fresh ahi tuna salads and sandwiches.

Kitexcite (☎ 809-571-9509; www.kitexcite.com; Kite Beach) This award-winning school uses radio helmets and optional offshore sessions to maximize instruction.

Laurel Eastman Kiteboarding (☎ 809-571-0564; www.laureleastman.com) Friendly, safety-conscious shop located on Bozo Beach and run by one of the world's top kiteboarders. Offers lessons in five languages. If you're walking along the beach from Cabarete, look for the canvas-sail roof of the restaurant next door.

Luciano Gonzalez Kite School (☎ 809-986-6454; lucianocabarete@hotmail.com) Two-time winner of the Master of the Ocean, Luciano now runs this small school opposite Kite Beach. Very patient with beginners. Offers a three-day, US$300 introductory course.

SURFING

Some of the best waves for surfing on the entire island – up to 4m – break over reefs 4km west of Cabarete on Playa Encuentro. The waves break both right and left and are known by names like El Canal, Encuentro, La Barca and Preciosa. Several outfits in town and on Playa Encuentro rent surfboards and offer instruction. Surfboard rental for a day is around US$25 to US$30; a three-hour course costs US$45 to US$50 per person, and five-day surf camps cost US$200 to US$225 per person. All the surf schools have small offices on Playa Encuentro.

Ali's Surf Camp (☎ 809-571-0733; alissurfcamp.com) Part of the hotel of the same name (opposite). Frequent shuttle service from Cabarete to Encuentro for surfers.

Buena Onda (☎ 829-877-0768; www.cabaretebuena onda.com) On Playa Encuentro.

No Work Team (☎ 809-571-0820; www.noworkteam cabarete.com) In the center of town. Also has a surf school on Encuentro.

Take Off (☎ 809-963-7873; www.321takeoff.com; Playa Encuentro) The German owner also organizes the Master of the Ocean competition.

WAKEBOARDING

Kitesurfers swear that this is a great way to develop your board skills, and on windless days you'll find more than a few out at La Boca going out for a tow or two. The river mouth at La Boca has more than 2km of flat, smooth water to play with, and attracts devoted wakeboarders from around the world.

Cabwake School (☎ 829-866-3929; www.cabwake .com; ☺ 9am-6pm), 6km east of town, is the only operator licensed to tow on the river. A 20-minute tow will set you back US$35, and week-long 'wake camps' – 10 to 15 tows in a week – are available at significant discount.

HORSEBACK RIDING

The fully equipped **Gipsy Ranch** (☎ 809-571-1373) riding stables are situated right near Playa Encuentro. Gipsy Ranch charges US$16 per person for an hour's ride on the beach, or US$52 for a longer, half-day ride. It can also organize longer excursions along the beach and in the nearby hills. The French owner is trilingual. From the entrance to Encuentro, continue down toward the beach and turn left. You'll find the stables opposite the Coconut Palms Resort.

DIVING

The well-respected Sosúa-based dive shop **Northern Coast Diving** (☎ 809-571-1028; www.northern coastdiving.com) has a representative in the offices of Iguana Mama (see below), and can organize excursions from Río San Juan in the east to Monte Cristi in the west. You're better off, though, popping over to Sosúa to compare prices and services (see p180).

MASSAGE

Michelle Bourdeau (☎ 809-851-9399; www.cabarete massagetherapy.com; massages per hr US$60; ☺ 10am-7pm Mon-Sat) is a highly recommended Canadian massage therapist. Perfect for those après-surf aches and pains. By appointment only.

Courses

Dance teacher **Tony Vargas** (☎ 809-916-4551; www .a-bailar.net; lessons per hr US$14) offers salsa, merengue and *bachata* (popular guitar music based on bolero rhythms) lessons in the dance studio in his home.

Tours

ourpick **Iguana Mama** (☎ 809-571-0908; www.iguana mama.com), the leading adventure-sports tour operator on the north coast, is in a class of its own. Its specialties are mountain biking (easy to insanely difficult, US$65) and cascading. It is the only operator that takes you to the 27th waterfall at Damajagua (US$85), and it has pioneered a new cascading tour to Ciguapa Falls, which only Iguana Mama offers. There's also a variety of hiking trips, including a half-day walk (US$45) into the hills behind Cabarete (Parque Nacional El Choco), and a full-day trip to Mount Isabel de Torres (US$80), just outside Puerto Plata. Its Pico Duarte trek is expensive, but handy if you want transportation to and from Cabarete (per person US$450). Iguana Mama can also arrange a number of halfday and full-day canyoning opportunities in the area (US$90 to US$125). Action and adventure junkies should ask about the oneweek 'Mama Knows Best' tour – seven days of nonstop adrenaline.

The owner of **Fun Tours** (☎ 809-571-0250), next door to Iguana Mama, will happily concede that with his tours, you get less than Iguana Mama, but he also charges you a lot less. Pay less, get less – your call. It offers the usual range of package tours, including a day trip to Cayo Arena (US$55), and an abridged version of the Damajagua Falls tour (you only go as far as the seventh waterfall).

If strapping a GPS and a machete to your bike and going out bush is your idea of a good time, hook up with **Max 'Maximo' Martinez** (☎ 809-882-5634; maxofthemt@yahoo.es), an intense, creative mountain-bike guide.

Festivals & Events

Master of the Ocean (☎ 809-963-7873; www.master oftheocean.com) is a triathlon of surfing, windsurfing and kitesurfing held in the final week of February. From the beach you can watch some spectacular performances.

Also in the last week of February, sandsculpture enthusiasts convene in Cabarete for the **International Sand Castle Competition**.

Held in Santiago and Cabarete in early November, the **Dominican Jazz Festival** (www.dr jazzfestival.com) attracts top musical talent from around the country and even abroad. A large stage and a beer tent are set up at the western end of the beach, and the players trumpet jazz into the night.

Sleeping

Cabarete's hotel rooms are slowly being condo-ized. In low season, you can pick up great deals on long-term rentals, but in high season – when condo owners return – hotel rooms can be hard to find. Book well in advance.

L'Agence (☎ 809-571-0999; www.agencerd.com; in Ocean Dream) Located in monster condo development Ocean Dream, L'Agence can help you find a condo rental.

BUDGET

Caribica Sanssouci Aparthotels (☎ 809-571-0755; www .caribica.com; r per person US$12-20; P ❊) The Sans Souci empire spans seven hotels and 75 apartments along the Cabarete strip. They're all clean and acceptable, if somewhat uninspired, but at this price, who cares? All have a small kitchenette, cable TV and a safe. The **Sans Souci Beach** property at the eastern end of the beach is the nicest. Ask for an ocean view.

our pick **Ali's Surf Camp** (☎ 809-571-0733; alis surfcamp.com; s US$29-44, d US$33-66, apt US$75-120; P ❊ 🖳 🛋) The closest thing Cabarete has to a backpackers, this place rocks – the German owner serves up great portions of barbecued meat for dinner, where guests sit at picnic tables and, as he put it, 'are forced to make friends.' (Even if you're not a guest,

it's worth the short walk here for dinner.) The rooms are rustic, there's no air-con and you'll want to use the mosquito net provided (it's south of town adjacent to the lagoon). Surf school on site.

Hotel Alegría (☎ 809-571-0455; www.hotel-alegria .com; Callejón 2; r US$35, with ocean view US$55, studio/ apt US$55/120; P 🖳) Hidden down one of Cabarete's few side streets, the Alegría may not have beach access, but from the wooden deck that towers from the top of the hotel you have an unrivalled view out over the beach and ocean. There's a small gym with treadmill and weights, and the studios and apartment each have kitchens.

MIDRANGE

Hotel Kaoba (☎ 809-571-0300; www.kaoba.com; s US$37-40, d US$47-52, ste US$65-85; P ❊ 🖳 🛋) The Kaoba has 25 charming bungalows set on lush grounds away from the main drag. Most rooms have kitchenettes; all have cable TV and minibars. The pool welcomes guests as they enter the complex and a restaurant/ bar at the front of the hotel is often hopping. Service tends to be a bit surly, though.

Hooked Cabarete (☎ 809-935-9221; hookedcabarete .com; Playa Encuentro; s/d/tr US$39/52/66; P ❊ 🖳 🛋) This small hotel feels like staying in someone's home. It offers five clean, self-contained apartments at Playa Encuentro, and is perfect for the hardcore surfer, or those wanting a bit more seclusion. It also rents scooters so you can get into town easily.

Albatros Hotel & Condos (☎ 809-571-0841; www .albatroscabarete.com; r US$45-70, apt US$96-145, penthouse US$145-165; P 🛋) Set back from the road at the west end of town, the Albatros offers clean and cheerful rooms amid a palm-tree-laden garden. Standard rooms come with a sitting area, a ceiling fan and a fridge. Studios and apartments come in various sizes: the smallest is a regular-sized room with a kitchenette; the largest is a two-story condo. A welcoming pool is the centerpiece of the grounds.

Kite Beach Hotel (☎ 809-571-0878; www.kite beachhotel.com; Kite Beach; s/d incl breakfast US$60/66, studio s/d US$70/80, apt US$90-240, penthouse US$450-600; P ❊ 🖳 🛋) This oceanfront hotel boasts well-appointed rooms with gleaming tile floors, good-sized bathrooms and satellite TV. All suites and apartments have balconies that afford at least partial ocean views. The laid-back pool area makes a great place to watch the action in the sky and on the water.

NORTH COAST

An extensive breakfast buffet is also included in the rate.

Agualina Kite Resort (☎ 809-571-0787; www .agualina.com; Kite Beach; r/studio/apt US$70/85/150; P ⊠ 🖳 🕿) Opened in 2004, this is the most comfortable lodging on Kite Beach. Studios and apartments have stylish, well-equipped kitchens – stainless-steel refrigerators are an especially nice touch – and large modern bathrooms with glass showers and gleaming fixtures. There's free wi-fi throughout the building.

TOP END

Hotel Villa Taína (☎ 809-571-0722; www.villataina.com; s incl breakfast US$109-142, d US$119-142; P ⊠ 🖳 🕿) This appealing boutique-y hotel at the western end of town has 55 tastefully decorated rooms, each with balcony or terrace, air-con, comfortable beds, in-room data ports and modern bathroom. There is a small, clean pool and a nice beach area fringed by palm trees. Suites and deluxe suites are also available.

ourpick Natura Cabañas (☎ 809-571-1507; www.naturacabana.com; s/d/tr/q US$120/160/210/240; P 🖳 🕿) Buried at the end of a McMansion subdivision just west of Cabarete, these marvelous eco-themed bungalows (think exposed freestone bathrooms) are right on the beach. Even if you aren't staying here, come for the day spa, one of the best on the north coast – yoga and massage on the beach are both on offer. The Chilean owners also serve excellent seafood in the on-site restaurant (mains US$15 to US$30). Very romantic spot.

Velero Beach Resort (☎ 809-571-9727; www .velerobeach.com; La Punta 1; s US$146, d US$173-185, ste US$200-252, penthouse US$326; P ⊠ 🖳 🕿) Set out on the point just east of the main Cabarete beach, these four-star digs are easily the best in town. All the rooms have a balcony or terrace and face the ocean. Sit poolside just steps from the sand, then walk west for five minutes to sample Cabarete's many excellent dining options. A fine choice.

Viva Wyndham Tangerine (☎ 809-571-0402, 809-686-5658; www.vivawyndhamresorts.com; s/d US$218/290; P ⊠ 🖳 🕿) One of the few all-inclusives in Cabarete, the Tangerine sits just a few hundred meters west of town. Built in 2003, this small-ish resort still maintains a sense of newness – the 222 rooms are tastefully decorated, and the bathrooms are tops. There's a gym, three bars and three restaurants, but the food has a poor reputation. Still, it's walking distance to all the great eating options in Cabarete, so who cares?

Eating

Dining out on Cabarete's beach is the quintessential Caribbean experience – paper lanterns hanging from palm trees, a gentle ocean breeze and excellent food (even if it does cost the same you'd pay back home). You can also find good, cheap Dominican set meals on the main street, if you're after a quick feed and aren't in the mood for anything fancy.

Several talentless local musicians may attempt to serenade you while you're eating dinner on the beach. Be kind to your fellow diners, and ask them not to.

ourpick Panadería Repostería Dick (☎ 809-571-0612; set breakfasts US$4-7; 🕑 7am-3pm, closed Wed) The undisputed champion of breakfast in Cabarete, Dick serves large set breakfasts with juice and strong coffee. The bakery does wholewheat bread and mind-blowing vanilla-cream Danish pastries.

La Casita de Juana 'El Tigre' (Callejón de la Loma; set meals US$4-8; 🕑 dinner, lunch in high season, closed Tue) The irrepressibly warm owner of this Dominican restaurant makes Dominican food memorable (no small challenge). Choice of chicken, goat or fish with rice, beans and salad. The specialty of the house is *arepita de yucca* (aniseed-flavored yucca pancakes).

Hexenkessel (☎ 809-571-0493; mains US$5-14; 🕑 24hr) After a night of debauchery, nothing hits the spot like a monstrous schnitzel (US$5) at this never-closed German eatery. Clients sit side by side at picnic tables. Other house specialties include potato pancakes with ground beef (US$6.50) and fried Bavarian bratwurst (US$4).

Pomodoro (☎ 809-571-0085; mains US$7-12; 🕑 lunch & dinner) Run by an Italian jazz fiend, this pizza joint makes the best crispy-crust pizza on the beach. It uses only quality toppings – including pungent, imported Italian cheese – and there's live jazz on Thursday nights.

ourpick Casanova (☎ 809-571-0806; mains US$12-25; 🕑 breakfast, lunch & dinner) This Asian-decorated restaurant has Buddha statues about the place, and plays funky house music. The food is the best you'll find directly on the beach – the usual suspects like surf and turf make an appearance, but also a goat's cheese salad and some mighty fine pizza, too. Dig your toes into the sand and relax with a beer. Now this is the life.

WHO'S YOUR MAMA – MAMAJUANA

You're on the beach, and some old guy is holding a bunch of empty bottles filled with leaves in your face asking you if you want to buy them.

A bottle full of leaves? What, are you kidding me?

Nope – it's *mamajuana*, the national hooch. Take a bottle, fill it with a variety of herbs and dried bark (the exact mixture depends on who's doing the mixing), top it up with rum, wine, and a bit of honey, and let it steep for a month or so.

Mamajuana is reputed to enhance male virility, and packs a punch. Most bars have a bottle somewhere, and quality can range from the revolting to the eye-poppingly good.

Bliss (☎ 829-865-6444; www.activecabarete.com/bliss; Callejón de la Loma; mains US$14-22; ✆ 4pm-midnight, closed Sun) It may not be on the beach, but sitting around the crystal-blue pool with a top-shelf cocktail in your hand, you can be forgiven for not caring. The food here is creative – think rack of lamb with thyme and bitter caramel sauce, shrimp with passionfruit sauce, or roasted duck breast with green pepper sauce.

Otra Cosa (☎ 809-571-0607; La Punta; mains US$15-35; ✆ dinner, closed Tue) This French-Caribbean restaurant, just across from Velero and with marvelous sea breezes at dusk, does some of the choicest food in town. The forbidden paste – foie gras (US$20) – features prominently on the menu, and it also serves filet mignon with duck liver, morels and cognac (US$33). Good fish, lobster and steak dishes, too.

Blue Moon Hotel & Restaurant (☎ 809-757-0614; www.bluemoonretreat.net; Los Brazos; mains US$18; ✆ dinner; **P**) Set in the mountains a short drive from Cabarete, this bungalow-style hotel and restaurant hosts family-sized Indian dinners (minimum eight people, reserve in advance). Food is quality South Asian fare, including two different veggie dishes, a main course such as tandoori or curried chicken or fish, rice, salad, coffee, tea and dessert. The bungalows (US$50 to US$60 per bungalow) include breakfast in the price, and are cool and comfortable, with inventive Indian-style decor. To get here from Cabarete, head east on the highway to Sabaneta and turn right on the road to Jamao al Norte. Proceed a few kilometers and you'll pass a bridge in the town of Los Brazos, where you should look for a sign to your left as you climb the hill.

Castle Club (☎ 809-223-0601; www.castleclubonline.com; Los Brazos; US$35 per person plus drinks; ✆ dinner) Just 200m past the Blue Moon on your left is this rambling, eccentric home – a castle of sorts, under continuous construction (and unlikely ever to be fully finished). The owners grow much of their own food on the property, and serve this superfresh produce in their restaurant, one of the very best in the country. Expect dishes like coconut sea bass, exquisite salads and cold lemon soufflé. Their schedule can be erratic, though – book at least two days in advance. They can cater for groups from six to 100.

There are three supermarkets in Cabarete. The biggest and best is **Janet's Supermarket** (☎ 809-571-0404) at the eastern end of town.

Drinking & Entertainment

Most people start out the night at Lax, and then move onto Onno's or Bambú until closing time. Friday night's bigger than Saturday.

our pick Lax (lax-cabarete.com; ✆ 9am-1am) This mellow bar and restaurant serves food until 10:30pm. In many ways it's the social headquarters of Cabarete. Try the *chinola mojito* – surprisingly good.

Onno's (☎ 809-571-0461; ✆ 9am-late) This edgy, foreign-owned restaurant and nightclub serves some of the cheapest food on the beach – a basic breakfast goes for just US$2, and salads for US$7. At night a DJ spins a decent set, and the party spills out onto the beach.

Bambú (✆ 6pm-late) Just 100m west of Onno's, this bar and disco plays loud house music and reggaeton, and the crowd spills out onto the beach until it merges with that at Onno's. Bring earplugs in case of rain (so you can stand inside).

Voy Voy (☎ 809-571-0805; ✆ 6pm-late) Vela Windsurf Center by day, bar by night, this small, hip café also serves sandwiches and snacks. Monday karaoke is a mandatory part of Cabarete beach life.

Latino Lounge (Callejón de la Loma; ✆ 6pm-late) Just inside Callejón de la Loma, this new spot is the best place in Cabarete to dance merengue or *bachata* (sorry salsa lovers, you picked the wrong country).

Ocean Sands Casino (☎ 809-571-0050; disco cover charge US$3; ✆ 4pm-very late) The on-site disco plays loud merengue and reggaeton, and doesn't begin to fill up till way past midnight.

One of your few options after the bars close. Moderate presence of sex workers.

El Rocón (☎ 809-462-9341; Antigua Calle de Canal; mains US$10-22; ☉ lunch & dinner) This secluded restaurant-cum-driving-range is just east of Encuentro. Great for a beachside lunch, it also sometimes holds after-hours parties that go till dawn – ask any DJ if it's on. Small, thatched chill-out shacks are a great place to watch the sun rise.

Getting There & Around

None of the main bus companies offers service to Cabarete – the closest bus depots are in Sosúa, where you can grab a *gua-gua* (US$0.30, 20 minutes) or taxi (US$12) to Cabarete. Heaps of *gua-guas* ply this coastal road, including east to Río San Juan (US$2.25, one hour) and west to Puerto Plata (US$1.75, one hour). Hail them anywhere along Cabarete's main drag.

Transportation in town is dominated by *motoconchos*, who will attempt to charge you two to three times the price you'd pay for a similar ride in Puerto Plata. Don't be surprised if you can't haggle them down. A ride out to Encuentro should cost US$1.50, but will probably cost more like US$3.

A popular option for the many visitors who stay a week or longer is to rent a scooter or a motorcycle. Expect to pay around US$10 to US$15 per day, less if you rent for a week or more. There are lots of scooter-rental shops along the main drag, and some hotels rent two-wheeled transport too. Be aware that helmets are pretty much nonexistent in this country, so if that's important to you consider bringing your own.

The motorcycle-shy can call a **taxi** (☎ 809-571-0767), which will cost US$8 to Encuentro, US$20 to the airport, and US$35 to Puerto Plata. There's also a **taxi stand** in the middle of town.

If you want to rent a car the best place to do so is at the Puerto Plata airport when you arrive (see p174). If you're already in town, you can take a *gua-gua* (US$0.60, 30 minutes) to the airport road (just past Sosúa), walk 500m to the terminal and shop around at the numerous car-rental agencies there.

RÍO SAN JUAN
pop 9000

So near, yet so far – this friendly, sleepy Dominican village is just an hour east of Cabarete, yet sees far fewer visitors than it actually deserves. It's a great base to explore two of the north coast's best beaches, including stunning Playa Grande, a 15-minute *gua-gua* ride east of town, and there's good diving and snorkeling nearby (although you'll need to organize it with a dive shop in Sosúa before you come). You can also go on a one-hour boat tour of adjacent Laguna Gri-Gri.

What you shouldn't miss, however, is spending the night at the Bahía Blanca Hotel (see p194), an ordinary-enough hotel that just happens to be built directly on the rocky shorefront, so that waves crash against the building as you go to sleep. It ain't luxury, but it's something special.

Information

Banco Progreso (☎ 809-589-2393; Calle Duarte 38)
Farmacia Reyes (☎ 809-589-2234; Calle Duarte 36)
Politur (tourist police; ☎ 809-754-3241) Located on the highway, 300m west of Calle Duarte.
Post office (Calle Duarte) Between Calles Mella and Rufino Bulbuena.
Solan@.com (☎ 809-549-2498; Calle 30 de Marzo 32; internet per hr US$1.80)
Tourist office (☎ 809-589-2831; cnr Calles Mella & 16 de Agosto) Staffers offer little information but there are plenty of maps and brochures on hand.

Sights & Activities
LAGUNA GRI-GRI

This lagoon at the northern end of Calle Duarte was once Río San Juan's claim to fame, drawing tourists from near and far for boat rides through its tangled mangrove channels. Unfortunately, overuse and the growth of Río San Juan have left the lagoon quite polluted – swimming is no longer recommended – and the water and mangroves are less picturesque than they once were. That doesn't prevent a dozen or more boatmen from offering tours of the lagoon, which typically cost US$35 for up to seven people and last around an hour, with visits to the mangrove forests, some interesting rock formations and a cave populated by hundreds of swallows. Look for a small **shack** (☎ 809-589-2277) next to the public bathrooms down by the Laguna – you'll find it easier to join a group on weekends, when Dominicans come to take this trip.

You can also visit the lagoon on foot – there's a path from the Hotel Bahía Blanca to the water's edge, where you turn right to head into the mangroves.

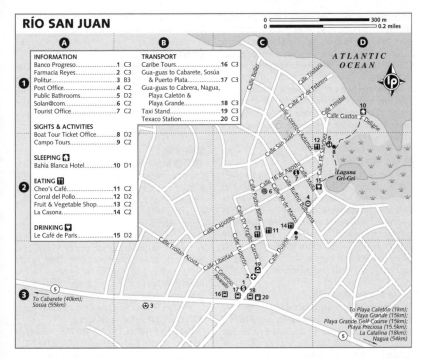

RÍO SAN JUAN

INFORMATION		TRANSPORT	
Banco Progreso	1 C3	Caribe Tours	16 C3
Farmacia Reyes	2 C3	Gua-guas to Cabarete, Sosúa	
Politur	3 B3	& Puerto Plata	17 C3
Post Office	4 C2	Gua-guas to Cabrera, Nagua,	
Public Bathrooms	5 D2	Playa Caletón &	
Solan@com	6 C2	Playa Grande	18 C3
Tourist Office	7 C2	Taxi Stand	19 C3
		Texaco Station	20 C3

SIGHTS & ACTIVITIES	
Boat Tour Ticket Office	8 D2
Campo Tours	9 C2

SLEEPING	
Bahía Blanca Hotel	10 D1

EATING	
Cheo's Café	11 C2
Corral del Pollo	12 D2
Fruit & Vegetable Shop	13 C2
La Casona	14 C2

DRINKING	
Le Café de Paris	15 D2

ATLANTIC OCEAN

Laguna Gri-Gri

To Cabarete (40km); Sosúa (55km)

To Playa Caletón (1km); Playa Grande (15km); Playa Grande Golf Course (15km); Playa Preciosa (15.5km); La Catalina (18km); Nagua (54km)

PLAYA CALETÓN

Located about 1km east of town, this small bay is a peaceful and beautiful place to spend an afternoon. The tawny sand is lapped by teal waters, and almond trees interspersed with towering palms provide plenty of shade. Food stands are near the entrance. The easiest way to get here is to take a *gua-gua* (US$0.45) or a *motoconcho* (US$1) to the turnoff, from which it's a 200m walk down a rocky access road past a goat farm to the beach. If you have a car, you can make it all the way to the beach, but take it slow on the rough parts.

PLAYA GRANDE

Just 15km east of Río San Juan is Playa Grande, one of the most beautiful beaches in the DR. Here, the long, broad, tawny beach has aquamarine water on one side and a thick fringe of palm trees on the other, with stark white cliffs jutting out into the ocean in the distance. It's a picture postcard everywhere you look. There is a number of facilities at the entrance – food stands selling snacks and beer; vendors renting beach chairs (per day US$2), umbrellas (per day US$7), snorkel equipment

(half-/full day US$12/17), body boards (hour/half-day/full-day US$7/12/22) and surfboards (hour/half-day/full-day US$12/22/27); plus a smattering of gift shops selling shell necklaces, bikinis and sunscreen. If you're interested in a quieter stretch of beach, walk east or west of the entrance – the beach goes on for ages and you're sure to find plenty of secluded spots.

A word about safety: Playa Grande has heavy surf and a deceptively strong undertow. Riptides – powerful currents of water flowing out to sea – do form occasionally, and tourists have drowned here in the past. Be conservative when swimming at Playa Grande, and children and less-experienced swimmers should probably not go in at all unless the surf is very low. If you do get caught in a riptide, swim parallel to the shore until you get out of the current and then swim in to shore.

The area all around Playa Grande has been bought by hotel developers, who have put a gate across the road to the beach, although it remains open to the public. If you take a *gua-gua* from town, most drivers will drive you right to the beach if you ask – it's not a detour for them as the beach road reconnects with the highway a couple of kilometers past the beach. Sometimes the gate is closed, however, in which case it's an easy 2km walk from the highway. You can also hire a *motoconcho* (US$2) or a taxi (US$8) to bring you directly to the beach.

At the west end of the beach you may notice the crumbling shell of the all-inclusive resort that used to be here – it is slated for demolition, and a new, lavish development is planned.

PLAYA PRECIOSA

Off the same access road to Playa Grande but 500m east of it is a steep path leading to a narrow and solitary beach known as Playa Preciosa. This spectacular stretch of sand is pounded by serious waves and few attempt to play in the surf. Those who do – typically surfers at dawn – do so for the thrill. A great place to relax and take in the sun, as long as you don't mind the relentless sea spray.

DIVING & SNORKELING

Río San Juan has a great variety of nearby dive sites, including **Seven Hills**, a collection of huge coral heads descending from 6m to 50m, and **Crab Canyon**, with a series of natural arches and swim-throughs. Twenty minutes east of Río San Juan is **Dudu Cave**, one of the best freshwater cavern dives in the Caribbean, where the visibility is almost 50m. Most dive shops require an Advanced Diver certificate or at least 20 logged dives to do these trips.

There was no dive center in Río San Juan when we were there. Your best bet is to organize something in Sosúa (see p180), where you'll pay roughly US$100 to US$120 per person for a full day of diving (minimum three people). You can also organize half-day snorkeling trips here (per person US$70 to US$85).

GOLF

Playa Grande Golf Course (☎ 809-582-0860; www .playagrande.com; Carretera a Nagua; 9/18 holes US$80/140; 🕑 7am-4:30pm) is a par-72 course built on a verdant cliff above Playa Grande. It is a well-tended course that boasts a spectacular ocean view from almost every hole. Caddies and carts are obligatory but not included in the rate (US$20 extra for 18 holes). Multigame discounts are also available. There were plans afoot to make the golf course available

to resident members only, and closed to the public, so be sure to call ahead.

Tours

The small **Campo Tours** (☎ 809-589-2550; Calle Duarte) agency sells predigested package tours to guests at the local all-inclusive, including a glass-bottomed boat tour (US$20) of the *laguna,* and a three-hour deep-sea fishing trip (US$70).

Sleeping

our pick **Bahía Blanca Hotel** (☎ 809-589-2563; Calle Deligne; bahia.blanca.dr@codetel.net.do; r US$15-35) Jutting out over turquoise blue waters, the Bahía Blanca has one of the best ocean views on the north coast. Rooms are decent – clean, tile-floored and with private bathroom – but are showing their age. All but two have at least partial ocean views and wide balconies on each of the three floors provide plenty of opportunities to enjoy the beauty. Rooms on the 3rd floor are the most spacious and have small private balconies. The hotel is also flanked by two calm bays, which are great for swimming.

Hotel La Catalina (☎ 809-589-7700; www.lacata lina.com; Cabrera; s/d incl breakfast US$78/98, apt USD$118-224; 🐱 P 🐟) Perched on a lush hill 18km east of town, La Catalina offers charming and airy rooms with modern amenities. All rooms and most common areas provide spectacular views of the sea and the palm-studded countryside. A full breakfast is included in the rate and is served in a classy, upscale restaurant. Free shuttles takes guests to and from Playa Grande.

Eating & Drinking

La Casona (☎ 809-589-2597; Calle Duarte 6; mains US$3-7; 🕑 lunch & dinner) This friendly Dominican restaurant does the best set meal in town. In the evening, the creative chef also serves up deep-fried pizza empanadas, of which he is inordinately proud.

Cheo's Café (☎ 809-589-2990; Calle Billini 6; mains US$4-15; 🕑 lunch & dinner) This friendly little café is off the main drag and has a palapa roof, wooden floor and walls, and plastic tables covered with tablecloths. The menu includes *conejo al coco* (rabbit in coconut sauce) and *parrillada de marisco* (large platter of grilled seafood, usually served for two people), in addition to the familiar beef, chicken and pasta dishes.

Le Café de Paris (☎ 809-844-4899; Calle FR Sánchez; mains US$7-23; ☺ breakfast, lunch & dinner) Directly in front of the lagoon, this French-owned café is a good spot to have a drink and watch boats launch from the pier. The food is varied – a little bit of Italian, lots of French and some seafood – but forgettable. Stick with the beer and catch up on your postcards.

Corral del Pollo (☎ 829-963-8269; cnr Calles 16 de Agosto & FR Sánchez; mains US$8-20; ☺ breakfast, lunch & dinner) This Spanish restaurant specializes in all things peninsular – paella, Spanish tortillas, even gazpacho. Lunch specials include salad, choice of main, drink and dessert for US$10. Linger afterwards at the stand-up bar with coffee and cigar (strictly for digestive purposes, of course).

Getting There & Around

Caribe Tours (☎ 809-589-2644), just west of Calle Duarte, on the coastal highway just outside town, provides a bus service between Río San Juan and Santo Domingo (US$8.20, 4½ hours) and stops along the way at Nagua (US$2, 45 minutes) and San Francisco de Macorís (US$3.25, 2½ hours). Buses depart at 6:30am, 8am, 9:30am, 2pm and 3:30pm.

Gua-guas come and go from the intersection of Calle Duarte and the coastal highway, known around town as simply *la parada* (the stop). West-bound *gua-guas* line up at the northwest corner of the intersection, departing every 15 minutes from 6am to 5pm for Cabarete (US$2.25, one hour), Sosúa (US$2.10, 1½ hours) and Puerto Plata (US$2.45, two hours).

Eastbound *gua-guas* line up on the northeast corner of the same intersection and leave every 10 minutes from 6:30am to 6pm for Playa Caletón (US$0.45, five minutes), Playa Grande (US$0.90, 15 minutes) and Nagua (US$2, 1¼ hours). From Nagua you can catch *gua-guas* to Samaná or 1st-class buses to Santo Domingo.

There's a **taxi stand** (☎ 809-589-2501) on Calle Duarte between Calles Luperón and Dr Virgilio García. The fare to Playa Caletón is US$10 and to Playa Grande is US$15.

NAGUA

pop 34,000

On the coastal highway 36km northwest of Sánchez and 54km southeast of Río San Juan, Nagua is a hot, dusty town whose interest to tourists is strictly as a transporta-

tion hub. It is the main transfer point for *gua-guas* heading in either direction along the coastal highway. The inland road to San Francisco de Macorís, Moca and Santiago begins here as well, meaning you can catch a *gua-gua* to just about anywhere from here.

To catch a coastal bus, simply walk to the coastal highway and wave down a *gua-gua* going in the direction you want. To catch an inland-bound bus, you must go to the intersection of the two highways and hail a bus that is turning off the coastal highway onto the inland highway. There are usually a few people waiting for the same bus there and they are usually happy to point you to the right bus. *Gua-guas* on the coastal road pass every 15 minutes, while inland buses can take up to half an hour.

Caribe Tours (☎ 809-584-4505; Calle Mella at Emilio Conde) has a dozen buses running to Santo Domingo (US$7.60, 3½ hours) every half-hour from 7am to 10am, and again from 1pm to 4pm

WEST OF PUERTO PLATA

The coastal area west of Puerto Plata remains largely undeveloped, and sees few foreign visitors. There's a couple of good day trips – the Damajagua waterfalls and Cayo Arena are popular – but otherwise there's not much reason to head this way. History buffs might like to visit Parque Nacional La Isabela, where Columbus founded the second settlement in the New World, but the shabby museum is hardly worth the trip. Boaters will already know of Luperón – famous as a 'hurricane hole' – but landlubbers have no reason to visit. If you're on your way to Haiti, Monte Cristi might be worth a day, but the lack of tourist infrastructure makes it very difficult to visit the outlying islands, where pristine coral lurks. The twice-weekly Haitian market at Dajabón may be of interest, if only to see how strikingly different the two peoples who share this island really are.

IMBERT

pop 8100

About 22km southwest of Puerto Plata, connected by a well-maintained highway that winds through sugarcane fields and rolling cattle country, is the small community of Imbert. The only reason to come here

TWENTY-SEVEN WATERFALLS & A KENNEDY

Travelers routinely describe the tour of the waterfalls at Damajagua as 'the coolest thing I did in the DR.' We agree. Guides lead you up, swimming and climbing through the waterfalls. To get down you jump – as much as 5m – down into the sparkling pools below.

It's mandatory to wear a helmet and a life jacket, and guides are trained in first aid and CPR. It wasn't always that way, however.

Flashback to 2004. A handful of unofficial guides led tours at the waterfalls. There were no safety measures, no visitors center, and the occasional minor injury. Then a young boy drowned.

Peace Corps volunteer Joe Kennedy – grandson of Robert F Kennedy and great-nephew of JFK – had just arrived. And there was nothing here. 'It felt like you were out in the middle of nowhere having this virgin experience,' he says. There was no visitors center, no restaurant, nothing. 'There simply wasn't any money for helmets or life jackets and training.'

Kennedy applied for and received grant money from both USAID (US$50,000) and the UN Development Program (US$30,000).

'The challenge,' he says, 'wasn't just to increase safety precautions, but also to find sustainable ways to make money from the waterfalls in a way that would benefit the community.'

The grant money was used to build the **visitors center** (☎ 809-635-1722; www.27charcos.com) and restaurant that are there now. With the help of several Puerto Plata area resorts, Kennedy raised upwards of US$10,000 to purchase life jackets and helmets.

These days it's mandatory to go with a guide, but there's no minimum group size, so you can go by yourself if you wish. You'll need around four hours to make it to the 27th waterfall and back. The falls are open from 8:30am to 4pm, but go early, before the crowds arrive, and you might just have the whole place to yourself.

To get to the falls, go south from Imbert on the highway for 3.3km (and cross two bridges) until you see a sign on your left with pictures of a waterfall. From there it's about 1km down to the visitors center. Alternatively, take a *gua-gua* from Puerto Plata and ask to get off at the entrance.

You can go up to the 7th, 12th or 27th waterfall. Most 'jeep safari' package tours only go to the 7th waterfall. You should be in good shape and over the age of 12. The entrance fee varies depending on your nationality and how far you go. Foreigners pay US$8 to the 7th waterfall, US$10 to the 12th, and US$14 to the highest waterfall, the 27th.

US$1 of every entrance fee goes to a community development fund. Eight people sit on the board, including the Secretary of Environment, to make sure the money gets spent wisely. Considering that an average of 3000 tourists go through the falls every month, the bank account is going well – plans are underway to build a library for the local school, fix a local church and build foot bridges over a nearby river.

And Kennedy? He finished his time in the Peace Corps and is back in Boston studying Law at Harvard. Other Peace Corps volunteers are continuing the project he began.

Any plans to go into politics?

He laughs. 'I just want to survive law school first.'

---

is the **27 waterfalls of Damajagua** (see boxed text, above).

The big Texaco station at Imbert serves as a crossroad for the entire area. There is a frequent *gua-gua* service to Santiago (US$2.50, 1¼ hours), Luperón (US$1.80, 40 minutes) and Puerto Plata (US$1.30, 30 minutes).

LUPERÓN
pop 4500

Luperón is famous among boaters as a 'hurricane hole' – a safe haven from rough seas.

There are two marinas here, and a third planned, and at some times of the year there are as many as 400 pleasure craft in harbor. Unless you're a boater, though, or a guest at the nearby all-inclusive resort, there's no reason to come here – it's a distant backwater with dirty, smelly, pitted streets, of no intrinsic interest.

If you do decide to come here, you'll definitely enjoy your stay more if you have your own vehicle, as things are kinda spread out.

Orientation

The road from Imbert enters Luperón from the south. Staying to your left, the highway becomes Calle Duarte and eventually intersects with Calle 27 de Febrero, Luperón's main east–west drag. This intersection is the commercial center of town. The town park is a few blocks east of there, the marinas a kilometer west and Parque Nacional La Isabela beyond that (see p198).

Information

BanReservas and **Politur** (tourist police; ☎ 809-581-8045) are across the street from each other on Calle Duarte at 16 de Agosto, four blocks south of town, near the *gua-gua* stop.

The **post office** (Calle Luperón) is on the east side of the park. **Farmacia Danessa** (☎ 809-571-8855; Calle Independencia) is on the west side of the park.

Sights & Activities

Luperón doesn't have much in the way of sights and activities, but it is the nearest town to Parque Nacional La Isabela (p198).

Luperón's beach, **Playa Grande**, is fronted by two large all-inclusive resorts, and as Dominican beaches go, is subpar – Playa La Isabela (see p198) is much prettier. The biggest drawback, though, are the sea urchins, which live in the large underwater patches of rock just offshore. Covered in spines, they are no fun to step on. There are two entrances to the beach – one is a path running beside the Luperón Beach resort and the other at the end of a well-marked dirt road off the highway another 700m further west. A *motoconcho* ride costs about US$1.80.

Sailing is on offer at Marina Puerto Blanco, 1km east of town. There are no official tours, but have a sit and a yak at the restaurant and someone is sure to take you out. Prices vary widely depending on the captain, but expect to pay US$40 to US$60 for a half-day trip, or US$70 to US$120 for a full day.

Sleeping

La Casa del Sol (☎ 809-571-8403; www.casadelsol.de.ms; Calle 27 de Febrero; r with fan/air-con US$24/30; 🐱) This German-run hotel, set on a leafy lot about 100m west of La Yola Bar Restaurant (right), features seven comfortable rooms, each with large firm beds and high ceilings and some with sofas or chairs and tables. The hotel is a 1.5km walk from town and 1.5km from the beach, and rents bikes and scooters to guests.

Pequeño Mundo (☎ 809-668-5043; La Rusia; d/q US$26/35; 🐱 🐱) A friendly German-Dominican couple runs this small hotel 2km west of town. All five rooms are spacious with small fridge, cold-water bathroom, high ceilings and a small table and chairs, but only two rooms have air-con. It's the furthest of the hotels from town, but the only one with a swimming pool.

Tropical Luperón & Luperón Beach (☎ 809-571-8303; www.besthotels.es; Carretera de las Américas; per person US$65-110; 🄿 🐱 🛏 🐱) These sister hotels facing Playa Grande share a number of the same facilities. The grounds are tidy though a bit plain, but the pool is very nice, and there's beach access (although it's nothing special). Like most all-inclusive places, the rooms and food service are OK but not terrific. All rooms have balconies either facing the ocean or the grounds. Windsurfing, sailing, horseback riding and scuba clinics in the pool are available.

Eating & Drinking

Captain Steve's Place (☎ 809-452-3612; captstevesplace@yahoo.com; Calle Duarte 47; mains US$4-12; 🛏 🐱) Honky-tonk food at honky-tonk prices, honky-tonk music – heck, the only thing missing here is a gum-snapping waitress with a chip on her shoulder. Former boater Steve makes great omelettes, burgers, even American-style onion rings, all to be washed down with his strong coffee (with added rum, if you've a mind). There's free internet with your meal, and the cheapest laundry in town (per kg US$0.80). There's also a small pool in back you can use (per person US$5).

La Yola Bar Restaurant (☎ 809-571-8511; Calle 27 de Febrero; mains US$5-20; 🕑 dinner, closed Tue) This pleasant, open-sided, thatch-roofed restaurant 500m west of the center isn't on the water yet always seems to catch a refreshing sea breeze. The most popular items here are seafood, but the goat, chicken and pork dishes are also good. Pizzas and pasta start at just US$5.

Getting There & Away

Gua-guas to Imbert (US$1.20, 40 minutes, every 15 minutes 5am to 6:30pm) leave from a stop on Calle Duarte at 16 de Agosto, four blocks south of Calle 27 de Febrero. From Imbert you can pick up *gua-guas* headed south to Santiago or north to Puerto Plata.

If you're driving, pick up the turnoff near Imbert on the Puerto Plata–Santiago highway.

NORTH COAST

PARQUE NACIONAL LA ISABELA

Unesco has been invited to step in and take over this slowly crumbling **national park** (admission US$3; ⊙ 9am-5pm), which marks Columbus' second settlement on Hispaniola. On his second voyage to the New World, Columbus found the first settlement at Cap-Haïtien in Haiti destroyed, so he shifted 110km east and set up a new camp here.

These days a shabby museum marks the occasion – its cheesiness is appropriate, considering that the majority of visitors are groups of Dominican primary-school students. There's some old coins, rings and arrowheads, and a small-scale replica of Columbus' house. All the exhibits are in Spanish, and guides speak very little English. You can see it all in half an hour, tops.

Across the road from the park is the mildly impressive **Templo de las Américas** (⊙ 9am-6pm; admission free). It's a loose replica – though much larger – of La Isabela's original church and was built as part of the settlement's 500th anniversary celebrations.

Also nearby is **Playa Isabela**, a broad outward-curving beach with coarse sand and beautiful, ultracalm water. There are a couple of small beach restaurants and usually at least one knick-knack stand that rents snorkeling gear (US$4) – ask the vendor to point you in the direction of the best coral patches. When swimming or wading, be alert for sea urchins lurking in the rock patches in the shallows.

The pleasant hillside **Miamar** (☎ 809-656-0732; El Castillo; r US$33; ⓅⒽⓈ) B&B has great views out over the national park. Rooms are comfortable and clean, and there are breezy chairs poolside to enjoy a sundowner. One of the owners is a French-trained chef, and if he's feeling well he might be persuaded to work some magic in the kitchen for you. Also of interest here is the private collection of Taíno artifacts, the largest of its kind, which includes some rare statuettes and a manatee-rib vomiting stick (don't ask). Miamar also has its own private Taíno cave, and the Belgian owners, who speak five languages, can take you there on weekends.

Located just outside the entrance to the national park, **Hostelería Rancho del Sol** (☎ 809-696-0325; Carretera las Américas; s/d incl breakfast with fan US$33/42, with air-con US$46/58; ⓅⒽⓈ) is an agreeable little hotel set on a large oceanfront plot. All eight rooms have a terrace with rocking chairs and ocean view, tile floor and hot water, and are big enough for a queen-sized bed, twin bed, plus a coffee table and chairs. The decor is a bit dated, but the rooms are very clean and comfortable and there's a swimming pool for guest use. As this place was for sale when we passed through, be sure to call ahead to see what the new owner's plans may be.

From Luperón, drive 11km west until you come to a T-junction. To your right lies Playa Isabela (1km), directly ahead the museum (100m), and to the left the church (500m). Turn left and keep going for 2km and you'll come to Miamar and Rancho del Sol.

It's possible, but somewhat harder, to get to La Isabela from the main highway between Santiago and Monte Cristi. Turn off at Laguna Salada and head north 25km to Villa Isabella, passing through Los Hidalgos on the way. (The signs can be a little confusing, so ask for 'El Castillo' – the town where the park is located – as you go.) The park is 7km from Villa Isabella, but the road is dirt and you have to cross two broad rivers; ask at a *motoconcho* stand in Villa Isabella how high the water is and if the car you're driving will make it across. After crossing the second river, turn right on the main road and you'll drive past the park – look for Templo de Las Américas on your right.

If you haven't got your own wheels, it's probably not worth coming here. If you're stubborn, however, a taxi from Luperón will set you back US$30 return, and a *motoconcho* around US$10.

PUNTA RUSIA
pop 200

This remote outpost exists solely to service the package tours coming to **Cayo Arena** (aka 'Paradise Island'). While the corals around the atoll are pristine and the snorkeling tops, the fact that you have to do so with 50 other people in the water at the same time definitely detracts from the experience.

There is no public transportation here, and the road is a muddy, rutted nightmare (25km, two hours). While the beach is pleasant enough, and you'll spot some wild orchids on a dirt track leading inland (5km west of town), the amount of effort required to get here doesn't really pay off once you arrive.

Sights & Activities
CAYO ARENA

Tour groups are shuttled by speedboat to this picturesque sandbar island about 10km northwest of Punta Rusia. You'll spend a couple of hours on the island, sunbathing and snorkeling, before returning via a fairly humdrum mangrove plantation (where you might spot a manatee). Unlimited drinks are included on the island, and there's an uninspired buffet lunch when you get back to town.

Lots of agents sell this tour, but the actual operator is **El Paraíso Tours** (☎ 809-320-7606; www .cayoparaiso.com). Expect to pay roughly US$50 per person, and be prepared to spend three hours each way in the back of a truck (if you're coming from the Puerto Plata region). If you're already in Punta Rusia it's US$35 per person. If you want to avoid the package tourists, hop the service and supply boat, which leaves Punta Rusia around 8:15am. You'll have the island to yourself for more than an hour. Otherwise, go on an afternoon boat, when there are fewer people.

Be warned: there is no bathroom on the island, so go before or be prepared to, err, fertilize the ocean.

BOAT TRIPS
El Paraíso Tours (☎ 809-320-7606; www.cayoparaiso .com) also offers a 'VIP' yacht tour (maximum 30 passengers) that includes a visit to Parque Nacional La Isabela, a champagne and oyster snack on board, a lobster lunch back at Punta Rusia, and the afternoon at Cayo Arena, including snorkeling and a return trip through the mangroves. The tour is normally US$140 per person, but those staying at Punta Rusia get it for US$95.

DIVING
There are more than two dozen great coral dive sites off Punta Rusia. There's no dive shop, but if the local expat-German diver happens to be around, he might take you out – ask at El Paraíso Tours (☎ 809-320-7606). Your best bet, though, is to contact the dive shops in Sosúa (p180), most of which offer this trip.

Sleeping & Eating
Casita Mariposa (☎ 809-325-2378; s/d incl breakfast US$15/24) A German-French couple runs this, the best lodging in Punta Rusia. Set on a bluff overlooking the ocean, it has great sea views, and it's just a short walk to a remote beach. Accommodation is in a handful of rustic cabins. To get there, just as you enter town look for a *gomero* (tire-repair shop) on your left, and turn right on the small road leading uphill just opposite.

El Paraíso Tours (r US$35) has a few rooms for rent in the large apartment complex across the street from its office. The rooms are basic, with private cold-water bath, two large beds and a small terrace.

For food, you can join one of the tour-group buffets for US$14, including drinks. There is also a number of modest **restaurants** (mains US$3-7) and beachside fish stands that serve basic, cheap meals.

Getting There & Away
There is no regular bus service to Punta Rusia. If you have a car, there are two routes – one a 25km dirt road from Villa Isabella, which can be reached by paved roads from either Imbert or Hwy 1 (turn off at Laguna Salada). You have to ford two rivers on this route, so ask in Villa Isabella about conditions. The other, and easier, route is from Villa Elisa, 20km west of Laguna Salada on Hwy 1. From there, the road north is paved for 8km and deteriorates steadily for the next 12km, but does not require you to cross any rivers.

MONTE CRISTI
pop 17,000
Welcome to the boonies. Were Monte Cristi about three hours' drive closer to Puerto Plata, it would be full of foreign tourists and profitable local businesses. As it is, this dusty frontier town offers only a few modest attractions, and serves principally as a jumping-off point to Haiti.

The lack of tourists mean residents continue to make their living fishing and tending livestock, just as they've done for generations. Another major source of revenue is salt, which is harvested from evaporation ponds north of town and sold in the USA by Morton Salt.

Monte Cristi celebrates what is considered the most brutal Carnival in the country – participants carry bullwhips and crack each other as they walk through the streets. I can hear my mother now: 'But you could lose an eye!'

Orientation
Hwy 1 enters Monte Cristi from the east, where it turns into Calle Duarte and becomes the main east–west road through town. Main intersections include the ones with Mella (which turns into Hwy 45 south to Dajabón), Benito Monción (with a hotel, a call center and several restaurants) and San Fernando (which runs along the far side of the park and leads to the beaches and El Morro).

Information

Just about everything you'll need is on or within a block or two of Calle Duarte.

BanReservas (Calle Duarte) Next to the post office.

Hospital Padre Fantino (☎ 809-579-2401; Av 27 de Febrero; ☾ 24hr) Located two blocks north of Calle Duarte, this modest hospital has a 24-hour emergency room.

Politur (tourist police; ☎ 809-579-3980) Office on the main beach.

Post office (cnr Calle Duarte & Colón; ☾ 8am-5pm Mon-Fri) Free internet on the second floor.

Sights & Activities

EL MORRO

Part of the 1100-sq-km **Parque Nacional Monte Cristi** (☾ 8am-5pm, admission free) that surrounds Monte Cristi on all sides, El Morro ('The Hill') sits 5km northeast of town – follow Av San Fernando north of town to the beach and continue to your right until the road dead-ends. Opposite the ranger station, 585 wooden stairs lead to the top (239m). The stairs are in disrepair and have been closed since 2002. Uniformed types say don't go, and for absolute safety you should heed the advice. If you do scramble over the rotting planks and loose gravel, you'll be rewarded with excellent views. It's about an hour return.

BEACHES

The main public beach is **Playa Juan de Boloños**, a kilometer north of town. **Playa Detras del Morro**, tucked behind the hill in the national park, is the prettiest beach in the area, a long slow curve of tan sand backed by a towering precipice. The beach is just past the ranger station.

PARQUE CENTRAL

Monte Christi's **city park** (cnr Calle Duarte & San Fernando) is notable for the 50m clock tower at its center. The tower was designed by French engineer Alexandre Gustave Eiffel and looks like a miniature version of the same engineer's more famous tower in Paris. It was imported from France in March 1895, reassembled and inaugurated by Monte Cristi's mayor three months later. The clock tower was allowed to deteriorate, but in 1997 the Leon Jimenez family, of Aurora cigar and Presidente beer fortune, financed the tower's restoration.

In the immediate vicinity of the park are several dilapidated Victorian homes. Some have been partially restored, in some cases enough for you to appreciate their one-time glory.

Tours

Most of the hotels in town organize snorkeling tours (per person $50), trips to the isolated beach at **Isla Cabra** ($30 up to four people), and boat tours to **Los Cayos de los Siete Hermanos** ($300 up to 12 people), a collection of seven uninhabited islands inside the national park.

So few people come here, though, that it can be expensive and difficult to arrange any of these tours – your best bet is to come on weekends in the high season (November to March) and ask at your hotel. Alternatively, ask **Politur** to recommend a boatperson and haggle with them directly.

Hostal San Fernando (see below) also runs a small dive center, and charges US$150 per person per day. **Northern Coast Diving** (see p181) in Sosúa may also be willing to take you out this way. The corals here make excellent diving, but then there are equally good corals more easily accessible elsewhere. Fortune-hunting wreck divers work this coastline, but the many wooden galleons that sank here have long since rotted away, leaving very little for the recreational diver to see.

Sleeping

Chic Hotel (☎ 809-579-2316; Benito Monción 44; s/d with fan US$18/25, s/d/tr/q with air-con US$27/30/33/40; ⓟ ⓧ ⓡ) 'Chic' might be wishful thinking. Perhaps the 'Undistinguished But Still Good Value Hotel' would be a better name. Still, this well-managed lodging offers 50 clean rooms right in the middle of town. The Chic empire includes neighboring bar, restaurant, ice-cream store and internet café. Check out the mango tree the hotel was built around – you'll pass the trunk in the hallway.

Hotel Montechico (☎ 809-579-2565; s/d/tw US$24/33/43; ⓟ ⓧ) You can't miss this one – take the road north to the beach, and you'll see a bright-yellow sign that says 'Restaurant.' There's no food, but the hotel is open. All rooms have a balcony: ask for one facing the ocean. It's about a 20-minute walk into town. Service can be lacking, however.

Hostal San Fernando (☎ 809-866-4511; www .ecomarinamontecristi.com; s/d/tr US$25/44/60; ⓧ ⓛ ⓡ) A drop of rain turns these otherwise pleasant bungalows into a mosquito-filled nightmare. In the dry season, though, it's the most pleasant accommodation in town. The rooms have high, sloped ceilings, whitewashed walls, firm beds, clean bathrooms and tile floors. From here it's a short walk to both the beach and

El Morro. There's a restaurant on site, but it's nothing special.

Eating & Drinking

Comedor Adela (☎ 809-579-2254; Alvarez 41; set meals US$5) This family-owned joint has a menu, but ignore it, and go for the day's special – rice and beans, salad, and some very tasty *chivo* (goat).

Ocean (☎ 809-579-3643; Calle Benito Monción 1; mains US$8-17; ☺ 9am-midnight) Four blocks south of Calle Duarte – look for the prominent red stairway – this restaurant and discotheque offers the diner loads of choices, from chicken dishes to lobster. The open-sided, fan-cooled dining area is situated under a large thatched roof, while the adjacent disco is a concrete structure that's packed with Dominicans on Friday and Saturday nights (free admission).

Super Fria Nina (Calle Duarte at Colón) and **Terraza Fedora** (Calle San Fernando), five blocks north of Duarte, are large beer gardens that get incredibly packed almost every evening, but especially on weekends. Also check out **New York New York** (opposite Parque 14 de Julio), where the cool kids go to bump and grind the night away.

Getting There & Away

Caribe Tours (☎ 809-579-2129; cnr Mella & Carmargo) has a depot a block north of Calle Duarte. Buses to Santo Domingo (US$8.50, four hours) leave at 7am, 9am, 1:45pm, 2:45pm and 4pm, with a stop in Santiago (US$3.65, two hours).

Monte Cristi's *gua-gua* terminal is on Calle Duarte near 27 de Febrero. There are *gua-guas* to Dajabón (US$1.50, 50 minutes, every 20 minutes from 7:30am to 10pm); for Puerto Plata, take any Santiago-bound *gua-gua* and get off at the junction in Navarrete ($3.70, 1½ hours, every 20 minutes), where you can

change for a Puerto Plata *gua-gua* ($1.80, one hour, every 20 minutes).

If you're driving, it's hard to get lost – Calle Duarte becomes Hwy Duarte to Santiago, while Av Mella becomes Hwy 45 to Dajabón. Avoid driving the Monte Cristi–Dajabón road at night, as assaults on cars have occurred in the past.

Getting Around

Most of Monte Cristi is navigable by foot. The exception is El Morro and the beach behind it – for those a car or a *motoconcho* is best.

DAJABÓN

pop 16,500

Most foreigners here are on their way to or from Haiti. Reaching the border is simple; coming from Monte Cristi on Hwy 45, as most people do, you'll come to a huge arch (the formal entrance to town) and a short distance afterwards the Parque Central on the east side of the street. Just past the park is Calle Presidente Henriquez; turn right (west) and the border is six blocks ahead. If you're arriving by Caribe Tours bus, the bus station is on Calle Presidente Henriquez. Just walk west from the bus station five blocks to get to the border.

If you're planning an early-morning border crossing, try the **Hotel Juan Calvo** (☎ 809-579-8285; Calle Presidente Henríquez 46; d/tw with fan US$12/15, with air-con US$15/20; ☒). Next to Parque Central, this hotel ('Bald John') is the best one in town, with 44 clean and comfortable rooms, and located just six blocks from the border.

For a bite to eat, there's lots of vendors selling grilled corn and hot dogs on the main park, and a few undistinguished eateries on the main road coming into town.

THE DAJABÓN MARKET – WHERE TWO NATIONS MEET

Crowds pushing and shoving, a sea of black faces, crates of eggs piled high on women's heads, wheelbarrows – so many wheelbarrows! – and your hands pressed hopelessly at your sides, trying to escape the crush of people.

This is the **Haitian market** at Dajabón, where Dominicans and Haitians come to trade. On Mondays and Fridays the border bridge opens, and Haitians pour across to buy fruit and vegetables from the DR and sell just about everything else.

Cursing at each other in Creole, the successful buyers attempt to return across the narrow bridge, the road clogged with people, advancing an inch per minute, motorcycles burrowing through the crowds – stand aside or get a handlebar in your gut.

Hands will grope your bottom now and then, but don't worry, they're not copping a feel – they're just trying to steal your wallet.

Caribe Tours (☎ 809-579-8554; cnr Calles Carrasco & Henríquez) has a depot five blocks from the border. Buses to Santo Domingo (US$8.50, five hours), with stops in Monte Cristi and Santiago, leave at 6:45am, 8:30am, 10:15am, 1pm, 2:25pm and 3:15pm

Gua-guas will also take you to Monte Cristi (US$1.50, 50 minutes). The terminal is just beyond the arch at the entrance to town on the east side of the road. The *gua-gua* station is just beyond it, also on the eastern side of the road.

There are taxis and *motoconchos* near the crossing point every day until the time the border closes. After that, taxis and *motoconchos* may still be found on the main road.

For information on crossing the border, see p256.

The Interior

Even the most diehard beach fan will eventually tire of sun and sand, and when you do, the cool mountainous playground of the interior is the place to come. Here you'll find the popular mountain retreats of Jarabacoa and Constanza – places where you might actually want a sweater – plus roaring rivers, soaring misty mountains and the only white-water rafting in the Caribbean. Below, on the plains, in the Valle del Cibao, is where merengue spontaneously erupted onto the musical landscape, and where you'll find some of the best Carnival celebrations in the country.

Jarabacoa (500m) is the Cabarete of the interior – a tourist town, and the center of a booming adventure-tour trade. Here you can go white-water rafting, visit waterfalls on horseback, and still party till the sun comes up, if you've a mind to do so. Even higher up is the less visited settlement of Constanza (1200m), a town unique in the Caribbean. Where else can you sit at dusk, huddled up in a sweater, watching the mist descend down into the valley as the sun sets behind the mountains?

Economic life in the interior revolves around Santiago, the DR's second-largest city. It is the capital of a vast tobacco- and sugarcane-growing region. No wonder, then, that the majority of the country's cigars – among the world's best – are processed and manufactured here. The Valle del Cibao, in which Santiago sits, is justly famous for its Carnival celebrations, the top bash in the country. Little La Vega frequently outdoes big city Santiago for both the scale and lavishness of the party – in particular, the ornate, handmade masks worn by participants.

HIGHLIGHTS

- Go **white-water rafting** (p213) on the Caribbean's only raftable river, the turbulent Río Yaque del Norte near Jarabacoa

- Party hearty with the locals in little La Vega in February, when it throws the country's biggest **Carnival celebrations** (p223)

- Light up a stogie and sample the local merchandise in **Santiago** (p207), capital of the cigar trade

- Watch the sunset as the mist descends into the valley in high-altitude **Constanza** (p220)

- Linger at the top of **Pico Duarte** (p217), taking in the views of the Atlantic and the Caribbean

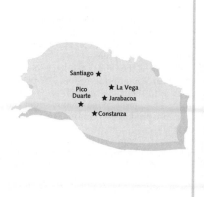

THE INTERIOR

GETTING THERE & AROUND

Santiago's **Aeropuerto Internacionál Cibao** (☎ 809-233-8000; www.aeropuertocibao.com.do) is the third-largest airport in the country, and offers frequent international air service to major destinations. There's a good selection of rent-a-car agencies at the airport, too.

Santiago sits on the main trunk highway that runs from Santo Domingo north to Puerto Plata, and has plenty of efficient bus service to all points of the compass. There's regular, first-class bus service to all destinations listed in this chapter, except for Constanza – you'll need to hop a *gua-gua* (local bus) to get up into the mountains.

As always, renting a car, preferably an SUV, will give you more freedom to explore the countryside.

SANTIAGO

pop 623,000

The second largest of the three city-states from which the DR was formed, Santiago maintains a distinct cultural flair that makes it not only uniquely Dominican, but also uniquely, err, Santiagan. The racial mix is noticeably different; fashions in clothing, facial hair and public transportation differ markedly from the rest of the country; and the citizens have a peculiar fetish for Confederate-style gazebos.

Santiago is often overlooked and even put down by travelers as a destination. This is largely unfair. It is a pleasant, livable city, with good restaurants and bars, a pleasant park, one of the country's six *beísbol* (baseball) teams, and best of all, few tourists, making this a good place to get to know the Dominican way of life.

The city is the capital of a large tobacco- and sugarcane-growing region. The plantations send their raw material to Santiago, where the majority of the country's rum and cigars are produced – Santiago is a must for cigar aficionados.

All buses from Santo Domingo to the north coast pass through Santiago. Consider getting off and staying for a day or two. There are some good hotels, a couple of interesting museums, and come Carnival time you'll be able to experience firsthand the region's tradition of ornate handmade masks.

HISTORY

Santiago was founded in 1495 by Christopher Columbus' elder brother, Bartholomew. However, the earthquake of 1562 caused so much damage to the city that it was rebuilt on its present site beside the Río Yaque del Norte. It was attacked and destroyed several times by invading French troops, as part of long-simmering tension between Spain and France over control of the island. Santiago also suffered terribly during the DR's 1912 civil war.

The years immediately following the civil war were some of the city's best. WWI caused worldwide shortages of raw tropical materials, so prices soared for products such as sugar, tobacco, cocoa and coffee – all of which were being grown around Santiago. From 1914 through the end of the war and into the 1920s, Santiago's economy boomed. Lovely homes and impressive stores, electric lighting and paved streets appeared throughout town. In May 1922, Hwy Duarte opened, linking Santiago with Bonao, La Vega and Santo Domingo.

Today, Santiago still relies on agriculture as its chief source of revenue, and is a noticeably wealthier city than most of the country.

ORIENTATION

The center of town is Parque Duarte, a busy, leafy park with a gazebo, the cathedral to its south side and Palacio Consistorial to its west. (A number of homeless people hang out here – expect to be aggressively panhandled if you sit down.) The park is at the corner of Av 30 de Marzo and Calle del Sol, both large commercial avenues with ATMs, hotels and assorted shops nearby. Av 30 de Marzo runs south to the Río Yaque del Norte and north to Av Las Carreras and Av 27 de Febrero, the main roads in and out of town.

Calle del Sol runs east to the Monument and the bar scene nearby – you can also take Av Restauración, two blocks north.

INFORMATION
Internet Access

Camber.Net (☎ 809-471-3917; Calle España 41; per hr US$1; ☼ 8am-10pm Mon-Sat) Doubles as a call center.
Centro de Internet Yudith (☎ 809-581-4882; Calle 16 de Agosto near Mella; per hr US$0.80; ☼ 8:30am-8:30pm Mon-Fri, to 5pm Sat)
Coffe Break Internet (☎ 809-724-1389; Cucurullo 61; per hr US$0.80) Has CD/DVD burners.

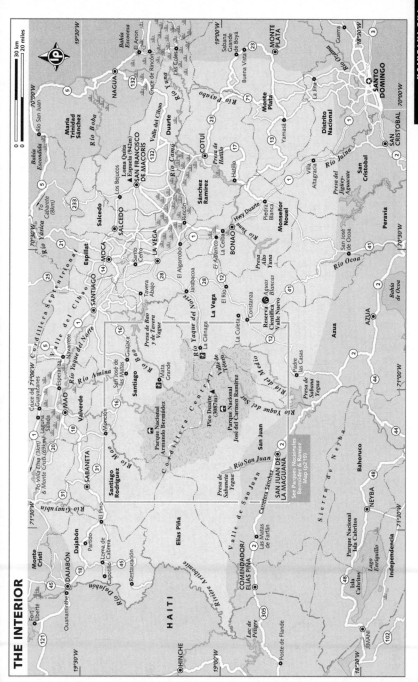

SANTIAGO

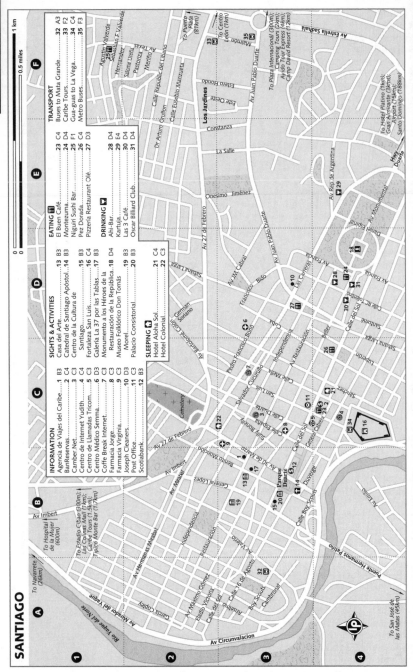

INFORMATION	
Agencia de Viajes del Caribe	1 B3
BanReservas	2 C4
Camber Net	3 C3
Centro de Internet Yudith	4 C4
Centro de Llamadas Tricom	5 C4
Centro Médico Semma	6 D3
Coffe Break Internet	7 C3
Farmacia Jorge	8 C3
Farmacia Virginia	9 C3
Joseph Cleaners	10 D3
Post Office	11 C3
Scotiabank	12 B3

SIGHTS & ACTIVITIES	
Casa del Arte	13 B3
Catedral de Santiago Apóstol	14 B3
Centro de la Cultura de Santiago	15 B3
Fortaleza San Luis	16 C4
Galería La 37 por las Tablas	17 B3
Monumento a los Héroes de la Restauración de la República	18 D4
Museo Folklórico Don Tomás Morel	19 B3
Palacio Consistorial	20 B3

SLEEPING	
Hotel Aloha Sol	21 C4
Hotel Colonial	22 C3

EATING	
El Buen Café	23 C4
Montezuma	24 D4
Niguirí Sushi Bar	25 F1
Pez Dorada	26 C4
Pizzería Restaurant Olé	27 D3

DRINKING	
Ahí-Bar	28 D4
Kartula	29 E4
Las 3 Café	30 D4
Oscar Billiard Club	31 D4

TRANSPORT	
Buses to Mata Grande	32 A3
Caribe Tours	33 F2
Gua-guas to La Vega	34 C4
Metro Buses	35 F3

1 km
0.5 miles

To Navarrete (16km)

To Hospital de la Mujer (600m)

To Estadio Cibao (300m); Las Colinas Mall (1km); Caribe Tours (1.5km); Típico Monte Bar (1.7km)

Av Imbert

Río Yaque del Norte

To Mirador del Yaque

Av Mirador del Norte

García Copley

Av Máximo Gómez

Eladio Victoria

Calle del Sol

Anselmo

Calle 16 de Agosto

Boy Scout

Cambronal

Av Circunvalación

To San José de las Matas (45km)

Av Hermanas Mirabal

Independencia

Restauración

General López

Benito Monción

Av Imbert

Av Mirabal

Av Valerio

Parque Duarte

Av 30 de Marzo

Av 27 de Febrero

Cementery

Salvador Cucurullo

San Luis

Calle España

Calle Duarte

Calle del Sol

Sabana Larga

Av JM Cabral

Francisco Bido

Las Carreras

Av Juan Pablo Duarte

Av Estrella Sadhalá

Av 27 de Febrero

Av Restauración

Benito Monción

Germán Soriano

Pedro Francisco Bonó

Av Bartolomé Colón

Cuba

Independencia

Duvergé

Central Cabral

Calle del Sol

Beller

Calle de Tolentino

Santomé

Sabana Larga

Lupéron

Sánchez

Av Francia

Av Monumental

Daniel Espinal

Av Texas

Agustín Valverde

Sebastián E Valverde

Hernández

Salomé Ureña

Pastoriza

Merino

Constanza

La Salle

Onésimo Jiménez

Dr Arturo Grullón

Av República del Líbano

Calle República del Líbano

Calle Eusebio Manzueta

Este Oeste

Estero Hondo

Los Jardines

Av Juan Pablo Duarte

Maimón

Av Rep de Argentina

To Centro León (1km)

To Puerto Plata (81km)

To Plaza Internacional (800m); Camping Tours (2km); Ayido Tour Express (4km); Camp David Resort (12km)

To Hotel Platino (1km); Gran Almirante (3km); Airport (15km); Santo Domingo (188km)

Hwy Duarte

Puente Hermanos Patiño

Av Estrella Sadhalá

Laundry

Joseph Cleaners (☎ 809-583-4880; Las Carreras near Duarte; ☽ 7am-7:30pm Mon-Fri, to 1pm Sat) US$1 per load (up to 9kg) and US$3 per load/half-hour to dry. Same-day service if you drop off early.

Medical Services

Centro Médico Semma (☎ 809-226-1053; Pedro Francisco Bonó btwn Sánchez & Cuba; ☽ 24hr) Free for local teachers and their families, this well-regarded hospital treats other patients at reasonable rates.
Farmacia Jorge (☎ 809-582 2887; cnr Calle España & Av Gómez)
Farmacia Virginia (☎ 809-582-4142; Av 30 de Marzo 48) Will deliver.
Hospital de la Mujer (☎ 809-575-8963; Av Imbert; ☽ 24hr) Specializes in women's care, but has a fully equipped emergency room.

Money

BanReservas (Calle del Sol 66)
Scotiabank (cnr Calle del Sol & 30 de Marzo)

Post

Post office (cnr Calle del Sol & San Luis) Three blocks east of Parque Duarte.

Travel Agencies

Agencia de Viajes del Caribe (☎ 809-241-1368; Av Restauración 123) Small, conveniently located agency that issues domestic and international air tickets and can book package tours in the area.

SIGHTS & ACTIVITIES
Centro León

The **Centro León** (☎ 809-582-2315; www.centroleon.org .do; Av 27 de Febrero 146, Villa Progreso; admission US$2.25, free Tue; ☽ 10am-7pm Tue-Sun, closed Mon) is a sprawling monument to the wealth of the León Jimenez empire, and has surprisingly little to offer the tourist. There are three **exhibition rooms** in the main building, and the emphasis here is on all things Dominican. One exhibition focuses on the local ecosystem, history and population; another displays contemporary Dominican art and photography; and the third (closed when we were there) houses temporary exhibits. A separate building houses a self-aggrandizing exhibit on the history of the Jimenez family, its beginnings in the tobacco industry, its break into the beer market, and its success in the banking world. For such a grand edifice it's all surprisingly mundane, and even the most tweedy of visitors will see everything in an hour or so.

Of moderately more interest is the working **cigar factory** on site, where you can watch a dozen cigar rollers making Aurora Preferidos, its premium brand. The adjoining cigar shop sells the complete range of smokes, including the Preferidos (a box of 25 costs US$420).

Guided tours are available in Spanish (per person US$4), English, French and German (per person US$5.50) and last about 1½ hours. Reservations are required three days in advance for tours. A taxi here will cost you US$3, or pick up a Ruta A *concho* (private car that follows a set route; US$0.39) along Calle del Sol – not all Ruta A *conchos* go as far as the Centro León, though, so be sure to ask.

A small **gift shop** sells books on Dominican history, art, culture and food, and there's a small cafeteria if you get the munchies. During the evenings, philistine insomniacs will find their cure – the center offers an ever-changing schedule of art appreciation classes, art-house cinema and sometimes live musical events.

Museo Folklórico Don Tomás Morel

Renowned poet and cultural critic Tomás Morel founded this eclectic, eccentric **folk art museum** (☎ 809-582-6787; Av Restauración 174; admission free; ☽ 9am-noon & 3:30-6pm Mon-Fri) in 1962, and helped operate it until his death in 1992. Considered by many to be the father of Santiago's modern Carnival, Morel was a tireless promoter and chronicler of the yearly celebration. He was especially fond of the distinctive *caretas* (masks), and since its founding the museum has displayed the best masks for visitors to enjoy. There's also information on the history of merengue, some Taíno artifacts, and with at least a week's notice you can organize mask-making classes (US$150 per group) at Carnival time, and dance classes (US$50 per group for two hours) the rest of the year. The brightly colored building is impossible to miss, and even those who may be dreading another museum will get a spark of astonishment out of this place.

Casa del Arte

Those interested in contemporary Dominican painting, photography and sculpture will find this small **gallery** (☎ 809-471-7839; Benito Moncón 46; admission free; ☽ 9am-7pm Mon-Sat) worth a visit. Some nights of the week a film club meets to screen good-quality Hollywood flicks (free

WHEN A CIGAR IS JUST A CIGAR

Despite the virulent antismoking campaigns faddish these days, a good cigar remains one of life's finest pleasures, and the DR – one of the world's largest producers of cigars – is the ideal place to sample a few.

Many of the world's top brands are made here – Aurora, Montecristo, Arturo Fuente, to name a few – but there are real bargains to be had on world-class cigars if you know where to look. Many of those name brands contract the work to local, Dominican cigar-makers, who then offer the 'label-less' cigar to locals and travelers at half the price.

It's critical when buying cigars to test whether they've been made well and stored properly. Pick up the cigar: it should have a springy tightness, indicating solid construction. If it's too soft or too hard it won't draw well. It shouldn't crackle under your fingers, either; that means it's too dry, and will smoke like kindling.

Look for dedicated cigar stores – don't buy from random vendors on the beach or on the street. The most important advice, though, is to always try the cigar before you splurge on a whole box. If they won't let you do that, go somewhere else.

admission), there's sometimes live music (US$10) and on Saturdays live theater (US$3 to US$5). Pass by for a copy of the gallery's latest monthly event calendar.

Galería LA 37 por las Tablas

Across the street from the Casa del Arte, **La 37** (☎ 809-587-3033; 37porlastablas.blogspot.com; Benito Monción 37; admission varies; ☺ 9am-7pm Mon-Sat) also hosts local art shows in its foyer, and has an outdoor stage for live music, dance and theater performances, both amateur and professional.

Centro de la Cultura de Santiago

Though not much to look at from the outside, the **Centro de la Cultura de Santiago** (☎ 809-226-5222; Calle del Sol; ☺ 9am-noon & 3-6pm Mon-Sat), a half-block from Parque Duarte, offers a regular program of musical and theatrical perform-ances, including plays, choral singing, chil-dren's theater and holiday concerts. There's also a rotating exhibition of Dominican paint-ing in the small gallery. Pass by for a copy of the monthly schedule.

Catedral de Santiago Apóstol

Santiago's **cathedral** (cnr Calles 16 de Agosto & Benito Monción; ☺ 7-9am Mon-Sat, to 8pm Sun), opposite the south side of Parque Duarte, was built between 1868 and 1895 and is a combination of Gothic and neoclassical styles. The cathedral contains the marble tomb of the late-19th-century dic-tator Ulises Heureaux, an elaborately carved mahogany altar and impressive stained-glass windows by contemporary Dominican artist Dincón Mora.

Palacio Consistorial

On the west side of Parque Duarte you'll find the former town hall, which now in-cludes a small **museum** (Parque Duarte; admission free; ☺ 9am-noon and 2-5pm Mon-Sat) devoted to the city's colorful history. If you're here during Carnival, don't miss the huge and stunning display of masks and *fichas* (posters), part of a yearly competition that draws entries from the top artists and mask-makers in Santiago and from across the country.

Monumento a los Héroes de la Restauración de la República

On a hill at the east end of the downtown area is Santiago's most visible and recogniz-able sight, the **Monument to the Heroes of the Restoration of the Republic** (Av Monumental; admission Dominicans/foreigners US$1/$2, Tue free; ☺ 9am-6pm Tue-Sun). Standing on the steps of the Monument, you begin to understand what it means to be Dominican – that final war against Spain, a war for identity, is commemorated here (for more history, see p46). Completely renovated and reopened in 2007, the site now boasts life-sized museum exhibits of Dominican history, and on Tuesdays you'll be joined by large groups of uniformed primary-schoolers being walked through the past. There are great views from the top of the eight-story base, but the spire has been permanently closed due to safety concerns. Large bronze statues of the celebrated gener-als gaze down upon Santiago from the steps, and in a corner of the grounds you'll find a bronze 'hall of fame' of former Águilas *beísbol* players (the local team).

Beísbol

Santiago's Águilas baseball team is one of the six baseball teams in the country, and watching the local fans root for the home side is almost as fun as the game itself. Games are played at **Estadio Cibao** (☎ 809-575-1810; Av Imbert), northwest of the city center; they're held two to three times a week in winter, and tickets cost US$8. It's wise to book in advance – stadium capacity is a mere 18,000 people, and the Águilas are the winning-est team in the league's history, making them very popular indeed. To get there, hop any Ruta A *concho* westbound on Calle del Sol.

Fortaleza San Luis

Built in the late 17th century, the **Fortaleza San Luis** (cnr Calle Boy Scouts & San Luis; admission free) operated as a military stronghold until the 1970s, when it was converted into a prison. Today it houses a small museum, with a strong emphasis on Dominican military history – ancient rusty weapons, a collection of 20th-century tanks and artillery, even three vials of sand from Iraq. There's a small collection of Taíno pottery, some paintings, and outdoors, in the middle of the fort, there are a few pleasant shady benches where you can sit and ponder the many busts of bygone Dominican generals.

TOURS

Camping Tours (☎ 809-583-3121; www.campingtours .net; Calle Two 2, Villa Olga) offers the cheapest trek to Pico Duarte. Expect Spanish-speaking guides and groups of 20 to 25 people. Prices per person are US$220 on foot, US$270 with a shared mule and US$320 for your own mule. (Go for the mule.)

SLEEPING

Hotel Colonial (☎ 809-247-3122; colonialdeluxe@yahoo .com; Salvador Cucurullo 113-115; s/d with fan US$12/19, with air-con US$16/27;) The Colonial has the most budget rooms in the center. The rooms are clean (the smell of disinfectant lingers in the military-barracks-style hallways); there's cable TV; and some rooms have fridges. The rooms in the hotel's **Colonial Deluxe** building next door are nicer, although the name might be a stretch.

Hotel Platino (☎ 809-724-7576; www.hotelplatinord.com .do; Av Estrella Sadhalá; s US$33-73, d US$61-106, ste US$97-124;) Set at the back of the Plaza Platinum shopping center a short ways out of town, this is the best-value midrange option in Santiago. The 92 rooms all have wired internet, reliable hot water, TVs and air-con, and rooms on the executive floor have wi-fi and plasma TVs. There's a small business center, a bar and restaurant, and plenty of parking. Avoid the basement standard rooms – they're a bit claustrophobic.

our pick Camp David (☎ 809-276-6400; www.camp davidranch.com; Carretera Luperón Km 71/2; s/d US$40/45;) Set on a mountain ridge about 30 minutes outside Santiago, at 923m Camp David offers sweeping vistas out over the city and the valley below. It was founded by an admirer of Rafael Trujillo; the lobby holds three of the former dictator's vintage cars. To say the rooms are spacious is an understatement – the bathrooms are as big as some hotel rooms – rooms 5, 6 and 7 in particular are enormous. As it's set several kilometers off the main road, you'll need your own car to get here (or helicopter – it has its own heliport), or take a taxi (US$10).

Hotel Aloha Sol (☎ 809-583-0090; www.alohasol .com; Calle del Sol 50; s US$56-70, d US$65-85 incl breakfast,

---

CARNIVAL IN SANTIAGO

Held in February, Carnival is big all over the country, but is especially so in Santiago. The city is famous for its incredibly artistic and fantastical *caretas* (masks) and hosts an annual international *careta* competition leading up to Carnival.

The Carnival parade here is made up of rival neighborhoods: La Joya and Los Pepines. Onlookers watch from overpasses, apartment buildings, even the tops of lampposts. Costumes focus on two images: the *lechón* (piglet), which represents the devil, and the *pepín*, a fantastical animal that appears to be a cross between a cow and a duck. The most obvious difference between the two is that *lechón* masks have two smooth horns and those of the *pepines* have horns with dozens of tiny papier-mâché spikes. All participants swing *vejigas* (inflated cow bladders) and hit each other – and onlookers – on the behind.

If you decide to come to Santiago for Carnival, be sure to make reservations – rooms fill up fast this time of the year.

ste US$155; (P) (X) (L)) This centrally located hotel is your best midrange option if you want to be within walking distance of almost everything. The rooms themselves are a bit past their due date, and many of the cheaper rooms lack exterior windows – and the air freshener they use here can be overpowering. Avoid the uninspired hotel restaurant, although the breakfast is good.

Gran Almirante (☎ 809-580-1992; www.hodelpa .com; Av Estrella Sadhalá; r/ste US$205/285; (P) (X) (L) (R)) The only five-star hotel in town, the Grand Admiral – a reference to Columbus – is the obvious choice for business travelers on an expense account. The rooms are top-notch, there's a variety of restaurants and bars, and the on-site casino will keep you bleary-eyed till late.

EATING

El Buen Café (☎ 809-582-6755; cnr San Luis & Calle del Sol; mains US$3-7; (Y) breakfast, lunch & dinner) This Dominican-style cafeteria has a menu, but ignore it – come for lunch and get a good set meal for US$3. It also delivers – the sandwiches, fried chicken and burritos are all good value (if not, perhaps, the height of culinary perfection).

Pizzería Restaurant Olé (☎ 809-582-0866; cnr Av Duarte & Independencia; mains US$7-14; (Y) breakfast, lunch & dinner) Dominican pizza is served with ketchup (pronounced ka-*choo*). Why? Coz there's no pizza sauce under the cheese. An oddly satisfying experience, and at the Olé you can squirt the red stuff to your heart's content, on, say, a medium pizza (US$10) that's big enough for two.

Niguiri Sushi Bar (☎ 809-581-1212; Calle Sebastian F Valverde 31; mains US$8-15; (Y) lunch & dinner) Well, we're pretty sure this ain't how they do it in Tokyo, but if you've been without for a while, the Niguiri really hits the sushi spot. It plays groovy electronic music, and on Wednesdays some dishes are two-for-one. Niguiri is set amid a small cluster of restaurants in a quiet residential neighborhood – look for the sailcanopy roof of the restaurant next door.

Montezuma (☎ 809-581-1111; cnr Av Francia & Beller; mains US$8-18; (Y) 11am-2am) Facing the Monument, this popular restaurant specializes in Mexican dishes, from tacos and burritos to filet of grouper grilled with chili and garlic. Prices are a bit high for the main dishes, but the smaller orders are reasonable and the restaurant itself – spread over three levels with patio seating, long bar tables and rusted steel stools – is worth a look. There's live mariachi music every Friday starting at 10pm.

ourpick Camp David (☎ 809-276-6400; www.camp davidranch.com; Carretera Luperón Km 71/2; mains US$10-18; (Y) breakfast, lunch & dinner) Sitting outside on the restaurant balcony, piano music on the stereo and the city spread out at your feet, there's only one thing to do: propose to your girlfriend (or to the waiter, who'll do in a pinch if you're single). This is easily the most romantic spot in town, and has service worthy of a resort called Camp David. Beef is the specialty here – go for the *filete generalissimo*, 8oz of Angus beef (US$15). Good wine list.

Pez Dorada (☎ 809-582-4051; Calle del Sol 43; mains US$15-40; (Y) 11:30am-11:45pm) This flashback to the '70s offers unrepentantly good, expensive food. There aren't too many restaurants left that still advertise 'London broil' (US$16) with pride. It also does a rabbit stroganoff (US$19) and lobster thermidor (US$38). The Chinese owners offer a small list of Chinese dishes.

DRINKING

Clustered around the Monument are a dozen or so bars, restaurants and late-night eateries (and one pool hall), making this Santiago's best place for bar-hopping, people-meeting and general revelry. When the bars close, head to the Monument, where vendors sell beer from coolers and locals blast music from their car stereos till dawn. Whenever you decide to stumble home, remember to take a cab – while not especially dangerous, the center can be dodgy in the wee hours.

Ahi-Bar (☎ 809-581-6779; www.ahi-bar.com; cnr Calle RC Tolentino & Av Restauración; (Y) 4pm-late) This is the biggest of a string of bars on Calle Tolentino, with a large patio set above street level featuring high bar tables and stools. Most people come to drink, but in case you missed dinner the food here is actually pretty good. There's live outdoor jazz on Mondays.

Kartuja (☎ 809-581-3107; Hotel & Casino Matum, Av Las Carreras 1; (Y) 8pm to very late) Set in the Matum casino, this place doesn't get thumping until 2am or 3am – as part of the casino, it is exempt from ever-changing local licensing laws. The bouncers and bar staff all inexplicably wear monk costumes, but the place has aircon – one of the very few clubs in the country that does.

ourpick Las 3 Café (☎ 809-276-5909; Calle RC Tolentino 38; (Y) 5pm-late) If a quiet drink with friends is what you're after, this is the place to go. The music is kept to a dull roar –although there's still enough space to dance merengue or *bachata* (popular guitar music based on bolero rhythms) – and the friendly owner will welcome you with a handshake and a smile. If you get peckish, the kitchen can set you up with *picaderas* – literally 'munchies' – a sampling of meats, cheeses and olives, perfect for sharing.

Oscar Billiard Club (☎ 809-241-4730; Beller btwn Calle RC Tolentino & Av Francia; tables per hr US$2; 🕑 2pm-4am) This club has 18 pool tables scattered through a large room with a bar fronting onto the street. The music is insanely loud – possibly the loudest on the street – so bring earplugs.

Tipico Monte Bar (☎ 809-575-0300; Av 27 de Febrero 18; www.tipicomontebar.com; admission varies; 🕑 5pm-late, closed Tue) For a taste of real merengue music and dancing, the Monte Bar is a must. There's frequent live music, and you'll spot some of the best merengue dancers in town. It even webcasts its musical events live on its website. As it's set amid a series of auto-repair shops in the Las Colinas neighborhood north of the city, you'll want a cab there and back (US$3 one way).

SHOPPING

Santiago has two large shopping malls.

Las Colinas Mall (Av 27 de Febrero; 🕑 8am-11pm) Anchored by the aptly named Supermercado Jumbo, one of the biggest supermarkets in Santiago. The **movie theater** (🕑 7pm-late Mon-Fri, 4pm-late Sat & Sun) has eight screens and shows the latest flicks for only US$3, the cheapest in town. The Ruta A *concho* passes right out front.

Plaza Internacional (Av Duarte; 🕑 8am-11pm) This decidedly more upscale shopping center, just a few kilometers east of the Monument, has a good food court, an excellent bookstore (very few English titles, unfortunately) and a movie theater. The Ruta A *concho* passes right out front.

GETTING THERE & AWAY

Air

Santiago's **Aeropuerto Internacionál Cibao** (☎ 809-233-8000; www.aeropuertocibao.com.do) is a 20-minute drive from the center. It is serviced by the following airlines:

Air Turks and Caicos (☎ 809-233-8262; www.airturksandcaicos.com)
American (☎ 809-200-5151; www.aa.com)
Continental (☎ 809-200-1062; www.continental.com)
Delta (☎ 809-200-9191; www.delta.com)
Jet Blue (☎ 809-200-9898; www.jetblue.com)

There are no buses or *gua-guas* convenient to the airport, so taxis are your only option (US$18 one way).

Bus

Caribe Tours (☎ 809-576-0790) has two terminals in Santiago: in Las Colinas on Av 27 de Febrero about 3km north of the center, and in Los Jardines, just steps from the competing Metro Buses terminal. All buses stop at both stations. Destinations include Santo Domingo (US$6.70, 2½ hours, 26 times daily from 6am to 8:15pm); Puerto Plata (US$2.75, 1¼ hours, hourly from 8:30am to 9:30pm); Monte Cristi (US$3.65, 1¾ hours, six departures from 9am to 6:15pm); La Vega (US$1.80, 45 minutes; take Santo Domingo bus); Dajabón (US$3.95, 2½ hours; take Monte Cristi bus); and Sosúa (US$3.05, two hours; take Puerto Plata bus).

Metro Buses (☎ 809-587-3837; cnr Av Duarte & Maimón) is located east of the center in the Los Jardines neighborhood. Buses to Santo Domingo (US$7, two hours, hourly from 6am to 7:45pm) leave from here, with a reduced schedule on Sundays. Buses to Puerto Plata (US$2.75, 1¼ hours) leave at 9am, 11am, 1pm, 4pm, 6pm and 9pm.

All three terminals are on or near the Ruta A *concho* line (US$0.39), or take a taxi (US3).

Ayido Tour Express (☎ 809-556-3082; Isla Instituto, Genaro Pérez) was launching a service to Cap-Haïtien in Haiti when we were there – worth checking out if you're headed that way.

Car

The airport has a good selection of reliable international rent-a-car companies, all open from 7am to 11pm.

Alamo (☎ 809-612-3602; www.alamo.com)
Avis (☎ 809-582-7007; www.avis.com)
Dollar (☎ 809-233-8108; www.dollar.com)
National (☎ 809-233-8158; www.nationalcar.com)

Alamo (☎ 809-583-5543; 🕑 8am-6pm Mon-Fri, to 4pm Sat, to noon Sun) and **National** (☎ 809-583-5543; 🕑 8am-6pm Mon-Fri, to 4pm Sat & Sun) also both have offices in the Gran Almirante.

GETTING AROUND

Transportation in Santiago, unlike most of the country, is dominated by *conchos* – not the *motoconchos* (motorcycle taxis) of Puerto Plata, but rather private cars that follow set routes around town, and charge US$0.39 (up to six passengers per vehicle). *Concho* drivers pay a weekly fee for a permit to slap a letter on their windshield and drive the route. After dark, however, the unlicensed *piratas* take over, and you should exercise caution before hopping into some random person's car.

The motorcycle-shy will be relieved to know that *motoconchos* are almost nonexistent in Santiago, and regular radio taxis ply the streets looking for passengers – the in-town fare when we were there was US$3.

That said, Santiago remains a fairly walkable city – those pedestrian-inclined will be able to walk to most of the major sites without engaging the services of a fiery four-wheeled beast of doom.

SOUTH OF SANTIAGO

SAN JOSÉ DE LAS MATAS
pop 36,000

This small mountain town is 45km southwest of Santiago, and is a jumping-off point for two major hiking trails in the Parque Nacional Armando Bermúdez. There's not much reason to come here otherwise, but it's a pleasant-enough town – a good place to linger the day before or after a long hike.

If you do happen to be out here for the day, follow the trail that starts behind the post office on Calle 30 de Marzo. It leads to a cliff-top park with great views of the surrounding mountains. It's about an hour return.

Only Camping Tours (p209) offers the trek to Pico Duarte starting from Mata Grande. From there it's a five-day trek to the summit and then down to Valle de Tétero and out at La Ciénega.

For an ATM, try **Asociación Cibao De Ahorros Y Préstamos** (☎ 809-578-8009; Morillo), just a few blocks from the park.

The **Policia Nacional** (☎ 809-578-8278; Calle San José) and the **post office** (Calle 30 de Marzo) are both just a few doors from the park.

Super Farmacia Bisonó (☎ 809-578-8206; Calle 30 de Marzo 38) is just two blocks from the park.

If you need a place to crash before or after a trek, try **Hotel y Restaurant San José** (☎ 809-578-8316; Calle 30 de Marzo; s/d US$12/21). The hotel also offers the best **restaurant** (mains US$7-15; ☯ 9am-11pm) in town.

Gua-guas leave opposite the Texaco station at the entrance of town. *Gua-guas* for Santiago (US$1.75, 45 minutes, from 6:15am to 7pm) leave whenever they fill up. Buses leave roughly every 15 minutes in the mornings, but you may have to wait an hour or more in the middle of the day. There is also a number of taxi stands around town, including **Sajoma Taxi** (☎ 809-578-8778).

Trillo de la Hispaniola

The Hispaniola Trail is reputedly the one used by Columbus to walk from the north coast to the interior. This may or may not be true, but a former environment minister – in a moment of political narcissism – announced the trail with great fanfare but little to no funding. The trail runs from here in Mata Grande to Río Limpio in the west.

The trek takes about eight days, on foot and by mule, and there are no cabins or support of any kind, although you do pass through a number of small villages. The trek should only be attempted in winter, as electrical storms in summer make crossing the high mountains dangerous. No tour companies offer this trip, so you'll need to speak sufficient Spanish to organize a guide and the mules on your own. Expect to pay roughly US$10 per day for a mule, US$10 per day for a muleteer, and US$15 per day for a guide. You'll also be expected to pay for everyone's food.

Few Dominicans, and even fewer foreigners, make this trip. If you do, drop us a line.

JARABACOA
pop 57,000

Nestled in the low foothills of the mountains at 500m, Jarabacoa likes to call itself the 'City of Eternal Spring.' This may be an exaggeration – you can still happily tan poolside if you wish – but in the evenings the climate is noticeably cooler. More importantly, Jarabacoa is the outdoor capital of the interior, a place to go white-water rafting, horseback riding or canyoning, and the base most people use to hike to Pico Duarte.

There are some excellent-value hotels in Jarabacoa, and a couple of good restaurants. Those wanting to party hearty can join the locals in the many *colmados* (combination corner store, grocery store and bar) that ring Parque Central, or practice your merengue steps in the handful of nightclubs in town.

Orientation

Av Independencia and Calle Marío N Galán, one block over, are Jarabacoa's main north–south streets – Parque Central is at one end of Av Independencia and the Caribe Tours bus terminal at the other. The city's major east–west street is Calle El Carmen, which borders Parque Central and is the road you take from Jarabacoa to get to Rancho Baiguate and Constanza.

Information

EMERGENCY

Politur (tourist police; ☎ 809-754-3216; cnr José Duran & Marío Galán) Located behind the Caribe Tours terminal.

INTERNET ACCESS

Internet shops cluster within a block or two of Parque Central.

Centro de Copiado y Papelería (☎ 809-574-2902; cnr Duarte & Av Independencia; per hr US$1) This busy copy shop also doubles as an internet center.

New York Net Café (Plaza Ramirez; per hr US$0.75; ⏰ 8am-midnight) Best hours and prices in town. Headphones and a fast connection.

MEDICAL SERVICES

The town has two private clinics that offer 24-hour medical services, and a pharmacy that can deliver to your door.

Centro Medico Dr Abad (☎ 809-574-2431; Calle El Carmen 40)

Clínica Dr Terrero (☎ 809-574-4597; Av Independencia 2A)

Farmacia Miguelito (☎ 809-574-2755; Calle Marío N Galán 70) Will deliver.

MONEY

Banco BHD (Galán near Carmen)
Banco Popular (Av Independencia) Near Herrera.
Banco Progreso (Calle Uribe near Av Independencia)
BanReservas (cnr Sánchez & Galán)

POST

Post office (Av Independencia) Located on the northern edge of town.

TELEPHONE

A&G Servicios Multiples (☎ 809-574-4044; genao tours@hotmail.com; Av Independencia 43; ⏰ 8am-10pm) This travel agency doubles as a telephone center.

TOURIST INFORMATION

Tourist office (☎ 809-574-7287; securja@hotmail .com; Plaza Ramírez, 2nd fl) On the west side of the central plaza, a small tourism office (Spanish only) shares basic information about the area's activities; if you're lucky, you may also be able to score a map or two.

Activities

White-water rafting is the star of the show here, followed closely by visiting the three waterfalls nearby. You can also go canyoning, and there are a few short hikes in the area.

WHITE-WATER RAFTING

The Río Yaque del Norte is the longest river in the country, and rafting a portion of it can be a fun day trip. A typical rafting excursion begins with breakfast, followed by a truck-ride upriver to the put-in. You'll be given a life vest, a helmet and a wetsuit (no elbow or knee pads, unfortunately) plus instructions on paddling and safety. Then everyone clambers into the rafts and sets off downriver. You're usually asked to paddle a fair amount of the time, both in the rapids to keep the boat on its proper line, and in the flatwater areas to stay on pace. You'll stop for a small snack about two-thirds of the way downriver, and then return to Jarabacoa for lunch.

The rapids are rated 2 and 3 (including sections nicknamed 'Mike Tyson' and 'the Cemetery') and part of the thrill is the real risk your raft may turn over, dumping you into a rock-infested surging river – ours did. A cameraman leapfrogs ahead of the group along the riverbank to film you going over each rapid, so you can watch the instant replay afterwards over a beer while rubbing your new lumps and bumps.

The Río Yaque del Norte has level 4, 5 and 6 rapids much further up in the mountains. No official tours go that far, but some guides raft it for fun on their own time. Ask around – if you don't mind paying a hefty premium you might be able to organize something.

A lot of people come from the north coast to do rafting, and then head straight back. This involves at least four hours each way on a bus. Consider spending a couple of nights in Jarabacoa – you'll enjoy your trip much more if you do.

WATERFALLS

So picturesque are the waterfalls near Jarabacoa that an opening scene of the movie *Jurassic Park* was filmed here, using **Salto Jimenoa Uno** as the backdrop. It's definitely the prettiest, a 60m waterfall that pours from

THE INTERIOR

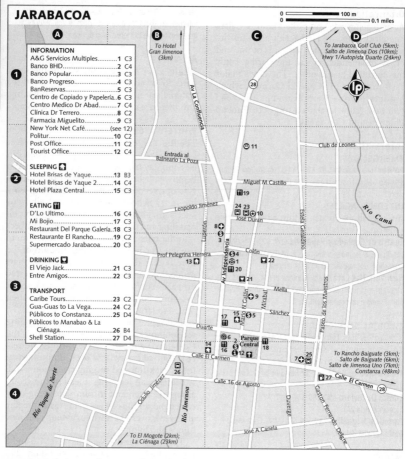

JARABACOA

0   100 m
0   0.1 miles

INFORMATION
A&G Servicios Multiples............**1** C3
Banco BHD................................**2** C4
Banco Popular...........................**3** C3
Banco Progreso.........................**4** C3
BanReservas..............................**5** C3
Centro de Copiado y Papelería..**6** C3
Centro Medico Dr Abad.............**7** C4
Clínica Dr Terrero......................**8** C2
Farmacia Miguelito....................**9** C3
New York Net Café...............(see **12**)
Politur.....................................**10** C2
Post Office...............................**11** C2
Tourist Office..........................**12** C4

SLEEPING
Hotel Brisas de Yaque..............**13** B3
Hotel Brisas de Yaque 2...........**14** C4
Hotel Plaza Central..................**15** C3

EATING
D'Lo Ultimo.............................**16** C4
Mi Bojio..................................**17** C3
Restaurant Del Parque Galería..**18** C3
Restaurante El Rancho.............**19** C2
Supermercado Jarabacoa.........**20** C3

DRINKING
El Viejo Jack............................**21** C3
Entre Amigos...........................**22** C3

TRANSPORT
Caribe Tours............................**23** C2
Gua-Guas to La Vega................**24** C2
Públicos to Constanza..............**25** D4
Públicos to Manabao & La
    Ciénaga..............................**26** B4
Shell Station............................**27** D4

a gaping hole in an otherwise solid rock cliff. (A lake feeds the waterfall via a subsurface drain.) There's a nice swimming hole, but the water is icy cold. The trail to the waterfall is 7.1km from the Shell station in Jarabacoa along Calle El Carmen, the road to Constanza. The road is paved and flat at first, then turns into a winding, hilly dirt road. Look for the access trail on your left opposite a small restaurant – it leads from the road down a steep canyon wall to the falls.

Salto de Jimenoa Dos is a 40m cascade with an appealing bathing pool – but don't, as the currents are sometimes quite strong. The turnoff to the falls is 4km northwest of Jarabacoa on the road to Hwy Duarte. Coming from town, you'll reach a major fork in the road with

a large bank of signs, one of which points to the right toward the falls. From there, a paved road leads 6km past the golf course to a parking lot. The waterfall is a 500m walk from there, over a series of narrow suspension bridges and trails flanked by densely forested canyon walls. The bridges were down when we were there (following Tropical Storm Noel) but should be back up by the time you read this.

Salto de Baiguate is also in a lush canyon but isn't nearly as impressive as the others, nor is the pool as inviting. To get there, take Calle El Carmen east out of Jarabacoa for 3km until you see a sign for the waterfalls on the right-hand side of the road. From there, a badly rutted dirt road, which at one point is crossed by a shallow creek, leads 3km to a parking lot. From there, a lovely 300m trail cut out of the canyon wall leads to the Salto. It's a pleasant walk from town, if you're not in a hurry.

The falls are easy to visit if you've got your own transportation. If not, a *motoconcho* tour to all three falls will set you back around US$15 to US$20, and a taxi US$60 to US$80. Either way you'll have to pay the park entrance fee (Dominicans/foreigners US$0.60/1.50).

HIKING

In addition to the trek to Pico Duarte, there are a number of shorter half-day and full-day walks you can take in the area.

The best day walk is to **El Mogote**, a short peak just 2km west of town. To get there, hop a *motoconcho* (US$3) or a taxi (US$7) to the entrance. Just past here you'll encounter a Salesian monastery, where the monks have taken a vow of silence, and who support themselves with a small pasta factory. From here it's a stiff 2½- to three-hour walk to the summit. Start early, wear boots if you have them, and bring plenty of water. It's a slippery walk, nay, slide, down from the top (at least the first half).

There are a couple of other shorter walks you can do in the area, including to La Jagua (around 4 hours; we estimate it's about 6km in distance) and Los Tablones (7 hours; it's about 10km). These trails are poorly marked and it's recommended to go with a local guide (US$35). You can also join a hiking group with Rancho Baiguate (right), which offers all of these excursions, ranging in price from US$25 to US$100 per person.

GOLF

Just outside of town, the **Jarabacoa Golf Club** (☎ 809-782-9883; ⌚ 7:30am-7pm) has a decent though rather nondescript nine-hole golf course that will do for anyone desperate for a golf fix. The course has two par-fives, the longest being 433m. Green fees are US$20 for two laps around the course. Club rental is US$10 with balls – oddly, rental is for one round only, so you have to pay it twice if you play 18 holes. To get there, take the turnoff to Salto de Jimenoa and look for signs for the *Campo de Golf,* about 3km down.

CANYONING

Canyoning is not especially popular in Jarabacoa, but there are a few places if you need an adrenaline fix. There are beginner and advanced options available.

Tours

Jarabacoa's biggest and best tour operator dominates the stage, leaving but crumbs for the rest. A few smaller outfits come and go, but for safety and reliability we recommend only **Rancho Baiguate** (☎ 809-574-6890; www.ranchobaiguate.com; Carretera a Constanza). While its main clientele are Dominican groups from the capital and foreign guests from the all-inclusive resorts near Puerto Plata, independent travelers are always free to join any of the trips, usually by calling a day or two in advance (except for Pico Duarte, which should be arranged weeks in advance).

Activities have the following prices, all including breakfast and lunch: rafting (US$50), canyoning (US$50), mountain biking (US$25). Rancho Baiguate also offers horseback/jeep tours to the waterfalls (US$16 to US$21 with lunch, US$9 to US$11 without lunch). Its Pico

---

THREE BEST HIKES

The interior has some great walking trails, both longer treks and day hikes.

■ The trek to Pico Duarte (p217) – This is the most popular multiday trek in the country. It can be walked in as little as two days or as many as five days, including some spectacular side trips.

■ Loma Quita Espuela (see boxed text, p225) – Rising out of the flat plains near San Francisco de Macorís, Loma Quita Espuela is surrounded by organic cocoa plantations and swimming holes. There's even a rustic cabin owned by a local farmer where you can stay the night.

■ El Mogote (above) – This small mountain outside Jarabacoa makes a great day outing. Climb past a Salesian monastery up to the top of the hill for great views of the surrounding mountain range.

Duarte trips range in price depending on the number of people and the side trips you take; a group of four people for three days with no side trips pays US$300 per person.

Sleeping

Jarabacoa's hotels are excellent value.

Hotel Plaza Central (☎ 809-574-7768; Marío N Galán; s/d US$17/34; P) The principal advantage of this run-down, linoleum-clad flophouse near Sánchez is that it's cheap. The hot water is unreliable and some rooms lack exterior windows, but the mattresses are new and there are ceiling fans. On weekends the disco downstairs plays loud music till late.

Hotel Brisas del Yaque (☎ 809-574-4490; cnr Luperón & Herrera; r US$33; 🎲) This small hotel offers eight excellent rooms, all with balconies, air-con and fridges. Ask for one facing west – the view of the surrounding mountains is excellent.

Hotel Brisas del Yaque II (☎ 809-574-2100; Independencia 13; d/tw US$45/75; P 🎲) From the creators of Hotel Brisas del Yaque comes a sequel: 20 rooms in this new, purpose-built hotel will take you on the nocturnal adventure of a lifetime, as you slumber in comfort in rustic surrounds. The twin rooms are distinctive in having two bathrooms, one for each guest. Ask for a mountain-facing room, if only to avoid the noisy streetside market. You'll laugh, you'll cry, you'll…sleep.

our pick Hotel Gran Jimenoa (☎ 809-574-6304; Av La Confluencia; www.granjimenoa.com; s/d/tr/ste incl breakfast US$50/74/95/117; P 🎲 🖳 🖼) Set several kilometers from town directly on the roaring Río Jimenoa, this is easily the best hotel in town. It may be neither on the beach nor an all-inclusive, but you could easily spend a week here without leaving the grounds (the restaurant is excellent). A new wing was under construction when we were there, and most of the old rooms are being remodeled – they may keep a couple unremodeled for budget travelers, so it's worth asking.

Rancho Baiguate (☎ 809-574-6890; www.rancho baiguate.com; Carretera a Constanza; s US$77-107, d US$126-163, tr US$170-220, q US$252; P 🖳 🖼) A cross between a summer camp and an all-inclusive resort, Rancho Baiguate offers plain but comfortable accommodations on its 72-sq-km complex, about 3km east of town. Three meals are included in the price. There's a beach volleyball court, a Ping-Pong table, and a pool table, and good bird life for those old enough to sit still. An on-site veggie garden supplies the competent Dominican cook, and a worm farm and a grey-water treatment plant reduce the resort's impact on the environment. Bring mosquito repellent. The hosts can pick you up from town.

Eating

D'Lo Último (☎ 809-574-7591; cnr Av Independencia & Duarte; mains US$3-10; 🕑 breakfast, lunch & dinner, closed Thu) This modest Dominican eatery offers reliable and tasty meals. Ask about the daily special; you can often get a salad, a meat-based main with a side of rice, and a dessert for US$3 to US$4.

Mi Bojio (☎ 809-574-2422; cnr Av Independencia & Duarte; mains US$8-15; 🕑 breakfast, lunch & dinner) Don't let the cheesy decor put you off – the cane chairs may be a little uncomfortable, and the reggaeton on the stereo may not be to everyone's taste, but the food itself is excellent. Go for the stewed guinea hen (US$12), a local specialty.

Restaurant Del Parque Galería (☎ 809-574-6749; cnr Duarte & Mirabal; mains US$8-15; 🕑 breakfast, lunch & dinner) Overlooking Parque Central, this open-air restaurant/bar serves up traditional Dominican meals as well as international favorites. If you're in the mood to try something a little different, the *conejo criollo* (rabbit prepared Creole-style, US$12) and the *cabrito al vino* (goat in wine sauce, US$9) are both excellent choices. A great place to people-watch – feel free just to order a drink and check out the goings-on in the park.

Restaurante El Rancho (☎ 809-574-4557; Av Independencia 1; mains US$8-15; 🕑 breakfast, lunch & dinner) Part of the Baiguate empire, El Rancho offers a varied menu of chicken and beef dishes, sushi-style wraps and excellent pizzas. The walls of this semidressy, open-sided restaurant are graced with handsome local paintings, although the *motoconcho* traffic outside detracts somewhat from the setting. Be sure to try the chili jam, served as an appetizer with yucca chips. Independent travelers can also inquire here about trips with Rancho Baiguate (p215).

Hotel Gran Jimenoa (☎ 809-574-6304; Av La Confluencia; www.granjimenoa.com; mains US$14-35; 🕑 7am-11pm) Jarabacoa's best hotel also offers one of the town's most notable dining experiences. The restaurant here occupies an open-air deck, shaded by low trees and perched right alongside the roaring Río Jimenoa. Tables along the edge have the best view – so close you may even feel some errant spray and have to speak loudly to be heard over the river's din. Dishes are fairly standard, though well prepared, including guinea hen or rabbit in wine sauce, and the local Jarabacoa specialty, chicken breast stuffed with cream cheese. Fight the Muzak menace – ask them to turn the stereo off.

Supermercado Jarabacoa (☎ 809-574-2780; Av Independencia; ⊙ 8am-10pm Mon-Sat, 9am-1pm Sun) A good-sized supermarket, this place has the best selection of canned food, produce and dry goods in town.

Drinking

Social life in Jarabacoa revolves around Parque Central. The church, the casino and restaurants are all here, and at night the numerous *colmados* pump loud merengue and beery customers onto the sidewalk, where the party really gets going.

El Viejo Jack (☎ 809-574-7536; cnr Marío N Galán & Mella; ⊙ 10:30am-10:30pm Sun-Thu, to midnight Fri & Sat) This liquor-store-cum-bar is full of enormous glass cases of dust-free premium booze, which Jarabacoa's elite quaff by the bottleful. Balloon wine glasses give a certain panache to sharing an entire bottle of cognac with friends. Big-screen projection TV too, and the beer is icy cold.

Entre Amigos (☎ 809-574-7979; Colón 182; ⊙ 9pm-late Fri-Sun) This thumping bar is the best party in town – expect merengue, salsa and reggaeton, and elbow-to-elbow service at the bar. There's often karaoke early in the evening, ending at 11pm. After that you'll need earplugs (and maybe before, depending on the karaoke).

Getting There & Away

Caribe Tours (☎ 809-574-4796; Calle José Duran near Av Independencia) offers the only first-class bus service to Jarabacoa. Four daily departures to Santo Domingo (US$5.40, three hours, at 7am, 10am, 1:30pm and 4:30pm) include a stop in La Vega (US$2.30, 1½ hours).

Next-door, a **gua-gua terminal** (cnr Av Independencia & Duran) provides frequent service to La Vega (US$1.40, 45 minutes, every 10 to 30 minutes from 7am to 6pm). If you prefer to hire a cab to La Vega, the ride costs around US$22.

Públicos to Constanza (cnr Deligne & El Carmen) leave from diagonally opposite the Shell gas station at around 9am and 1pm daily (US$2.80, two hours). It's a scenic but rough ride in the back of a pickup truck; the first 29km are on a badly rutted road that winds around denuded mountains, but once you hit El Río, the remaining 19km are on a paved road that passes through a lush valley.

Públicos to La Ciénaga (US$2.25, 1½ hours) leave roughly every two hours from Calle Jiménez near Calle 16 de Agosto. It's 42km long, of which the first 33km are paved. Returning can be more of a challenge, especially if you return from your hike in the afternoon. Don't hesitate to hail down any truck heading toward Jarabacoa. Chances are the driver will allow you to hop aboard.

Getting Around

The town of Jarabacoa is easily managed on foot, but to get to outlying hotels and sights you can easily flag down a *motoconcho* on any street corner during the day. If you prefer a cab, try **Taxi Jarabacoa** (☎ 809-574-7474), or a good place to hail one is at the corner of José Duran and Av Independencia.

CAR

There are several car-rental agencies in Jarabacoa. We had bad experiences with two of them, and strongly recommend that you bring a car with you if you need one (preferably an SUV). The nearest reliable, trustworthy rent-a-car agencies are in Santiago.

PARQUES NACIONALES BERMÚDEZ & RAMÍREZ

In 1956 the Dominican government established Parque Nacional Armando Bermúdez with the hope of preventing the kind of reckless deforestation occurring in Haiti. The park encompasses 766 sq km of tree-flanked mountains and pristine valleys. Two years later, an adjoining area of 764 sq km was designated Parque Nacional José del Carmen Ramírez. Between them, the parks contain three of the highest peaks in the Caribbean, and the headwaters of 12 major rivers, including the Río Yaque del Norte, the country's only white-water and most important river.

Activities
CLIMBING PICO DUARTE

Pico Duarte (3087m) was first climbed in 1944, as part of a celebration commemorating the 100th anniversary of Dominican independence. During the late 1980s, the government began cutting trails in the parks and erecting cabins, hoping to increase tourism to the country by increasing the accessibility of its peaks. These days about 3000 people a year ascend Pico Duarte.

For all the effort involved to reach the summit, there actually isn't a great deal to see. Up to around 2000m you travel through rainforest, passing foliage thick with ferns and some good bird life. You quickly pass above this limit, however, and spend most of the trip in a wasteland of burnt-out *pino caribeño* – a monoculture plantation that looks suspiciously like Monterey pine (the stuff loggers like because of its spindly, knot-free branches). Numerous forest fires have left the landscape barren, and the only animals you're likely to see are marauding bands of cawing crows. Amid the bleakness you may see the occasional colorful epiphyte.

You'll enjoy this trip much more if you spend all or part of the journey on the back of a mule – we certainly wish we had.

Orientation & Information

There are **ranger stations** (park admission Dominicans/foreigners US$1.50/3; 8am-5pm) near the start of the major trails into the parks – at La Ciénaga, Sabaneta, Mata Grande, Las Lagunas and Constanza. As a safety precaution, everyone entering the park, even for a short hike, must be accompanied by a guide.

What to Bring

Cold-weather and rain clothing are musts for anyone intending to spend a night in either park. While the average temperature ranges between 12°C and 20°C most of the year, lows of -5°C are not uncommon, especially in December and January. Rainstorms can happen at any time during the year. While the soil is sandy and drains well, you'll still want a good raincoat plus study shoes or boots.

If you're not climbing Pico Duarte as part of an organized tour, you'll also need to discuss with your guide what supplies to bring.

Tours & Guides

The easiest way to reach the summit of Pico Duarte is to take an organized tour. Prices vary widely and depend on how many people are going and for how long. Expect to pay roughly US$80 to US$100 per person per day. Be sure to book at least a month in advance.

Camping Tours (p209) in Santiago is the cheapest, as it caters primarily to Dominicans,

but its guides speak only Spanish. Camping Tours is also your only option if you want to walk Mata Grande to Pico Duarte and exit at La Ciénaga. Rancho Baiguate (p215) is the best overall choice for non-Spanish speakers, as it is based in Jarabacoa, and also offers the detour through Valle de Tétero. Iguana Mama (p188) in Cabarete is good if you're in a hurry and want transportation to and from the north coast.

Your other option – assuming you speak good Spanish and you're not in a hurry – is to go to the trailhead in person and organize mules, food and a guide on your own. Mules and muleteers go for around US$10 per day each, and the lead guide around US$15 per day (minimum one guide for every five hikers). Be aware also that if you walk out a different entrance than where you came in, you'll have to pay them several days' extra wages for them to get back to the starting point (where they live). Guides can organize basic provisions for you. There is a small spring of drinking water halfway up the trail from La Ciénaga, but you're well advised to pack in your own water (water-cooler-sized bottles, which the mules carry).

Attempting to climb Pico Duarte without mules is neither possible nor desirable – you can't enter the park without a guide, and a guide won't go without mules. Plus walking with a full pack in this heat would drain whatever enjoyment you might get from the walk. Mules are also essential in case someone gets injured.

Routes to the Top

There are two popular routes up Pico Duarte. The shortest and easiest route (and by far the most used) is from **La Ciénaga**, reached via Jarabacoa. It is 23km in each direction and involves approximately 2275m of vertical ascent en route to the peak. It's recommended to do this route in three days – one long day to arrive at the La Compartición campground, one easy day to hike up and enjoy the views, and one long day back out again. The trip can be done in two days by getting up at 4am for a dawn summit, but afterwards it's a grueling, hot slog down the mountain. Consider also adding a fourth day to your trip to do the side trip to the **Valle de Tétero**, a beautiful valley at the base of the mountain. Three tour companies – Camping Tours (p209), Rancho Baiguate (p215) and Iguana Mama (p188) – offer the trek from La Ciénaga.

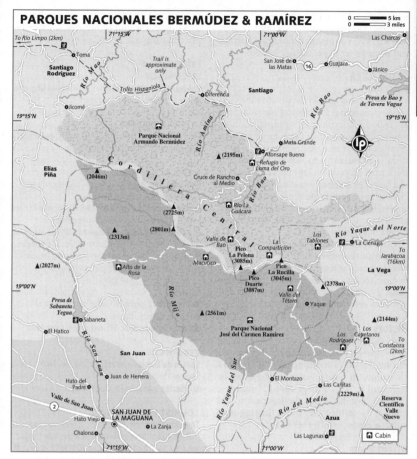

PARQUES NACIONALES BERMÚDEZ & RAMÍREZ

The second most popular route is from **Mata Grande**. It's 45km to the summit and involves approximately 3800m of vertical ascent, including going over La Pelona, a peak only slightly lower than Pico Duarte itself. You'll spend the first night at the Río La Guácara campground and the second at the Valle de Bao campground. You can walk this route return in five days, but far more interesting is to walk out via the Valle de Tétero and La Ciénega (also five days). Camping Tours offers the trek from Mata Grande.

It is also possible to reach the peak from **Sabaneta** (via San Juan de la Maguana), **Las Lagunas** (via Padre las Casas) and **Constanza**. These routes are little traveled and significantly more difficult, and no tour companies

offer this trek – you'll need to organize a guide and mules yourself.

Sleeping

There are approximately 14 campgrounds in the parks, each with a first-come, first-served cabin that hikers can use free of charge. Each cabin can hold 20 or more people and consists of wood floors, wood walls and a wood ceiling, but no beds, cots, mats or lockers of any kind. That wouldn't be so bad except that the most-frequented cabins have developed a somewhat unnerving rat problem – if you have a tent, consider bringing it along so you can avoid using the cabins altogether.

Most of the cabins also have a stand-alone 'kitchen': an open-sided structure with two or three concrete wood-burning stoves. Fallen dead wood is usually abundant near the camp-sites – be sure you or your guide bring matches and some paper to get the fire started.

CONSTANZA
pop 43,000

There's a saying here in the mountains: 'God is everywhere, but he lives in Constanza.' Set at 1200m in a fertile valley and walled in by towering mountains, you can see why – it's a breathtaking spot. Dusk, especially, is awesome – as the sun sets behind the peaks, a thick mist sinks down into the valley floor.

The valley is full of wonderful smells – the chief crops here are potatoes, strawberries, apples, lettuce and garlic, and at certain times of the year the air is filled with the pungent aroma of fresh garlic.

Constanza makes a fine weekend getaway, and during the week you're likely to have the whole place to yourself. There isn't a whole lot do here, though, and the tourist attractions are of far less interest than the cooler climate and the sheer remoteness of it all.

History

Also calling Constanza home are a couple of hundred Japanese farmers who arrived during the 1950s at dictator Rafael Trujillo's invitation. In return for providing superior farmland at dirt-cheap prices to 50 Japanese families, Trujillo hoped the Japanese would convert the fertile valley into a thriving agricultural center, which they did.

Orientation

The main street is one-way Calle Luperón, which runs from east to west and has a prominent Isla gas station – also known as *la parada* (the stop) – at its eastern end. Most of Constanza's hotels and restaurants are on or near Calle Luperón, although the best hotels are several kilometers outside the city limits. Constanza has a tall radio tower poking up in the middle of town – it's right next to the tourist office and is a useful landmark if you ever get turned around. The *mercado municipal* (municipal market) is at the far western end of town, a few blocks north of Calle Luperón.

Constanza's Parque Central represents the center of town and may be reached by proceeding three or four blocks down Calle Luperón from the Isla station and turning left.

On weekends the park comes alive with locals drinking at the end of the day – a sociable place to hang out for an hour or two.

Information

EMERGENCY
Politur (tourist police; ☎ 809-539-3020) Two kilometers east of town, just opposite the airport.

INTERNET ACCESS
Cyber Bibiloteca Emy (☎ 809-539-1372; per hr US$2) Located across from the baseball diamond.

MEDICAL SERVICES
Farmacia San José (☎ 809-539-2516; Miguel Abreu 87) At the northeast corner of the park.
Farmacia Yazdana (☎ 809-539-1142; Luperón 38) Two blocks east of the Isla gas station. Free delivery.
Hospital Pedro Antonio Cespede (☎ 809-538-2420, 809-539-3288; Calle Antonio Isacc; � 24hr) This small hospital has a fully equipped emergency room. On your right as you come into town, just past the airport.

MONEY
Banco Léon (Luperón 19) On the main drag. Also exchanges traveler's checks.
BanReservas (Luperón 18) Next door to Banco Léon.

TELEPHONE
Centro de Llamada Israel (☎ 809-539-2160; Libertad 21)
Mi Plazita (☎ 809-539-3239; cnr Luperón & Libertad)

TOURIST INFORMATION
Tourism office (☎ 809-539-2900; www.constanza .com.do; Calle Viña near Abreu) Next to the radio station, this office has lots of helpful information and friendly staff. Spanish only. Good website (in English and Spanish).

Sights & Activities

Though Constanza is surrounded by mountains, there aren't many established hikes or excursions in the area. The main sights are all quite distant, and require a 4WD to get there. Most hotels in the area can organize ad hoc tours in their own vehicles – ask.

AGUAS BLANCAS
These impressive **waterfalls** are a beautiful but difficult 16km drive from Constanza, and are reputedly the largest falls in the Greater Antilles. The falls – actually one cascade in three different sections – crash some 135m down a sheer cliff into a pretty pool. You'll need a 4WD to get there: turn north at the

Isla gas station and continue past Colonia Japonésa. If you haven't got your own vehicle, many hotels can take you there for around US$10 per person. The road was washed out when we were there (following Tropical Storm Noel), but will likely be repaired by the time you read this.

LA PIEDRA LETRADA

Meaning 'Inscribed Stone,' **Piedra Letrada** is a shallow cave containing scores of Taíno petroglyphs and pictograms, mostly depicting animals and simplistic human-like figures. The site is a good 30km from Constanza via the town of La Culeta. The road to La Culeta is paved, but it deteriorates quickly after that. Ask for directions in La Culeta, as the road is easy to miss. You'll need a 4WD.

SANCTUARÍO DE LA VIRGEN DE ALTAGRACIA

If you're driving the main Constanza–Santo Domingo highway, look for this **small church** by the side of the road. It's perched at the top of the highest pass (1300m), and devout travelers frequently stop to light a candle and utter a word of prayer. Those less devout will still welcome the views and the opportunity to stretch their legs. It's about 38km east of Constanza.

SOFTBALL GAMES

One of the most enjoyable things to do in Constanza is to attend one of the friendly **softball games** held almost every night all year long at the local baseball diamond. Games begin at 7pm; there is no admission fee and you can usually find someone selling beer, soda and odd snacks from a cooler in the stands. The stadium is located several blocks west of the Parque Central.

Festivals & Events

Every September – the date varies – Constanza goes nuts during **Fiestas Patronales**, a nine-day-long party that is nominally in honor of the Virgen de las Mercedes, the town's patron saint. There are live music events, beer tents in the park, and the whole shebang culminates in the crowning of the new *reina* – a Miss Constanza pageant, of sorts.

Sleeping

Only two to three hours from Santo Domingo by car, Constanza fills up on weekends and holidays and empties during the week. Many establishments operate with skeleton staffs in off-peak periods, and prices vary accordingly. You'll enjoy your stay a great deal more if you stay outside of town – the center of Constanza is dirty and noisy, and clogged with the constant din of motorcycles and scooters.

Hotel Aguas Blancas (☎ 809-539-1561; García near 14 de Julio; s with fan US$15, d with air-con US$18; P) Near the *mercado municipal*, this small hotel offers seven spotless rooms with tiled floors and private hot-water baths. Some have air-con.

Hotel Restaurant Mi Casa (☎ 809-539-2764; cnr Luperón & Sánchez; r/tw US$15/26; P) A block west from the Isla gas station; rooms here are basic and clean. Only some are tiled but all have private bathrooms. Some rooms lack good ventilation; request one with an outward-facing window for a breeze. The on-site restaurant is decent for breakfast.

Rancho Macajo (☎ 809-707-3805; Carretera Duvergé; half cabin US$24, whole cabin US$46, house US$136; P) What is surely unique accommodation in the entire region, this homey retreat-cum-zoo is perched on a ridgeline several kilometers outside of town, and offers four cabins, each with two bedrooms and a kitchen. The eccentric Dominican owner – she calls herself the 'old monkey lady' – keeps a small menagerie of pet primates and parrots. The rooms are nice, the views stunning, and the on-site bar and restaurant serves acceptable if not particularly exciting food. The driveway is a steep, first-gear-only climb in a good 4WD. Coming from town, at the fork in the road in Colonia Japonésa go right (the official tourist map is confusing on this point).

our pick Alto Cerro (☎ 809-539-6192; www.alto cerro.com; s/d/ste US$24/30/39, villas for 2/5/7 people US$52/100/167, camping per person US$10; P) Easily the best accommodation in Constanza, this large, family-owned complex is 2km east of town off the road toward Hwy Duarte. Perched partway up a high bluff, the rooms have terrific views of the whole valley, the bright green fields of carrots and strawberries spread out like a patchwork quilt below. Rooms have high ceilings and comfortable beds; the suites and two-story villas are larger and convenient for their kitchens. Other than the restaurant at the hotel, there are no places to eat without going into town, but the hotel has a small market, where you can buy pasta and other basics for a simple meal. If the hosts like the look of you, there's a small campground with a bathroom and a wood-fired barbecue.

Eating

Foodies will be somewhat disappointed in Constanza, as there is nothing truly top end.

Restaurant Aguas Blancas (☎ 809-539-1561; Espinosa 54; mains US$4-9; ⌚ lunch & dinner) With a pleasant dining room and excellent food, this is the best value in town. The set meals at lunchtime (US$4) prove our theory that the smaller the town, the better the rice and beans.

Lorenzo's Restaurant Pizzería (☎ 809-539-2008; Luperón 83; mains US$5-14; ⌚ breakfast, lunch & dinner) Towards the western edge of town, Lorenzo's does good-value steaks, pizzas and sandwiches. At lunchtime it sometimes offers a hearty *sancocho* (US$4) – a stew of meat, sausage, plantain and potato.

Alto Cerro (☎ 809-539-6192; www.altocerro.com; mains US$10-25) Located 2km east of town on the highway. The balcony of this hotel's restaurant-cum-bar is the best spot in town to watch the sunset. Beef is the specialty here; go for the *churrasco* (US$18).

Mercado Municipal (cnr Gratereaux & 14 de Julio; ⌚ 7am-6pm Mon-Sat, to noon Sun) A good-sized market near the north end of town, here you'll find a wide variety of locally grown produce.

Super El Económico (☎ 809-539-2323; Luperón; ⌚ 7:45am-noon & 1:45-8pm Mon-Sat, 9am-noon Sun) Across from Isla gas station, this medium-sized grocery store has canned food, snacks, water, produce and more.

Getting There & Away

The Jarabacoa–Constanza road is worse than your favorite SUV commercial: it's jaw-rattlingly bad. You should not attempt it without a good 4WD and a lot of patience. That said, we saw a lot of Photoshopped images of what the planned new highway will look like – with a 50-year guarantee, or so claims the Brazilian company building it. Should this actually take place, travel times will be cut drastically, making Constanza a feasible day trip from Jarabacoa, and an easy drive in a regular car.

If you're coming from Hwy Duarte, the turnoff at El Albanico is 89km north of Santo Domingo, and from there it's 51km on a well-paved, twisty mountain road. You'll enjoy your time in Constanza more if you come in an SUV, though, as the roads once you get here are pretty bad.

Gua-guas regularly service El Albanico (US$5, 1½ hours), where you can change for a *gua-gua* to Santo Domingo and La Vega (US$6.20, two hours). If you're in a hurry, bus company **Linea Junior** (☎ 809-539-2177) offers a commuter service from Santiago to Constanza ($US7, 3½ hours, via La Vega and El Albanico) at 5am and noon, returning from Constanza at 1pm and 6pm. Call ahead and they'll pick you up from your hotel (US$1 extra).

You'll pass a small **airstrip** as you come into town. There were no commercial flights when we were there, and it's used more often for *draguero* (drag racing) than for winged flight.

LA VEGA

pop 220,000

About halfway between Santo Domingo and Santiago, La Vega is a small farming town famous principally for its Carnival celebration, the biggest and most lavish in the country (see boxed text, opposite).

The main street is Av Antonio Guzman, which runs north–south and intersects Hwy Duarte on the north side of town. On the northern end of the avenue, there are two hotels and a Santiago-bound *gua-gua* stop; near the central part, you'll find the main plaza, the cathedral, food stands and a bank.

History

La Vega dates to the late 1490s, at which time Christopher Columbus ordered a fort be built to store gold mined in the area. During the next 50 years, the first mint in the New World was established here; the nation's first commercial sugar crop was harvested in the vicinity; and the first royally sanctioned brothel in the western hemisphere opened its doors for business.

But this prosperity came to an abrupt end in 1562, when an earthquake leveled the city. So severe was the damage that the city was moved several kilometers to its present site on the banks of the Río Camú. You can visit what remains of the old city near the town of Santo Cerro.

Information

BanReservas (Adolfo 24) A half-block from the cathedral.

Red Cross (☎ 809-277-8181; ⌚ 24hr) Your best bet in a medical emergency.

Sights & Activities

Other than during Carnival, there's no real reason to stop in La Vega. If you do happen

---

LET THERE BE LENT

La Vega hosts the largest and most organized Carnival in the country. Townspeople belong to one of numerous Carnival groups, which range from 10 to 200 members and have unique names and costumes. The costumes (which can cost up to US$1000) are the best part of Carnival here – a colorful baggy outfit (it looks like a clown, but is supposed to represent a prince), a cape and a fantastic diabolic mask with bulging eyes and gruesome pointed teeth.

Groups march along a long loop through town, and spectators either watch from bleachers set up alongside or march right along with them. The latter do so at their own risk – the costume also includes a small whip with an inflated rubber bladder at the end, used to whack passersby on the backside. The celebration has been criticized lately for being overly commercialized. Indeed, you'll see booths and VIP viewing areas hosted by Orange, Presidente and other companies, and some Carnival groups stitch the name of sponsors onto their costumes (which are themselves typically bought, as opposed to handmade as in Santiago and elsewhere). But for now, the celebration is still more personal than corporate, and the high level of organization and security are certainly a plus.

---

to find yourself in town, however, there are a few things worth checking out.

CATEDRAL DE LA CONCEPCIÓN
La Vega's infamous **cathedral** (cnr Av Guzman & Adolfo; ⊙ varies) is a fascinating eyesore that looks more like a set of smokestacks than a place of worship. It is an odd mixture of Gothic and neoindustrial style constructed of concrete and decorated with sculpted metal bars and pipes alongside random ornamental windows. It faces the main park and it is impossible to miss.

SANTO CERRO
Just north of La Vega, and several kilometers east of Hwy Duarte along a well-signed road, is Santo Cerro (Holy Hill). Santo Cerro acquired its godly name the old-fashioned way – through a miracle. Legend has it that Columbus placed a cross he received as a bon-voyage gift from Queen Isabela atop the hill, which commands a sweeping view of the Valle del Cibao. During a battle between Spaniards and Taínos, the latter tried to burn the cross but it wouldn't catch fire. And then, with Taíno warriors looking on, the Virgen de las Mercedes appeared on one of its arms. The Taínos are said to have fled in terror.

Today the cross is gone – supposedly it's in private hands, but it is unclear whose – but you can still see the Santo Hoyo (Holy Hole) in which the cross was allegedly planted. The hole is inside the **Iglesia Las Mercedes** (⊙ 7am-noon & 2-6pm), covered with a small wire grill and tended by nuns and Jesuit priests. The beige-and-white church with its red-tile roof is a major pilgrimage site, drawing thousands of believers every September 24 for its patron-saint day. Be sure to look for a fenced-off tree near the steps leading to the church – it is said to have been planted in 1495.

LA VEGA VIEJA
If you continue a few kilometers on the same road that brought you to Santo Cerro, you'll come to **La Vega Vieja** (admission Dominicans/foreigners US$0.60/1.50; ⊙ 8am-5pm), the original site of the city. All that's left are the ruins of the fort Columbus ordered built, as well as a church. Little of either actually survived the great earthquake of 1562 and most of what remained of the structures was taken to the latter-day La Vega, where it was used in construction.

Sleeping & Eating
Unless you're in La Vega for Carnival, there is no real reason to stay the night. If you do end up needing a place to crash, there's one good, regular hotel and lots of little love motels whose principal business is *de paso* – a few hours' rental – but which may rent you a room for the night.

Hotel Rey (☎ 809-573-9797; Calle Restauración 3; s/d/ste US$33/49/82; Ⓟ 🅿 ✗) This is a modern hotel with clean though somewhat dated rooms. Each has cable TV. Ask for a room towards the back – those facing the road can get loud. There's an on-site restaurant that serves decent Dominican fare.

Food stands serving fried chicken and *pastelitos* (flaky fried dough stuffed with meat, cheese or veggies) can be found in front of the cathedral.

Getting There & Away

La Vega is a regular stop on the well-covered Santo Domingo–Santiago route. **Caribe Tours** (☎ 809-573-2488; Av Rivera) has its terminal on the main highway 1.5km from the center of La Vega. From there, buses depart for Santo Domingo (US$4.55, 1½ hours, every 30 to 60 minutes from 6:30am to 7:45pm) and north to Sosúa (US$5, 2½ hours, hourly from 7:30am to 8:30pm) with stops at Santiago (US$1.85, 40 minutes) and Puerto Plata (US$4.55, two hours). Santiago-bound *gua-guas* (US$1.80, 50 minutes) leave from a terminal on the main road into town about five blocks from Parque Central.

For Jarabacoa, the Caribe Tours bus from Santo Domingo passes the La Vega terminal at roughly 8:30am, 11:30am, 3pm and 6pm (US$2.30, one hour). Alternatively, *gua-guas* and pickups leave whenever they're full from a stop called Quinto Patio (about a kilometer from the center, US$2 in a taxi) from 7am to 6pm.

For Constanza, there are two direct buses (US$5.50, two to three hours) leaving from the *mercado público* (public market) at around 8am and 2pm, though the actual departure times can vary widely. Otherwise, you can catch a Bonao-bound *gua-gua* on Av Gregorio Riva south to El Albanico (US$2.25, 45 minutes), and hail a passing *gua-gua* there (US$3, 1½ hours).

EAST OF SANTIAGO

MOCA
pop 132,000

The country town of Moca has prospered in recent decades as a result of its production of coffee, cocoa and tobacco. The tallest building in town is also its only tourist attraction, the **Iglesia Corazón de Jesus** (admission free; ☿ varies), with a panel of beautiful stained glass imported from Turin, Italy.

During the 18th century, Moca was one of the Spanish colony's chief cattle centers. Then in 1805 an invading Haitian army took Moca, killed virtually the entire population and burned the town to the ground. Moca struggled back, and in the 1840s began to raise tobacco as a commercial crop; now, some of the world's finest cigars contain tobacco grown on the hillsides around the town.

Moca is on the road heading south from Sabaneta, just east of Cabarete. There's not much point coming here if you haven't got your own car, but there is frequent *gua-gua* service from Santiago (US$1.75, 45 minutes) and La Vega (US$2.10, one hour).

If you're driving, be sure to check out **El Molino de la Cumbre** (☎ 809-781-1256; Sabaneta-Moca hwy Km 34; mains US$8-15); 14kms before you hit Moca on the road from Sabaneta you'll come to this restaurant perched on the edge of a cliff. The views down to Santiago are amazing, and for the nondriver the cocktail list is extraordinary. Crêpes are the specialty of the house. It's a 45-minute drive from Cabarete.

SAN FRANCISCO DE MACORÍS
pop 157,000

San Francisco de Macorís is a bustling, prosperous place in the heart of the Valle del Cibao. It draws much of its prosperity from the fields of cocoa and rice that grow around it in all directions. (It may also derive some trickle-down effect from the wealthy drug lords who reputedly own some of the huge barricaded mansions visible around town.) There are a number of colonial buildings about the place, and a large, pretty plaza. San Francisco is also home of one of the DR's six baseball teams, the Gigantes (Giants).

There isn't a whole lot to do or see in San Francisco, and very few tourists come here. Probably the best reason to venture out this way is a day trip to Loma Quita Espuela (see boxed text, opposite).

Sleeping & Eating

There's one good hotel in town, and a small rustic cabin inside the national park. A number of budget options also cluster around the main square.

Rancho Don Lulú (r US$10; ℗) This simple accommodation is just 1km from the Quita Espuela trailhead. There's one double bed in a rustic cabin a couple of hundred meters from the owners' home, where you eat (meals US$2 to US$5). Ideal for a taste of country life. Contact the Fundación Loma Quita Espuela (opposite) at least a day or two in advance to reserve the cabin.

Hotel Las Caobas (☎ 809-290-5858; cnr Calle Carrón & Av San Diego; s/d/ste per person US$50/60/100; ℗ 🛰 🖳) The 'Mahogany Hotel' lives up to its name, at least in the lobby and the on-site restaurant – mahogany furniture and paneling everywhere. The rooms themselves are pungent with air freshener, but all have a safe, fridge and TV.

RESERVA CIENTÍFICA LOMA QUITA ESPUELA

The 'Mountain of the Missing Spur' – a reference to the dense underbrush that ripped boot spurs from cowboys, not the *espuela* (fighting claw of a cock, also frequently removed) – is a remote and lovely (and definitely off the beaten track) national park. The NGO **Fundación Loma Quita Espuela** (☎ 809-588-4156; www.flqe.org.do; Urbanización Almánzar, cnr Calle Luis Carrón & Av del Jaya; ⏰ 8am-noon & 2-5pm) runs the national park on behalf of the government, and is actively involved in developing sustainable ways for the local farmers to use this natural resource.

Many of the local, small cocoa growers whose land borders the national park now produce organic cocoa, and the Foundation helps them achieve organic certification. A beekeeping project is also encouraging locals to keep bees in the national park – having more bees helps the endemic plants fertilize better, and it's extra income for the locals at minimal cost to the environment.

The national park contains the largest rainforest on the island, and is full of endemic species, both plant and animal, that are on the point of extinction. Additionally, more than 60 streams flow from these mountains and provide water to the cities and towns surrounding, making the foundation's efforts critical to the survival not only of the park but also the hundreds of thousands of people who live nearby.

Visiting Quita Espuela makes a pleasant day trip from Santiago or Santo Domingo. The Foundation offers a number of tours, including the hike to the top of **Loma Quita Espuela** (942m, 2½ hours), where an observation tower commands excellent views out over the Valle del Cibao. A guide is mandatory (Spanish only), and can explain the flora and fauna you see along the way. The tour costs US$12 for a group of up to 15 people. You'll also have to pay the park entrance fee (Dominicans/foreigners US$0.60/1.50).

For those less actively inclined, there's a shorter walk that tours several cocoa plantations, where you can buy *bola de cacao* – crude chocolate balls that the local housewives grate and sweeten to make hot chocolate. The tour ends at a local *balneario* (swimming hole), where you can take a dip. There are several Taíno caves nearby, too, and, if you're driving, the Foundation staff can take you there for free (or, if not, for the price of the gasoline).

The entrance to Loma Quita Espuela is 14km (30 minutes) northeast of San Francisco de Macorís on a rough road that gets progressively worse. From the center of town, take Calle Salcedo to Av Libertad and turn left. Continue three blocks until you see the *mercado municipal* (municipal market) on your left. Then turn right on Calle Castillo and follow the road out of town as it bends around to the east. The entrance will be on your left, and from there it's two rough kilometers to the trailhead, including crossing a small river. Don't try this without a good 4WD.

The restaurant is open all day, and a pleasant pool beckons out back. Conveniently located just a few hundred meters from the offices of Fundación Loma Quita Espuela.

Getting There & Away

For such a large city, it's flabbergasting that not a single highway is marked 'to San Francisco de Macorís.' The turnoff from Hwy Duarte is about 15km (10 minutes) south of La Vega. The tangle of unmarked country roads that crisscross the lowland marshes east of the main Santo Domingo–Santiago highway is quite confusing – expect to make frequent stops to ask for directions. It's possible but much more difficult (and on much worse roads) to come south from the coast via Nagua.

Caribe Tours (☎ 809-588-2221; cnr Calle Castillo & Hernández) runs more than a dozen buses daily from Santo Domingo (US$6.70, 6am to 7pm).

The Southwest

Few travelers come to the southwest. There's a reason for that: it's remote, and its treasures yield themselves only to those who apply the effort. It's worth it, though – miles of pristine, empty beaches, twittering birdsong in the cloud forests of the mountains, and the striking dry desert landscape of cactus stretching all the way to the border.

The remoteness and loneliness add savor and spice to the adventure. Bahía de Las Águilas is a stunning stretch of 10km of yellow sand. That you have to take a boat to get there – and that there won't be any tourists there except for you – transform it into one of the most beautiful beaches in the country.

The infrastructure here remains poor – roads are bad and telephone service sketchy. But for those looking to disconnect from the wired world, this may be a blessing in disguise. Where else can you sleep in a cabin on top of a fog-bound mountain in the Caribbean and be completely confident that your BlackBerry won't work?

Towards the Haiti border you'll find Lago Enriquillo, an inland sea and remnant of the strait that once divided the island from Barahona to Port-au-Prince. Everywhere you'll see rocks of fossilized coral and, in the middle of the lake, Isla Cabritos, a national park where unique, endemic varieties of plants and animals thrive.

Last but not least, the larimar mine just south of Barahona is the only larimar mine in the country and, indeed, the world. You can visit the mine and buy crude stones directly from the miners or purchase cut-price jewelry from the small workshops that cluster both at the mine and the coastal towns nearby.

HIGHLIGHTS

- Savor the coolness and tranquility of the cloud forest at the remote cabins of **Cachóte** (p235)

- Delight in the untouched beauty of deserted **Bahía de Las Águilas** (p237), the most remote beach in the country

- Spot flamingos and turtles on a boat tour to super-salty **Laguna Oviedo** (p236)

- Marvel at cactus flowers, butterflies and beefy iguanas on **Isla Cabritos** (p240), the lowest point in the Caribbean

- Get caffeinated at the **Polo Organic Coffee Festival** (p240) on the first weekend in June

★ Isla Cabritos

★ Polo

★ Cachóte

Bahía de
las Aguilas ★

★ Laguna Oviedo

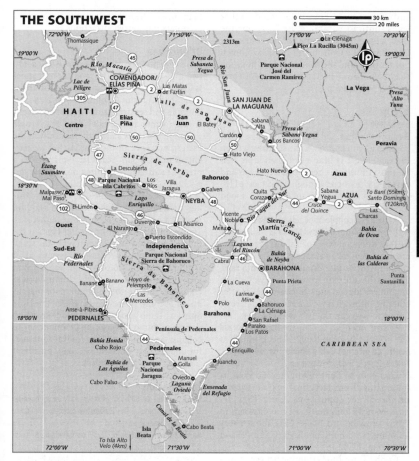

GETTING THERE & AROUND

Although there's one nominally international airport just outside of Barahona, no commercial airlines fly there, so your only way to get here is by bus or car. Caribe Tours has regular service to Barahona and San Juan de la Maguana, but after that only *gua-guas* (small buses) transit the rest of the region. Because of union agreements, *gua-guas* plying the coastal highway do not stop at every town along the way, even though they pass right through them. Be careful to get on the right bus, or else you'll be let off outside of town and you'll have to walk or catch another ride in.

If you're thinking of renting a car, be warned on two counts: there are no rental car agencies of any kind in the southwest, so rent

something in Santo Domingo; and two, if you plan on going even 100m off the side of the highway, you're going to want a really good 4WD – the roads here are astonishingly bad.

The coastal road between Barahona and Pedernales is one of the few places in the country where hitchhiking is common and reasonably safe. Only hitchhike during daylight hours, and offer the driver a buck or two (although he'll probably refuse it).

INLAND

Three highways lead west to the Haitian border. Fifteen kilometers west of Ázua the highway branches west to San Juan de la Maguana and the border at Elías Piña, and the other leads south to Barahona. At Barahona the road splits again – the interior road runs past Lago Enriquillo to the highly trafficked Jimaní border post, and the southern road hugs the coast before dead-ending at Pedernales (where there is no border post).

ÁZUA
pop 88,000

Ázua is the first and largest town you'll encounter as you approach the southwest from the east, but it is little more than a pit stop for most travelers. There are a few hotels and basic services here, though Baní (see p115) is a much more pleasant place to spend the night.

Ázua has a couple of beaches: **Playa Río Monte** is the most popular; **Playa Blanca** is a kilometer further west along the coastal dirt road. There are also a few nice vantage points where you can sometimes spot dolphins or manta rays. The beaches are 6km from the highway, down an unmarked road a few hundred meters after entering the town from the east. If you haven't got your own car, though, don't bother.

If you need an ATM, try **Banco Progreso** (☎ 809-521-2592; 19 de Marzo). Check email at **Centro de Internet Gente Online** (☎ 809-521-2362; Av Mella 2; per hr US$1; ☺ 8am-8pm).

Gua-guas to Santo Domingo (US$2, 1¾ hours) leave from a terminal on Calle Duarte, on the corner opposite the park. They depart every 15 minutes from roughly 5am to 7pm. West-bound buses pass about every 15 minutes, to both San Juan (US$2.45) and Barahona (US$2.15).

Caribe Tours buses running between Santo Domingo and Barahona stop in Ázua, arriving and departing from the Parque Central. If you're already in Ázua and headed to Santo Domingo, buses depart at 7:15am, 7:30am, 10:45am, 11:15am, 2:30pm, 2:45pm and 6:15pm.

SAN JUAN DE LA MAGUANA
pop 73,000

San Juan de la Maguana is known as *La Ciudad de los Brujos,* the City of Shamans. Haitians are increasingly taking the places of Dominicans who move to the big city, and the Vodou influence lurks just under the Dominican-Catholic exterior. That said, if you really want to put a hex on your ex, you might have to do a little digging – most shamans live in the hills outside the city, and are definitely not tourist attractions.

Orientation

When the highway hits the town, it splits into two one-way streets – the west-bound street is Calle Independencia, and the east-bound is Calle 16 de Agosto. All of the city's hotels, restaurants and services are on those two streets. A large white arch modeled on the Arc de Tríomphe in Paris stands dramatically at the eastern entrance of the city. At the western end of town is San Juan's large plaza, with a pretty cream-colored church on one side and a school of fine arts on the other.

Sometime in May – the date varies according to the date Easter falls – San Juan's faithful mount a unique procession that showcases, among other things, the strong Haitian influence in this region. Beginning in the small town of El Batey, a procession carries a small religious figurine to San Juan, some 15km away. The procession includes drumming and chanting, and it's not uncommon for marchers to become possessed by either the Holy Spirit or Taíno ghosts, and to suddenly begin dancing around or speaking in tongues or to collapse on the ground. The festival continues for another day or so in San Juan, mostly in the plaza around the church.

Information

Banco León (☎ 809-557-6094; cnr Calle Independencia & Mariano Rodríguez) This bank is two blocks west of the arch, across from a gas station.

BanReservas (☎ 809-557-2230; cnr Calle Independencia & 27 de Febrero) A bank.

Cetecom (☎ 809-557-4353; Calle 16 de Agosto 49A btwn Mella & Colón; per hr US$0.90; ☺ 8am-7pm Mon-Sat) This rambling copy shop has three computers with internet access.

Codetel (☎ 809-220-7890; Calle Nuestro Señora de Rosario No 136; ☺ 8am-7pm Mon-Fri, 8am-2pm Sat) Provides telephone services.

Data Center (☎ 809-557-6190; cnr Capotillo & Colon; per hr US$0.90; ☺ 8am-10pm) Biggest and fastest internet in town, two blocks south of the main drag.

Farmacia Inmaculada (☎ 809-557-2801; Calle Independencia 45; ☺ 8am-10pm) A pharmacy.

Policia Nacional (national police; ☎ 809-557-2380; cnr Calle Independencia & Dr Cabral; ☺ 24hr) Located one block west of the large white arch at the east entrance of town.

Viajes Vimenca (☎ 809-557-2100; cnr Calle 16 de Agosto & 27 de Febrero) Travel agent; located inside a money exchange office.

Sleeping & Eating

Hotels in San Juan are generally full of Dominican business travelers, and for this reason are mildly good value.

Hotel y Supermercado El Detallista (☎ 809-557-1200; cnr Calle Trinitaria & Puello; s/d US$29/37; P) This hotel and supermarket is one street up from Calle Independencia. Rooms are on the 3rd and 4th floors, surrounding a large common area with couches and tables. Rooms are a little small, but comfortable and clean. The supermarket downstairs has a payphone, ATM, plus all the produce, snacks and other foods you may need.

Hotel Maguana (☎ 809-557-2244; Av Independencia 72; s/d/tr/ste incl breakfast on weekends US$29/39/49/55; P) Built at dictator Trujillo's request in 1947, the Maguana's imposing façade suggests a grandeur that has now faded. All the rooms have hot water and TV, although some lack windows – look before you leap. If you can afford it, ask for the Trujillo suite – the biggest of the bunch, and where his highness used to lay his head.

Rincón Mexicano (☎ 809-557-3713; cnr Calle 27 de Febrero & Capotillo; mains US$2-8; dinner to late on weekends) Owned by a real live Mexican, this large, airy restaurant pumps out authentic, bite-size Mexican tacos (US$1.80), all served with spicy salsa. Choose from white flour or yellow maize tortillas, with beef, chicken, or pork. The generous sides of guacamole (US$1) are a bargain. You'll want three or four of these to make a meal, and the beer here is so cold it's slushy.

Il Bocconino (☎ 809-557-1616; Calle 2 No 13; pizzas US$10-15; lunch & dinner) This top-shelf pizzeria also runs a public swimming pool next door, where you can sit around in your swimsuit eating pizza and drinking beer. There's a quieter, more refined dining area on the 2nd floor, where you can enjoy quality pasta and a huge cocktail menu. It delivers (US$1 extra), and charges US$5 per person to use the pool.

Getting There & Around

Caribe Tours (☎ 809-557-4520) has a terminal 75m west of Hotel Maguana in the town's Caribe Tours depot. Buses to Santo Domingo (US$6.70, 2½ hours) depart at 6:45am, 10am, 1:45pm and 5:15pm.

Gua-guas for Santo Domingo (US$5.50, three hours, every 20 minutes from 7am to 6:30pm) leave from a terminal three blocks east of the arch, across from the baseball field. There are three express buses (US$5.50, 6:30am, 9:30am and 3pm), which make the trip a half-hour faster because they don't make a food stop along the way. If you're really in a hurry, **Transporte de Valle** (☎ 809-557-6200) runs a bus (US$6.50) at 3am to Santo Domingo, arriving around 6:30am, and can pick you up from your hotel.

If you are going to Barahona, you can take any of the four Caribe Tours buses to Ázua (US$2.15, one hour) and catch a Barahona-bound bus there. Alternatively, take a Santo Domingo *gua-gua* and get off at Cruce del Quince (US$2, 50 minutes), the main highway intersection 15km west of Ázua, and catch a south-bound *gua-gua* from there.

For Comendador/Elías Piña (US$3, 1½hrs, every 30 minutes from 7am to 6pm), the *gua-gua* terminal is at the far western end of Calle Independencia, past the Texaco gas station. *Motoconchos* (motorcycle taxis) may tell you that the only bus stop is outside of town – ignore them. Additionally, make absolutely sure your bus is going all the way to Elías Piña: if there aren't enough passengers, they may dump you halfway (at Las Matas) and you'll have to wait for another bus to come through (or pay a premium for a taxi).

Taxis and *motoconchos* may be found near Parque Central. You can also call a **taxi** (☎ 809-557-6400).

COMENDADOR DEL REY (ELÍAS PIÑA)
pop 26,000

Comendador del Rey, or Comendador for short, is the official name of the border town west of San Juan. However, almost everyone who doesn't live there calls it Elías Piña, which is the name of the state, and you'll have more luck using that name anywhere but in town. Comendador is best known for the Haitian market held there every Monday and Friday, when hundreds of Haitians arrive on donkeys and on foot to sell their wares.

Comendador also has a major military base and a police headquarters, and security (aimed at preventing illegal Haitian immigration) is tight. Even white travelers may find themselves detained and questioned if not carrying their passport (it happened to us).

For more information on crossing the border see p256.

Orientation

The highway splits into two one-way streets when it enters town. The west-bound street is Calle Santa Teresa and the east-bound is Calle 27 de Febrero. Almost everything you need is on or near those two streets. The park is at the eastern end of town, between Calles Las Carreras and Las Mercedes. There's a large roundabout at the western end of town, at which point the roads merge again and lead to the Haiti–DR border, about 1.5km away.

Information

For emergencies, contact the **Policía Nacional** (☎ 809-527-0290; cnr Calles 27 de Febrero & Las Mercedes; ✆ 24hr). There is no tourist police office here. **BanReservas** (☎ 809-527-0907) has a 24-hour ATM at its branch office located at a traffic circle near the market on the west end of town. **Médicos Del Mundo** (☎ 809-527-0369; ✆ 24hr) is near the eastern entrance of the town, set 30m off the south side of the street, across from the military base. Inside there's a pharmacy that's also open 24 hours. There's a small **taxi service** (☎ 809-839-4420; ✆ 5am-midnight).

Sights

The **Haitian market** is impossible to miss; just stay on the main road through town until you run into it. Vendors lay their goods out on the ground, shaded by large plastic tarps suspended from every available tree, road sign and telephone pole. Cooking utensils, clothing, shoes, fruits and vegetables are the primary items, sold for as little as 50% of the normal price. There's not much in the way of handicrafts, since few tourists attend the market, but just wandering around and taking in the scene is worthwhile. (And who knows, maybe you'll see a colander you like.)

Sleeping

If you get stuck here there's one serviceable hotel-cum-hardware store.

Casa Teo Hotel y Ferretería (☎ 809-527-0392; cnr Calles Santa Teresa & Las Mercedes; s/d/tr US$10/17/22) Every border town should have one of these places – for all your holiday hardware needs! It faces the park and is predictably grubby. A last resort (and not the all-inclusive kind, either).

Getting There & Away

The main *gua-gua* terminal is on Av 27 de Febrero, at the eastern end of the main park.

Buses for Santo Domingo (US$7.50, four hours, every 30 minutes from 2am to 6pm). If you're just going to San Juan (US$2.60, one hour), take one of the *gua-guas* parked just outside the terminal, as the Santo Domingo bus doesn't officially stop in San Juan. For Barahona, take a Santo Domingo bus to Cruce del Quince (the main highway intersection 15km west of Ázua; US$4.25, two hours) and then catch a south-bound bus from there. Or use Caribe Tours – see (p229) for details.

PENÍNSULA DE PEDERNALES

The Península de Pedernales contains some of the most outstanding attractions of the southwest: Bahía de Las Águilas, Laguna Oviedo and Parque Nacional Jaragua; Cachóte; and world-class bird-watching in the Parque Nacional Sierra de Bahoruco. It's also home to Barahona, and a number of small, friendly coastal towns.

The peninsula was once originally a separate island, but tectonic movement pushed it north and upward into Hispaniola, closing the sea channel that once ran from Port-au-Prince to Barahona, and creating many of the unique geographical features you'll see today.

The southwest is the best place on the island to go bird-watching, as you can see nearly all the endemics here. There are roughly 306 known birds in the DR and 31 endemic birds on the island. Half of these birds are migratory, making winter the best time to spot them.

Tours

our pick **Eco Tour Barahona** (☎ 809-243-1190; www.ecotour-repdom.com; apt 306, Carretera Enriquillo 8, Paraíso) This experienced, professional French-owned tour company has been pioneering tourism in the southwest since 2004. It offers good day trips to Bahía de Las Águilas, Isla Cabritos, Laguna Oviedo, Cachóte and Hoyo de Pelempito. It also offers a handful of day hikes in the hills around Paraíso, and can organize one-day and multiday horseback-riding tours. The owners and their small group of guides are trilingual. All day trips cost US$70 and include an excellent three-course picnic lunch.

THREE BEST PLACES TO DISCONNECT

Telephone and internet service in the southwest is sporadic at best. If you want to completely unplug, here's three places where your BlackBerry will make an elegant paperweight.

- Cachóte (p235) – At 1400m and nestled on top of a fog-bound mountain, these rustic cabins are perfect for a secluded, information-highway-free break from the world.

- Rancho Platón (p235) – Get the kids away from the Xbox at this place, halfway down the mountain of the same name. There's horseback riding, dune buggies, a Ping-Pong table, trampoline, river tubing and a wicked, 25m water slide, all included in the price.

- Villa Barrancoli (p239) – Stalk the local endemics at this remote bird-watching camp on the north slope of the Sierra de Bahoruco. Bring your binoculars, and leave your consumer electronics at home.

THE SOUTHWEST

Those seeking to leave the beaten path in the dust will be interested in the 14-day treks, which take you to some of the most remote and beautiful portions of the southwest, places that require several days' walk or mule-ride to get to. These run three to four times a year (usually Christmas, February and Easter), and aren't cheap, but they will give you a comprehensive survey of all the best of the southwest (including everything you'll read about in this book). Eco Tour Barahona also offers a number of shorter, three- to four-day trips, including one to Isla Beata and Alto Velo (see p238).

Tody Tours (☎ 809-686-0882; www.todytours.com; Santo Domingo) is the only bird-watching tour company based in the DR. The expatriate American owner lives in Santo Domingo but runs tours on demand to the southwest. She has more than 10 years' experience as a guide and charges US$200 per day plus expenses; she organizes all transportation, food and accommodation for you. She prefers a minimum booking of a week. She also owns and runs a remote bird-watching camp, Villa Barrancoli (see p239).

BARAHONA
pop 78,000

Barahona is an unpleasant, industrial settlement of little interest to the traveler. Fortunately, though, a growing number of quality accommodation options have sprouted along the coastal road between here and Paraíso, making this a good base for exploring the region.

Barahona has the only ATMs for 100km and more, so you'll need to come here to get cash. It's also a necessary transfer point if you're traveling by bus.

History
By Dominican standards, Barahona is a young city, founded in 1802 by Haitian general L'Ouverture as a port to compete with Santo Domingo. For over a century, residents mostly made their living taking what they could from the Caribbean Sea, but today fishing accounts for only a small part of Barahona's economy. The dictator Rafael Trujillo changed everything when he ordered many square kilometers of desert north of town converted into sugarcane fields for his family's financial benefit. More than three decades after his assassination, the thousands of hectares of sugarcane continue to be tended, only now they are locally owned and benefit the community.

Orientation
The highway enters town from the west; after a large roundabout with a prominent square arch, it becomes Av Luís E Delmonte and Barahona's main drag. Av Delmonte continues straight as a sugarcane stalk downhill to the sea or, more exactly, to the seaside sugarcane refinery. From here, you can turn right or left onto Av Enriquillo. Left leads to an industrial area; right is the continuation of the coastal highway, leading another 75km down the east coast of the peninsula.

An extensive network of industrial train-tracks once linked most of the country. There was never a passenger service and during the economic crash of the 1950s and 1960s the trains all but disappeared. Only one track remains: leading from the cane refinery several kilometers north of town to Barahona's port. If you walk down to water, you can't miss seeing it.

Information

Banco Popular (☎ 809-524-2102; cnr Calles Jaime Mota & Padre Billini) Right at Parque Central. Has a 24-hour ATM.

BanReservas (☎ 809-524-4006; cnr Av Uruguay & Calle Padre Billini) Around the corner from Banco Popular. Has a 24-hour ATM.

Centro Médico Regional Magnolia (☎ 809-524-2470; cnr Av Uruguay & Fransisco Vásquez; ⏰ 24hr emergency room) Medical services; serious cases generally get sent to Santo Domingo.

Codetel (☎ 809-220-7979; Av Uruguay; per hr US$1) Internet access; also a call center.

Farmacia Dotel (☎ 809-524-2394; cnr Av Delmonte & Duverge) Pharmacy.

GigaNet (Mota at Móntez; per hr US$0.80) Biggest and best internet in town.

Sleeping

Unless you're after dirt-cheap budget accommodation, there's no reason to stay in the city itself (and even then…). Far better are the numerous hotels that string themselves along the coast south of Barahona on the road to Paraíso (see p234).

Hotel Cacique (☎ 809-524-4620; Av Uruguay 2; s with fan US$11, s/d/tr with air-con US$20/29/38; ❄️) We don't reckon the *cacique* (headman of the tribe) would have stayed here. The rooms are clean enough, there's cable TV and hot water, but there are better-value air-con rooms elsewhere, and when the power goes out – which is almost always – the on-site generator makes a dreadful din.

Gran Hotel Barahona (☎ 809-524-2415; Calle Jaime Mota 5; s/d/tr/ste US$27/36/43/47; 🅿️ ❄️) Masochists intent on staying in Barahona will want to stay here, the best-value option in town. Rooms are clean, with hot-water bathrooms and cable TV. Some of the mattresses are better than others, so ask to see a few if that's an important issue. The higher-priced rooms aren't much larger, but have nicer furnishings. The ones on the top floor have high, sloped ceilings. It's near Parque Central and several restaurants, banks and internet cafés.

Hotel Costa Larimar (☎ 809-524-5111; Av Enriquillo 6; costalarimar@codetel.net.do; s/d/tr/q incl breakfast US$48/79/109/133; 🅿️ ❄️ 💻 🍽️) The closest thing to an all-inclusive resort in the southwest, the Costa Larimar is at the southern end of town, with beach access and a pool with a swim-up bar. On the weekends it fills up with Dominicans from the capital, but during the week it echoes with emptiness. Basic price includes breakfast, and an all-inclusive plan (per person US$20) is available.

Eating

Restaurant Pizzería D'Lina (☎ 809-524-3681; cnr Av 30 de Mayo & Calle Anacaona; mains US$3-14; ⏰ breakfast, lunch & dinner) Even with the chain pizza and chicken places down the street, this Barahona institution has a loyal clientele who come for good pies and friendly family service. Large pizzas start at around US$10; there are also sandwiches and various meat, chicken and seafood dishes. Filling egg breakfasts go for around US$4. Convenient location.

Los Robles (☎ 809-524-1629; cnr Nuestra Senora del Rosario & Av Enriquillo; mains US$3-16; ⏰ breakfast, lunch & dinner) Among the best value in town for size, taste and price; you can have sit-down service at picnic tables on a pleasant outdoor patio, or order hefty grilled sandwiches from a stand-alone to-go shack. There's a little of something for everyone – including pizzas (US$8 to US$12), grilled beef and chicken plates (US$9 to US$11) and of course plenty of seafood (US$10 to US$16).

OUR PICK Brisas del Caribe (☎ 809-524-2794; restbrisas@codetel.net.do; Av Enriquillo 1; mains US$8-18; ⏰ breakfast, lunch & dinner) Add this restaurant to your list of essential services, somewhere after ATMs and before the medical clinic. It's one of the few reasons worth making the trip to Barahona (assuming you're already in the region). The kitchen offers some of the best seafood in the area – fresh, local sea creatures captured and cooked for your pleasure, as the seasons dictate. Set on a small rise about 500m north of Av Delmonte, the open-sided restaurant catches a cool breeze and most of the tables have a view of the green-blue Caribbean (and smoke stacks from nearby processing plants, but what can you do?).

Drinking

Los Robles (☎ 809-524-1629; cnr Nuestra Senora del Rosario & Av Enriquillo; ⏰ 9am-2am) and other nearby open-air restaurants are popular spots for a beer.

Entertainment

There is one disco in town – **Lotus** (cnr Calle Padre Billini & Nuestra Senora del Rosario; ⏰ 7:30pm-2am Wed-Sun) – but the *puta* (prostitute) factor may be too high for some. For more wholesome, authentic Dominican party-time, check out the various no-name discos in Paraíso and Bahoruco.

Getting There & Away

AIR

Aeropuerto Internacional María Móntez (☎ 809-524-4144) is located 10km north of town. There were no commercial flights when we were there.

BUS

Caribe Tours (☎ 809-524-4952; Av Uruguay) has first-class service to Ázua (US$2.15, one hour) and Santo Domingo (US$6.70, 3½ hours) departing at 6:15am, 9:45am, 1:45pm and 5:15pm.

There is frequent *gua-gua* service to all points of the compass during daylight hours. All *gua-guas* leave from near the corner of Av Delmonte at Calle Padre Billini. You can also pick up south-bound *gua-guas* at a stop on the highway at the southern end of town. *Gua-guas* generally leave every 15 to 30 minutes during daylight hours.

There's frequent service to Santo Domingo (US$6, 3½ hours; every 15 minutes from 4am), and plenty of *gua-guas* ply the route south and west along the coastal highway, passing through Paraíso (US$1.80, 40 minutes) on the way to Pedernales (US$5, two hours, until 3pm). *Gua-guas* head west to the border at Jimaní roughly every 45 minutes (US$3.70, 2½ hours) until 3pm. It's also possible but difficult to visit Isla Cabritos via *gua-gua* – take any bus to Neyba (US$2.40, 1¾ hours) and transfer for a La Descubierta–bound bus (US$0.70, 40 minutes).

For San Juan de la Maguana, take any non-*expreso* Santo Domingo–bound *gua-gua* and get off at the Cruce del Quince (15km west of Ázua), and wait at the junction for a west-bound bus to San Juan (US$3, 1½ hours). There are several small eateries if you missed breakfast, and you'll find a fair number of people waiting with you.

Getting Around

Barahona is somewhat spread out, though the area around the center is navigable by foot. For points further afield, taxis and *motoconchos* can be found beside the Parque Central and along Av Delmonte, or call the local **taxi association** (☎ 809-524-4003). If you want to go off-road, you may be able to hire a 4WD and driver by contacting Eco Tour Barahona (p230), whose own stable of drivers occasionally freelance.

Don't take *motoconchos* after dark along the coastal road – that's just asking for trouble.

SOUTH OF BARAHONA

Information

One of the few reliable places for internet outside of Barahona, **Guanaba.net** (Calle Duarte 35, La Ciénaga; www.guanaba.net; per hr US$1; 8am-8pm Mon-Sat, 8am-9:30pm Sun) has 10 computers with a good satellite link, plus a few headphones.

The **Internet Café de Paraíso** (Calle Arzobispo Noel; per hr US$1; 9am-6pm), next to the market, has a few computers. For medical emergencies, there's the **Clínica Amor el Prójimo** (☎ 809-243-1208; Calle Arzobispo Noel), also in Paraíso, with a doctor and nurse on call 24 hours per day.

Sights & Activities

BAHORUCO & LA CIÉNAGA

The adjoining seaside villages of Bahoruco and La Ciénaga are 17km south of Barahona, and are typical of the small communities along the east coast of the Península de Pedernales, with friendly local residents and a gravelly beach used more for mooring boats than bathing.

Especially in La Ciénaga, after dark almost any night of the week you're likely to find small, no-name *colmados* (small bars) and discos pumping the merengue out to the stars, and people drinking and dancing out of doors. If you decide to join them you'll likely be the only gringo in the place.

SAN RAFAEL

Three kilometers south of Bahoruco and La Ciénaga is the town of San Rafael (population 5300), notable for several awesome highway **vista points** on either side of town, and for Balneario San Rafael – natural and artificial **swimming holes** in the river, which are popular with local kids and families. You'll see one set of pools right alongside the highway – 100m north (downhill) from there is an unmarked dirt road leading to a second set of pools nearer the ocean. Fifty meters in the other direction, a steep paved road leads to **Villa Miriam** (8am-6pm; admission US$5), another swimming area that has several natural pools (with some help from sandbags) and a regular swimming pool.

PARAÍSO

About 35km south of Barahona is the aptly named town of Paraíso (population 13,500), with a spectacular beach and mesmerizing ocean – who knew there could be so many shades of blue?

Paraíso is a good budget alternative to Barahona, and is walking distance (or *moto-concho* distance) to the *balneario* (swimming hole) at Los Patos (see below). If you're driving, be sure to check out the *mirador* (lookout) just north of town – the views of the beach and ocean are jaw-dropping.

The **beach** directly in front of town has a fair amount of litter and numerous boats moored there. There are much better spots several hundred meters outside of town – follow the shady coastal road south and look for small paths through the brush. As elsewhere, much of the beach is covered in white stones, but there are several patches of fine sand where you can lay out a towel.

LOS PATOS

Several kilometers south of Paraíso is the hamlet of Los Patos, which is notable mostly for **Playa Los Patos,** a pretty white-stone beach, and for the adjacent *balneario*. Larger and more attractive than Balneario San Rafael, the water here flows clear and cool out of the mountainside, forming a shallow lagoon before running into the ocean. Small shacks serve good, reasonably priced food, making this a nice place to spend a couple of hours. On weekends it's crowded with Dominican families, but is much less busy midweek. There is a cave on the other side of the highway with what are supposedly Taíno petroglyphs, but we have our doubts.

Sleeping & Eating

Given the overall sense of isolation in this part of the country, it makes sense that most of the hotels along the Barahona–Paraíso coastal highway also have their own restaurants, which are generally open to the public, and not just guests.

Note that we've listed the following hotels in geographical order as you go south from Barahona; restaurants are listed in geographical order at the end of the section.

Hotel Casablanca – Campo Suizo (☎ 809-471-1230, 829-975-5291; www.hotelcasablanca.com.do; Carretera Km 10, Juan Esteban; d/tr US$35/40; ⓟ) This small, Swiss-owned B&B offers the most personalized style and service on this stretch of coast. Six simple but comfortable rooms are set on a well-tended garden. All rooms have a fan, clean bathroom and either a king-size bed or a queen and twin. Fifty meters away, a beautiful curving cliff provides a dramatic view of the Caribbean, and stairs down one side lead to a narrow beach that's mostly rocky but has some nice sandy spots. There's a larger beach a 10-minute walk away. Breakfast (US$7) isn't included, but it's one of the best breakfasts you'll have in the entire country. Ditto for dinner – even if you aren't staying here, consider phoning ahead in the morning to reserve a spot – the owner is an excellent cook.

our pick Playazul (☎ 809-454-5375; Carretera Km 7; s incl breakfast US$36-46, d US$55-64; ⓟ ⓧ ⓡ) 'Refined' is the key word at this new, French-run miniresort, easily the best-value hotel on the coast. Rooms are tastefully decorated and floored in blue tile, the beds comfortable and the shower has reliable hot water. The hotel is built on a bluff with great ocean views, and sturdy concrete slabs lead down to a pretty, private beach. Room price includes breakfast in the French-influenced restaurant (mains US$5 to US$15)– worth visiting even if you're staying elsewhere – where the chef's specialty is anything with shrimp. The *crêpes de ca-marónes* (US$7) are especially good, and make a great light meal.

Hotel Pontevedra (☎ 809-341-8462; www.pon tevedracaribe.com; Carretera Km 15; s/d/tr incl breakfast & dinner US$33/64/70; ⓟ ⓧ ⓡ) Four kilometers north of Bahoruco is this Dominican-run semi-all-inclusive hotel. Each of the 16 self-contained apartments is spacious, if not the cleanest, has a sofa, coffee table, and a kitchen with two electric burners, sink, fridge, and a small breakfast bar. The restaurant (mains US$8 to US$14) is open to the public – although we can't recommend the food. There are two pools, one for the kiddies, and steps lead down to a yellow pebble beach. Popular with Dominicans.

Casa Bonita (☎ 809-476-5059; www.casabonitadr .com; Carretera Km 17; r incl breakfast US$130 Sun-Thu, US$170 Fri & Sat; ⓟ ⓧ ⓓ ⓡ) Formerly the vacation retreat of a wealthy Dominican family, Casa Bonita is set on a hill overlooking the north end of Bahoruco. It is easily the most expensive hotel in the southwest, and the restaurant (mains US$7 to US$22) arguably one of the best. Under renovation when we were there, the 12 rooms – six with king-size beds, six with two full-size beds – were being redone in coral stone, and balconies have been added to all the rooms (which

---

CACHÓTE – FOGGY MOUNTAIN BREAKDOWN

About 25km (1½ hours' drive) west of Paraíso on an impressively bad road – you ford the same river half a dozen times – sit the remote cabins of **Cachóte**. At 1400m you're in the heart of Caribbean cloud forest. It's here that seven rivers spring from the ground to supply the coastal towns below.

In order to protect the water supply, coffee growing was ended in the 1990s, and today, with the help of Peace Corps volunteers, cabins have been constructed and short trails built in the regenerating forest. More cabins are planned, and at Easter time you may well stumble upon a swarm of volunteers from the University of Dayton, Ohio building them.

The cabins themselves are rustic but comfortable, and each has one large queen-size bed and a triple-decker dormitory-style bunk. Prices include accommodation, pickup from Barahona or Paraíso, three Dominican-style meals and Spanish-speaking guide, and are skewed toward large groups – one to four people pay US$100 per person per night, dropping to US$50 per person per night for groups of five to nine, and US$33 per person per night for groups of 10 to 20. Be sure to give them at least two weeks' notice that you're coming. Contact **Ecoturismo Comunitario Cachóte** (☎ 809-899-4702; soepa.paraiso@yahoo.com).

Eco Tour Barahona (p230) also runs a day trip to Cachóte (US$70), stopping at the small communities along the way. You'll pass from dry coastal plains up through a large coffee-, citrus- and mango-growing region into cloud forest at the top.

Unless you're a professional off-road rally driver we don't recommend trying to drive here yourself. Those sufficiently foolhardy, however, should look for the turnoff in the village of La Ciénega (see p233). There is no sign but it's the only road leading west into the mountains.

---

are otherwise a bit small). The tropical-themed bar and restaurant suggests colonial Malaysia under the British, and the food is Asian/fusion – think tuna steak with soy sauce and ginger (US$17). There's an 'infinity' pool, Jacuzzi, free wi-fi, and fridges in the rooms.

Coral Sol Resort (☎ 809-233-4882; www.coralsolresort .com; Carretera Km 21, south end of La Ciénega; **P** **⚡**) This small resort has 10 large cabins, each with two double beds and two bathrooms, set on a tree-filled hillside sloping down to a pebbly beach protected from the pounding sea by a rocky strip. It's ideal for families – rooms aren't particularly lavish so there's nothing for kids to break, and the restaurant's focus is on quantity, not quality, so the rugrats can fling spaghetti at the wall to their hearts' delight. Three of the cabins have a good ocean view – ask for one of these. Prices include all meals: for one person US$65, two people US$55 each, three or more people US$45 each. A breakfast-only plan is available.

Rancho Platón (☎ 809-683-1836; per person all-inclusive US$75; **P** **⚡**) Owned by a wealthy Dominican family and managed by Eco Tours Barahona, this rustic country retreat sits about 7km west of Paraíso on a rough road that crosses several rivers. A 20m-high waterfall drops right next to the main building, where

an artificial pool has been built. There are enormous stands of bamboo, and ducks and guinea hens wander about. Perfect for families, the price includes all the horseback riding, tubing (down to Paraíso beach, no less), hiking, 25m-high water sliding, dune buggying and Ping-Pong playing you can handle. There are five double rooms for the adults, and a smaller adjacent building offers dorms for the kids. There's no phone or internet, and a small hydro generator produces power from the adjacent waterfall. Minimum group size of six. Transportation included in price. Bring mosquito repellent.

Hotel Paraíso (☎ 809-243-1080; Carretera Km 34, Paraíso, cnr Av Gregorio Luperón & Calle Doña Chin; r with fan US$15-21, with air-con US$25; **P** **⚡**) This small hotel in the center of Paraíso offers the best budget digs on the coast. It's an easy walk to the area's best beaches. The rooms themselves are fairly spacious, but are otherwise nothing special – some have air-con and TV, and most have bathtubs. Those on the top floor have peaked ceilings. There is a pool but it was empty when we were there. Be sure to call ahead – Habitat for Humanity sometimes does projects in Paraíso, and books out the entire hotel.

Hotelito Oasi Italiana (☎ 829-918-6969; www.lospa tos.it; Carretera Km 37, Los Patos, Calle José Carrasco; mains US$7-14; **P** **⚡** **⚡**) While this Italian-owned hotel does offer a few rooms (singles/doubles including breakfast US$36/46), the real star of the show here is the food. It's not gourmet, but simple food, well prepared – fresh fish, soups, salads, even homemade polenta (the owner/chef is from Verona). Set on a rise a few hundred meters from the beach, the restaurant has great views over the sea – a choice spot to sit with an iced martini, catching those cooling breezes and watching the sun set. Additional rooms were under construction when we were there, but the ones already built were poorly thought out – come for the food, stay somewhere else.

Restaurante Luz (☎ 809-630-9861; mains US$5-9; ☯ breakfast, lunch & dinner) On the coastal road in the adjoining villages of Bahoruco and La Ciénaga, this good option has a tidy 2nd-floor dining room overlooking the shore, and a nice ocean breeze. Seafood is the main option here, including grilled fish and *lambi* (conch). All dishes come with rice and beans.

Sea View (☎ 809-243-1045; Malecón; mains US$15-25; ☯ lunch & dinner) One of a couple of good options in Paraíso, Sea View faces the ocean. The menu is fish, fresh and well prepared. This place also does a paella and a *cazuela de mariscos* (seafood stew).

Getting There & Away

The *gua-gua* stop in Paraíso is on the highway at Calle Enriquillo, 1km uphill from the beach. From here you can get buses to Barahona (US$1.80, 40 minutes, every 25 minutes), and south-bound *gua-guas* to Enriquillo (US$1.30, 15 minutes), Laguna Oviedo (US$1.80, 45 minutes) and Pedernales (US$3.50, 1½ hours) pass by roughly every 15 minutes. A Santo Domingo–bound express bus from Pedernales passes through here at around 4am (US$8, four hours).

LARIMAR MINE

All larimar in the DR – and, indeed, the world – comes from this one mine. Discovered in 1974 by Miguel Méndez, the name comes from Larissa (Méndez's daughter) plus *mar* (sea). Its scientific name is blue pectolite.

The mining operations are done not by a large mining concern but by a small collective of individual miners. You can visit the mines and even go down some of the mine shafts. A small group of basic shacks sells cut-rate larimar jewelry at the mine, and a few no-name eateries sell food and drink to the miners.

The tunnels had collapsed and the road was washed out when we were there (after Tropical Storm Noel), but by the time you get there things should be back to normal.

To get there, look for the turnoff in the small hamlet of El Arroyo, 13km south of Barahona (3km north of Bahoruco). It's an hour's drive on a rough SUV-only road. Eco Tour Barahona (p230) offers a tour here (US$70). Alternatively, take a *gua-gua* to the turnoff early in the morning; you may be able to hitchhike in with one of the miners.

A Peace Corps volunteer was attempting to organize a community-driven tour to the mine and local workshops when we were there; these may well be up and running by the time you read this. Contact the **Asociación de Artesanos de Bahoruco** (☎ 829-633-8018; larimarexperience@gmail.com).

ENRIQUILLO
pop 13,500

Fifteen kilometers south of Paraíso (and 54km south of Barahona) is this typical Dominican town, which is notable for having the last two hotels and gas station until Pedernales, some 82km away. There is no ATM.

PARQUE NACIONAL JARAGUA

The **Parque Nacional Jaragua** (admission Dominicans/foreigners US$0.60/1.50; ☯ 8am-5pm) is the largest protected area in the country. Its 1400 sq km include vast ranges of thorn forest and subtropical dry forest and an extensive marine area that spans most of the southern coastline, including Laguna Oviedo, Bahía de Las Águilas, and the islands of Isla Beata and Alto Velo.

Laguna Oviedo

This hypersalinic lake, separated from the ocean by a thin 800m-wide strip of sand, is a popular bird-watching destination, and home to a small colony of flamingos, which swells in population during winter. You're also likely to spot ibis, stork and spoonbills, especially in late spring and early summer. The enormous, one-ton *tinjlare* turtle comes here from April to June to lay and hatch its eggs, but can only be seen very late at night.

A new visitors center has been built at the entrance, plus two viewing platforms – one at the shore, another on the biggest of the 24 or so islands in the lake, where you'll also find lots of big, beefy iguanas. So salty

THE SOUTHWEST

THE SOUTHWEST

WHERE TO FIND THE BLUE STUFF

There are two good artisan shops selling handmade larimar jewelry along the coastal road. The first, **C & A Larimar Gift Shop**, is located just off the main coastal highway as you drive south, about 17km south of Barahona, near Bahoruco. It's just before the little baseball diamond, not far from Casa Bonita.

The other, **Vanessa's Gift Shop**, is along the beachside road that goes through Bahoruco and La Ciénega. Once you enter Bahoruco on the main highway, you'll pass the baseball diamond, cross a bridge and there will be a road that goes to your left along the beach (there's a small sign that says 'Bahoruco'). Follow that road to the beach for a half-mile, pass the Restaurant Luz on your left, and you'll come to the gift shop on your right.

In addition to the handmade larimar jewelry they both have for sale, for an additional US$15 they'll admit you to their workshop out back and let you make your own larimar souvenir. An artisan will use a wet saw to cut a general shape to your taste, then guide you in shaping and polishing the stone.

Beachcombers may also find their own larimar stones on the beach. The river that runs near the mine meets the sea at Playa Bahoruco, a short walk from town. After heavy rains especially, there's a good chance you'll find a larimar stone or two washed up onto the sand.

is the lake that in the dry season you'll see crystallized salt mixed with the sand on the islands.

You can take a boat tour from the **visitors center** (☎ 829-305-1686, or Areas Protegidas in Santo Domingo 809-472-4204; ☼ 8:30am-4pm). A two-hour tour costs US$60 per boat (up to 10 people), a Spanish-speaking guide costs US$10, plus there's the national park entrance fee (Dominicans/foreigners US$0.60/1.50). The tour includes a brief visit to a small Taíno cave, plus a short walk across the dividing strip to the ocean and the beach there, a beautiful yellow strand marred by an unbelievable quantity of plastic flotsam and jetsam – broken buckets, empty bleach bottles and the occasional light bulb. Wear shoes.

Eco Tour Barahona (p230) offers a day trip here (US$70). It is also considering starting a late-night turtle watching tour in springtime – worth asking about.

There's a well-marked entrance to the park and lagoon off the coastal highway about 3km north of the town of Oviedo. Oviedo and Pedernales buses can drop you at the park entrance. The last bus back to Barahona passes by around 4pm, but try not to cut it that close.

Bahía de Las Águilas

Bahía de Las Águilas is a pristine and extremely remote beach in the far southwestern corner of the DR. It's not on the way to anything else, and getting there is something of an adventure, but those who do make it

are rewarded with 10km of nearly deserted beach forming a slow arc between two prominent capes.

To get there, take the dirt road turnoff to Cabo Rojo, about 12km east of Pedernales. The Aluminum Company of America (Alcoa) used to mine bauxite here (a key ingredient for aluminum), and even though a new company has taken over, this is still called 'the Alcoa road.' You'll pass huge mountains of bauxite ore along the way – do drive carefully, as the road is used mainly by huge, fast-moving dump trucks.

You'll reach the town of Cabo Rojo after 6km, and a tiny fishing community called Las Cuevas 3km after that. Note the namesake cave in the middle of the settlement – fishing folk used to live inside it, and now store their fishing gear there. There are two ways to get to Las Águilas from here. One is to have a really good 4WD (and a driver with significant off-road experience) and attempt to drive there on a steep, pockmarked track through the coastal cactus forest.

The far more relaxing, enjoyable alternative is to go on a boat tour run by the owner of the restaurant **Rancho Tipico** (☎ 809-474-3408, 809-753-8058; rodriguezsantiago3@hotmail.com; mains US$10-15; ☼ breakfast, lunch & dinner) in Las Cuevas. Prices are as follows: for groups of one to five, US$46 per boat; six to eight, US$9 per person; nine to 12, US$8 per person; 13 to 30, US$6 per person; 30 to 35, US$5 per person. He also rents goggles and fins (at outrageous prices) so you can go 'snokling' – groups of one to five, US$150; six to eight, US$30 per person; nine to 12, US$25 per person. Bring your own snorkeling gear if at all possible. You'll also need to pay the national park entrance fee (Dominicans/foreigners US$0.60/1.50).

Eco Tour Barahona (p230) runs a day trip here (US$70). It organizes all the logistics, picks you up and drops you off at your hotel, supplies lunch, and can show you where the best corals are to go snorkeling.

A small tourist center was being built by the Pedernales guide association (AGUINAPE; see right) when we passed through. Several kilometers south of the turnoff on the Alcoa road, you'll come to a fork in the road. The better road turns left and inland (the normal route to Las Cuevas). Continue straight east for a few kilometers and you'll come to it. The association plans to rent snorkeling gear (US$5 per day), tents (US$10 per day), coolers with ice (US$5 per day), beach chairs (US$2 per day) and life jackets (US$2 per day). They can also provide transport here from Pedernales if you're coming by gua-gua.

There's a very small shelter (little larger than a phone booth) on the beach, but otherwise no facilities. Camping is permitted, but be sure to bring plenty of water, food and insect repellent, and take your garbage out with you. A national park visitors center was planned, and there were rumors the road would be paved. We sincerely hope not – part of the beauty here lies in its remoteness.

ISLA BEATA & ALTO VELO

These are end-of-the-world spots, difficult to access but seductive because of their remoteness. They are challenging for independent travelers to visit, and can be enjoyed more fully by taking a tour.

Isla Beata, once home to a prison for political dissidents under the dictatorship of Trujillo in the 1950s, remains under joint management of the military and the Parque Nacional Jaragua. The small fishing village of **Trudille** sits directly on **Playa Blanca**, a 40km-long white sand beach full of iguanas. The prison was destroyed after Trujillo's assassination but you can still visit the ruins.

Alto Velo is a smaller, uninhabited island 1½ hours further south of Isla Beata. It's the southernmost point in the DR. Windswept and covered in bird droppings (from the swarms of seagulls that live there), there's a lighthouse at the highest point of the island

(250m). It's a two-hour return walk (about 2.5km each way) with amazing views. There's no beach though.

The best way to visit the islands is to take a tour with Eco Tours Barahona (p230), which offers a three-day trip (US$460 per person, minimum six) that includes a night at both Bahía de Las Águilas and Isla Beata. An extra day (US$120 per person) can be tacked on if you also want to visit Alto Velo.

PEDERNALES
pop 14,000

The coastal highway dead-ends in Pedernales. There's no road here to Haiti, nor border post, and is principally of interest to those wanting to linger at Bahía de Las Águilas or in the national parks nearby. There are several quite acceptable places to lay your head for the night, and the seafood you'll eat in the local restaurants comes fresh off the boat.

With the help of a local Peace Corps volunteer and a World Bank grant, a small guide association is just getting on its feet. The **Associación de Guias de Naturaleza de Pedernales** (AGUINAPE; ☎ 809-214-1575; www.nuestra frontera.org/aguinape) will be of most interest to travelers without their own vehicles, as the group can organize transport to and from both Bahía de Las Águilas and Hoyo de Pelempito (US$15 each way). The guides are enthusiastic (if not yet supremely knowledgeable) and can discuss the local flora and fauna along the way (per day/half-day US$24/18). They were building a small tourist center off the main road to Las Águilas when we passed through, from which they plan to rent camping equipment, snorkeling gear, beach umbrellas etc.

The well-recommended **Hostal Doña Chava** (☎ 809-524-0332; hostalchava@hotmail.com; Calle 2, BarRío Alcoa; s/tr with fan US$12/17, s/d/tr with air-con US$18/21/23; P 🐾) offers clean, simple rooms with tidy bathrooms and cable TV. There's a pleasant patio out back, and breakfast (US$3) is available.

You wouldn't expect to find such grandmotherly accommodation as **Hostal D'Óleo Méndez** (☎ 809-524-0416; Calle Antonio Duvergé; s with fan US$14, s/d with air-con US$24/30; P 🐾) in what is, really, the middle of nowhere, but the D'Óleo Méndez offers just that. Sixteen of the rooms have aircon and TV, and it offers cheap Dominican lunch specials (US$3). It has a secure parking lot just a block down.

There are a couple of good seafood restaurants in town. **King Crab** (☎ 809-256-9607; Calle Dominguez 2; mains US$3-15; ☉ breakfast, lunch & dinner) and **Jalicar** (☎ 809-524-0350; Calle Libertad; mains US$3-15; ☉ breakfast, lunch & dinner) are both recommended.

BanReservas (☎ 809-524-0549; Calle Duarte) has the only ATM in town, but it empties out fast, especially on weekends.

Gua-guas go back and forth between Pedernales and Barahona (US$4.25, two hours, hourly from 2am to 3pm).

PARQUE NACIONAL SIERRA DE BAHORUCO

This **national park** (admission Dominicans/foreigners US$0.60/1.50; ☉ 8am-5pm) directly west of Barahona covers 800 sq km of mostly mountainous terrain and is notable for the rich variety of vegetation that thrives in its many different climates, from lowland desert to cloud forest. Valleys are home to vast areas of broad-leafed plants, which give way to healthy pine forests at higher elevations. In the mountains the average temperature is 18°C, and annual rainfall is between 1000mm and 2500mm.

Within the national park there are 166 orchid species, representing 52% of the country's total. Thirty-two percent of those species are endemic to the park. Flitting about among the park's pine, cherry and mahogany trees are 49 species of bird. These include the white-necked crow, which can only be seen on Hispaniola. The most common birds in the mountains are La Selle's thrush, white-winged warblers, Hispaniolan trogons and narrow-billed todies. At lower elevations, look for white-crowned pigeons, white-winged doves, Hispaniolan parakeets, Hispaniolan lizard cuckoos and Hispaniolan parrots.

Tody Tours runs a bird-watching camp near Puerto Escondido called **Villa Barrancoli** (☎ 809-686-0882; www.todytours.com; Santo Domingo; camping US$2-10, food per day US$20 per group). When the camp is not otherwise in use independent travelers are welcome – be sure to give several days' notice. You'll want a good 4WD (and know how to use it). To get there from Barahona, head to the town of Duvergé along the southern side of Lago Enriquillo. In town, turn left on an unmarked road about three corners after the gas station. Follow this to Puerto Escondido (30 minutes). You'll see

the **park office** (no phone; admission Dominicans/foreigners US$0.60/1.50) on your right as you enter. Continue to a 'T' intersection, then turn left, following the sign to Rabo de Gato. Turn right and cross the canal. At the next fork turn right again and follow the signs to Rabo de Gato until you come to the campsite.

Hoyo de Pelempito

Part of Parque Nacional Sierra de Bahoruco, the 'hole' at Pelempito is actually a deep gorge formed when the Península de Pedernales jammed itself up into Hispaniola umpteen million years ago. The brand-new visitors center, perched on the edge of a cliff at 1450m, offers breathtaking views, north and east, of completely untouched national park. The cliff itself is a 600m drop.

The visitors center has information (in Spanish) on the various flora and fauna in the area, and a number of short nature walks have small signs identifying the various plants. Serious bird-watchers scoff that this is a poor bird-watching location, but for the casual tourist the views make it worth the drive.

Pelempito sits on the south side of the Sierra de Bahoruco. The road to get here is ridiculously well paved by Dominican standards. The turnoff is about 12km east of Pedernales, before the road to Bahía de Las Águilas. You'll come to a **ranger station** (☎ no phone; admission Dominicans/foreigners US$0.60/1.50) about halfway up the mountain. Eventually the highway-like road turns into a rutted, 4WD track. It's about 30km (1½hrs) from the turnoff.

POLO
pop 9500

The small town of Polo, nestled on the south slopes of the Sierra de Bahoruco, is the center of a major coffee- and vegetable-growing region. It's principally famous for the optical illusion on the highway 20km north of town (see p240), and more recently for the **Festival de Café Orgánico**, which happens on the first weekend of June (see the boxed text, p240).

From Barahona, drive 12km west to Cabral and look for the unmarked southbound turnoff in the middle of town (where all the *motoconchos* hang out). From there it's about a 30km (45-minute) drive to Polo.

THE SOUTHWEST

THE POLO ORGANIC COFFEE FESTIVAL

Started in 2004, the **Festival de Café Orgánico de Polo** (☎ 809-682-3877; www.festicafe.org) is held on the first weekend in June. From Friday to Sunday, local coffee growers celebrate the end of the coffee-harvesting season. There's live merengue and *bachata* in the evenings, and during the day stands sell coffee and typical southwestern arts and crafts. There's a 'coffee parade,' and lots of (decaffeinated) games for the kids. The organizers also lead hiking trips to remote coffee plantations in the mountains.

There's no real hotel in town, but during the festival the organizers can put you up in a spare room in someone's house – be sure to call several weeks ahead, as rooms fill up fast. You can also drive out from Barahona; it's about an hour each way.

POLO MAGNÉTICO

Twelve kilometers west of Barahona is the town of Cabral and the turnoff for the town of Polo. About 10kms south from the turnoff you'll encounter a famous mirage. Put your car in neutral, let go of the brake and watch your car get 'pulled' uphill. The effect is best between the towns of El Lechoso and La Cueva, and works on a smaller scale, too – get out of the car and put a water bottle on the road. It, too, will show a mysterious desire to climb uphill.

NORTH OF PEDERNALES

LAGO ENRIQUILLO & ISLA CABRITOS

Parque Nacional Isla Cabritos (☎ 809-996-3649; admission Dominicans/foreigners US$0.60/1.50; ⏰ 7am-5pm) is named after the 12km-long desert island in the center of Lago Enriquillo, an enormous saltwater lake 40m below sea level. The lake is the remains of an ancient channel that once united the Bahía de Neyba to the southeast (near Barahona) with Port-au-Prince to the west. The accumulation of sediments deposited by the Río Yaque del Sur at the river's mouth on the Bahía de Neyba, combined with an upward thrust of a continental plate, gradually isolated the lake. Today it is basically a 200-sq-km inland sea.

The park includes, oddly, just the island, and not the rest of the lake, where fishermen cast nets for tilapia, an introduced fish. The highlights are the lake's creatures, including an estimated 200 American crocodiles that can be seen at the edge of the lake. From December to April you'll also see flamingos and egrets.

The island, which varies in elevation from 40m to 4m below sea level, is a virtual desert,

supporting a variety of cacti and other desert flora. In summer, temperatures of 50°C have been recorded – go early. It is home to Ricord iguanas and rhinoceros iguanas, some more than 20 years old and considerably beefier than most house cats. The island also has lots of scorpions, not to mention plenty of cacti, so wear covered shoes if possible.

There is a small **visitors' center** on the island, with information on the history and geology of the island. From March to June you'll see a blooming of cactus flowers, and June sees a small swarm of butterflies.

The **park entrance** is about 3km east of La Descubierta. A boat tour of the park costs US$110 for up to eight people – expect a sore, wet bum (and salt stains). Be sure to call ahead – if a tour group has the boat reserved, you might be out of luck (although if there's empty spaces they'll usually let you join for US$35 per person). The boat will take you to the mouth of the Río de la Descubierta – where the most crocodiles and flamingos are visible – and Isla Cabritos. The tour usually lasts one to two hours. Bring a hat and plenty of water.

A short distance east of the park entrance, look for **Las Caritas** (The Masks). On the north side of the highway, brightly painted green and yellow handrails lead up to a small rock overhang with what are believed to be pre-Taíno petroglyphs. A short but somewhat tricky climb up the hillside – you'll need shoes or decent sandals – affords a close look at the pictures and a fine view of the lake. Very little is known about the meaning of the figures. Note that much of the rock here is actually petrified coral, remnants of the time the entire area was under the sea.

If you're driving, be sure to stop at the junction at the southeast corner of the lake to check out the statue, 'Monumento del Cacique.'

Nearly 500 years ago, somewhere in the Sierra de Bahoruco, the Taíno chief Enriquillo chose to fight the conquistadores. The battle raged off and on for 14 years – from 1519 to 1533 – during which time the Spaniards came to respect the *cacique* and finally made peace with him. The chief declared a small free republic in the highest reaches of the Sierra de Bahoruco. The statue honors these deeds with the words, chiseled in stone, 'the first cry of freedom for the whole continent.'

Eco Tour Barahona (p230) offers a popular day trip to Isla Cabritos (US$70), including a visit to Las Caritas, the Haitian market at Jimaní, and the swimming hole at La Descubierta.

Sleeping & Eating

About 3kms west of the park entrance lies the small town of La Descubierta, which is popular for its large swimming hole right in the middle of town. There's not much reason to spend the night here, but if you get stuck, the **Hotel Iguana** (☎ 809-301-4815; d/tw US$10/20; ✂) on the main road west of the park will do in a pinch. Rooms are small and simple, but also clean and quiet. Three rooms have air-con, but are stuffier than the fan-cooled ones, which have private bathrooms and surprisingly comfortable beds. The Iguana's friendly proprietor prepares excellent home-cooked meals, but needs a day's notice. Otherwise, there are **food shacks** in town, near the park and swimming hole.

Getting There & Away

You're better off driving if you're coming out this way, but you can also grab a *gua-gua* from Barahona to Neyba, and then change for any west-bound *gua-gua* to the ranger station. Be sure to tell the driver that that's where you want to go, or he'll drive right past it.

JIMANÍ

pop 6700

This dusty border town is on the most direct route between Santo Domingo to Port-au-Prince, and is therefore the busiest of the three official border crossings. Dominicans from as far away as Santo Domingo come here for the Monday and Friday markets, where they can buy humanitarian aid (giant sacks of rice and beans and jugs of cooking oil), meant for Haitians, at rock-bottom prices. There are also a few *tiendas* selling Haitian beer (Prestige)

and rum (Rhum Barbancourt), both arguably better than their Dominican counterparts. The market is just past the Dominican border post in no-man's-land.

A hurricane in 2004 destroyed the La Cuarenta neighborhood, killing more than 800 people. Today you can see hundreds of small, new cinderblock houses erected to house the surviving population.

For information on crossing the border see p256.

Information

BanReservas (☎ 809-248-3373) has a 24-hour ATM and is at the west end of Calle 19 de Marzo, the main road from Neyba just before it leaves town for the Haitian border. **Farmacia Marian** (☎ 809-248-3304; ☽ 8am-10pm) is on the uphill road to/from Duvergé.

Sleeping & Eating

Hotel Jimaní (☎ 809-248-3139; Calle 19 de Marzo 2; r US$23; ✂ ✎) On the right side of the road as you enter town from La Descubierta, Jimaní's best hotel looks a little like a small high school, but is surprisingly comfortable. Each of the 10 rooms has both a twin and queen-size bed, plus cable TV and a private cold-water bathroom. The hotel is showing its age and the bathrooms could stand to be remodeled, but this is much better than you'd expect for a border town.

The hotel has a somewhat popular **restaurant** (☽ breakfast, lunch & dinner). Otherwise, the eating options are slim, limited to several small, forgettable eateries along the road to Duvergé.

Getting There & Away

Jimaní is served by *gua-guas* from Santo Domingo, passing La Descubierta, Neyba and Baní along the way; and from Barahona via Duvergé and the south side of Lago Enriquillo. Both bus stops are on the dusty sloping road that enters town from the Duvergé side. The Santo Domingo route has a proper terminal near the bottom of the hill (US$9, five hours, every 30 to 45 minutes from 1am to 5pm). For La Descubierta, it's US$1.30 and takes 30 minutes. *Gua-guas* to Barahona (US$4.25, two hours, every 45 minutes from 4am to 3pm) leave from a shady corner about 200m up the hill, across from a small supermarket. Caribe Tours has a direct service from Santo Domingo to Port-au-Prince, with a stop in Jimaní (see p102).

THE SOUTHWEST

Dominican Republic Directory

CONTENTS

ACCOMMODATIONS

Compared to other destinations in the Caribbean, lodging in the Dominican Republic is relatively affordable. That said, there is a dearth of options for independent travelers wishing to make decisions on the fly and for whom cost is a concern. All the room rates listed in this book are for the high season, which varies slightly from region to region. Sometimes a price range is indicated for those properties where the low- or medium-season rates are significantly reduced – otherwise assume that low-season rates are from 20% to 50% less than high-season rates. More so than other destinations, hotel rooms booked a minimum of three days in advance on the internet are shockingly cheaper, especially so at the all-inclusive resorts the country is famous for, than if you book via phone or, worst-case scenario, simply show up without a reservation.

For the purposes of this book, budget is any room that's US$40 and under. Most hotels at this level are fairly basic with few amenities, though most will have private bathroom, hot water and 24-hour electricity. Cable TV and air-con are less common, and the latter may not function when the hotel is using its generator. Breakfast is generally not included, and public spaces like lobbies and lounges are either absent or uninviting. You won't feel like you're on vacation necessarily, especially in the cities, but there are a few exceptions, including Las Terrenas on the Península de Samaná and Bayahibe in the southeast, which have several good-value budget options. The DR has no proper hostels, and very little backpacker culture of the sort found in the rest of Latin America, Europe and elsewhere. The few extremely cheap hotels (US$20 and under) are often either unpleasant or unwise to stay in – the prevalence of prostitution is part of the problem. The walled compounds with names suggestive of intercourse or romantic love on the outskirts of most large towns, especially Santo Domingo, are short-time hotels for couples seeking privacy.

We've used the fairly large range, US$40 to US$80 per night, to group accommodation in the midrange category – the majority of hotels in the DR. On the plus side this means that you can find a room with clean linens, air-con, cable TV, off-street parking, sometimes breakfast, internet access and a swimming pool and much more in resort areas, for rather inexpensive rates. However, it also means that you may find rooms with ordinary, sometimes old furniture, fixtures in need of updating and, in the case of all-inclusive resorts, decidedly midrange food. In

---

BOOK YOUR STAY ONLINE

For more accommodation reviews and recommendations by Lonely Planet authors, check out the online booking service at www.lonelyplanet.com/hotels. You'll find the true, insider lowdown on the best places to stay. Reviews are thorough and independent. Best of all, you can book online.

PRACTICALITIES

- *El Listín Diario* (www.listin.com.do), *Hoy* (www.hoy.com.do), *Diario Libre* (www.diariolibre.com), *Ultima Hora* (www.ultimahora.com) and *El Nacional* (www.elnacional.com.do), plus *International Herald Tribune*, the *New York Times* and the *Miami Herald* can be found in many tourist areas.

- There are about 150 radio stations, most playing merengue and *bachata* (popular guitar music based on bolero rhythms); and seven local TV networks, though cable and satellite programming is very popular for baseball, movies and American soap operas.

- The DR uses the same electrical system as the USA and Canada (110 to 125 volts AC, 60 Hz, flat-pronged plugs). Power outages are common but many hotels and shops have backup generators.

- The DR uses the metric system for everything except gasoline, which is measured in gallons, and at laundromats, where laundry is measured in pounds.

some places like Santo Domingo, you can stay in restored colonial-era buildings with loads of character with comfortable accommodation for less money than you would spend for a night at a bland international-chain-style hotel. Most have websites where you can make reservations in advance and you can often pay with a credit card, though it's a good idea to check in advance. A good number of all-inclusives, especially outside the holidays and the high season, fall into this category and can be remarkably good deals considering what you get. It's important, however, to keep in mind the peculiar nature of this style of accommodation; see right for more details.

Top-end lodging, US$80 and up, refers mostly to a handful of upscale hotels in Santo Domingo and Santiago and a good chunk of the all-inclusive resorts. For the former, in addition to all of the amenities listed in the midrange category, you can expect at least one on-site restaurant, shops, a swimming pool, gym, professional service and sometimes an attached casino. All-inclusives at the low end of this category certainly aren't luxurious but you can generally count on better food and service than those charging midrange rates. From US$200 and up (the ceiling is high for the most exclusive resorts) there's a big jump in terms of the quality of furnishings, food and service, and in the Dominican Republic, maybe more than elsewhere, you truly get what you pay for.

Seasons

The DR has two main high seasons – from December to March, when Canadians and Americans do most of their traveling, and from July to August, when many Europeans

and Dominicans are on holiday. Semana Santa (Holy Week, ie the week before Easter) is also an extremely busy time, as all local schools, universities, government offices and many businesses are closed and Dominicans flock to beaches and riverside areas. Carnival is celebrated every weekend in February, and hotels can fill up in the most popular areas, like La Vega, Santiago and Santo Domingo. During all these times expect prices to rise by about one-third. Reservations are recommended during these periods, especially at beach areas, and you may have less luck bargaining for a reduced rate. No matter what season, weekend and weekday rates are generally uniform, but always ask for a discount if you'll be staying for more than a couple of days.

All-Inclusive Resorts

Easily the most popular form of lodging in the DR is the all-inclusive resort. In some people's minds they're synonymous with tourism here and for good reason – much of the prime beachfront property throughout the country is occupied by all-inclusives. The largest concentrations are at Bávaro/Punta Cana in the east and Playa Dorada in the north, though their numbers are growing in areas around Bayahibe, Río San Juan, Sosúa and Luperón. Boca Chica and Juan Dolio, both within easy driving distance of Santo Domingo, have small concentrations as well. Because of its relative inaccessibility, the Península de Samaná was largely free of all-inclusives until recently; a handful are in operation now and more are likely in the near future.

If you're looking for a hassle-free vacation, it's easy to understand the appeal of the

DOMINICAN REPUBLIC DIRECTORY

SORTING THROUGH ALL THE ALL-INCLUSIVES

Consider the following questions if you're trying to choose an all-inclusive resort:

■ Location: What part of the country is the resort in? What sights are nearby?

■ The fine print: Are all the restaurants included? How about alcoholic beverages? Motorized water sports?

■ Ocean front: Is the resort on the beach, across the street, a bus ride away?

■ Size of the resort: Do you need to rent a golf cart to get from your room to the buffet?

■ Variety of restaurants: Do you have options other than the same old buffet?

■ Accommodations: When were the rooms last updated?

■ Children: Is this a kid-friendly resort? Is there a kids' club? Babysitting service?

■ Pools: How many pools are there? Is loud music piped in the pool area all day?

■ Drinks: Is top-shelf alcohol included? What about bottled beer?

■ Entertainment: Are there nightly performances or live-music venues? How about a disco?

---

all-inclusive. Everything you could want, from food and drink to activities and entertainment, are all available in a single self-contained destination. The majority offer at least one all-you-can-eat buffet and several stand-alone restaurants (these sometimes require reservations once you've arrived and sometimes cost extra) and food is usually available virtually around the clock. Drinks (coffee, juice, soda, beer, wine, mixed drinks) are also unlimited and served up almost 24/7 from restaurants, beach and pool bars, cafés, discos etc. Most are located on the beach and have lounge chairs and towels, as well as several pools. A variety of tours are on offer daily, including snorkeling, diving, trips to parks and sights in the surrounding area, city tours and horseback riding. If there isn't a golf course on the property, no doubt the concierge can arrange a tee time. The average stay at an all-inclusive leaves little time or room to explore or learn much about the country or its people, but it does make for a relaxing and indulgent week.

Several companies dominate the resort landscape in the Dominican Republic. Names like Melia, Barcelo and Wyndham are plastered on signs everywhere from Puerto Plata to Bávaro. Often there will be several Melias, Barcelos or Wyndhams in the same area, ranging widely in terms of quality and costs – it can get confusing. While choosing the best resort for you or your family requires some homework, it's well worth the effort. Too often people's vacations are ruined by unrealistic expectations fostered by out-of-focus photos and inaccurate information found online. And if it's your first time visiting the Dominican Republic, it's difficult to have a sense of the geography of the area you're considering. For example, the Bávaro/Punta Cana region is quite large, and while some resorts are within walking distance of one another and local restaurants and shops, others are isolated and without a rental vehicle you might end up feeling stranded. Websites like **dr1.com** (www.dr1.com) and **Debbie's Dominican Republic Travel Page** (www.debbiesdominicantravel.com) can be useful: posting detailed, first-person reviews from travelers who have stayed recently at various resorts.

All-inclusive resorts, per person, range from solidly midrange to luxury top end. Cable TV, hot water, 24-hour electricity and air-con are standard. More expensive resorts generally have better buffets and one or more à la carte restaurants, and food quality is one of the most obvious and significant reasons to spend a few more bucks. More expensive resorts also tend to have nicer and larger pool areas and prime beachfront locations. Unless you're paying top dollar, odds are room furnishings and mattress quality won't be highlights. Loud, throbbing dance music is commonly piped in the pool and beach areas – whether this is a plus or minus is an important determining factor in where you stay.

Camping

Other than the none-too-appealing free cabins en route to Pico Duarte, there are no formal campgrounds and the whole idea of camping is peculiar to a majority of Dominicans. If you are dead set on sleeping in a tent, you'll have the most luck in rural mountain areas or along deserted beaches – inland, you should ask the owner of the plot of land you are on before pitching a tent, and on the beach ask the Politur (tourist police) or local police if it is allowed and safe.

Rental Accommodations

If you'll be in the Dominican Republic for long – even a couple weeks – renting an apartment can be a convenient and cost-effective way to enjoy the country. There are a number of homes that can be rented by the week or month; alternatively, look for 'apartahotels,' which have studio, one-bedroom and two-bedroom apartments, usually with fully equipped kitchens. This book lists a number of apartahotels in areas where long-term units are popular, such as Cabarete (p189). A number of hotels have a small amount of units with kitchens – such cases are also indicated in the listings.

ACTIVITIES

For many people, a trip to the Dominican Republic equals lazy days spent doing nothing on the beach. This certainly is an option, but there's also a wide range of sports and ecoactivities, enough to leave little time for sunbathing, for those looking for more excitement and activity. Because of its geographic diversity and relatively small size, it's possible to combine everything from mountaineering to snorkeling and kitesurfing in a single vacation. Many of the sports and activities listed here are covered in more detail in the Dominican Republic Outdoors chapter (p59).

Diving & Snorkeling

The Dominican Republic has excellent and varied options for diving and snorkeling. Because it has the Caribbean to the south and the Atlantic to the north and east, the DR offers divers and snorkelers a number of distinct underwater environments and conditions. The southern coast faces the Caribbean and the water is typically warmer and clearer here than anywhere else. It's best reached using dive shops in Boca Chica and Bayahibe. The north coast has cooler Atlantic waters with somewhat less visibility, but makes up for that with more varied underwater formations. You can explore this area from Las Galeras, Las Terrenas, Río San Juan and Sosúa, all of which have recommended dive shops. A bit off the beaten path are the diving and snorkeling opportunities in the northwest, specifically Monte Cristi – the national park of the same name there has the DR's most pristine coral formations – and the small fishing village of Punta Rusia. The DR also has two cave dives – one near Río San Juan can be done by skilled divers with just Open Water certification, while the second, deep inside Parque Nacional del Este, is for advanced cave divers only.

Golf

Known as one of the premier golf destinations in the Caribbean, the DR has more than two dozen courses to choose from. Signature courses by high-profile designers like Tom Fazio, Robert Trent Jones Sr, Pete Dye, Jack Nicklaus, Nick Faldo and Arnold Palmer are being built at a steady pace. The majority are affiliated with (or located nearby) the top all-inclusive resorts, but are open to guests and nonguests alike. Many consider Teeth of the Dog at the Casa de Campo resort near La Romana the finest course in the country. Almost all take advantage of their Caribbean setting (of course, this means many were built on former mangrove areas) and feature fairways and greens with spectacular ocean views. Green fees range from under US$30 to over US$200, plus caddie and/or cart fees. Reservations are essential in the high season at the top courses. Green fees are reduced when booked through many hotels and resorts, and golf vacation packages are available.

Hiking

The Caribbean, a region not known for its high peaks, isn't generally considered a hiking destination, so many people are surprised by the wealth of opportunity in the Dominican Republic. Pico Duarte, at 3087m, the tallest peak in the Caribbean, is the most obvious choice; it's challenging aerobically, though not technically, and while the scenery along the ascent isn't especially stunning, the views from the top are worth the effort. If you're not up for the summit, the highland town of Jarabacoa, where many hikes begin, has several rewarding circuits to area waterfalls. In the southwest there are several recommend hikes best done on a tour, and coastal walks in the Península de Samaná (especially Las Galeras), which end at beautiful isolated beaches.

Mountain Biking

Road cycling in the DR is a challenging, even dangerous, activity, whereas mountain bikers avoid the number one hazard – cars. Organized tours cover the miles of back roads and dirt paths in the central highlands and the north and southwest. Iguana Mama in Cabarete (p188) is without question your best bet; trips can be customized for just about any length or skill level. There are also tours and bike rentals in Las Galeras and Las Terrenas in the Península de Samaná. With a good map, Spanish-speaking skills and a definite sense of adventure, it's possible to head out on your own.

River Rafting

Jarabacoa is the jumping-off point for trips down the Dominican Republic's longest river, the Río Yaque del Norte. While relatively mild as white-water adventures go, this portion of the river does have some nice rolls and rapids as it winds through an attractive gorge, making it a fun half-day excursion.

Surfing

Cabarete, better known as a place to go windsurfing and kiteboarding, is also one of the country's best places for surfing. In fact, there are great breaks to be found all along the north coast. In addition to Cabarete, there are some good spots west of Sosúa and east of Río San Juan, near Playa Caletón and Playa Grande, and Playa Bonita near Las Terrenas in the Península de Samaná.

Whale-Watching

From mid-January to mid-March the Samana Bay becomes the whale-watching capital of the Caribbean. In fact, they come in such high numbers and with such regularity that the DR is considered one of the best places in the world to observe humpbacks (see p145). Most tours depart from the town of Samaná, and guests are treated to numerous sightings, sometimes at very close range. Reservations are a good idea – the tours are very popular and the season overlaps with Carnival and Independence Day.

Wind Sports

The DR is one of the top places in the world for windsurfing and kiteboarding, and the wind blows hardest in Cabarete, which hosts major annual competitions in both sports and has numerous schools for those who want to learn. Las Terrenas on the Península de Samaná, a growing destination for enthusiasts for both windsurfing and kiteboarding, has good conditions for much of the year. Most people need a minimum of six hours' instruction to pick up kiteboarding, but nine or 12 hours is recommended. The basics of windsurfing can be grasped in a few hours, though it is a sport that takes months or years to master. Cabarete is also an excellent place for sailing.

BUSINESS HOURS

Banks are typically open from 8am to 4pm Monday to Friday and 9am to 1pm Saturday, but almost all of them offer 24-hour ATM access. Government offices keep short hours – 7:30am to 2:30pm Monday to Friday. Stores and shopping malls tend to open from 9am to 7:30pm Monday to Saturday and supermarkets from 8am to 10pm Monday to Saturday. Restaurants keep the longest hours, typically staying open from 8am to 10pm or later Monday through Saturday, although most close between lunch and dinner. Liquor-licensing laws, and hence bar opening and closing times, were in flux at the time of research; however, you can expect bars, nightclubs and casinos to be open from 6pm to late or until the early morning. Internet cafés and call centers are open 9am to 6pm Monday to Saturday and also half-days on Sunday. Most tourist attractions, tour operators and car-rental agencies are open from 9am to 6pm (or later) daily, although museums, galleries and some historical monuments may close one weekday, usually Monday.

CHILDREN

All-inclusive resorts can be a convenient and affordable way for families to travel, as they provide easy answers to the most vexing of travel questions: When is dinner? Where are we going to eat? What are we going to do? Where's the bathroom? Can I have another Coke? For independent-minded families the DR is no better or worse than most countries – its small size means no long bus or plane rides, and the beaches and outdoor activities are fun for everyone. At the same time, there are few kid-specific parks or attractions, and navigating the cities can be challenging for parents and exhausting for children.

Practicalities

All-inclusive resorts have the best child-specific facilities and services, from high chairs in the restaurants to child care and children's programming. That said, not all resorts cater to families with young children, so be sure to choose a place that does. Independent travelers will have a harder time finding facilities designed for children and few smaller restaurants will have high chairs.

Child safety seats are not common, even in private cars, and are almost unheard of in taxis or buses. Seatbelts are required by law, however, so if you bring your own car seat – and it's one that can adapt to a number of different cars – you may be able to use it at least some of the time.

Breast-feeding babies in public is not totally taboo, but nor is it very common. It is definitely not done in restaurants, as in the US and some other countries. If necessary, nursing mothers should find a private park bench and use a shawl or other covering. Major grocery stores sell many of the same brands of baby food and diapers (nappies) as in the US. For excellent general advice on traveling with children, check out Lonely Planet's *Travel with Children*.

Sights & Activities

Some places in the DR are better suited for kids than others. Santo Domingo, while big and busy, does have a number of sights kids will like (p89), including a terrific children's museum, an interesting colonial-era fort, a huge botanic garden and an aquarium.

The central highland town of Jarabacoa has a plethora of outdoors activities suitable for hardy children, including hiking, horseback riding and river-rafting.

A number of schools in Cabarete on the north coast give safe and reliable windsurfing and kiteboarding lessons to kids. Cabarete also has some good tour operators with a number of fun, outdoorsy options for children.

Samaná offers whale-watching tours from mid-January to mid-March, amazing excursions even for jaded teenagers.

And, of course, the all-inclusive resorts at Bávaro and Punta Cana are excellent for children and families, with myriad activities and programs for young people of all ages. Outside of Bávaro and Punta Cana, the resorts in Playa Dorada and Luperón have large beaches and mild surf, an easy-to-reach marine park, and good outdoor excursions in the nearby mountains.

CLIMATE CHARTS

Looking at the accompanying charts, it's not hard to see why the Dominican Republic is sometimes said to have an 'eternal summer.' Month to month, region to region, temperatures remain fairly steady. Rainfall varies much more and travelers should note that although it's a small country, the rainy season peaks in different months in different parts of the country. In Santo Domingo, summer is the rainy season, with strong daily rains from May to October. The north coast's rains generally come later, beginning around October and sometimes lasting until March. Samaná is the wettest region, with on and off rain most of the year (February and March are the driest months). The southeast is much drier, and the

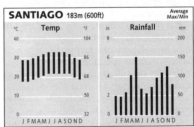

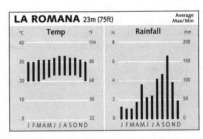

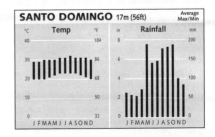

southwest even drier still – in both areas the months from May to October have the most rain. But like many places in the tropics, rain storms in the DR tend to be heavy but last only an hour or so.

Hurricane season, roughly August to October (though storms can occur in November and even December), can bring intense rain storms and the occasional hurricane, which typically affect the eastern part of the country. The big ones don't hit every year, though they are becoming more frequent – 2007 was a particularly tough year, as the country was devastated by Tropical Storm Noel and then later in mid-December by Tropical Storm Olga (see boxed text, p36). Of course, sunny days outnumber stormy ones, even in hurricane season – as long as a storm doesn't hit, it can be a pleasant and affordable time to travel.

CUSTOMS

Customs regulations are similar to most countries, with restrictions on the import of live animals, fresh fruit or vegetables, weapons and drugs, and the export of ancient artifacts and endangered plants or animals.

Other than the obvious, like weapons and drugs, there are only a few specific import restrictions for foreigners arriving in the Dominican Republic. Visitors can bring up to 200 cigarettes, 3L of alcohol and gifts not exceeding US$100 duty-free. It's best to carry a prescription for any medication, especially psychotropic drugs.

It is illegal to take anything out of the DR that is over 100 years old – including paintings, household items and prehistoric artifacts – without special export certificates. Mahogany trees are endangered and products made from mahogany wood may be confiscated upon departure. Black coral is widely available and, although Dominican law does not forbid its sale, international environment agreements do – avoid purchasing it. The same goes for products made from turtle shells and butterfly wings – these animals are facing extinction. It is illegal to export raw unpolished amber from the DR, though amber jewelry is common and highly prized.

Most travelers run into problems with the export of cigars, and it's not with Dominican customs as much as their own. The USA allows its citizens to bring up to 100 cigars duty-free. Canada and most European countries only allow 50 cigars before duty taxes kick in.

DANGERS & ANNOYANCES

The Dominican Republic is not a particularly dangerous place to visit. Street crime is rare in most tourist areas, especially during the day, but you should always be alert for pickpockets and camera snatchers. Avoid walking on beaches at night, and consider taking a cab if you're returning home late from clubs and bars. Prostitution is dangerous mainly to those participating in it, although solo men may get annoyed by persistent propositioning and some readers have reported being pick-pocketed by prostitutes. See p344 for information on reporting child prostitution in the DR. Car theft is not unheard of – this author had his rental vehicle stolen from right in front of his hotel in Boca Chica – so it's best to not leave any valuables inside your car.

Perhaps the number one annoyance is not being given the proper change after a purchase. In many cases it is a legitimate error in math. But it's not entirely uncommon for waiters, taxi drivers and shop owners to 'accidentally' give you 120 pesos when you're owed 220. If something's missing, say so right away.

EMBASSIES & CONSULATES

Embassies vary greatly in terms of the services they offer to their citizens. That said, citizens should not hesitate to contact their embassy for help; at the very least, they can direct you to appropriate third-party agencies or services. All of the following are located in Santo Domingo.

Canada (Map p77; ☎ 809-685-1136; sdgo@dfai-maeci .gc.ca; Av Eugenio de Marchena 39)

Cuba (Map pp74-5; ☎ 809-537-2113; Calle FP Ramírez 809)

France (Map pp80-1; ☎ 809-687-5270; www.amba france-do.org; Calle Las Damas 42)

Germany (Map pp74-5; ☎ 809-542-8949; Torre Piantini, 16th fl, Av Gustavo A Mejía Ricart)

Haiti (Map p77; ☎ 809-686-5778; Calle Juan Sánchez Ramírez 33)

Italy (Map p77; ☎ 809-682-0830; Calle Rodríguez Objío 4)

Japan (Map pp74-5; ☎ 809-567-3365; Torre BHD office Bldg, 8th fl, cnr Calle Luís Thomen & Av Jiménez Moya)

Netherlands (Map pp74-5; ☎ 809-565-5240; Mayor Enrique Valverde)

Spain (Map pp74-5; ☎ 809-535-6500; Torre BHD office Bldg, 4th fl, cnr Calle Luís Thomen & Av Jiménez Moya)

UK (Map pp74–5; ☎ 809-472 7111; Av 27 de Febrero 233)
USA (Map p77; ☎ 809-221-2171; www.usemb.gov.do;
cnr Av César Nicolás Penson & Av Máximo Gómez)

FESTIVALS & EVENTS
February
CARNIVAL
Carnival (or Carnaval, in Spanish) is celebrated with great fervor throughout the country every Sunday in February, culminating in a huge blow out in Santo Domingo on the last weekend of the month or the first weekend of March. Almost every major city (and many minor ones) has Carnival celebrations, each lending unique twists and traditions to the event. Masks and costumes figure prominently in all – Santiago even hosts an international *caleta* (Carnival mask) competition, and the craftsmanship is truly astounding. The largest and most traditional Carnivals outside of Santo Domingo (p90), all of which are held in February or March, are celebrated in Santiago (p209), Cabral, Monte Cristi and La Vega (p223).

INDEPENDENCE DAY
The Dominican Republic declared its independence from Spain in November 1821, but only a year later submitted to Haitian rule to avert reinvasion by Spain (or else Haiti itself). February 27 is the day, in 1844, that the DR regained independence from its neighbor, making it the only Latin American country whose independence celebration does not mark a break from European colonial rule. The day is marked by street celebrations and military parades.

March
SEMANA SANTA
Any place that has access to water – mainly the beach towns, but also those near lakes, rivers or waterfalls – is thoroughly inundated with Dominican vacationers during 'Holy Week,' the biggest travel holiday in the country and much of Latin America. Many foreign travelers may find the crowded beaches, innumerable temporary food stands and loud music day and night a bit off-putting. Others, including most Dominicans, revel in the lively atmosphere. However, most water sports are prohibited during Semana Santa, including scuba diving and windsurfing. Inland is somewhat less crowded than the beaches, but make reservations early, no matter where you end up.

June
PUERTO PLATA CULTURAL FESTIVAL
This weeklong festival brings merengue, blues, jazz and folk concerts to the Puerto Plata's Fuerte San Felipe at the end of the Malecón. Troupes from Santo Domingo perform traditional songs and dances, including African spirituals and famous salsa steps.

July–August
SANTO DOMINGO MERENGUE FESTIVAL
Santo Domingo hosts the country's largest and most raucous merengue festival. For two weeks at the end of July and the beginning of August, the world's top merengue bands play for the world's best merengue dancers. While the Malecón is the center of the action, you'll find dance parties in hotel ballrooms and private terraces, on city squares and public parks, and in restaurants and makeshift bars throughout town.

October
PUERTO PLATA MERENGUE FESTIVAL
The country's other merengue festival is held in Puerto Plata during the first week of October. The entire length of Puerto Plata's Malecón is closed to vehicular traffic. Food stalls are set up on both sides of the boulevard and famous merengue singers perform on a stage erected for the event. This festival is different from the one in Santo Domingo in that it also includes a harvest festival and an arts-and-crafts fair.

LATIN MUSIC FESTIVAL
This huge, annual three-day event – held at the Olympic Stadium in Santo Domingo – attracts the top names in Latin music, including jazz, salsa, merengue and *bachata* (popular guitar music based on bolero rhythms) players. Jennifer Lopez, Marc Anthony, Enrique Iglesias and salsa king Tito Rojas have been featured in the past.

FOOD
Some visitors to the Dominican Republic never experience a meal outside of their all-inclusive resort and when all the food you can eat is calculated into the room price, eating can seem like a bargain. For travelers hoping to eat out on their own, food can be surprisingly expensive. Of course, prices tend to be much higher in heavily touristy areas, such as the Zona Colonial in Santo Domingo

(comparable to US and European prices), and cheaper in small towns and isolated areas. However, outside of informal food stands and cafeteria-style eateries, a meal without drinks at most restaurants will cost a minimum of $6. Many restaurants have a range of options, from inexpensive pizza and pasta dishes to pricey lobster meals. The listing categories in this book refer to the cost of a main dish with tax: budget (less than US$5), midrange (US$5 to US$15) and top end (US$15 and above). For more information on food and drink in the DR, see p66.

GAY & LESBIAN TRAVELERS

As a whole, the Dominican Republic is quite open about heterosexual sex and sexuality, but still fairly closed-minded about gays and lesbians. Gay and lesbian travelers will find the most open community in Santo Domingo, though even its gay clubs are relatively discreet. Santiago, Puerto Plata, Bávaro and Punta Cana also have gay venues, catering as much to foreigners as to locals. Everywhere else, open displays of affection between men or women are rare and quite taboo. Two men may have trouble getting a hotel room with just one bed, even though you'll pay more for a room with two. Two good websites with gay-specific listings and information for the Dominican Republic are **Guia Gay** (www.guiagay.com, in Spanish) and **Planetout.com** (www.planetout.com).

HOLIDAYS

Other than Samana Santa, most holidays should not disrupt your travel plans much – banks, government offices and some museums and galleries may be closed, and parades (especially on Independence Day) can block traffic. Carnival processions are held every weekend in February and are a highlight of any trip to this holiday-happy island.

New Year's Day January 1
Epiphany/Three Kings Day January 6
Our Lady of Altagracia January 21
Duarte Day January 26
Independence Day, Carnival February 27
Semana Santa March/April
Pan-American Day April 14
Labor Day May 1
Foundation of Sociedad la Trinitaria July 16
Restoration Day August 16
Our Lady of Mercedes September 24
Columbus Day October 12

UN Day October 24
All Saints' Day November 1
Constitution Day November 6
Christmas Day December 25

INTERNET ACCESS

The Dominican Republic has no shortage of internet cafés, where high-speed broadband connections are increasingly the norm, as well as CD burners, high-speed USB compatibility, even webcams for phone and chat programs. Most cafés charge US$1 to US$4 per hour to access the internet, more for additional services like printing or burning CDs. Rates can be higher in resort areas. Most of these cafés also operate as call centers.

Wi-fi access is becoming more and more prevalent, especially in top-end hotels and resorts throughout the country. Travelers with laptops won't have to go far before finding some place with a signal. However, the majority of the all-inclusives charge daily fees (around US$12) for access. Many others that offer the service free for guests only have a signal in public spaces like the lobby or the café and not in guest rooms. Certain towns, Las Terrenas on the Península de Samaná for example, tend to be more connected than others and many hotels here, the majority midrange, offer free wi-fi access for guests.

LAUNDRY

Most laundromats and hotels in the DR charge per piece, which adds up very fast. Expect to pay US$0.75 to US$1.50 per piece, for even underwear and T-shirts. Some charge by the load, rather than by the pound or kilo – a load is usually up to 14lb (sometimes 18lb), and can cost US$2 to US$7. Same-day service is usually available if you drop your clothes off early.

LEGAL MATTERS

The Dominican Republic has two police forces – the Policía Nacional (national police) and the Policía Turística (tourist police, commonly referred to by its abbreviation 'Politur'). The Policía Nacional are not as corrupt and unreliable as their counterparts in other Latin American countries, but you still want to have as little interaction with them as possible. If a police officer stops you, be polite and cooperate. They may ask to see your passport – you're not required to have it on you, but it's always a good idea to carry a photocopy.

Politur officers, on the other hand, are generally friendly men and women whose job is specifically to help tourists. Many speak a little bit of a language other than Spanish. They wear white shirts with blue insignia and can usually be found near major tourist sights and centers. You should contact Politur first in the event of theft, assault or if you were the victim of a scam, but you can equally ask them for directions to sights, which bus to take etc. Many cities have a Politur station, which you will find listed in the destination chapters throughout this book.

Prostitution is big business in the DR. Tourists picking up willing men or women is common and, evidently, there is no law that is enforced against it, even if money changes hands. But there is no law expressly legalizing prostitution, either. It is definitely illegal to have sex with anyone under the age of 18, even if the offender didn't know the prostitute's real age. Encouraging or aiding prostitution is illegal, and the law, while targeted at pimps or brothel owners, is obviously open for some interpretation. In fact, the Dominican consulate will tell you that prostitution in all forms is illegal. In any case, walking the line between what is legal and illegal, especially as a foreigner, is definitely risky.

MAPS
If you rent a car, it's worth buying a good map to the area you'll be driving in. You should also get in the habit of asking directions frequently. Not only will this prevent you from getting off track, but it's also a good time to ask about road conditions – in some cases rain or construction have made the roads very difficult to pass, especially if you're driving a compact car. The easiest way to ask directions if you're going to, say, Punta Rusia is to ask '¿Para Punta Rusia?,' literally 'For Punta Rusia?' To ask about conditions, you can say '¿El camino está bien o malo?' (Is the road good or bad?) or '¿Se puede pasar mi carro?' (Will my car be able to pass?). Of course, understanding the directions you're given is half the battle; some key words to listen for are *derecho* (straight), *derecha* (right), *izquierdo* (left), *desvío* (turnoff), *letrero* (sign), *mucho pozo* or *mucha olla* (lots of potholes or holes) and *vaya preguntando* (ask along the way).

In Santo Domingo, **Mapas GAAR** (Map pp80-1; ☎ 809-688-8004; www.mapasgaar.com.do; Espaillat;

☒ 8:30am-5:30pm Mon-Fri) publishes and sells the most comprehensive maps of cities and towns in the DR. Borch produces a high-quality map of the DR available online and in bookstores. For a frame-quality map, the **Instituto Geográfico** (Map pp80-1; ☎ 809-682-2680; El Conde btwn Las Damas & Av del Puerto; ☒ 8am-6pm Mon-Fri), sells a great five-panel, 1m-by-1.5m map for US$35.

MONEY
The Dominican monetary unit is the peso, indicated by the symbol RD$ (or sometimes just R$). Though the peso is technically divided into 100 centavos (cents) per peso, prices are usually rounded to the nearest peso. There are one- and five-peso coins, while paper money comes in denominations of 10, 20, 50, 100, 500 and 1000 pesos. Many tourist-related businesses, including most midrange and top-end hotels, list prices in US dollars, but accept pesos at the going exchange rate.

ATMs
ATMs are common in the Dominican Republic and are, without question, the best way to obtain Dominican pesos and manage your money on the road. Banks with reliable ATMs include Banco Popular, Banco Progreso, Banco de Reservas, Banco León and Scotiabank. As in any country, be smart about where and when you withdraw cash – at night on a dark street in a bad part of town is not the ideal spot. Most ATMs are not in the bank itself, but in a small booth accessible from the street (and thus available 24 hours). Unless otherwise indicated all banks listed have ATMs.

Credit Cards
Credit and debit cards are becoming more common among Dominicans (and more widely accepted for use by foreigners). Visa and MasterCard are more common than Amex but most cards are accepted in areas frequented by tourists. Some but not all businesses add a surcharge for credit-card purchases (typically 16%) – the federal policy of withdrawing sales tax directly from credit-card transactions means merchants will simply add the cost directly to the bill.

Moneychangers
Moneychangers will approach you in a number of tourist centers. They are unlikely

to be aggressive. You will get equally favorable rates, however, and a much securer transaction, at an ATM, a bank or an exchange office.

Taxes & Tipping

There are two taxes on food and drink sales: a 16% sales tax (ITBIS) and a 10% service charge. The latter is supposed to be divided among the wait and kitchen staff; some people choose to leave an additional 10% tip for exceptional service. There's a 23% tax on hotel rooms – ask whether the listed rates include taxes. It's customary to tip bellhops for carrying your bags and to leave US$1 to US$2 per night for the housecleaner at resorts. You should also tip tour guides, some of whom earn no other salary.

Traveler's Checks

With the advent of reliable ATM networks, traveler's checks have lost much of their usefulness. That said, traveler's checks can be exchanged at most banks and *casas de cambio* (exchange booths) in tourist centers. You may be required to show your passport and, in some cases, the receipt from when you purchased the checks.

POST

There are post offices in every town and hours are typically 8am to noon and 2pm to 5pm Monday to Friday, and 8am to noon only on Saturday. It costs about US$0.75 to send a postcard to North and Central America, slightly more for Europe. Service is relatively reliable – postcards are more likely to arrive than letters – but by no means foolproof. For important documents and packages, definitely go with an international courier, such as UPS, DHL or Federal Express. They each have stand-alone offices in Santo Domingo; in smaller towns, they are usually affiliated with Metro Pac or another local delivery agency, which will have all the packaging and tracking materials.

SHOPPING

The DR is one of the largest producers of cigars in the world; some of the better-known brands are Macanudo, Davidoff, Fonseca, Montecristo and Preferidos. Santiago is the center of tobacco plantations and a good place to experiment with different brands to find your favorite.

Dominican rum is a popular item, available everywhere, from the most modest *col-mado* (combination corner store, grocery and bar) to airport duty-free shops. For more on brands and varieties, see p67.

Dominican amber is among the best in the world, both for its variety of color and the high number of 'inclusions' (insects, plant material and other things trapped inside). The quality of the jewelry made from amber varies widely, but if you look around enough, you'll find an excellent piece that's in your price range. For help on choosing a piece, see boxed text, p173. Larimar is another beautiful material – a blue mineral with white streaks – and is found only in the DR. Amber and larimar are typically sold together, so a shop that's good for one is likely to be good for the other. You can also find objects made of horn, wood and leather.

You can't possibly miss the Haitian-style paintings that are for sale in virtually every tourist destination in the country. Most are very generic and formulaic, unsurprising since their production resembles a car-parts factory. More professional pieces can be found in several galleries in Santo Domingo (p99) or the Haitian Caraibes Art Gallery in Las Terrenas (p161).

Many souvenirs sold in the DR are made from endangered plant and animal species, and you should avoid buying them. All species of sea turtles are endangered, so steer clear of any item made of turtle shell – typically combs and bracelets – or food dishes made from *carey* (turtle meat). The same goes for products made from American crocodiles and black or white coral, despite what some store owners say.

TELEPHONE

There has been some flux regarding telecommunications companies and there could be more mergers, acquisitions and divestments in the future. In 2007 Verizon changed the name of its services to Claro (wireless division) and CODETEL (fixed line and broadband market). Orange, Tricom and Centennial are the other companies and competitors.

The easiest way to make a phone call in the DR is to pay per minute (average rates per minute to USA US$0.20; per minute to Europe US$0.50; per minute to Haiti US$0.50) at a Codetel Centro de Comunicaciones call center or an internet café – virtually all operate as dual call centers.

Cell (mobile) phones are very popular and travelers with global-roaming-enabled phones can often receive and make cell-phone calls. It's worth checking with your cell-phone carrier for details on rates and accessibility – be aware that per-minute fees can be exorbitant. If you have a GSM phone, and you can unlock it, you use a SIM card bought from Orange or Claro (prepaid startup kit US$10). If it's CDMA, it will work with Claro, Tricom or Centennial. New cell phones can be bought at Orange with a prepaid SIM card for less than US$30; used phones at Claro can be bought for US$10.

Phone cards to be used at public phones are available in denominations of RD$50, RD$100, RD$150, RD$200 and RD$250. Remember that you must dial ☎ 1 + 809 for all calls within the DR, even local ones. There are no regional codes. Local calls cost US$0.14 per minute and national calls are US$0.21 per minute. Toll-free numbers have ☎ 200 for their prefix (not the area code).

TIME
The DR is four hours behind Greenwich Mean Time. In autumn and winter it is one hour ahead of New York, Miami and Toronto. However, because the country does not adjust for daylight saving time as do the USA and Canada, it's in the same time zone as New York, Miami and Toronto from the first Sunday in April to the last Sunday in October.

TOURIST INFORMATION
Almost every city in the DR that's frequented by tourists has a tourist office, and a number of less-visited towns do as well. Whether they are actually helpful is another question entirely. In general, treat the information you get at tourist offices skeptically and double-check with other sources. Some tourist offices offer maps, bus schedules or a calendar of upcoming events, which can be handy.

A service-oriented tourist office is located in the heart of the Zona Colonial, on Calle Isabel La Católica beside Parque Colón (for more details, see p78). The location and business hours of tourist offices throughout the country, where they exist, are listed in the appropriate Information sections within the destination chapters.

There are also information counters at both Aeropuerto Internacional Las Américas and at Aeropuerto Internacional Gregorio Luperón near Puerto Plata.

TRAVELERS WITH DISABILITIES
Few Latin American countries are well suited for travelers with disabilities, and the Dominican Republic is no different. On the other hand, all-inclusive resorts can be ideal for travelers with mobility impairments, as room, meals, and day- and nighttime activities are all within close proximity, and there are plenty of staff members to help you navigate around the property. Some resorts have a few wheelchair-friendly rooms, with larger doors and handles in the bathroom. And, it should be said, Dominicans tend to be extremely helpful and accommodating people. Travelers with disabilities should expect some long and curious stares, but also quick and friendly help from perfect strangers and passersby.

VISAS
The majority of would-be foreign travelers in the Dominican Republic do not need to obtain visas prior to arrival. Tourist cards (you don't need to retain this for your return flight) are issued for US$10 upon arrival to visitors from Argentina, Australia, Austria, Belgium, Brazil, Canada, Chile, Denmark, France, Germany, Greece, Ireland, Israel, Italy, Japan, Mexico, the Netherlands, Portugal, Russia, South Africa, Spain, Sweden, Switzerland, the UK and the USA, among many others. Whatever your country of origin, a valid passport is necessary.

Tourist Card Extensions
A tourist card is good for up to 30 days from the date of issue, though the exact length depends on what the officer writes on the card when you enter. If you need just a little extra time, it's usually unnecessary to formally extend – instead you'll be charged a 'fine' of about US$5 for every month you overstayed when you depart from the country. Another easy way to extend your time is to leave the DR briefly – most likely to Haiti – and then return, at which point you'll be issued a brand-new tourist card. (You may have to pay entrance and departure fees in both countries, of course.)

To extend your tourist card anywhere from 15 days to three months the official way, you must apply in Santo Domingo at the **Dirección General de Migración** (Map pp74-5; ☎ 809-508-2555; www.migracion.gov.do; cnr Av 30 de Mayo & Héroes de Luperón; ☺ 8am-2:30pm Mon-Fri) at least two weeks before your original card expires. You'll be required to fill out a form – usually available in Spanish only – and to present your passport, a photocopy of your passport's information page(s) and two passport-size photos of yourself. The fee is US$10; your passport and new tourist card will be ready for pickup at the same office two weeks later. The process is a good way to blow an entire day.

VOLUNTEERING

Many of the NGOs are primarily community networks attempting to develop sustainable ecotourism. There are no formal volunteering programs, but if you speak good Spanish and don't mind some elbow grease (or office work), you may be of some use to them. You should have at least a month to play with. Be sure to contact them well ahead of time. There is occasionally some wildlife volunteering on offer – helping biologists hatch turtle eggs, for instance – and the best months for field work are February, April, May, August and October. Several of the more established organizations that accept volunteers include the following:

CEDAF (Centro para el Desarrollo Agropecuario y Forestal; ☎ 809-894-0005; www.cedaf.org.do; José Amado Soler 50, Ensanche Paraíso, Santo Domingo) This nationwide NGO helps local farmers develop sustainable ways to use the land, including market gardening on mountainside terraces to reduce erosion. Few volunteers make their way here, and capacity is limited. If you're looking for an internship and speak good Spanish, it's worth making contact.

DREAM Project (Dominican Republic Education & Mentoring; ☎ 809-571-0497) Nonconformists will want to avoid this rigidly managed NGO, which otherwise does excellent work in the Cabarete schools.

Grupo Jaragua (www.grupojaragua.org.do) The largest and oldest NGO in the southwest. Based in Santo Domingo, it concentrates on biodiversity and conservation through microfinancing as little as US$300 to assist locals with bee farming etc.

Punta Cana Ecological Foundation (☎ 809-959-9221; www.puntacana.org) One of the pioneers of sustainable development in the DR; projects targeted at restoring and preserving natural environment in Punta Cana area.

REDEC (Red Enriquillo de Ecoturismo Comunitario; ☎ 809-913-1587; Barahona) Founded in 2006, this is a network of small NGOs.

REDOTUR (Red Dominicana de Turismo Rural; ☎ 809-487-1057; tinglar@yahoo.com) Promotes alternative and sustainable tourism projects.

SOEPA (☎ 809-899-4702) Its biggest project is maintenance and development at Cachóte (see boxed text, p235).

WOMEN TRAVELERS

Women traveling without men in the Dominican Republic should expect to receive a fair amount of attention, usually in the form of stares and admiring comments like 'Hola, preciosa' (Hello, beautiful). Dominican men are also consummate butt-lookers, no matter what the age, size, shape or nationality of the woman passing by. Then again, women's fashion in the DR is all about accentuating what you've got, and having your backside checked out by men is clearly more bothersome to foreign women than it is to many Dominicans. Indeed, much of what women travelers experience as unwanted attention is fairly ordinary male–female interaction among Dominicans. Many Dominicans, male and female, are somewhat baffled by the strong negative reaction some foreign women have to men's 'appreciation.'

But that is not at all to say that women travelers shouldn't take the same precautions they would in other countries, or ignore their instincts about certain men or situations they encounter. Robbery and assaults, though rare against tourists, do occur and women are often seen as easier targets than men. In much the same way, it isn't a good idea to flash money, jewelry or electronics. Foreign women who don't want extra male attention should dress a little conservatively to avoid sending the wrong message.

Beyond that, simply follow basic commonsense precautions when traveling by yourself; avoid isolated streets and places, especially at night, and don't hitchhike or camp alone.

Dominican Republic Transportation

CONTENTS

GETTING THERE & AWAY

Flights and tours can be booked online at www.lonelyplanet.com/travel_services.

ENTERING THE COUNTRY

The vast majority of tourists entering the Dominican Republic arrive by air. Independent travelers typically arrive at the main international airport outside of Santo Domingo, Aeropuerto Internacional Las Américas. Flights from Boston, Fort Lauderdale, New York, Newark, Miami, Philadelphia, San Juan (Puerto Rico) and various European countries arrive there daily. Passing through immigration is a relatively simple process. Once

---

THINGS CHANGE...

The information in this chapter is particularly vulnerable to change. Check directly with the airline or a travel agent to make sure you understand how a fare (and ticket you may buy) works and be aware of the security requirements for international travel. Shop carefully. The details given in this chapter should be regarded as pointers and are not a substitute for your own careful, up-to-date research.

DEPARTURE TAX

The US$20 departure tax is usually already included in the cost of your airline ticket, and exceptions are rare. Those leaving by land or sea are routinely charged US$25. You don't need to retain your tourist card if you are leaving the country by air.

---

disembarked, you are guided to the immigration area where you must buy a tourist card (US$10). You're expected to pay in US dollars. Euros and GBP are accepted, but you lose out substantially on the rate; a few people report that DR pesos (RD$) are accepted, though this is not official policy. Once you've filled in the card, join the queue in front of one of the immigration officers. They will often assume you are visiting for two weeks or less, and give you just 15 days, so if you plan on staying longer, let the officer know this right away – he is allowed to give you up to 30 days on a tourist card. In general, entering is a breeze. The procedure is the same if you arrive at one of the smaller airports like Puerto Plata or Punta Cana, though the latter is easily the busiest airport in the country in terms of tourist arrivals. Officers are even less scrutinizing there, but the queues may become backed up as you are asked to pause for an obligatory photograph with two woman dressed in some kind of garish island costume reminiscent of the Chiquita Banana mascot.

Passport

All foreign visitors must have a valid passport to enter the DR. Be sure you have room for both entry and exit stamps, and that your passport is valid for at least six months beyond your planned travel dates. See p253 for information on visas.

AIR
Airports & Airlines

The DR has 10 international airports, though at least three of them are primarily used for domestic flights (Aeropuerto Internacional Herrera outside of Santo Domingo closed in 2006).

Aeropuerto Internacional Arroyo Barril (ABA; ☎ 809-248-2718) West of Samaná, a small airstrip used mostly during whale-watching season (January to March) that handles only propeller aircraft.

Aeropuerto Internacional Cibao (STI; ☎ 809-581-8072) Serves Santiago and the interior.

Aeropuerto Internacional El Catey (AZS; ☎ 809-338-0094) New airport 40km west of Samaná that handles international flights from various European cities and San Juan, Puerto Rico.

Aeropuerto Internacional El Portillo (EPS) Airstrip only a few kilometers from Las Terrenas that gets busiest during whale-watching season. Used mostly for domestic flights.

Aeropuerto Internacional Gregorio Luperón (POP; ☎ 809-586-1992) Serves Playa Dorada and Puerto Plata.

Aeropuerto Internacional La Isabela (JBQ; aka DR Joaquin Balaguer, Higuero; ☎ 809-567-3900) Located 16km north of Santo Domingo in Higuero, this airport services domestic airlines.

Aeropuerto Internacional La Romana (LRM; aka Casa de Campo; ☎ 809-689-1548) Modern airport near La Romana and Casa de Campo; handles primarily charter flights from the US, Canada and Europe.

Aeropuerto Internacional Las Américas (SDQ; ☎ 809-549-0081) Located 20km east of Santo Domingo. The country's main international airport, with modern facilities, including a strong wi-fi signal once past security.

Aeropuerto Internacional María Montez (BRX; ☎ 809-524-4144) Located 5km from Barahona; does not have a regular commercial passenger service.

Aeropuerto Internacional Punta Cana (PUJ; ☎ 809-959-2473) Serves Bávaro and Punta Cana, and is the busiest airport in the country.

AIRLINES FLYING TO/FROM THE DOMINICAN REPUBLIC

International carriers with services to the DR:

Aeropostal (VH; ☎ 809-549-8067; www.aeropostal.com; hub: Caracas)

Air Canada (AC; ☎ 809-541-2929; www.aircanada.ca; hub: Toronto)

Air Europa (AEA; ☎ 809-683-8020; www.aireuropa.com; hub: Mallorca)

Air France (AF; ☎ 809-686-8432; www.airfrance.com; hub: Paris)

Air Jamaica (JM; ☎ 809-872-0080; www.airjamaica.com; hub: Kingston)

American Airlines (AA; ☎ 809-542-5151; www.aa.com; hub: New York) Flies to Samaná via San Juan (Puerto Rico); also flies to Santo Domingo, Santiago and Puerto Plata.

Condor (DE; ☎ 809-689-9625; www.condor.com; hub: Munich)

Continental Airlines (CO; ☎ 809-262-1060; www.continental.com; hub: Newark)

COPA Airlines (CM; ☎ 809-472-2672; www.copaair.com; hub: Panama City) Several flights a week from Santo Domingo to Havana, Kingston and Port of Spain (Trinidad).

Cubana Air (CU; ☎ 809-227-2040; www.cubana.cu; hub: Havana) Twice-weekly direct flights between Santo Domingo and Havana.

Delta (DL; ☎ 809-200-9191; www.delta.com; hub: Atlanta)

Iberia (IB; ☎ 809-508-7979; www.iberia.com; hub: Madrid)

Jet Blue (B6; ☎ 809-549-1793; www.jetblue.com; hub: New York) Nonstop service between JFK and Puerto Plata, Santiago and Santo Domingo. Also nonstop service from Orlando to Santo Domingo.

Lan Chile (LAN; ☎ 809-689-2116; www.lan.com; hub: Santiago)

LTU (LT; ☎ 809-586-4075; www.ltu.com; hub: Dusseldorf) Flights from Germany and Austria to Samaná.

Lufthansa (LH; ☎ 809-689-9625; www.lufthansa.com; hub: Frankfurt)

Martinair Holland (MP; ☎ 809-621-7777; www.martinair.com; hub: Amsterdam) Flights from Amsterdam and Frankfurt to Puerto Plata and Punta Cana.

Mexicana (MX; ☎ 809-541-1016; www.mexicana.com; hub: Mexico City)

Spirit Airlines (NK; ☎ 809-381-4111; www.spiritair.com; Fort Lauderdale) Nonstop flights from Fort Lauderdale to Santo Domingo and Punta Cana.

Swissport (☎ 809-508-2277; www.swissport.com) Handles ticketing and other ground services of various airlines and charters.

US Airways (US; ☎ 809-540-0505; www.usair.com; hub: Philadelphia)

Varig (RG; ☎ 809-563-3434; www.varig.com; hub: Sao Paolo)

LAND

There are three points where you can cross between Haiti and the DR. The most trafficked is at the Jimaní–Malpasse crossing in the south, on the road that links Santo Domingo and Port-au-Prince. Also busy is the northern crossing at Dajabón–Ouanaminthe, which is on the road between Santiago and Cap-Haïtien (only a six-hour drive with the completion of a new highway on the Haitian side); however, you should try to avoid crossing on market days (Monday and Friday) because of the enormous crush of people and the risk of theft. The third border crossing is at Comendador (aka Elías Piña) and Belladère, which sees few foreign travelers. It's the least trafficked of the three and certainly the dodgiest; having to wade the river or cross it on a motorcycle is also a nuisance. Only Haitians and Dominicans are permitted to use other border crossings, including the one at Pedernales–Ainse-a-Pietre in the far south, a popular route for smugglers.

Immigration offices on the Dominican side are usually open 8am to 6pm, and 9am to 6pm on the Haitian side. It's always a good idea to arrive as early as possible, so you are sure to get through both countries' border offices and onto a bus well before dark. When deciding whether either crossing in the late afternoon or staying an extra night and crossing in the morning, choose the latter. Also, long lines and immigration officials who leave early or take long lunch breaks can cause delays at the border.

Tourists leaving the DR will be asked to produce their passports and their tourist cards and are likely to be asked more questions than if they were leaving via an airport. However, this shouldn't be a concern since it's usually only out of curiosity that a tourist would travel this way. Officially, you are supposed to pay US$25 to leave the DR, which gives you the right to reenter at the same point for no extra charge. However, border officials have been known to ask for an extra US$5 to US$10 to leave, and the full US$10 to reenter for no other reason than they can. It's worth politely pointing out that you have already paid the full fee. In the end, however, you may have to cough up the extra cash.

When you enter Haiti, you pay a US$10 fee. Leaving Haiti, you must present your passport and yellow entry card, but are not supposed to have to pay anything. That said, it's wise to have small bills on hand (US cash is always best) to smooth your passage if need be. As with Dominican officials, you don't have much recourse if they decide to charge you extra 'fees.' Unless the fees are exorbitant, the best thing to do is simply pay up and move on.

Caribe Tours, Capital Coach Lines and Terra Bus service the Santo Domingo–Port-au-Prince (see p102) route daily; it's the most convenient way to reach Haiti via public transportation. From the north coast it's easy enough to reach Dajabón, but then you have to transfer to a Haitian vehicle on the other side.

Ayido Tours runs a bus service from Cap-Haïtien to Santiago; see p336 for details.

Rental vehicles are not allowed to cross from one country into the other, and you need special authorization to cross the border with a private vehicle. For specific information about the border facilities and services in individual towns, check the relevant destination chapters in this book.

SEA

The only regularly scheduled international ferry service is between the DR and Puerto Rico. However, international cruise ships on Caribbean tours commonly stop in Santo Domingo, Cayo Levantado in the Península de Samaná and elsewhere. Sans Souci, the Santo Domingo port, is undergoing a massive renovation, including new docking areas, terminals, hotels and a convention center.

Ferries del Caribe (www.ferriesdelcaribe.com); Santo Domingo (☎ 809-688-4400); Santiago (☎ 809-724-8771); Mayagüez, Puerto Rico (☎ 787-832-4400); San Juan, Puerto Rico (☎ 787-725-2643) offers a passenger and car ferry service between Santo Domingo and Mayagüez, Puerto Rico. The trip takes about 12 hours and departs three times weekly. See Santo Domingo (p101) for details.

GETTING AROUND

AIR

The DR is a fairly small country, so in theory at least it's easy to drive or take public transportation from one side of the country to the other. In practice, however, the inadequate road network will behoove some with limited time to consider flying. It's a more expensive option, but often a convenient and logical one that can save you an entire day of road rage. Most one-way flights cost US$35 to US$170. The main domestic carriers and air taxi companies include the following:

AeroDomca (☎ 809-567-1195; www.aerodomca .com) Scheduled flights between La Isabela outside Santo Domingo to El Portillo near Las Terrenas (US$75). Charter flights can be booked to almost any airport.

Air Century (☎ 809-826-4222; www.aircentury.com) Charter flights from La Isabela outside Santo Domingo.

Take Off (☎ 809-552-1333; www.takeoffweb.com) Offers the widest selection of scheduled flights, including Las Americas in Santo Domingo to El Portillo near Las Terrenas ($80), Punta Cana to El Portillo (US$116) and Puerto Plata to La Romana (US$170). There's a small, efficient office with English speakers in the Plaza Brisas in Bávaro. As of yet there is no office at the Aeropuerto Internacional Las

Américas; ask at the 2nd-floor information booth to be directed to personnel.

BICYCLE

The DR's undermaintained highways are not well suited for cycling, and Dominican drivers are not exactly accommodating to people on bikes. Add to that the high number of motor-cycles (which move faster than bikes but slower than cars), and *gua-guas* (local buses) and *públicos* (private cars operating as taxis) making frequent unannounced stops, and the situation on the side of the road is hectic to say the least. However, mountain biking on the DR's back roads and lesser-used high-ways can be very rewarding, and a number of recommended tours are available from Jarabacoa and Cabarete for just that (p64).

There are very few places where you can rent a bike, and none are for long-distance travel. If you're planning a multiday ride, definitely consider bringing your own bike. If you're joining a bike tour, most tour op-erators will provide you with a bike as part of the price. You'll find bike-rental outfits in Las Terrenas, Las Galleras and at some of the resort areas. (A number of resorts and a few independent hotels offer bicycles for guests' use.) Expect to pay around US$5 to US$15 per day. There are a few agencies that offer multi-day mountain bike tours; see p189 and p215.

BOAT

The only regularly scheduled domestic pas-senger boat route in the DR is the ferry serv-ice between Samaná and Sabana de la Mar, on opposite sides of the Bahía de Samaná in the northeastern part of the country. The journey is subject to weather and departures are frequently cancelled. There is no car ferry service here, so unfortunately, if you arrive in Sabana de la Mar with a rental vehicle, you'll have to leave it behind and return by the same route you arrived.

BUS

The DR has a great bus system, with frequent service throughout the country. And since it's relatively small in size, there are none of the epic overnight journeys travelers often encounter in places like Mexico or Brazil. There are two classes of bus service in the DR: *primera* (1st class) utilizes large air-conditioned buses simi-lar to Greyhound buses in the US. Virtually all 1st-class buses have toilets in the back and TVs in the aisles showing movies en route. Fares are low – the most expensive 1st-class ticket is less than US$10. Unfortunately, there are no central bus terminals in the majority of cities and each company has its own station location.

Second-class service is on minibuses known as *gua-guas*, which are more frequent than 1st-class buses but go much more slowly as they stop to pick up and drop off passengers along the way. *Gua-guas* are divided into two types – the majority are *caliente* (literally 'hot'), which don't have air-conditioning, naturally. For every four or five *caliente* buses there is usu-ally an *expreso*, which typically has air-condi-tioning, makes fewer stops and costs slightly more. Within these two categories there's a virtual rainbow of diversity in terms of vehicle quality and reliability.

Classes
FIRST CLASS

First-class buses leave from designated ter-minals and you must buy your ticket before boarding. They almost never stop along the road to pick up passengers but drivers are often willing to drop passengers off at various points along the way; they will not, however, open the luggage compartment at any point other than the actual terminal. If you plan on getting off early, bring your bags onboard with you. This is actually a very good idea, as you generally won't have to worry about your bag being stolen or accidentally unloaded along the way. That said, there are usually intermediate bathroom and snack stops, and it's a good idea at those times to check that your bag did not get removed.

First-class carriers include the following:

Caribe Tours (Map pp74–5; ☎ 809-221-4422; cnr Avs 27 de Febrero & Leopoldo Navarro, Santo Domingo) The most ex-tensive bus line, with service everywhere but the south east.

El Canario (☎ 809-291-5594) Not exactly 1st-class vehicles, but the only daily direct service between Puerto Plata and Samaná (US$7, 3½ to four hours), with stops in Nagua and Sánchez.

Expreso Santo Domingo Bávaro (Map p77; ☎ 809-682-9670; cnr Juan Sánchez Ruiz & Máximo Gómez, Santo Domingo) Connects Santo Domingo and Bávaro with a stop in La Romana.

Metro (Map pp74–5; ☎ 809-566-7126; Calle Francisco Prats Ramírez, Santo Domingo) Located behind Plaza Central Shopping Mall in Santo Domingo, Metro serves nine cities, mostly along the Santo Domingo–Puerto Plata corridor.

Terra Bus (Map pp74–5; ☎ 809-531-0383; Plaza Lama, cnr Avs 27 de Febrero & Winston Churchill, Santo Domingo) Air-con service from Santo Domingo to Port-au-Prince, Haiti.

GUA-GUAS

Wherever long-distance buses don't go, you can be sure a *gua-gua* does. *Gua-guas* are typically midsize buses holding around 25 to 30 passengers. They rarely have signs, but the driver's assistant (known as the *cobrador,* or 'charger' since one of his jobs is to collect fares from passengers) will yell out the destination of the bus to potential fares on the side of the road. Don't hesitate to ask a local if you're unsure which one to take. *Gua-guas* pick up and drop off passengers anywhere along the route – to flag one down simply hold out your hand – the common gesture is to point at the curb in front of you (as if to say 'stop right here') but just about any gesture will do. Most *gua-guas* pass every 15 to 30 minutes and cost US$1 to US$2, but unless you have the exact amount some *cobradors* may pocket the change of unwary foreigners. It's a good idea to carry change or small bills and to find out the exact cost in advance by asking a local waiting with you at the stop.

Reservations

Reservations aren't usually necessary and rarely even taken, even on 1st-class buses. The exceptions are the international buses to Port-au-Prince, Haiti, operated by Caribe Tours and Terra Bus. During Dominican holidays you can sometimes buy your ticket a day or two in advance, which assures you a spot and saves you the time and hassle of waiting in line at a busy terminal with all your bags. Finally, there are a few routes where you should arrive early to secure a spot, either because the bus fills up or because it may leave early. Those cases are noted in the appropriate chapters.

CAR & MOTORCYCLE

Though the DR's bus and *gua-gua* system is excellent, having your own car is invariably faster and more convenient. Even if renting a car isn't in your budget for the entire trip, consider renting one for a select couple of days, to reach sights that are isolated or not well served by public transportation.

Driver's License

For travelers from most countries, your home country driver's license allows you to drive in the DR. Be sure it's valid.

Fuel & Spare Parts

Most towns have at least one gas station, typically right along the highway on the outskirts of town. There are a couple of different companies, but prices are essentially the same for all. The base price of gasoline is regulated by the federal government, but has fluctuated wildly in recent years. At the time of research, gas prices had just been hiked to US$4.50 to US$5 and were still on the rise.

Play it safe and always keep your gas tank at least half full. Many *bombas* (gas stations) in the DR close by 7pm, and even when they are open they don't always have gas. If you're traveling on back roads or in a remote part of the country, your best bet is to buy gas from people selling it from their front porch. Look for the large pink jugs sitting on tables on the side of the road.

The most common car trouble is to end up with a punctured or damaged tire caused by pot holes, speed bumps and rocks or other debris in the road. The word for tire is *goma* (literally 'rubber') and a tire shop is called a *gomero,* which are even more common than gas stations. If you can make it to one on your busted tire, the guys there can patch a flat (US$5 to US$8), replace a damaged tire (US$10 to US$50 depending on type of tire and whether you want a new or used replacement), or just put the spare on for you (US$1 to US$2).

Insurance

The multinational car-rental agencies typically offer comprehensive, nondeductible collision and liability insurance for fairly small daily fees. Smaller agencies usually offer partial coverage, with a deductible ranging from US$100 to US$2000. Several credit-card companies, including Amex, offer comprehensive coverage for rentals, but you should check your own insurance policy before declining the rental company's.

Rental

Familiar multinational agencies like Hertz, Avis, Europcar, Alamo and Dollar all have offices at Aeropuerto Internacional Las Américas (and pickup service at airports like Punta Cana), as well as in Santo Domingo and other cities. Not only are their rates usually much less than those of local or national agencies, but their vehicles are of much better quality and they provide reliable and comprehensive service and insurance. If you plan to do any driving outside major cities, it's highly recommended, if not necessary, to rent a 4WD. Rates typically cost US$40 to US$100 per day, but if you make a reservation in advance via the internet discounts are substantial. Motorcycles can also be rented, but only experienced riders should do so because of poor road conditions. It's usually possible to pick up and drop off the car at different locations for an additional fee.

Road Conditions

Roads in the DR range from excellent to awful, sometimes along the same highway over a very short distance. The *autopista* (freeway) between Santo Domingo and Santiago has as many as eight lanes and is fast moving and in excellent condition. However, on the rest of the highways, be alert for potholes, speed bumps and people walking along the roadside, especially near populated areas. On all roads, large or small, watch for slow-moving cars and especially motorcycles. Be particularly careful when driving at night, as potholes and speed bumps are harder to spot and many motorcycles and pedestrians don't have lights or reflectors. Better yet, *never drive at night*. Even the most skilled person with the reflexes of a superhero will probably end up in a ditch by the side of the road.

Several new highways were under construction at the time of research and scheduled to be completed in the near future. Most important of these is the one that will cut the driving time between Santo Domingo and Samaná nearly in half. There's a major new road being built in the Punta Cana area to alleviate the heavy traffic and the long commute between the airport and resort areas.

Some of the highways, including Hwy 3 heading out of Santo Domingo to the east and Hwy 2 leaving the city to the west, have toll fees of fairly nominal amounts (around US$1). It's best to have exact change that you can simply toss into the basket and quickly move on. If not, there are booths and collectors who can give change.

Road Rules

First rule is there are none. In theory, road rules in the DR are the same for most countries in the Americas, and the lights and signs are the same shape and color you find in the US or Canada. Seatbelts are required at all times. That said, driving in the DR is pretty much a free-for-all, a test of ones' nerves and will, a continuous series of games of chicken

where the loser is the one who decides to give way just before the moment of impact.

In small towns, nay in all towns, traffic lights are frequently ignored, though you should always plan to stop at them. Watch what other drivers are doing – if everyone is going through, you probably should, too, as it can be even more dangerous to stop if the cars behind you aren't expecting it.

HITCHHIKING

Though hitchhiking is never entirely safe anywhere in the world, Dominicans hitch all the time, both men and women, especially in rural areas where fewer people have cars and *gua-gua* service is sparse. It's also very common in resort areas like Bávaro, where a large number of workers commute to Higüey or other towns nearby every morning and evening. And the *motoconcho* (motorcycle taxi) and *público* systems in cities of all sizes are themselves essentially hitchhiking, since there is little formal regulation. That said, it is rare to see foreigners hitchhiking, and doing so (especially if you have bags) carries a greater risk than for locals.

LOCAL TRANSPORTATION
Bus

Large cities like Santo Domingo and Santiago have public bus systems that operate as they do in most places around the world. Many of the larger city buses are imported from Brazil, and are the kind in which you board in the back and pay the person sitting beside the turnstile. Other city buses are more or less like *gua-guas*, where you board quickly and pay the *cobrador* when he comes around. In general, you will probably take relatively few city buses, simply because *públicos* follow pretty much the same routes and pass more frequently.

Motoconcho

Cheaper and easier to find than taxis, *motoconchos* (motorcycle taxis) are the best and sometimes only way, to get around in many towns. An average ride should set you back no more than US$1.50. However, a high number of riders have been injured or killed in *motoconcho* accidents; ask the driver to slow down (*¡Más despacio por favor!*) if you think he's driving dangerously. Avoid two passengers on a bike since not only is the price the same as taking separate bikes but the extra weight makes most scooters harder to control. For longer trips, or if you have any sort of bag or luggage, *motoconchos* are usually impractical and certainly less comfortable than the alternatives.

Públicos

These are banged-up cars, minivans or small pickup trucks that pick up passengers along set routes, usually main boulevards. *Públicos* (also called *conchos* or *carros*) don't have signs but the drivers hold their hands out the window to solicit potential fares. They are also identifiable by the crush of people inside them – up to seven in a midsize car! To flag one down simply hold out your hand – the fare is around US$0.30. If there is no one else in the car, be sure to tell the driver you want *servicio público* (public service) to avoid paying private taxi rates.

Taxi

Dominican taxis rarely cruise for passengers – instead they wait at designated *sitios* (stops), which are located at hotels, bus terminals, tourist areas and main public parks. You also can phone a taxi service (or ask your hotel receptionist to call for you). Taxis do not have meters – agree on a price beforehand.

THE 2010 EARTHQUAKE

On 12 January, 2010, an earthquake measuring 7.0 on the Richter scale hit Haiti, with its epicenter near the town of Leógâne, 25km west of Port-au-Prince. The earthquake devastated swathes of the capital, Leógâne and Petit-Goâve, and badly damaged Jacmel. The final death toll may never be exactly known, but it's estimated that around 200,000 people lost their lives. The earthquake caused over US$7 billion damage to Haiti's infrastructure. The Inter-American Development Bank reported the earthquake to be the most devastating natural disaster of modern times.

The international community responded with a massive relief effort, but the speed of the response was initially hampered by the fact that the earthquake had not only put Port-au-Prince's airport and port out of action, but also leveled the centers of government, from the Palais National and Parliament down. Similarly, the UN headquarters was destroyed and its chief of mission killed. The transport hubs were soon reopened by the US military, who sent thousands of personnel, but a lack of agency coordination (later criticized by senior UN staff) further contributed to delays, and even a month after the earthquake there were areas that had yet to receive any relief or assistance

The immediate needs were immense. A million people were rendered homeless and up to 250,000 buildings in the capital alone were estimated to be damaged or destroyed. Those who had swelled Port-au-Prince's shanties in recent decades were particularly affected, with whole neighborhoods of cheaply built shacks flattened in an instant. In the aftermath, tented camps sprang up across the city wherever there was space. Shelter was a huge priority, with the need for adequate tents essential in the face of the rains and hurricane season. At the same time, the destruction saw a large-scale exodus from Port-au-Prince, with people leaving to stay with relatives in the provinces. One of the lasting legacies of the earthquake is the high number of amputees among survivors.

Rebuilding will take a matter of years, not months. With the emergency medical emergency phase of the relief operation over, the new priorities are longer-term primary care and public health, particularly for those living in crowded temporary shelters. Rubble clearance for rebuilding is also a high priority.

Travel to Haiti?

While as of March 2010 non-essential travel to the affected areas was not advised, tourism income can undoubtedly play a part in Haiti's economic recovery. Volunteer tourism, of the sort that was seen after the 2004 Asian Tsunami and in post-Katrina New Orleans, will also have its part to play, although at time of publication organized volunteer programs were yet to fully take shape. It should be noted that away from the center, places like Cap-Haïtien, the northern coast and the southwest were largely untouched by the earthquake, although most towns have received influxes of those displaced by the quake.

The following sights in Port-au-Prince are known to have been destroyed: Palais National, Marché de Fer, Centre d'Art, Sainte Trinité Episcopalian Cathedral and Notre Dame Catholic Cathedral. Grand Rue was leveled, although the artists' community survives, as do the majority of the historic gingerbread houses. In Fermathe, Fort Jacques was damaged. Jacmel's historic core was also badly damaged.

In Port-au-Prince, St Joseph's Home for Boys Guest House and the Hotel Montana were flattened, while the El Rancho and Villa Creole hotels were damaged and closed after the quake. In Jacmel, the Hôtel Florita was severely damaged. In Petit-Goâve, Le Relais de l'Empereur was completely destroyed. In the short term, hotel space is likely to remain at a premium, and advance booking essential.

For updated information on the earthquake, a good place to start is ReliefWeb (www.reliefweb. int/haiti). Many major international relief and development NGOs such asOxfam (www.oxfam.org) and Médecins Sans Frontières (Doctors Without Borders; www.msf.org) have had a long-term presence in Haiti, but there are also plenty of local NGOs doing valuable work within their own communities, such as Partners in Health (www.pih.org), Lambi Fund (www.lambifund.org), Konbit Pou Ayiti/KONPAY (www.konpay.org) and Fonkoze (www.fonkoze.org).

Further updates are available from www.lonelyplanet.com/haiti.

Haiti

WAYNE WALTON

HAITI

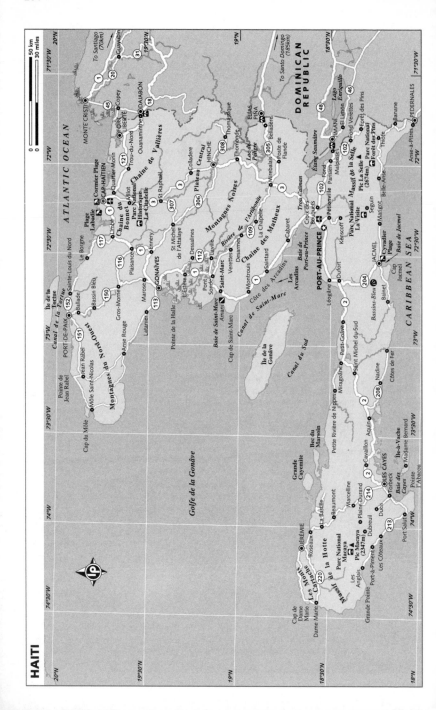

Haiti History

THE HAITIAN SLAVE REVOLUTION

At the end of the 18th century, Haiti – the French colony of St-Domingue – was the 'Pearl of the Antilles.' The most valuable colony in the world, it was flush with sugar and coffee wealth, produced by the sweat and blood of half a million African slaves. But France itself was on the cusp of revolution, and when the Bastille was stormed in 1789, the struggle for *liberté* also opened the door for Haitian slaves to grab their independence.

The French Revolution didn't initially abolish slavery, but it inspired St-Domingue's growing mulatto class to travel to Paris to demand political representation. White colonists were already split between revolutionaries and royalists, the government was threatening to turn into anarchy and the country was a tinderbox. A mulatto uprising led by Vincent Ogé was crushed, but the revolutionary fires had spread beyond the slave owners to their slaves. At Bois Caïman, the Vodou priest Boukman led a ceremony that saw the north erupting into a full-blown slave revolt (see the boxed text, p335). Lasting two years, the revolt saw slaves, mulattoes and whites both fighting and forming brief alliances against each other.

For the history of Hispaniola prior to Haitian independence, see p29.

Out of the chaos stepped François Dominique Toussaint Louverture. His slave army had sought support from Santo Domingo, which sought to weaken France's hold on the island. St-Domingue's planters were so wedded to slavery that they turned to the hated British for support against the revolution, who landed a massive invasion force from Jamaica. But when Revolutionary Paris formally abolished slavery, Toussaint allied his slave army to the motherland. With his generals Jean-Jacques Dessalines and Henri Christophe, he crushed the British and brought the colony under his firm control.

Toussaint didn't stop there, and in 1801 he invaded Santo Domingo to free the Spanish slaves. Napoleon, who had taken control in France, saw that as a step too far and divined that the free slaves would eventually want complete freedom from France. He wanted a return to slavery instead, and a year later the French invaded. The guerrilla war was immensely costly. Over half the soldiers died of tropical diseases, with losses reaching 40,000 before a truce was agreed. Toussaint again pledged allegiance to France if slavery was forever abandoned, but was imprisoned and shipped to France.

'In overthrowing me, you have cut down in St-Domingue only the trunk of the tree of liberty. It will spring up by the roots again for they are numerous and deep.'

TOUSSAINT LOUVERTURE FOLLOWING HIS ARREST BY THE FRENCH, 1802

It was France's final gambit. Dessalines raised the country in anger again, promising full independence as the slaves' reward. In a bloody campaign he beat the French for a final time at Vertières, and on New Year's Day 1804 in Gonaïve proclaimed St-Domingue dead. Haiti, the old Taíno name for the island, was chosen for the world's first black republic, and only the second modern nation (after the USA) to break the yoke of European colonialism.

TIMELINE

1791	1793	1794-96
A Vodou ceremony held by slaves at Bois Caïman near Cap-Haïtien preaches the message of emancipation, sparking a slave rebellion that sets St-Domingue's plantations ablaze.	Toussaint Louverture, Henri Christophe and Jean-Jacques Dessalines lead slave armies against the French and mulattoes. Amid the confusion, Britain invades, hoping to grab the island for itself.	Slavery is abolished in the colony, and Toussaint Louverture rejoins French forces to repel the British. After bringing St-Domingue under his control, Toussaint is appointed governor-general.

TOUSSAINT LOUVERTURE

The son of an African chief, yet born into slavery near modern Cap-Haïtien, François Dominique Toussaint Louverture was one of the most remarkable figures of the 18th century. He worked as a steward and, unusually, was granted something of an education. He read voraciously, although was never a competent writer. When the fires of rebellion reached St-Domingue he was ready to grab their ideals and lead the slaves to liberty.

Although untrained militarily, he was a naturally gifted tactician and inspired great successes against the colonist militias, and both the invading English and French armies. Toussaint was astute enough to try to keep the valuable plantations intact and went out of his way to woo the white planters to his cause, and for a while was feted by revolutionary whites, blacks and mulattoes alike. But he could be ruthless, too – ordering the torching of Cap-Français to prevent it falling into enemy hands, and enacting forced labor to prop up the economy (thus alienating many of his followers).

Toussaint was a product of the French Revolution as much as Robespierre was. For a long time he saw a free St-Domingue as part of France, and only late in the day saw that independence was the only option for the slaves. It took the more ruthless Dessalines to declare a free Haiti, one reason why he, rather than Toussaint, is often more celebrated in modern Haiti. But Toussaint was the real architect of the revolution. Even as Napoleon was deriding him as 'the gilded African' and leaving him to rot in jail, the poet Wordsworth was dedicating sonnets to him. Today Toussaint's statue stands aptly in Port-au-Prince between the National Palace and the statue of the Marron Inconnu, 'Unknown Slave'.

Haiti was ravaged. In 13 years of war the economy was shattered and nearly a third of the population dead or displaced. Dessalines followed up by massacring the remaining whites, for fear of being reconquered. To take full charge he announced himself emperor and ruled as a dictator. Free, educated mulattoes were spurned, and the laborers forced back onto the plantations to rebuild the economy. His rule was brutal, and the reaction inevitable. In 1806, after being born free in Africa and having endured the Middle Passage, Dessalines died an emperor in a murderous ambush outside Port-au-Prince.

The Louverture Project (http://thelouverture project.org) is a highly useful online resource covering the history of the Haitian revolution.

NORTH AGAINST SOUTH

Dessalines was the glue holding Haiti together, and on his death the country promptly split in two. General Alexandre Pétion took control of Port-au-Prince and became president of the mulatto-dominated southern Republic of Haiti. Henri Christophe, who saw himself as Dessaline's rightful successor retreated to the north and crowned himself king. The two rulers had very different ideas on how to rule.

Christophe ruled with absolute power, but was an enlightened and effective monarch. Within a year, he had stabilized the economy with a new

1802	1804	1807
France invades St-Domingue. Invited to a parley with the French general Leclerc, Toussaint Louverture is clapped in irons and shipped to prison in France, where he dies of neglect the following year.	Following his overwhelming victory at the Battle of Vertières, Jean-Jacques Dessalines declares Haitian independence, and rips the white stripe from the French Tricolour to create the new country's flag.	Haiti splits in two. Henri Christophe crowns himself ruler of the new Kingdom of Haiti in the north, while Alexandre Pétion is declared president of the southern Republic of Haiti.

currency, the gourde, and reformed the judicial system. Seeing education as pivotal, he constructed several schools, backed up with a state printing press. He built a splendid palace at Sans Souci and the awesome Citadelle la Ferrière (p338) near Cap-Haïtien, and created an instant nobility, parceling out land to the new dukes and barons.

All this was supported by serfs, who weren't particularly happy that Christophe had kept them tied to the hated plantations, even if they were now earning a wage. As time went on and the building of the Citadelle progressed, Christophe's megalomania increased and his nobles began to plot against him. But as revolt began to spark in 1820, Christophe suffered a massive stroke. Rather than face the dual indignities of infirmity and rebellion he shot himself in the heart with a silver bullet.

Pétion's south took a different direction altogether. A political liberal, he faced black guerillas, a secessionist movement in the far southwest and a restive army. His answer was massive land reform. Recognizing the plantation system was no longer feasible, he divided and distributed the land into small plots. While many of his generals grabbed the largest slices of land, redistribution allowed Pétion to resettle his soldiers and, even more importantly, placate the peasantry. Liberty was associated with the possession of a small plot of land, and Pétion is still remembered as 'Papa Bon-Coeur' (Papa Good-Heart) for his actions.

Land reform had unforeseen consequences. The move to subsistence peasant farming meant loss of revenues for the state, and the republic stagnated in comparison to the north. The mulattoes became mercantilists and frequently saw government as a way of enriching their own pockets. Haiti's two classes began to take separate paths.

UNITED, BUT NOT FREE?

It took the deaths of both Pétion and Christophe for Haiti to be joined again under one flag. Jean-Pierre Boyer, Pétion's chosen successor, was the man to do it. Christophe's kingdom in the north was abolished and the republic began to look to the future. Unfortunately, Boyer's rule laid many of the foundations of Haiti's current problems.

Born a free mulatto, Boyer had no great love for the blacks, and immediately wrecked Christophe's vision of an educated black ruling class by dismantling his education system, thus consolidating mulatto rule. Christophe's economic plans met with more approval, and Boyer sought to maintain the plantation system of forced labor until a shortage of soldiers to back up his plans demanded a change of heart. Haitian peasantry had become wedded to the idea of land-ownership, turning into sharecroppers selling their surplus at local markets. Sugar cultivation virtually disappeared, and as the population increased so did the demand for land, opening the door to forest clearance, soil erosion and ultimate environmental degradation.

'The freedom of the negroes, if recognized in St-Domingue and legalized by France, would at all times be a rallying point for freedom-seekers of the New World'.

NAPOLEON BONAPARTE COMMENTS ON THE SLAVE REVOLUTION

When Christophe became king he created an instantly nobility among his followers, including such luminaries as the Count of Limonade and the Duke of Marmalade, each with their own coat of arms.

'Pluck the chicken but make sure it doesn't squawk.'

JEAN-JACQUES DESSALINES FREQUENTLY FOLLOWED ADVICE ON HOW TO RULE (AND PLUNDER) HAITI

1820	1825	1844
Henri Christophe commits suicide in Sans Souci. The president of the south, Jean-Pierre Boyer, reunites the country as one republic. Two years later, the Haitian army invades Santo Domingo and abolishes slavery, unifying Hispaniola.	France finally recognizes Haitian independence, after Port-au-Prince agrees to reparations for French slavers' losses incurred during the revolution. The indemnity accounts for 10 times Haiti's annual revenue, turning Haiti into a debtor nation.	Following years of suppression of Spanish culture and the Catholic Church, Santo Domingo takes advantage of the confusion following President Boyer's ouster, and declares independence as the Dominican Republic.

But economics would be for nothing if Haiti couldn't remain independent, and so Boyer sought rapprochement with France. The deal eventually struck was Faustian. The old colonial planters were still smarting from their losses, and demanded compensation of 150 million francs. Although this was reduced to 60 million, it bankrupted the state, which was forced to take out huge loans (from French banks) to pay the debt. The world's first black republic took on the first Third World debt.

It took the rest of the century to pay off the loan. Exporting coffee, cocoa and tropical hardwood spurred further land clearance. The rest of the world hardly rushed to follow France's recognition. Haiti was the ultimate bad example – black slaves kicking out their masters to run their own affairs. Boyer advertised in American newspapers for runaway slaves to settle in Haiti, and the USA only recognized Haiti in 1862 during its own civil war, when American slave emancipation was finally on the cards.

Boyer was overthrown in 1843, having presided over Haiti's bankruptcy, a weakening of state machinery and the entrenchment of the rich mulatto/poor black divide. Haiti slipped into a political morass, with a revolving door of short-lived presidents, political generals and even 10 years as an 'empire.' Of the 22 heads of state between 1843 and 1915, only one served his full term in office; the others were assassinated or forced into exile.

In the 1990s President Aristide campaigned (unsuccessfully) for France to repay the 'blood money' it demanded for recognition of Haiti's independence in 1825.

AMERICAN OCCUPATION

Haiti's strategic proximity to the newly opened Panama Canal reignited the USA's interest in Haiti in the early 20th century. Political instability and increased German interests in the country led the US to take its chance. When President Vilbrun Guillaume Sam was killed by a Port-au-Prince mob in 1915, the US sent in the marines.

The USA immediately began to remodel Haiti in line with its own interests. Dessalines' constitutional ban on foreign land ownership was ripped up and American companies flooded in. The country was declared open for business, and to aid investment a massive infrastructure building program was begun. The army was abolished and replaced with an American-trained force.

First published in 1938, *The Black Jacobins*, by CLR James, remains the classic work describing the Haitian slave revolt and the path to independence.

Unfortunately for the Americans, the Haitians didn't take to being turned back into a colony. To build the public works, the Americans instituted the hated *corvée*, labor gangs of conscripted peasants, roped together and forced to work. It was all too reminiscent of slavery, and provoked the two-year Chacos Rebellion led by Charlemagne Péralte. It was brutally suppressed, with the new US air force used to support the marines fighting in the mountainous interior. Only the mulattoes, mindful of their economic supremacy, dealt openly with the occupiers.

The media played an important role on both sides. From the US came waves of dime-store novels and the new movies playing up Haiti as primi-

1847	1915	1918
Head of the presidential guard Faustin Soulouque crowns himself emperor, in imitation of Jean-Jacques Dessalines. His failed attempts to reconquer the Dominican Republic bankrupt the state and, in 1860, cost him his crown.	The USA invades Haiti, starting a 20-year occupation. Aimed at stabilizing the country, US marines introduce forced labor gangs to build infrastructure and realign the economy toward American interests.	Charlemagne Péralte launches the Cacos Rebellion, a peasant uprising across northern Haiti aimed at ending the US occupation. It lasts two years, finally ending with the capture and execution of Péralte.

tive, black and Vodou-ridden. The black middle classes responded with the development of the Noirisme (or Indigeniste) movement. Simultaneously a literary and political movement, it rejected the 'European' values of the mulatto elite and advocated that Haitian citizens take pride in their African heritage. Creole and Vodou were reclaimed as sources of inspiration and cultural identity. Noirisme was hugely influential. One of its leading proponents was Dr François Duvalier (later to reappear as Haiti's most notorious president). It reverberates even today on the canvases on Haitian's leading naïve painters.

The US pulled out in 1934. Stability had apparently been returned, but puppet presidents and a pro-American military were to be more lasting legacies. Most Haitians remained no better off than before, and thousands migrated to seek work in sugarcane fields in the Dominican Republic. Dominican memories of Haiti's own occupation of their country preceded them. Competition for jobs and institutional racism culminated in the killing of around 20,000 Haitians by the Dominican army in 1937. Many of the deaths occurred along the tragically named Rivière Massacre on the border.

Edwidge Danticat's novel *The Farming of Bones* movingly recreates the events around the 1937 massacre of Haitians in the Dominican Republic.

PAPADOCRACY: HAITI & THE DUVALIERS

Economic disarray continued into the 1940s. The elite squashed the attempts of progressive black president Dumarais Estimé to redress Haiti's inequalities, and corrupt military-backed rule remained the order of the day. In 1957, however, a black country doctor named François 'Papa Doc' Duvalier swept national elections on a Noiriste platform. The masses thought salvation lay ahead, while the elite saw another potential front man to do their bidding. Both were cruelly mistaken.

Power was Duvalier's raison-d'être, and his soft-spoken demeanor belied a ruthless streak. Knowing real power lay with force of arms, he set up his own gangs of thugs that eventually evolved into the feared Tontons Macoutes militia. He led attacks on vested mulatto interests, the church and the unions, and practiced divide-and-rule among the military. Government was eviscerated, with local rule devolved to loyal section chiefs who acted as feudal lords over the population. At the same time Cold War hysteria allowed Papa Doc to paint himself as a brave anticommunist and gain the grateful support of the US. Anyone who stood in his way – whether officers considering a coup or simple peasants sick of extortion – was open to a visit from the Tontons Macoutes. Thousands were killed or simply disappeared.

In 1964 Papa Doc declared himself President for Life. His coterie enriched themselves at Haiti's expense, while the rest of the country lived in fear and paranoia – the 'nightmare republic' of Graham Greene's novel *The Comedians*.

The joke turned even blacker in 1971 when Papa Doc died, leaving his playboy son Jean-Claude as his successor. The new president for life was less

'When [Haitians] ask me, 'Who is our Mother?' I tell them, 'The Virgin.' But when they ask, 'Who is our Father?' then I must answer, 'No one – you have only me'.'
FRANÇOIS 'PAPA DOC' DUVALIER, 1963

Papa Doc's feared security thugs were named after Tonton Macoute ('Uncle Knapsack'), the childsnatching bogeyman of Haitian folklore.

1928-31	1937	1957
The novel *Ainsi parla l'oncle* (Thus Spoke the Uncle) by Jean-Price Mars and the writings of Jacques Roumain spark the politically important Noiriste movement to reclaim Haiti's African heritage.	Dominican dictator Rafael Trujillo orders the massacre of 20,000 Haitian migrant workers in the Dominican Republic. After an outcry, compensation is later paid to the Haitian state at US$29 per victim.	François 'Papa Doc' Duvalier becomes president, and begins his project to turn Haiti into a totalitarian dictatorship, using a blend of terror, patronage, Vodou and economic cronyism.

A PRAYER FOR PAPA DOC

Papa Doc was never shy of promoting himself as Haiti's spiritual leader as well as its secular one. He managed to convince the Pope to allow him to appoint the Archbishop of Port-au-Prince, while simultaneously painting himself as the image of Baron Samedi to followers of Vodou. He even had the *Lord's Prayer* rewritten in his honor, dubbing it the *Catechism of the Revolution:*

'Our Doc, who art in the National Palace for life, hallowed be Thy name by present and future generations. Thy will be done in Port-au-Prince as it is in the provinces. Give us this day our new Haiti and forgive not the trespasses of those antipatriots who daily spit upon our country. Lead them into temptation, and poisoned by their own venom, deliver them from no evil. Amen.'

---

sure of his powerbase, and any hint of sticking to his father's Noiriste rhetoric was forgotten with his marriage to a wealthy mulatto, realigning himself with the traditional elite. Michele Duvalier was a conspicuous consumer who thought nothing of dropping a million dollars on a shopping trip to Paris – all paid for by the Haitian people, of course. Jean-Claude (who was inevitably dubbed Baby Doc) made some token concessions to human rights long enough to attract American factories back to Haiti, but followed up with periodic bouts of brutal repression.

In the mid-1980s protests began to erupt against the regime. The inept handling of a swine-fever outbreak that led to the eradication of the Creole pig that peasants depended on was only one spark to the fire. Despite being fired on by the army, mass protests toppled Baby Doc from power, who fled to a life of gilded exile in Paris.

ARISTIDE'S RISE & FALL

During the mid-1980s, a young priest named Jean-Bertrand Aristide, influenced by Latin American liberation theology, had begun preaching incendiary sermons, advocating a rebalancing of power away from the traditional elites toward the poor. Despite the optimism following Baby Doc's ouster, it soon became clear that even without the Tontons Macoutes it was business as normal. General Namphy seized power at the head of a military junta – Duvalierism without Duvalier.

Aristide's burgeoning Ti Legliz (Little Church) movement stepped up its campaign for reform, despite repression and cosmetic elections in 1987. These saw voter massacres and the generals entrenched even further, lining their pockets in the cocaine-smuggling business. Namphy was replaced by General Prosper Avril, who was persuaded to hold elections in the face of increasing unrest across Haiti. Aristide stood as a surprise last-minute candidate with the slogan 'Lavalas' (Flood) and won a landslide victory. His outspoken criticism of the junta had won him a huge following among the poor, who came out in force to support him.

1977	1982	1986
François Duvalier dies. His son Jean-Claude 'Baby Doc' Duvalier is inaugurated as president for life at the age of 19, with the national treasury as his personal piggy bank.	In response to the presence of African Swine Fever, the USA pressures Haiti into eradicating its entire population of Creole pigs, the economic mainstay of the Haitian peasantry. The pig-replacement program is a complete failure.	Popular protests force Jean-Claude Duvalier to flee Haiti into exile in France. A turbulent period of *dechoukaj* (uprooting) follows, to remove the influence of Duvalierism from the Haitian body politic.

Aristide took power with an audacious program. At his inauguration he publicly retired most of the army's remaining generals, and proposed separating the army and the police to depoliticize them. But just seven months into his term, an alliance of rich mulatto families and army generals, worried about their respective business and drug interests, staged a bloody coup. General Raoul Cédras, the one general Aristide trusted, seized the reins of power.

International condemnation was swift, but it wasn't until floods of Haitian boat people started arriving in the USA a year later that efforts to resolve the situation stepped up. More than 40,000 refugees fled the widespread violence and repression in Haiti, only to be intercepted by the US Coast Guard and repatriated via the US naval base at Guantánamo Bay, Cuba – an act widely criticized internationally.

The Uses of Haiti by Paul Farmer is an angry and impassioned take on Haiti's often tortured relationship with the USA, leading up to the coup against Aristide in 1991.

Newly elected Bill Clinton helped bring about an oil embargo against the regime, although the US government turned a blind eye to American companies breaking it. A plan was eventually brokered to allow Aristide to return in 1993, but when a US navy vessel arrived in Port-au-Prince to support a transition, it was prevented from docking by gangs of thugs from the right-wing FRAPH (Front for the Advancement and Progress of Haiti) militia who had been menacing and killing Lavalas supporters.

Sanctions were promptly tightened, and black American political groups kept up the pressure for a resolution to the crisis. Although American support for Aristide was crucial, it wasn't unconditional. Many had seen the priest as a radical socialist, so when a plan was finally brokered for his return the next year, it was only on his agreement to sign up to a World Bank and International Monetary Fund economic restructuring plan that eviscerated his original ideas for Haitian reform. Aristide signed, after three years of exile, and was returned cheering, backed by a UN mandate and 20,000 US army troops.

COUPS & INTERVENTIONS, REDUX

Aristides's return wasn't all roses. Cédras was allowed to slip quietly into exile in Panama, and many of the FRAPH leaders (who had CIA contacts) were given refuge by the USA. Back in office, Aristide choked on implementing the imposed economic reforms and the promised foreign aid vanished as a result. Constitutional rules bar two successive presidential terms, so in 1995 Lavalas party prime minister René Préval was returned as president.

In opposition, Aristide was free to criticize, and Lavalas fell apart. The privatization of state utilities and lowering of tariffs to allow cheap imports laid off workers and devastated national food production. Aristide's new party, Fanmi Lavalas, split parliament and left the government without a prime minister for almost two years. In the end Préval was forced to call elections. The poll was marked by unrest, violence and allegations of vote rigging, but in 2001 Aristide returned to the presidential palace.

1990	1991	1994
Radical priest Jean-Bertrand Aristide wins a landslide presidential election with support from his grassroots Lavalas movement, promising economic reform for the poor and plans to strip the Haitian army of its political powers.	A military coup overthrows Aristide, followed by violent repression against the population. An international embargo is declared against the junta, while thousands of Haitians attempt to flee in boats to the USA.	Backed by US Marines, Aristide returns to office. He abolishes the army and serves out the remainder of his term, though his social reforms are hobbled by the economic deals he struck to win international support for his return.

Michael Deibert's *Notes from the Last Testament* is a gripping eye-witness account of the chaos of the final years of Aristide's rule, up to the 2004 coup.

Aristide's second term was hardly a success. The opposition, which had boycotted the elections, refused to accept the result and the country again looked chaos in the face. The police were ineffectual against violence from both sides: opposition agitators, and the *chimeres,* armed gangs loyal to Aristide. Haiti's bicentennial in 2004 was marked by bloodshed.

The end came just a month later, when rebels captured Gonaïves and Cap-Haïtien. For the second time, Aristide's presidency ended in exile, as he fled to the Central African Republic and finally South Africa. Claims to his flight vary – Aristide himself maintains he was effectively kidnapped by US agents and bundled out of Port-au-Prince; the US denies this but maintains that his overthrow was necessary to return stability to Haiti. Either way, the US favorite Gerard Latortue took power and formed an interim administration, with peacekeepers from the UN Stabilization Mission for Haiti (MINUSTAH) sent to the island.

THE ROAD AHEAD

The instability of the coup period continued throughout Latortue's government. Repression against Lavalas supporters was matched by the violence of the *chimeres.* Port-au-Prince, in particular, was hit by a rash of gang violence and kidnappings. It wasn't until René Préval returned to office in 2006 that things started to calm down. MINUSTAH launched a controversial but largely successful military campaign to uproot the gangs, and finally brought a modicum of normality to the streets of the capital.

MINUSTAH has its own website (www.minustah .org, in French) covering all aspects of the UN's involvement in Haiti.

The path ahead remains tricky – evident in early 2008, when demonstrations against rocketing food prices turned briefly violent. Repeatedly battered from the time that St-Domingue's slaves threw off their shackles, Haiti has entered its third century as an independent nation mixing guarded optimism with a tired hope for lasting stability.

2001	**2004**	**2006**
Aristide wins a second term as president, against a backdrop of increasing instability and an opposition boycott of the election. Chaos paralyses Haiti, making effective government impossible.	Armed rebels force Aristide from office, in disputed circumstances. Violence continues under the interim government, exacerbated by the havoc wreaked by Hurricane Jeanne later in the year.	René Préval re-elected as president. In response to gang warfare and kidnappings, UN-mandated troops lead the campaign against Port-au-Prince gangs, improving security but resulting in civilian deaths.

Haiti Culture

THE NATIONAL PSYCHE

For many Haitians, their national identity is something they are both proud of and vilified for. Haiti's history as the first independent black republic is something to be continuously celebrated, yet Haitians are keenly aware that this is not how most of the world sees them. Instead, images of boat people, misunderstandings about Vodou and a history of US interventions cloud popular perceptions, and inevitably some of this is reflected back on the Haitian self-image. Most visitors are likely to receive a warm welcome and a strong dose of national pride (particularly if you can manage a few words of Creole), as Haitians are keen to counter their media stereotypes.

Life in Haiti is communal and based on extended families. In the country this takes the form of the *lakou*, a grouping of half a dozen or so houses in a shared compound, allowing labor and materials to be pooled. Although urban drift challenges this model, community spirit is remarkably strong in the shanties of Port-au-Prince, where unemployment is rife and residents have to support each other to survive. Religion plays a correspondingly strong role in binding Haitians together, whether through Vodou or the traditional church.

LIFESTYLE

Life in Haiti has always been sharply divided between the tiny urban elite and the poor rural bulk of the population.

Most Haitians are peasants practicing subsistence farming. Beans, sweet potatoes, maize, bananas or coffee are grown on small plots, while along the coast fishermen take their catch from simple sailboats. Division of labor is clear – men plant and harvest the crops and women care for the children and prepare meals. In rural areas, women usually sell the crops and are more economically active (see p276).

Rural life is hard. Electricity is often a distant aspiration and food is cooked over charcoal, the production of which is a major cause of environmental damage. Food insecurity is high, and usually only two meals a day are eaten. Community spirit isn't wanted for, however, and large-scale jobs are tackled by communal work teams called *kombits,* with neighbors pooling labor and sweating and singing together. In the evenings, groups often relax by playing *Krik? Krak!*, an oral game of riddles, or men gather by oil lamp to drink rum and play dominoes.

According to city dwellers, the rural poor live in the *peyi andeyò* (outside country), totally removed from the economic and political levers of power. Peasants are either mocked as yokels or mythologized in folkloric art and dances as the noble poor. But as demands on the exhausted land have reached breaking point, increasing numbers of peasants have sought a better life in Port-au-Prince. The result are the teeming *bidonvilles* (slums) of areas like Cité Soleil, shanties of cinder-block houses reinforced with abandoned metal sheeting and cardboard packing cases. Drinking water has to be brought in on tankers, and open ditches serve for sewers. During heavy rains, the *bidonvilles* regularly flood and raw sewage rages through the shacks.

For the elite 1% of the population who own half the country's wealth, life could hardly be more different. The mainly mulatto family oligarchies disdain Creole in favour of speaking French, dominate manufacturing and import/export, and have traditionally been the powers that stood behind the president's throne. Behind the high walls of Pétionville are the best French

Libeté: A Haiti Anthology, edited by Charles Arthur and Michael Dash, is an excellent primer on Haitian history, society, culture and politics, collecting writings on the country from Columbus to the present day.

French has always been Haiti's literary language. The first novel published in Creole was *Dézafi* by Franck Etienne, published in 1975.

The online Haitian Book Centre (www.haitian bookcentre.com) is a fantastic resource for tracking down hard-to-find books about Haiti.

restaurants and boutiques, the most imposing SUVs and riches unimaginable by the vast majority of Haitians.

ECONOMY

Starring Charlotte Rampling, *Heading South* (2005) is a compelling drama about power relationships and sex tourism in Baby Doc's Haiti, based on the short stories of Haitian writer Dany Laferrière.

Haiti is the poorest country in the Western hemisphere and its economy lags far behind those of its nearest neighbors, including the Dominican Republic. Haiti is a major recipient of international aid.

In the 1980s Haiti became a major center for assembly factories, producing sporting goods, clothing and electronic components for the US market. Despite the work being generally very low paid, these factories were important job creators, many of which pulled out during the turmoil of the 1990s. To revive the industry, Haiti has been granted tariff-free clothing exports to the USA, but is hampered by poor infrastructure. Removal of tariffs in the opposite direction has damaged local economies further – rice farming has been devastated by cheap imported American rice.

The majority of urban Haitians are underemployed and scraping by on minimal incomes. Even the *bouretye,* the cart pullers in every city working as beasts of burden, have to rent their handcarts, while the lack of access to capital means that the *marchands* (female market sellers) find it hard to expand their businesses.

Women are often more economically active in the countryside, responsible for selling farm goods at the markets. Rural *revendeuses* (saleswomen) travel great distances between markets, buying and selling staples. The peasant economy largely exists outside the formal economy.

Remittances from the Haitian diaspora were worth an estimated US$1.65 billion in 2006 – 35% of Haiti's GDP.

The huge number of Haitians living outside Haiti are important contributors to the economy, with remittances to families helping more directly than much international aid. Foreign money plays a less positive role in other spheres though, with Haiti remaining a major transshipment center for drug trafficking from South America to the USA, with narco dollars corrupting state machinery.

POPULATION

Haiti is home to almost 8.4 million people, of whom three-quarters are rural, living off agriculture. People of African origin make up about 95% of Haiti's population. The other 5% is made up of mulattos, Middle Easterners and people of other races. It is believed that some of the population are descendants of the union between the Arawak and Taíno peoples, the original indigenous population, and African slaves. Members of the mulatto class, which constitutes half of the country's elite and controls most of the country's economy, are the descendants of African slaves and French plantation owners.

In the small town of Cazales, north of Cabaret, one can find the anomaly of dark-skinned, blue-eyed people who sing and dance to traditional Polish

---

RESTAVEKS

It's a sad irony that in a country that won its freedom in a slave rebellion, child slavery is still endemic. A *restavek* is a bonded child domestic laborer, three-quarters of whom are girls. There are around 200,000 *restaveks* in Haiti. The children are given up by their destitute parents, who are unable to feed them, to urban families, where they live as domestic servants. Although some are well cared for, they are frequently barred from attending school and physically or sexually abused. Fetching water and cleaning during 18-hour days are common tasks, and to encourage hard work, small whips called *martinets,* often sold in the markets and specially designed to be used on children, are used. Many children run away and prefer life on the dangerous streets to living with their 'adoptive' parents.

LUCKY NUMBERS

See those brightly painted shacks called 'bank' on every street in Haiti? They're hardly safe places for your money – they're selling *borlette* (lottery) tickets. Everyone bets on the lottery. Tickets cost a couple of gourdes, with prizes of just a few dollars. Numbers are taken from the New York State lottery, with just three needed to scoop some cash. Everyone has their own system of picking a winner, and there's even a pocketbook called a *tchala* that allows players to interpret dreams and symbols as winning numbers.

---

folk music. These are descendants of a Polish regiment from Napoléon's army who were so sickened by the war against the slaves in Haiti that they deserted in 1802, establishing a small community in the countryside.

SPORTS

In most of the Caribbean, there's only one question: 'Cricket or baseball?' In Haiti you'll just meet a blank stare, because this country is all about soccer. You can see impromptu games everywhere, but the big matches are in the Digicel Première Division, which runs from November to May. The most successful sides are Racing Club Haïtien from Port-au-Prince, and Saint-Marc's Baltimore Sportif Club. Most clubs lack investment, but the talent is there – in 2008 English Premiership sides sent scouts to the country looking for promising youth players, a first in the Caribbean. The Sylvio Cator Stadium in Port-au-Prince is a great place to see a match, usually raucous affairs. Its biggest day out in years was in 2004 when world champions Brazil played here to promote the Brazilian leadership of the UN Stabilization Mission for Haiti (MINUSTAH) mission.

Cockfighting is popular across Haiti, and *gallera* (cockfighting rings) are hidden away in the back streets of most towns. Unlike in the DR, the birds neither wear spurs nor fight to the death. Before a fight, the two cocks are paraded in the pit, although there's usually more strutting done by the owners than the cocks. Everyone bets. If you favor one bird, you point it out to someone next to you. If they prefer the other, your neighbor will take your money, usually about a dollar, and keep hold of all the cash throughout the fight. If your bird wins, you've doubled your money. Expect a very macho atmosphere and a lot of shouting – it's best to attend with a local.

In 1974 Haiti became the first Caribbean country to qualify for the soccer World Cup. Although the team failed to win a single match, it did at least score a famous goal against the great Italian goalkeeper Dino Zoff. For soccer results, see www.haitifoot.com.

MULTICULTURALISM

One of the main threads of Haitian history since independence has been the cleaving of the blacks and the mulattoes into two largely separate social classes. The mulattoes have formed the business and military elites, holding power over the black majority. Mulatto society has tended to be European in outlook, keeping French as its mother tongue and distancing itself from its African roots. In contrast, the traditions of Vodou and the Creole language have allowed black Haitians to maintain their African heritage, although it wasn't until the Noirisme movement of the 1920s that this was given a formal voice.

Haiti's foreign ties have always been strongest with the USA, a country that has frequently involved itself directly in Haitian political life. The largest populations of Haitians outside Haiti are in the US, mainly in New York and Miami. Haitians often maintain contradictory views about the USA. On the one hand, it is seen as having a malign influence on Haitian life on everything from supporting coups to the Creole pig fiasco, while on the other hand it remains a major economic draw for many Haitians seeking a better life.

Haitians in the DR aren't always welcomed, often facing racism and discrimination. For more information, see p52.

HAITI & HIV

HIV is a contentious topic in Haiti. In the early 1980s a number of AIDS cases in south Florida were linked to Haitian immigrants. In the resulting furor, Haiti was accused in the international media of being the crucible for HIV/AIDS in North America. Although scientific evidence for this was swiftly retracted, the label stuck and had a devastating effect on the country's international image, and effectively wiped out the tourism industry overnight. In late 2007 genetic research repeated this claim, causing a similar uproar, although again the results of the research were disputed with many Haitians claiming this was another stick the media would use to beat them. Away from the controversy, Haiti's HIV infection rate has actually dropped in recent years due to safe-sex education and increased condom use.

MEDIA

Radio is the most important media in Haiti. Traditionally French-only, many stations now broadcast in Creole. Independent media continues to face a number of challenges. Many radio and print media outlets are owned by people operating in Haitian politics, and are not always welcoming of investigative journalism. The Association of Haitian Journalists, which bravely speaks up for independent reporting, regularly receives death threats against its members, and many journalists have either been killed or have had to flee Haiti for filing reports that offended vested interests.

Most Haitian websites are written in French. News sites in English are often highly partisan, with pro- and anti-Aristide websites shouting loudly for attention.

Directed by Jonathan Demme, *The Agronomist* (2003) is a powerful documentary about the life (and eventual murder) of Haitian journalist and activist Jean Dominique.

RELIGION

A popular maxim has it that Haiti is 80% Catholic, 20% Protestant, but 100% Vodou. This uniquely Haitian religion, blending many traditional African religions with Catholic elements, permeates the country – for more information, see p279.

Catholicism dominates public life, and has frequently found itself swimming in the murky currents of Haitian politics. François 'Papa Doc' Duvalier (see p269) exiled many Catholic orders and created his own loyal clergy, who remembered him in their prayers and stayed silent over the regime's excesses. On a grassroots level, the Ti Legliz (Little Church) movement took inspiration from the 1980s Latin American liberation theologists, and was instrumental not only in ousting the Duvaliers but sweeping Father Jean-Bertrand Aristide into power in 1991.

The word *teledjol* means 'word of mouth' – the traditional medium for carrying the news (in a country where rumor is often truth).

Protestantism is a relatively new import into Haiti, arriving in an evangelical wave in the 1970s. Many churches from North America, mainstream and otherwise, continue to pour missionaries and money into the country, and own numerous radio stations. Evangelicals are usually fiercely opposed to Vodou, often claiming that Haiti's myriad problems are punishment by God for the sins of following Vodou.

WOMEN IN HAITI

Women are often referred to as the central pillar, or *poteau mitan*, of Haitian life, but it's an honor not always borne out by reality. In a poor country, women are the poorest citizens. In some ways, women are often highly visible being economically active, such as the *marchands* on every street, and the traveling *revendeuses* who stitch the rural economies together. But lack of access to education prevents most women from stepping above these simple market activities. In the cities, the problem may be more acute, especially in the slum areas of Port-au-Prince, where endemic unemployment, poverty and gangs have created a rape problem of massive proportions.

ARTS
Painting & Sculpture

The visual arts of Haiti – mainly paintings but also sculpture and Vodou flags – are an outpouring of creative force unmatched in the Caribbean.

Painting under early leaders like President Boyer followed the European portrait tradition, but parallel to this artists had always been active painting murals to decorate the walls of Vodou temples and making elaborate sequined flags for use in ceremonies. The link to the *lwa* (Vodou spirits) with their visual language of Vévé signs is central to Haiti's artistic vision.

In the 1920s Port-au-Prince artists started the Indigéniste movement, the visual equivalent to literature's Noirisme (see p278), seeking to reclaim Haiti's African roots. Subject matter switched from literal representation to idealized subjects, such as peasant life and landscapes. This style of art is often dubbed 'naive' or 'primitive,' partly due to its simple style and avoidance of classical perspective.

The Indigénistes paved the way for the arrival of the American De Witt Peters in Port-au-Prince. Trained in the arts, Peters recognized the extraordinary flavor of the primitivist work and helped artists to develop their skills by setting up the Centre d'Art in Port-au-Prince (p296). Here he discovered Hector Hyppolite, a Vodou priest now considered Haiti's greatest painter. A flood of stunning painters soon arrived at the Centre d'Art, all untutored but producing incredible work that stunned the international art world. As one critic noted, 'generous nature was their one and only instructor.' At the same time, Peters also discovered Georges Liautaud, the carved iron sculptor of Croix des Bouquets (p311).

Throughout the 1950s naive art became standard, pressed into easily recognizable images to serve the booming tourist market (the same paintings are still offered today). The Foyer des Arts Plastiques movement, led by Lucien Price, reacted against this by injecting a social ethic into Indigénisme. This moved away from magic realism to portray the harsh realities of Haitian life. The next great theme arose with the Saint-Soleil group of the 1970s. Spontaneity was key for artists like Tiga and Louisianne St Fleurant, often painting *lwa* as abstract forms or bursts of energy.

Modern Haitian art continues to go from strength to strength, from young painters, such as Pascal Monnin, to the inspired junkyard Vodou sculptures of the Grand Rue artists (p297).

Music

Haitian music has been used for many things – as an accompaniment to Vodou ceremonies, as a form of resistance in politics, or even just to dance the night away.

One of the most popular forms of Haitian music is *rara*. During Carnival, Port-au-Prince and Jacmel fill with rivers of people who come to hear the *rara* bands traveling the streets on floats. Most bands compete for the song prize with a specially composed song, each of which has been recorded and played constantly on the radio during the lead-up to Carnival. In the country, *rara* bands march for miles, with percussionists and musicians playing *vaskins* and *kònets* (bamboo and zinc trumpets, respectively). They create an otherworldly sound, with each instrument playing just one note, but together creating mesmerizing riffs with the drummers.

Dance music has always taken in foreign sounds. Cuban *son* has influenced the troubadour bands that entertain in restaurants and hotels, singing and

Gérald Alexis's monumental *Haitian Painters* is a comprehensive and gorgeously illustrated book that should grace the coffee table of anyone with even a passing interest in the Haitian art scene.

The Centre d'Arts' biggest project was the murals of Port-au-Prince's Sainte Trinité Episcopalian Cathedral (p295), an astonishing showcase of Haiti's naive masters.

Ghosts of Cité Soleil (2006) by Asger Leth is a slick (if partisan) documentary about gangs in the aftermath of Aristide's 2004 ouster, viewed through a lens of bad-boy hip-hop imagery.

gently strumming guitars. Merengue, the Dominican big-band sound (see p55), has always been played enthusiastically on dance floors, and in the 1950s evolved into *compas direct* (or just *compas* for short), with its slightly more African beat. A joy to dance to, its greatest exponents are Nemours Jean-Baptiste and the late Coupé Cloué.

Racines (roots) music grew out of the Vodou-jazz movement of the late 1970s. Vodou jazz was a fusion of American jazz with Vodou rhythms and melodies. For many *racines* bands, this new music reflected the struggle for change in Haiti. The lyrics were a clarion call for change and for a reevaluation of the long-ignored peasant culture. *Racines* was propelled by Vodou rhythms overlaid with electric guitars, keyboards and singing. The most notable *racines* bands are Boukman Eksperyans, Boukan Ginen and RAM. During the military dictatorships of the late 1980s and the coup years of the 1990s, many of these bands endured extreme harassment and threats from the military. For more on RAM, see the boxed text (p304). In recent years musicians like Wyclef Jean have refreshed Haitian music once more, with American-influenced Creole hip-hop.

> Song and dance are integral to any Vodou ceremony, with the *lwa* greeted and saluted by their own songs, and constant drumming marking out the pace of ritual. For more, see p281.

Literature

Haiti's literary scene is almost as rich as its visual arts. The American Occupation from 1915 to 1934 was its main creative spur, as black Haitians sought to create a strong independent cultural identity through literature. The resulting Noiriste movement had a big impact on Haitian politics (see p268). Important novels were *Ainsi parla l'oncle* (Thus Spoke the Uncle) by Jean-Price Mars, which sought to reclaim the voice of the Creole peasantry, and Jacques Roumain's *Les gouverneurs de la rosée* (Masters of the Dew), generally recognized to be Haiti's finest work of literature.

Writers like Roumain were influenced by the international Surrealist movement, which in the late 1940s was responding to the newly discovered Haitian naive painters. Stéphen Alexis and poet René Depestre thrived in response.

The rise of the ostensibly Noiriste 'Papa Doc' Duvalier saw intellectual and literary life come under attack. Alexis was murdered by Duvalier's henchmen and Depestre went into exile. Probably the most famous book on Haiti, *The Comedians*, by Graham Greene, was a horrifically comic response to Papa Doc's vicious rule.

> Unsurprisingly, 'Papa Doc' Duvalier hated Graham Greene's satirical novel *The Comedians*, banning it and raging against the author who he dubbed 'a conceited scribbler' and 'a chimerical radicalist.'

Many of the best contemporary Haitian writers have come from the diaspora. Most celebrated is Edwidge Danticat, writer of *Breath, Eyes, Memory*, *The Farming of Bones* and *Krik? Krak!*, all written in English. Dany Laferrière *(An Aroma of Coffee)* is another noted Haitian novelist.

> Gingerbread Houses: Haiti's Endangered Species by Anghelen Arrington Phillips contains dozens of beautiful line drawings of the best gingerbreads in Port-au-Prince, Cap-Haïtien, Jacmel and Jérémie.

Architecture

Very few examples of French colonial architecture have survived Haiti's tempestuous history. The best are found in the north, such as at Fort Liberté (p339). Many forts were also built in the immediate years following independence, the most stupendous of which is easily the Citadelle (p338), along with the palace of Sans Souci (p337), both built during the reign of Henri Christophe.

In the late 19th century, Parisian style met the requirements of tropical living in the so-called gingerbread houses and mansions, characterized by their graceful balconies, detailed wooden latticework and neo-Gothic designs. For a walk through Port-au-Prince's gingerbread architecture, see p297 Fine examples can also be found in Cap-Haïtien and Jacmel.

Haiti Vodou

It's hard to think of a more consistently maligned and misunderstood religion than Vodou. The name itself sparks an instantly negative word-association game of voodoo dolls, zombies and black magic – less a religious tradition than a mass of superstitions based on ignorance and fear. The truth is somewhat distant from the hype. Vodou is a complicated and sophisticated belief system with roots in Haiti's African past and the slave rebellion that brought the country's independence in 1804. Central to Haiti's national identity, these roots have also led to the demonization of Vodou in the West.

For three centuries slaves were shipped to Haiti from the Dahomey and Kongo kingdoms in west and central Africa. The slaves brought their traditional religions with them as well as their labor; beliefs in the spirit world helped sustain them through their bondage. Vodou as practiced today is a synthesis of these religions, mixed with residual rituals from the Taínos along with Catholic and Masonic regalia, and symbols inherited from the colonial plantation era.

This rich mix of traditions is what makes Haitian Vodou unique. Conversion of slaves to Christianity was an active policy in the colony, as the salvation of one's 'heathen soul' was seen as ample reward for being worked to death on a plantation. Many slaves, however, had other ideas, and saw in the icons of Catholic saints their own African spirits, represented in new forms and as new ideas, and appropriated the images as their own. Vodou thrived both clandestinely on the plantations and among bands of runaway slaves in secret hill camps. Forming a wholly new religion, it bound together the slaves from disparate parts of Africa, now incorporated into the Vodou pantheon as the spirits of the 21 Nations of Africa.

Vodou played a large part in both the inspiration and organization of the struggle for independence. The Vodou ceremony at Bois Cayman in 1791, presided over by the slave and priest Boukman, is considered central to sparking the first fires of the Haitian slave rebellion that led to eventual independence. However, Vodou's relationship to power has always been a rocky one. Both Toussaint Louverture and Jean-Jacques Dessalines outlawed Vodou during their reigns, fearing its political potential. Ironically, the killing and expulsion of whites under Dessalines removed the influence of the Catholic priesthood and allowed Vodou to develop without external influences. Overseas, the 'bad example' of slaves emancipating themselves led to Vodou being castigated in the USA and Europe throughout the 19th century. The bad press went into overdrive during the US occupation of Haiti from 1915 to 1934. Coinciding with the advent of Hollywood and the dime-store pulp novel, the Western public eagerly ate up concocted stories of darkest Africa in the Caribbean, all witch doctors and child sacrifice.

Haitian governments have played their part, too, with several ruthless anti-superstition campaigns in the 20th century egged on by the Catholic Church

First published in 1953, Maya Deren's *Divine Horsemen: The Living Gods of Haiti* is a classic work. If you only read one book on Vodou, make it this one.

WHAT'S IN A NAME?

Vodou is the officially recognized name of Haiti's religion. The word is from the Fon word *vodu* (divine spirit), from modern-day Benin. As the ancient kingdom of Dahomey, Benin provided many of the slaves transported to Haiti, and Vodun remains the national religion of the country. Modern practitioners tend to avoid the Anglicized 'voodoo', because of its lurid associations in popular culture.

and the government. In the 1930s and early '40s Vodou altars were burned and Mapou trees (sacred trees where spiritual offerings are made) were cut down. 'Papa Doc' Duvalier chose to co-opt the Vodou priests instead, which led to a violent backlash against some practitioners after the fall from power of his son in 1986. By this time, however, more-progressive Catholics in the Haitian church had begun to reach an accommodation with Vodou, and in 1987 a new constitution guaranteed freedom of religion. In 1991 President Aristide formally ranked Vodou as a national religion alongside Christianity.

PRACTICE & CEREMONIES

Vodou is not an animist religion of worshipping spirits. Followers of Vodou (Vodouisants) believe in one God, Gran Met (Great Master), whom they worship. Gran Met is seen as being distant from the physical plane, so lesser spirit entities called *lwa* are approached in ceremonies as interlocutors. Summoned through prayer, song, drumming and dance, the *lwa* are the spirits left to help followers in their journey back to the divine. During ceremonies, the *lwa* possess or 'mount' participants. Being possessed is central to a ceremony and is the ultimate purpose for initiates as they experience absolute communication with the God and their ancestors. Possession is analogous to the speaking in tongues in Christian spiritualism, or the rapture of Muslim Sufism. *Lwa* possession manifests itself in song, dance, the offering of advice or healing illnesses.

There are many branches (or houses) of *lwa*, which are called upon in different orders according to ritual. The most popular invoked *lwa* are the Rada, also known as the 'sweet' or 'cool' spirits. Rada summoning accounts for more than 90% of Vodou ceremonies. In contrast, the 'hot' or 'angry' Petro *lwa* are rarely invoked, due to their links with black magic. Those that summon the Petro are said to practice their religion with the left hand. Other families of *lwa* include the Gédé, spirits associated with death and the transition to the next world, and the *lwa* of the African nations, such as the Ibo, Senegal and Kongo.

Ceremonies are generally held in dedicated temples, called peristyles. Each peristyle contains an altar, decorated with paintings of *lwa* and images of Catholic saints alongside rocks, bottles of liquor and packets of herbs. At the center of the peristyle is a *poto mitan,* a pole representing a tree that provides a focus for ceremonies. Peristyles are dedicated to a particular house of *lwa,* and decorated accordingly, with paintings on doors and walls and the hanging of bunting. Each peristyle is maintained by a priest – either a *houngan* or *mambo* depending on whether they are male or female. Each carries an *asson* (ceremonial rattle) as a symbol of their priesthood.

Followers of Vodou don't talk of practicing Vodou, instead referring to it as 'serving the *lwa*.'

Initiation

There are different levels of participation in Vodou ceremonies and religions. An uninitiated adherent, known as a Vodouisant (a general term such as Christian or Muslim), can attend ceremonies, seek advice and medical treatment from a *houngan* or *mambo,* and take part in Vodou-related activities.

For a Vodouisant to become a *houngan* or *mambo,* he or she must first go through a series of initiations. Those preparing for the first level of initiation are sometimes called *hounsi bossale.* All wear white clothing in ceremonies to show humility. Forming a choir, the *hounsis* can be possessed by *lwa.* After their first mounting, initiates are regarded as *serviteurs* or *hounsi kanzo,* marked by a ritual washing of the head *(lave tet).*

Those willing or able to progress take the *asson* at a *si pwen* ritual. Held in secret, the *serviteur* becomes a *houngan* or *mambo.* These practitioners lead prayers and songs, conduct rituals and are those most likely to be possessed by *lwa.* They often act as choirmasters in ceremonies, and may become leaders of their own temples. The final level of initiation is Asogwe.

ARE ZOMBIES REAL?

The dead that walk are a key part of popular media voodoo imagery, but do they have any basis in Vodou fact?

Many Haitians believe in the existence of the *zombi* (the Creole spelling): a person brought back from the grave to do the bidding of another. The practice is the alleged providence of a *bokor* (sorcerer), who serves the *lwa* 'with both hands.' A potion is secretly given to a victim, which induces a deathlike state to such an extent that they are actually given a funeral. The *bokor* then exhumes and revives the person, and induces a trance, under which the victim can be controlled, most usually to do manual labor.

Fact or horror story? Researchers have claimed that the poison tetrodotoxin is the key ingredient in the potion, as it can induce such states. Vodouisants claim the potion causes the victim to lose its *ti-bonanj* (a person's 'good angel', similar to the conscience), turning them into a shell. Salt apparently can revive a *zombi*. Modern reports of *zombis* are incredibly uncommon and are rarely verified. Zombification remains a criminal offence under Haitian law.

These are the ultimate human authority, with the power to initiate others, and are called upon when others are unable to summon a particular *lwa*.

Beating the Drums

Vodou services are highly developed rituals to pleasure, feed and ultimately summon the *lwa* through the possession of a human body. Ceremonies are called to order through singing and drums, struck in tattoos of 13 beats. These symbolize knocking on the door of Ginen (ancestral Africa), with the entire congregation matching the beat with handclaps. After this, the Asogwe sing the Priye Ginen (prayer of Africa). It begins with Catholic hymns in French before segueing into Creole prayers, lists of ancestors and *lwa*, and finishing in *langaj*, the forgotten tongues of the 21 African nations.

All ceremonies begin this way, but what comes next depends on the *lwa* being summoned. For Rada services, there are usually three drums: the *mamman*, the *segon* and the *boula*. The *mamman* is the largest drum, which the leading drummer beats fiercely with a single stick and one hand. The *segon* player provides hypnotic counter-rhythms, while the *boula* drummer plays an even rhythm that holds all the others together. The *houngan* or *mambo* then takes the *asson* from the altar and the *hounsis* start to dance and sing ritual songs. The spirits appear in strict order and are summoned by their own particular drum rhythms and songs.

Before any *lwa* can be summoned, Legba (the spirit of the crossroads; see boxed text, p282) must open the gates to the spirit world. Then the four cardinal points are saluted, acknowledging the rising and setting sun, and birth and death.

At the top of the spirit listing, the ceremony honors Papa Loko Attisou (the ancestral spirit of Vodou's original priest), who is greeted through song. The *houngan* then traces out the *vévé* (sacred symbol) for Ayizan (the first Vodou priestess) in cornmeal or flour on the floor. Thought to be the legacy of the Taínos, the ephemeral and delicate *vévés* are pounded into the earth by dancers' feet. These spirits preside over the ceremony as a whole rather than manifesting through mounting.

Next Damballah may be greeted – a participant possessed by Damballah will writhe around the floor in a serpentine manner. The congregation then continues to salute a host of spirits with individual rhythms and songs.

The first group of *lwa* is the Rada, and their main ceremonial color is white. This is the most disciplined and restrained part of the ceremony as participants seeking particular services make their requests.

In *The Serpent and the Rainbow*, ethnobotanist Wade Davis searches for the truth behind Haiti's *zombi* phenomenon. A gripping mix of science and travelogue, although the author isn't afraid of painting himself as the next Indiana Jones.

THE VODOU PANTHEON

There are a dizzying number of *lwa*, each with well-defined characteristics, including sacred numbers, colors, days, ceremonial foods and ritual objects. These are some of the most important *lwa*:

Legba

The master of passageways, who guards entrances and crossroads and the doors between the physical and spirit worlds. Often portrayed as a crippled wanderer, he can offer directions or equally misdirect you. His counterparts include St Peter and St Lazarus, and offerings include green bananas, bones, toys and cigars.

Damballah

Depicted as a snake biting its tail, the master of the sky and *grande zombi* represents the ordering of chaos and the creation of the world, as well as the dualities of death/rebirth, sickness/health and male/female. His counterpart is St Peter, and he is offered white chickens, eggs, rice and milk.

Marasa

These *lwa* twins represent love, truth and justice. Often paid respect at the opening of ceremonies, they are associated with procreation and children, who are usually invited to feast on their offerings. Their counterparts are St Comas and St Daman; their offerings are piles of food.

Baron

Also known as Baron Samedi, this *lwa* is the master of the dead and keeper of the cemeteries. His powers are equally responsible for procreation of the living and putrefaction of the dead. Often depicted as a swaggering skeleton with top hat, cane and purple cape, his offerings include black roosters, rum, cigars and black coffee. St Gerard is his counterpart.

Maman Brigitte

The wife of Baron, Maman Brigitte has similar curative powers and is a foul-mouthed *lwa* with sexually suggestive dances. She's known to press hot peppers on her genitals, the test to which

The ceremony transitions through the Doubja *lwa*, the Ibo, Senegal and Kongo before arriving at the Petro *lwa*. Their ceremonial color of red reflects their fierce, magical and aggressive characters, and creates a fast-paced and exciting atmosphere.

The last family to appear is the Gédé, which includes Baron and Maman Brigitte, the keepers of the dead. With instantly distinguishable colors of violet and black, they appear in any order they like and their degenerate and bawdy behavior instantly changes the mood of any ceremony.

When the last repetitions of the final song are finished, the ceremony is over. Sometimes, however, enthusiastic participants may continue singing and dancing along to songs that relate to the *lwa*. This is the party that follows the service, called a *bamboche* in some parts of the country. The party can last until the wee hours of the dawn.

Voodoo in Haiti, by anthropologist Alfred Metraux, is another key work for understanding the centrality of Vodou in the national culture.

Attending a Ceremony

There are various levels of participation in a Vodou ceremony. Anyone may enter the peristyle and join a ceremony, and singing and dancing are encouraged. Most Vodou practitioners also welcome tourists to attend ceremonies in the hope that they will take a more positive view of the practice back to their home country, although it's essential to check instead of turning up unannounced.

It's advisable to arrive with a guide anyway – most ceremonies take place without fanfare in locations that would be hard to stumble upon randomly.

women suspected of 'faking' possession are subjected. Her counterpart is St Brigitte, and her offerings the same as Baron.

Erzuli Dantor

Comparable to Venus, and with the Virgin Mary as her counterpart, Erzuli Dantor is the *lwa* of love. She's also represented as La Sirene, a mermaid who enchants with her beauty and her trumpet. Perfume, wine, cakes and jewelry are all preferred offerings.

Erzuli Freda

The heart and the knife are the symbols of Erzuli Freda, the *lwa* of motherhood. A strongly passionate figure, she is represented everywhere by the image of the Black Madonna. She is voiceless, and carries facial scars from her African homeland. Her offerings include Creole pigs and rum.

Ogou

This warrior spirit of steel and iron was invoked by slaves fighting for freedom, and his strength means people call on him for support in physical and legal struggles. He takes offerings of all things red, especially roosters. His counterparts are St James and St Jacques.

Zaka

Zaka the farmer is the *lwa* of agriculture and harvest, usually depicted as a hard-working peasant in denims and red scarf, with a *macoute* (straw bag) – a look appropriated by Duvalier's Tontons Macoutes militia. His counterpart is St Isodor, and he is offered bread, sugar, tobacco and *klerin* rum.

Agwe

Agwe is the master of the sea. He not only provides passage across water but assists people as they emerge from water at birth and are reimmersed at death. He is offered rams, cakes and rum, and his counterpart is St Ulrich.

You should treat the *houngan* or *mambo* with respect by offering a gift, traditionally a bottle of five-star Barbancourt rum or a few good cigars. When you're introduced to the *houngan* or *mambo*, make sure you show appropriate reverence and, should you want to take photos or join in with the dancing, obtain permission beforehand. You may also be asked for a cash donation – to make an offering to the *lwa*, to pay the drummers and the *houngan* or *mambo*, and to contribute to the upkeep of the peristyle.

Certain elements of ceremonies are extremely secret and take place behind closed doors. Once they have advanced to the open they can still remain very intimate affairs. While tourists are usually warmly welcomed, in many cases it may be best to sit on the sidelines. It's definitely worth being aware that most services also involve animal sacrifice of some kind. The killing of an animal releases life, which the *lwa* receive to rejuvenate themselves during the rapture of the ceremony. Chickens are the most common offering.

Ceremonies are commonly held at night, starting any time from sunset on and often lasting all the way through to dawn. You might want to pace yourself, although it's acceptable to wander in and out of the sidelines. If you're staying late, try to arrange transport home before attending, as taxis start drying up late at night.

Baron Samedi is the last resort against magic, because even if a spell should bring a person to the point of death, he can refuse to 'dig the grave', meaning the person cannot die.

Haiti Food & Drink

Haitians love to eat. Everywhere you go in Haiti you can see food being prepared and eaten, from quick snacks cooked on the street and heaped plates of rice and beans being carried onto buses by hungry passengers, to liveried waiters serving high cuisine in the capital's swankiest restaurants. Haitian – that is to say Creole – cuisine is fairly simple, with a heavy reliance on starches, such as rice and plantains, and a selection of hearty sauces, complemented by the local catch from the Caribbean and a great array of refreshing tropical fruit.

STAPLES & SPECIALTIES

Main Dishes

Chronic malnourishment is widespread in Haiti. It's estimated that around 2.4 million people (a quarter of the population) can't afford to consume the minimum 2240 daily calories recommended by the World Health Organization.

If you walked into a restaurant anywhere in the country and asked for the most typical Creole dish, it's likely that the waiter would bring you a *plat complet*. In a single serving it gives a tour of the key elements of Haitian cuisine. The first element is *diri ak pwa* (rice and red beans), the staple that seems to power half the country. Next up is *bannann peze* (fried plantain), cut into thick slices. These starchy elements are balanced by your choice of meat – or just as often, whatever is available. Commonly this is *poule* (chicken), *griyo* (fried pork), *kabrit* (goat) or *tasso* (jerked beef). Also very popular is *lambi,* the conch harvested in huge numbers across Haiti and the Dominican Republic (see the boxed text, p38).

The meal is accompanied by a sauce, often served in a separate dish. This is usually the simple *sòs kreyol,* a tomato-based Creole sauce, but may also be the much livelier *ti malice* sauce, made with a liberal dose of chilies. A thin sauce is *bouillon,* more like a soup. Haitian food is generally more peppery than the Creole food found elsewhere in the Caribbean.

Soup jomou is a traditional pumpkin soup, and Haitian country cooking at its best. The proper time to eat it is on New Year's Day, when the entire country appears to tuck into a bowl.

Haiti's long coastline means that seafood is widely available, and is very reasonably priced. The fish, garlicky *crevettes* (shrimp) and lobster can all be fantastic.

More often cooked at home than served in restaurants, *diri djon djon* is a Haitian twist on risotto. Dried *djon djon,* black mushrooms, are left to soak, and the soaking water is then used as a stock to cook rice, imparting a delicate smoky flavor to the meal. Another home-cooking favorite you can sometimes find is *mayi moulen* (cornmeal porridge), often cooked with kidney beans and flavored with peppers and coconut – a lifesaver for vegetarians when served with half an avocado. It's a staple dish for peasants, who often cannot afford anything grander. Yams and manioc (cassava) are another countryside staple. Every November village harvest festivals celebrate the new yam crop across the country.

Haiti's geography gives it enough microclimates to grow a staggering array of fresh produce, including both tropical and temperate varieties. Fruit is widespread, from citrus, coconuts and papaya to guava. King of all Haitian fruits, however, is the mango. Over 140 varieties are recorded but the most important is the Madame Francis, which is a major export crop for the country.

Most hotels offer a free breakfast of bread, jam, eggs, juice and coffee, but you'll occasionally be offered heartier fare such as spaghetti, soup or boiled potatoes.

Snacks

You won't have to look far to find cheap and good street food. It can seem like there are women cooking and selling food on most street corners, with the concentration increasing the closer you get to a market or a bus station. When food is cooked like this at street level on charcoal braziers it's known

---

INDULGING YOUR SWEET TOOTH

One of the highlights of Haiti is *dous*, a term that covers a delightful range of sticky treats for anyone in need of a sugar rush. The ingredients vary, from coconut or peanut to molasses, made into cookies, fudge or brittle candy. Most areas of the country have their own special types of *dous*. One of the most famous is *dous macoss* from Petit Goâve, a milky sweet slab sold by so many shops you'd think it was the only thing for sale in the town. Alternatively, go for *pain patate,* a cake-bread made with milk, cinnamon, nutmeg and sweet potato.

---

as *chenjanbe* – 'crossed by dogs,' although the food is more appetizing than the name. The most common sight is a large pan of oil, used to produce *fritay*. More a technique than a particular menu item, anything can be fried up and offered in a roll of paper – wedges of plantain or breadfruit, knuckles of pork or, on the coast, a handful of tiny battered fish. *Accra* is a *fritay* made from grated *malanga*, a starchy root similar to yam. *Fritay* is often sold with a helping of *pikliz* (spicy pickled carrots and cabbage).

Bananas can also be thinly sliced and sold salted in bags like potato chips (*papite*) – ideal snacks on bus trips. Another filling snack is *pate* (*pate cho* when sold hot), savory pastries stuffed with beef, fish or chicken. Any of these snacks will cost just a few gourdes.

DRINKS

Haiti is blessed with an abundance of fruit, much of which is turned into delicious juice. Citrus varieties are the most commonly available, including freshly squeezed orange, lemon and *shadek,* a local cross between a grapefruit and a lemon. Servings come with a bowl of sugar to sweeten the taste. Grenadine, papaya and cherry also make popular juices. Fruit syrups are also slathered over crushed ice to make a *fresco* – great on a hot day, although the provenance of the ice can't always be guaranteed.

Coffee has consistently been an important export for Haiti, and good coffee is served everywhere. The best (and most expensive) variety is Haitian Blue.

Everyone who can afford it drinks treated water, and delivery trucks carrying plastic barrels of it are everywhere. Culligan is the longest-established brand, such that its name is synonymous with treated water in general. Other brands include Crystal and Aquafine. As well as being sold in smaller bottles, you'll see street vendors hawking sealed plastic bags of water for a few gourdes. Either way, the resulting plastic waste is a major contributor to Haiti's refuse mountain. Restaurants automatically provide jugs of treated water with meals; hotels similarly oblige. Never drink the tap water.

Most Caribbean countries proclaim that their rum is the best in the world, and Haiti is no exception. The main producer is Barbancourt, established in 1862. It's possible to visit the distillery just outside Port-au-Prince for a tour (see p312). Haitian rum is unique in that it is made direct from sugarcane, rather from the molasses left over during sugar production used elsewhere. Barbancourt ages its rum for up to 15 years in oak barrels. Both the three- and five-star rums are excellent, with the latter being a favored offering to Vodou priests. Most good hotel bars offer rum punches to their own recipe, and it's an essential travel experience to road test a few to discover the best. Rum sours (mixed with sugar and lime) are a refreshing alternative.

Haitians are also partial to *klerin,* a cheaper white rum produced in small distilleries for the local market. It can be ferocious stuff, but is renowned for it's health-giving properties (see the boxed text, p286).

To ask for Coca-Cola say 'Koka' not 'Coca-Cola', otherwise you'll receive the sweet fizzy Haitian drink called Kola.

Mirta Yurnet-Thomas's comprehensive *A Taste of Haiti* is the ideal cookbook to help you recreate your Haitian culinary adventure at home.

GOOD FOR WHAT AILS YOU

Although the strong kick of *klerin* (white rum) can sometimes be too much for visitors, for many Haitians, who well know the restorative powers of a good stiff drink, it's an essential part of their medicine cabinet. Look in the markets for small stalls carrying an interesting array of jars and bottles containing brightly colored liquids. This is the *klerin* pharmacy. With the skill of a herbalist, the vendor makes *trempé*, soaking carefully chosen leaves, bark, spices and fruits in *klerin* to produce remedies for almost any ill under the sun. Headaches, fits, stomach upsets and even problems in the bedroom can all be cured, it is claimed, by a well-made *trempé*.

The locally produced beer is Prestige, of which Haitians are deservedly proud. It was awarded a Médaille d'Or at the 2000 World Beer Cup. Presidente beer from the Dominican Republic is widely available, along with international brands like Heineken. The Prestige brewery also makes bottled Guinness under license, but it's more readily available in shops rather than bars.

WHERE TO EAT & DRINK

There's a gradation in eating establishments in Haiti. At the top there are restaurants, although you'll just as often eat in less formal bar-restaurants (or bar-restos), which span the divide between eating and drinking establishments. Breakfasts can be a big affair, and as most Haitians tend to eat their main meal of the day at lunchtime, it's not uncommon for places to open early but be closed by 9pm. Eating out in the evening can sometimes be a case of asking what's actually available in the kitchen rather than what's listed on the menu.

Except at the cheaper end, most restaurants add a 10% service charge to the bill, so further tipping is discretionary.

Most bar-restos offer only a handful of dishes, with variations on the pork/chicken with beans/rice/plantain theme. On the coast you can expect a wider choice, with plenty of seafood. Midrange restaurants usually carry menus mixing French and Creole dishes. Apart from pizza, pasta and burgers, international cuisine is virtually impossible to find outside the Port-au-Prince area. Haiti's best restaurants are all found in Pétionville.

VEGETARIANS & VEGANS

Haiti isn't a terrifically kind country for vegetarians. Most dishes are meat-based to some degree, and pork fat is used widely to cook with, even in dishes that don't contain meat. If you ask to skip the meat, you'll just get the same dish with the meat fished out, often accompanied by a quizzical look. There are enough side dishes to keep you filled up, although the repetition of beans, rice and plantain may quickly have you on a carbohydrate overdose. Salads are common and avocadoes often accompany many dishes, but green vegetables are harder to find. Only the restaurants of Port-au-Prince and Pétionville really offer any decent selection of vegetarian food, although pizza and pasta are good meat-free standbys, and widely available. Be thankful for the surfeit of fresh fruit.

EAT YOUR WORDS

For pronunciation guidelines, see p369.

Useful Phrases

I'd like ...	*Mwen ta vle ...*
I'd like what he/she is having.	*Mwen ta vle sa l-ap manje la.*
I don't eat meat.	*Mwen pa janm manje viann nan.*
What do you have to drink?	*Ki sa w gin pou bwe, souple.*

Very good/tasty.   *Sa te bon anpil/li te tre bon mèsi.*
The bill, please.   *Ou kap ban-m fich la, silvouple.*

Food Glossary

akra	fried malanga (yamlike tuber)
bannann	plantain
bannann peze	fried plantain slices
bonbon dous	cookie
bonbon sèl	salty/savory biscuit
boutèy dlo	bottled water
byè	beer
diri	rice
diri ak sòs pwa	rice cooked with beans
diri djon djon	rice with dried mushrooms
dlo	water
fig	banana
fresco	iced fruit syrup
fritay	fried snack food
griyo	pork
gwayav	guava
kabrit	goat
kafe	coffee
kann	sugarcane
kasav	cassava
klerin	white rum
kokoye	coconut
lambi	conch
mango	mango
mayi moulen	cornmeal porridge
oma	lobster
pain patate	cake-bread of milk, cinnamon, nutmeg and sweet potato
papay	papaya
papita	salted banana slices
pate	hot savory pastry
pen	bread
piman	hot pepper
plat complet	complete menu (consisting of rice and beans, salad, plantains and meat of your choice)
poule	chicken
pwason	fish
rom	rum
seriz	cherry
shadek	grapefruit
sitwon	lemon/lime
sòs kreyol	tomato-based sauce
sték	beef
tasso	beef dish with the meat cut into strips
ti malis	hot pepper sauce
zaboka	avocado
ze	egg
zoranj	orange

Port-au-Prince

Let's admit the obvious: Port-au-Prince doesn't have the image of somewhere you'd visit purely for fun. A true Third World city just one hour by air from Miami, the city has a reputation for impoverished chaos that precedes it. But look behind this and something altogether different is revealed: one of the most vibrant and exciting cities in the Caribbean, with a fantastic arts scene, good restaurants and live music, and an irrepressible spirit. Like a bottle of local *klerin* rum, Port-au-Prince takes all the raw energy of Haiti and distils it down into one buzzing shot.

You should be prepared, however. Port-au-Prince's infrastructure has never kept pace with its rapid growth. Electricity supply and garbage collection are massively inadequate, and whole districts flood whenever a hurricane blows through the Caribbean. The gap between the haves and have-nots is remarkable, with the poorest slums in the Americas overlooked from the cool hills of Haiti's richest suburbs.

Amid all this, the streets are mobbed with colorful painted buses, street vendors, impromptu art galleries and music. The calm heart of the city is the Champs de Mars district, with its parks, museums and memorials to the country's turbulent history. Nearby, many streets are still lined with instantly recognizable 'gingerbread' houses, while even the cathedrals stand as painted monuments to a rich artistic heritage. In the markets and cemeteries, the older spirits of Vodou come to the fore. Away from the hustle of the center is the suburb of Pétionville, where you'll find another Port-au-Prince altogether with expensive restaurants and five-star hotels.

Port-au-Prince has many faces. Its poverty can be distressing, but witnessing the self-sufficiency and spirit of its people might be the most life-affirming experience you will have on your travels. It's a chaotic, exhilarating and compelling place. We'd encourage you to jump right in.

HIGHLIGHTS

- People-watch amid the parks, avenues and statues of **Champs de Mars** (p293)
- Stand in awe at the Haitian art masterpieces decorating the interior of **Sainte Trinité Episcopalian Cathedral** (p295)
- Look for arts and crafts bargains at the **Marché de Fer** (p296), Port-au-Prince's splendidly chaotic covered market
- Visit the **Grand Rue artists** (p297) to see where the Haitian art of the past collides with the art of the future
- Dance late into the night at a **RAM concert** (p304) at the Hôtel Oloffson

HISTORY

Port-au-Prince was founded in 1742 during the boom years of French rule, when it was decided that St-Domingue needed a new central port, and was given its royal charter as capital seven years later. The broad bay in the Golfe de la Gonâve was the ideal location; its name taken from the French ship *Prince* that had first moored there in 1706.

During the slave revolution Port-au-Prince was a key strategic target. Jean-Jaques Dessalines rejected it as his new capital, seeing it as a mulatto stronghold (Pétionville, in particular), and was assassinated on its outskirts in 1806. When Haiti was reunited in 1820, Port-au-Prince returned to its capital status and has dominated the country ever since.

The initial site of the city was confined to the modern Bel Air district. In 1831 Pétionville, located in the cleaner hills above the city, was considered as a possible alternative capital but the idea never stuck. During the 19th century Port-au-Prince grew rapidly, its expansion only occasionally halted by the periodic fires that razed it to the ground. The wealthier residents moved to the rural east of the city, creating the suburbs of Turgeau and Bois Verna, where many of Port-au-Prince's best gingerbread houses can now be found. The poor found themselves pushed to the less salubrious marshy areas of La Saline in the north, the beginning of the city's *bidonvilles* (shanty towns).

The 20th century saw a push for modernization. The US occupation of 1915 improved the city's infrastructure and hygiene through its drain-building program. In 1948 the Estimé government built a link road to Pétionville, spurring the growth of the Delmas suburb. A year later the waterfront area just south of the docks was remodeled to celebrate the city's bicentennial. During the Duvalier period anarchic growth was more the order of the day, as vast numbers of country dwellers flocked to the city. The model development of Cité Simone (named for Papa Doc's wife) soon lapsed into slums, and was subsequently renamed Cité Soleil, while the sprawl of Carrefour similarly lacked state services or infrastructure.

Port-au-Prince continues to grow like a wild plant. The rich have largely retreated to Pétionville and other upscale suburbs, while the poorest areas such as Cité Soleil have proved the breeding ground for both popular political movements like Jean-Bertrand Aristide's Lavalas, and the armed gangs that prospered in the period preceding and following his 2001 ouster. The presence of UN troops, while not without controversy, has at least brought a semblance of order back to the streets.

ORIENTATION

Port-au-Prince's unrestricted growth, its hilly position and lack of street-grid system means that getting your bearings can take a while for first-time visitors. To add confusion, many streets have two names (see the boxed text, p292).

The old commercial centre, Centre Ville (or downtown), lies east of the dockside area, Bicentenaire, bisected north–south by Blvd Jean-Jacques Dessalines (Grand Rue). A central reference point for visitors is Champs de Mars. A large park area (and the cleanest, most open part of Port-au-Prince), this is where you'll find the Palais National, museums, and most of the downtown hotels and restaurants. Just north of here is the cathedral, Sainte Trinité Episcopalian Cathedral, and the Marché de Fer (Iron Market).

Grand Rue runs the length of Port-au-Prince, joining Rte National 1 to Cap Haïtien and other points north, and to the south Rte National 2 to Jacmel and Les Cayes, through the chaotic Carrefour suburb. Two main roads run southeast from Grand Rue, both ultimately leading to Pétionville: Ave John Brown (Lalue) and Rte de Delmas. Several hotels are found off Lalue, which skirts the Nazon and Bourdon districts before changing its name to Ave Pan Américaine before it arrives in Pétionville. All of the side roads that join Rte de Delmas are numbered sequentially, odd to the north and even to the south, increasing toward Pétionville. Delmas 13 is an important junction – south is Ave Martin Luther King (Nazon), which joins Delmas to Lalue, while Blvd Toussaint Louverture (Rte de l'Aéroport) is the main road to the airport.

A third route to Pétionville is along Ave Lamartinière (Bois Verna), via Canapé Vert. Pétionville itself is relatively easy to navigate, as it has both a grid system and street signs.

Maps

Guides Panorama produces the best up-to-date map of Port-au-Prince (US$5). A decent alternative is the street map produced by the Association of Haitian Hoteliers, which is

PORT-AU-PRINCE

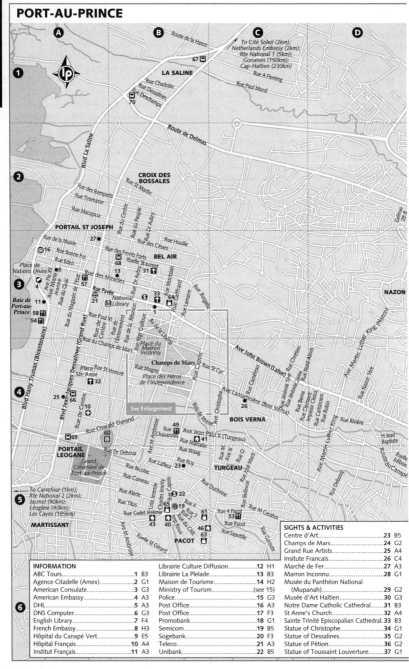

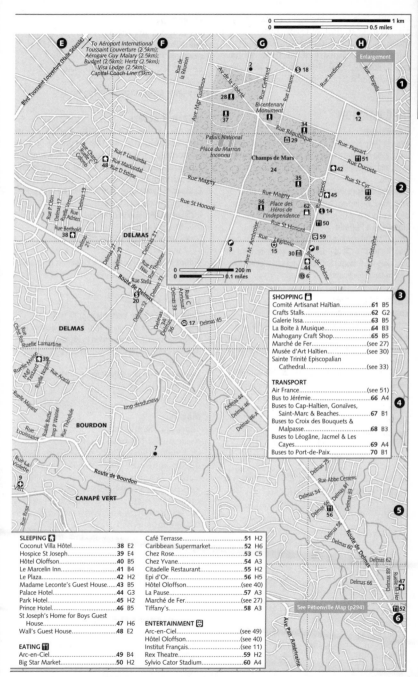

0 _____ 1 km
0 _____ 0.5 miles

Enlargement

To Aéroport International
Toussaint Louverture (Haïle Sélassié);
Aérogare Guy Malary (2.5km);
Budget (2.5km); Hertz (2.5km);
Visa Lodge (2.5km);
Capital Coach Line (3km)

Rue de la Réunion

Ave de la Liberté

Rue Geffrard

Rue Lamarre

Rue Jardines

Rue Borgella

Bicentenary Monument

Rue République

Palais National

Place du Marron Inconnu

Champs de Mars

Rue Piquart

Rue Ducoste

Rue Magny

Rue Magny

Rue St Honoré

Rue St Cyr

Rue St Honoré

Place des Héros de l'Independance

Rue Lépitinie

Rue M. Ambroise

Bois de Rhène

Ave Christophe

Blvd Toussaint Louverture (Haïle Sélassié)

Rue Chery Rue Ble C Colmar

Rue P Lumumba

Rue Mackindal

Rue D Estine

DELMAS

Rue Berthold

Rue P Obin

Rue Verna

Rue Adrien

Delmas 19

Delmas 17

Rue 72

Delmas 23

Rue Fze Nau

Rue Stella

Rue Thimène

Delmas 31

Delmas 31

Delmas 33

Delmas 53

Delmas 52

Delmas 39

Rue C Ambroise

Delmas 45

DELMAS

Route de Delmas

Ruelle Lamartine

Ruelle Meyer Rue Acacia

Ruelle Piquant

Ruelle Magloire

Rue Magny

Rue Théodule

Imp desduness

Delmas 44

Delmas 46

Delmas 4

BOURDON

Rue Butte

Imp P Warner

Rue Louisiana

Rue La Violette

Rue Roux

Route de Bourdon

CANAPÉ VERT

Rue Abbé Cessens

Delmas 75

Delmas 83

Delmas 81

Delmas 54

Delmas 66

Delmas 85

Delmas 58

Route de Delmas

Delmas 60

Delmas 62

Delmas 88

Ruelle St Her

Delmas 66

See Pétionville Map (p294)

Ave Pan Américaine

0 _____ 200 m
0 _____ 0.1 miles

available free from most car-rental companies. Harder to find, but with a useful street index, is the *Haïti Carte Touristique*, produced by the Ministry of Tourism. All have major routes highlighted and are indispensable if you're spending any length of time in the city.

INFORMATION
Bookshops

Asterix (Map p294; ☎ 2257-2605; cnr Rues Grégoire & Ogé, Pétionville) Has a large selection of French-language books and magazines, plus some in English, along with postcards.

Librairie Culture Diffusion (Map pp290-1; ☎ 2223-9260; Ave John Brown) Just off Champs de Mars, with a decent selection of US magazines.

Librairie La Pléïade Port-au-Prince (Map pp290-1; ☎ 2510-0016; cnr Rue Bois-Patate & Ave Martin Luther King) Pétionville (☎ 257-3588; Complexe Promenade, cnr Rues Grégoire & Moïse) Port-au-Prince's best choice for English-language books.

Cultural Centers

English Library (Map pp290-1; ☎ 2249-6177; Pétionville Club, Rue Métreaux, Bourdon; ☺ library 4-6pm Fri) For long-term residents, this English library has annual membership costs of US$30, and a social scene attached.

Institut Français (Map pp290-1; ☎ 2244-0014/0015; www.ifhaiti.org; 99 Ave Lamertinière; ☺ 10am-4pm Tue-Fri, 9am-5pm Sat) Port-au-Prince's major cultural center. Holds regular music concerts, lectures, exhibitions and literary events.

Institut Haitiano-Americain (Map pp290-1; ☎ 222-2947, 222-3715; cnr Rues Capois & St Cyr; ☺ 8am-noon & 1-5pm Mon-Fri) Has a decent English library, but few events.

KNOW YOUR STREET NAMES

Some official street names don't match the names used by locals. The following are some of the most common roads (listed first) with preferred colloquial names following:

Blvd Harry Truman	Bicentenaire
Ave Martin Luther King	Nazon
Ave John Brown	Lalue
Ave Lamartinière	Bois Verna
Blvd Toussaint Louverture	Rte de l'Aéroport
Ave Jean Paul II	Turgeau
Rue Paul VI	Rue des Casernes
Blvd Jean-Jacques Dessalines	Grand Rue
Delmas 105	Fréres

Emergency

Fire Brigade (☎ emergency 115)
Police Port-au-Prince (Map pp290-1; ☎ 2222-1117, emergency 117; 4 Rue Légitime); Pétionville (Map p294; ☎ 2257-2222; emergency 117; Place Saint-Pierre)
Red Cross ambulance (☎ emergency 118)

Internet Access

Internet cafés are plentiful, often opening and closing at the drop of a hat. Concentrations are found downtown along Lalue, around Delmas 85, and Rue Grégoire in Pétionville.

Companet Cyber Café (Map p294; Rue Lamarre; per hr US$1.20; ☺ 9am-7pm)
DNS Computer (Map pp290-1; Rue Capois; per hr US$0.80; ☺ 8am-9pm)
Semicom (Map pp290-1; Rue Capois; per hr US$1; ☺ 7am-9pm)
Vidnet (Map p294; Rue Grégoire, Pétionville; per hr US$3; ☺ 8am-10pm)

Medical Services

Hôpital du Canapé Vert (Map pp290-1; ☎ 2245-0984/0985; 83 Rte de Canapé Vert) Excellent doctors and emergency service, recommended by expats.
Hôpital Français (Map pp290-1; ☎ 2222-2323, 2222-4242; 378 Rue du Centre)
Hôpital François de Sales (☎ 2223-2110, 2222-0232; 53 Rue Charéron)

Money

Sogebank, Scotiabank and Unibank are the most useful for travelers, as long as you're exchanging US dollars cash. All attract long queues, however, so an equally good alternative is to change money at a supermarket, such as Caribbean, Big Star or Eagle, most of which have dedicated counters. Midrange hotels and above will normally change money, but check the rates first. At the bottom of the rank are the street money-changers, often to be found in the vicinity of the large post offices.

Agence Citadelle (Map pp290-1; ☎ 2222-5004, 2222-1938; 35 Place du Marron Inconnu) Agent for Amex.
Promobank (Map pp290-1; cnr Ave John Brown & Rue Lamarre)
Scotiabank (Map p294; cnr Rues Geffrard & Louverture, Pétionville) Has an ATM.
Sogebank Port-au-Prince (Map pp290-1; Rte de Delmas 30); Pétionville (Map p294; Rue Lamarre) Both have ATMs.
Unibank (Map pp290-1; 118 Rue Capois)

Post

DHL (Map pp290-1; ☎ 2223-8133; 29 Ave Marie Jeanne, Bicentenaire)

Post office Port-au-Prince (Map pp290-1; Rue Bonne Foi, Bicentenaire; ☺ 8am-4pm Mon-Sat); Delmas (Map pp290-1; Delmas 45; ☺ 8am-4pm Mon-Sat); Pétionville (Map p294; Place Saint-Pierre; ☺ 8am-4pm Mon-Sat)

UPS (Map p294; Rue Geffrard, Pétionville)

Telephone

There are plenty of phone shops selling cell (mobile) phones, and street phone merchants for making calls and buying top-up cards.

Teleco Port-au-Prince (Map pp290-1; cnr Rue Pavée & Blvd Jean-Jacques Dessalines); Pétionville (Map p294; ☎ 2257-8651; cnr Rues Magny & Rigaud)

Tourist Information

There is currently no good state-run tourist information center in Port-au-Prince. For up-to-date tourist information, your best bet is to contact the local private tour operators (see Tours, p298).

Maison de Tourisme (Map pp290-1; ☎ 2222-8659; Rue Capois; ☺ 8am-4pm Mon-Fri) In a white gingerbread building by Champs de Mars, but currently closed with any reopening uncertain.

Travel Agencies

ABC Tours (Map pp290-1; ☎ 2223-8705, 2223-9244; 156 Rue Pavée)

Agence Citadelle (Map pp290-1; ☎ 2222-5004, 2222-1938; www.agencecitadelle.com; 35 Place du Marron Inconnu) Reliable and well-established travel agent.

DANGERS & ANNOYANCES

Popular conceptions hold that just to visit Port-au-Prince is to take one's life in one's hands, an image bolstered by the violence and kidnappings that followed the 2004 coup. Thankfully, the reality is a little calmer than the perception and visits by foreigners overwhelmingly pass without incident. Operations by the UN Stabilization Mission for Haiti (MINUSTAH) have largely neutralized the gang problem, and although kidnappings do still occasionally occur, targets are almost exclusively rich Haitians.

However, street crime is a fact of life in Port-au-Prince, so take sensible precautions. Don't be ostentatious with valuables, carry only what money you need and don't keep your cash in your back pocket as the pick-pockets are skilful.

Rather than crime or gang violence, Port-au-Prince's worst problem for visitors is actually the traffic. The jams, the drivers treating the roads like a war zone, the potholes and the endless procession of vendors, beggars and street kids all conspire to make getting from A to B an exhausting process. Sidewalks are jam-packed, frequently forcing pedestrians onto the roads and into the paths of oncoming taptaps (local buses or minibuses).

Avoid walking at night where possible. Aside from the crime risk, streetlights are almost nonexistent, so broken pavements (and open sewer channels) present a genuine accident risk.

Unless you have a valid reason and are accompanied by a local, avoid visiting the *bidon-villes*, such as Cité Soleil and Cité Liberté.

SIGHTS
Champs de Mars

The neat order of **Champs de Mars** (Map pp290–1), Port-au-Prince's largest open area, is a marked contrast to the rest of the city. Originally the site of a racetrack, it was built in 1954 to mark the 150th anniversary of independence, and gets further additions every time there's a significant anniversary to commemorate. A pleasant place to relax, it comprises a series of parks split by wide boulevards that collectively make up the **Place des Héros de l'Independence**. Champs de Mars runs from the Palais National to Rue Capois, and also takes in the Musée du Panthéon National and Musée d'Art Haïtien.

As the president's official residence, the **Palais National** is the focus of national politics and traditional host to coups d'état. It stands on the same site as its two predecessors, each destroyed during political unrest in 1869 and 1912 respectively. The three-domed, pristinely white building was completed in 1918 and modeled on the White House in Washington, DC. The palace is always under armed guard and is not open to the public.

Two statues stand in front of the Palais. **Toussaint Louverture** takes pride of place, and faces the **Marron Inconnu** across the road on Ave de la Liberté. This statue of the Unknown Slave by sculptor Albert Mangonès depicts a runaway slave blowing a conch-shell trumpet as a call to begin the revolution. Next to the statue is the scroll-like monument of the Eternal Flame erected in honor of 'Baby Doc' Duvalier; it was extinguished almost the moment he fled the country in 1986.

PORT-AU-PRINCE

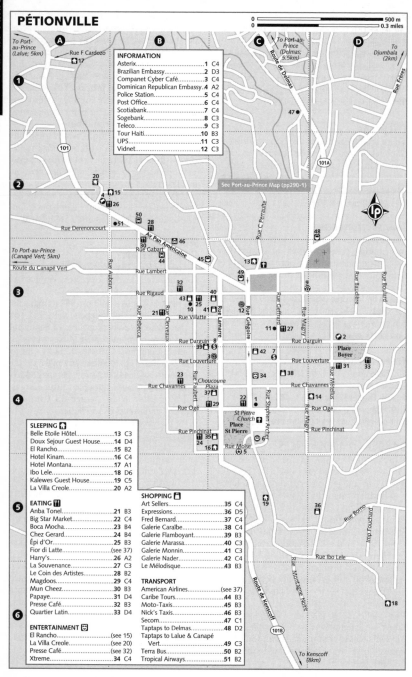

PÉTIONVILLE

Near the Marron Innconu, the huge monument for Haiti's bicentenary erected by Aristide squats ugly and unmissable, a gray monolith resembling an oil derrick. It stands four floors high, each with 50 steps for every year of independence, leading to another (unlit) eternal flame. The 2004 coup meant it was never finished, nor is it likely to be.

East of the Palais, separate parks each contain statues of the remaining founders of independent Haiti: Jean-Jacques Dessalines (on horseback), Alexandre Pétion and Henri Christophe.

The area is a popular promenading spot, especially around sunset and on Sunday. It's also the one part of Port-au-Prince with reliable streetlights – visit of an evening and you'll see students with their books taking advantage of the light to do their homework. Food stalls are set up opposite the Musée d'Art Haïtien each evening and there are a couple of craft stalls, as well as a few would-be guides and street kids trying their luck.

Musée du Panthéon National

The **Musée du Panthéon National** (Mupanah; Map pp290-1; ☎ 2222-8337; Place du Champs de Mars; adult/student US$1.40/0.70; ☻ 8am-4pm Mon-Thu, to 5pm Fri, 12-5pm Sat, 10am-4pm Sun) is a modern, mostly subterranean museum set in its own gardens. Its unusual design echoes the houses of Haiti's original Taíno inhabitants, a motif repeated by the conical central 'well' bringing light to illuminate the gold monument recreating the cannons and banners found on the national flag. The bodies of Toussaint Louverture, Dessalines, Christophe and Pétion are interred below, and the names of further heroes of the independence struggle marked on the surrounding walls.

The museum's permanent exhibition chronicles Haiti's history, from the Taínos, through slavery to independence and the modern era. There are some fascinating exhibits. Exquisite Taíno pottery faces the rusting anchor of Columbus' flagship, the *Santa María*; slave shackles nod toward a copy of the fearsome *Code Noir* that governed the running of the plantations; while the silver pistol with which Christophe took his life leads past Emperor Faustin's ostentatious crown to 'Papa Doc' Duvalier's trademark black hat and cane. A further gallery holds a good cross-section of modern Haitian art, but it suffers from poor labeling.

Musée d'Art Haïtien

The **Musée d'Art Haïtien** (Museum of Haitian Art; Map pp290-1; ☎ 2222-2510; 16 Rue Légitime; admission US$1.40; ☻ 10am-5pm Mon-Sat, to 4pm Sun), on the southern edge of Champs de Mars, is something of a curate's egg. It holds probably the largest collection of Haiti's naive art, with masters like Hector Hyppolite, Préfète Duffaut, Philomé Obin and Robert St Brice well represented. Unfortunately the works aren't hung well, and the permanent collection isn't always on display. Instead you have to take potluck as to what's on show, although the rotating exhibitions can be very good and sometimes branch out into photography. There's a small craft shop at the right-hand side of the building.

Sainte Trinité Episcopalian Cathedral

From the outside, this **cathedral** (Map pp290-1; cnr Ave Mgr Guilloux & Rue Pavée; donation requested), just north of Champs de Mars, doesn't look architecturally inspiring – a large but essentially unimpressive pale brick building. But the quiet exterior hides an amazing secret, as the inside is covered with joyously exuberant murals marking out the life of Christ, executed by the great masters of Haitian painting.

In 1950 the cathedral commissioned artists from the Centre d'Art (p296) to decorate the interior. The results are astonishing, as the artists chose to interpret the Bible stories through their own experience, placing Christ in easily recognizable Haitian situations. The apse contains the first paintings to be completed: three huge murals depicting the *Nativity* (painted by Rigaud Benoît), the *Crucifixion* (by Philomé Obin, who places himself at the foot of the cross with his back to the viewer), the *Ascension* (by Castera Bazile) and above them all Gabriel Lévéque's *Heaven*.

To the right of the apse is Wilson Bigaud's striking *Wedding of Cana*, with Jesus turning water to wine. It's a fantastic snapshot of Haiti – a *rara* (festival music used in street processions) band plays for the party, a pig is slaughtered, chickens peck about the scene – all executed in wild naive colors. On the opposite side of the cathedral, Bazile shows Jesus' baptism, next to women washing clothes in the river, such as you might see anywhere in the country. Elsewhere, Duffaud reimagines the procession of the Cross through his native Jacmel instead of Jerusalem, while other murals show the Last Supper, the flight to Egypt, and Adam and Eve. Hyppolite contributed with his clay apostles near the rear door, where visitors enter when there are no services.

As well as offering a masterclass in the Haitian masters, the cathedral also has a well-regarded philharmonic orchestra that plays regular concerts.

Notre Dame Catholic Cathedral

Two blocks north of Sainte Trinité in Bel Air this **cathedral** (Map pp290-1; cnr Rues Dr Aubry & Bonne Foi) is the city's largest ecclesiastical building. Completed in 1912, the pink-and-yellow structure has two domed towers on its west face. The cathedral itself was one of the first in the world to be built from reinforced concrete, and as such had to receive special dispensation from the Vatican to be consecrated. Worshippers fervently pray on the cathedral steps, at the gates and around the walls, alongside beggars and small stalls selling Catholic ephemera.

Centre D'art

The **Centre d'Art** (Map pp290-1; ☎ 2222-2018; 58 Rue Roy; ☺ 9:30am-5pm Mon-Fri, 9am-3pm Sat) is in a two-floor gingerbread house on a quiet street south of Champs de Mars. It was opened in 1944 by De Witt Peters as both school and exhibition space to encourage the new breed of Haitian painters. Through its work the Centre d'Art helped give painters such as Hyppolite, Obin and Bigaud the recognition they deserved, and was of such importance in the development of Haitian art that its opening is often referred to as 'the miracle of 1944.'

COLONIAL PORT-AU-PRINCE?

The district of Bel Air, named for its healthy climate, was once the heart of French St-Domingue, but you'll be hard pressed to find much of it left. Just about all that remains is the esplanade wall of Notre Dame Catholic Cathedral, built in 1788 as part of a never-completed governor's residence. An older cathedral once sat next door. Built in 1771 on the ruins of the city's first church, this elegant structure was razed by fire in 1991 just before President Aristide's inauguration, torched by a mob protesting against the pro-Duvalierist Archbishop of Port-au-Prince's alleged involvement in an attempted coup.

The Centre d'Art was the first art gallery in Haiti and remains a commercial venture, although there's more than an air of museum about the place. The downstairs is given over to current exhibitions (both paintings and the cream of Croix des Bouquets metal sculptures), while the upstairs rooms are stacked high with canvases in a manner more akin to a treasure trove than a formal gallery. It would take hours to go through everything, and it's an exciting place for art lovers to browse. Almost all pieces are for sale. Compared to the galleries in Pétionville, it's a sleepy place, but the staff are very knowledgeable, and there are sometimes artists working on-site.

For more galleries, see p305.

Marché De Fer

Several of Haiti's cities have Iron Markets, but the original and best is in central Port-au-Prince. The **Marché de Fer** (Iron Market; Map pp290-1; cnr Grand Rue & Rue des Fronts Forts; ☺ daily) is an exuberant and exotic red-metal structure dating from 1889, which looks more akin to something from the *Arabian Nights* than tropical Haiti. In fact, it was originally destined to be the main hall of Cairo train station (hence its minarets), but when the sale from the Parisian manufacturers fell through, President Florvil Hyppolite snapped it up as part of his plan to modernize Port-au-Prince.

The market is roughly divided into two sections. The southern hall is the food market, a full-on assault on the senses, with the stifling air buzzing with the noise of traders and the tang of fruit, vegetables, meat and unknown scents. All the produce of Haiti is here, from piles of dried mushrooms and yams, heaps of millet and more different types of mango than you've ever seen, along with charcoal braziers and various cooking implements made from old oil cans.

The northern hall is given over to a giant craft market, with the biggest selection of local arts in the country. It's all here, from naive paintings and Vodou flags to wood and metal sculptures. The market is especially rich in Vodou paraphernalia.

Marché de Fer is open every day, although there are fewer vendors on Sundays. Be prepared for plenty of bustle, and a little hustle, too – you'll attract plenty of would-be guides and should also keep a close watch on your possessions.

PORT-AU-PRINCE'S GINGERBREAD ARCHITECTURE

The vast majority of Haiti's unique gingerbread buildings are in Port-au-Prince, almost entirely the product of just three Parisian-trained Haitian architects: Georges Baussan, Léon Mathon and Joseph-Eugèe Maximilien. There are a couple of hundred gingerbreads, although many are now falling into disrepair, being expensive to maintain.

The key gingerbread characteristics are brick-filled timber frames adorned with lacy wooden latticework, high ceilings, and graceful balconies set over wide porches – all designed to take advantage of the prevailing winds. The old Palais National, built in 1881 (and blown up in 1912), was an early model, and its style was quickly appropriated as the height of bourgeois tropical living. The residential areas of **Pacot** (Map pp290–1) and **Bois Verna** (Map pp290–1) saw gingerbread houses reach their zenith during a 30-year spree that ended in 1925 when Port-au-Prince's mayor stifled wooden buildings as a potential fire hazard.

The **Hôtel Oloffson** (Map pp290–1) on Ave Christophe is Port-au-Prince's most photographed example of gingerbread. Built in 1887, it served as the family home to the son of President Sam, then as a military hospital during the American Occupation before being converted to a hotel in 1936. A walk along **Ave Lamartinière** (Map pp290–1) in Bois Verna reveals a parade of great gingerbreads: the twin witch's-hats towers of No 15; President Tancrède Auguste's 1914 mansion at No 46; No 48 with its strange room over the porch; the impossibly narrow No 52; and the one-story house at No 84 with its elaborate roof. Other notables are Le Manoir at 126 Ave John Brown (Lalue), with its four towers and grand bishop's-hat roof, and the four-story Villa Miramar at 2 Rue 4 in Pacot.

There are few gingerbreads in Pétionville. The loveliest by far is the **Hotel Kinam** (Map p294), although this was built in the 1950s, long after the original gingerbread boom.

Grand Rue Artists

While most of Haiti's artists are represented in the rarified air of Pétionville's galleries, a collective of sculptors and installation artists is producing spectacular work in the unlikeliest of settings, squeezed into the cinderblock houses backing onto the mechanics and body workshops on Grand Rue. The **Grand Rue artists** (Map pp290-1; 622 Blvd Jean-Jacques Dessalines; www.atis-rezistans.com) are unlike anything you've seen in Haiti, turning scrap and found objects into startling Vodou sculpture. The results are a heady mix of spirit, sex and politics – a Caribbean junkyard gone cyberpunk, yet one very much grounded in the preoccupations of daily Haitian life.

Three main artists make up the endeavor. André Eugène is the founder and elder member, a one-time housebuilder who has turned to sculpting in wood, plastic and car parts to produce his vision of the *lwa* (Vodou spirits). Doll's heads and human skulls abound, alongside the earthy humor of highly phallic Gédé pieces.

Jean Hérard Celeur trained as a sculptor, and has done many of the largest pieces, life-sized statues of twisted wood and parts of car chassis, hubcaps, old shoes and a liberal application of twisted nails.

The youngest of the artists is known simply as Guyodo and is never seen without a pair of big sunglasses. Of all the artists, Guyodo favors painting his sculptures with metallic spray, and his workshop (artfully lit using car batteries for power) glitters silver and gold like a weird Vodou grotto.

The artists have exhibited across the USA, and in 2006 collaborated with the local community to build a sculpture for Liverpool's International Slavery Museum in the UK. Pieces are for sale, but sadly most are too large for easy transportation.

This urban museum is near Ciné Lido on Grand Rue. Set slightly back from the road, look for the giant Gédé statue made from car parts and with a giant spring-loaded penis guarding the way. Just beyond this, Eugène's house-museum is surrounded by statues, with the motto 'E Pluribus Unum' ('Out of many, one') hung over the door. Guyodo and Celeur's workshops are in the narrow lanes beyond – you'll need to be accompanied.

Grand Cimetière De Port-au-Prince

A vast necropolis of raised tombs, Port-au-Prince's **Grand Cimetière De Port-au-Prince** (Map pp290–1) sprawls itself out between Grand

Rue and Silvio Cator Stadium, bound by walls with often lurid Vodou murals. Many of the elevated sarcophagi more closely resemble houses, bigger and more elaborate than many of the shanties in the *bidonvilles*. It's a fascinating but weird place, littered with broken graves and old beer bottles left behind from late-night offerings to Baron Samedi and Maman Brigitte, guardians of the deceased.

'Papa Doc' Duvalier, who so consciously portrayed himself as an incarnation of the Baron, was buried here in 1971. Fifteen years later during the reaction against Duvalierism, his tomb was sacked to desecrate his body, dooming him on Judgment Day. But his coffin had been mysteriously spirited away, and the final resting place of his body remains unknown.

The cemetery is the main focus for the Fet Gédé celebrations every November 1 and 2 (see p346) and is well worth checking out, although it's best to attend with a local. Funeral processions are a public affair here, regularly taking place in the late afternoon with marching jazz bands and troops of majorettes, with several funeral parties marching together from nearby St Anne's church to the cemetery gates.

Pétionville

The suburb of Pétionville (Map p294) was founded by President Boyer and named for his predecessor. It never became the replacement capital he hoped for, but from the mid-19th century it became a popular getaway from Port-au-Prince. Urban sprawl has long incorporated Pétionville into greater Port-au-Prince, but the district has maintained its own identity as the center of gravity for Haiti's elite, and a hub for many businesses and banks.

Place Saint-Pierre (Map p294) is at the heart of Pétionville, a shady square featuring a bust of Pétion with an allegorical figure representing Haiti, and the Saint-Pierre church. The action naturally flows downhill from here, with streets laid out in a grid (surprisingly well signed for Haiti). This is where you'll find the best restaurants, galleries and upmarket shops. At the bottom of the hill a large street market spills along Rue Grégoire toward Rte de Delmas.

TOURS

Haiti's two main tour operators can organize guided tours around Port-au-Prince, as well as excursions beyond the capital:

Tour Haiti (☎ 3457-5242, 3746-8696; info@tourhaiti .net, ccchauvel@hotmail.com) Day tour per person US$90, minimum two people.
Voyages Lumière (☎ 2249-6177, 3557-0753; www .voyagelumierehaiti.com) Day tour per person for one/ two/three people US$125/100/90.

A good local guide who can be found in his small Mahogany Craft Shop (Map pp290–1) outside the Hôtel Oloffson in Port-au-Prince is Milfort Bruno, who knows a lot of artists and is a useful fixer.

FESTIVALS & EVENTS

Port-au-Prince's main festival, and one of the biggest in the Caribbean, **Carnival** takes place during the three days before Ash Wednesday, its highpoint being the huge parade of floats, music and carnival queens that winds its way downtown through an immense crush of people before climaxing at Champs de Mars. Taking most of the afternoon, the revelries continue late into the night. For many people, the best part of Carnival is the bands, who either play on floats or walk through the crowds. Carnival bands are fiercely competitive, each devising their own new merengue song that they hope will become the theme to the entire festival, played on the radio in the run-up to the parade. But whoever comes out on top, all strike up the 'Ochan' (Carnival Theme) at the drop of a hat to pay tribute to the partying masses.

SLEEPING

There's essentially one main choice when choosing a bed for the night: whether you want to stay downtown or above it all in more upscale Pétionville. Both have their advantages. Staying downtown puts you in the heart of the action, for the liveliest (and unsanitized) Port-au-Prince experience; it has some good cheap guesthouses as well as one of Haiti's most iconic hotels. Pétionville is quieter with less hustle but has a better selection of hotels at the higher end of the price bracket, as well as putting you closer to the best eating options, which tend to congregate in the suburb.

Port-au-Prince
BUDGET
Hospice St Joseph (Map pp290–1; ☎ 2245-6177, 3550-5230; www.hospicesaintjoseph.org; 33 Rue Acacia, Nazon;

r US$30 per person, incl breakfast & dinner) One of the Christian guesthouses Port-au-Prince seems to specialize in. The hilltop location of the hospice (not to be mistaken for St Josephs Home for Boys Guest House) gives great views over the city. There's a relaxed atmosphere and good, clean rooms, with your rent helping support local health care, feeding, human-rights and education programs.

Wall's Guest House (Map pp290-1; ☎ 2249-4317, 2249-0505; www.wallsguesthouse.org; 8 Rue Mackandal, Delmas 19; shared r per person with fan/air-con US$30/35, incl breakfast & dinner; P 🛇 🖳) A friendly guesthouse run with a strong Christian ethic; you're likely to find yourself sharing with missionaries, aid workers and adopting families. Rooms are basic and bathrooms shared, there's a tiny pool and everyone eats together (but early – dinner is served at 5pm).

our pick St Joseph's Home for Boys Guest House (Map pp290-1; ☎ 2257-4237; sjfamilyhaiti@hotmail.com; 3rd street on right, Delmas 91; shared r per person US$35, incl breakfast & dinner) You've never stayed anywhere like this before, a guesthouse also operating as a highly regarded home for ex-street boys, and a fantastic Haitian experience. Spread over several stories, the house has lots of hidden corners with terraces and views, as well as a chapel and performance area for the music and dance recitals the boys regularly perform. Most rooms contain two bunk beds, and you may be expected to share depending on availability; meals are also taken together. For water conservation, buckets are used to flush the toilets. From Delmas 91 (opposite Radio Haiti Inter), take Rue La Plume (third right) and turn left at the end of the road. St Joe's is the last house, marked by a bright mural.

Madame Leconte's Guest House (Map pp290-1; ☎ 2222-9703; 54 Rue Cadet Jérémie; r US$35) If you're on a tight budget but need to stay close to Champs de Mars, this guesthouse-cum-family-home may be your best option. Facing the park near the Oloffson hotel, there are a few comfy rooms sharing a bathroom, although the nearby bars can be noisy. Breakfast is included but a generator is not, so prepare for the power cuts.

MIDRANGE

Palace Hotel (Map pp290-1; ☎ 2222-3344, 2223-4455; hotellepalace@yahoo.fr; 55 Rue Capois; s/d/tr US$40/50/60; P 🛇) Next to Champs de Mars are the wide verandahs of the Palace Hotel. Everything is whitewashed, contrasting with the black-and-white tiled entrance and the funky Haitian art

everywhere. Rooms are decent enough but could be a bit sharper – the overall effect is a little tired, but certainly fun.

Park Hotel (Map pp290-1; ☎ 2222-4406, 2222-8721; www.parkhotel.homestead.com/park2.html; 23 Rue Capois; s/d US$53/70; P 🛇 🖳) An old townhouse-hotel facing Champs de Mars, the Park aspires to faded grandeur but ends up just feeling a bit sleepy. Rooms are simple but well turned out, set around the pool at the back or in the block alongside. The gardens are shady, adding to the quiet atmosphere – not bad considering the location. Breakfast isn't included in the rate.

Coconut Villa Hôtel (Map pp290-1; ☎ 2246-1691, 2246-0234; www.coconutvillahotel.com; 3 Rue Berthold, Delmas 19; s/d US$65/77; P 🛇 🖳) The Coconut Villa is set in large and leafy grounds, with quick and easy access to Rte de Delmas. Rooms in the main block are comfy and fair value, with the green calm of the surroundings (and the cool blue of the pool) making this hotel a welcome retreat.

Le Marcelin Inn (Map pp290-1; ☎ 2221-8233, 2221-9445; www.marcelin.com; 29 Rue Marcelin; r US$76-86; P 🛇 🖳) This hotel is tucked off Ave Christophe, a modern building that's been 'gingerbreadized' to pleasing effect. The rooms are very nice with brand-new fixtures and fittings, although it's a shame a few lack external windows. There's a decent restaurant and a small pool, and good-quality art on the walls. Good value for both price and location.

Prince Hotel (Map pp290-1; ☎ 2223-0100, 2245-2764; princehotelha@yahoo.com; 30 Rue 3, Pacot; s/d from US$77/91; P 🛇 🖳) Placing yourself in Pacot should give the advantage of views across Port-au-Prince, and this hotel doesn't disappoint. A charming-enough option, with pool, bar and restaurant, although some of the rooms are in need of a refit.

our pick Hôtel Oloffson (Map pp290-1; ☎ 2223-4000, 2223-4102; oloffsonram@aol.com; 60 Ave Christophe; s/d US$80/92, ste US$130-146, bungalow US$101/118; P 🛇 🖳 🖳) Immortalized as the Hotel Trianon in Graham Greene's *The Comedians*, the Oloffson remains for many people the quintessential Port-au-Prince hotel. We can understand why: the elegant gingerbread building is one of the city's loveliest, further tricked out with paintings and Vodou flags. There's a very sociable bar for your rum punches, and every Thursday the house band RAM plays up a storm until the small hours (see the boxed text, p304). The Oloffson isn't beyond trading on its name (some of the rooms are certainly a bit creaky, although the suites are very good), but its charms always seem to win out at the end of the day.

TOP END

Visa Lodge (off Map pp290-1 ☎ 2250-1561, 2249-1202; www .visalodge.com; Rte des Nimes; s/d US$85/96; P ✜ 🖳 🖢) This is certainly one of Port-au-Prince's better hotels, a relaxed high-quality hideaway in large grounds off Blvd Toussaint Louverture, near the airport. A number of buildings are arranged around a central pool, plus there's a tennis court and a gym if you're feeling energetic (and two restaurants and a bar if you're not). Rooms are very spacious and comfy, and there are weekly rates for long-term guests. The only drawback is the location – super-handy for flights, but a significant drive from the rest of the city.

Le Plaza (Map pp290-1; ☎ 2224-9310, 3510-4594; hiplaza@acn2.net; 10 Rue Capois; s/d from US$97/108; P ✜ 🖢) The unobtrusive main entrance opposite Champs de Mars (you'll walk past it twice) hides the fact that this is downtown's largest and most high-class hotel. The hotel was originally the Holiday Inn, and some people still refer to it thus. Rooms have balconies facing inward to a central quadrangle and, while well fitted out with all mod-cons, are best described as business-class bland. A good-quality (if not very exciting) choice.

Pétionville

BUDGET

Kalewes Guest House (Map p294; ☎ 2257-0817; 99 Rue Grégoire; r US$40; 🖢) This gingerbread in lush grounds is a short walk uphill from Place Saint-Pierre on the main (and busy) road to Kenscoff. Rooms are pretty basic, although not lacking for space. There are some nice verandas around the garden and pool, and colorful murals provide a bright contrast to the dark antique furniture in the communal areas.

Belle Etoile Hôtel (Map p294; ☎ 2256-1006; Rue C Perraulte; s/d US$40/43) Some of Pétionville's budget hotels tread an uneasy line between cheap and cheerful and overflowing with prostitutes. The Belle Etoile manages just fine – threatening to be grimy from the outside, but actually hosting bright and clean rooms that have been recently kitted out, with friendly staff.

Doux Sejour Guest House (Map p294; ☎ 2257-1533, 2257-1560; www.douxsejourhaiti.com; 32 Rue Magny; s/d from

US$40/50; ✜ 🖳) A fun little guesthouse painted lobster pink, the Doux Sejour has a series of airy rooms interestingly laid out (ascending the balcony terrace feels like climbing into the trees). Staff are helpful, and the attached restaurant (Le Bistro; mains US$8 to US10) serves tasty, filling meals.

MIDRANGE

Hotel Kinam (Map p294; ☎ 2257-0462, 2257-6525; www .hotelkinam.com; Place Saint-Pierre; s/d from US$76/112, ste from US$120; P ✜ 🖳 🖢) A large gingerbread hotel right in the center of Pétionville, the Kinam is something of a winner. Rooms are well sized and modern, while the hotel as a whole offers quality that goes beyond its price tag. The whole effect is charming, particularly of an evening when the pool is lit up and guests congregate for the renowned rum punches.

Ibo Lele (Map p294; ☎ 2257-8500, 2257-8509; Rte Ibo Lele; s/d US$78/97; P ✜ 🖢) The Ibo Lele was a big player in the 1960s tourist years, but today it feels a bit lifeless. Rooms still maintain some quality, and the huge pool can be a draw for nonguests to use. There are stunning views as the hotel is perched high on the slopes above Pétionville proper.

TOP END

El Rancho (Map p294; ☎ 2256-9870, 2256-9873; www .hotelelrancho.com; Rte El Rancho; s/d from US$121/143, ste from US$174; P ✜ 🖳 🖢) Entering this hotel through its dramatic canopied lobby-walkway, you'd be forgiven for thinking you were part of a Golden Age Hollywood premiere. Interiors do their best to carry on the glitz, with marble floors, large luxurious rooms and not one but two swimming pools. The fitness center has saunas and offers massage, where you can shirk off your losses from the hotel casino. A couple of restaurants and bars seal the deal.

La Villa Creole (Map p294; ☎ 2257-1570, 2257-0965; www.villacreole.com; Rte El Rancho; s/d from US$132/165, ste from US$185; P ✜ 🖳 🖢) Measuring itself confidently against Port-au-Prince's other top hotels, the Villa Creole carries a slightly more relaxed air than its competitors. It's nicely laid out, with the open reception area flowing down to the exceedingly pleasant bar and pool area, beyond which are most of the rooms and an elegant restaurant. Rooms are medium to large, superbly appointed and comfortable, and the staff are well known for their service and attention to detail.

Hotel Montana (Map p294; ☎ 2229-4000, 3510-9495; www.htmontana.com; Imp Cardozo, Ave Pan Américaine; s/d from US$133/165, ste from US$330; P ⚡ ⬜ ☀) The Montana is the hotel of choice for Port-au-Prince's great and good, and carries off its air of international professionalism with some aplomb. It has all one could want for the price tag: two restaurants, several bars and coffee-shops, a business center and a gym. Rooms are excellent, and the hotel's commanding location means that its views over the city are justly famous.

EATING

There's a wide range of restaurants in Port-au-Prince, with the default menu being Creole with a smattering of French and American dishes. If you're downtown, you should also consider the hotel restaurants – many restaurants close on Sundays and lots of places only open in daytime hours during the week (lunch is the big meal of the day). For a wider range of eating options, head up the hill to Pétionville, Haiti's undisputed fine-dining capital.

Port-au-Prince
RESTAURANTS

Arc-en-Ciel (Map pp290-1; 24 Rue Capois; mains around US$5; ⏱ 9am-2am) This is a decent no-frills sort of a place, serving up healthily large portions of Creole standards. Along with platters of *griyo* (pork), plantain and the like, there's good jerked chicken and a dash of American fast food. Later in the evening, diners compete with dancers as the music and atmosphere crank up a pitch.

Chez Yvane (Map pp290-1; ☎ 3512-7182; 18 Blvd Harry Truman; mains US$5; ⏱ 8am-6pm) It looks like a bright American diner, but Creole is the order of the day here. It's good, too, going beyond *plat complet* (complete menu; consisting of rice and beans, salad, plantains and meat of your choice) for some interesting stews and soups. Also known locally as Chauffeur Gide.

La Pause (Map pp290-1; ☎ 2222-9382; 14 Rue des Miracles; mains US$5; ⏱ 8am-4pm Mon-Fri) La Pause is a successful minichain, with branches on Delmas 32 and in Pétionville. Swift service and good value is what's done – Creole, pastas and other international dishes fly over the counter to customers who'll no doubt be back for a return visit.

Citadelle Restaurant (Map pp290-1; 4 Rue St Cyr; mains US$7; ⏱ 9am-2pm) Down a road to the right of

Le Plaza Hotel, Citadelle is a lovely dilapidated red-and-white gingerbread. The food is all Haitian and can be eaten inside, on the veranda or in the courtyard. All very friendly and relaxed.

Hôtel Oloffson (Map pp290-1; ☎ 2223-4000; 60 Ave Christophe; snacks/mains from US$4/8; ⏱ 7am-11pm) A lazy lunch on the veranda of the Oloffson is one of central Port-au-Prince's more pleasurable dining experiences, and lit up at night its equally charming. A mixed international and Creole menu, dishes can sometimes be a bit hit and miss, although the salads and club sandwiches are always reliable. On Thursdays, stay to watch the owner's band RAM play from around midnight (see boxed text, p304).

Chez Rose (Map pp290-1; ☎ 2245-5286; cnr Rues 4 Pacot & Bellevue; mains from US$8; ⏱ 11am-9pm) The service and setting in this converted gingerbread are worth a detour. The menu is the expected mix of Creole and French dishes, nicely presented and with accompanying ambiance.

Tiffany's (Map pp290-1; ☎ 2222-3506; 12 Blvd Harry Truman; mains around US$11; ⏱ 9am-6pm Mon-Sat) This well-regarded restaurant in Bicentenaire has a cool, dark interior that attracts a slightly more well-heeled crowd, making this one of the few higher-end downtown restaurants to hold its own against the gravitational pull of the Pétionville dining scene. The French-influenced menu and good wine list are equally attractive draws here.

QUICK EATS

There are plenty of quick and informal cheap eats to be had in Port-au-Prince, with food stalls around Champs de Mars in the evening, and bar-restos extending down Rue Capois. Street corners and transport junctions attract plenty of women selling *fritay* (fried snack food).

Épi d'Or (Map pp290-1; ☎ 2246-8560; Rte de Delmas, Delmas 56; sandwiches around US$2.50; ⏱ 6am-9pm) This Haitian take on the Subway-style sandwich outlet was taking Port-au-Prince by storm when we visited. As well as fantastic sandwiches, it also serves crepes, pizza and 'MacEpi' burgers, and there's an inhouse patisserie, all in bright surroundings and with cool air-con. Pay first, then present your ticket to complete the order. Be prepared for lengthy lunchtime queues.

Café Terrasse (Map pp290-1; ☎ 2222-5648; 11 Rue Capois; lunches around US$4-9; ⏱ 10am-4pm Mon-Fri)

Enter this café on Rue Ducoste to the side of Le Plaza hotel. For such a small place it has a broad international menu, and there is a couple of dining options – in the upstairs salon or on the terrace café, designed for quick refueling. Good salads and crepes.

GROCERIES

Big Star Market (Map pp290-1; Rue Capois) Next to the Rex Theatre, this is the most central supermarket for downtown hotels, with several other options along Lalue.

Caribbean Supermarket (Map pp290-1; Delmas 95) The country's largest supermarket, with a huge selection of imported goods.

Marché de Fer (Iron Market; Map pp290-1; cnr Grand Rue & Rue des Fronts Forts; ⊙ daily) Shopping for fresh produce at this market (p296) is always an adventure.

Pétionville

RESTAURANTS

Anba Tonel (Map p294; ☎ 2257-7560; cnr Rues Clerveaux & Vilatte; ⊙ 5-11pm, closed Mon-Wed) Most people hit Pétionville's restaurants for an alternative to Creole cuisine, but Anba Tonel may be the place to change minds. *Kibby* (fried stuffed meatballs) is the highlight here, along with the winning (and unlikely) *lambi* (conch) kebabs. It's all served amid wonderfully kitsch decor, quite unmissable.

Harry's (Map p294; ☎ 2257-1885; 97 Ave Pan Américaine; mains around US$5; ⊙ 10am-4am) A popular extended bar-resto, Harry's is one for the nightbirds. Pizzas are the thing, but there are sandwiches and a smattering of Creole dishes, too. It's unconventionally cool, and when you've eaten, grab a beer and challenge the locals to a game of pool on one of the tables.

Quartier Latin (Map p294; ☎ 3455-3325; 10 Place Boyer; mains US$5-22; ⊙ 10:30am-11pm) A newer restaurant that's proving itself popular, Quartier Latin throws French, Italian and Spanish dishes into the mix, and serves up generous and tasty dishes as a result. There are a few tables outside around a tiny pool, and a generally relaxed ambiance – further exhibited by the encouragement of its diners to write reviews and other messages on the walls at the entrance.

Le Coin des Artistes (Map p294; ☎ 2257-2400; Ave Pan Américaine; fish US$6-15; ⊙ noon-10pm, closed Sun) Come here if you're after seafood. It's an informal sort of an affair, with an open-air grill in its terraced garden. The catch of the day is cooked over coals and served with Creole accompaniments, tasty and highly enjoyable with a cold one from the bar.

Magdoos (Map p294; ☎ 3552-4040; 30 Rue Oğe; mains around US$9; ⊙ 11am-11pm) The best place in Pétionville for Lebanese food, Magdoos also doubles as one of the places to be seen: check out the young, beautiful and rich here every Friday night. While you're at it, enjoy the spread of Middle Eastern mezze, kebabs, and the Arabic music on Friday and Saturday evenings.

Fior di Latte (Map p294; ☎ 2256-8474; Choucoune Plaza; salads from US$5, mains US$9-17; ⊙ 11am-10pm, closed Mon) Fior di Latte is not particularly well signed (it's next to the American Airlines office). This restaurant's vine-covered canopy is a lovely place to take an extended lunch break. The menu is Italian, with great plates of pasta and pizza, and some really tasty quiches thrown in, too. Finishing a meal with a bowl of homemade ice cream is a must.

Presse Café (Map p294; ☎ 2257-9474; 28 Rue Rigaud; light bites US$3-7, buffet US$10, mains US$10-13; ⊙ 7:30am-midnight Tue-Sat, to 7pm Mon, closed Sun) We like Presse Café for its casual bistro air. Decorated with old newspapers and photos of jazz heroes, it's a great place for a relaxed snack and drink, and even better for its lunchtime buffet. On Thursday and Friday evenings there's usually live music.

Papaye (Map p294; ☎ 3513-9229; 48 Rue Métellus; mains around US$18-28; ⊙ noon-2:30pm & 7-11pm, closed Sun-Mon) 'Caribbean fusion' aren't words you expect to see written in a Haitian restaurant review, but Papaye carries off the idea with considerable aplomb, taking Creole dishes and jamming them up against Asian, European and other culinary influences. Somehow it works, and is worth repeated investigation.

La Souvenance (Map p294; ☎ 2257-7688; 42 Rue Geffrard; mains from US$20; ⊙ 6:30-11pm, closed Sun-Mon) For years La Souvenance has been regarded as one of Haiti's best restaurants. It's certainly its poshest. The menu is extensively French high dining, and the service impeccable.

Chez Gerard (Map p294; ☎ 2257-1949; 17 Rue Pinchinat; mains around US$25; ⊙ noon-3pm & 7:30-10:30pm, closed Sun-Mon) One of the places you dress up for, Chez Gerard is in a verdant covered garden hidden behind grand wooden doors. There are liveried waiters and dripping candles galore, and a Cordon Bleu menu of the highest order. If you want France in Haiti, look no further.

QUICK EATS

Épi d'Or (Map p294; ☎ 2257-5343; 51 Rue Rigaud; sandwiches around US$2.50; ☷ 6am-9pm) This new branch of the popular Haitian franchise serves up more of its successful mix of sandwiches, burgers, crepes and pastries to the Pétionville crowd.

Mun Cheez (Map p294; ☎ 2256-2177; 2 Rue Rebecca; burgers/pizza from US$2.50/6; ☷ 11am-11pm Mon-Sat, 2-10pm Sun) A long-established and popular 1st-floor fast-food joint with good food, overlooking the junction with Ave Pan Américaine. It's a cheery spot; you can sit with a beer and burger and watch the world go by.

Boca Mocha (Map p294; ☎ 3656 7369; Rue Chavannes; sandwiches around US$5; ☷ 8am-4pm Mon-Fri, to 2pm Sat; 🖳) Expats call Boca Mocha the Haitian Starbucks, but it's nicer than the epithet suggests. Coffee is the order of the day – we fell for the white-chocolate mochaccinos – but there are some refreshing smoothies and a suitably fortifying selection of sandwiches and cakes. There's wi-fi, the art on the wall is for sale and the air-con is positively arctic.

GROCERIES

There are plenty of supermarkets in Pétionville, including a couple of branches of Big Star, one on Place Saint-Pierre. The side streets of the main square usually attract plenty of fruit and vegetable sellers, while **Épi d'Or** (Map p294; ☎ 2257-5343; 51 Rue Rigaud; ☷ 6am-9pm) has the best bread and pastries in town.

ENTERTAINMENT
Music

You don't have to go far to hear music in Port-au-Prince: many taptaps have their own mega soundsystems blasting tunes out to the world. If you want something a little more organized, look out for the billboards posted on major junctions advertising forthcoming concerts. Cover charges cost about US$7 to US$20 for really big names. As well as venues in Port-au-Prince (most bands play in Pétionville), large concerts and music festivals are regularly held at Canne á Sucre (p312) just outside the city. **Kiprogram** (www.kiprogram) also lists upcoming gigs and festivals.

Several bands play regular concerts that are worth checking out. Foremost of these is RAM at the **Hôtel Oloffson** (Map pp290-1; ☎ 2223-4000; 60 Ave Christophe) every Thursday from midnight (see the boxed text, p304). Also worth checking out are the troubadour band Macaya at **La Villa Creole** (Map p294; ☎ 2257-1570, 2257-0965; www.villacreole

.com; Rte El Rancho) and the *compas* (traditional music) outfits Jukann and Mamina most Friday and Saturday nights at **Presse Café** (Map p294; ☎ 2257-9474; 28 Rue Rigaud; ☷ 7:30am-midnight Tue-Sat, to 7pm Mon, closed Sun). There's no admission fee for these shows.

Bear in mind that if you're out dancing all hours, taxis can be extremely hard to find late at night.

Xtreme (Map p294; ☎ 2257-0841; 64 Rue Grégoire, Pétionville) Home most Saturdays to the fantastic Orchestre Super Choucoune, a big-band orchestra whose blend of *compas*, merengue, Cuban *son* and troubadour styles is tailor-made to get you dancing.

Djumbala (off Map p294; ☎ 2257-4368; cnr Ave Boisand Canal & Rue Frères, Pétionville) A large and always popular open-air club, leaning heavily on *compas*, with regular live bands.

Institut Français (Map pp290-1; ☎ 2244-0014/0015; www.ifhaiti.org; 99 Ave Lamertinière, Port-au-Prince) Holds regular concerts of classical, folkloric and modern Haitian music.

El Rancho (Map p294; ☎ 2256-9870; Rte El Rancho, Pétionville; ☷ from 9pm Friday) The El Rancho hosts one of Pétionville's more popular dance clubs – if you want tips on how to dance to *compas* or are ready to rumba, head here.

Less formal are the plentiful bar-restos that often feature live music on the weekend. Rue Capois off Champs de Mars has several decent places – head for **Arc-en-Ciel** (Map pp290-1; 24 Rue Capois, Port-au-Prince; ☷ 9am-2am), or just follow your ears.

Cinema

Because of the popularity of pirate DVDs, there are only a couple of cinemas, typically costing US$2 a seat and showing a mix of Hollywood and Haitian Creole movies:

Ciné Capitol (☎ 2221-3820; Rue Lamarre, Petionville)

Rex Theatre (Map pp290-1; ☎ 2222-1848; 41 Rue Capois, Champs de Mars)

Sports

Soccer matches are regularly played at **Sylvio Cator Stadium** (Map pp290-1; cnr Rue Oswald Durand & Ave Mgr Guilloux; admission US$1.50). It hosts international matches as well as being the home ground for Port-au-Prince's two main clubs, Racing Club Hätien and Violette Athletic. The atmosphere can be frenzied, with lots of music, drumming and Prestige beer.

Port-au-Prince has several *gaguères* (cockfighting arenas). They're low-key and often

RAM – THE BEST HOUSE BAND IN THE CARIBBEAN?

Every Thursday night between 11pm and midnight, crowds gather at the Hôtel Oloffson (p299) to dance until the small hours to the Vodou rock 'n' roots music of RAM. A potent blend of African rhythms, *rara* horns, guitar and keyboards, the shows have an irresistible atmosphere. At the center of everything is band leader (and Oloffson owner) Richard A Morse. We caught up with him after a show.

How would you describe RAM's music?

When Haiti became independent back in 1803–04, half the population had been born in Africa. Because it was a slave revolt, the surrounding countries ostracized Haiti to try to keep the revolution from spreading. That isolation kept Haiti's roots intact. We take those African roots as a starting point to our music, hence the word *racines* or 'roots.'

How long have you been playing?

I thought about the RAM project as early as 1983–84. I was still in my [New York] punk band. A French producer heard some tropical influences in our music, found out my mother was from Haiti and told me to get down here. It took me five years, plus taking over the Oloffson, before forming RAM in 1990.

RAM's music often has a strong political element, and you've had some run-ins with the authorities in the past...

When you write love songs, people want to get involved in your personal life. In the long run giving someone a positive message is probably the way to go. I've been grabbed by authorities, and some band members were once arrested during a show. If I get into more detail, perhaps we'll lose our 'tourist' audience!

But you still had the most popular merengue of the 2008 Carnival?

We were champions of Carnival. Corporate sponsorship, government recognition...I don't know what my friends back home would say!

Do you really play every single Thursday at the Oloffson?

If we're on tour, we might miss a Thursday or so and we often take the month of October off before starting up again in November. But the party here on Thursdays is always new and fresh. People join in, people dance, some are off in the corners making deals or exchanging stories. It's quite a phenomenon. Sometimes I can't believe I'm in the middle of it. When I read Quincy Jones' description of a 'juke joint,' I thought, 'I live in a juke joint!'

We heard you bought the Oloffson in a slightly unorthodox manner.

I was coming back from a friend's house one Saturday morning with a *houngan* [male Vodou priest] I had met. He asked me, 'Do you want the hotel?' to which I replied 'No.' Once again he asked me, 'Do you want the hotel?' and once again I said 'No.' His eyes were getting wider and he was getting more excited as he said, 'Say yes! Say yes! Do you want the hotel???' To which I resigned myself and said, 'OK, I want the hotel' and he snapped back, 'GIVE ME TWENTY DOLLARS!...'

How would Thursday nights with RAM have played in the Hotel Trianon in Graham Greene's The Comedians?

Well, if the Trianon had had RAM, then perhaps he wouldn't have had to sell!

Finally, what other Haitian bands should we have on our iPods?

I'm old-school – I like Coupe Cloué, Tropicana, Gerard Dupervil, Jazz Des Jeunes. But you've also got to check out Tabou Combo and Boukman Eksperyans.

macho affairs, hosting bouts most days. If you want to see a fight, it's best to get a local to take you; entrance is usually about US$0.30.

SHOPPING

Port-au-Prince is Haiti's market place. For a full-on sensory shopping experience, head for the **Marché de Fer** (Iron Market; Map pp290-1; cnr Grand Rue & Rue des Fronts Forts; ⌣ daily), where you'll find everything from paintings and *artisanat* (handicrafts) to Vodou flags, and a heady slice of Haitian life. Have your bargaining wits about you. For more details, see p296. Alternatively, head for some of the more specialist options following.

Crafts

There are some good *artisanat* (craft) stalls outside **Sainte Trinité Episcopalian Cathedral** (Map pp290-1; cnr Ave Mgr Guilloux & Rue Pavée). The following places have fixed prices unless noted.

Comité Artisanat Haïtien (Map pp290-1; ☎ 2222-8440; 29 Rue 3, Pacot; ☿ closed Sun) Established in 1972, this craftmakers' cooperative has worked to promote Haitian crafts and provide fair wages for its artisans. The shop here is strong on well-priced metalwork, stone sculptures, lively painted boxes and miniature taptaps.

Musée d'Art Haïtien (Map pp290-1; 16 Rue Légitime, Port-au-Prince; ☿ closed Sun) This shop is part of the Saint-Pierre art college attached to the museum, and sells paintings and various *artisanat* produced by the students.

Mahogany Craft Shop (Map pp290-1; Rue Capois, Pacot) Near the gates of Hôtel Oloffson is this tiny, brightly painted shop, packed with jolly woodcarvings, paintings and painted metalwork. Prices are set by haggling.

Fred Bernard (Map p294; ☎ 2256-2282; Choucoune Plaza, Pétionville; ☿ closed Sun) A more upmarket Pétionville interpretation of an *artisanat* shop, here you'll find painted boxes and papier mâché, metalwork and other delights, along with current Haitian fashions.

Art

Impromptu open-air art galleries can be found throughout Port-au-Prince, with canvases hung on fences and walls, all quickly executed copies of the Haitian masters. Large congregations are found downtown near the main post office on Rue Bonne Foi, and along the wall of the Hotel Kinam in Pétionville. Prices should never really top US$15.

If you're after something more specific. try the following galleries, all but one in Pétionville (and the district has plenty more to discover). Staff are knowledgeable and will be able to give more information about specific artists and schools of painting. Prices range from reasonable to astronomical depending on the artist. Galleries tend to close on Saturday afternoons and Sundays, but have regular exhibitions and openings that are worth attending if you can. In central Port-au-Prince, the Centre d'Art (p296) is worth a detour for anyone interesting in shopping for canvases.

Galerie Issa (Map pp290-1; ☎ 2222-3287; 17 Rue du Chili, Pacot) Set up by the late Issa el Saieh, one of Haiti's most important art collectors (and sometime jazz musician). The gallery, with everything piled up in one huge room, has a wide collection of artwork on sale, plus some of the best metal art from Croix des Bouquets.

Galerie Caraïbe (Map p294; ☎ 2256-2659; 56 Rue Geffrard, Pétionville) Set in a courtyard with a restaurant, this gallery has a small and specialized collection of contemporary works.

Galerie Flamboyant (Map p294; ☎ 3555-9398; 9 Rue Darguin, Pétionville) A small gallery with a nice mix of naives and moderns.

Galerie Marassa (Map p294; ☎ 2257-5424; galerie marassa@hotmail.com; 17 Rue Lamarre, Pétionville) This is a quite specialized and exclusive gallery exhibiting a good base of contemporary and naive Haitian artists, as well as metalwork, crafts and Vodou flags.

Galerie Monnin (Map p294; ☎ 2257-4430; galerie monnin@hotmail.com; 23 Rue Lamarre, Pétionville) Port-au-Prince's oldest private art gallery, in a lovely building. Lots of landscapes, but with a wide selection of different Haitian schools.

Galerie Nader (Map p294; ☎ 2257-5602; galerienader@ hotmail.com; 50 Rue Grégoire, Pétionville) A huge gallery over two floors, with a large collection of mostly moderns and some naives. The owner has an extensive private collection housed as a museum at a separate address.

Expressions (Map p294; ☎ 2256-3471; 55 Rue Métellus, Pétionville) A well-regarded Pétionville gallery.

Music

Along with the shops listed here (which also sell concert tickets), there are plenty of street stalls in the markets selling pirated CDs of some of Haiti's more popular musicians.

La Boite à Musique (Map pp290-1; 11 Rue Pavée, Port-au-Prince) Close to the intersection with Rue Montalais, La Boite à Musique is a good downtown music choice.

Le Mélodisque (Map p294; cnr Rues Rigaud & Faubert, Pétionville) Has the best selection of Haitian music CDs in Pétionville.

GETTING THERE & AWAY
Air

International flights depart from **Aéroport International Toussaint Louverture** (off Map pp290-1; ☎ 2250-1120) and domestic flights from **Aérogare Guy Malary** (off Map pp290-1; ☎ 2250-1127), next to each other on the northern outskirts of Port-au-Prince.

The following airlines have offices in Port-au-Prince:

Air Canada (☎ 2250-0441, 2250-0442; www.aircanada .ca; Aéroport International Toussaint Louverture)

Air France (Map pp290-1; ☎ 222-1078, 222-4262; www
.airfrance.com; 11 Rue Capois, Champs de Mars)
American Airlines (Map p294; ☎ 2246-0100, 3510-
7010; www.aa.com; Choucoune Plaza, Pétionville)
Caribintair (☎ 2250-2031, 2250-2032; caribintair@
accesshaiti.com; Aérogare Guy Malary)
Tortug Air (☎ 2250-2555, 2250-2556; tortugair@
yahoo.com; Aérogare Guy Malary)
Tropical Airways (Map p294; ☎ 2256-3626, 2256-
3627; Ave Pan Américaine, Pétionville)

Bus & Taptap

Port-au-Prince has no central bus station;
instead there is a series of mildly anarchic
departure points according to the destination.
Timetables are generally absent, with buses
and taptaps leaving when full – exceptions
are for Cap-Haïtien and Jérémie, which you
can buy seats for in advance.

For destinations in the south and southwest, go to Estation Port au Léogâne, Les
Cayes and Jacmel (its name depends on your
destination; Map pp290–1), at the junction of
Rue Oswald Durand and Blvd Jean-Jacques
Dessalines (Grand Rue). Here you'll find
buses and taptaps to Jacmel (US$2.70, three
hours), Les Cayes (US$8, four hours), Petit-
Goâve (US$4, two hours) and all points in
between. For Jérémie (US$14, 11 hours) there
are several bus offices on Grand Rue near
the Ciné Lido. Buses usually depart between
5am and 7am.

For Cap-Haïtien (US$12, seven hours) go to
Estation O'Cap (Map pp290–1), at the corner
of Grand Rue and Blvd La Saline. Transport to
Gonaives (US$6, three hours) and the Côte des
Arcadins also leaves from here (see p315).

To make your way to Croix des Bouquets
(US$1, 30 minutes), there are taptaps that de-
part from Carrefour Trois Mains near the airport. If you're heading to Kenscoff (US$0.30,
30 minutes) and the mountains above Port-
au-Prince, taptaps leave from Place Saint-
Pierre in Pétionville.

Three companies offer direct services to
Santo Domingo in the DR: **Caribe Tours** (Map
p294; ☎ 2257-9379; cnr Rues Clerveaux & Gabart, Pétionville),
Terra Bus (Map p294; ☎ 2257-2153; Ave Pan Américaine,
Pétionville) and **Capital Coach Line** (off Map pp290-1;
☎ 3512-5989; www.capitalcoachline.com; Rte de Tabarre),
departing from the northern Tabarre district.
All have daily departures at around 8am, arriving in Santo Domingo nine hours later,
with tickets costing around US$40. For more
on crossing into the DR, see p352.

Car

Many of the car-rental companies are based
along Blvd Toussaint Louverture near the
airport. Among the more reliable:
Budget (off Map pp290-1; ☎ 2250-0554; www.budget
haiti.com; Blvd Toussaint Louverture)
Hertz (off Map pp290-1; ☎ 2250-0700; hertz@dynamic
-haiti.com; Blvd Toussaint Louverture)
Secom (Map p294; ☎ 2257-1913; www.secomhaiti.com;
Delmas 68, Rte de Delmas)

GETTING AROUND
To/From the Airport

From the northern edge of Port-au-Prince,
it takes around 30 to 45 minutes to reach the
airport from the city center depending on the
time of day. Badged and cream-shirted taxi
drivers from the **Association des Chauffeurs Guides**

VODOU FLAGS

Brightly sparkling Vodou flags are one of Haiti's more unusual and eye-catching art creations.
Used during Vodou ceremonies, the flags (drapo) are magnificent affairs, made of thousands
of sequins sewn onto sacking, catching the light from every angle. Each flag is dedicated to a
particular lwa (Vodou spirit), often depicted through its Catholic saint counterpart or with its
personal vévé (sacred symbol).

Flags are highly collectable, and many of the most celebrated artists' flags are sold in Pétionville's
art galleries. But it's fun to go direct to the artists themselves, who mostly live in the Bel Air
district just north of Notre Dame Catholic Cathedral. A guide is recommended, as many of the
workshops are down narrow alleys and impossible to find alone (the Hôtel Oloffson, which also
sometimes sells flags, is a good place to ask). Artists to look out for are Edgar Jean Louis, an
urbane Vodou priest and coffin-maker, on Rue des Césars; Silva Joseph, also a Vodou priest, at
the top of Rue Houille; and Yves Telemacque, on Rue Tiremasse.

There are also a couple of good flag artists in Nazon, such as Ronald Gouin, off Rue Christ Roi,
and Georges Valris, in the same area.

ART ON WHEELS

Haitian art isn't just found on the walls of galleries – it weaves through the streets picking up passengers. Painted taptaps (local buses or minibuses) are one of Port-au-Prince's delights. While some owners are content to just paint their routes on the doors, others really go the distance by adding extra bumpers and mirrors and repainting the whole vehicle until it looks like a fairground ride. Slogans and Biblical verses typically decorate the windshield, while the rear serves as a canvas for paintings both sacred and profane: in five minutes between downtown and Carrefour we spotted the Nativity, Daniel in the lion's den, two Ché Guevaras, Tupac Shakur and a Ronaldinho!

---

d'Haïti (ACGH; ☎ 2222-1330, 3402-7706) will approach you in the arrival hall. The fare should be fixed at US$20, but make sure this is clear before getting in the vehicle.

It's possible to take a taptap to or from the airport (US$0.15); they wait outside the terminal and drop passengers off at the corner of Blvd Toussaint Louverture and Rte de Delmas (Delmas 13), from where it's possible to get a shared taxi into town.

Taptap

Port-au-Prince's taptaps run along set routes and are a very cheap and convenient way of getting around. The usual fare is five gourdes (US$0.15) per trip. Routes are painted on the side of the cab doors, sometimes abbreviated (eg 'PV' for Pétionville). They all stop on request if they have space for more passengers – standing on the edge of the sidewalk with a wave of the hand or a loud 'psst!' usually does the trick. Shouting 'Merci chauffeur!' or

banging on the side of the vehicle will stop the driver, whom you pay as you alight.

Particularly useful routes include Ave John Brown (Lalue) to Pétionville, Rte de Delmas to Pétionville and Canapé Vert to Pétionville. Routes running north–south include Aéroport to Nazon (crossing Delmas and Lalue), and Saline to Martissant (running along Grand Rue).

Taxi

Collective taxis called *publiques* ply Port-au-Prince's streets. Invariably beaten-up saloon cars, they're recognizable from the red ribbon hanging from the front mirror and a license plate starting with T (for transport). Hail one as you would a taptap, and squeeze in with the other passengers. Fares are set at 25 gourdes (US$0.75). Like taptaps, *publiques* stick to set routes, so if your destination doesn't suit the driver will refuse you, otherwise beckoning you in with what looks like a dismissive tilt of the head. If you get into an empty *publique* and the driver removes the red ribbon, he's treating you as a private fare and will charge accordingly – up to US$20 if you're going a long way. State clearly if you want to ride *collectif* and share the ride with others.

Publiques don't tend to travel between Port-au-Prince and Pétionville, so hiring is often the best option. There are a couple of radio-taxi firms, especially useful if you're out late: **Nick's Taxis** (Map p294; ☎ 2257-777) and **Taxi Rouge** (☎ 3528-1112). Both charge around US$10 between downtown and Pétionville, or US$15 per hour.

Both Port-au-Prince and Pétionville have moto-taxis, if you're up for weaving through the insane traffic. They cost around 30 gourdes (US$0.80) for short trips, with prices hiking steeply for long distances. The best place to find a moto-taxi is around a bus or taptap station.

Around Port-au-Prince

For all its buzz, Port-au-Prince can sometimes be a tiring place to stay. When city life gets too much, it's time to get out of the urban sprawl and recharge your batteries. Whether you want to laze on a beach, hike in pine-clad mountains or buy a piece of art, all options are within easy striking distance of the capital.

As the suburb of Pétionville peters out above the city, the Route de Kenscoff sweeps you up through increasingly dramatic mountain scenery toward the Massif de la Selle. The small town of Fermathe holds a couple of old forts built to safeguard Haiti's precarious independence, with commanding views out to sea. Beyond here, the air cools and the area becomes forested with pines, culminating in Parc National la Visite. This offers some of the best hiking in Haiti – you can even walk halfway to Jacmel from here if you've strong legs.

Down on the flat, the Plaine du Cul-de-Sac east of Port-au-Prince hosts the metal artists of Croix des Bouquets, who turn out beautiful sculptures from scrap iron. The Plaine is also important historically and culturally. A restored sugar plantation gives an insight into the past, while the Barbancourt Rhum Distillery offers a different taste of where the sugar goes. Those of a more spiritual bent may be drawn to Ville-Bonheur, where every summer the Saut d'Eau Vodou pilgrimage draws devotees from across the country. There's bird-spotting (and crocodiles, too) at Lac Azueï nearby. But if that's too much to choose from and you can't decide, take yourself to the Côte des Arcadins, where you'll find plenty of sand and sun lounges at the beach resorts – the only decision you'll need to make there is whether to have that second rum punch before dinner.

HIGHLIGHTS

- Shop for the intricate beaten metalwork from the craftsmen of **Croix des Bouquets** (p311)

- Take in the breathtaking views from Fermathe's **Fort Jacques** (opposite) over Port-au-Prince to the sea

- Hike through the mountain woods and rock formations of **Parc National la Visite** (p310)

- Follow the faithful to the water on the annual Vodou pilgrimage to **Saut d'Eau** (p313), outside Ville-Bonheur

- Catch some rays while lazing on the beaches of the **Côte des Arcadins** (p314)

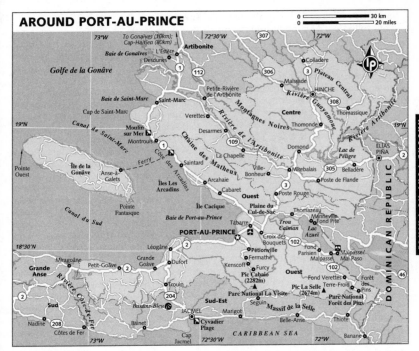

AROUND PORT-AU-PRINCE

SOUTH OF PORT-AU-PRINCE

ROUTE DE KENSCOFF

The main road from Pétionville's Place St Pierre winds steeply uphill toward the cool of the mountains. After just a few kilometers you're in a rich agricultural area, with steep terraced fields clinging to the sides of the mountains, and the fug of the city replaced by sweet cool breezes.

GETTING THERE & AWAY

Taptaps (local buses or minibuses) leave throughout the day from Pétionville's Place St Pierre to Kenscoff, departing when full (US$0.30, 30 minutes), and pass through Fermathe. Change at Kenscoff for Furcy.

Fermathe

The small town of Fermathe is 13km above Pétionville. The main attraction is **Fort Jacques** (admission US$0.70; ☼ sunrise-sunset), erected during the burst of fort-building following

independence in 1804. Well preserved, it was built by Alexandre Pétion and named after Jean-Jacques Dessalines. **Fort Alexandre**, a short walk away but ruined, was named by Pétion after himself. Both protected the Massif de la Selle overlooking Port-au-Prince, and now offer very grand views. The fort is usually locked – a guardian will open it on payment, though he won't help with the kids who try to attach themselves to you as guides. The fort is a 3km walk from the main road – take the sharp uphill road opposite Fermathe's covered market.

Fermathe also has the **Mountain Maid Gift Shop & restaurant** (☼ 8.30am-5pm, closed Sun) located near the entrance to the town. Run as part of the Baptist Mission, it sells crafts and produce from local cooperatives and self-help groups – everything from greeting cards and carvings to jams and cakes (the granola cookies here are famous). The restaurant is more a burger bar–cafeteria joint, but it has good sandwiches and great views. Next door is an interesting **museum** (donation requested; ☼ 8.30am-5pm, closed Sun), with a large and well-labeled array of artifacts from Haitian history, and a small ethnographic collection. Free English tours are worth taking.

A few doors up from the Mountain Maid shop, **Wings of Hope** (☎ 3449-9942; sjfamilyhaiti@hotmail.com; Fermathe; per person half-board US$35) is part of the same organization as St Joseph's Home for Boys (p299) in Port-au-Prince. With the same deal and appeal as its partner, it has the advantage of a much more spectacular setting perched above a terraced valley. With three six-bed dorms and one double room, all with private bathroom and balcony to soak up the stunning views, it's an ideal getaway from the city chaos.

Kenscoff

The cool of Kenscoff makes it a popular weekend destination for city dwellers – at 1980m above sea level, it's often referred to as the Switzerland of the Caribbean (there are even a few weird Caribbean-Alpine architectural hybrids). With sweeping views everywhere you look and the brooding cloud-capped backdrop of Massif de la Selle behind you, it's tailor-made for day walks or horseback riding (see Ranch Le Montcel, below). A highly productive area, coffee and vegetables are grown in great quantities here, giving Kenscoff an interesting local market.

Le Florville (☎ 3512-3535; 19 Rte de Kenscoff, Kenscoff; s/d US$40/60; P) is a popular hotel and restaurant on the left as you drive up from Pétionville. There is only a couple of rooms, tidily appointed, but some virtually open out onto the restaurant. Eating here is actually the big draw, with the restaurant's high wooden ceiling and well-set tables serving a mix of French and Creole dishes (mains US$12 to US$22). The baby ribs are a particular hit. The outside terrace offers fine views, and at weekends live music frequently livens things up further with the crowds from the city.

Set 9km above Kenscoff, **Ranch Le Montcel** (☎ 3510-4777; www.montcelhaiti.com; Belot-Kenscoff; tent US$45, s/d/tr US$60/110/150; P ⌘ ▭ ⌕) bills itself at Haiti's only ecotourist hotel. Around 90% of its electricity is generated by wind or solar power, food is locally grown, and recycling and water conservation is encouraged. The ranch is spread over several acres, with delightful Swiss chalets giving tremendous views to sea, and a host of activities, including horseback riding, tennis and wild camping, in the nearby plantations and mountains.

Furcy

To continue to the smaller and even more picturesque village of Furcy, turn left at Kenscoff Commissariat, then right after the fast-food places and continue uphill. Locals will rent out horses here (per hour around US$3), making it easy to reach the Bassins Bleu waterfall, 1½ hours above the village by foot. Continuing on from Furcy, you reach the entrance to Parc National la Visite, from where you can hike over the mountains to Seguin (below).

Whatever your plans, don't forget some warm clothes – temperatures drop once the sun starts to dip.

A Canadian-style stone-and-wood cottage seems incongruous in Haiti, but the **Lodge** (☎ 3510-9870; www.thelodgeinhaiti.com; Furcy; s/d/tr ind breakfast US$45/75/90; P ⌘ ▭), set amid the trees, has been finished with a keen eye for details. As well as standard rooms, there are a couple of apartments, some with saunas. The menu (mains from US$15) makes a big thing of imported dishes like Alaskan king crab, but while the food is excellent, the welcome from staff and management often tends to discourage repeat visits.

PARC NATIONAL LA VISITE

The Massif de la Selle divides Haiti's southeast, a series of spectacular ridges still dotted with pine forest. You can do one of Haiti's best hikes here, a day of trekking that takes you across the western section of the mountains toward the Caribbean. The route traverses four mountains and takes in some truly beautiful terrain, from wooded slopes to almost rolling green hills, as well as lovely views out to sea. Once you reach Seguin you'll find the weird *kraze dan* (broken teeth) rock formations, great slabs of karst jutting up from the ground like so many discarded giant dentures.

A decent degree of fitness is required to do the trek, which usually takes six to eight hours. Take plenty of water and some food, as well as suitable clothing: the altitude ascends above 2000m in places, so there can be strong sun and wind as well as unexpected rain and chill. You won't be always be alone on the trek, however; although this is rugged terrain, the route is also a well-used pedestrian highway, traveled primarily by women on their way to market balancing their produce on their heads. The sight of foreigners walking for fun always seems to raise a friendly smile.

To reach the trailhead, take a taptap from Pétionville to Kenscoff, from where you change for Furcy. From there, you can walk to Carrefour Badyo, then bear left to follow the track to Seguin. By 4WD, you can drive 15 minutes to Badyo, from where you must start hiking. Once at Seguin, you descend to Marigot (a further couple of hours), from where it is a taptap ride to Jacmel (US$1, one hour). At Furcy it's possible to hire horses with guides, but you'll have to pay for the return trip from Seguin.

In Seguin, the **Auberge de la Visite** (☎ 2246-0166, 257-1579; tiroyd@yahoo.com; r full board US$50) is a delightful place to rest up after the trek. There are two low stone buildings with cozy rooms and porches, where you can sit in a rocking chair and enjoy views to the Caribbean. The owner is Haitian-Lebanese, a fact further reflected in the food served. The auberge can also arrange guides and horses for further exploration of the area.

EAST & NORTH OF PORT-AU-PRINCE

PLAINE DU CUL-DE-SAC

The fertile Plaine du Cul-de-Sac runs east from Port-au-Prince toward the Dominican Republic. Once the heart of the colonial plantation system, it's of interest to visitors for its metalworking community in Croix des Bouquet, its bird-watching sites at Trou Caïman, and the brackish waters of Lac Azueï, which straddles the border. To the northwest, the road leads into Haiti's central district, where every year the village of Saut d'Eau becomes the focus of a major Vodou pilgrimage.

Croix des Bouquets

An important market town east of Port-au-Prince, Croix des Bouquets is the setting for both one of Haiti's largest livestock markets, and one of its most vibrant art scenes. Although threatening to be sucked in by the capital's inexorable urban sprawl, it has a proud identity of its own, with a strong tradition of Vodou secret societies, such as *zobób* and *bizango*. During the Haitian revolution, the victory of the slave and free black army in the Battle of Croix des Bouquets in March 1792 was the turning point that allowed the capture of Port-au-Prince.

Every Friday the town is filled with a cacophony of braying cattle, goats, pigs and horses accompanied by the cries of hawkers. The Noialles district is a bigger draw for visitors, home to the *boss fé* (ironworkers), who hammer out incredible decorative art from flattened oil drums and vehicle bodies. It's great fun to wander around and talk to the artisans, who are willing to demonstrate their skills.

SIGHTS

Croix des Bouquet's metal-art tradition was begun by the blacksmith George Liautaud, who made decorative crosses for his local cemetery. In the early 1950s he was encouraged by De Witt Peters, the founder of the Centre d'Art in Port-au-Prince (p296), to make freestanding figures and incorporate Vodou iconography into his work. The result was an explosion of creativity, with Liautaud and his apprentices creating a uniquely Haitian form of art: carved iron. Although Liautaud died in 1991, his legacy is the thriving community of artists in Croix des Bouquets that he originally inspired.

Steel drums are the most common material for the art. Cut in half and flattened, paper templates are laid down and the designs chalked onto the metal. Then begins the laborious task of cutting out with chisels. Once free, the edges are smoothed and relief work beaten out. The smallest pieces are the size of this guidebook; the most gloriously elaborate can stand over 2m. Popular designs include the Tree of Life, the Vodou *lwa* La Siren (the mermaid), birds, fish, musicians and angels.

It's worth spending time in Noailles wandering between **artists' workshops** to get an idea of what different artists are producing. One of the first workshops belongs to Serge Jolimeau, one of Liautaud's apprentices and the current master of the scene. His designs verge on art deco, and are frequently sold in American galleries. John Sylvestre is another imaginative artist, frequently drawing on Haitian folklore for inspiration. Many pieces depict particular *lwa* (Vodou spirits), so don't be afraid to ask about specific meanings.

There's a complete absence of hard sell from the artists, so take your time to browse. The smallest pieces can usually be picked up for US$3 to US$4, while the most expensive pieces from the most celebrated artists can stretch into the hundreds or even thousands.

GETTING THERE & AWAY

Taptaps from Port-au-Prince (US$1, 30 minutes) leave from Carrefour Trois Mains near the airport. Get out at the police post, where the road splits left to Hinche and right to the DR. Take the right-hand road, then turn right at Notre Dame Depot. For Noailles, turn right at the Seventh Day Adventist Church, then follow the sound of hammered metal – a 10-minute walk from the main highway. The main workshops are on Rte Noailles and Rte Remy. Transport to Port-au-Prince leaves from the police post.

Parc Historique de la Canne á Sucre

At the outbreak of the Haitian Revolution, the Plaine du Cul-de-Sac was one of the richest parts of Saint-Domingue. The building of irrigation canals and watermills had turned it into one of the largest industrial centers in the Western world, with a series of huge sugar plantations feeding Europe's sweet tooth, all on the back-breaking labor of tens of thousands of slaves.

The plantation system was largely destroyed in the turmoil that followed independence, and little visible remains of this period. One important sugar mill constructed at the end of the 19th century was built on the site of Chateaublond Plantation and now stands as a **museum** (☎ 2298-3226; Blvd 15 Octobre, Tabarre; admission U$7; ❧ 9am-1pm Mon-Fri, to 5pm Sat & Sun) to the period. Exhibits are mainly open air, surrounded by low colonial buildings that comprised factories and shops. In the grounds there is a collection of sugarcane presses, boilers and part of the aqueduct used to drive the mills. Sitting incongruously among such neatly clipped surroundings, there's also a train for the narrow-gauge railway laid to carry sugarcane to the factories.

The park is also a popular outdoor venue for music concerts.

Barbancourt Rhum Distillery

In such a rich sugar-producing area, it should be no surprise that Plaine de Cul-de-Sac is also home to Barbancourt, Haiti's most celebrated rum. Over 600 hectares of sugarcane from 200 local growers is used to produce the rum. After fermentation, the rum is aged in oak barrels from Limousin in France to give

it its distinctive flavor. The best Five Star rum sits patiently for 15 years before it's ready.

Group tours of the **Barbancourt Rhum Distillery** (☎ 2250-6335; www.barbancourt.net; Damien, Plaine du Cul-de-Sac) are available by prior arrangement. As well as seeing the process from cane cutting to bottling, there's also plenty of opportunity for tasting and buying, including some unusual blends hard to find elsewhere, like mango and coffee. The rum punches are, unsurprisingly, excellent.

Ville-Bonheur

An otherwise unprepossessing town, Ville-Bonheur becomes the focus of Haiti's largest Vodou pilgrimage every July 16. True to form, elements of Catholicism and Vodou have been blended to produce something uniquely Haitian (see boxed text, opposite).

During the pilgrimage the area around the Church of Our Lady of Mt Carmel is turned into a huge campsite for pilgrims. The few guesthouses are inundated. A decent option is the bright and clean **Hotel Villa Marie Robenson & Georges** (☎ 2245-2212; www.sautdeauinfo.com; Rue Clerveaux, Saut d'Eau; r US$40; ℗ ⌘ 🖳), in the town center. Alternatively, there is accommodation in nearby Mirebalais. The **Wozo Plaza Hôtel** (☎ 4455-07730; wozoplazahotel@yahoo.fr; Rte National 3, Mirebalais; s/d incl breakfast US$70/100; ℗ ⌘ 🖳 🍸) on the outskirts of town gets consistently good reviews for its service.

Buses and taptaps leave from Estacion Mirebalais in Port-au-Prince (US$2.50, 2½ hours) between Grand Rue and the cathedral, at the junction of Rue de Fronts Forts and Rue du Centre. Taptaps run throughout the day between Ville-Bonheur and Mirebalais (US$0.30, 45 minutes).

Trou Caïman

The best place to see waterbirds in Haiti is northeast of Croix des Bouquets, off the main road to the Plateau Central. Also known as Eau Gallée by locals, Trou Caïman is a large marshy lake surrounded by rice plantings and saltbush flats. The name literally means 'crocodile hole,' although the scaly inhabitants have long since been hunted out. The lake is home to a resident colony of at least 150 greater flamingos, seven species of heron, beautiful bronze-gold glossy ibis and uncommon ducks, such as white-cheeked pintails and fulvous whistling ducks. From September until April the area hosts many visiting shore-

SAUT D'EAU VODOU PILGRIMAGE

In 1847 a vision of the Virgin Mary appeared in a palm tree in Ville-Bonheur, and began to draw pilgrims who were convinced of its healing abilities. A church was built on the site, but local devotees soon linked it to the nearby waterfall of Saut d'Eau, which was sacred to Erzuli Dantor – the *lwa* (Vodou spirit) often represented as the Virgin. As a result, both Catholic and Vodou adherents now make the pilgrimage in huge numbers to spiritually cleanse themselves. A Catholic Mass is said in the church and a statue of the Virgin Mary is carried around town. The white of the Vodou adherents is augmented by the red and blue colors of Erzuli. People can be seen holding up photos of loved ones to be healed, or passports praying for US visas. Vodou pilgrims then trek the 4km to the Saut d'Eau waterfalls, a series of shallow pools overhung by greenery, where they bathe in the sacred waters, light candles and whisper requests to those adherents lucky enough to become possessed by Erzuli herself.

birds and the raptors that hunt them, such as the low-flying merlin falcon.

To get there from Port-au-Prince, drive to Croix des Bouquets and bear left at the main intersection by the police post. Continue toward the main church and turn left onto Rue Stenio Vincent, the start of Rte Nationale 3, to Mirebalais and Hinche. Continue several kilometers across the dry plains. Just before the road begins to climb up into the mountains, turn right on the dirt track to Thomazeau. This leads to the northern edge of the lake, where local villagers will eagerly offer to arrange a boat trip. Taptaps travel irregularly from Croix des Bouquets to Thomazeau.

Lac Azueï

Also called Étang Saumâtre (Brackish Pond), the intense blue Lac Azueï is Haiti's largest lake and, as its name suggests, a slightly salty one. It stretches into the DR, and until end of the 19th century was used as an important trade route between Port-au-Prince and Santo Domingo. Today the lake is an important center for wildlife, home to over 100 species of waterfowl. Colonies of pink flamingos are its most emblematic sight, along with a small population of caimans that can sometimes be seen basking on the shores. Fishing is also popular, due to introduced species like tilapia.

The southwest edge of the lake is bound by savannah, and is skirted by the road from Croix des Bouquets to the border crossing at Malpasse – a very picturesque drive. Bird-spotters should head to the northern shores, however, at Fond Pite. Also nearby at Manneville is a cold freshwater spring that empties into the warm lake waters. A sandy beach here is ideal for swimming.

You get to Lac Azueï from Port-au-Prince via Croix des Bouquets. To reach Manneville, take Rte National 3 toward Mirebalais, turning east to Thomazeau. Manneville is a further 6km. There are occasional taptaps to Thomazeau, with the possibility of onward moto-taxis to Manneville, although a 4WD is recommended (allow 1½ hours from Port-au-Prince).

Any transport from Port-au-Prince to the Dominican border will be able to drop you on the southern shore at Ganthier or Fond Parisien. At Ganthier, huge numbers of pilgrims climb the Kalvé Mirak (Calvary Miracle) hill here every Good Friday to retrace the Stations of the Cross, one of the largest religious gatherings in the region.

Parc National Forêt des Pins

When you're sweltering in Port-au-Prince, the idea of cool mountain pine forests can seem a world away, but driving three hours east to the Massif de la Selle near the Dominican border can have you pleasingly reaching for another layer to ward off the cool.

The road is very poor as it winds up the mountains, but the views are spectacular. Sadly, it's also a textbook illustration of deforestation and erosion; many towns beyond Forêt des Pins are regularly damaged during hurricanes. Large-scale logging persisted here until the early 1980s, and although it's nominally protected under law, cutting for wood and charcoal continues to be a problem.

From Fond Parisien on the Croix des Bouquets–Dominican Republic highway, the road turns south. It's a 50km drive to the village of **Fond Verettes** (which has its market day on Tuesday), and as the road climbs the climate gets colder and mistier. Four hours' drive from Port-au-Prince, the park entrance is just beyond the suitably named village of Terre-Froide. A checkpoint for the **Ministry of Agriculture, Natural Resources and Rural Development** (MARNDR; ☎ 2250-0867) is here. There is no entrance fee to the park. Just past the entrance there is a cluster of basic cabins (per person US$11). Prebooking with MARNDR is advisable, and you should be self-sufficient down to your (warm) bedding. The village of Forêt des Pins is a short walk beyond the cabins and has an interesting Saturday market.

The park is perfect for hiking. The denser parts of the forest are cool and tranquil, with birdsong and sunlight filtering through the trees. Good hikes from the park entrance include the gentle 5km walk to Chapotin, from where views stretch to the sea and to Lake Enriquillo in the Dominican Republic, or the stiff climb to Do Gimbi ridge for more fantastic views of the mountains, forest and sea (around four hours' walk round-trip). You'll meet plenty of locals on the tracks along both routes, so you shouldn't get lost.

CÔTE DES ARCADINS

From Port-au-Prince, Rte National 1 stretches north along the coast before switching inland toward Gonaïves and Cap-Haïtien. The deforested Chaine des Matheux mountains descend almost to the sea here, looking out toward Île de la Gonâve, Haiti's largest island. The coast itself is named for the Arcadins, a trio of sand cays surrounded by coral reefs in the channel between the mainland and Gonâve.

The first main town after leaving the capital is **Cabaret**, 'Papa Doc' Duvalier's modernist construction built to order as a symbol of his regime, and ruthlessly satirized for its pretensions in *The Comedians*. The futuristic (and unused) cock-fighting stadium on the main road is the main relic of this time; instead look out for the merchants selling local *tablet* (peanut brittle) to passing vehicles for US$0.30 a bag – it's delicious. Just beyond is **Arcahaie**, where Dessalines created the Haitian flag in 1804 from the rags of the Tricolor.

Beyond Arcahaie are the beach resorts. The beaches themselves aren't too inspiring, but offer safe, shallow swimming and snorkeling in clear water. During the week they're almost completely deserted but on weekends they come alive with visitors from the capital, and it's worthwhile booking accommodation in advance (although there are rates for day

visitors). The coast also has Haiti's best diving sites and one of the largest underwater sponges in the world. Kaliko Beach Club can arrange dives (for details, see below).

The **Plage Publique** (Km 62, Rte National 1; admission US$1) is tucked in between the Kaliko Beach Club and Wahoo Bay. There are basic facilities, food sellers, sound systems and booze – it's a great picture of regular Haitians at play.

North of Montrouis, at Moulin sur Mer, is the **Musée Colonial Ogier-Fombrun** (☎ 2278-6700; Km 77, Rte National 1; admission free; ◷ 10am-6pm) in a restored colonial plantation and sugar mill. It's definitely worth a look: there's an eclectic collection of exhibits, from a reconstruction of a colonist's room to slave shackles. At the entrance is a framed letter from Toussaint Louverture to the present owner's ancestors. Official opening hours are optimistic, however – if you visit during the week, you'll probably have to ask for it to be opened.

Sleeping & Eating

Beach hotels are the order of the day along the Côte des Arcadins, and are listed here in order of their distance from Port-au-Prince.

Kaliko Beach Club (☎ 3513-7548; www.kalikobeach club.com; Km 61, Rte National 1; s/d full board US$110/150, day pass US$25; P ⊠ ▣ ⊛) A modern all-inclusive-style resort, with a series of linked pools and cute octagonal bungalows set amid shady grounds. There are various water-sports options along the pebbly beach. Also based at Kaliko, **Pegasus** (☎ 3624-9486/9411/4775; nicolemarce linroy@yahoo.com) can arrange diving charters for qualified divers.

Wahoo Bay (☎ 2298-3410; www.wahoobaybeach .com; Km 62, Rte National 1; s/d from US$65/80, ste US$130; P ⊠ ▣ ⊛) Set in lush gardens and skirting a sandy beach, Wahoo wears a slightly more laid-back air than its neighbors. Rooms are decent, and there's the expected complement of restaurant, bar, pool and water sports. It's a long walk down to the beach, though, so don't expect waiter service.

Ouanga Bay (☎ 2257-6347; ouanga@hotmail.com; Km 63, Rte National 1; r incl breakfast US$77; P ⊠ ⊛) A relatively small hotel, but with a cute and immaculate beach and breezy rooms. The palm-thatched restaurant extends over the water, making it an ideal place to laze over fresh seafood (mains US$12 to US$16) and watch the boats go by.

Moulin Sur Mer (☎ 2222-1918; www.moulinsurmer .com; Km 77, Rte National 1; s/d full board US$100/160, day

AN AMERICAN KING IN HAITI

Barren Île de la Gonâve has always been set slightly apart from the mainland. A refuge for Taínos from the Spanish and for runaway slaves from the French, it was on its reefs that the ghost ship *Marie Celeste* was abandoned in 1884. But the island's strangest story came with the US occupation in 1915, when a Polish-American marine sergeant named Faustin Wirkus was appointed administrator of the island. Popular with the locals, he came to be seen as the reincarnation of Emperor Faustin Soulouque, who ruled in the mid-19th century. At his police station he was crowned King Faustin II with great ceremony, and decorated with hummingbird and macaw feathers. He ruled to local acclaim for four years until 1929, when he was faced with an army transfer; he resigned his commission and left Haiti for the more prosaic occupation of bond broker. Wirkus wrote a regal memoir, *The White King of La Gonave,* and died in 1945.

A daily ferry crosses to Île de la Gonâve from a jetty 500m north of Ouanga Bay hotel (US$6, one hour), departing early in the morning for the port of Anse-á-Galets and returning late afternoon. There's a very basic hotel here and not much else, but some good beaches on the west side of the island.

pass US$9; (P) (X) (Q) (R)) This charming large complex was undergoing extensive renovations when we visited. Rooms nearest the beach had been 'gingerbreadized,' while those further back leaned more toward a Spanish hacienda style. Both are well appointed, and are augmented by a pool, beachside **Boucanier** (mains US$10-18) seafood restaurant, and gardens full of sculptures. The Musée Colonial Ogier-Fombrun is in the same grounds, a (complimentary) golf-buggy ride away.

Club Indigo ((☎) 3442-9999; www.clubindigo.net; Km 78, Rte National 1; s/d US$121/176, day pass US$35; (P) (X) (Q) (R)) Everything at this former Club Med hotel is bright and breezy, with huge grounds and whitewashed buildings centered on the pool and restaurant-bar area. The beach is lovely, and a good job, too, as you'll only want to sleep in the frankly tiny rooms. At weekends Club Indigo heaves with UN Stabilization Mission for Haiti (MINUSTAH) staff and Port-au-Prince's hip set.

Xaragua Hôtel ((☎) 3510-9559; Km 80, Rte National 1; s/d full board US$71/128; (P) (X) (R)) Big rooms

all offer sea views here. Rates are very reasonable, so you can happily ignore the tired 1970s architecture and decor inside. Instead, look to the pool terrace and the beach. The hotel is owned by a local aid organization, and all profits go toward running five rural hospitals in Haiti.

Cabaret and Montrouis are good places to stop if you want to buy cheap eats, where there are food stalls selling fruit, pâté, beans and rice along the roadside.

Getting There & Away

By public transportation from Port-au-Prince, catch a bus or taptap to Gonaïves or Saint-Marc (US$3.50, 2½ hours) from Estation O'Cap beside the Shell gas station, at the confluence of Blvd Jean-Jacques Dessalines (Grand Rue) and Blvd La Saline in Port-au-Prince, and advise the driver where you want to be dropped. Return transport is a lot more hit and miss, as you're reliant on flagging down passing buses – don't leave it too late in the afternoon.

Southern Haiti

Haiti's south is all about taking it easy. Pulling out of Port-au-Prince on Rte National 2, the urban hustle is soon replaced by a much more relaxed air and rightly so – you're heading toward the Caribbean Sea.

Of the towns strung along the coast, Jacmel is the gem. It's an old coffee port full of pretty buildings, with a chilled yet friendly welcome. Most people take quickly to its charms. Some hit the many handicrafts shops to load up on the painted wood and papier-mâché that the town is famous for. Others try to time their visit for the renowned Carnival festivities, when the whole town seems to turn into a giant masked street party.

Further west, things get pretty sleepy. The town of Les Cayes seems to be permanently in a contented half-yawn, and doesn't seem to mind that visitors prefer to use it as an embarkation point for Île-à-Vache. This island is blessed with possibly Haiti's best beaches and a couple of its nicest hotels. If you can tear yourself away, there are more palm-fringed sandy delights for all budgets in nearby Port Salut.

The southern 'claw' is bisected by the rugged Massif de la Hotte, home to some of the last remaining cloud forest, and the stunning Parc National Macaya. It's a bird-watchers dream, and a visit here can be hugely rewarding, although the logistics are extremely challenging. After a spectacular mountain crossing, the road just about gives up when it reaches the sea at half-forgotten Jérémie, the sometime City of Poets and the most isolated town in Haiti.

HIGHLIGHTS

- Shop for handicrafts in **Jacmel** (p324), the south's most charming and laid-back port town

- Groove to the musical beat of *rara* and *compas* during **Carnival** (p322), Jacmel's – and Haiti's – best street party

- Chill out in style on the island getaway and former pirate stronghold of **Île-à-Vache** (p325)

- Bump over some spectacular mountain roads to reach **Jérémie** (p327) on Haiti's isolated southwestern tip

- Make a real expedition by exploring the hard-to-reach cloud forests of **Parc National Macaya** (p327)

★Jérémie

★ Parc National Macaya

★Jacmel

★ Île-à-Vache

JACMEL

pop 40,000

Sheltered by a beautiful 3km-wide bay, the old coffee port of Jacmel is one of the most friendly and tranquil towns in Haiti. Little more than a couple of hours drive south from Port-au-Prince, it's a popular weekend destination for city dwellers, and hosts one of the country's best Carnivals every Lent. But at any time of year, Jacmel is a great place for recharging the batteries.

Part of Jacmel's charm is down to its old town center, full of mansions and merchants' warehouses with a late-Victorian grace poking out from behind the wrought-iron balconies and peeling façades.

If some of the buildings need a lick of paint, Jacmel's artists could hardly be described as slouches. The town is the undisputed handicrafts capital of Haiti, with dozens of workshops producing hand-painted souvenirs, from wall decorations to the elaborate papier-mâché masks produced for the Carnival festivities. It's the birthplace of two hugely influential creative forces, both of whom have created inspiring works depicting the town, the artist Préfète Duffaut, who contributed to the amazing murals of Sainte Trinité Episcopalian Cathedral in Port-au-Prince (p295), and the novelist and poet René Dépestre.

HISTORY

Founded by the French in 1698, the exact origins of Jacmel's name remain a mystery. The Arawak settlement it replaced is believed to have been called Yaquimel, although other sources point to Jacques Melo, an alleged colonial founding father. Either way, Jacmel was a prosperous port by the close of the 18th century, when the town's large mulatto population began demanding equality with the whites. Soon after, Jacmel became an important battleground in the swirl of the Haitian independence struggle, with the mulattoes under André Rigaud initially siding with the colonists against the slave armies. The black general Lamour Derance from Jacmel more successfully led the struggle from the other side, eventually uniting the two sides, although Jacmel again became a center of mulatto power when Haiti split into two following Dessaline's death in 1806.

Jacmel also played a small role in the South American independence movement. Pétion hosted Simón Bolívar here in 1816 when the Venezuelan revolutionary leader was assembling his army, hospitality that Bolívar returned by abolishing slavery after liberating his country.

By the middle of the 19th century, Jacmel served as a major Caribbean loading point for steamships bound for Europe, and many European names can be found on the gravestones in the cemetery from this time. Jacmel was the first town in the Caribbean to have telephones and potable water, and when the cathedral was lit up on Christmas Eve 1895, Jacmel became the first town to have electric light. The town center was destroyed by a huge fire in 1896 and then rebuilt in the unique Creole architectural style that remains to this day. Port trade, however, began to dry up following WWII and the Duvalier era, leaving the annual Carnival the one time of year when Jacmel truly recreates its glory days.

ORIENTATION

Most people enter Jacmel on Rte National 2 from Port-au-Prince and Léogane; it is known as Portail Léogâne as it enters town and then turns into Ave de la Liberté, which heads toward the sea. Close to the town center it is met by Ave Barranquilla, Jacmel's second main street, which eventually leads east out of town toward the main beaches, the airport and Marigot. A turning west from Ave de la Liberté along Rue Comedie heads toward Bassins-Bleu.

Jacmel is built on three small hills, with its streets running down to the sea. From Ave de la Liberté, steep lanes lead up to the Place Toussaint L'Ouverture (also sometimes called Place d'Armes). East of the square on Rue de l'Eglise are the Marché de Fer (Iron Market) and the Cathédrale de St Phillippe et St Jacques. Rue St-Anne runs parallel to the seafront, and is where you'll find many of the artisans' shops.

INFORMATION

Emergency

Police (Ave de la Liberte)

Internet Access

Jacmel Cybernet (Ave Baranquilla; per hr US$1.10; ☼ 7am-10pm Mon-Sat, 9am-10pm Sunday) Has good electricity supply.

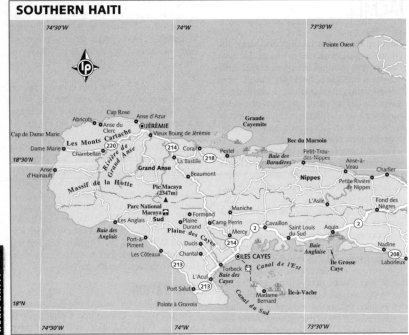

Oasis Cybercafe (Ave de la Liberté; per hr US$0.85; 10am-10pm)

Medical Services
Hôpital St Michel (☎ 2288-2151; Rue St-Philippe) For emergencies, but not brilliant.
Pharmacie St-Cyr (48 Ave Barranquilla)

Money
Banque Nationale de Crédit (Grand Rue)
Dola Dola (cnr Ave Barranquilla & Ave de la Liberté) Moneychanger.
Philippe Agent de Change (Ave Barranquilla) Changes euros and Canadian dollars.
Unibank (Ave de la Liberté) Gives Visa advances.

Post
Post office (Rue du Commerce; 8am-4pm Mon-Sat)

Telephone
Teleco (Ave Barranquilla)

Tourist Information
There are plenty of freelance guides in Jacmel, most of whom you'll find around the entrance to the Hôtel la Jacmelienne sur Plage. They can organize tours of the *artisanats* (craft workshops) and where the carnival masks are made, as well as arrange trips to Bassins-Bleu (p321). Expect to pay around US$20 to US$30 for a full day. One highly regarded English-speaking guide is **Michel Jean** (☎ 3693-3425).
Associations des Micro-Enterprises Touristiques du Sud'Est (Amets; ☎ 2288-2840; amets_service@ yahoo.fr; 40 Rue d'Orléans; 8am-4pm Mon-Fri, to 2pm Sat) Has maps of Jacmel, and can arrange car and horse rental. Also arranges homestays with local families.

SIGHTS
Old Jacmel
Running parallel to the seafront, Rue du Commerce is the heart of old Jacmel and has many splendid (if slightly run-down) examples of 19th-century warehouses and merchants' residences. Key characteristics are the high-shuttered doors and windows, shaded by wide balconies with filigree railings. Of these, the house of the influential Vital trading family has been turned into the **Hôtel Florita**. At the eastern end of the street are some of the oldest surviving buildings, including the **Customs House** next to

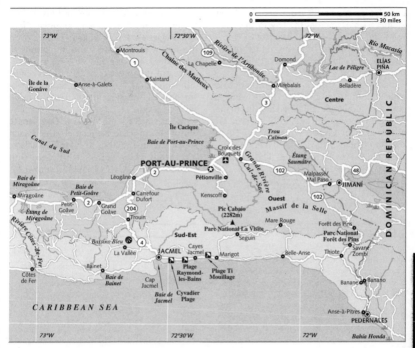

SOUTHERN HAITI

the wharf on Place de la Douane, and the 18th-century **prison**.

The Vital family also owned the **Manoir Alexandre**, between Rue du Commerce and Place Toussaint L'Ouverture, during WWI. This white-and-green building is probably the most famous in Jacmel, once a hotel and the fictional residence of Hadriana Siloé (see boxed text, p321). Other key buildings to look out for are the grand **Maison Cadet** (cnr Ave de la Liberté & Grand Rue), with its red-iron 'witch's hat,' and **Maison Boucard**, near Rue Seymour Pradel, which has an intricate wrought-iron gallery façade.

Near Maison Boucard is the **Salubria Gallery** (☎ 2288-2390; 26 Rue Seymour Pradel; ❧ by appointment), an eclectic gallery in a blue-and-white fin-de-siècle house owned by American professor Robert Bricston. The walls are packed with paintings, even the bathrooms and bedrooms; you trail around the whole house, looking at a collection that includes most of the masters of Haitian art.

East of Place Toussaint L'Ouverture is the red-and-green baroque **Marché de Fer**, built in 1895 as a scaled-down version of the grand iron market in Port-au-Prince. Closed Sundays, at all other times local produce spills out of every side of the market, jamming the surrounding streets.

The pretty white **Cathédrale de St Phillippe et St Jacques** (Rue de l'Eglise) built in 1859 is close to the market. The ostentatious tombs in the rambling **cemetery** at the eastern end of Rue Alcius Charmant, one block north of Rue de l'Eglise, include those of many early European settlers.

Beaches

The beachfront along Jacmel is sandy but also a little dirty – it's worth making the effort to head a little further out to enjoy more pleasant surroundings. Note that the undertow is especially strong along this coastline and can be fatal; don't venture out too far.

The closest beach to town is **La Saline**, a small cove with crystal-clear water that's a 30-minute walk from the town center past the cemetery (US$0.40 by moto-taxi). If you're lucky, you might find a fisherman here who'll catch and grill you a lobster and sell you some cold beer to boot. You can also arrange a lift from here (or from Jacmel's wharf) across the bay to the large sand-and-pebble beach of **Baguette** (30 minutes by boat) where, once you've tired of sun and sea, you can hike up to the ruins of an old French fort.

East of town, there is a succession of fine beaches leading toward Cayes Jacmel village. A taptap (local bus or minibus) heading in the Marigot direction will be able to drop you off at any of them. **Cyvadier Plage** is about 10km outside of Jacmel, down a small track leading from the Cayes Jacmel road. The beach is part of the Cyvadier Plage Hôtel (see p322). The small half-moon-shaped cove flanked by rocky cliffs has a protected beach, making the undertow less of a problem here.

About 13km from Jacmel and just before Cayes Jacmel lies the very popular **Plage Raymond-les-Bains**. This is another long stretch of sand, with palm trees and mountains as a backdrop. Parking and showers are available, and it can get crowded at weekends, although eating freshly caught seafood here surrounded by holidaying Haitians can make for a great time.

In the small fishing village of **Cayes Jacmel**, about 14km east of Jacmel, the beach spreads a further 3km to **Plage Ti Mouillage**, a gorgeous white-sand stretch fringed with coconut palms. Cayes Jacmel is known for making the rocking chairs seen throughout Haiti, while other artisans make wooden model boats.

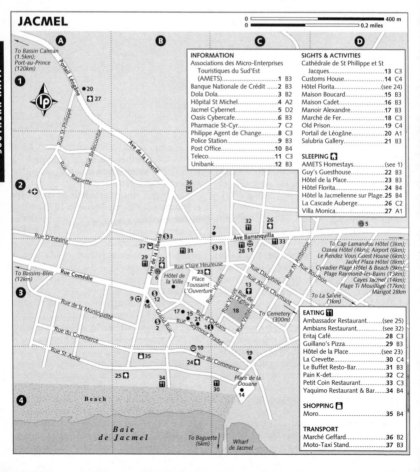

JACMEL

0 — 400 m
0 — 0.2 miles

INFORMATION
Associations des Micro-Enterprises
  Touristiques du Sud'Est
  (AMETS)...................................1 B3
Banque Nationale de Crédit 2 B3
Dola Dola...................................3 B2
Hôpital St Michel........................4 A2
Jacmel Cybernet.........................5 D2
Oasis Cybercafe..........................6 B3
Pharmacie St-Cyr........................7 C2
Philippe Agent de Change...........8 C3
Police Station..............................9 B3
Post Office................................10 B4
Teleco.......................................11 C3
Unibank....................................12 B3

SIGHTS & ACTIVITIES
Cathédrale de St Phillipe et St
  Jacques..................................13 C3
Customs House..........................14 C4
Hôtel Florita.........................(see 24)
Maison Boucard.........................15 B3
Maison Cadet............................16 B3
Manoir Alexandre......................17 B3
Marché de Fer...........................18 B3
Old Prison.................................19 C4
Portail de Léogâne....................20 A1
Salubria Gallery........................21 B3

SLEEPING
AMETS Homestays.................(see 1)
Guy's Guesthouse......................22 B3
Hôtel de la Place.......................23 B3
Hôtel Florita.............................24 B4
Hôtel la Jacmelienne sur Plage...25 B4
La Cascade Auberge..................26 C2
Villa Monica..............................27 A1

EATING
Ambassador Restaurant.........(see 25)
Ambians Restaurant..............(see 32)
Eritaj Café................................28 C3
Guillano's Pizza........................29 B3
Hôtel de la Place..................(see 23)
La Crevette...............................30 C4
Le Buffet Resto-Bar..................31 B3
Pain K-det................................32 C2
Petit Coin Restaurant................33 C3
Yaquimo Restaurant & Bar......34 B4

SHOPPING
Moro..35 B4

TRANSPORT
Marché Geffard.........................36 B2
Moto-Taxi Stand.......................37 B3

To Bassin Caïman
(1.5km);
Port-au-Prince
(120km)

SOUTHERN HAITI

Portail Léogâne
Rue St-Phillipe
Rue Bellecombe
Rue Raquette
Ave de la Liberté
Rue D'Estaing
Rue de la Liberté
To Bassins-Bleu   Rue Comédie
(12km)
Rue Claire Heureuse
Hôtel de
la Ville   Place
Toussaint
L'Ouverture
Rue de la Municipalité
Grand Rue
Rue du Commerce
Rue St-Anne
Rue du Commerce
Ave Barranquilla
Ave Ambroise
Rue M Bourbon
Rue Dauphine
Rue Aldus Charmant
Rue Yvonne
Rue de
l'Église
Rue Vallière
Rue d'Orléans
Rue Seymour Pradel
Place de la
Douane
Beach
Baie
de Jacmel
To Baguette
(6km)
Wharf
de Jacmel
To Cap Lamandou Hôtel (3km);
Ozama Hôtel (4km); Airport (6km);
Le Rendez Vous Guest House (6km);
Cyvadier Plage Hôtel & Beach (9km);
Plage Raymond-les-Bains (13km);
Cayes Jacmel (14km);
Plage Ti Mouillage (17km);
Marigot 28km
To La Saline
(1km)
To Cemetery
(300m)

HADRIANA DREAMING

Jacmel's most famous resident exists purely in the imaginative hinterland of the Haitian psyche. Hadriana Siloé is the troubled heroine of *Hadriana dans tous mes rêves* (Hadriana in all My Dreams) by Reńe Depestre, one of Haiti's most celebrated novelists.

On her wedding day during Carnival, Hadriana dies at the altar, and her body is displayed at a public wake before burial. But after her funeral she is found to have been turned into a *zombi* (Creole spelling of zombie) and is exhumed by the witch doctor who poisoned her. Hadriana escapes and flees to the mountains where she is mistaken for a freshwater *lwa* (Vodou spirit), and is invited to seek a new life in Jamaica.

Although the Manoir Alexandre, which served as Hadriana's home, is now closed as a hotel, visitors to Jacmel can still see it – and if you come during Carnival, you might even catch a glimpse of a *zombi* in the procession, although Hadriana herself has long since fled to a happier life.

Bassins-Bleu

Bassins-Bleu is tucked into the mountains 12km northwest of Jacmel, a series of three cobalt-blue pools linked by waterfalls that make up one of the prettiest swimming holes in the country.

The three pools are Bassin Clair, Bassins-Bleu and Bassin Palmiste. Bassin Clair is the most beautiful of the three, deep into the mountain at the bottom of the waterfall, sheltered and surrounded by smooth rocks draped with maidenhair and creeper ferns. You'll undoubtedly share the pool with local kids, who will be initially curious to see you, before encouraging you to go into the small cave behind the falls so they can scream past you as they lunge into the pool from the higher rocks. You're sadly less likely to see the nymphs that according to legend live in the grottoes, although be warned that they've been known to grab divers attempting to discover the true depth of the pool.

Any guide in Jacmel can arrange a trip to Bassins-Bleu, which takes about two hours each way, usually by horse. Expect to pay around US$20. The road is accessible most of the way by 4WD. Doing the trip without a guide is quite possible, but expect other 'guides' and hangers-on to attach themselves to you.

From Jacmel, walk to the western end of Rue Comédie and follow the road across the river. About 800m beyond the river you'll reach the place where you meet the horse handlers. From here follow the track to the left as it climbs the hill steeply, remembering to take in the spectacular views of the Baie de Jacmel behind you. A hat and sunblock are recommended for the walk. There is a small hamlet close to the pools where the horses are watered and rested. The self-appointed guardian of the falls normally meets you here and leads you deeper into the woods to the pools (he'll expect a tip of around US$3 to US$4). The path is a little uneven, and at one point you must climb down a steep rock face (with carved footholds) by rope. From here, you're ready to dive in.

While the mineral-rich waters of Bassins-Bleu are a delight at most times of the year, it's worth noting that they turn a muddy brown after heavy rainfall, slightly dampening the experience.

FESTIVALS

Jacmel's Carnival celebrations (see boxed text, p322) are famous across Haiti, and people come from across the country and the diaspora to join in the party. The city also hosts two other big festivals worth checking out.

Since 2004 **Jacmel Film Festival** (www.festivalfilmjakmel.com) has been one of Haiti's biggest cultural events. Taking place over a week every November, Jacmel hosts movie screenings by Haitian and international directors as well as film-making workshops. The festival takes place in several venues, including an open-air cinema erected on the wharf.

The first **Jacmel Music Festival** (www.jacmelmusicfestival.com) was held in May 2007, featuring bands from across Haiti and the Caribbean and (if funding permits) was planned to be an annual event. A three-day open-air concert on the beach, the festival helped further cement Jacmel's reputation as Haitian's festival capital.

CARNIVAL IN JACMEL

Every year, thousands of partygoers descend on Jacmel to take part in Carnival, one of Haiti's most fantastic spectacles. At this time, Jacmel turns into one giant street theater, with participants and the audience playing their part, and the whole thing a world away from the sequins and sparkle of Carnival in Rio de Janeiro.

The Carnival season starts its build up on Epiphany (January 6), with events every Sunday leading up to the giant celebrations and procession on the Sunday the week before Shrove Tuesday (it's held a week earlier than other Carnivals so it doesn't clash with Port-au-Prince's party). The streets suddenly swell and everywhere you look are strange figures in fantastical papier-mâché masks – the signature image of Jacmel Carnival. You can see the masks being made and on display in the ateliers year-round. Jungle animals jostle with mythical birds, giant fruit and *lwa* (Vodou spirits). Mixed in with the procession are celebrants dressed as Arawaks and colonists, and horned figures covered in molasses and soot, who tease revelers with their sticky grab. St Michael and his angels ritually fight the devil, while gangs of *chaloskas* – monsters caricaturing military misrule – growl scarily at the crowds. There's even (an old Carnival favorite, this) a donkey dressed up in peasant clothes and sneakers. Music is everywhere, from bands on organized floats to *rara* (one of the most popular forms of Haitian music) outfits on foot. It's an enormous party. The procession kicks off roughly around noon, with celebrations continuing late into the night.

SLEEPING

Despite its obvious tourist attractions, Jacmel isn't overendowed with hotel beds. Many of the midrange and top-end hotels are actually outside Jacmel, heading out from Ave Baranquilla to Cyvadier Plage. Whatever your budget, if you plan on visiting during Carnival, advance booking is absolutely essential. Unless noted, all hotels listed include breakfast.

Budget

Guy's Guesthouse (☎ 2288-2569, 2288-9646; Ave de la Liberté; s US$25-40, d US$40-50, tr US$55; P 🍴 🖥 🐾) There are invariably a few NGO workers staying at Guy's and it's easy to see why it remains popular. Although bathrooms are shared, everything is kept very clean, the rooms are comfy, and the staff friendly and helpful. Breakfasts are huge, and the restaurant out the front is a good place for lunch or dinner.

Villa Monica (☎ 2288-2380, 3703-5560; Ave de la Liberté; r US$30; P) A homey little guesthouse a few minutes' walk from Marché Geffrard, Villa Monica has fairly basic rooms in a bungalow set in a shady garden. Bathrooms are shared, and there's no breakfast or any food options.

Le Rendez Vous Guesthouse (☎ 3541-3044; lerendez_vousrestobar@yahoo.fr; Route de Cyvadier; r US$35; P) Outside the center of Jacmel and opposite the airstrip, you'll find this friendly, simple place. There are nine uncluttered rooms, an open-sided bar-restaurant, and lots of greenery with chickens and ducks pecking about. The man-

ager also has a house to rent that sleeps four (per night US$200).

La Cascade Auberge (☎ 2288-4197, 3525-6834; cascadauberge@yahoo.fr; 63 Ave Barranquilla; r US$40; 🍴) A new guesthouse that's a great deal: the large and spotless rooms have gleaming private bathrooms. The management speaks some English; the only drawback is that some of the rooms don't have external windows, making them a bit gloomy.

Midrange & Top End

Hôtel de la Place (☎ 2288-3769; 3 Rue de l'Eglise; r US$45; P 🍴) A pleasant old building overlooking Place Toussaint L'Ouverture, and a popular place to enjoy Carnival. Rooms are modern, although some are a little on the small side; most manage a view. The ground-floor terrace bar seems designed for hours of people-watching.

Cyvadier Plage Hôtel (☎ 2288-3323; www.hotelcyvadier.com; Route de Cyvadier; s US$61-72, d US$82-104, tr US$158; P 🍴 🖥 🐾) Off the main highway, this is the furthest of the beach hotels from the center of Jacmel, but also one of the best. Rooms in a cluster of buildings face the terrace restaurant and out to the private cove of Cyvadier Plage (nonresidents are welcome). Rooms are good, if nothing spectacular, but the whole deal is very professionally run and welcoming.

Jaclef Plaza Hôtel (☎ 3757-6818; www.jaclefplazahotel.com; Route de Cyvadier; s/d US$65/75; P 🍴 🖥 🐾) A brand-new hotel just outside town trying to decide if it wants to pitch to the business traveler or the tourist. There's a good range of facilities and a bar, plus conference rooms. Guest rooms are very well sized but a shade characterless, something that's overcompensated for with a reckless love of chintz.

Hôtel Florita (☎ 2288-2805; www.hotelflorita.com; 29 Rue du Commerce; r US$66; 🐾) A converted mansion from 1888, the Florita oozes charm. There are polished floorboards, period furniture and comfy chairs aplenty, while rooms are whitewashed and airy, with mosquito net and balcony. Extra rooms at the back overlook the courtyard garden and are a bit more cramped, but still quite stylish.

Hôtel la Jacmelienne sur Plage (☎ 2288-3541; Rue St-Anne; r US$75-100; P 🐾 ⬛) Once Jacmel's most celebrated hotel, the Jacmelienne is now sadly a little past its best. The large rooms command good views to sea from their balconies, and although adequately appointed, are in need of some maintenance. The service and restaurant are decent enough.

Ozana Hôtel (☎ 3703-7463, 3542-0487; Rue St Cyr Imp Prophéte; r US$77; P 🐾 ⬛ ⬛) A bright, clean and very modern hotel, with nice rooms, satellite TV, a restaurant and everything kept spotlessly clean. The drawback? The location, down a long dirt track off the highway, makes your own vehicle pretty much essential.

Cap Lamandou Hôtel (☎ 3720-1436, 3920-9135; www.lamandouhotel.com; Route de Lamandou; r US$93; P 🐾 ⬛ ⬛) On the edge of Jacmel but a bit of a hike off the main road, the Cap Lamandou is Jacmel's glitziest hotel. Rooms are immaculate, with wi-fi throughout and all with possibly the best views over the bay in Jacmel. The bar leads onto the central terrace and pool, which has more steps descending to the sea if you're in need of a further dip.

EATING

Hôtel de la Place (☎ 2288-2832; 3 Rue de l'Eglise; mains US$3-9; 🕙 10am-10pm) The menu at this hotel inclines more to Western fast food with a few Creole dishes thrown in, but the main reason to eat here is to sit on the terrace and watch life unfold on the town square before you.

Pain K-det (Ave Baranquilla; burgers, pizzas & sandwiches US$4-7; 🕙 10am-late) Near Rue Veuve, this is a pleasant bar with a good line in sandwiches, ice cream and other snacks. It's a popular hangout, especially on Friday when it has a

happy hour between 7pm and 9pm, and blasts music out of the speakers on its terrace.

Yaquimo Restaurant & Bar (Grand Rue; prices US$4-10; 🕙 11am-11pm) Something of a beach bar, the Yaquimo has a bit of everything, mixing good food with decent music and plenty of drinks. It's a popular place for bands to play at weekends, when there's an admission charge of around US$6.

Ambians Restaurant (Ave Barranquilla; mains US$4-11) A bar-resto with a terrace to relax with a drink and take the town's temperature. It has a varied Creole-French menu; the food is good, but can sometimes take a while to materialize.

Le Buffet Resto-Bar (Ave Baranquilla; mains US$5; 🕙 9am-11pm) Typical of the bar-restos along Ave Baranquilla, Le Buffet is a hole-in-the-wall place serving simple but satisfying Creole dishes. Ask what's available that day – usually chicken, *griyo* (pork) or *kabrit* (goat) with plantains, undoubtedly washed down with a cold Prestige and accompanied by a tomato and avocado salad.

Guillano's Pizza (☎ 2288-2695; Ave de la Liberté; pizzas US$5-15) Part of Guy's Guesthouse opposite (you can equally order and eat in its restaurant), this place does better than average pizzas, coming in very generous sizes.

Petit Coin Restaurant (☎ 2288-3067; Rue Bourbon; mains around US$7; 🕙 12pm-11pm) A cozy little restaurant, with a hint of French bistro. Three tables on a tiny terrace allow you to catch the last of the day's sun and people-spot, before retiring to the interior. The menu is Creole, with a couple of French dishes, all of it tasty.

Eritaj Café (50 Ave Barranquilla; fish US$7-12; 🕙 12pm-midnight) A great new seafood place on the main drag, the Eritaj has a shady courtyard with bright murals on the wall, a chilled atmosphere and a well-stocked bar. Locally caught fish is the order of the day, but there are some interesting pasta dishes also on offer.

Cyvadier Plage Hôtel (☎ 2288-3323; Route de Cyvadier; mains around US$13; 🕙 11am-11pm) The lobster at this hotel-restaurant is worth making a detour for, served up on a terrace that catches a cool sea breeze. There are plenty of other good fish dishes to choose from, although we'd recommend you go easy on the lethal house rum punch.

La Crevette (☎ 2288-2834; Rue St-Anne; mains US$6-14; 🕙 12pm-late) This place has a long covered dining area that overlooks the wharf and sea, so you'll be unsurprised to find seafood playing heavily on the menu. It's particularly

SOUTHERN HAITI

busy at weekends, when locals also come for the cocktails and the dance floor to get the party going.

Ambassador Restaurant (☎ 2288-3451; Hotel la Jacmelienne sur Plage, Rue St-Anne; mains US$8-14; ✆ 11am-11pm) The Jacmelienne's hotel leans toward the formal, trying to echo Pétionville's finer dining establishments with French gastronomy and a wine list to match.

For self-caterers, the markets in the streets around the Marché de Fer are the place to head for; a local specialty is tiny sweet *ti malice* (bananas). There's plenty of street food around here, too. Between July and January look out for women selling *pisquettes*, tiny fish sautéed in huge numbers.

SHOPPING

Jacmel is a souvenir buyer's paradise. Its most famous output are the papier-mâché Carnival masks, unique to the town, that you can see being made in the months before the festival. More portable handicrafts include hand-painted placemats and boxes, wooden flowers, and models of taptaps, jungle animals and boats. Prices are cheap, starting at a couple of dollars for the smallest items, with a complete absence of hard sell. Most of the shops can be found on Rue St-Anne in the vicinity of the Hôtel la Jacmelienne sur Plage, along with a number of galleries showcasing Jacmel's art scene. One of the better *artisanat*-galleries is **Moro** (21 Rue du Commerce), although it's not the cheapest.

GETTING THERE & AROUND

The airline **Caribintair** (☎ 2250-2531) runs a popular daily flight from Port-au-Prince to Jacmel (US$80; 15 minutes). The **airport** (☎ 2288-2888; Route de Cyvadier) is about 6km east of town.

Buses to Port-au-Prince (US$2.70, three hours) leave from the Bassin Caïman station 2km out of town. Some taptaps (US$3, 2½ hours) also leave from Marché Geffrard, closer to the town center. From either place, transport runs from before dawn until about 5pm, departing when full. The ride along Rte National 4 (Rte de l'Amité) is one of the best roads in Haiti and particularly scenic. At Carrefour Dufort the road joins Rte National 2 to the capital. If you want to travel west, get off here by the Texaco gas station and flag down passing buses before noon, as there are no direct buses from Jacmel in this

direction. Change at Grand Goâve or Petit Goâve if necessary.

A moto-taxi around town costs around US$0.40. Even trips as far as Cyvadier Plage should give change from US$1. Taptaps run all day along Ave Barranquilla. **Chery's Taxis** (☎ 2288-3717) has metered taxis, and will do charters to Port-au-Prince for around US$80.

THE SOUTHWEST

RTE NATIONAL 2

From Port-au-Prince, Rte National 2 runs the length of Haiti's southern 'claw' to Les Cayes. Traffic whizzes through a succession of medium-sized towns along the coast: **Léogâne**, which is known for its distilleries and stone sculptors; **Petit-Goâve**, famous for its sweet *dous macoss* (see boxed text, p285); and the port of **Miragoâne**, its streets brimming over with imported (and often smuggled) goods, home to a large cathedral. The coastal road used to be popular for weekend beach visits from the capital before snarling traffic made the resorts of Côte des Arcadins a more attractive prospect. From Miragoâne the road cuts inlands and heads across the mountains westward to Les Cayes.

If you want to break your journey, Petit-Goâve has one of Haiti's most splendidly eccentric hotels.

Built in 1849 as a residence for Emperor Faustin Soulouque, **Le Relais de l'Emperor** (☎ 3462-3793; cnr Rues Républicaine & Louverture; r US$65; ✪) is faded grandeur personified. Rooms are ostentatious, with high ceilings, four-poster beds and huge baths with gold taps in the bedrooms. In the 1970s Hollywood's brightest propped up the bar, while the manager paraded his pet jaguar on a leash. There's a feeling of arriving slightly too late for a really great party, but anywhere else in the Caribbean this would be a boutique hotel to die for.

Buses and taptaps ply the highway all day between Port-au-Prince and Les Cayes.

LES CAYES
Pop 46,000
You'd be hard pressed to find a sense of urgency in Haiti's fourth-largest city, lulled into a sense of torpor by the gentle Caribbean breeze. More popularly known

---

OK IN AUX CAYES?

According to legend, the term 'OK' was born in Les Cayes. When high-quality rum was exported to the USA, Haitian packers would mark the crates 'Aux Cayes' to note its point of origin. American stevedores, charged with inspecting goods arriving at port, knew the contents would always be top-quality booze, so would let them pass without having to open them up. Thus 'Aux Cayes' was abbreviated as port slang to 'OK,' the word then spreading to the rest of the world through the merchant shipping lanes.

---

as Aux Cayes, Les Cayes is an old rum port sheltered by a series of reefs that has sent many ships to their graves (its first recorded victim was one of Columbus' ships on his final voyage to Hispaniola). Pirates were another treat, notably from nearby Île-à-Vache (right). John James Audubon, the naturalist and painter, was born here in 1785. Today Les Cayes has little to offer the visitor, although it's a good stopping-off point for other destinations in the south.

Les Cayes is laid out in a grid. Rte National 2 turns into Ave des Quatre Chemins upon entering the town, bisected by Rue Général Marion. Two main roads lead south from here to the town center – Rue Nicholas Geffrard and Rue Stenio Vincent. The former leads to the wharf, while the latter takes you to the main square with its easily spotted Notre Dame Cathedral, a whitewashed copy of the Parisian original.

Sleeping & Eating

There isn't a huge range of sleeping options in Les Cayes. For something fancier, head across the water to Île-à-Vache.

Le Meridien des Cayes (☎ 2286-0331; info@hotel meridiendescayes.com; 15 Rte National 2; s/d with fan US$34/48, with air-con US$58/76; 🅿 🖳 🔊) A fair if slightly bland choice. Rooms vary but are mostly spacious; some face onto the internal courtyard and restaurant, and lack external windows. Staff are brisk rather than friendly, although the restaurant is good, both for the breakfasts and the Creole dinner menu.

Concorde Hôtel (☎ 2286-0079; Rue Gabions des Indigenes; s/d with fan US$40/47, with air-con US$45/57; 🅿 🖳 🔊) Centrally located, the Concorde has two buildings set in large and pleasant gardens. Rooms are slightly quaint but decent enough (those in the main building are nicer), there's a pool, and the manager is very helpful. There's an extra supplement for breakfast.

Cayenne Hôtel (☎ 2286-0770; Rue Capitale; r with fan US$56, with air-con US$68-114; 🅿 🖳 🔊) This is the closest thing Les Cayes gets to a beach hotel: the sea is on the other side of the Cayenne's boundary wall. There's nothing wrong here – rooms are standard– but the whole place carries a slightly weary air that makes the prices seem a little on the steep side.

Bay Klub (☎ 2286-0544; Les Cayes wharf; mains around US$5; 🕙 9am-10pm) Looking out to sea, this is a good place to chill. During the day you're better off sticking to drinks as service is incredibly laid-back; food – griyo, kabrit, lambi (conch) and the like – comes once the sun starts dipping.

Nami Restaurant (☎ 2286-1114; 15 Rue Nicholas Geffrard; mains US$5-7; 🕙 8am-10pm) This little restaurant is a happy incongruity in Les Cayes, and has some really good Chinese dishes for those whose palettes need refreshing from Creole (which is also served, along with Continental selections).

Getting There & Around

There's a daily flight to Port-au-Prince with **Caribintair** (US$80, 30 minutes). **Nami** (☎ 2286-9898; 15 Rue Nicholas Geffrard) is the agent for both Caribintair and Tortugair, as well as running the restaurant next door.

Buses and taptaps leave from the area around Carrefour des Quatre Chemins, leaving when full. Port-au-Prince transport is the most common (US$8, four hours), stopping at Petit-Goâve and Léogâne. Get off at the latter to change for Jacmel, or just before at Carrefour Dufort. Taptaps to Port Salut (US$1, 45 minutes) are plentiful. To get to Jérémie (US$10, eight hours), you have to wait for the bus from Port-au-Prince to pass through around mid-morning, or go to Camp Perrin (US$2, 1½ hours) and hope to get something from there.

Moto-taxis around town cost US$0.30.

ÎLE-À-VACHE

The so-called 'Island of Cows,' Île-à-Vache lies about 15km south of Les Cayes. In the 16th century it was a base for the Welsh pirate Henry Morgan as he terrorized Santo Domingo and Colombia. Three centuries later

Abraham Lincoln tried to relocate emancipated black American slaves here, but it was a short-lived and ill-provisioned experiment. The island today is scattered with rural houses, plantations, mangroves, the odd Arawak burial ground and some great beaches.

The only accommodation options are two contrasting upmarket resorts, although some islanders in the village of Madame Bernard have been known to rent rooms to foreigners for around US$10.

Abaka Bay Resort (☎ 3721-3691; www.abakabay .com; Anse Dufour; s/d US$98/195; ✗ ▣) This hotel must have one of the most fabulous beaches in the Caribbean, a smooth white curve of a bay, met by lush foliage and a series of pleasant bungalows and villas. The atmosphere is laid-back, but the service manages good attention to detail.

Port Morgan (☎ 3921-0000; www.port-morgan.com; Cayes Coq; s/d incl full board from US$225/420, 2 nights min; ℗ ✗ ▣ ▣) Served by a yacht harbor, Port Morgan is all bright-and-breezy gingerbread chalets with lovely views out to sea. There's a small beach, a really excellent restaurant serving French-influenced cuisine, and various kayaks and other water-sports equipment for rent.

Both resorts include transfers from Les Cayes wharf in their rates and can organize other boat excursions, including to nearby Ilet des Amoreux (Lover's Island). Otherwise, the Île-à-Vache *bateaux-taxi* (water taxi) leaves from the wharf several times daily (US$2, 30 minutes) for Madame Bernard. Getting around by foot is easy; you can do a pleasant day walk in a loop between the two resorts via Madame Bernard, taking in the viewpoints of Pointe Ouest and Pointe Latanier.

PORT SALUT

An excellent new road leads west from Les Cayes to the spectacular beaches of Port Salut. A one-street town strung for several kilometers along the coast, it's best known as the birthplace of the former president Aristide. The beach is the main reason to come here: kilometers of palm-fringed white sand with barely a person on it, and the gorgeously warm Caribbean to splash around in.

Sleeping & Eating

Hotels are presented in the order they appear on the main road when arriving from Les Cayes. All have their own restaurant unless noted.

Arada Inn (☎ 3754-6956; r US$28; ℗ ✗ ▣ ▣) The first hotel on the main road, and the cheapest decent sleeping option in Port Salut, there are just five rooms, simply presented but well maintained. Food is available on request, and the beach is a short walk away.

Relais du Boucanier (☎ 3558-01806; s/d US$70/80; ℗ ✗) You could hardly be closer to the Caribbean in this coral-pink hotel. The waves almost break into the open-sided dining room, while in any of the large and fine rooms you'll be pleasantly lulled to sleep by the sound of the sea.

Hôtel du Village (☎ 3779-1728; portsaluthoteldu village@yahoo.fr; r with fan/air-con US$40/65; ℗ ✗) A government-owned hotel comprising a series of chalets, which was getting a facelift when we visited. The results are excellent value – airy rooms nicely turned out, although you're not likely to spend much time in them since the front doors open straight onto the sand.

Auberge du Rayon Vert (☎ 3713-9035; auberge durayonvert@yahoo.fr; s/d US$79/112; ℗ ✗) Stylish and immaculate rooms are the order of the day here, with locally made furniture and very modern bathrooms, and the beach seconds away. The restaurant-bar is the best in Port Salut, with a range of seafood and other French-influenced dishes and a good wine list. Very hospitable.

Two new high-specification hotels beyond the Auberge du Rayon Vert were due to open soon after this book's publication, both worth investigating: Creek Bay Hotel, with its own tiny bay, and the Chambres d'Hôtes, which promised to be run on ecofriendly lines.

Chez Guito (mains US$4-9) Opposite Hôtel du Village, this decent beach bar (albeit sitting on the opposite side of the road) is the place to head for fish and *lambi*, a cold Prestige and a sweet *compas* soundtrack.

Getting There & Around

Taptaps to Les Cayes (US$1, 45 minutes) leave throughout the day, while moto-taxis zip up and down the length of the town.

CAMP PERRIN

At the foot of the Massif de la Hotte range in lush surroundings en route to Parc National Macaya and Jérémie, Camp Perrin is where the south's good roads give out: from here on it's rough and rocky. The town is little more than two streets with a few shops and barrestos. It was founded in 1759 by the French,

SOUTHERN HAITI

who left behind a network of irrigation canals. A different watery attraction not to be missed is the beautiful **Saut Mauthurine waterfall** *('les chutes')* with its deep green pool, a 15-minute moto-taxi ride away.

Auberge La Distribution (☎ 2286-0899; Zone Lévy; d with fan/air-con US$25/40; ℗ ✷) Standing next to one of the irrigation canals, this hotel is better than one might expect for such a small town. There is a number of buildings set in a large and rambling garden, with tidy rooms and a palm-shaded terrace bar and restaurant. It's fairly well signed from the main road.

Taptaps to Les Cayes (US$2, 1½ hours) leave several times daily, picking up passengers along the main street. Buses to Jérémie usually pass through in the middle of the day.

PARC NATIONAL MACAYA

The 5500-hectare Parc National Macaya contains Haiti's last region of cloud forest, spread across the mountain ridges of the Massif de la Hotte. It has an extremely rich biodiversity, particularly birds and amphibians, with a high number of endemic species. One in every 10 plants is only found inside the park, with orchids notably represented.

The near-permanent cloud cover brings around 4000mm of rain per year, which goes on to water the Plaine des Cayes, Haiti's most productive agricultural region. But Macaya itself is desperately poor, and not immune to the pressures of tree felling for charcoal and land clearance, particularly the largest broadleaf and pine trees, some of which tower 45m high. The Société Audubon Haïti, Haiti's leading conservation organization, is working to promote the long-term conservation of the park. Macaya has a huge future potential as an ecotourism destination, but right now potential is almost all there is, as nothing is easy about organizing a visit.

As well as its biodiversity, Macaya has several potential treks. The most challenging, taking four days there and back, is to the top of Pic Macaya (2347m). You must cross over a 2100m ridge and descend another 1000m before attempting the mountain itself. The trails are barely existent, so a knowledgeable guide and a machete to cut the way are both essential.

The main starting point for entering the park is Formond. The road from Les Cayes is extremely tough, and you'll need a 4WD with high clearance, a couple of spare tires

and at least four hours. Along the way you'll pass the overgrown Citadelle des Platons, one of Dessalines' network of defensive forts built after independence.

If you're planning a trip, we'd advise getting in touch with **Philippe Bayard** (pbayard@ societeaudubonhaiti.org), president of the Société Audubon Haïti. A good guide based in Camp Perrin is **Jean-Denis Chéry** (☎ 3766-4331), who has worked with many international organizations in Macaya. There is no accommodation, so tents are necessary. As the region is so poor, employing locals to cook or as further guides is a good way of spending money locally – a guide is recommended to help arrange this equitably. Bring food, water purification paraphernalia and wet-weather gear.

JÉRÉMIE

Jérémie, the capital of Grand Anse Départment, is about as close to the end of the road as you can get in Haiti. The journey here amply demonstrates its isolation, with a terrible road crawling over the mountains to Les Cayes in rough (albeit truly spectacular) fashion. Once here, it seems to fulfill the cliché of a forgotten tropical port, with abandoned warehouses, little traffic and a sense of torpor in the air – a town whose best days are behind it.

By contrast, Jérémie has a rich history. In 1793 it was the landing point for Britain's short-lived invasion of Haiti. After independence it was a major center for mulatto power, and its inhabitants grew rich on the coffee trade, sent their children to be educated in Paris and wore the latest French fashions. Jérémie was known as the 'City of Poets' for its writers. Its most famous sons are the mulatto general Alexandre Dumas, whose son wrote *The Three Musketeers,* and the poet Emile Roumer. Such heritage is hard to find these days, however. In 1964 the town was the focus of an attempt to overthrow 'Papa Doc' Duvalier, who responded in murderous fashion by ordering the massacre of virtually Jérémie's entire mulatto population of around 400 men, women and children, along with the closure of the port (yet to fully reopen).

Politically and economically isolated, Jérémie is a sleepy, pretty place to spend a few days. There's little to occupy yourself with except soaking in the atmosphere, but there's no rush…

Information

Alliance Française (☎ 2286-6573; 110 Rue Stenio Vincent; internet per hr US$1.70; ☼ 9am-1pm & 4-8pm) Excellent internet connection. Also hosts concerts, films and an annual cultural festival every April.

Martha Cybernet (Place Alexandre Dumas, 1st fl; internet per hr US$1.40; ☼ 9am-8pm)

Soleil Levant (Ave Emile Roumer) Moneychangers inside handy Lebanese supermarket.

Teleco (Rue Eugène Margron)

Unibank (Place Alexandre Dumas)

Sights

The town is centered on Place Alexandre Dumas, with its red-and-white cathedral, inaugurated in 1893, on its western edge. On the eastern side, Rue Stenio Vincent runs parallel to the sea, with many interesting old buildings and coffee warehouses, almost all sadly neglected. Continuing past the grubby beach takes you to Fort Télémargue, a crumbling fort that makes an excellent spot to watch the sunset.

About 5km northwest of Jérémie is the beach of **Anse d'Azur**, a gorgeous sandy bay with several caves that any Caribbean country would envy. A return moto-taxi will cost around US$3 to US$4.

Sleeping

There are several insalubrious cheapies on Rue Stenio Vincent near Place Alexandre Dumas. The better hotels are all uphill along Ave Emile Roumer in the Bordes district.

La Patience Hôtel (☎ 2284-6290; Rue Stenio Vincent; s/d US$25/35) Immediately east of Place Alexandre Dumas, between the street and the sea, this is the best of a gang of unimpressive budget hotels. Reasonably clean, reasonably welcoming and reasonably acceptable for the price.

Hôtel La Cabane (☎ 2284-5128; Ave Emile Roumer; s US$30-40, d US$50-60, tr US$70, incl breakfast; P ⊠ ▯) A bright and clean hotel. Some rooms are a little small, or maybe they just feel that way because of the ostentatious dark-wood furniture squeezed in. The airy restaurant is decorated with paintings of Jérémie's famous literary and political sons.

our pick **Auberge Inn** (☎ 3727-9678, 3465-2207; aubergeinn@netscape.net; 6 Ave Emile Roumer; s US$45-54, d US$72-84, tr US$90-108, incl breakfast; P ⊠ ▯) The decor and welcome make the Auberge Inn feel more like a home than a guesthouse. Very charming, rooms have mosquito nets, the food is excellent, and there's a selection of books, maps and handicrafts on sale. The only drawback is that bathrooms are shared.

Hôtel le Bon Temps (☎ 2284-9148; hotelbontemps@ yahoo.fr; 8 Ave Emile Roumer; s US$65-75, d US$100-110, incl breakfast; P ⊠ ▯) Next door to the Auberge Inn, this is a modern, well-appointed hotel, run with an efficient smile. The whole place is spotless, although some of the (cheaper) rooms have skylights rather than windows.

Next door to Hôtel La Cabane, the Hotel des Trois Dumas has had good reviews in the past, but was temporarily closed when we visited. When it reopens, expect to pay around US$40 a head.

Eating

The midrange hotels all have restaurants, but usually demand advance warning if you're eating in.

Chouconne (☎ 2286-6573; 110 Rue Stenio Vincent; meals US$1.50-7; ☼ 9am-1pm & 4-8pm) Located inside the Alliance Française, this small cafeteria-restaurant is a relaxing place to take a meal, and you'll often find yourself striking up a conversation with the students. Food is simple (sandwiches, pasta dishes etc) but tasty.

Chez Patou (Rue Monseigneur Boge; snacks/mains from US$2/4; ☼ 8am-3pm & 6-9pm) A great place to fill up, this airy red-and-white building has a decent range of sandwiches and burgers, along with hearty servings of Creole standards, spaghetti and the like.

Le Boucanier (Rue Stenio Vincent; mains from US$5; ☼ 6-11pm) A typical bar-resto, Le Boucanier has a wide-ranging Creole menu, but there are usually only one or two dishes available, typically barbecued chicken or *griyo* (pork) served with plantain and salad.

L'Oasis Restaurant (☎ 2284-4757; mains around US$7-10; ☼ 6pm-late) Popular with Jérémie's youth, this large restaurant is a lively place at weekends, when the drinks flow and the sound system is cranked up (there's often live music). Expect no surprises from the menu (although the fish and *lambi* are good), but go for the atmosphere. It's located near Rue la Source Dommage.

You can buy fruit, vegetables and bread at the market north of the main square, along Rue Alexandre Pétion and Rue Monseigneur Boge.

Getting There & Around

Jérémie feels a long way from just about anywhere else in Haiti. The quickest way in and

SOUTHERN HAITI

out is the daily **Tortugair** (☎ 2250-2555) flight from Port-au-Prince (US$90, 45 minutes). Demand is high, so book as far in advance as possible. The grassy airstrip is 5km northwest of Jérémie.

Buses leave every afternoon for Port-au-Prince (US$14, 11 hours) from a lot on the southern outskirts. The road gives literal meaning to the Haitian proverb 'After the mountains, more mountains,' and can be treacherous during the rains. Buses stop at all main towns en route, but you'll be asked to pay the full Port-au-Prince fare irrespective of your destination.

A ferry sails from Jérémie wharf every Friday evening to Port-au-Prince (US$14, 12 hours), although the boat is very creaky and often dangerously overloaded.

Moto-taxis ply the streets, charging around US$0.40 for most rides (US$0.60 to the bus station from the town center).

AROUND JÉRÉMIE

About 20km west of Jérémie is the startlingly beautiful cove of **Anse du Clerc**. It's pretty much as far as the road goes and you need a 4WD to get here, although a moto-taxi can just do it if it hasn't rained recently (US$8.50,

one hour). There's a small village on the pebble beach, and a charming hotel. **Anse du Clerc Beach Hotel** (☎ 2246-3519; per person half-board US$55) has half-a-dozen thatched bungalows surrounded by lawns and palm trees right on the beach, one of the most picturesque spots in Haiti.

Contrary to many maps, the road does not continue west from here to Dame Marie and Anse d'Hainault.

PESTEL

The pretty port village of Pestel is three hours east of Jérémie along the Grand Anse coast. It's a charming place once you're here, with its French fort, old wooden houses and some of Haiti's most wonderful (and wonderfully untouched) beaches. Until recently Pestel hosted a great **Festival of the Sea** every Easter, with regattas and *rara* bands; plans are afoot to restart it in the near future.

Hotel Louis & Louise (☎ 2284-6191; r US$35) is a yellow-and-blue gingerbread-style building with cozy rooms and home-cooked food.

The easiest way to get to Pestel from Jérémie is by boat (US$7), but they're often worryingly overloaded. There's daily transport, but the road is terrible.

SOUTHERN HAITI

Northern Haiti

If you're interested in how Haiti came to be as it is today, head for the north coast. It all happened here, from Columbus' first landfall on Hispaniola to the key events of the Haitian slave revolution, and there are still many monuments left to mark out this path of history.

Everything starts at Cap-Haïtien, Haiti's second city. Now a quiet sort of a place, it was once one of the richest colonial ports in the world. Its central square and wide gridded streets with high-shuttered doors and balconies make it the ideal base from where you can explore the region.

Cap-Haïtien is just an hour away from what has to be Haiti's most stupendous tourist attraction. The magnificent Citadelle la Ferrière is the mother of all Caribbean forts – a true castle perched high on a mountain and the master of all it surveys. Built in the early years of independence, it's a monument to the vision of a short-lived king, whose ruined palace of Sans Souci sits below, looking like something from a tropical Hollywood adventure movie. There are more forts further to the east, including Fort Liberté, part of France's futile attempts to keep hold of its colony – independence was declared in Gonaïves, on the road back to Port-au-Prince. Haiti's history reaches back even further to the west, where Île de la Tortue evokes memories of the golden age of piracy.

History is well and good, but the crashing Atlantic waves give the north some spectacular coastline and great beaches as well. Cormier Plage and Plage Labadie are a stone's throw from Cap-Haïtien and are ideal places to unwind – even in the years of turmoil, Labadie was one place the cruise lines couldn't bear to give up.

HIGHLIGHTS

- Take a breathtaking trip through the past at **La Citadelle la Ferrière** (p338), one of the Caribbean's most awesome historic sites
- Explore the wide boulevards of **Cap-Haïtien** (opposite), Haiti's second city
- Chill on the beach with a rum punch at **Cormier Plage** or **Plage Labadie** (p338)
- Explore the Vodou heritage of the festivals of **Souvenance** and **Soukri** (p341), held at Souvenance and Les Poteaux

CAP-HAÏTIEN

pop 130,000

Haiti's second city feels a world away from the throng and hustle of Port-au-Prince. During the French colonial era it was the richest city in the Caribbean, and even if that grandeur has long since faded, the city still maintains a relaxed and parochial atmosphere. Its streets are laid out in a grid system that make it difficult to get lost, and the old port architecture of high shop fronts and balconies makes it a pleasant place to wander. Most people refer to the city simply as 'Cap,' or 'O'Kap' in the high-lilting local Creole accent of its residents.

Despite its rich history, there is still plenty of poverty in Cap-Haïtien, although recent efforts to improve municipal facilities, water supply and rubbish collection are slowly beginning to have their effect.

There isn't too much to do in Cap-Haïtien beyond enjoy the atmosphere, but it's an ideal place to base yourself to enjoy the nearby attractions, including the amazing La Citadelle la Ferrière and the beaches around Plage Labadie.

History

The currently sleepy nature of Cap-Haïtien belies a turbulent past. It has been razed to the ground five times by man and nature alike, and had four changes of name. Its history is inextricably linked to Haiti's colonial past and struggle for independence.

Cap-François was founded in 1670 by Bertrand d'Ogeron, who recognized the superb natural harbor of its location. It was a refuge for Calvinists fleeing religious turmoil in France, but as Saint-Domingue grew as a colony, the port soon became its most important possession. Renamed Cap Français, it sat at the hub of the booming plantation economy of the 18th century. Sugar, coffee, cotton and indigo swelled its coffers, and all fed by the African slave trade. By the middle of the century, Cap Français was displaying its wealth through its grand buildings and the fine dress of the colonists, the 'Paris of the Antilles.'

This Paris was destined to burn in the great slave revolution. Early rebellions had been squashed here, the inhabitants witnessing the executions of Mackandal in 1758, Vincent Ogé, who had agitated for mulatto's rights, in 1790 and Boukman a year later. The city was sacked when the full revolution erupted, then completely torched in 1803 on the orders of Toussaint Louverture, who preferred to see it burn rather than fall into the hands of Napoleon's invading army. At Vertières on its outskirts Dessalines won the final victory that brought independence, and renamed the city Cap-Haïtien as a symbol of freedom. In a gesture of vanity, when Christophe became king he renamed it Cap Henri, but the name reverted on his death in 1820.

From then Cap-Haïtien ceded its central political and economic role to Port-au-Prince, and never fully recovered from the earthquake that leveled it in 1842. Charlemagne Péraulte, the hero of the Caco rebellion against the US military occupation in 1915, is buried here, but even he couldn't stop the Americans forcing one last name change on the city, when they reordered the street plan for their own convenience.

Orientation

Cap-Haïtien is laid out in a grid pattern. Streets parallel to the sea are lettered Rue A through Q, A being the closest to the sea; those running perpendicular are numbered Rue 1 to 24, starting from the southern end of the city. If a building is on the corner of Rues 15 and L, its address is written as Rue 15L, while if the building is along Rue 14 between Rues A and B, the address is written Rue 14A-B (if the building is on Rue A between Rues 13 and 14, its address is Rue 13-14A). The streets were renamed in this utilitarian fashion by the US Marines in 1915, who couldn't pronounce the French originals.

The wide avenue running the length of the seafront is simply called the Boulevard (or Boulevard de Mer). The area to the north of the city, across a water canal, is called Carenage.

Information

CULTURAL CENTERS

Alliance Français (☎ 2262-0132; Rue 15B-C; ☽ 8am-4:30pm Mon-Fri) Runs regular cultural events.

EMERGENCY

Police (Rue A)

INTERNET ACCESS

Discount Cybercafé (Rue 14H; per hr US$1.15; ☽ 8am-8pm)

Pale Klè Net (Rue G14; per hr US$1.25; ☽ 8am-8pm)

NORTHERN HAITI

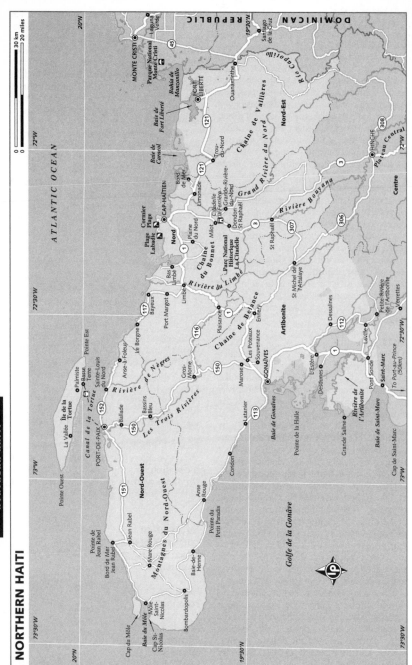

MEDICAL SERVICES

Hôpital Justinien (☎ 2262-0512, 2262-0513; Rue 17Q) Cap-Haïtien's main hospital.

Rien Que Pour Vos Yeux (82 Rue 17Q) Well-stocked pharmacy.

MONEY

There's a useful cluster of banks along Rue10-11A. When the banks are closed, you can change money on the street outside the Universal Hotel – moneychangers call to attract your attention.

Banque de L'Union Haïtienne (BUH; Rue 17A)

Sogebank (Rue11A) Has an ATM open during banking hours.

Unibank (cnr Rue 11 A)

POST

Post Office (Rue 16-17A)

TELEPHONE

Teleco (Rue 17) Located between Rue A and the Boulevard.

TOURIST INFORMATION

Bureau du Tourisme (☎ 262-0870; cnr Rue 24 & the Boulevard)

TRAVEL AGENTS

Up 2 Date Travel (☎ 2262-5545; Rue 17L) Useful for domestic flight tickets.

Sights

CITY CENTER

Cap-Haïtien in centered on **Place d'Armes**, a wide and pleasant square between Rues 18 and 20. A statue of Dessalines stands guard over the square, which is liberally tricked out with red-and-blue Haitian flags on holidays. At other times it's a popular meeting place for students from the Roi Christophe University, on the southeast corner of the square. The **Notre Dame Cathedral** otherwise dominates proceedings, a simple and airy white basilica with pretty, abstract, stained-glass windows.

The earthquake of 1842 left few colonial-era buildings in Cap-Haïtien, and its streets are now lined with an amalgam of styles. Most common are the old commercial buildings, with high shop fronts and tall shuttered doors and windows. The floors above are residential and support wide balconies with ornate iron railings that give the sidewalks shade at almost all times of day.

The best architectural gems are in the immediate vicinity of the cathedral. On the corner of Rue 16F is a tremendous (if slightly worn) red-brick Gothic mansion built in 1898, while on Rue 15 behind the cathedral are some charming gingerbread houses. The oldest accessible building is the Hostellerie du Roi Christophe, now a hotel (see p336), whose oldest parts were built in 1724.

Like Port-au-Prince and Jacmel, Cap-Haïtien has a **Marché de Fer** (Iron Market). This forms the hub of commercial activity, with market vendors spilling out in the streets around it to bring traffic to a halt, easily the most boisterous part of this otherwise laid-back city.

FORTS

As a major port, Cap-Haïtien has had a number of important forts to defend its harbor, all originally built by the French and found looking out to sea on the way to Plage Rival. All are ruins, but offer nice views and a chance to get out of the city center.

If you follow the Boulevard through Carenage, you'll quickly arrive at **Fort Etienne-Magny**, about 500m past the Hôtel Les Jardins de l'Ocean. Only the foundations remain, but five cannons are still in place. Several benches have also been installed there, and the spot is a popular place for Haitian kids to meet and kick a football around. The next is **Fort St Joseph**, on the right on the edge of the cliff. There are more ruins here, but they aren't easily accessible.

If you continue until the road peters out at Plage Rival, then continue along the sand, you'll reach **Fort Picolet**, about 1.5km from Fort Etienne-Magny. Although the fort itself is in ruins, some quite large walls and brick staircases are still standing, and you'll find an amazing array of cannons. The view is perfect, and the spot is often deserted. It's a peaceful place to watch the sunset, although it's a dark walk home.

Sleeping

Cap-Haïtien has a shortage of midrange beds. Rooms fill fast at the weekend, so advance booking is advised.

BUDGET

Hôtel la Sargesse (☎ 2262-2116; Rue 9A; r US$12) Most of Cap-Haïtien's cheapies are fairly grim affairs, but this one just about makes the grade. Bathrooms are shared. Don't expect any frills, and bring some earplugs if

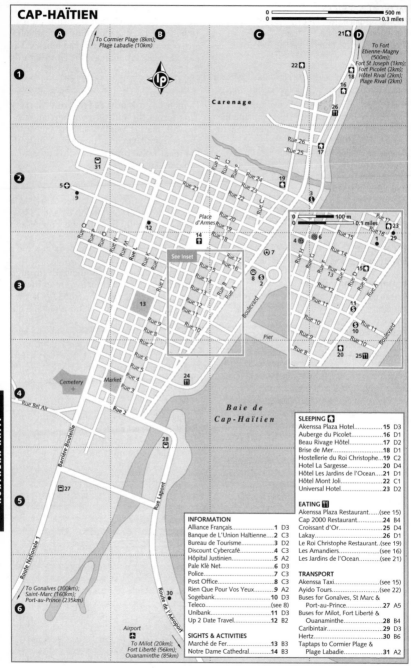

CAP-HAÏTIEN

0 ————— 500 m
0 ————— 0.3 miles

NORTHERN HAITI

To Carmier Plage (8km);
Plage Labadie (10km)

To Fort
Etienne-Magny
(500m);
Fort St Joseph (1km);
Fort Picolet (2km);
Hôtel Rival (2km);
Plage Rival (2km)

Carenage

Rue 26
Rue 25

Rue 24
Rue 23
Rue 21
Rue 22

Place
d'Armes
Rue 20
Rue 19
Rue 18
Rue 17
Rue 16
Rue 15
Rue 14
Rue 13
Rue 12
Rue 11
Rue 10
Rue 9
Rue 8
Rue 7
Rue 6
Rue 5
Rue 4
Rue 3
Rue 2

Cemetery
Market

Rue Bel Air

*Baie de
Cap-Haïtien*

Pier

See Inset

0 ————— 100 m
0 ————— 0.1 miles

Rue 17
Rue 16
Rue 15
Rue 14
Rue 13
Rue 11
Rue 10
Rue 9
Rue 8

Boulevard

Route Nationale 1

Barrière Bouteille

Rue Lapont

Route de l'Aéroport

Airport

To Gonaïves (100km);
Saint-Marc (160km);
Port-au-Prince (235km)

To Milot (20km);
Fort Liberté (56km);
Ouanaminthe (85km)

INFORMATION

Alliance Français..................**1**	D3
Banque de L'Union Haïtienne...**2**	C3
Bureau de Tourisme..............**3**	D2
Discount Cybercafé..............**4**	C3
Hôpital Justinien.................**5**	A2
Pale Klè Net.......................**6**	D3
Police..............................**7**	C3
Post Office........................**8**	C3
Rien Que Pour Vos Yeux........**9**	A2
Sogebank.........................**10**	D3
Teleco...........................(see 8)	
Unibank..........................**11**	D3
Up 2 Date Travel.................**12**	B2

SIGHTS & ACTIVITIES

Marché de Fer...................**13**	B3
Notre Dame Cathedral..........**14**	B3

SLEEPING

Akenssa Plaza Hotel............**15**	D3
Auberge du Picolet..............**16**	D1
Beau Rivage Hôtel...............**17**	D2
Brise de Mer.....................**18**	D1
Hostellerie du Roi Christophe...**19**	C2
Hotel La Sargesse...............**20**	D4
Hôtel Les Jardins de l'Ocean...**21**	D1
Hôtel Mont Joli..................**22**	C1
Universal Hotel..................**23**	D2

EATING

Akenssa Plaza Restaurant......(see 15)	
Cap 2000 Restaurant............**24**	B4
Croissant d'Or....................**25**	D4
Lakay............................**26**	D1
Le Roi Christophe Restaurant...(see 19)	
Les Amandiers.................(see 16)	
Les Jardins de l'Ocean.........(see 21)	

TRANSPORT

Akenssa Taxi....................(see 15)	
Ayido Tours.....................(see 22)	
Buses for Gonaïves, St Marc &
Port-au-Prince...................**27**	A5
Buses for Milot, Fort Liberté &
Ouanaminthe....................**28**	B4
Caribintair.......................**29**	D3
Hertz............................**30**	B6
Taptaps to Cormier Plage &
Plage Labadie...................**31**	A2

THE NIGHT OF FIRE

On the night of August 14, 1791, just outside Cap-Français in the woods of Bois Caïman, a gathering of slaves held a Vodou ritual, sparking the fire that eventually erupted into the slave revolution. The ceremony was led by Boukman, the headman from a local plantation and *houngan* (Vodou priest). Against a thundering sky, a pig was sacrificed, binding the slaves to the *lwa* (Vodou spirits) of Africa through Boukman's incendiary freedom cry:

'The god who created the sun which gives us light, who rouses the waves and rules the storm, though hidden in the clouds, he watches us. He sees all that the white man does. The god of the white man inspires him with crime, but our god calls upon us to do good works. Our god who is good to us orders us to revenge our wrongs. He will direct our arms and aid us. Throw away the symbol of the god of the whites who has so often caused us to weep, and listen to the voice of liberty, which speaks to the hearts of us all.'

Within weeks, the plantations of the north were ablaze, their ashes falling like snow on Cap-Français like snow. Although this stage of the rebellion was crushed and Boukman executed, Toussaint Louverture participated in the uprising and used his experience in the final struggle for independence. Bois Caïman is now a national monument, and remains an auspicious Vodou site to this day.

you're a light sleeper. There's an OK restaurant out front.

Akenssa Plaza Hotel (☎ 2262-4354; Rue 14B; r US$15-45; 🟦) The rooms here are better than the slightly depressing gray concrete entrance (on Rue 14 next to the restaurant). Rooms are simple, with lots of tiling that at least helps keep the place clean.

Universal Hotel (☎ 2262-0254; Rue 17B; r US$22-30, with shared bathroom US$18; 🟦) Definitely one of the better budget options. A large hotel with several terraces, its rooms are simple and clean. The management is helpful and pious, too: Bible passages remind guests that the meek shall inherit the earth. A handy sentiment if you're staying in the budget category.

Brise de Mer (☎ 2262-0821; 4 Carenage; r US$30-50; 🟦) This hotel has just celebrated its centenary. It's a sweet place, but is slightly feeling its age. Rooms are fairly basic, although several are blessed with sea views and balconies, and the agreeable air in the garden complements the salty breeze from the ocean.

MIDRANGE & TOP END

Hôtel Rival (☎ 2262-0977; hotelrival@hotmail.com; Rte de Rival; s US$45-65, d US$51-71; 🅿 🟦 🖥 🖂) On the outskirts of the city by the sea near Fort Picolet, you can't miss this orange hotel. It's a bright option, and agreeably self-contained given its location. Rooms are fine (ask for a sea view), and it's the one place in Cap where you can happily dip your toes in the sea.

Hôtel Les Jardins de l'Ocean (☎ 2262-2277; 90 Carenage; r with fan/air-con US$50/80; 🅿 🟦) This French-run hotel seems to ramble up the side of the hill it sits on, so there's no shortage of terraces offering views to sea (the rooms themselves have none). Rooms come in a variety of shapes and sizes, all individually decorated to the owner's taste – we loved the one with the mosaic wall of broken mirror. Its restaurant is recommended.

Beau Rivage Hôtel (☎ 2262-3113; beaurivage@yahoo .com; 25 Blvd de Mer; s/d US$60/80; 🅿 🟦 🖥) A new hotel facing the seafront, the Beau Rivage is a good addition to Cap's sleeping options. Service is good, and if some rooms are a little on the small and boxy side, they're all well appointed with modern fixtures and fittings.

Hôtel Mont Joli (☎ 2262-0300; www.hotelmontjoli .com; Rue B, Carenage; s/d US$78/96; 🅿 🟦 🖥 🖂) On a hill overlooking Cap, the Mont Joli easily has the best views in the city. It's also the best standard hotel, and great value for the price. Rooms are generously sized, the restaurant has a good bar, and there's an exceedingly pleasant pool and terrace to chill out on.

Auberge du Picolet (☎ 2262-5595; Blvd de Mer; s/d US$86/110; 🅿 🟦) A new kid on the block, this hotel is proving popular. Spacious rooms are uncluttered and centered on a small shady courtyard. Sympathetically designed, it feels more Dominican colonial than brand-new Haitian.

NORTHERN HAITI

ourpick **Hostellerie du Roi Christophe** (☎ 2262-0414; Rue 24B; s/d US$96/120, ste US$132; P ✕ ⌨ ⏣) Cap-Haïtien's most charming hotel, this French colonial building has something of the Spanish hacienda about it. Set within lush gardens, there's an elegant, leafy central courtyard with plenty of rocking chairs, and a terrace restaurant. The rooms are large and comfy with plenty of period furniture and art; many have balconies. The story that Henri Christophe worked in the kitchens as a slave is sadly apocryphal.

Eating

Most restaurants in town serve Creole food, with a couple of French dishes thrown in. The fanciest options are all hotel restaurants, while at the other end of the scale, there are plenty of nondescript bar-restos where you can fill up on a cheap plate of rice and beans with chicken or fish.

Croissant d'Or (Rue 8 Blvd; ☖ 8am-4pm Mon-Sat) This small bakery sells fresh baguettes, cakes and savory pastries. It always seems packed out and one visit will explain why – it's the best bakery in town. Load up on sticky treats, or go for the quiche or pizza slices as filling snacks.

Cap 2000 Restaurant (Rue 5 Blvd; prices US$4-8; ☖ 7am-11pm) This restaurant has a friendly atmosphere and good cheap Creole dishes at reasonable prices. The chicken *plat complet* (set meal) is well prepared, and tasty fish and chips and pasta dishes are also available.

Akenssa Plaza Restaurant (Rue 14B; mains around US$5-8; ☖ 6am-11pm) This is a cheap and cheerful place in the town center, although busier during the day than in the evening, when beer tends to win out over food in the ordering stakes. All the Creole standards are here, such as *griyo* (pork) and *lambi*, piled high with rice and plantain. Pasta dishes and burgers cater to other tastes.

Le Roi Christophe Restaurant (☎ 2262-0414; Rue 24B; mains US$6-11; ☖ 11am-3pm & 6-10.30pm) Relaxing on the terrace of this hotel restaurant is an great way to spend a meal. There are some tasty sandwiches that make ideal lunchtime fillers, and a good range of pasta dishes. French and Creole round out the menu, along with a decent wine list.

ourpick **Lakay** (☎ 2262-1442; Blvd de Mer; mains from US$8; ☖ 5-10pm) One of the busiest restaurants in Cap-Haïtien, and it's not hard to see why. There are tables facing the seafront where you can enjoy a drink, otherwise you

step inside to eat under bamboo thatch and load up on generous plates of Creole food, plus a few pizzas. The atmosphere is lively, and at weekends there are often bands (an admission charge of US$4 applies).

Les Jardins de l'Ocean (☎ 2262-2277; 90 Carenage; mains US$8-15; ☖ 12-3pm & 6-10pm) With its French owner, the menu here is decidedly Gallic. The menu is ambitious, including lamb with green herbs, Provençal shrimp and carpaccio of *lambi* (conch), but you're better off asking what's available before drooling over the menu too much. The resulting meals, however, are delicious.

Les Amandiers (☎ 2262-5595; Blvd de Mer; mains US$8-15; ☖ 6-10pm) This pleasant restaurant at the Auberge du Picolet serves mainly French cuisine, with a couple of Creole classics in the mix. There are plenty of seafood options, or go for more unusual dishes such as duck with olives or chicken *confit d'ail*. All dishes come with a salad entrée.

Getting There & Away

The airport is 3.5km east of the city (US$5/1.25 by taxi/moto-taxi). Both **Tortugair** (☎ 2250-2555) and **Caribintair** (☎ 2262-2300; Rue 16B) fly twice daily to Port-au-Prince (US$85, 30 minutes).

Buses for Port-au-Prince (US$12, seven hours) leave from near the Barrière Bouteille (City Gates) on Rue L from around 5am. Leave in good time as buses terminate in La Saline on the edge of Cité Soleil – not recommended after dark. Buses travel via Gonaïves (US$6, three hours) and Saint-Marc (US$7, four hours).

For Cormier Plage and Plage Labadie, taptaps (local buses or minibuses) leave regularly from Rue 21Q (US$0.75, 30 minutes). For the Citadelle, taptaps to Milot (US$0.40, one hour) leave from Rue Lapont on the eastern edge of town near the main bridge. The road is bad, especially after rain. Transport to Fort Liberté (US$1.60, two hours) and Ouanaminthe (US$2.50, three hours) also leaves from here.

Ayido Tours (☎ 3729-8711, 556-3082) runs a direct coach service to Santiago in the Dominican Republic every Wednesday and Saturday from the Hôtel Mont Joli. Buy tickets at the hotel shop.

Getting Around

Publiques (collective taxis) have a set rate of US$0.30 anywhere in town – a few are signed as taxis, otherwise look for the red ribbon hanging from the front windshield mirror. Taptaps (US$0.15) run two main routes along Rue L (also called Rue Espanole) from Rue 15L to the Barrière Bouteille, and along Rue A from Rue 10A to the airport.

Moto-taxis here should never cost more than US$0.40. They're weedy scooters, and coupled with the pot-holed roads are the most uncomfortable moto-taxis we found in Haiti. The Akenssa Plaza Hôtel runs a metered taxi service, **Akenssa Taxi** (☎ 2262-4934). For care hire go to **Hertz** (☎ 2262-0369; Rte de l'Aéroport).

AROUND CAP-HAÏTIEN

THE CITADELLE & SANS SOUCI

The awe-inspiring mountain fortress of La Citadelle la Ferrière is a short distance from Cap-Haïtien on the edge of the small town of Milot. Built to repel a possible French attack, it also stands as a monument to the vision of Henri Christophe, who oversaw its construction. A visit here is an essential part of any trip to Haiti, and actually takes in two sites – the Unesco World Heritage–listed fortress itself and the no-less amazing palace of Sans Souci. The Citadelle sits high above the town, and can be reached either on foot or horseback. Visiting in the morning is preferable, before the views are obscured by haze.

Information

The entrance to the site, formally known as the Parc National Historique La Citadelle, is at the far end of Milot town, next to an unmissable white church with a huge dome, and facing the ruins of Sans Souci. Opposite this is the **ticket office** (admission US$5, horse rental US$10; ☽ 8am-5pm). This is the one place in Haiti where tourist hassle is guaranteed, and the sight of a *blanc* (generic word for a foreigner; not color-specific) invariably attracts a throng of would-be guides and horse wranglers eager for your custom. Most of the guides can only parrot the most self-evident features of the site; one that comes recommended is **Maurice Etienne** (☎ 3667-6070), who really knows his history and also runs the Lakou Lakay cultural center (see p338). A reasonable fee for a good guide is US$20 to US$30, plus the hire of his horse.

Horses are the normal method of reaching the Citadelle, although they struggle on the

cobbled path after heavy rain. Each generally comes with two handlers (both of whom expect a tip of US$4 to US$5), one of whom is employed to help push the beast along. It's not always a pretty scene. From Sans Souci to the Citadelle takes a couple of hours by horse, although a 4WD can make it to a parking area 30 minutes' walk short of the top. There are further offers of horse rental here, as well as local women selling trinkets.

Sights

SANS SOUCI

Built as a conscious rival to the splendors of the Versailles in France, Henri Christophe's palace of Sans Souci has lain abandoned since it was ruined in the 1842 earthquake. The years of neglect have left it partially reclaimed by the tropical environment, creating a wonderfully bizarre and evocative monument at once elegant and truly alien.

Finished in 1813, Sans Souci was more than just a palace, but designed to be the administrative capital of Christophe's kingdom, housing a hospital, a school and a printing press, as well as an army barracks.

The palace sits on a wide terrace, and is approached by a grand staircase once flanked by bronze lions. You enter a series of rooms – the throne room, banqueting halls and private apartments, even a billiards room. Although the walls are now bare brick, during Christophe's reign they would have been hung with rich tapestries and paintings, all designed to show that although Haitians had once been slaves, they were now a cultured nation. Open to the sky, the palace originally had four stories and huge French picture windows. From his apartments, Christophe maintained correspondences with world figures of the day, from the Czar of Russia to the English abolitionist William Wilberforce.

Behind the palace are the remains of the King's and Queen's Gardens with their ornamental fountains and channels that brought cool mountain water into the palace. To one side are the remains of the hospital and, opposite, the old barracks. The Royal Corps were stationed here, originally slaves from Dahomey who were freed by Christophe when their slave ship (bound for the USA) was forced into port at Cap-Haïtien.

Just above the palace site, a roughly paved road winds up the mountain to the Citadelle.

NORTHERN HAITI

CAVES, BATS & ANCIENT SCULPTURES

If you fancy yourself as Indiana Jones, head well off the beaten track to the caves of Dondon St Rafaël. This small town surrounded by coffee, cocoa and vanilla plantations is home to a series of caves once used by the Taínos for refuge. From Dondon it's a two-hour hike up the mountain to the caves (Des Grottes), but you'll probably require a local guide to show you the way, and possibly rent you a horse. The caves are now home to large numbers of bats, but the Taínos have left their mark on many of the stalagmites, the tops of which have been carved to resemble skulls. It's one of the most intriguing – and remote – Arawak sites in the country

It takes a 4WD one hour to reach Dondon St Rafaël from Cap-Haïtien; there are daily taptaps from Rue Lapont (US$1.50, two hours).

LA CITADELLE LA FERRIÈRE

Haitians call the Citadelle the eighth wonder of the world, and having slogged to the 900m summit of Pic la Ferrière, which the fortress crowns, you may be liable to agree. This astounding structure with a battleship-like appearance overlooks Cap-Haïtien, the northern plain and routes leading to the south, giving astonishing views in every direction. It was completed in 1820, employing 20,000 people over 15 years. It held enough supplies to sustain the royal family and a garrison of 5000 troops for a year. With 4m-thick walls that reach heights of 40m, the fortress was impenetrable, although the French attack it was meant to repel never materialized and its cannons were never fired in anger.

Inside the ramparts, the fort has a series of further defensive entrances with drawbridges and blind corners to fox attackers. These lead through a gallery containing the first of several cannon batteries. The Citadelle contains over 160 cannons, mostly captured in battle from the English, the Spanish, and the French (look for the royalist cannons with their insignia scratched out by revolutionaries). Throughout the fort are huge piles of cannonballs – 50,000 in total – all neatly stacked and waiting patiently for Napoleon.

At the heart of the fort is the central courtyard, with its officers' quarters. Christophe himself was buried here after his suicide – his grave is under a huge boulder that forms part of the mountain. On the level above is the whitewashed tomb of his son Prince Noel, killed in an explosion in the gunpowder store in 1818.

It's easily possible to spend a couple of hours exploring the site, which constantly reveals hidden passages, halls, new views from its ramparts or down into the huge cisterns designed to collect water. Sheer drops protect the Citadelle from every angle except its rear, where you can look south to Site des Ramiers, a huddle of four small forts protecting its exposed flank.

In the main courtyard there's a small shop that sells postcards and drinks; the caretaker will open it for you.

Sleeping & Eating

Most people visit the Citadelle as a day trip from Cap-Haïtien, but if you're here overnight there's one good sleeping and eating option.

Lakou Lakay (☎ 2262-5189, 3667-6070; Milot; meal US$10) This cultural center is a delight. Run by guide Maurice Etienne and his family, visitors are welcomed by traditional dancing and serenaded with folk songs and drumming while enjoying a huge Creole feast. Rooms for visitors are under construction and should be open by this book's publication. The whole center is also used for community celebrations and other events, so your visit is certain to get you close to traditional Haitian life.

Getting There & Away

A taptap from Cap-Haïtien costs US$0.45 (one hour), and drops you a short walk from Sans Souci. Don't leave the return too late, as transport dries up by late afternoon.

BEACHES WEST OF CAP-HAÏTIEN

A rough road leads west from Cap-Haïtien, winding through the hills to the northwest coast of the cape. If you've been disappointed by the beaches surrounding Cap-Haïtien, you're heading in the right direction, toward some of the loveliest coastal scenery in the country, where richly wooded hills tumble straight into the Atlantic, the two divided by sheer cliffs or stretches of delicious golden sand.

The road hits the north coast of the cape near **Cormier Plage**, the picture of a Caribbean beach and resort, where white breakers roll in to shore and rum punches are the order of the day. Further around the point is **Plage Labadie**, a small walled-off peninsula rented by Royal Caribbean Lines for its cruise-ship guests three or four times a week.

If you've been in Haiti for any length of time, the sight of a giant white ship with up to three thousand passengers – a sight common anywhere in the Caribbean – seems like a surreal event. Ferries shuttle guests back and forth all day, and the sea buzzes with jet skis and holidaymakers leaping from giant inflatable toys. During the rest of the week the place is empty, and you can pay US$3 to enter and enjoy the place yourself and take out a sea kayak. Locals sell food and drink.

Royal Caribbean Lines is the single biggest contributor to Haitian tourism, with the ships worth an estimated US$2 million to the economy. Although the company contributes to local education projects, little of the revenues are spent locally – the nearby Labadie village lacks decent electricity and the road to Cap-Haïtien remains a complete nightmare.

From Plage Labadie, *bateaux-taxis* (water taxis) ferry passengers to the beaches further west. Just around the cape is **Plage Belli**, from where the view of ocean-washed headland after headland fading into the far distance is spectacular. The village of **Labadie**, a small collection of rural dwellings, is a nice place to wander around watching kids playing basketball and women washing clothes. There are a few small shops, places to buy drinks and snacks, and fishermen selling their catch.

Sleeping & Eating

Hotels are listed in order of their distance from Cap-Haïtien.

Cormier Plage Resort (☎ 3528-1110; cormier@ hughes.net; Route de Labadie; s/d US$106/168 half-board; P X 🖳) One of the loveliest resorts in Haiti, Cormier Plage has 36 big and airy rooms dotted amid palm trees looking out to sea, all with terrace and wi-fi, and meters from the gently shelving golden beach. The restaurant is one of the best seafood places in the country, and worth making a detour to from Cap-Haïtien.

Belli Beach Bar (☎ 2262-2338; Plage Belli; s/d US$20/30) As the road west of Plage Labadie peters to an end, follow the narrow, steep steps leading down to Plage Belli. The tiny beach is lovely, but the hotel is exceedingly basic, with spartan rooms and frequent problems with

water supply. A restaurant serves seafood and Creole dishes.

Norm's Place (www.normsplacelabadee.com; Labadie; per person US$25; P X 🖳 🎧) A *bateau-taxi* hop between Plage Belli and Labadie village (ask for 'Kay Norm'), this charming guesthouse was built from a restored French fort by an American who came to Haiti in the early 1970s and never quite left. Large rooms have four-poster beds with mosquito nets, there's a garden for lounging and a warm welcome throughout. Meals are home-cooked on request.

Getting There & Away

Taptaps going to Cormier Plage and Plage Labadie (both US$0.80, 30 and 40 minutes respectively) leave regularly from Rue 21Q in Cap-Haïtien. Taptaps terminate (and leave from) the western side of Plage Labadie by the boundary fence of the Royal Caribbean Lines compound, from where brightly painted *bateaux-taxis* ferry passengers to Plage Belli and Labadie village. With other passengers, expect to pay around US$0.30, and several times that if you have the boat to yourself.

THE NORTHEAST

The Nord-Est Department borders the Dominican Republic. In the colonial era it was a major plantation area, and remains an important coffee-producing area. Its pine forests are heavily exploited for charcoal but are hanging in there. In addition to the border area, there are several colonial forts of interest to visitors.

FORT LIBERTÉ

It's quiet now, but Fort Liberté was once one of France's most strategically important bases in Saint-Domingue, at the center of a wide bay with a natural harbor. Inaugurated as Fort Dauphin by the French in 1731, a huge fortress was built here, once four bases that guarded the bay like beads on a string. They couldn't withstand Toussaint Louverture, however, who captured the port in 1796 and renamed it Fort Liberté, before continuing into Santo Domingo to conquer the Spanish. In the 1860s Fort Liberté served as a meeting place for the world's antislavery movement. The area is now economically depressed, the huge sisal plantations it once sustained long closed.

Fort Français (the fort's current name) is intact, and is one of the best French forts along the coast, with its ramparts, batteries and magazines. If the guardian is there, you'll be asked to pay a US$0.70 entrance fee. The remains of the fort surrounding the Baie de Fort Liberté can also be visited in a couple of hours – the easiest way is by moto-taxi. Fort Labouque and the Batterie de l'Anse are on the eastern lip of the bay guarding its entrance. Between here and the town are Fort St-Charles and Fort St-Frédéric.

There are two hotels. The **Hôtel Bayaha** (Rues Vallières et Bourbon; s/d US$35/60) is the better option, overlooking the bay. It has reasonable rooms and a restaurant. Cheaper and simpler is the **Hôtel La Sirene** (Rue Bory; r US$12) near the main school. It's just about adequate.

Fort Liberté can be visited as a day trip from Cap-Haïtien (US$1.60, two hours). It's about 5km off the main road to Ouanaminthe.

OUANAMINTHE

The very picture of a dusty border town, Ouanaminthe is an important trading centre across the Massacre River from Dajabón (p201) in the Dominican Republic. It's alive with small traders hurrying across to the Dominican side to buy goods, particularly on the market days of Monday and Friday. The contrast between the rubbish-strewn anarchy of Ouanaminthe and the paved streets and order of Dajabón is striking.

The border is open from 8am to 4.30pm. On arrival in Ouanaminthe, continue until the road splits in two. The left road leads to the bridge across the river that marks the border; the right to the customs and passport office. For more on crossing between the two countries, see p352.

Hôtel Paradis (Rue St-Pierre; s/d US$10/16) hardly lives up to its name, but it's just about bearable if you get stranded in town. You're better off sleeping in Dajabón if you can.

Taptaps to Cap-Haïtien (US$2.50, three hours) are plentiful.

THE NORTHWEST

Heading north from the Côte des Arcadins, you'll find the departments of Artibonite and Nord-Ouest. This is the birthplace of Haitian

independence, but its history extends to the earliest European contacts – Columbus first set foot on Hispaniola here, and the island of Île de la Tortue (Tortuga) was a free port during the golden age of piracy.

GONAÏVES

At first glance, Gonaïves looks like any other large town in Haiti, but it holds a very close place in the nation's heart. On January 1, 1804, Dessalines signed the act of Haitian independence here, creating the world's first black republic, and his wife, Claire Heureuse, is buried in the local cemetery. Gonaïves has played a revolutionary role in more recent years as well – it was rioting here in 1985 that showed the writing was on the wall for 'Baby Doc' Duvalier, while the rebel capture of Gonaïves in 2004 marked the beginning of the end for Aristide.

The town is a handy breaking point when traveling between Port-au-Prince, Cap-Haïtien and Port-de-Paix. Place de l'Indépendance is the town's focus, with its striking triangular modernist cathedral. In front of this is a martial statue of Dessalines in the prow of a ship, as if willing independence by the force of his presence alone. If you continue west from here, you'll reach the port and grubby beach – locals will tell you that toxic ash from Philadelphia is buried beneath the sand.

Sleeping & Eating

Family Hotel (☎ 2274-0600; Ave des Dattes; d with fan/air-con US$35/50; P ⊠) This is a decent medium-sized hotel, with a restaurant. Rooms are good value, although the service can be a bit poor.

Chachou Hôtel (☎ 3547-0172; 145 Ave des Dattes; s/d US$60/80; P ⊠ ⊡ ⊠) Gonaïve's best hotel, and frequently full of UN staff. Rooms are large and comfortable with satellite TV, and the restaurant is well recommended.

There are several cheap bar-restos near the main bus station and on Rue L'Ouverture.

Getting There & Away

Gonaïves is roughly halfway between Port-au-Prince and Cap-Haïtien. The bus station is east of the main square next to the Texaco gas station on the main highway. There are regular buses to Port-au-Prince (US$7, 3½ hours) and Cap-Haïtien (US$6, three hours). Buses south also stop at Saint-Marc (US$1.30, one hour); there are also plenty of

---

SOUVENANCE & SOUKRI

Souvenance and Soukri are major dates on the Vodou calendar. People from all over Haiti congregate near Gonaïves to take part in these marathon ceremonies, used by celebrants for spiritual cleansing and revival.

Souvenance begins on Good Friday, and continues for a week, accompanied by the constant sound of *rara* music. During the week prayers are offered to a sacred tamarind tree, initiates bathe in a sacred pond, libations are poured and bulls are sacrificed for the Vodou spirits. Ceremonies include singing and dancing and go on every night, while the celebrants rest by day. The rituals are three centuries old and are said to have originated in the maroon camps, the secret communities of runaway slaves. Ogou, the warrior *lwa* who helped inspire slaves during the revolution, is particularly revered here.

Soukri is a ritual dedicated to the Kongo *lwa*. The service is divided into two branches: 'the father of all Kongo,' which takes place on January 6, and the second, larger ceremony, 'the mother of all Kongo,' occurs on August 14. The rituals last a mammoth two weeks each, a true test of endurance. Many of the celebrations are similar to those in Souvenance. If you wish to visit these ceremonies, you should introduce yourself to the head of the Vodou society when you arrive.

Souvenance is held off the road between Gonaïves and Cap-Haïtien, about 20km north of Gonaïves. The festival has become well-known enough that the place where it is held is also now known as Souvenance. As you leave Gonaïves on the road to Cap-Haïtien, you cross over the Rivière Laquinte on a bridge called Mapou Chevalier. The first immediate right after the bridge will take you to Souvenance. There are small houses for rent around the temple, although many of the participants just sleep on straw mats in the shade.

Soukri takes place off the same road from Gonaïves to Cap-Haïtien. Continue northward past the turnoff for Souvenance until you reach a small market town, Les Poteaux. A turning opposite the Saint-Marc Catholic Church leads to the *lakou* (a collection of dwellings) known as Soukri.

---

taptaps here. The highway to Cap-Haïtien is a microcosm of environmental climates. Having followed the road from the capital through banana plantations and the beaches of Côte des Arcadins, around Gonaïves the land turns to semidesert, with cacti the size of trees. Turning inland from here the road climbs through green mountains before finally descending to the coast. The highway is in definite need of improvement, but the ever-changing views are always interesting.

Buses to Port-de-Paix (US$8, five hours) also leave from the bus station. The road is poor.

PORT-DE-PAIX & ÎLE DE LA TORTUE

Nord-Ouest Department, of which Port-de-Paix is the capital, is the most deforested and arid part of Haiti. The main reason to come here is to visit Île de la Tortue, the sliver of an island that forever seems to be on the cusp of development as the Caribbean's next big tourist thing. Although the island is covered with rocky hills, it also holds some glorious beaches, particularly the truly gorgeous Pointe-Ouest (although you really need your own boat to get there).

Île de la Tortue is famous for its piratical associations (see boxed text, p32). The contraband heritage continues into the 21st century, as the island (and Port-de-Paix) are well-known smuggling transshipment points to Miami, from duty-free goods to cocaine.

Boats sail every morning from Port-de-Paix to Basse-Terre on Île de la Tortue (US$4, one hour). From here you can get transport to the capital, Palmiste. Unfortunately there is no accommodation on the island. The **Hôtel Brise Marina** (☎ 2239-4648; Rte de St-Louis-du-Nord; r US$60; P ✗ ⬛) just outside Port-de-Paix is the best accommodation option in the region. Decent rooms have sea views and there's a restaurant.

There's regular transport to Gonaïves (US$8, five hours), from where you must change for onward travel.

Haiti Directory

CONTENTS

ACCOMMODATIONS

Most levels of accommodation are available in Haiti, from top-end hotels and beach resorts to complete fleapits, with everything in between. Port-au-Prince naturally has the widest choice of available options, along with Cap-Haïtien and Jacmel. You should be able to find the right accommodation for you, although there is often a shortage of midrange beds on offer.

In the Haiti guide we have defined budget as up to US$40, midrange as up to US$80 and top end as anything above this. Rooms come with private bathroom unless noted in the text. Prices are for doubles, but in many places you'll just be quoted a flat rate for the room irrespective of occupancy. As a general rule, only in midrange places and above can you expect to have breakfast thrown in. Even cheap hotels usually have a ceiling fan, with air-conditioning more or less standard above this price range.

Whatever level you pitch for, bringing a torch (or candles) is recommended. Power cuts can be both frequent and long. At the budget level you just have to ride out the cut, while more expensive places tend to have their own generators, even if they don't always run them during daylight hours. Many hotels add an electricity surcharge of US$5 to US$10 to the daily rate, included in the prices listed where possible. Midrange and top-end rates also include the 10% government tax added to the bill.

Guesthouses

Port-au-Prince has a number of small private guesthouses that cater primarily to visiting church groups, volunteers and aid workers. They offer a homey alternative to hotels, with a modest price tag attached. Standard rates are around US$35, including breakfast and dinner, which are eaten together to give a highly sociable atmosphere. Bathroom facilities are invariably shared. These places usually have a strong Christian ethic attached, and sometimes operate night curfews. As they cater to visiting groups, booking in advance is recommended where possible.

Camping

Pitching a tent isn't really an option in Haiti, and most Haitians would find the idea of voluntarily sleeping under canvas eccentric in the extreme. On top of this, with people everywhere in Haiti, finding a private pitch is nigh on impossible. The only likely options

---

BOOK YOUR STAY ONLINE

For more accommodation reviews and recommendations by Lonely Planet authors, check out the online booking service at www.lonelyplanet.com/hotels. You'll find the true, insider lowdown on the best places to stay. Reviews are thorough and independent. Best of all, you can book online.

are for full-on expeditions, such as in Parc National Macaya, where the terrain demands that you be completely self-sufficient. We found just one campsite in the country, in the extensive grounds of Ranch Le Moncel on the slopes above Port-au-Prince (p310).

Hotels

While hotels in Haiti come in all stripes, in comparison to the DR rooms can feel a little expensive, particularly in the midrange bracket, where even at this price you're not always guaranteed hot water.

At the budget end, hotels can be dreary, although we've tried to pick the best of the bunch. Some hotels double as brothels, with room rates quoted by the hour rather than the night. Known locally as *suivants* (for 'next!'), they're not particularly female friendly, although the turnover of guests means that their rooms are cleaned more regularly and efficiently than comparative hotels.

At the other end of the market, wi-fi access is becoming more standard. Expect good fixtures and a decent electricity supply. Most hotels of all ranges have attached restaurants or bars. Mosquito nets are rare.

Room rates don't change according to season, although at peak times – Jacmel during Carnival, for example – prices go up with demand.

Resorts

Beach resorts don't feature in Haiti to the extent they do in the DR, but there are a string

of them along the Côte des Arcadins north of Port-au-Prince. Prices are all-inclusive, usually with a couple of bars and restaurants to choose from, along with water sports and other activities. If you arrive during the week, you'll virtually have them to yourself, while the city's well-heeled inhabitants descend en masse at weekends.

ACTIVITIES

Compared to the DR, Haiti isn't a hugely rich activity-centered destination. Instead, traveling in Haiti itself becomes the activity. However, there are a few good options if you want a particular focus for your trip. It's possible to go scuba diving and snorkeling along the Côte des Arcadins, where there is good sea life, as well as along the Atlantic coast. Haiti's mountainous terrain lends itself well to hiking. A short drive from Port-au-Prince, Parc National La Visite and Parc National Forêt des Pins both offer good trekking country, with superb views and cool pine forests to explore. Both are also ornithologically rich. Birders will be amply rewarded by a visit to Trou Caïman and the wild Parc National Macaya.

BUSINESS HOURS

Banks are usually open from 8:30am to 1pm weekdays, but some of the more central branches are also open from 2pm to 5pm weekdays. Shops and offices usually open at 7am and close at 4pm weekdays, but many close earlier on Friday; most shops are also open on Saturday. Government offices are open 7am to 4pm weekdays, closing for an hour at noon. Sunday is very quiet, with many restaurants and most businesses closed.

CLIMATE CHARTS

Tropical Haiti enjoys pretty steady temperatures throughout the year. The main variation is due to altitude – while you'll get by

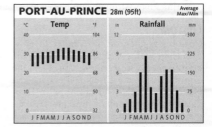

PREVENTING CHILD-SEX TOURISM IN THE DOMINICAN REPUBLIC & HAITI

Tragically, the exploitation of local children by tourists is becoming more prevalent throughout the Dominican Republic and Haiti. Various socioeconomic factors make children susceptible to sexual exploitation, and some tourists choose to take advantage of their vulnerable position.

Sexual exploitation has serious, lifelong effects on children. It is a crime and a violation of human rights.

The Dominican Republic and Haiti have laws against sexual exploitation of children. Many countries have enacted extraterritorial legislation that allows travelers to be charged as though the exploitation happened in their home country.

Responsible travelers can help stop child-sex tourism by reporting it. It is important not to ignore suspicious behavior. **Cybertipline** (www.cybertipline.com) is a website where sexual exploitation of children can be reported. You can also report the incident to local authorities and if you know the nationality of the perpetrator, report it to their embassy.

Travelers interested in learning more about how to fight against sexual exploitation of children can find more information through **ECPAT International** (End Child Prostitution & Trafficking; www.ecpat.org).

ECPAT – USA (☎ 718 935 9192; www.ecpatusa.org) is part of a global network working on these issues with over 70 affiliate organizations around the world. The US headquarters is located in New York.

Beyond Borders (www.beyondborders.org) is the Canadian affiliate of ECPAT. It aims to advance the rights of children to be free from abuse and exploitation without regard to race, religion, gender or sexual orientation.

---

with short sleeves most of the time, once you start climbing into the mountainous interior temperatures can take on a slight chill and you'll need an extra layer. Along the coast, humidity is more likely to be a problem.

Rainfall varies greatly, and depends both on your location and the time of year. Port-au-Prince gets most of its rain between April to November, easing off for drier July. The south more or less follows suit, while the north is wetter between November and March. Rains tend to fall heavily but stop abruptly, so are easy to work around. Look for *marchands* (female street vendors) suddenly appearing selling umbrellas and shower caps to keep hairdos dry! Travel in rural areas can be difficult after heavy rains due to rough roads and mudslides.

Hurricane season traditionally runs from August to October, although the winds sometimes blow strongly into November.

CUSTOMS

Customs regulations are similar to most countries, with restrictions on the import of live animals, weapons and drugs, and the export of ancient artifacts and endangered plants or animals. You can bring in 1L of liquor and one carton of cigarettes or 50 cigars. Customs inspections can be vigorous.

DANGERS & ANNOYANCES

Haiti has rarely enjoyed a popular media image abroad. Poverty and regular political turmoil play their part, and many governments currently advise against nonessential travel to the country. And yet, for the traveler, Haiti really can seem like one of the friendliest and most welcoming countries in the Caribbean. Navigating these apparently contradictory states is the key to getting the most out of your visit.

The presence of large numbers of UN troops under the auspices of the Stabilization Mission for Haiti (MINUSTAH) have done much to bring stability to Haiti, especially in dealing with the large-scale gang and kidnapping problems. But you should always keep your ear to the ground for current developments before traveling – trouble generally occurs around elections, although it's incredibly rare for foreigners to get caught up in it. Avoid demonstrations, and if you come across one, turn in the opposite direction. In the event of real trouble, listen to the advice of embassy and hotel staff and follow it.

A weak state and high poverty levels can foster street crime. Take advantage of hotel safes and don't carry anything you're not willing to lose (or money in your back pocket). There are plenty of people on the streets during the day, and should you encounter trouble it's quite likely that someone will come to your aid.

For all this, the main annoyances travelers are likely to face are the poor electricity supply and crazy traffic. A lack of street lights is as good a reason not to walk at night as any risk of being mugged – no one wants to fall into a sewer hidden in the darkness. Beggars can be persistent in some places, and at tourist spots, such at the Citadelle, expect persistent attention from faux guides. Try to discourage them before you set off – their only function seems to be to tell you how much tip you're going to have to pay at the end – as it's very hard to not pay them after they've run up a mountain alongside you.

On a less obtrusive note, all foreigners should get used to being stared at out of curiosity. You'll be called *blanc* a lot, too. This is the generic word for a foreigner and is not color-specific: we've even met Nigerians in Haiti utterly bemused at being called *blanc*! If someone gestures to you with what looks like a throat-slitting action, they're telling you they're hungry and want food – not that you're for the chop.

Finally, while taking care to be sensible, it's important not to get too hung up on Haiti's bad name. Many travelers fear the worst and avoid the country; those who do make it here are more likely to come away with positive impressions than horror stories.

EMBASSIES & CONSULATES

All of the embassies and consulates listed following are in Port-au-Prince or Pétionville. Australia, New Zealand and Ireland do not have diplomatic representation in Haiti.

Brazil (Map p294; ☎ 2256-6206; fax 2256-6206; 168 Rue Darguin, Place Boyer, Pétionville)

Canada (☎ 2249-9000; fax 2249-9920, btwn Delmas 75 & 76, Rte de Delmas, Port-au-Prince)

Cuba (☎ 2256-3811; fax 2257-8566; 3 Rue Marion, Pétionville)

Dominican Republic (Map p294; ☎ 2257-9215; fax 2257-0568; 121 Ave Pan Américaine, Pétionville)

European Union (☎ 2249-0142; fax 2260-0544; 1 Impasse Brave, Delmas 60, Port-au-Prince)

France (Map p290-1; ☎ 2222-0951; fax 2223-9858; 51 Rue Capois, Port-au-Prince)

Germany (☎ 2256-4131; fax 2257-4131; 2 Impasse Claudinette, Bois Moquette, Pétionville)

Mexico (☎ 2257-8100; fax 2257-6783; 2 Delmas 60, Musseau, Port-au-Prince)

Netherlands (off Map pp290-1; ☎ 2222-0955; fax 2222-0955; Rue Belleville, Parc Shodecosa, Port-au-Prince) Located off Rte Nationale 1.

UK (Map pp290-1; Hotel Montana, Rue F Cardoza, Port-au-Prince) Currently closed, but with possible plans to reopen it during the lifetime of this book.

USA Embassy (Map pp290-1; ☎ 2222-0220, 2222-0269; fax 2223-1641; Blvd Harry Truman, Port-au-Prince); Consulate (Map pp290-1; ☎ 2223-0989, 2223-8853, 2223-9324, 2223-7011; fax 2223-5515; 104 Rue Oswald Durand, Port-au-Prince)

Venezuela (☎ 2222-0971; fax 2222-3949; 2 Cité de l'Exposition, Blvd Harry Truman, Port-au-Prince)

FESTIVALS & EVENTS

There are plenty of festivals throughout the year that can be tied into your trip with a bit of planning. Most are based on religious feasts – either Christian or Vodou. In addition to those listed here, each town celebrates its patron saint's day (Fête Patronale; see boxed text, p346). This is marked by a Catholic Mass, but is often an excuse for a parade, music and late-night revelries – great fun if you happen to be in town on the day.

If you plan on attending one of the Vodou festivals, it's definitely a good idea to go with a local guide or Vodou follower, to ensure you adhere to local etiquette (and to explain to you what's happening).

January
SOUKRI

There are two Soukri celebrations, held in January and August. Both are dedicated to the Kongo *lwa* (Vodou spirits), and are fortnightlong events, marked by music and ritual. They're held between Gonaïves and Cap-Haïtien – for details, see boxed text, p341.

February
CARNIVAL

Flush with color, music, dancing and rum, Carnival, or Mardi Gras – celebrated countrywide on the three days leading up to Ash Wednesday – is a great experience.

The main Carnival venue is Port-au-Prince. Here music is the main attraction, so you'll see few of the traditional costumes that characterize other Caribbean carnivals. There are often free open-air concerts on Champs de Mars during the run. For the main event, there are stands set up around the Plaza Hotel where, for a couple of dollars, you can watch the activity from a 'safe' distance. Haiti's main

---

FÊTES PATRONALES

The following towns and cities celebrate their patron saint's day (Fêtes Patronales) on these days:

- Port-de-Paix – April 28 (St Louis Marie de Monfort)
- Jacmel – May 1 (St Jacque & St Philippe)
- Pétionville – June 29 (St Pierre)
- Cap-Haïtien – July 25 (St Jacque)
- Fermathe – July 25 (St Jacque)
- Camp Perrin – July 26 (St Anne)
- Port-au-Prince – July 26 (St Anne), August 15 (Virgin Mary)
- Les Cayes – August 15 (Virgin Mary)
- Ounaminthe – August 15 (Virgin Mary)
- Mirabelais – August 25 (St Louis)
- Croix des Bouquets – 1st Sunday of October (Our Lady of the Rosary)
- Gonaïves – November 1 (St Charles)

---

bands cram onto decorated floats with massive sound systems playing specially composed merengue songs that are all vying to be the anthem of the year. There are also roving bands that draw swarms of revelers in their wake. Most of the action takes place late at night, and it's all a bit hectic: a great party but possibly not for the claustrophobic.

During the week before Carnival, slightly more traditional celebrations take place in Jacmel. These are based around costumes and street theater rather than music, and are the most colorful in Haiti. In the months running up to Jacmel Carnival it's possible to see craftsmen making the papier-mâché masks that make the parade so famous. For more information, see boxed text, p322.

Easter
RARA

Sometimes dubbed the 'rural Carnival,' Rara takes place in the week leading up to Easter, when roads all over Haiti swell with bands of revelers, percussionists and players of bamboo and tin trumpets. The bands are led by 'presidents,' 'colonels,' 'queens' and other members of complex Rara band hierarchies. It's easy to become immersed in the band's groove of wild, spiraling rhythms as it moves slowly along the road visiting temples and saluting dignitaries – before you know it, you've followed the band for kilometers. Finally, exhausted, the band will reach its climax by performing the *salute,* the cue for a fierce dance by the Major Jonc (lead male dancer).

SOUVENANCE

Held at the site of the same name between Gonaïves and Cap-Haïtien, Souvenance is one of the biggest Vodou festivals, running for a week from every Good Friday. The *lwa* Ogou is celebrated here, accompanied by music and bathing in sacred pools (for details, see boxed text, p341).

July
SAUT D'EAU PILGRIMAGE

The largest Vodou pilgrimage of the year is at the Saut d'Eau waterfall near Ville-Bonheur, where a 19th-century sighting of the Virgin Mary has become fused with her *lwa* counterpart Erzuli Dantor. It's an incredible and powerful sight, with white-clad adherents bathing in the sacred pools to cleanse themselves. For more information, see boxed text, p313.

November
FET GÉDÉ

Fet Gédé takes place on November 1 and 2. The Gédé spirits (see p281) serve as both the guardians of the cemetery and the lords of the erotic. For this festival, people pile into the cemeteries to pour libations for Baron Samedi around blackened crosses festooned with candles, skulls and marigolds. A person possessed by a

Gédé will whiten his or her face with powder to resemble a corpse, and act lasciviously toward other onlookers, especially foreigners. The uniform of Gédé is black and purple clothes, a top hat and mirrored shades, matched with lewd behavior and omnipresent bottles of *klerin* (white rum). Rituals usually start late at night and continue into the small hours.

FOOD

You can eat on any budget in Haiti, spending just a few gourdes on filling *fritay* (fried street food) eaten on the hoof compared to dining in the posh restaurants of Pétionville, where a main course might set you back US$20. The most typical experience is eating in a bar-resto, with a plateful of fried pork or chicken with plantains, salad and a beer, all for around US$4. Vegetables aren't high on the agenda, but there's plenty of fresh fruit. Excellent seafood abounds along the coast.

For more information on Haitian food and drink, see p284.

GAY & LESBIAN TRAVELERS

Haiti isn't as homophobic as some other places in the Caribbean, including macho Spanish DR. There are no dedicated gay venues, however; these were clamped down on in the 1980s following negative publicity about HIV/AIDS in Haiti. While you may commonly see friends of the same sex holding hands and being openly affectionate with each other throughout the country, any tourists doing this will attract attention. Same-sex couples sharing a room should have no problem, although some discretion, especially in the more religious establishments, is advisable.

HOLIDAYS

Government offices and most businesses will be closed on the following public holidays:

Independence Day January 1
Ancestors' Day January 2
Carnival January/February (three days before Ash Wednesday)
Good Friday March/April
Agriculture and Labor Day May 1
Flag and University Day May 18
Anniversary of Jean-Jacques Dessalines' Death October 17
Anniversary of Toussaint Louverture's Death November 1
Anniversary of the Battle of Vertières November 18
Christmas Day December 25

INSURANCE

It's always unwise to travel without insurance. Policies vary widely, but it's essential to have as much medical cover as possible (including emergency evacuation cover). Medical services insist on payment on the spot, so collect all the paperwork you can when being treated so you can claim later. Some policies ask you to call them (they'll usually call you back) so that an assessment of your problem can be made. Check excess fees for lost, stolen or damaged luggage.

An important point to note is that some governments issue travel warnings advising against nonessential travel to Haiti. Some insurance policies (or certain areas of their cover) may be invalidated in such circumstances, so discuss this with your broker before signing up.

INTERNET ACCESS

Online access isn't a problem in any decently sized Haitian town, and internet cafés open and close frequently. Broadband connections are increasingly standard, along with webcams, CD burning and USB connections for uploading digital photos. Prices cost US$0.80 to US$3 per hour. The more expensive the joint, the better the electricity supply is likely to be. Cheap places don't run generators, making them highly susceptible to the regular power cuts.

If you're bringing a laptop, top-end (and some midrange) hotels often provide wi-fi access.

LEGAL MATTERS

One of the key tasks of the UN presence in Haiti has been to train and reorganize the Haitian National Police (HNP). It's a mammoth task, as the police are spread thin and corruption is rife, with the judiciary burdened with similar problems.

Drugs are illegal in Haiti, and you will be jailed for possession of marijuana or cocaine. If you are involved in a car accident, the law requires you to stop your car and call the police as soon as possible. In general, Haitian law presumes innocence until guilt is proven, and it's unlikely that you'll actually be arrested unless there are supportable charges against you. Always try to contact your embassy without delay, and keep its contact details on your person. If the 'problem' is an imaginary one, the ability to be extremely patient may eventually see the issue disappear.

MAPS

Of most use to travelers is the *Haïti Carte Touristique,* which can be found in Port-au-Prince bookshops. On one side there is a detailed country map with lots of tourist information, while on the reverse there are street plans of Port-au-Prince, Cap-Haïtien, Jacmel and all the other departmental capitals.

A decent alternative is the map produced by the Association of Haitian Hoteliers, which is available free from most car-rental companies, also with a map of Port-au-Prince. Guides Panoramas produces the best up-to-date map of Port-au-Prince (US$5), as well as a street plan of Jacmel.

MONEY

The Haitian currency is the gourde, usually seen written gde. The gourde is divided into 100 centimes, although the smallest coin you're likely to see is the 50 centimes, followed by the one and five gourde coins. Bank notes come in denominations of 10, 25, 50, 100, 250, 500 and 1000 gourdes, all with a revolutionary hero on one side and a historic fort on the other. There are still a few very grubby one, two and five gourde notes in circulation, although these are no longer issued.

Where matters get confusing is that most Haitians refer to the Haitian dollar (H$) when quoting costs. The gourde used to be tied to the US dollar at a rate of one to five, with the result that five gourdes is universally known as one Haitian dollar. It's a system seemingly designed to perplex short-term visitors. When buying something, always check what people mean when quoting the price, whether a hundred is in gourdes or dollars (in which case it's 500 gourdes). To make things even more confusing, prices for expensive goods (or tourist souvenirs) are sometimes listed in US dollars.

The way to minimize headaches is to choose one system, either the Haitian dollar or the gourde, and stick with that. If you choose to work in Haitian dollars, you must divide prices in gourdes by five; if you choose to think in gourdes, you must multiply all Haitian dollar prices by five. You'll eventually be able to make price comparisons to your home currency, which is nearly impossible if you keep slipping between the two systems.

ATMs

Automatic teller machines are increasingly common in Port-au-Prince and Pétionville, but yet to catch on elsewhere in the country (we found just one, in Cap-Haïtien). They're the simplest and most secure way to manage your money on the road, although obviously you'll need to make sure you're liquid when heading out of the capital. Most ATMs are directly on the street, with some in secure booths. Always be aware of your surroundings when using an ATM and pocketing a wad of cash.

Cash

Cash is king in Haiti. With the exceptions noted for credit cards (below), almost everything you buy will be with folding stuff. Traveling outside Port-au-Prince, you're likely to be carrying plenty of money, but there are a few precautions to reduce the risk of losing your stash to misadventure.

It's unwise to carry wads of money in your wallet, and you're similarly more prone to being robbed if you carry valuables in a shoulder bag, which can easily be snatched. Keep a small amount of money for the day in a handy but concealed place (eg in an inner pocket), and the bulk of your resources more deeply hidden. A well-concealed money belt is one of the safest ways to carry your money as well as important documents, such as your passport. It's also a good idea to have emergency cash (say US$100 in small bills) stashed away from your main hoard, as a backup.

For many purchases – hotel rooms, for instance – it's acceptable to pay in US dollars instead of gourdes.

Credit Cards

Most midrange and all top-end hotels (and Port-au-Prince restaurants) will happily let you flash the plastic. Visa, MasterCard and (to a slightly lesser extent) American Express will all do nicely. With an accompanying passport, cash advances on credit cards can generally be made in the larger banks.

Moneychangers

Haiti must be one of the few countries where if you want to change money, the simplest option is to go to a supermarket. These generally have a separate counter near the cashier where you can top up your gourdes. In Haiti, the US dollar rules supreme, although Canadian dollars and euros are usually accepted, along with Dominican pesos. Try not to bring any other currency. Where there are street moneychangers, they're only interested in US dollars.

Traveler's Checks

These are a nonstarter in Haiti. Bank tellers will almost look at them with some curiosity before pushing them back over the counter for you to take elsewhere, possibly mumbling something about having to go to the 'head office.' Persistence to the point of tears might get you somewhere (make sure you also have the purchase receipts with you), but we'd really advise against it.

PHOTOGRAPHY & VIDEO

As in many developing countries, taking photos of airports and police buildings is forbidden. It's a bad idea to snap a policeman without obtaining permission first, and UN soldiers can be similarly sensitive.

Haitians are well aware of their country's poverty, and often hate to be photographed in work or dirty clothes. Always ask permission – whether you're in a market or the countryside, producing a camera out of the blue can occasionally provoke a reaction. Discretion is key. This goes double at Vodou ceremonies, where you should always check with the *houngan* or *mambo* (respectively male or female Vodou priest) before you start clicking away.

Most internet cafés allow you to upload photos and burn CDs, and digital supplies are easy to come by in Port-au-Prince.

POST

There are post offices in every town. Postcards to North America cost 25 gourdes (US$0.70) to send, or 50 gourdes (US$1.40) to Europe and Australia. It's generally better to send from a postbox, although the larger towns also have mailboxes dotted around. The service is reasonably reliable, although hardly superfast.

If you're in Haiti long-term and want to receive mail, you can have it addressed to Poste Restante at the central post office where you're based. Senders should underline your name and you should bring your passport identification when collecting mail for. A better, although more pricey, alternative is to set up a *boîte postale* (post box) at your local post office. Receiving mail is never fast in Haiti.

Faster in both directions are the international couriers. DHL, UPS and TNT are all represented in Port-au-Prince and Pétionville, with a few offices elsewhere noted throughout this book.

TOP HAITIAN SOUVENIRS

Here are some of our favorite souvenirs from Haiti:

- Paintings by Haiti's most exciting artists from the galleries of Pétionville.
- Papier-mâché masks from Jacmel.
- Painted wooden boxes and place mats from Jacmel.
- Sequined Vodou flags from Port-au-Prince's Bel Air district.
- Intricate metal sculptures made from old oil drums in Croix des Bouquets.
- *Compas* (Haitian dance) and *racines* (roots) CDs, available everywhere.
- A bottle of Barbancourt Five Star rum.
- Rada drums as used in Vodou ceremonies.
- Carved wooden statues.
- Straw hats, worn everywhere in the countryside.

SHOPPING

With its renowned arts scene, Haiti is filled with enough interesting handicrafts and souvenirs to have you worrying about your baggage allowance on the plane home. Port-au-Prince has the widest choice, with good shopping areas including the Marché de Fer and the Pétionville galleries. Jacmel, the so-called handicrafts capital of Haiti, also offers a comprehensive (and more laid-back) shopping experience. Often you'll be able to buy direct from the artists or artisans.

Except in galleries and a few shops, prices are never fixed, so be prepared to haggle. There's no rule on how much to offer, but it's best to treat the deal-making as a game rather than becoming obsessed with driving the price into the ground. Both sides will take it in turns to be uninterested and then outraged at the prices offered before finding common ground.

TELEPHONE

Landline connections in Haiti can sometimes be patchy, and most businesses list several numbers on their cards and many people carry two cell phones of different networks.

Haiti uses the GSM system for cell phones. The two main operators are Digicel and Voila, with HaiTel coming a fairly distant third. Coverage is generally good. The providers have international roaming agreements with many foreign networks, but it can work out cheaper to buy a local handset on arrival in Haiti for about US$20 (including several hundred gourdes credit). Take a copy of your passport to the dealer for identification. Calls within Haiti cost around US$0.10 per minute according to the network, and around US$0.90 per minute overseas. Top-up scratch cards for more credit are available from shops and the ubiquitous street vendors.

To make a call, the quickest option is to find a phone 'stand,' usually a youth on the street with a cell phone that looks like a regular desk phone, who will time your call and charge accordingly. Alternatively, look for a central Teleco office, which has booths where you can place your call.

Haiti's international telephone code is ☎ 509. There are no area codes. To make an international call, dial ☎ 00. The annually updated **Haiti Business Directory** (www.haiti-business .com) is useful for tracking down numbers.

TIME

Haiti runs on Eastern Standard Time (GMT minus five hours), putting it in the same time zone as New York, Miami and Toronto. Haiti doesn't adjust for daylight saving time, so from the first Sunday in April to the last Sunday in October it's actually an hour ahead of eastern USA and Canada.

TOURIST INFORMATION

Haiti's moribund tourist industry has left visitors scrabbling around for information. Port-au-Prince's main information center, the **Maison de Tourisme** (Map pp290-1; ☎ 2222-8659; Rue Capois, Champs de Mars, Port-au-Prince; ✆ 8am-4pm Mon-Fri), had been closed for some time when we visited, with no plans to reopen. You may have more luck contacting the **Ministry of Tourism** (Map pp290-1; ☎ 2223-2143; 8 Rue Légitime, Champs de Mars, Port-au-Prince) direct, but we make no promises. There's an occasionally staffed information booth at the international airport, Aéroport International Toussaint Louverture. Instead, the private tour operators (see p353) are the best source of up-to-date information.

Outside the capital, the **Associations des Micro-Enterprises Touristiques du Sud'Est** (Amets; ☎ 2288-2840; amets_service@yahoo.fr; 40 Rue d'Orléans; ✆ 8am-4pm Mon-Fri, to 2pm Sat) in Jacmel has good informa-

tion, and the **Bureau du Tourisme** (Map p334; ☎ 2262-0870; cnr Rue 24 & the Blvd, Cap-Haïtien) can also sometimes help. There are no tourist offices abroad.

TOILETS

There are no public toilet facilities in Haiti, but you can use the toilets in hotels or restaurants. The Haitian sewerage system is overstretched so, where supplied, dispose of toilet paper in a bin. Most Haitian men think nothing of urinating in the streets and, on long journeys, relieving oneself at the side of the road is usually the only option. For women, this is more easily accomplished if you're wearing a loose-fitting skirt or dress, although you'll see plenty of local women yanking down their trousers in such situations.

TRAVELERS WITH DISABILITIES

Haiti is going to be hard going for travelers with disabilities. Crowded and broken streets, anarchic traffic and the absence of wheelchair-accessible buildings all pose serious problems. However, travel is possible for those with an iron will, plenty of stamina and the willingness to adapt to whatever hurdles present themselves. Traveling with an able-bodied companion can immensely help in overcoming these obstacles. At the very least, hiring a vehicle and a guide will make moving around a great deal easier. Travelers with disabilities shouldn't be surprised at stares from Haitians, but they'll often also receive offers of assistance where needed.

For more information, consider contacting **Mobility International USA** (MIUSA; ☎ 3541-343 1284; www.miusa.org; 132 E Broadway, Ste 343, Eugene, OR 97401), which offers general travel advice for travelers with physical disabilities.

VISAS

Unless you're a citizen of the DR, Colombia, Panama or Taiwan, no visa is needed to visit Haiti, just a passport valid for six months and a return ticket. Your entry stamp entitles you to stay for up to 90 days. You'll also be given a green entry card that must be given up on departure from Haiti, so keep this safe.

If you wish to stay in Haiti for longer than 90 days, you must apply for a visitor/resident visa at your nearest embassy before you travel, a process of several months involving letters of support from your employer or a Haitian resident.

WOMEN TRAVELERS

Haiti is an easier place for a woman to travel alone than many countries in the region (see also p254). The catcalls, whistles and leering that females may experience in many other places seem to be at a minimum. Haitian men do enjoy flirting and complimenting, but it usually isn't too overbearing and should be taken in good humor.

Haitian roads are abysmal and, as public transport is extremely bouncy, consider wearing a sports bra, especially on longer journeys, where you should also wear a skirt to allow for roadside toilet breaks. It's not a problem for women to wear modest shorts or sleeveless tops in and around town. A sarong is recommended for wrapping over a swimsuit at a hotel pool or the beach.

WORK

Paid work is in short supply in Haiti. Official unemployment estimates mask far higher figures, and wages are desperately inadequate. Competition for jobs is enormous, so to find work you need to be able to demonstrate you have skills that no one in the domestic market possesses. Fluency in French and/or Creole is virtually essential. After you've been in the country for 90 days you must register as a resident with the **Department of Immigration** (171 Ave John Brown, Port-au-Prince), for which you'll need a letter from your embassy and your employer, a health check and a Haitian bank account proving solvency.

Many foreigners working in Haiti and not in business are involved in aid and development. **ReliefWeb** (www.reliefweb.int) and **DevNet** (www.devnetjobs.org) are good places to look for jobs in the development sector in Haiti.

Volunteer work in Haiti has traditionally been dominated by two strands – the Peace Corps and churches. The Peace Corps pulled out of Haiti following the 2004 coup, and it's not known if it will be returning. Church groups regularly send charitable missions to Haiti, but it's essential to know the work they'll be doing is both wanted by local communities and sustainable. The NGO **Healing Hands for Haiti** (www.healinghandsforhaiti.org) sends medically trained volunteers to work with Haitians with disabilities through local partner organizations. These type of volunteer trips are usually quite short – often less than a month. If you want to get a taste of life as a volunteer, the web has scores of blogs from volunteers (including church groups) recounting their experiences. **Haiti Innovation** (www.haitiinnovation.org), a blog run by former Peace Corps workers, has an interesting commentary on the state of development and aid in Haiti, and is worth checking out.

Haiti Transportation

CONTENTS

GETTING THERE & AWAY

Flights and tours can be booked online at www.lonelyplanet.com/travel_services.

ENTERING HAITI

The vast majority of travelers enter Haiti by air through Port-au-Prince, with the most common flight routes all being from the USA – Miami, Fort Lauderdale and New York. The international airport at Cap-Haïtien also handles a small number of incoming flights.

By land, there are several border crossings with the Dominican Republic, and direct bus services linking Port-au-Prince and Santo Domingo, and Cap-Haïtien with Santiago. There are no international boat services to Haiti.

Passport

All foreign visitors must have a valid passport to enter Haiti. Be sure you have room for both entry and exit stamps, and that your passport is valid for at least six months beyond your planned travel dates. See (p350) for information on visas.

AIR
Airports & Airlines

Haiti has just two international airports.
Aéroport International Toussaint Louverture
(PAP; off Map pp290-1; ☎ 2250-1120) The main international airport, in Port-au-Prince.

DEPARTURE TAX

All departure taxes for leaving Haiti are included in the cost of your air ticket.

Aéroport International Cap-Haïtien (CAP; ☎ 2262-8539) In Cap-Haïtien, but currently only has flights with Lynx Air to Florida, USA.

AIRLINES FLYING TO/FROM HAITI
International carriers with services to Haiti:
Aerocaribbean (7L; ☎ 2222-5004; www.aero-caribbean.com; Havana, Cuba) Flights from Havana and Santiago, and Punta Cana (DR) and Port-au-Prince.
Air Canada (AC; ☎ 2250-0441, 2250-0442; www.aircanada.ca; Toronto, Canada) Direct flights from Montreal.
Air France (AF; ☎ 2222-1078, 2222-4262; www.airfrance.com; Paris, France) Flights from Paris via Pointe-á-Pitre, Guadeloupe or Miami.
Air Santo Domingo (EX; ☎ 2244-4897; http://airsantodomingo.com.do; Santo Domingo, Dominican Republic)
American Airlines (AA; ☎ 2246-0100, 3510-7010; www.aa.com; New York, USA) Direct flights from Miami, Fort Lauderdale and New York.
Caribintair (CRT; ☎ 2250-2031, 2250-2032; caribintair@accesshaiti.com; Port-au-Prince, Haiti) Flights to Santo Domingo.
Copa Air (CM; ☎ 2223-2326; www.copaair.com; Panama City, Republic of Panama)
Lynx Air (LY; ☎ 3513-2597, 2257-9956; www.lynxair.com; Fort Lauderdale, USA)
Spirit Airlines (NK; ☎ in Dominican Republic 809-381-4111; www.spiritair.com; Fort Lauderdale, USA)

LAND

The Haitian–Dominican border has three official crossing points open to foreigners. Of the most use to travelers is the Malpasse–Jimaní crossing between Port-au-Prince and Santo Domingo, followed by the northern Ouanaminthe–Dajabón crossing on the road between Cap-Haïtien and Santiago. A third, and little used, crossing is from Belladère to Comendador (aka Elías Piña).

There are direct coach services linking the two capitals, and Cap-Haïtien to Santiago; see p306 and p336 respectively for more details. Included in the cost of the ticket are border fees that all travelers have to pay.

Entering the DR you must pay US$10 for a tourist card. The situation with fees entering/leaving Haiti by land is fluid – these are meant to have been abolished, but border officials may still ask for US$10 to stamp you in or out. It remains unclear whether this is a legitimate fee or just a 'gratuity.'

The Haitian border can be slightly chaotic if you're traveling independently, particularly at Ounaminthe with its sprawling local market. Onward transport is plentiful, however, along with the occasional hustle – any tourist is going to stand out in this scenario. For more on the Dominican side of the border, see p256.

TOURS

Haiti has three local tour operators, all offering excellent packages and services if you don't want to strike out on your own.

DOA/BN (☎ 3510-2223; www.haititravels.org)

Tour Haiti (Map p294; ☎ 3457-5242, 3746-8696; info@tourhaiti.net, ccchauvel@hotmail.com; 115 Rue Faubert, Pétionville)

Voyages Lumière (☎ 2249-6177, 3557-0753; www.voyagelumierehaiti.com)

GETTING AROUND

AIR

There are three airlines running domestic services in Haiti: **Caribintair** (☎ 2250-2031, 2250-2032; caribintair@accesshaiti.com), **Tortug Air** (☎ 2250-2555, 2250-2556; tortugair@yahoo.com) and **Tropical Airways** (☎ 2256-3626, 2256-3627) linking Port-au-Prince to several departmental capitals. Caribintair flies to Cap-Haïtien, Les Cayes, Jacmel and Jérémie. Tortug Air serves Cap-Haïtien, Les Cayes, Jérémie and Port-de-Paix, while Tropical Airways flies to Cap-Haïtien

---

THINGS CHANGE...

The information in this chapter is particularly vulnerable to change. Check directly with the airline or a travel agent to make sure you understand how a fare (and ticket you may buy) works and be aware of the security requirements for international travel. Shop carefully. The details given in this chapter should be regarded as pointers and are not a substitute for your own careful, up-to-date research.

---

and Port-de-Paix, with a route to Jacmel on the cards. Haiti's small size means that flights are short (just 15 minutes to Jacmel), saving hours on bad roads. The planes are small and demand can be high, especially for destinations like Jérémie, so book as far in advance as possible. One-way tickets usually cost around the US$85 mark.

BUS

Getting around Haiti by bus isn't always terrifically comfortable, but it's the cheapest way to travel within the country and services run to most places you'll want to get to. Sturdy beasts, buses have the advantage of taking you to places that you'd usually need a 4WD to reach. They are mostly secondhand American school buses, colorfully repainted, with more Haitian liveries for bus lines like L'Ange de Dieu and Dieu Qui Decide.

Seating is designed to squash in as many people as possible, with six or seven across being the norm. Your space is numbered, however, so look for the numerals painted above your head as you clamber through the bus over the assembled passengers and their bags (and occasionally chickens, too). When buying your ticket it's worth asking for a window seat to give yourself some extra air. Try not to sit too far back either – suspension is not the vehicle's strong suit, and the state of Haiti's roads means that passengers sitting behind the rear axle are regularly bounced unceremoniously into the air. The front cab has several seats next to the driver. These are the most comfortable of all, but attract an extra premium of around two-thirds of a standard ticket.

With a few exceptions noted in the text, there are no timetables; buses leave instead when they've collected their quota of passengers. There's a tricky payoff for travelers here: arrive too early and you'll sit for hours waiting for the bus to fill, arrive too late and you'll be stuck with a terrible seat. Buying a ticket in advance is sometimes possible for long distances (Port-au-Prince to Cap-Haïtien or Jérémie, for example), but be advised that the hour you're told to be at the bus station will invariably be at least an hour before the bus pulls onto the road. If you're 'lucky,' the driver will be playing deafeningly loud music to help pass the time. Overhead racks and space below the seats should be sufficient for most bags, otherwise they'll have to go on the roof (the baggage handler will want his tip). Although baggage is usually covered, rainstorms can still soak through, so keeping your belongings in plastic bags inside your luggage is a good idea.

Each town has a departure point for buses, known as 'estacion' followed by the destination name (Estacion Port-au-Prince, for example). They're not proper bus stations, rather sprawling, chaotic and noisy conglomerations of vehicles and people and market stalls: Haiti in microcosm. Touts shout out destinations, which are also painted on bus fronts. While you're waiting for the bus to leave, there's a constant procession of hawkers and street-food vendors, so you won't go hungry. Some even travel with the bus – travelling goods salesmen selling everything from toothpaste to miracle cures (we've experienced pitches lasting a good hour into a journey).

Upon arrival in their destination, buses turn into pseudo-taxi services, stopping at the roadside at passengers' request. This can be done by pressing a buzzer or yelling 'merci, monsieur' to the driver. While this may be great for getting dropped right outside your chosen hotel, it can be maddeningly frustrating as the bus stops every 50m or so to drop off yet more people and their assorted baggage.

Breakdowns aren't uncommon, but can sometimes provide relief from the terrible roads, or allow a much-needed toilet or food stop (women are advised to wear a skirt to allow for roadside squatting). Otherwise food or rest stops can be rare, although brave food and drink vendors do hang perilously from the windows and doors as buses pass through towns and villages. When road conditions allow it, buses love to get up a head of steam, forcing all comers to scatter before them.

CAR & MOTORCYCLE

Although having your own wheels is a convenient way of seeing Haiti, be aware that you need both nerves of steel and a sense of humor. Terrible roads, a lack of road signs, and the perils of wayward pedestrians and oncoming traffic are all part of the mix. But if you're up for the challenge, you might find yourself driving with a flair and aplomb you never knew you possessed before.

Driver's License

In order to drive or rent a vehicle in Haiti, you need either a valid International Driving Permit or a current license from your home country. It is an offense to drive without a valid driver's license on your person. Carry your passport with you at all times, as the police will want to see it if they stop you for any reason.

Rental

Many international car-rental companies operate in Haiti, mostly based near Port-au-Prince's international airport; see p306. Rates are pricey due to the high rate of accidents and road conditions that cause a lot of wear and tear. Although fees vary from company to company, don't be surprised to be quoted around US$70 for a saloon, or US$150 for a 4WD per day. Although insurance is offered, it isn't always comprehensive and often carries high deductibles; furthermore, foreign drivers are often held liable for accidents whether they are at fault or not.

Road Conditions

It's best not to come with high hopes of Haiti's roads to avoid bad surprises. With the notable exception of the well-maintained highway from Port-au-Prince to Jacmel, the main roads are potholed and cracked. Secondary roads are worse, with some becoming impassable, especially after rain, except in a 4WD. Wherever tarmac allows drivers to get some speed up, accidents are common, so it's sometimes worth thinking of the broken roads as an efficient traffic-calming system.

Avoid driving at night if at all possible. Many drivers are allergic to using headlights, and animals and pedestrians are hard to see in the dark.

Road Rules

Road rules are extremely lax, but most vehicles at least aspire to drive on the right. Drivers rarely signal, so expect cars to swerve out in front of you suddenly, usually to avoid a hole. When overtaking, use your horn liberally. Many drivers far prefer the horn instead of the brakes, so take heed. Always beep to warn people walking that you're coming, and they will make way – even in the most congested street, you can usually miraculously slip through.

If you have an accident, you must to stop your car and call the police as soon as possible.

In cities, watch out for parking restrictions. Instead of issuing tickets, police are liable to remove your license plates, returnable from the local police station on payment of a fine. When parking, kids or men may approach you to be a *gardien* and watch your vehicle for you for a small fee.

HITCHHIKING

It's extremely unusual to see foreigners hitchhiking in Haiti, but due to the low rate of car ownership and unreliable transport systems, Haitians are used to asking for a *rue libre* (free ride). As with hitchhiking anywhere in the world, there's a small but potentially serious risk in flagging down a ride. If you do get picked up, don't be surprised if the driver asks for some money – keep public-transport fares in mind so that, should you strike someone trying to extort silly amounts from you, you'll know what not to give and what you'll be expected to pay for the ride. However, some Haitians will be baffled by the sight of a foreigner without a vehicle and will just pick you up out of curiosity.

TAPTAP & CAMIONETTE

Smaller vehicles than buses ply the roads carrying passengers. A taptap is a converted pickup, often brightly decorated, with bench seats in the back. Fares are slightly cheaper than a bus. The same rules for buses apply to taptaps, which leave from the same *estacion*: they go when full, the comfy seats next to the driver are more pricey, and you can hail one and get off where you like. They're usually packed like sardines (the answer to how many people you can fit in a taptap is invariably 'one more'), so carrying luggage places you at a disadvantage. Expect a few bruises from the hard bench seats, bouncy roads and sharp elbows.

Taptaps are better suited for short trips, and in many areas are likely to be the only feasible way of getting around. In Port-au-Prince, taptaps run within the city along set routes and are by far the cheapest and easiest way of getting from A to B.

Halfway between a taptap and a bus is the *camionette*. This is a larger truck designed primarily for transporting goods, but which also takes human cargo. Often open sided, or with crude windows cut out of the truck body, these are very cheap and as basic as they come. There are no seats, just a few ropes dangling

from the ceiling for people to hold on to. A foreigner riding in a *camionette* will get such looks of incredulity from a Haitian that it's worth trying one for the response alone. Certainly, don't do it for a smooth ride.

LOCAL TRANSPORTATION
Moto-taxis

The quickest and easiest way to get around any town is to hop on the back of a moto-taxi (motorcycle taxi), often just referred to as a 'moto.' As with *publiques* (collective taxis), these have transport license plates, and in some towns the drivers wear colored bibs. A trip will rarely cost more than about 20 gourdes/US$0.45, although rates can climb steeply if you want to travel any serious distance.

Moto-taxis can have two passengers riding pillion, although it's not recommended. If you have luggage, get the driver to place it between his handlebars, rather than unbalancing yourself with it on your back. Although pot-holed roads don't always allow the bikes to attempt high speeds, many drivers seem to have a fatalist's view of their own mortality, so don't be afraid to tell them to slow down.

Taxi

Port-au-Prince and Cap-Haïtien operate collective taxis called *publiques* for getting around town. You might find them hard to spot initially, as they look like any other battered car, but look for the red ribbon hanging from the front mirror and license plates starting with 'T' for transport. Once you spot one, they're everywhere. Charging set fares (usually about 25 gourdes/US$0.70), they roughly stick to particular routes. After you hail a *publique*, the driver will let you know if he's going your way (minor detours are usually fine). The usual tight seating arrangement is two in the front and four in the back.

When you get into an empty *publique*, the driver will sometimes remove the ribbon, indicating a private hire with resulting increased charge. If you want to ride *collectif* (with other passengers), now is the time to let him know. Alternatively, settle the fee before he drives off, not on arrival.

Most major towns have radio-taxi firms with meters.

HAITI TRANSPORTATION

Health David Goldberg MD

CONTENTS

From a medical standpoint, the DR and Haiti are generally safe as long as you're reasonably careful about what you eat and drink. The most common travel-related diseases, such as dysentery and hepatitis, are acquired by consumption of contaminated food and water. Mosquito-borne illnesses are not a significant concern, although there is a small but significant malaria risk in certain parts of both countries. By following common sense and keeping your vaccinations topped up, the worst complaint you might come down with on your trip is a bad stomach.

BEFORE YOU GO

Since most vaccines don't provide immunity until at least two weeks after they're given, visit a physician four to eight weeks before departure. Ask your doctor for an International Certificate of Vaccination (otherwise known as 'the yellow booklet'), which will list all the vaccinations you've received. It's a good idea to carry it wherever you travel.

INSURANCE

Many health insurance plans provide coverage while you are traveling abroad, but it is important to check with your provider before leaving home. Some travel-insurance policies include short-term medical and life insurance, even emergency evacuation, in addition to the standard trip-cancellation and lost-luggage coverage. Ask your travel agent or current insurance provider about travel insurance plans, or check the internet for providers in your area. As always, spend some time reading the fine print to be sure you are clear what the plan does (and does not) cover. Scuba divers should consider obtaining dive insurance from \DAN (Diver Alert Network; www.diversalertnetwork .org); many standard insurance plans do not cover diving accidents, and even when they do, cannot compare to the specialized coverage and experience DAN offers.

MEDICAL CHECKLIST

Following is a list of other items you should consider packing in your medical kit when you are traveling.

- antibiotics (if traveling off the beaten track)
- antibacterial hand gel
- antidiarrheal drugs (eg loperamide)
- paracetamol (eg Tylenol) or aspirin
- anti-inflammatory drugs (eg ibuprofen)
- antihistamines (for hay fever and allergic reactions)
- antibacterial ointment (eg Bactroban; for cuts and abrasions)
- steroid cream or cortisone (for allergic rashes)
- bandages, gauze, gauze rolls
- adhesive or paper tape
- scissors, safety pins, tweezers
- thermometer
- pocket knife

TRAVEL HEALTH WEBSITES

The following government travel-health websites are useful resources to consult prior to departure:
Australia (www.smartraveller.gov.au)
Canada (www.hc-sc.gc.ca/english/index.html)
UK (www.doh.gov.uk/traveladvice/)
United States (www.cdc.gov/travel/)

RECOMMENDED VACCINATIONS

No vaccines are required for DR or Haiti but a number are recommended.

Vaccine	Recommended for	Dosage	Side effects
Chickenpox	Travelers who've never had chickenpox	Two doses 1 month apart	Fever; mild case of chickenpox
Hepatitis A	All travelers	One dose before trip; booster 6-12 months later	Soreness at injection site; headaches; body aches
Hepatitis B	Long-term travelers in close contact with the local population	Three doses over 6-month period	Soreness at injection site; low-grade fever
Rabies	Travelers who may have contact with animals and may not have access to medical care	Three doses over 3 to 4-week period	Soreness at injection site; headaches; body aches; expensive
Tetanus-diphtheria	All travelers who haven't had a booster within 10 years	One dose lasts 10 years	Soreness at injection site
Typhoid	All travelers	Four capsules by mouth, one taken every other day	Abdominal pain; nausea; rash

- DEET-containing insect repellent for use on the skin
- permethrin-containing insect spray for clothing, tents and bed nets
- sun block
- oral rehydration salts
- iodine tablets (for water purification)
- syringes and sterile needles (if traveling to remote areas)

INTERNET RESOURCES

There is a wealth of travel-health advice on the internet. For further information, the Lonely Planet website (www.lonelyplanet.com) is a good place to start. The World Health Organization (www.who.int/ith/) is an excellent resource for travel health information, along with MD Travel Health (www.mdtravelhealth.com), which provides complete travel-health recommendations for every country.

FURTHER READING

Lonely Planet's *Healthy Travel* is packed with useful information including pretrip planning, emergency first aid, immunization and disease information, and what to do if you get sick on the road. Other recommended references include *Travellers' Health* by Dr Richard Dawood (Oxford University Press) and *The Travellers' Good Health Guide* by Ted Lankester (Sheldon Press), an especially useful health guide for volunteers and long-term expatriates working in the field and away from the cities.

IN TRANSIT

DEEP VEIN THROMBOSIS (DVT)

Deep vein thrombosis (DVT) occurs when blood clots form in the legs during plane flights, chiefly because of prolonged immobility. The longer the flight, the greater the risk. Though most clots are reabsorbed uneventfully, some may break off and travel through the blood vessels to the lungs, where they may cause life-threatening complications.

The chief symptom of DVT is swelling or pain in the lower leg, usually but not always on just one side. When a blood clot travels to the lungs, it may cause chest pain and difficulty breathing. Travelers with any of these symptoms should immediately seek medical attention.

To prevent the development of DVT on long flights you should walk about the cabin, regularly contract your leg muscles while sitting and drink plenty of fluids. Recent research also indicates that flight socks, which gently compress the leg from the knee down, encourage blood to flow properly in the legs and reduce the risk of DVT by up to 90%.

JET LAG & MOTION SICKNESS

Jet lag is common when crossing more than five time zones, resulting in insomnia, fatigue, malaise or nausea. To avoid jet lag try drinking plenty of fluids (nonalcoholic) and eating light meals. Upon arrival, get exposure to natural sunlight and readjust your schedule (for meals, sleep etc) as soon as possible.

HEALTH

Antihistamines such as dimenhydrinate (Dramamine) and meclizine (Antivert, Bonine) are usually the first choice for treating motion sickness. Their main side effect is drowsiness. A herbal alternative is ginger, which works like a charm for some people.

IN HISPANIOLA

AVAILABILITY & COST OF HEALTH CARE

In the DR, medical care is variable in Santo Domingo and limited elsewhere, although good cover can be found in many of the more heavily touristed towns. The picture is even more pronounced in Haiti. Although Port-au-Prince has a number of good hospitals, medical facilities even in provincial capitals can be lacking. If you're visiting a clinic don't be surprised to be treated by a Cuban doctor, as many are sent to Haiti as part of a medical aid program. Recommended hospitals are listed under Information in the major-city sections of regional chapters in this book; your embassy may also be a useful contact.

In both countries, many doctors and hospitals expect payment in cash, regardless of whether you have travel-health insurance. If you develop a life-threatening medical problem, you'll probably want to be evacuated to a country with state-of-the-art medical care. Since this may cost tens of thousands of dollars, it's essential that your travel insurance will cover you for this.

Pharmacies are denoted by green crosses (or red in the DR). Most are well supplied, though it is always preferable to bring along an adequate supply of any medications you may need.

TRAVELER'S DIARRHEA

The strains of travel – unfamiliar food, heat, long days and erratic sleeping patterns – can all make your body more susceptible to upset stomachs.

In terms of prevention, eat only fresh fruits or vegetables if they are cooked or if you have washed or peeled them yourself. Water should be treated before drinking (see p362). Meals freshly cooked in front of you (like much street food) or served in a busy restaurant are more likely to be safe. It's also essential to pay close attention to personal hygiene while on the road, particularly after toilet breaks. Antibacterial hand gel, which cleans without needing water, is a real traveler's friend.

If you develop diarrhea, drink plenty of fluids, preferably an oral rehydration solution – readily available in pharmacies. Avoid fatty food and dairy products. A few loose stools don't require treatment but, if you start having more than four or five watery stools a day, you should start taking an antibiotic (usually a quinolone drug) and an antidiarrheal agent (such as loperamide). If diarrhea is bloody, persists for more than 72 hours, is accompanied by fever, shaking, chills or severe abdominal pain you should seek medical attention.

Amoebic Dysentery

Amoebic dysentery is actually rare in travelers but is often misdiagnosed. Symptoms are similar to bacterial diarrhea, ie fever, bloody diarrhea and generally feeling unwell. You should always seek reliable medical care if you have blood in your diarrhea. Treatment involves two drugs: tinidazole or metroniadzole to kill the parasite in your gut, and a second drug to kill the cysts. If left untreated, complications such as liver or gut abscesses can occur.

Giardia

Giardia is a parasite that is relatively common in travelers. Symptoms include nausea, bloating, excess gas, fatigue and intermittent diarrhea. 'Eggy' burps are often attributed solely to giardia, but recent research has shown they're not specific to giardia. The parasite will eventually go away if left untreated, but this can take months. The treatment of choice is tinidazole; metronidazole is a second option.

INFECTIOUS DISEASES
Hepatitis A

Hepatitis A is the second most common travel-related infection (after traveler's diarrhea). It occurs throughout both the DR and Haiti. Hepatitis A is a viral infection of the liver that is usually acquired by ingestion of contaminated water, food or ice, though it may also be acquired by direct contact with infected persons. Symptoms may include fever, malaise, jaundice, nausea, vomiting and abdominal pain. Most cases will resolve without complications, though hepatitis A occasionally causes severe liver damage. There is no treatment.

The vaccine for hepatitis A is extremely safe and highly effective. If you get a booster six to 12 months later, it lasts for at least 10 years. Because the safety of the hepatitis A vaccine has not been established for pregnant women or children under age two, they should instead be given a gammaglobulin injection.

Hepatitis B

Like hepatitis A, hepatitis B is a liver infection that occurs worldwide but is more common in developing nations. Unlike hepatitis A, the disease is usually acquired by sexual contact or by exposure to infected blood, mainly through blood transfusions or contaminated needles. The vaccine is recommended only for long-term travelers (on the road more than six months) who expect to live in rural areas or have close physical contact with the local population. Additionally, the vaccine is recommended for anyone who anticipates sexual contact with the local inhabitants or a possible need for medical, dental or other treatments while abroad, especially if a need for transfusions or injections is expected.

The hepatitis B vaccine is safe and highly effective. However, a total of three injections are necessary to establish full immunity. Several countries added hepatitis B vaccine to the list of routine childhood immunizations in the 1980s, so many young adults are already protected.

Dengue Fever

Dengue fever is a viral infection found in the DR and, to a lesser degree, Haiti. Dengue is transmitted by *Aedes* mosquitoes, which bite preferentially during the daytime and are usually found close to human habitations, often indoors. They breed primarily in artificial water containers, such as jars, barrels, cans, cisterns, metal drums, plastic containers and discarded tires. As a result, dengue is more common in densely populated urban environments.

Dengue usually causes flu-like symptoms, including fever, muscle aches, joint pains, headaches, nausea and vomiting, often with a rash following. The body aches may be quite uncomfortable, but most cases will resolve uneventfully in a few days. Severe cases usually occur in children under age 15 who are experiencing their second dengue infection.

There is no treatment for dengue fever except to take analgesics such as acetaminophen/paracetamol (Tylenol) and drink plenty of fluids. Severe cases may require hospitalization for intravenous fluids and supportive care. There is no vaccine. The cornerstone of prevention is avoiding being bitten – for more on insect bites, see below.

HIV/AIDS

HIV is spread via infected blood and blood products and through sexual intercourse with an infected partner. While sexual encounters abroad can be fun they can also be risky, so practicing safe sex (with a condom or nonpenetrative) is essential. There is a small risk of infection through medical procedures, such as blood transfusion and improperly sterilized medical instruments.

The DR and Haiti together account for around three-quarters of all HIV/AIDS cases in the Caribbean, although a 2007 UN report states that infection levels have recently stabilized in both countries. The regional origins and transmission of HIV/AIDS is a highly politicized topic in Haiti (see boxed text, p276).

Malaria

Malaria occurs in several ports of Hispaniola. Spread by a parasite transmitted by the bite of an infected *Plasmodium falciparum* mosquito (usually between dusk and dawn), the main symptoms are high spiking fevers, which may be accompanied by chills, sweats, headache, body aches, weakness, vomiting or diarrhea. Severe cases may involve the central nervous system and lead to seizures, confusion, coma and death. In the DR, malaria occurs chiefly in the western provinces and La Altagracia (including Punta Cana). In Haiti, malaria is primarily found in the central mountains around Hinche and Gros Morne but has been reported throughout the country, including Jacmel and along the Côte des Arcadins.

Two strategies should be combined to prevent malaria – prophylactic antimalarial medication and mosquito avoidance.

All travelers should consider malaria prophylaxis. The first-choice malaria pill is chloroquine, taken once weekly in a dosage of 500mg, starting one to two weeks before arrival and continuing through the trip and for four weeks after departure. Chloroquine is safe, inexpensive and highly effective, and no drug resistance has been reported in either country. Side effects are typically mild and may include nausea, abdominal discomfort, headache, dizziness, blurred vision or itching. Severe reactions are uncommon, but remember that malaria can be fatal and the risk of contracting the disease far outweighs the risk of any antimalarial-tablet side effects.

However, no pills are 100% effective, so travelers are advised to prevent mosquito bites by taking these steps:

- Use a DEET-containing insect repellent on exposed skin. Adults should use preparations containing 25% to 35% DEET, reduced to 10% DEET for children under 12. DEET should never be used on children under two. Natural repellents like citronella or eucalyptus can be effective, but must be applied more frequently than those containing DEET.
- Mosquitoes bite between dusk and dawn: sleep under a permethrin-impregnated mosquito net.
- Wear long sleeves and trousers in light colors. Permethrin can also be used on clothes, but it should never be applied to skin.
- Use mosquito coils.
- Spray your room with insect repellent.

If you may not have access to medical care while traveling, you should bring along additional pills for emergency self-treatment. If you were taking malaria pills when you were infected, you should switch to a different medication for treatment, as it is likely you were infected with a resistant strain. Since you will likely be taking chloroquine as a preventative pill, one treatment option is to take four tablets of Malarone once daily for three days. You should begin self-treatment if you can't reach a doctor and you develop symptoms that suggest malaria, such as high spiking fevers. However, professional medical attention is much preferred, and it is unlikely you will be out of reach of a hospital considering the relatively small size of Hispaniola. If you do start self-medication, you should try to see a doctor at the earliest possible opportunity.

Remember to continue taking malaria pills for four weeks after you leave an infected area. If you develop a fever after returning home, see a physician, as malaria symptoms may not occur for months.

Rabies

Rabies is a viral infection of the brain and spinal cord that is almost always fatal. The rabies virus is carried in the saliva of infected animals and is typically transmitted through an animal bite, though contamination of any break in the skin with infected saliva may result in rabies. Rabies occurs in both the DR and Haiti, with most cases in related to bites from street dogs or wild animals, particularly the small Indian mongoose.

The rabies vaccine is safe, but a full series requires three injections and prices range from being free to staggeringly expensive. Public hospitals in the DR give the vaccine (and post-infection treatment) for no charge, including to tourists; however, if the nearest public facility doesn't have the vaccine on hand, a private facility can charge up to US$350 per injection. Only hospitals in the major cities in Haiti are likely to carry the vaccine. Those at high risk for rabies, such as animal handlers and spelunkers (cave explorers), should certainly get the vaccine. In addition, those at lower risk for animal bites should consider asking for the vaccine if they might be traveling to remote areas and might not have access to appropriate medical care if needed. The treatment for a possibly rabid bite consists of a vaccine with rabies immune globulin. It's effective, but must be given promptly. Most travelers don't need rabies vaccine.

All animal bites and scratches must be promptly and thoroughly cleansed with large amounts of soap and water, and local health authorities contacted to determine whether or not further treatment is necessary (see Animal Bites, opposite).

Typhoid Fever

Typhoid fever is caused by ingestion of food or water contaminated by a species of Salmonella known as *Salmonella typhi*. Fever occurs in virtually all cases. Other symptoms may include headache, malaise, muscle aches, dizziness, loss of appetite, nausea and abdominal pain. Either diarrhea or constipation may occur. Possible complications include intestinal perforation, intestinal bleeding, confusion, delirium or (rarely) coma.

Unless you expect to take all your meals in major hotels and restaurants, typhoid vaccine is a good idea. It's usually given orally, but is also available as an injection. Neither vaccine is approved for use in children under age two. If you get typhoid fever, the drug of choice is usually a quinolone antibiotic such as ciprofloxacin (Cipro) or levofloxacin (Levaquin), which many travelers carry for treatment of traveler's diarrhea.

Other Infections

Leptospirosis may be acquired by exposure to water contaminated by the urine of infected animals. Outbreaks often occur at times of flooding, when sewage overflow may contaminate water sources. The initial symptoms, which resemble a mild flu, usually subside uneventfully in a few days, with or without treatment, but a minority of cases are complicated by jaundice or meningitis. There is no vaccine. You can minimize your risk by staying out of bodies of fresh water that may be contaminated by animal urine. If you're visiting an area where an outbreak is in progress, you can take 200mg of doxycycline once weekly as a preventative measure. If you actually develop leptospirosis, the treatment is 100mg of doxycycline twice daily.

Brucellosis is an infection of domestic and wild animals that may be transmitted to humans through direct animal contact or by consumption of unpasteurized dairy products from infected animals. In both Hispaniola countries, most human cases are related to infected cattle. Symptoms may include fever, malaise, depression, loss of appetite, headache, muscle aches and back pain. Complications may include arthritis, hepatitis, meningitis and endocarditis (heart-valve infection).

Leishmaniasis has been reported in the eastern part of the DR. The infection is transmitted by sandflies, which are about one-third the size of mosquitoes. Most cases are limited to the skin, though symptoms are often diffuse. Leishmaniasis may be particularly severe in those with HIV. There is no vaccine. To protect yourself from sandflies, follow the same precautions as for mosquitoes (see Malaria, p359), except that netting must be finer mesh (at least 18 holes to the linear inch).

Schistosomiasis, which is a parasitic infection acquired by skin exposure to contaminated fresh water, occurs in the DR mainly in the eastern lowlands and as far west as Jarabacoa. The parasite can be contracted while swimming, wading, bathing or washing in bodies of fresh water, including lakes, ponds, streams and rivers. That said, the overwhelming majority of travelers do not get infected from the many water activities around Jarabacoa.

Conjuntivitis is common in Haiti, where it is called *pish-pish*. Symptoms are swelling and redness in the white of the eyes, with a yellowish discharge and soreness. Pharmacies are used to dealing with this and can sell medicated eyedrops (regularly bathing the eye in tea also helps). In tandem, washing the eye area with soap, and removing discharge with tissues or cotton wool (discarding after use) is essential, along with always washing hands after touching your eyes.

ENVIRONMENTAL HAZARDS
Animal Bites

Do not attempt to pet, handle or feed any animal, with the exception of domestic animals known to be free of any infectious disease. Most animal injuries are directly related to a person's attempt to touch or feed the animal.

Any bite or scratch by a mammal, including bats, should be promptly and thoroughly cleansed with large amounts of soap and water, followed by the application of an antiseptic such as iodine or alcohol. Go to the nearest hospital or clinic for possible postexposure rabies treatment, whether or not you've been immunized against rabies. It may also be advisable to start an antibiotic, since wounds caused by animal bites and scratches frequently become infected. One of the newer quinolones, such as levofloxacin (Levaquin), which many travelers carry in case of diarrhea, would be an appropriate choice.

Snakes are a minor hazard on Hispaniola. In the event of a venomous snake bite, place the victim at rest, keep the bitten area immobilized and move the victim immediately to the nearest medical facility. Avoid tourniquets, which are no longer recommended. Spiny sea urchins and coelenterates (coral and jellyfish) are a hazard in some areas.

Sun

Along with diarrhea, sunburn is the most common traveler's health concern. To protect yourself from excessive sun exposure, you should stay out of the midday sun, wear sunglasses and a wide-brimmed sun hat, and apply sunscreen with SPF 15 or higher, with both UVA and UVB protection. Sunscreen should be generously applied to all exposed parts of the body approximately 30 minutes before sun exposure and should be reapplied after swimming or vigorous activity. Travelers should also drink plenty of fluids and avoid strenuous exercise when the temperature is high.

HEALTH

Water

Tap water in the DR and Haiti is not reliably safe to drink. Bottled water is preferable and widely available; in Haiti water is often sold in sealed plastic bags. Untreated river and lake water should also be avoided.

If you need to drink tap water or river or lake water, vigorous boiling for one minute is the most effective means of purification. Another option is to use iodine-based water-purification pills. Follow purification instructions carefully – pregnant women, those with a history of thyroid disease and those allergic to iodine should avoid water treated this way.

A number of water filters are on the market, and help avoid the environmental cost of mountains of discarded plastic water bottles. Those with smaller pores (reverse osmosis filters) provide the broadest protection, but they are relatively large and are readily plugged by debris. Those with somewhat larger pores (microstrainer filters) are ineffective against viruses, although they remove other organisms such as bacteria and amoebae.

TRAVELING WITH CHILDREN

All travelers with children should know how to treat minor ailments and when to seek medical treatment. Make sure the children are up to date with routine vaccinations, and discuss possible travel vaccines well before departure, as some vaccines are not suitable for children aged under a year.

Upset stomachs are always a risk for children when traveling, so take particular care with diet. If your child is vomiting or experiencing diarrhea, lost fluid and salts must be replaced. It may be helpful to take rehydration powders for reconstituting with sterile water. Ask your pediatrician about this. In hot weather, keep a close watch for sunburn or dehydration.

Lonely Planet's *Travel with Children* and *The ABC of Healthy Travel*, by E Walker et al, are both valuable resources if your little ones are traveling with you.

WOMEN'S HEALTH

Emotional stress, exhaustion and traveling through different time zones can all contribute to an upset in the menstrual pattern. If using oral contraceptives, remember that some antibiotics, diarrhea and vomiting can stop the pill from working and lead to the risk of pregnancy, so remember to take condoms with you just in case.

Pads, panty liners, tampons and other women's sanitary products are generally available in both countries. Large pharmacies and supermarkets tend to have the best selection, including a number of internationally recognized brands. The same applies for contraceptives (both birth control pills and condoms).

Traveling during pregnancy is usually possible but there are important things to consider. Have a medical checkup before embarking on your trip. The most risky times for travel are during the first 12 weeks of pregnancy, when miscarriage is most likely, and after 30 weeks, when complications such as high blood pressure and premature delivery can occur. Most airlines will not accept a traveler after 28 to 32 weeks of pregnancy, and long-haul flights in the later stages can be very uncomfortable. Taking written records of the pregnancy, including details of your blood group, is likely to be helpful if you need medical attention while away. Ensure your insurance policy covers pregnancy delivery and postnatal care, but remember that insurance policies are only as good as the facilities available.

Malaria is a high-risk disease in pregnancy. None of the more effective antimalarial drugs is completely safe in pregnancy, which should be borne in mind if traveling to Haiti.

Traveler's diarrhea can quickly lead to dehydration and result in inadequate blood flow to the placenta. Many of the drugs used to treat various diarrhea bugs are not recommended in pregnancy. Azithromycin is considered safe.

Language

CONTENTS

> ### TALKING LIKE A REPUBLICAN
> Here are some Dominicanisms you should wrap your head (and tongue) around.
>
> | | |
> |---|---|
> | **apagón** | power failure |
> | **apodo** | nickname |
> | **bandera dominicana** | rice and beans (lit: Dominican flag) |
> | **bohío** | thatch hut |
> | **bulto** | luggage |
> | **carros de concho** | routed, shared taxi |
> | **chichi** | baby |
> | **colmado** | small grocery store |
> | **fucú** | thing that brings bad luck |
> | **guapo** | bad-tempered |
> | **guarapo** | sugarcane juice |
> | **gumo** | (a) drunk |
> | **hablador** | person who talks a lot |
> | **papaúpa** | important person |
> | **pariguayo** | foolish |
> | **pín-pún** | exactly equal |
> | **una rumba** | a lot |
> | **Siempre a su orden**. | You're welcome. |
> | **tiguere** | rascal |
> | **timacle** | brave |

WHO SPEAKS WHAT WHERE?
Dominican Republic
The official language of the Dominican Republic is Spanish, and it's spoken by every Dominican. Some English and German are also spoken by individuals in the tourist business.

Dominican Spanish is much like Central America's other varieties of Spanish. One notable tendency is that Dominicans swallow the ends of words, especially those ending in 's' – *tres* will sound like 'tre' and *buenos días* like 'bueno día.' For some other regionalisms, see boxed text, opposite.

If you don't already speak some Spanish and intend to do some independent travel outside Santo Domingo or Puerto Plata, you'd be well advised to learn at least some basics in the lingo. For a more detailed guide, get a copy of Lonely Planet's compact *Latin American Spanish Phrasebook*.

Haiti
While for many years French has been considered the official language of Haiti, only 15% of the population can speak it, mainly the educated elite, who these days also have very good English. The majority of the population speaks only Creole, and beyond the major centers it's the only sure means of communication. Language in Haitian society deepens the already massive divisions between social classes, as the government and the judicial system operate in French. The Creole-speaking and mostly illiterate masses are in this way excluded from civil society, leaving the control in the hands of the upper and middle classes. Most schools teach in French, which further disadvantages those who only speak Creole. Since the 1980s there has been a movement among reformists toward the increased use of Creole in civil society. Politicians have begun to make more speeches in Creole, musicians sing in it, more radio stations broadcast in it and there is now a weekly Creole-language paper, *Libète* (Liberty).

There is some debate as to the roots of the Creole language. The vocabulary is predominantly French, with some English and Spanish thrown in, but the structure is considered closer to that of West African languages. The most popularly held belief is that it's the synthesis of 18th-century French with many African languages, Spanish and English.

It is worth learning a few Creole phrases to use in smaller restaurants and for greetings. If you wish to learn Creole, the best book is *Ann Pale Kreyòl*, published by the **University of Indiana Creole Institute** (http://www.indiana.edu/~creole/), who also offer a bilingual Haitian Creole–English dictionary. Its website is an excellent source of information on Haitian Creole. Another good source of language books and self-guided language courses is **Educa Vision Inc** (www.educavision.com), based in Florida, USA.

With the ever increasing number of aid and church workers traveling throughout the country, and Haitians repatriated from the US, the number of English-speaking Haitians is on the rise. While you won't find them everywhere, they will seek you out and, in the larger cities, a combination of English and pidgin French will get you from A to B and enable you to order a beer when you get there.

SPANISH

PRONUNCIATION

Pronunciation of Spanish isn't difficult. Many Spanish sounds are similar to their English counterparts, and the relationship between pronunciation and spelling is clear and consistent. Unless otherwise indicated, the English examples used below take standard American pronunciation.

Vowels & Diphthongs

a	as in 'father'
e	as in 'met'
i	as in 'police'
o	as in British English 'hot'
u	as in 'rude'
ai	as in 'aisle'
au	as the 'ow' in 'how'
ei	as in 'vein'
ia	as the 'ya' in 'yard'
ie	as the 'ye' in 'yes'
oi	as in 'coin'
ua	as the 'wa' in 'wash'
ue	as the 'we' in 'well'

Consonants

Spanish consonants are generally the same as in English, with the exception of those listed below.

The consonants **ch**, **ll**, **ñ** and **rr** are generally considered distinct letters, but in dictionaries **ch** and **ll** are now often listed alphabetically under **c** and **l** respectively. The letter **ñ** still has a separate entry after **n** in alphabetical listings.

b	similar to English 'b,' but softer; referred to as 'b larga'
c	as in 'celery' before **e** and **i**; elsewhere as in 'cot'
ch	as in 'choose'
d	as in 'dog'; between vowels and after **l** or **n**, it's closer to the 'th' in 'this'
g	as the 'ch' in the Scottish *loch* before **e** and **i** ('kh' in our pronunciation guides); elsewhere, as in 'go'
h	invariably silent
j	as the 'ch' in the Scottish *loch* ('kh' in our pronunciation guides) or, often, the 'h' in 'how'
ll	as the 'y' in 'yellow'
ñ	as the 'ni' in 'onion'
r	as in 'run,' but strongly rolled
rr	very strongly rolled
v	as for **b**; referred to as 'b corta'
x	as English 'h' when it follows **e** or **i**, otherwise like 'taxi'; in some place-names it can also be pronounced as the 'sh' in 'ship'
z	as the 's' in 'sun'

Word Stress

In general, words ending in a vowel, an **n** or an **s** are stressed on the second-last syllable, while those with other endings stress the last syllable. Thus *vaca* (cow) and *caballos* (horses) are both stressed on the next-to-last syllable, while *ciudad* (city) and *infeliz* (unhappy) are stressed on the last syllable.

Written accents generally mark stress on words that don't follow these rules, eg *sótano* (basement), *América* and *porción* (portion).

GENDER & PLURALS

In Spanish, nouns are either masculine or feminine, and there are rules to help determine gender (there are, of course, some exceptions). Feminine nouns generally end with -**a** or with the groups -**ción**, -**sión** or -**dad**. Other endings typically signify a masculine noun. Endings for adjectives also change to agree with the gender of the noun they modify (masculine/feminine singular -**o**/-**a**). Where both masculine and feminine forms are included in this language guide, they are separated by a slash, with the masculine form first, eg *perdido/a* (lost).

If a noun or adjective ends in a vowel, the plural is formed by adding **s** to the end. If it ends in a consonant, the plural is formed by adding **es** to the end.

ACCOMMODATIONS

I'm looking for ...
Estoy buscando ...   e·stoy boos·kan·do ...
Where is ...?
¿Dónde hay ...?   don·de ai ...
   a hotel
   un hotel   oon o·tel
   a boarding house
   una pensión   oo·na pen·syon
   a youth hostel
   un albergue juvenil   oon al·ber·ge khoo·ve·neel

Are there any rooms available?
¿Hay habitaciones   ay a·bee·ta·syon·es
   libres?   lee·bres

I'd like a ... room.
Quisiera una habitación ... kee·sye·ra oo·na a·bee·ta·syon ...
   single
   individual   een·dee·bee·dwal
   double
   doble   do·ble
   twin
   con dos camas   kon dos ka·mas

How much is it per ...?
¿Cuánto cuesta por ...?   kwan·to kwes·ta por ...
   night
   noche   no·che
   person
   persona   per·so·na
   week
   semana   se·ma·na

Does it include breakfast?
   ¿Incluye el desayuno? een·kloo·ye el de·sa·yoo·no
May I see the room?
   ¿Puedo ver la   pwe·do ver la
   habitación?   a·bee·ta·syon
I don't like it.
   No me gusta.   no me goos·ta

MAKING A RESERVATION

For phone or written requests:
To ...   A ...
From ...   De ...
Date   Fecha

I'd like to book ... Quisiera reservar ...
                          (see the list under
                          'Accommodations' for bed
                          and room options)
in the name of ...   en nombre de ...
for the nights of ... para las noches del ...
credit card ...   ... tarjeta de crédito
   number   número (de)
   expiry date   fecha de vencimiento (de)

Please confirm ...   Puede confirmar ...
   availability   la disponibilidad
   price   el precio

It's fine. I'll take it.
   OK. La alquilo.   o·kay la al·kee·lo
I'm leaving now.
   Me voy ahora.   me voy a·o·ra

private/shared baño privado/   ba·nyo pree·va·do/
   bathroom   compartido   kom·par·tee·do
full board   pensión   pen·syon
                    completa   kom·ple·ta
too expensive   demasiado caro de·ma·sya·do ka·ro
cheaper   más económico   mas e·ko·no·mee·ko
discount   descuento   des·kwen·to

CONVERSATION & ESSENTIALS

Hello.   Hola.   o·la
                      Saludos.   sa·loo·dos
Good morning.   Buenos días.   bwe·nos dee·as
Good afternoon.   Buenas tardes. bwe·nas tar·des
Good evening/   Buenas noches. bwe·nas no·ches
   night.
Bye/See you   Hasta luego.   as·ta lwe·go
   soon.
Yes.   Sí.   see
No.   No.   no
Please.   Por favor.   por fa·vor
Thank you.   Gracias.   gra·syas
Many thanks.   Muchas gracias. moo·chas gra·syas
You're welcome.   De nada.   de na·da
Pardon me.   Perdón.   per·don
Excuse me.   Permiso.   per·mee·so
   (used when asking permission)
Forgive me.   Disculpe.   dees·kool·pe
   (used when apologizing)

EMERGENCIES

Help!	¡Socorro!	so·ko·ro
Fire!	¡Incendio!	een·sen·dyo
I've been robbed.	Me robaron.	me ro·ba·ron
Go away!	¡Déjeme!	de·khe·me
Get lost!	¡Váyase!	va·ya·se

It's an emergency.
Es una emergencia.   es oo·na e·mer·khen·sya
Could you help me, please?
¿Me puede ayudar,   me pwe·de a·yoo·dar
  por favor?   por fa·vor
I'm lost.
Estoy perdido/a. (m/f)   es·toy per·dee·do/a
Where are the toilets?
¿Dónde están los baños?   don·de es·tan los ba·nyos

Call ...!
¡Llame a ...!   ya·me a
  an ambulance
  una ambulancia   oo·na am·boo·lan·sya
  a doctor
  un médico   oon me·dee·ko
  the police
  la policía   la po·lee·see·a

How are you?
¿Cómo está usted? (pol)   ko·mo es·ta oos·ted
¿Cómo estás? (inf)   ko·mo es·tas
What's your name?
¿Cómo se llama? (pol)   ko·mo se ya·ma
¿Cómo te llamas? (inf)   ko·mo te ya·mas
My name is ...
Me llamo ...   me ya·mo ...
It's a pleasure to meet you.
Mucho gusto.   moo·cho goos·to
The pleasure is mine.
El gusto es mío.   el goos·to es mee·o
Where are you from?
¿De dónde es? (pol)   de don·de es
¿De dónde eres? (inf)   de don·de e·res
I'm from ...
Soy de ...   soy de ...
Where are you staying?
¿Dónde está alojado/a? (pol) don·de es·ta a·lo·kha·do/a
¿Dónde estás alojado/a? (inf) don·de es·tas a·lo·kha·do/a
May I take a photo (of you)?
¿Puedo sacar una foto   pwe·do sa·kar oo·na fo·to
  (de usted)?   (de oos·ted)

DIRECTIONS

How do I get to ...?
¿Cómo puedo llegar a ...? ko·mo pwe·do ye·gar a ...

Is it far?
¿Está lejos?   es·ta le·khos
Go straight ahead.
Siga derecho.   see·ga de·re·cho
Turn left.
Voltée a la izquierda.   vol·te·e a la ees·kyer·da
Turn right.
Voltée a la derecha.   vol·te·e a la de·re·cha
Can you show me (on the map)?
¿Me lo podría indicar   me lo po·dree·a een·dee·kar
  (en el mapa)?   (en el ma·pa)

SIGNS

Entrada	Entrance
Salida	Exit
Información	Information
Abierto	Open
Cerrado	Closed
Prohibido	Prohibited
Comisaria	Police Station
Servicios/Baños	Toilets
Hombres/Varones	Men
Mujeres/Damas	Women

north	norte	nor·te
south	sur	soor
east	este	es·te
west	oeste	o·es·te
here	aquí	a·kee
there	allí	a·yee
avenue	avenida	a·ve·nee·da
block	esquina	es·kee·na
street	calle	ka·ye

HEALTH

I'm sick.
Estoy enfermo/a.   es·toy en·fer·mo/a
Where's the hospital?
¿Dónde está el hospital? don·de es·ta el os·pee·tal
I'm pregnant.
Estoy embarazada.   es·toy em·ba·ra·sa·da
I've been vaccinated.
Estoy vacunado/a.   es·toy va·koo·na·do/a

I'm allergic to ...	Soy alérgico/a a ...	soy a·ler·khee·ko/a a ...
antibiotics	los antibióticos	los an·tee·byo·tee·kos
nuts	las nueces	las nwe·ses
penicillin	la penicilina	la pe·nee·see·lee·na

I'm ...	Soy ...	soy ...
asthmatic	asmático/a	as·ma·tee·ko/a
diabetic	diabético/a	dee·ya·be·tee·ko/a
epileptic	epiléptico/a	e·pee·lep·tee·ko/a

LANGUAGE

I have ...	Tengo ...	ten·go ...
a cough	tos	tos
diarrhea	diarrea	dya·re·a
a headache	un dolor de	oon do·lor de
	cabeza	ka·be·sa
nausea	náusea	now·se·a

LANGUAGE DIFFICULTIES

Does anyone here speak (English)?
¿Hay alguien que hable (inglés)?
ai al·gyen ke a·ble (een·gles)
Do you speak (English)?
¿Habla (inglés)?
a·bla (een·gles)
I speak a little Spanish.
Hablo un poco de español.
a·blo oon po·ko de es·pa·nyol
I (don't) understand.
(No) Entiendo.
(no) en·tyen·do

Could you please ...?
¿Puede ..., por favor?   pwe·de ... por fa·vor
  repeat that
  repetirlo   re·pe·teer·lo
  speak more slowly
  hablar más despacio   a·blar mas des·pa·syo
  write it down
  escribirlo   es·kree·beer·lo

How do you say ...?
¿Cómo se dice ...?   ko·mo se dee·se ...
What does ... mean?
¿Qué quiere decir ...?   ke kye·re de·seer ...

NUMBERS

0	cero	ce·ro
1	uno/a	oo·no/a
2	dos	dos
3	tres	tres
4	cuatro	kwa·tro
5	cinco	seen·ko
6	seis	seys
7	siete	sye·te
8	ocho	o·cho
9	nueve	nwe·ve
10	diez	dyes
11	once	on·se
12	doce	do·se
13	trece	tre·se
14	catorce	ka·tor·se
15	quince	keen·se
16	dieciséis	dye·see·seys
17	diecisiete	dye·see·sye·te
18	dieciocho	dye·see·o·cho
19	diecinueve	dye·see·nwe·ve
20	veinte	vayn·te
21	veintiuno	vayn·tee·oo·no
30	treinta	trayn·ta
31	treinta y uno	trayn·tai oo·no
40	cuarenta	kwa·ren·ta
50	cincuenta	seen·kwen·ta
60	sesenta	se·sen·ta
70	setenta	se·ten·ta
80	ochenta	o·chen·ta
90	noventa	no·ven·ta
100	cien	syen
200	doscientos	do·syen·tos
1000	mil	meel

SHOPPING & SERVICES

I'd like to buy ...
Quisiera comprar ...   kee·sye·ra kom·prar ...
I'm just looking.
Sólo estoy mirando.   so·lo es·toy mee·ran·do
May I look at it?
¿Puedo mirarlo?   pwe·do mee·rar·lo
How much is it?
¿Cuánto cuesta?   kwan·to kwes·ta
That's too expensive for me.
Es demasiado caro   es de·ma·sya·do ka·ro
para mí.   pa·ra mee
Could you lower the price?
¿Podría bajar un poco   po·dree·a ba·khar oon po·ko
el precio?   el pre·syo
I don't like it.
No me gusta.   no me goos·ta
I'll take it.
Lo llevo.   lo ye·vo

Do you accept ...?	¿Aceptan ...?	a·sep·tan ...
credit cards	tarjetas de	tar·khe·tas de
	crédito	kre·dee·to
traveler's checks	cheques de	che·kes de
	viajero	vya·khe·ro

less	menos	me·nos
more	más	mas
large	grande	gran·de
small	pequeño	pe·ke·nyo

I'm looking for the ...
Estoy buscando ...
es·toy boos·kan·do ...

ATM	el cajero	el ka·khe·ro
	automático	ow·to·ma·tee·ko
bank	el banco	el ban·ko
bookstore	la librería	la lee·bre·ree·a
embassy	la embajada	la em·ba·kha·da

exchange office	la casa de cambio	la *ka*·sa de *kam*·byo
general store	la tienda	la *tyen*·da
laundry	la lavandería	la la·van·de·*ree*·a
market	el mercado	el mer·*ka*·do
pharmacy	la farmacia	la far·*ma*·sya
post office	los correos	los ko·*re*·os
supermarket	el supermercado	el soo·per·mer·*ka*·do
telephone centre	el centro telefónico	el *sen*·tro te·le·*fo*·nee·ko
tourist office	la oficina de turismo	la o·fee·*see*·na de too·*rees*·mo

What time does it open/close?
¿A qué hora abre/cierra?
a ke o·ra a·bre/sye·ra

I want to change some money/traveler's checks.
Quiero cambiar dinero/cheques de viajero.
kye·ro kam·byar dee·ne·ro/che·kes de vya·khe·ro

What's the exchange rate?
¿Cuál es la taza de cambio?
kwal es la ta·za de kam·byo

I want to call ...
Quiero llamar a ...
kye·ro ya·mar a ...

| airmail | correo aéreo | ko·re·o a·e·re·o |
| stamps | estampillas | es·tam·pee·yas |

TIME & DATES

When?	¿Cuándo?	kwan·do
What time is it?	¿Qué hora es?	ke o·ra es
It's (one) o'clock.	Es la (una).	es la (oo·na)
It's (seven) o'clock.	Son las (siete).	son las (sye·te)

midnight	medianoche	me·dya·no·che
noon	mediodía	me·dyo·dee·a
half past two	dos y media	dos ee me·dya
now	ahora	a·o·ra
today	hoy	oy
tonight	esta noche	es·ta no·che
tomorrow	mañana	ma·nya·na

Monday	lunes	loo·nes
Tuesday	martes	mar·tes
Wednesday	miércoles	myer·ko·les
Thursday	jueves	khwe·ves
Friday	viernes	vyer·nes
Saturday	sábado	sa·ba·do
Sunday	domingo	do·meen·go

| January | enero | e·ne·ro |
| February | febrero | fe·bre·ro |

March	marzo	mar·so
April	abril	a·breel
May	mayo	ma·yo
June	junio	khoo·nyo
July	julio	khoo·lyo
August	agosto	a·gos·to
September	septiembre	sep·tyem·bre
October	octubre	ok·too·bre
November	noviembre	no·vyem·bre
December	diciembre	dee·syem·bre

TRANSPORTATION
Public Transportation

What time does ... leave/arrive?	¿A qué hora sale/llega?	a ke o·ra ... sa·le/ye·ga
the bus	el autobus	el ow·to·boos
the plane	el avión	el a·vyon
the ship	el barco	el bar·ko

airport	el aeropuerto	el a·e·ro·pwer·to
bus station	la estación de autobuses	la es·ta·syon de ow·to·boo·ses
bus stop	la parada de autobuses	la pa·ra·da de ow·to·boo·ses
luggage-check room	la guardería de equipaje	la gwar·de·ree·a de e·kee·pa·khe
ticket office	la boletería	la bo·le·te·ree·a

I'd like a ticket to ...
Quiero un boleto a ...
kye·ro oon bo·le·to a ...

What's the fare to ...?
¿Cuánto cuesta hasta ...?
kwan·to kwes·ta a·sta ...

student's (fare)	de estudiante	de es·too·dyan·te
one-way	ida	ee·da
return	ida y vuelta	ee·da ee vwel·ta

Private Transportation

pickup (truck)	camioneta	ka·myo·ne·ta
truck	camión	ka·myon
hitchhike	hacer dedo	a·ser de·do

I'd like to hire ...
Quisiera alquilar ...
kee·sye·ra al·kee·lar ...

a bicycle	*una bicicleta*	oo·na bee·see· kle·ta
a car	*un auto/un coche*	oon ow·to/oon ko·che
a 4WD	*un todo terreno*	oon to·do te·re·no
a motorbike	*una moto*	oo·na mo·to

Where's a gas/petrol station?
¿Dónde hay una bomba? don·de ai oo·na bom·ba

ROAD SIGNS

Acceso	Entrance
Ceda el Paso	Give Way
Dirección Única	One-Way
Mantenga Su Derecha	Keep to the Right
No Adelantar/	No Passing
No Rebase	
Peligro	Danger
Prohibido Aparcar/	No Parking
No Estacionar	
Prohibido el Paso	No Entry
Pare	Stop
Salida de Autopista	Exit Freeway

I've run out of gas/petrol.
Me quedé sin gasolina. me ke·*de* seen ga·so·*lee*·na

Please fill it up.
Lleno, por favor. ye·no por fa·*vor*

I'd like (20) liters.
Quiero (veinte) litros. kye·ro (vayn·te) lee·tros

diesel	*diesel*	dee·sel
gas/petrol	*gasolina*	ga·so·*lee*·na

Is this the road to ...?
¿Se va a ... por esta se va a ... por es·ta
carretera? ka·re·te·ra

(How long) Can I park here?
¿(Por cuánto tiempo) (por *kwan*·to *tyem*·po)
Puedo aparcar aquí? pwe·do a·par·*kar* a·*kee*

Where do I pay?
¿Dónde se paga? don·de se *pa*·ga

I need a mechanic.
Necesito un mecánico. ne·se·*see*·to oon me·*ka*·nee·ko

The car has broken down in ...
El carro se ha averiado el *ka*·ro se a a·ve·*rya*·do
en ... en ...

The motorbike won't start.
No arranca la moto. no a·*ran*·ka la *mo*·to

I have a flat tyre.
Tengo una goma ten·go oo·na *go*·ma
pinchada. peen·*cha*·da

I've had an accident.
Tuve un accidente. *too*·ve oon ak·see·*den*·te

TRAVEL WITH CHILDREN

I need ...
Necesito ... ne·se·*see*·to ...

Do you have ...?
¿Hay ...? ai ...

  a car baby seat
  un asiento de seguridad para bebés
  oon a·*syen*·to de se·goo·ree·*da* pa·ra be·*bes*

  a child-minding service
  un servicio de cuidado de niños
  oon ser·*vee*·syo de kwee·*da*·do de *nee*·nyos

  (disposable) diapers/nappies
  pañales (de usar y tirar)
  pa·*nya*·les (de oo·*sar* ee tee·*rar*)

  infant formula (milk)
  leche en polvo para bebés
  le·che en *pol*·vo pa·ra be·*bes*

  a highchair
  una trona
  oo·na *tro*·na

  a potty
  una pelela
  oo·na pe·*le*·la

  a stroller
  un cochecito
  oon ko·che·*see*·to

HAITIAN CREOLE

PRONUNCIATION

Creole pronounciation is fairly intuitive. There are no silent consonants – a hard 'c' is only ever represented by a **k**, and **g** is always hard, as in 'go.' There is no silent **e** and all instances of **e** are pronounced as acutes (**é**) unless they have a grave accent (**è**). For example, *pale* (to speak) is pronounced like *palé* ('pa-lay') The word for 'me' is *m* and is pronounced 'um.'

CONVERSATION & ESSENTIALS
Be Polite!

When you're introduced to someone, you give your name and say *anchante*. Polite greetings when out and about are very important. When you are addressing people you don't know, you should always say *bonjou* (good morning) or *bonswa* (good afternoon/evening) – see below for the various polite forms of address.

To get someone's attention you say 'psst.' This isn't rude, but clicking your fingers to someone is; 'psst' is the best way to stop a taxi or a taptap.

Good day ...	Bonjou .... (used before noon)
Good afternoon/	Bonswa .... (used after 11am)
evening ...	
Good night ...	Bonnwit .... (used when taking
your leave at evening's end)	
Sir	Msye
Madam	Madam
Gentlemen	Mesye

Ladies	*Medam*
Ladies and Gentlemen	*Mesye e Dam*
See you later.	*Na wè pita.*
Yes.	*Wi.*
No.	*Non.*
Please.	*Silvouple/Souple.* (In the capital you'd use *silvouple*; *souple* is used more for the provinces.)
Thank you.	*Mèsi anpil.*
Sorry/Excuse me.	*Pàdon.*
How are you?	*Ki jan ou ye?*
Not bad.	*M pal pi mal.*
I'm going OK.	*M-ap kenbe.*
What's your name?	*Ki jan ou rele?*
My name is ...	*M rele ...*
I	*m/mwen*
you	*ou/w*
he/she/it	*li*
you (plural)/we	*nou*
they	*yo*
I'm ...	*Mwen se ...*
American	*ameriken/amerikenn* (m/f)
British	*anglèz*
I'm from ...	*Mwen sòti ...*
Australia	*ostrali*
France	*lafrans*
May I take your photograph?	*Eske m ka fè foto ou?*
Do you speak English?	*Eske ou ka pale angle?*
I don't understand.	*M pa konprann.*

I'm looking for ...	*M'ap chache ...*
Where does the bus leave from?	*Kote taptap pati?*
What's the time?	*Kilè li ye?*
I'd like to change money.	*Mwen ta vle chanje lajan.*
Is that local dollars or US dollars?	*Eske se dola ayisyen ou dola ameriken?*
How much is it?	*Konbyen?*
How many?	*Konbyen?*
Let's go.	*Ann ale.*
I'd like to go (visit, speak with) ...	*M ta vle ale (vizite, pale ak) ...*
I'm lost.	*M pèdi.*
Where is ...?	*Kote ... ye?*
Can you help me, please?	*Eske ou kap ede mwen silvouple/souple?*
Help!	*A mwen!*
to stop	*rete*
to wait	*tann*
Where is/are ... ?	*Kote ... ?*
the toilets	*twalèt yo*
the hospital	*lopital la*
I have ...	*M gen ...*
chills	*lafièv*
cramps/diarrhea	*vant fè mal*
fever	*fyèv*
headache	*tèt fè mal*
I keep vomiting.	*M'ap vomi.*

Fè mal is a general word for 'ache', eg *tet fè mal* (headache), *pye fè mal* (sore foot).

Also available from Lonely Planet:
Latin American Spanish Phrasebook

Glossary

This glossary is a list of Creole (C), English (E), French (F), Spanish (S) and Taíno (T) words you may come across in the Dominican Republic and Haiti. See p70 and p286 for a list of culinary terms.

artisanat (C) – craft workshop
asson (C) – sacred rattle used in Vodou ceremonies
ayuntamiento (S) – local unit of government

bahía (S) – bay
baie (F) – bay
bateye (S) – community of Haitian sugarcane workers
bidonville (C) – urban slum area
boula (C) – drum used in Vodou ceremonies; provides an even rhythm, holding all the other drums together

camionette (C) – form of public transportation; large trucks piled with people and sacks of goods
caréy (S) – local turtle
carita (S) – mask for Carnival

cimetière (F) – cemetery
cobrador (S) – conductor who takes money for fares on *gua-guas*
colmado (S) – combination corner store, grocery store and bar
comedor (S) – eatery
compas (C) – traditional Haitian music; fusion of dance band and merengue beats

dechoukaj (C) – literally 'uprooting'; refers to the systematic destruction of remnants of Jean-Claude Duvalier's dictatorship after the leader's flight
department (C) – administrative province of Haiti
draguero (S) – drag racing

estacion (C) – bus station

fôret (F) – forest

galerie (F) – art gallery
gédé (C) – pronounced gay-day; family of *lwa* that includes Baron Samedi and Maman Brigitte
gingerbread (E) – Haitian architectural style of the late 19th and early 20th centuries
gua-gua (S) – local bus

houngan (C) – Vodou priest
hounsi (C) – initiate in Vodou ceremony

île (F) – island
isla (S) – island

kombit (C) – communal work team
kònet (C) – trumpet made from hammered zinc, ending in a flared horn
Krik? Krak! (C) – oral game of riddles played in the Haitian countryside

lakou (C) – communal rural housing
Lavalas (C) – pro-Aristide political movement
liberté (F) – liberty, freedom
lwa (C) – Vodou spirits

mambo (C) – Vodou priestess
mamman (C) – largest drum used in Vodou ceremonies, which the leading drummer beats fiercely with a single stick and one hand
marchand (C) – female market vendor
marché (F) – market
MINUSTAH (E) – UN Stabilization Mission to Haiti
musée (F) – museum

Noirisme (C) – literary-artistic movement reclaiming Haiti's African heritage

peristyle (C) – Vodou temple or ceremonial altar
plage (F) – beach
playa (S) – beach

racines (C) – literally 'roots'; type of Haitian music reflecting increased political-cultural consciousness
rara (C) – performance ritual during Lent when temple ceremonies are taken to the streets by marching bands of musicians, singers and dancers
restavek (C) – bonded child worker
rue (F) – street

segon (C) – drum used in Vodou ceremonies; provides hypnotic counter rhythms

taptap (C) – local bus; minibus
Tontons Macoutes (C) – notorious guards created under François Duvalier, named for a child-stealing traditional bogeyman character; also known as Volontaires de la Sécurité Nationale

vaskin (C) – bamboo trumpet
vevé (C) – sacred Vodou symbol
Vodouisant (C) – follower of Vodou

The Authors

PAUL CLAMMER
Coordinating Author, Port-au-Prince, Around Port-au-Prince, Southern Haiti, Northern Haiti

Molecular biologist, tour leader and now travel writer, Paul has a penchant for heading to places many people head away from – on this trip he added Haiti to his previous work for Lonely Planet in Afghanistan and Nigeria. Getting behind the headlines, he's happy to report these places are never as bad as the papers would have us believe – something a tour of Port-au-Prince's nightlife happily bore out. He'd like to think that Haiti first came to his attention while reading Graham Greene's *The Comedians*, but secretly wonders if childhood viewings of *Live and Let Die* didn't also play their part. He's already planning his next trip for Carnival. Paul also wrote Destination Dominican Republic & Haiti, Getting Started, Itineraries, Hispaniola History, Hispaniola Environment, Haiti History, Haiti Culture, Haiti Vodou, Haiti Food & Drink, Haiti Directory and Haiti Transportation.

MICHAEL GROSBERG
Santo Domingo, Around Santo Domingo, the Southeast, Península de Samaná

Michael was raised in the Washington, DC, area, studied philosophy in Michigan and Israel, and then worked in business on a small island in the Northern Marianas. After a long trip through Asia and then across the US, he worked as a journalist in South Africa. Michael's interest in Latin America began in earnest while pursuing work in literature in New York City, and his Spanish-language skills were improved by long and short trips in the region, including to Panama, Mexico, Ecuador, Puerto Rico and, of course, the Dominican Republic. More recently he has taught literature and writing in several NYC colleges, and other Lonely Planet assignments have taken him around the world. Michael also wrote Dominican Republic History, Dominican Republic Culture, Dominican Republic Food & Drink, Dominican Republic Directory and Dominican Republic Transportation.

LONELY PLANET AUTHORS

Why is our travel information the best in the world? It's simple: our authors are passionate, dedicated travelers. They don't take freebies in exchange for positive coverage so you can be sure the advice you're given is impartial. They travel widely to all the popular spots, and off the beaten track. They don't research using just the internet or phone. They discover new places not included in any other guidebook. They personally visit thousands of hotels, restaurants, palaces, trails, galleries, temples and more. They speak with dozens of locals every day to make sure you get the kind of insider knowledge only a local could tell you. They take pride in getting all the details right, and in telling it how it is. Think you can do it? Find out how at **lonelyplanet.com**.

JENS PORUP
North Coast, the Interior, the Southwest

Jens is a playwright, novelist, essayist and guidebook author who lives in Cali, Colombia. He doesn't believe in taking holidays (it's better to live the life you want every day), but his curiosity got the better of him when Lonely Planet offered to send him to the Dominican Republic, where he found there's far more to this tiny nation than just beaches. He still doesn't believe in holidays, but if he did, he'd head to the southwest, his favorite part of the country. His website is www.jensporup.com. Jens also wrote Dominican Republic Outdoors.

Behind the Scenes

THIS BOOK

This 4th edition of *Dominican Republic & Haiti* was written by Paul Clammer, Michael Grosberg and Jens Porup. Paul coordinated the book. The 3rd edition was written by Gary Prado Chandler and Liza Prado Chandler. Previous editions were written by Scott Doggett, Leah Gordon and Joyce Connolly.

This guidebook was commissioned in Lonely Planet's Oakland office and produced by the following:

Commissioning Editors Jay Cooke, Erin Corrigan, Jennye Garibaldi

Coordinating Editors Susan Paterson, Laura Stansfeld, Louisa Syme

Coordinating Cartographer Owen Eszeki

Coordinating Layout Designer Wibowo Rusli

Managing Editor Imogen Bannister

Managing Cartographer Alison Lyall

Managing Layout Designer Adam McCrow

Assisting Editors Peter Cruttenden, Chris Girdler, Penelope Goodes, Kim Hutchins, Kristin Odijk, Kirsten Rawlings

Assisting Cartographers Barbara Benson, Karen Grant, Lyndell Stringer

Cover Designer Pepi Bluck

Project Manager Craig Kilburn

Language Content Coordinator Quentin Frayne

Thanks to Rachel Imeson, Lisa Knights, Jacqualine Labrom, Katy Murenu, Malcolm O'Brien, Celia Wood

THANKS
PAUL CLAMMER

Krik? Krak! Above all, thanks to the fabulous Jacqualine Labrom, in Port-au-Prince, for far too many things to list. Extra thanks also to Céline Chauvel, Jean Cyril Pressoir, Michael Geilenfeld, Richard Morse and Leah Gordon (who proved that the Oloffson bar remains the best place for serendipitous encounters). *Mési anpil* to André Eugene and the Grand Rue artists, along with Maurice Etienne in Milot, Mary at Radio Ibo, Toni Monnin in Pétionville and Christian Barriere in Port Salut. Off stage, *merci* to Rebecca Hurrell for French assistance. Finally, thanks to Jo for holding the fort at home.

MICHAEL GROSBERG

Special thanks to my fellow author Paul Clammer for his patience and cooperation; the same for Lonely Planet editor Erin Corrigan. To Rafael Antonio, my personal guide to the culture and politics of the Dominican Republic. To Kim Bedall for sharing her knowledge of humpback whales. To Joseph who spent hours with me and the police after my car was stolen. To Paul and Kate Hayes in Las Galeras; to Emily Maguire for her advice on Dominican lit-

---

THE LONELY PLANET STORY

Fresh from an epic journey across Europe, Asia and Australia in 1972, Tony and Maureen Wheeler sat at their kitchen table stapling together notes. The first Lonely Planet guidebook, *Across Asia on the Cheap,* was born.

Travelers snapped up the guides. Inspired by their success, the Wheelers began publishing books to Southeast Asia, India and beyond. Demand was prodigious, and the Wheelers expanded the business rapidly to keep up. Over the years, Lonely Planet extended its coverage to every country and into the virtual world via lonelyplanet.com and the Thorn Tree message board.

As Lonely Planet became a globally loved brand, Tony and Maureen received several offers for the company. But it wasn't until 2007 that they found a partner whom they trusted to remain true to the company's principles of traveling widely, treading lightly and giving sustainably. In October of that year, BBC Worldwide acquired a 75% share in the company, pledging to uphold Lonely Planet's commitment to independent travel, trustworthy advice and editorial independence.

Today, Lonely Planet has offices in Melbourne, London and Oakland, with over 500 staff members and 300 authors. Tony and Maureen are still actively involved with Lonely Planet. They're traveling more often than ever, and they're devoting their spare time to charitable projects. And the company is still driven by the philosophy of *Across Asia on the Cheap*: 'All you've got to do is decide to go and the hardest part is over. So go!'

erature; and to Juan Herrera for his tips on Santo Domingo. And most importantly to Rebecca Tessler: we will both remember this trip always.

JENS PORUP

'Boldness has power, genius and magic in it,' said Goethe. Just when things seem darkest, sheer determination attracts those who will aid you – and so too in a mammoth undertaking like this. Without the aid of numerous unexpected smiles and handshakes along the way, this project would have been doomed from the start. In particular, I wish to thank Marco and his maps, tight-lipped Michael, the Spaniard in the mountains, a Canadian by the sea, the gaggle of girls in Santiago, and a Frenchman or three in Paraíso. Special thanks, as always, go to *mi cresposita conejita*, who was there when I got back.

OUR READERS

Many thanks to the travelers who used the last edition and wrote to us with helpful hints, useful advice and interesting anecdotes:

A John A Adams, Paul Alper, Fabian Andersson, Juha Asikainen **B** Hauke Baeumel, Emilio Baldi, Gabriele Bapst, Claudia Barchiesi, Dyanne Bax, Rosemary Beattie, Johannes Beck, Danielle Bedard, Jorg Beyeler, Leander Bindewald, Linda Gray Biok, Mme Blanca, Dan Broockmann, Peace Corps Broockmann, Thomas Brooks, Heather Buck, Philippe Bélisle **C** Andrew Campbell, Barb Campbell, Robert Carbo, Bonnie Carpenter, Olivia Carrescia, Robert Chaleff, Jodi Chen, Karen Cheung, David Church, Ann Cleary, James Cocks, Jeffrey Cohen, Dan Coplan, H Crighton, Michael Critchley, Margaret Cunningham **D** Edward William Dadswell, Robert D'Avanzo, Susan Davis, Chad Degroot, Ruud Dirksen, Daniel Dolan, Faye Donnaway, Joseph Dragon, Sheila Duncan **E** Susana Echeverria, Frank Ehrlicher, Nils Elvemo, Silje Førland Erdal, Patricia Fobare Erickson, Dimos Ermoupolis, Ana Escorbort, Rhian Evans **F** Maria Falgoust, Hanne Finholt, Jude Raymond Fish, Muriel Foucher, Eric Franco, Jonathon Frisbee **G** Jean Marc Gaude, Mordecai Gemer, Mylene Gibbs, Patrick Glynn, Stephan Gorthner, Maarten Gresnigt, Robert Göller **H** Ronald Hakenberg, David Hall, Jean-Lou Hamelin, Thomas Hill, Bill Hoppe, Caroline Houde, Frans Huber, Olivia Hung, Maggie Hurchalla **I** John Ide **J** Ellen James, Volkmar E Janicke, Fausto Jimenez, Neysha Jimenez, Joey Johnson **K** Linda Karlbom, Kevin Keller, Lisa Kirkman, Toni Klein, Cara and Sam Kolb, Richard Kowalczyk, Jack Kravitz, Dennis Kroeger, Irina Kuha **L** Andy Lam, Michelle Lewis, Paul Luchessa **M** Fulvio Maccarone, Andre Marcil, Anna Marfitt, Judit Marothy, Volker Maschmann, Sara Mason, Christian Massetti, Nick Massey, Michael Mayan, Theresa McDonald, John McEnroe, Jeanette McGarry, Liam McKnight, Iris Metawi, Ryan Miller, Helen Miner, Landon M Modien, Denise Molina, Dennis Mooij **N** Akanksha Naik, Peter Necas, Leah Nichols, Sally Nowlan **O** Marielle Ogor, Rob Ostrowski, Todd Owens **P** Rolf Palmberg, Wolfgang Pannocha, Carlos Paz-Soldan, Matt Pearce, Muriel Michele Peretti, Leslie Petri, Johnathan Pierce, Robert Pinckney, Tom Pisula, Sonya N Plowman, Sergio Prescivali, Sylvie Proidl, Peter Puranen **R** Helen Rankin, Ken Reed, Riikka Reunanen,

SEND US YOUR FEEDBACK

We love to hear from travelers – your comments keep us on our toes and help make our books better. Our well-traveled team reads every word on what you loved or loathed about this book. Although we cannot reply individually to postal submissions, we always guarantee that your feedback goes straight to the appropriate authors, in time for the next edition. Each person who sends us information is thanked in the next edition – and the most useful submissions are rewarded with a free book.

To send us your updates – and find out about Lonely Planet events, newsletters and travel news – visit our award-winning website: **lonelyplanet.com/contact**.

Note: we may edit, reproduce and incorporate your comments in Lonely Planet products such as guidebooks, websites and digital products, so let us know if you don't want your comments reproduced or your name acknowledged. For a copy of our privacy policy visit www.lonelyplanet.com/privacy.

Eddie Reynoso, John Riley, David Roach, Claudia Rogoff, Bruce Rumoga **S** Aaron Sainer, Loeve Saint-Ourens, Michelle Salazar, Gabriele Schenk, Beate Schmahl, Mark Schuler, Sheila Sedgwick, Brigitte Seidel, Travis Smith, Karen Söderberg, Ioannis Sofilos, Mitzi Stein, Paul Stevenson, Gordon Stewart, Margaret Stewart, Ben Stubenberg **T** Gerard Tarly, Erin Taylor, Helen Temple, Suzanne Teune, Rosalie Thanh, Peter Theglev, Betty R Theriault, Heather Thoreau, David Thornton, Armin Timmerer, Patrick Traynor, S P Tschinkel, Le Tu, Leo Tucker, Jack Tyler **V** Jorgen Vandewoestijne, Adrie van Sorgen, Monika Vetsch, Eric Viel, Jorge Alvar Villegas, Giacomo Volpi **W** Eunice Walaska, Clive Walker, Richard Walton, Garth Ward, Doug Wilkins, Michael Wilson, E Winmill, Ruth Wise, Swiatoslaw Wojtkowiak, Ute Wronn **Y** Elaine Yong **Z** Karen Zabawa, Harald Zahn, Ondrej Zapletal, Baerbel Zimmer, Marshall Zipper, John Zubatiuk

ACKNOWLEDGMENTS

Many thanks to the following for the use of their content:

Globe on title page ©Mountain High Maps 1993 Digital Wisdom, Inc.

Internal photographs p5 Vova Pomortzeff/Alamy; p6 Thony Belizaire/AFP/Getty Images; p7 Leah Gordon; p8 PCL/Alamy; p10 Reinhard Dirscherl/Alamy; p11 (#2) Nick Hanna/Alamy; p11 (#3) Wilmar Photography/Alamy; p12 Massimo Borchi/Atlantide Phototravel/Corbis. All other photographs by Lonely Planet Images, and by Margie Politzer p9; Alfredo Maiquez p43; Wayne Walton p263.

BEHIND THE SCENES

Index

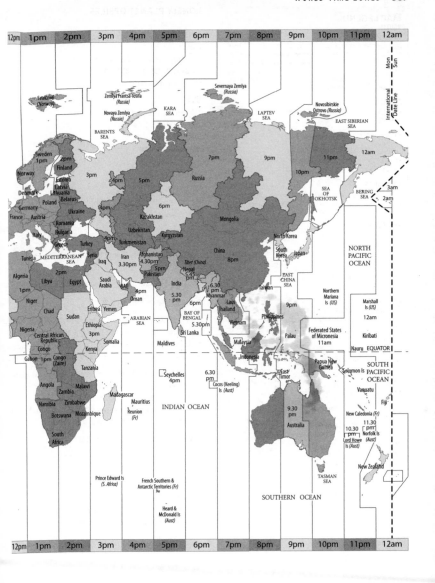

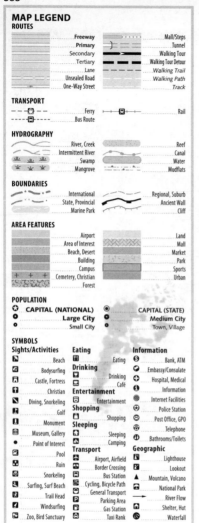

MAP LEGEND
ROUTES

Freeway	Mall/Steps
Primary	Tunnel
Secondary	Walking Tour
Tertiary	Walking Tour Detour
Lane	Walking Trail
Unsealed Road	Walking Path
One-Way Street	Track

TRANSPORT

Ferry	Rail
Bus Route	

HYDROGRAPHY

River, Creek	Reef
Intermittent River	Canal
Swamp	Water
Mangrove	Mudflats

BOUNDARIES

International	Regional, Suburb
State, Provincial	Ancient Wall
Marine Park	Cliff

AREA FEATURES

Airport	Land
Area of Interest	Mall
Beach, Desert	Market
Building	Park
Campus	Sports
Cemetery, Christian	Urban
Forest	

POPULATION

○ CAPITAL (NATIONAL)	◉ CAPITAL (STATE)
● Large City	◎ Medium City
○ Small City	○ Town, Village

SYMBOLS

Sights/Activities
- Beach
- Bodysurfing
- Castle, Fortress
- Christian
- Diving, Snorkeling
- Golf
- Monument
- Museum, Gallery
- Point of Interest
- Pool
- Ruin
- Snorkeling
- Surfing, Surf Beach
- Trail Head
- Windsurfing
- Zoo, Bird Sanctuary

Eating
- Eating

Drinking
- Drinking
- Café

Entertainment
- Entertainment

Shopping
- Shopping

Sleeping
- Sleeping
- Camping

Transport
- Airport, Airfield
- Border Crossing
- Bus Station
- Cycling, Bicycle Path
- General Transport
- Parking Area
- Gas Station
- Taxi Rank

Information
- Bank, ATM
- Embassy/Consulate
- Hospital, Medical
- Information
- Internet Facilities
- Police Station
- Post Office, GPO
- Telephone
- Bathrooms/Toilets

Geographic
- Lighthouse
- Lookout
- Mountain, Volcano
- National Park
- River Flow
- Shelter, Hut
- Waterfall

LONELY PLANET OFFICES

Australia
Head Office
Locked Bag 1, Footscray, Victoria 3011
☎ 03 8379 8000, fax 03 8379 8111
talk2us@lonelyplanet.com.au

USA
150 Linden St, Oakland, CA 94607
☎ 510 250 6400, toll free 800 275 8555
fax 510 893 8572
info@lonelyplanet.com

UK
2nd fl, 186 City Rd,
London EC1V 2NT
☎ 020 7106 2100, fax 020 7106 2101
go@lonelyplanet.co.uk

Published by Lonely Planet Publications Pty Ltd
ABN 36 005 607 983

© Lonely Planet Publications Pty Ltd 2008

© photographers as indicated 2008

Cover photograph: Cracking open a coconut beachside in Dominican Republic, Konrad Wothe/Look-foto. Many of the images in this guide are available for licensing from Lonely Planet Images: www.lonelyplanetimages.com.

Printed by Toppan Security Printing Pte. Ltd., Singapore.